CRIME IN AMERICA:
The War At Home

CRIME IN AMERICA: The War At Home

AN EDITORIALS ON FILE BOOK

EDITOR: Oliver Trager

Facts On File®
New York • Oxford

CRIME IN AMERICA: The War At Home

Published by Facts On File, Inc.
460 Park Ave. South, New York, N.Y. 10016
© Copyright 1988 by Facts On File, Inc.

Library of Congress Cataloging-in-Publication Data
Main entry under title:

Crime in America: the war at home/
editor, Oliver Trager

p. cm.—(An Editorials On File book)
Includes Index
1. Crime and criminals—United States—Juvenile literature.
2. Criminal justice, Administration of—United States—Juvenile literature. I. Trager, Oliver. II. Series.
HV6789.C692 1988
364'.973—dc19 88-11259
CIP
AC
ISBN: 0-8160-1591-0

Printed in the United States of America

9 8 7 6 5 4 3 2 1

Contents

Preface

Crime is rising in America. According to the Federal Bureau of Investigation's most recent crime figures, one violent crime is committed in the United States every 21 seconds, one property crime every three seconds, one robbery every minute and a murder every 25 minutes. In addition, the F.B.I. says that there were 13.2 million reported crimes in 1986, a 6% increase over 1985. Since 1977, the bureau reported, violent crimes as a whole have risen 20%.

Criminal behavior is often viewed as limited to certain social classes and ethnic groups. It has been argued for decades that crime rates have gone up because of economic deprivation, family disintegration, population changes, or judicial leniency. Crime projections predict that 40% of all male children will be arrested at least once during their lifetimes for non-traffic offenses. Additional numbers of people who do not define themselves as criminal will commit crimes and not be arrested.

Behind these figures lie real lives and difficult questions with no simple answers. How does America deal with the problem of crime? What is the relation between juvenile delinquency and drug abuse? Have we gone too far on defendants' rights? Have prison reform and alternative sentencing been successful? Has capital punishment served as a deterrent for murder and is it a humane response for a progressive society? What are the ramifications of corporate crime? How have recent Supreme Court decisions affected law enforcement's ability to control crime? How powerful is the Mafia?

Crime in America: The War At Home examines these questions and the stories that have made them major issues. The Bernhard Goetz case, the devastating emergence of 'crack' cocaine, the Ivan Boesky insider stock trading scandal, the recognition of child abuse as a national issue, the death penalty and the moves to privitize the federal prison system.

As law enforcement agencies and civic groups around the country organize themselves to battle crime in their communities, *Crime in America: The War At Home* explores this ongoing crisis.

July, 1988   Oliver Trager

Part I:
A Statistical and Legal Overview

A series of landmark decisions by the Supreme Court in the 1960's extended the fundamental due process rights to criminal defendants. Though most of these rights had long been available to defendants in federal courts through the Bill of Rights, sharp judicial conflict marked the debate as to which sections of the Bill of Rights were guaranteed to citizens in state courts through the application of the 14th Amendment right to equal protection under the laws. A consensus was formed in the Court that held that the constitutional guarantees basic to due process, such as the 4th Amendment protection against illegal search and seizure, the 5th Amendment right against self-incrimination and the 6th Amendment right to counsel and trial by jury should apply uniformly to start court proceedings.

The 1970s and 1980s have marked a turning point in the due process activism of the Supreme Court. The retirement of Chief Justice Earl Warren and the advent of the Burger and Rehnquist courts have brought a halt to the Supreme Court's willingness to correct practices in state criminal proceedings through a liberal interpretation of the 14th Amendment and the Bill of Rights. Though the Supreme Court has not reversed the rulings of the Warren Court, it has narrowed them and carved out critical areas where they do not apply.

The controversial *Miranda* ruling has suffered dilution in the 1980s. The 1966 ruling requires police to inform suspects in custody of their right to remain silent, of the right to counsel and to appointed counsel if they are indigent and the fact that any statements they made could be held against them. If police obtain statements in violation of this rule the statements must be suppressed and cannot be used at trial. *Miranda* not only involves the area of confessions, but limits police misconduct and prevents the use of forced confessions that are inherently suspect. The Burger Court's 1977 ruling in *Oregon v. Mathieson* said that the police were under no obligation to inform a suspect of his right against self-incrimination prior to arrest if he had not been placed under arrest or was in custody. By 1985, *Miranda* was under severe attack by Attorney General Edwin Meese 3rd, who argued that the ruling did not protect innocent people, only guilty ones.

Another key feature of the Warren Court that has been under constant attack is the so-called exclusionary rule. The exclusionary rule forbids the use of any evidence in state criminal trials that was seized in violation of the 4th Amendment's search and seizure requirements. Though the rule has no basis in the 4th Amendment itself, it was formulated by the court to serve as a deterrent to illegal police practices. It was reasoned that if the police are unable to benefit by the fruit of their unconstitutional activity they will take pains to adhere to lawful procedures in their work. Chief Justice Burger long opposed the exclusionary rule on the ground that it has little or no effect in halting illegal police conduct but does allow the guilty to go free because of police bungling. While Chief Justice Burger failed to succeed in scuttling the entire rule, the court, under his leadership, whittled away at it by redefining the scope of illegal police conduct. The Court's 1984 decision on the exclusionary rule said that criminal evidence illegally gathered by police was admissible at a trial if the police could prove the evidence would have inevitably been discovered by lawful means.

The larger questions involving crime, the law and their relation to society as a whole are perhaps even more difficult than the complex minutia that mark Supreme Court decisions. The average citizen perceives that crime rates will grow if, other things being equal, crime becomes more profitable compared with other ventures. Accordingly, the average citizen thinks it obvious that one major reason why crime has gone up is that people have discovered that it is easier to get away with it. By the same token, the average citizen thinks a good way to reduce crime is to make the consequences of crime to the would-be defender more costly, such as making penalties more severe and certain, or to make the alternatives to crime more attractive, such as increasing the availability and pay of legitimate jobs, or both.

The average citizen, however, may be surprised to discover that social scientists who study crime are deeply divided over the correctness of such views. Some scholars believe the popular is also the scientifically correct one: becoming a criminal can be explained in much the same way we explain becoming a carpenter or buying a car. But to other scholars, especially sociologists, the popular view is wrong: crime rates do not go up because people discover they can get away with it and will not come down just because society decides to get tough on criminals. The debate over the effect on crime rates by changing the costs and benefits of crime is usually referred to as a debate over deterrence, that is, the attempt to prevent crime by making would-be offenders more fearful of committing crime.

Complicating this is that the principal method by which scholars and law enforcement agencies have attempted to measure the effect on crime involves using data about aggregates of people (entire class, counties, states and nations) rather than on individuals. For instance, a typical statistical study will show that the rate at which robbery is committed in each state is explained by means of a statistical procedure in which the analyst takes into account both the socioeconomic features of each state that might affect the supply of robbers (for example, the percentage of persons with low incomes, the unemployment rate, or the population density in big cities) and the criminal justice system of each state as it attempts to cope with robbery (for example, the probability of being caught and imprisoned for a given robbery and the length of of the average prison term for robbery). Most such studies find that, after controlling for socioeconomic differences among the states, that the higher the probability of being imprisoned, the lower the robbery rate.

However, studying the effect of sanctions on crime rates using aggregate data of this sort is not without its problems. One is that many of the most important factors are not known with any accuracy. For example, the dependency on police reports for the measure of the robbery rate which undoubtedly vary from place to place. This would not be important if all police departments were inaccurate to the same degree. It is probable that some police departments are less accurate than others, and this variable error can introduce a serious bias into the statistical estimates of the effect of the criminal justice system.

Crime Stats Show Big Drop in '83; Serious Crime Down 7%

The number of serious crimes reported to law enforcement authorities in 1983 fell 7% from 1982, according to FBI figures released April 19, 1984. The 7% drop was the largest since 1960. Reported serious crimes had fallen 3% in 1982 and by a statistically insignificant amount in 1981. Approximately 12,857,200 crimes had been reported in 1982. The recent FBI report gave only percentage changes for 1983.

Attorney General William French Smith said the new crime data showed "we are beginning to win the battle against crime with some of the most significant initiatives and results in years." French later added that the data showed "we are turning back crime, not just holding our own against it." FBI Director William H. Webster said the crime data could mean that crime was "being managed effectively by the nation's law enforcement community." Webster also cited "greater citizen involvement" in anticrime programs for the fall in reported crime. Another reason given for reduced crime was that members of the postwar baby boom generation were now reaching ages at which they were less likely to commit crimes. Patrick Murphy, former New York City police commissioner and currently head of the Police Foundation, said a major reason for the falling crime rate was "the shrinking of the population in the crime-committing age—the late teens and early 20s."

For violent crimes, the FBI figures showed a 9% drop in murder, no reduction in forcible rape, a 9% reduction in robbery and a 3% decline in aggravated assault. For property crimes, the statistics showed a 10% drop in burglary and 6% reductions in larceny-theft and motor vehicle theft. The FBI data, based on reports from 16,000 law enforcement agencies covering 97% of the U.S. population, showed decreases in every category of serious crime except forcible rape. Statistics compiled by United Press International using new FBI data showed that among the nation's 10 largest cities, Detroit had the highest crime rate, with 133 crimes per 1,000 residents. Philadelphia, with 54 crimes per 1,000 residents, had the lowest 1983 crime rate of any of the 10 most populous cities, according to U.P.I.

WORCESTER TELEGRAM
Worcester, MA, April 22, 1984

Crime is bad news, but there is good news about crime.

The FBI says serious crimes fell off 7 percent in 1983, the largest drop in 23 years. The experts are saying the drop in serious crime will continue through the decade.

That's no surprise to those who have been saying for some time that crime is a function of age. Most street crime is committed by those in the 14- to 21-year-old age group. As the baby-boom generation moves beyond that range, the size of the group has been shrinking. That may be one explanation of why serious crimes seem to be diminishing.

If the trend moves forward as predicted, the pressure should eventually start coming off the court system and the jails and prison system. At the moment, criminals are behind bars in record numbers.

Any drop in the crime rate will be a relief for states and counties that have been pressed to the wall in a search for affordable lock-up space.

Even more encouraging for the Northeast, the decline in serious crime was 8 percent in these parts as compared with 6 percent in the West.

The crime rate report is certainly good news and portends a trend that we hope will continue. Now we can start worrying about the baby boomerang — the time when the baby-boom generation's children reach those troublesome teen years.

The Washington Post
Washington, DC, April 23, 1984

THE FBI RELEASED some encouraging figures last week. Serious crimes are down significantly; the numbers for 1983 represent the sharpest drop since the bureau began keeping comparable statistics in 1960. In every region of the country and in every category of serious crime—murder, rape, robbery, aggravated assault, burglary, larceny and motor vehicle theft—there were dramatic declines. In this city, reported crimes were down 12 percent last year, as compared with a national decline of 7 percent.

The attorney general believes that some of this improvement is due to federal law enforcement efforts, and so it may be. In the last three years, 1,000 new FBI and Drug Enforcement Administration agents have joined the ranks. The federal law enforcement budget is up 50 percent, and a major effort has been mounted to combat organized crime and the drug traffic. The narcotics trade remains a priority problem, mainly because of the high volume of violent crime generated by addiction. And because these criminal enterprises are organized, international in scope and extremely profitable, the federal government must take the lead in fighting them.

Most of the offenses on the FBI's serious crimes list however, fall within the jurisdiction of state and local police forces. No amount of federal effort will account for the statistical fall-off in these areas. Demographics play the most important role. It is well known that most violent crimes are committed by young men between the ages of 18 and 26. There have simply been fewer of them in recent years, and the size of this cohort will continue to diminish. Birthrates in this country began to decline in the early 1960s. Men born before then are now past the dangerous years and have settled either into law-abiding useful lives or long prison terms. There are now more 22-year-olds in this country than people of any other age: 4,451,724. The number at each age declines steadily all the way down to the 15-year-olds—there are only 3,518,982 of them—before leveling off. The prospects are good, therefore, that crime figures will continue to decline for a number of years because there will be fewer potential criminals.

Two points should be kept in mind on these new statistics. First, they challenge the idea that hard times produce increased criminal activity. We have, in the past three years, seen some of the highest unemployment figures in modern times, while crime went down, not up. Second, we will have an unprecedented opportunity, in the next 10 years, to devote increased resources to the war on crime and problems of dealing with offenders. Prison conditions and alternative sentencing for nonviolent offenders are two projects that need attention; drug-traffic control and addict treatment and rehabilitation can use a larger share of law enforcement resources. Falling crime rates can make these innovations and budget shifts possible.

The News American

Baltimore, MD, October 22, 1984

There are two ways of looking at the new statistics showing that Baltimore ranked second among the nation's 15 largest cities when calculating violent crime per resident.

One response, which we heard plenty of, was to howl about the inaccuracy of the numbers and the unfairness of the calculation, including the notion offered by City Hall that the statistics were wrong because they didn't include tourists, whatever that meant.

The second is to accept the numbers for what they are — a snapshot of a moving target, a one-dimensional view of a much more complex issue, and a point of departure in formulating a proper response. As the wise bureaucrat once said, "You can't see a problem until you can put a number on it."

What's accurate is that the city is second among the nation's 15 largest cities when you look at the number of violent crimes committed per city resident. In Baltimore last year, according to data city police provided the FBI, there were 201 murders, 6,267 assaults, 497 rapes and 9,167 robberies committed. In all, there were 20 violent crimes for each 1,000 residents.

What was also right is that the trend of violent crime is declining. That is because some of the worst criminals are behind bars; tough laws and tougher judges are imposing longer and longer sentences on criminals. Further, the number of people in the younger, more crime-prone ages is declining rapidly. As a result, the number of violent crimes committed in Baltimore fell nearly 6 percent, though the comparable drop across the nation was nearly 9 percent.

Has Baltimore been hit by a crime wave? No. Is Baltimore making progress and reducing the level of crime? Yes.

Still, the numbers demand attention. Properly, City State's Attorney Kurt Schmoke recognizes the reality. "It is a disturbing statistic, and it is one that will probably come as a surprise to some people. We're one of the poorest cities in the nation. And urban poverty is going to breed a fair amount of crime."

The reality is that there is simply too much crime in our community. It is an urban problem. It is also suburban problem; the entire Baltimore area ranks third, behind Los Angeles and New York, when calculating violent crimes per resident. It is a problem that requires attention from all of the major institutions of government and private enterprise, from schools, from law enforcement agencies, from legislators, from neighborhood organizations and corporations alike.

It may have been a surprise, as Mr. Schmoke noted. But it no longer can be ignored.

THE ATLANTA CONSTITUTION

Atlanta, GA, April 23, 1984

This much is clear: From New York City to Atlanta, from Columbus to Savannah, the problem of serious crime is now firmly on the mend. For the second consecutive year, the total number of crimes reported to police has dropped. The national index declined 7 percent for 1983 (the steepest fall since 1960), following a 3-percent fall for 1982.

It is a welcome glimpse of daylight after a long night of national distress. For Atlanta last year, there were fewer reported murders, robberies, assaults, burglaries, larcenies and auto thefts. Only the number of reported rapes rose, from 613 in 1982 to 619 in 1983.

Less clear are the reasons *why* these statistics have plunged. The prevailing theory these days pins the salutary trend to the maturation of the vast Baby Boom generation. As more Americans rendezvous with middle age, fewer folks are left in the crime-prone age bracket (late teens and early 20s).

There are other ideas. U.S. Attorney General William French Smith gives voice to a belief that is prominent among Reagan administration hard-liners: "It is no coincidence that the decreases in our crime rate come at a time when more criminals are behind bars than ever before." (Many experts insist, however, that this might indeed be coincidental.)

Still others point to the ounce of prevention that millions of worried Americans have taken. Citizens have upgraded their home security and joined neighborhood-watch groups. Many have become more guarded in their personal habits, carefully selecting where they choose to walk and with whom they choose to converse.

Some studies praise the police for providing communities with a pound of cure. Electronic record-keeping can identify repeat offenders faster and electronics can more quickly spread the word on fugitives. Local police forces have stepped up their patrols and many departments have worked to become symbols of trust in their communities. Police officers, like citizens, now put more emphasis on crime prevention.

Are these the only reasons for a falling crime rate? Probably not. The complete explanation doubtless lies with these and many other factors.

For now, perhaps, it is best simply to savor the good news in what is, at bottom, a bittersweet message. That message adds up to this: As a people, we have grown older and warier; we trust our neighbors more, we trust the police more, and we trust strangers less. And we are safer.

The Boston Herald

Boston, MA, May 12, 1984

THE homespun advice that "if it ain't broke don't fix it" makes so much sense that it just isn't very smart to go against it — which brings us to the House Judiciary Subcommittee on Constitutional Rights.

For some time now the FBI has been running "sting" operations so successfully that, in the 12-month period which ended last Sept. 30 they produced 1328 indictments, 816 felony convictions, more than $81 million in court-ordered forfeitures and restitutions, and nearly $3 million in fines.

Obviously the strategy "ain't broke," but the subcommittee, which spent four years studying it, has decided to fix it anyway. It has recommended a series of restrictive changes which, the FBI says, would put three-fourths of its undercover investigations out of business and severely hamper those that survive.

The fact that a special Senate committee studied the bureau's undercover operations two years ago and found them legal and proper hasn't made the slightest difference to its counterpart in the House. That body is recommending that the FBI be required to obtain court warrants before even starting a "sting," that even the disguises its agents use be subject to review, and that a number of administrative changes be made in the bureau.

Intended or not, the changes could have the effect of crippling FBI probes of political corruption, such as Abscam. That will make them more attractive to some members of Congress who oppose or have reason to fear such "stings." The majority of reps and senators, who have no cause to worry on that score, will — we hope — vote against this ill-considered attempt to fix the FBI's most successful strategy against crooks in public life.

It just "ain't broke."

Burger Report Restates Themes

Chief Justice Warren E. Burger devoted most of his 1983 year-end report on the legal system to previously stated concerns. The report, sent to members of Congress and to federal judges, was made public Jan. 2, 1984. Burger reiterated his belief that there were far too few judges and far too many lawyers in the nation, creating a huge backlog of litigation in the courts. The failure of Congress to establish new federal judgeships, he said, had pushed the judiciary to the "verge of collapse." The chief justice urged Congress to immediately create 51 new federal district judgeships and 24 new federal appeals court judgeships. He argued that the openings should be first filled in those judicial districts with the heaviest caseloads, as determined by the U.S. Judicial Conference. Burger noted that while the average judicial district had 200.6 criminal cases pending at the end of 1983, the Southern District of Florida had 1,368 cases pending, most of them drug-related.

Restating previous requests, the chief justice asked Congress to:

■ Create a temporary "intercircuit tribunal" to weigh appeals court decisions before they reached the Supreme Court. Such a bill had failed to advance past the subcommittee level when Congress adjourned in November 1983.

■ Allow the Supreme Court broader discretion in the types of cases it was required by law to review.

■ Eliminate the legal barriers that prevented the production and sale of most goods by inmates in prisons.

■ Give trial judges increased power to penalize lawyers who unnecessarily prolonged pretrial proceedings.

Richmond Times-Dispatch

Richmond, VA, January 5, 1984

Chief Justice Warren E. Burger is generally regarded as one of the two or three most "conservative" members of the U.S. Supreme Court when it comes time for the high court to make its calls on what the Constitution (dis)allows. But when it comes down to the chief justice's role as manager of the whole federal system of courts — a role this chief justice takes quite seriously — the Burger blend is one part fiscal conservatism, one part judicial and penal innovator.

His latest "Year-End Report on the Judiciary" again demonstrates a keen eye for seemingly small court savings that can add up. For instance, the chief justice endorses recent moves to reduce a federal-court juror summons to a standard-sized envelope, at savings of 9 cents per each piece of mail and $58,000 a year; and to mail the summons first class rather than by certified mail or other special handling, at a savings of $1.25 per summons and approximately $250,000 a year.

Much greater savings, however, could be realized by structural changes in the judicial system, Mr. Burger points out. He notes that the drain on the public treasury of private lawsuits is "enormous"; often such suits can cost taxpayers "more to process than is at stake in the litigation." These are the civil suits, some 8 million of which were filed in 1982 alone, on which Americans increasingly (and lamentably) are depending to settle their disputes. Processing of these cases costs taxpayers more than $2 billion a year. A study in California indicated that the average jury trial in a tort case costs $8,300 in tax money, while other surveys in Illinois and Wisconsin showed that half of plaintiffs wind up winning no money and those who do win typically receive less than $5,000.

The chief justice recommends settlement of many of these cases through "alternative dispute resolution" short of full-blown trials. The use of court-sponsored non-binding arbitration prior to judicial involvement is one such alternative. In Allegheny County, Pa., about 60 percent of civil cases in recent years have been assigned to arbitration, about half of these have been settled without an arbitration hearing, and the average cost to the public per case has been only $65. The chief justice also cited approvingly the "mini-trial" in which two disputants submit their cases to a neutral third party. The Wisconsin Electric Power Co. and American Can Co. recently settled a multi-million-dollar contract clash "at substantial savings to both sides and to the public."

Another cost that catches the chief justice's eye is the $17 million a day that it takes to house 400,000 prisoners in state and federal prisons. He notes that the states may spend another $10 billion over the next 10 years to build still more prisons. As we read it, the Burger year-ender does not declare that all plans for new prisons ought to be scrapped; rather, he questions the building of more that will serve merely as "human warehouses." The need, as he sees it, is for new kinds of penal institutions that will not only punish but also "train prisoners with marketable skills and let them engage in meaningful productive work to help pay the cost of prisons." Toward that end, he endorses repeal of laws that discriminate against the products of prison labor.

The chief justice makes points worth pondering. Ultimately, the social costs of idling the hands of warehoused humans, most of whom eventually will be turned back into society, could far out-run all the other accumulated inefficiencies within the nation's judicial system.

THE BLADE

Toledo, OH, January 7, 1984

CHIEF Justice Warren Burger in his annual plea for more help for the judiciary says that the growth of the lawyer population has rapidly outstripped that of judges who must hear the cases these attorneys bring and that the imbalance should be corrected.

This sounds like a chicken-versus-egg argument. Does the presence of more lawyers create a need for more judges or does the presence of more judges inspire more litigation by lawyers? It seems to work both ways.

Congress created new 152 new judgeships in 1978, bringing the total to 659 trial and appellate judge posts. It took more than 3½ years to fill these positions, the chief justice noted, adding the comment: "Creation of many judgeships following a lengthy period of demonstrated need is not an effective way to respond to the judgeship problem." He suggests that fewer positions be created periodically as the need arises.

There is merit in this, just as there is in his other suggestions that more cases be submitted to informal arbitration and that ad hoc tribunals of sitting federal circuit court judges be created to resolve conflicting legal decisions between two or more federal judicial circuits. This would relieve pressure on the Supreme Court and, as an additional bonus, might head off efforts to create a new and costly level of appellate courts interposed between federal circuit courts and the Supreme Court itself.

Implicit in these proposed reforms always seems to be the notion that the way to relieve clogging of court calendars is to create more courts. Why should not judges instead try to discourage the litigation that gives rise to the clogging and crack down on the foot-dragging by lawyers that is so cherished as a legal tactic?

The nation turns out far too many lawyers for its own good. As the old saw has it, one lawyer in a town will starve to death, but two will prosper nicely as each creates work for the other. No civilized society depends upon legal jousting to the extent that ours does.

Perhaps the chief justice, who recently visited courts and penal systems in Europe, should pay a visit to Japan where litigation generally is frowned upon by a society which values consensus building more than legal strife.

If the United States keeps on its present course, there will be an endless parade of requests for more judges and courtrooms, all couched, of course, in terms of the need for efficiency, fairness and equity.

The Salt Lake Tribune
Salt Lake City, UT, January 5, 1984

Chief Justice Warren Burger has not enjoyed notable success in bringing about improvements in the American criminal justice system. But that doesn't mean his annual evaluation of its faults and recommendations for its improvement are without value.

A system as complex and diverse as criminal justice needs constant surveillance and prodding just to keep it from sliding backwards. Mr. Burger has contributed mightily to that task.

In his latest Year-end Report on the Judiciary, the chief justice cited some different shortcomings such as the high cost to taxpayers of civil lawsuits. But it was an old Burger standby — prisons — that again drew his special attention. He urged the nation to "stop building human warehouses" for prisoners and confine them instead to facilities where they can learn useful trades. It's a recurring theme that sounds so rational but isn't as good as it seems.

Let's concede right away that there undoubtedly are prisoners who could and would go straight if they were trained in a speciality that was in demand at the time of their release. But how many of this type are there? Our guess is, not many.

If a job skill will keep an ex-convict on the beam, how is it that people with job skills end up in prison along with the others? A marketable skill is a factor in individual conduct but it is no guarantee of salvation. So, it can be assumed that some of the newly trained prisoners will not be saved although some will be.

What about the rest of the prisoner pool? In 1967 the task force on corrections of the President's Commission on Law Enforcement and the Administration of Justice drew up this profile:

"Individual offenders differ strikingly. Some seem irrevocably committed to criminal careers; others subscribe to quite conventional values or are aimless and uncommitted to goals of any kind. Many are disturbed and frustrated boys and men.

"Still others are alcoholics, narcotic addicts, victims of senility, or sex deviants. This diversity poses immense problems to correctional officials, for in most institutions or community treatment caseloads a wide variety of offender types must be handled together."

The task force's profile doesn't include many types likely to profit from job training.

There is another obstacle to achieving the chief justice's "object all sublime." Prison inmates these days are increasingly two and three time losers before they ever see a state or federal cell. By the time many of them get to prison they have already run the gamut of lesser forms of punishment and established themselves as unlikely to change their antisocial ways.

We share the chief justice's dislike of "warehousing" these troubled people but, as the task force profile plainly shows, much more than job training facilities will be needed to make even a small advance toward meaningful rehabilitation.

Herald News
Fall River, MA, January 6, 1984

Once again Chief Justice Warren Burger has urged the government to increase the number of federal judges. The Chief Justice has been stressing the need for more judges for years as part of his running campaign for reform of the nation's judicial and penal systems.

In his latest statement on the subject the Chief Justice referred to the "glut of lawyers" and at least implied that the number of lawyers is to some degree responsible for the extraordinary growth in the amount of litigation in this country in recent years.

Be that as it may, it has been true for a long time that delays in hearing cases have been so protracted that by the time many of them are finally heard, it is very difficult to deal with them justly.

Furthermore, the increase in the case load for judges on almost every level has been so extreme that it is taking longer and longer for many cases to be heard.

It is this combination of the number of cases and the consequent delays in hearing them that has prompted the Chief Justice to undertake his campaign to persuade the government to expand the number of federal judges.

No one can accuse Chief Justice Burger of being inconsistent. He has been harping on the need for more judges for years without, apparently, getting very far.

Yet surely he is right. Judges are needed for the administration of justice, and the more cases there are, the more judges are required.

The reasoning in back of Chief Justice Burger's campaign is as simple and as unanswerable as that.

Yet he seems to be unable to convince the administration and Congress to act on his repeated pleas for more judges.

In a sense it is understandable that the government, with its annual, sky-high deficits, is unwilling to undertake the extra expense that a major increase in the number of federal judges would entail.

Yet the administration of justice is being seriously hampered by the shortage of judges and the constantly increasing number of cases.

And no one has ever questioned that the country's legal system depends on the efficiency of its courts.

Chief Justice Burger has repeatedly pointed out that present conditions seriously impair that efficiency. In other speeches he has even warned of a possible breakdown in the operations of the courts if something is not done to remedy the situation.

Now, at the beginning of a new year, he is once again issuing the same plea.

Once again his message is receiving considerable publicity, as it certainly should.

But will it have any effect?

There is no indication that it will, even though the Chief Justice, by virtue of his high office, is automatically the nation's principal authority on the administration of justice.

What he needs is the active seconding and cooperation, not only of other judges, but of bar associations everywhere.

Presumably it is in their interest to facilitate the administration of justice.

They should echo Chief Justice Burger's plea for more federal judges. He should not be waging his campaign alone.

If he had enough support, sooner or later the public, too, would be convinced that more judges are needed, and when the public is convinced of something, the government acts.

The expansion of the judiciary is a matter of some urgency, as Chief Justice Burger has made clear. It should not be neglected any longer.

The News and Courier

Charleston, SC, February 26, 1984

Chief Justice Warren C. Burger of the U.S. Supreme Court delivered his 16th annual address to the American Bar Association earlier this month and it was the most scathing assessment of lawyers since 1977, when he said half the nation's lawyers may not be qualified to represent their clients in court. This time he said:

— Lawyers are abusing the justice system, their motivation more geared to lucrative fees rather than to the promotion of justice.

— The public's view of justice and the courts is soured by such frivolous law suits as a father suing a school board to raise his son's grades and a football fan suing to reverse a referee's ruling.

— The willingness of some lawyers to advertise their services like used car dealers is related to the nondisciplining of unethical attorneys.

— That loss of confidence in the system is a product of the high cost of legal services and the slow pace of justice. The United States, with 650,000 lawyers, has two-thirds of all the attorneys in the world, more per capita than any other nation, but it has fewer judges per capita than some European countries.

The public costs of private litigation "are enormous," he said. In 1982, more than 8 million lawsuits were filed in state and federal courts — that's 8 million plaintiffs and 8 million defendants. Counting all class action suits and those with multi-party actions, there are over 20 million Americans suing someone every year. The taxpayers foot a $2 billion bill just to process the paper work involved.

The judge also came down heavily on "absurd lawsuits" initiated by unscrupulous attorneys promoting fat fees. He called on the judges to regain control of their courtrooms by using their powers to levy $5,000 or $10,000 penalties on those who litigate in bad faith. Such fines will "help focus attention on the matter of abuses by lawyers," he added. He then went on to warn, perhaps a little naively, that if lawyers don't straighten themselves out, somebody else will. "State legislatures may move independently if our profession does not act," he said.

But that's part of the problem. Many seats in state legislatures, especially ours, are traditionally filled by lawyers, certainly more than their proportion of the population. That's why reforms unpopular with lawyers rarely pass.

We think the chief justice hit the nail on the head, especially when he complained about the absurd lawsuits. Our courtrooms should be reserved for more important cases. Also we recommend that those found at fault in civil actions be required to pick up the exorbitant court costs rather than turning them over to the taxpayers. That threat not only might slow down those who would sue at the lifting of an eyebrow but also the lawyers standing behind them anxious to pick up a quick fee.

The Knickerbocker News

Albany, NY, February 20, 1984

When it comes to reducing the strain on the nation's courts, Chief Justice Warren Burger has the right motive but the wrong method.

He would encourage prompt settlements by making it costly for stubborn litigants to refuse good faith offers from their courtroom opponents. Those who refuse the offer and press on would do so at their own risk: They would be liable for the attorney fees of the opponents if their case is finally found without merit, or if they are awarded damages below the amount they sued for.

If that were the only way to reduce courtroom overload, then Congress, which must approve the chief justice's proposal in order for it to take effect, would be well advised to consider it.

But it's far from the only way. There's a much more sensible method for clearing dockets, one both Congress and the chief justice ought to support wholeheartedly: Keep out those who would use the system for petty or selfish ends.

The Burger proposal is faulty because it would substitute chance for fair treatment. If a claimant had a good case but guessed wrong on the amount of damages he or she could collect, the results could be punishing. Instead of receiving any damages, the claimant might wind up owing huge legal bills. That would turn on its head the principle that any claimant is entitled to fair compensation for wrongs suffered at the hands of others.

A more constructive way to help beleaguered judges would be to raise the standards for filing suits in the first place. As recent experience in this area shows, the courts are often quick to listen to the wrong parties, while legitimate cases sometimes aren't heard for years.

Consider the recent case involving the parents of the severely deformed "Baby Jane Doe." When the parents elected to forgo life-extending surgery for their daughter, they were dragged through all three levels of the state judicial system, and later into Federal District Court, by an attorney with no relation to the family or the case. His sole interest was in pressing right-to-life causes.

Consider the recent controversy surrounding the proposed civic center in Albany County. Rensselaer County Executive William Murphy, an outsider, threatens court action to force planners to consider his county as a possible site. If he's allowed to proceed, valuable court time will be consumed to settle a political issue.

Add these cases to thousands of similar ones nationwide and it's easy to see why the courts are strained. Ironically, meritorious cases are often more rigidly scrutinized.

Consider the case of the former security guard at Rensselaer Polytechnic Institute, who was falsely accused of rape in 1977. It took six years of litigation before the state's highest tribunal, the Court of Appeals, affirmed his right to sue, but even then it termed excessive the $15,000 in damages he was awarded from the Court of Claims.

By contrast, the late Isidore Zimmerman, who was falsely imprisoned by the state for 24 years, had no standing to file suit for damages until former Governor Carey signed enabling legislation.

There's no defensible reason for letting the outsider have a hearing while denying the truly aggrieved. If Chief Justice Burger and Congress really want to clear the dockets, they should start by being more selective about who is entitled to a day in court. That would surely make our system more efficient — and more just.

The Birmingham News

Birmingham, AL, February 14, 1984

Supreme Court Chief Justice Warren Burger is on to something, whether the American Bar Association wants to admit it or not.

In a speech to the ABA's winter convention over the weekend, Burger jumped on the current evolution of the American legal system with both judicial feet. Lawyers, he said, should be "healers," not "hired guns," working to find ways to bring society together rather than tear it apart.

(It is interesting to recall that Lt. Gov. Bill Baxley, defending himself for criticism he received for representing the Alabama Education Association in a court case, described himself as only a "hired gun.")

Burger went on to tell the ABA that "the entire legal profession — lawyers, judges, law teachers — have become so mesmerized with the stimulation of the courtroom contest that we tend to forget that we ought to be healers of conflict." The present system, he said, has become "too costly, too painful, too destructive, too inefficient for a civilized society."

This was not the first time that the chief justice has leveled harsh criticism at the ethics of the legal profession, of course. Indeed, his opinions on the matter have earned him the resentment of many lawyers who hail the American adversary system as the final safeguard of freedom.

While that is true, to be sure, these advocates would do well to heed Burger's insights as in accord with the thinking of many Americans today who see the legal system as the playground of "hired guns" who pay too little attention to justice and too much to technicalities.

As was well stated in a recent *News* Op-Ed piece by Samford law professor Nicholas L. Chiarkas, the American legal system is founded on the concept of the accused's innocence until proven guilty, with the safeguards of due process flowing from that basic presumption of innocence. Yet it should also be recognized by the legal profession that, rightly or wrongly, much of the public feels that "due process" in criminal cases has evolved into an undue concern for the criminal's welfare and that civil law has become an apparatus designed for the collection of legal fees.

The best antidote for that perception, as suggested by Chief Justice Burger, is renewed legal attention to the ideal of justice — for true justice in fact should involve a healing of society's wounds, and not further division.

Rockford Register Star

Rockford, IL, February 20, 1984

Since juries don't render findings of guilt by consensus, we can't agree with Chief Justice Warren Burger's recent condemnation of the American legal profession inasmuch as it was based on the public's general disdain for lawyers.

In an address to a convention of the American Bar Association, Burger blasted lawyers for the contempt with which much of the public regards them. He faulted the legal community for the high fees it charges, the frivolousness of much of its litigation, the delays of justice it fosters, the laxity of its self-discipline, and the tone of some of its advertising.

There is much truth in what the chief justice says, and lawyers would do well to heed his admonitions. But we would remind Burger that public esteem should not be the ultimate objective of the legal profession. Lawyering is a means of resolution of conflict and dispute and as such it is bound to offend certain segments of the public.

As a member of the highest judicial tribunal in the land, Burger should know as well as anyone that justice doesn't always sit well with all of the populace. The chief justice himself has written court decisions that were unpopular among the general public.

We would also remind Burger that the legal profession is not unlike many another American institution in the decline it has experienced in public confidence in recent years. Ours is a society in an increasingly higher state of flux. Hence, many of its institutions are subjects of disenchantment among segments of the public buffeted by the winds of change.

The point should also be made that some of Burger's charges against lawyers are vague, undocumented generalizations. For example, it would be difficult to prove that the rapid pace at which court dockets are growing is entirely the fault of lawyers.

In Burger's defense, however, we note that the point he made about frivolous litigation certainly is not without merit. For example, two lawyers from Houston who were upset with the chief justice's tirade against their profession say they are considering suing Burger unless he issues a retraction.

Exceptions to Miranda Warning, 'Exclusionary Rule' Upheld

The Supreme Court June 11 and June 12, 1984 issued two rulings that could have a significant impact on the outcome of a broad range of criminal trials. In the first decision, the high court ruled that criminal evidence illegally gathered by police was admissible at trial if the the police could prove the evidence would have inevitably been discovered by lawful means. The case centered on the so-called "exclusionary rule," under which judges were required to bar evidence gathered in violation of the constitutional rights of criminal suspects. The principal figure in the case was Robert Anthony Williams, who had also been the defendant in a 1977 Supreme Court case concerning the rape and murder of a 10-year-old girl. In that case, the high court had ruled that the conviction was invalid because Williams had been illegally questioned by police seeking the location of the victim's body. Williams had then been retried and convicted but the conviction was overturned by a court of appeals. The Supreme Court in its June 11 ruling overturned the appeals court and, in so doing, established an "inevitable-discovery" exception to the exclusionary rule. Chief Justice Warren E. Burger wrote: "If the prosecution can establish by a preponderance of the evidence that the information ultimately or inevitably would have been discovered by lawful means...then the deterrence rationale has so little basis that the evidence should be received." In this case, the evidence was the victim's body and clothing, and the lawful means by which it was assumed they would have been found was a massive search party, some of whom were near the body when Williams told police where it was.

The second case stemmed from the arrest in New York City of a rape suspect, and involved the "Miranda warning," a legal principle established by a landmark Supreme Court ruling in 1966. Since that decision, arrested suspects were entitled to be advised of their right to remain silent, to have a lawyer present during questioning and to have a court-appointed lawyer if they could not afford counsel. In the present case, New York police officers cornered the rape suspect in a supermarket and noticed that he wore an empty gun holster. They questioned the suspect about the location of his gun without first advising him of his Miranda rights, and the suspect answered the questions. Three New York State courts subsequently ruled that neither the suspect's responses nor the gun itself could be used as evidence in prosecution for possession of an illegal firearm. The Supreme Court reversed the state courts on a 5-4 ruling, concluding for the first time that there was a "public safety exception" to the Miranda doctrine. Justice William H. Rehnquist, writing for the majority, argued that: "We do not believe that the doctrinal underpinnings of Miranda require that it be applied in all rigor to a situation in which police officers ask questions reasonably prompted by a concern for public safety...The need for answers to questions in a situation posing a threat to public safety outweighs the need for the prophylactic rule protecting the Fifth Amendment's privilege against self-incrimination."

The Supreme Court ruled July 5, 1984 that there was a good-faith exception to the so-called "exclusionary rule." Both of the cases at issue in the July 5 decision dealt with searches by police who had been armed with search warrants that were later ruled invalid. In one case, a federal judge ruled that a magistrate in California had issued a warrant without the sufficient probable cause required by the Fourth Amendment, which prohibits unreasonable searches and seizures. An indictment for drug-trafficking conspiracy was dismissed in the case. In the second-case, a Massachusetts court overturned a murder conviction on the ground that a search warrant used to obtain the evidence was flawed, because it was of the wrong type and improperly filled out. Justice Byron R. White, writing for the 6-3 majority, held that the exclusionary rule was a "judge-made" device that was not an intrinsic part of the Fourth Amendment. The rule had been created by the Supreme Court in 1914 and extended to the states by the high court in 1961. Therefore, he said, judges had to weigh the "social costs" of tossing out "inherently trustworthy tangible evidence." White continued: "Particularly when law enforcement officers have acted in objective good faith or their transgressions have been minor, the magnitude of the benefit conferred on such guilty defendants offends basic concepts of the criminal justice system." They key overall dissent was authored by Justice William J. Brennan Jr., who blasted the majority for its "gradual but determined strangulation" of the exclusionary rule.

The Virginian-Pilot

Norfolk, VA, June 15, 1984

"You have the right to remain silent. . ." and so on is a staple of cops-and-robbers television dramas. It is also the real-life statement of rights required to be read to criminal suspects by arresting police officers. For 16 years, this procedure has strictly protected a defendant's Fifth Amendment right against self-incrimination — occasionally at the expense of court convictions. But that was a cost the court was willing to pay when it decided the so-called Miranda case.

But the court drew the line this week in the case of Benjamin Quarles. When New York City police Officer Frank Kraft arrested Quarles in a supermarket late one night in 1980 and found an empty shoulder holster, the officer posed this question: "Where is the gun?" The handcuffed rape suspect nodded toward some cardboard cartons and replied, "The gun is over there." The officer reached over and pulled out a loaded revolver. Then he read Benjamin Quarles his Miranda rights.

In court, the defendant's lawyer argued that the arresting officer failed to follow the prescribed Miranda procedure before obtaining the gun and therefore Benjamin Quarles should be tried on the weapons charge against him without the gun entered as evidence. (The rape charge was dropped because the victim did not press it.)

Reason prevailed in the Supreme Court's 5-4 decision. In overruling three lower state courts, the high court ordered Quarles to stand trial with the gun as incriminating evidence.

It was particularly interesting to the Supreme Court's majority, in an opinion written by Justice William H. Rehnquist, that the defense lawyer did not contend that his client was coerced into self-incrimination. Police brutality, beatings, whippings and the third degree were a concern of the court debate that produced the 1966 Miranda decision. Miranda rights were designed to curtail such police rough stuff.

No police mistreatment was evident in the case of Benjamin Quarles. Instead, in searching for the gun, the arresting officer demonstrated an overriding concern for public safety. A loaded revolver in a public supermarket is an obvious hazard in the hands of a child, a shopper or, for all the officer knew, an accomplice.

Furthermore, after Officer Kraft recovered the gun and advised the suspect of his Miranda rights, the suspect declined to remain still and continued to answer still more police questions: Did he own the gun? Yes. Where did he get it? Miami. No evidence of coercion there.

The Supreme Court's decision, therefore, upholds common sense as it makes its first exception to the Miranda rule. The decision will be welcome especially in police work, where procedural technicalities sometimes spring otherwise guilty suspects. It will be worrisome to civil libertarians, who fear a revival of rogue police. But, as one prosecutor observed, the decision's value will be "limited" and its application "extremely rare." And the court's narrow majority suggests no willingness to reverse the basic tenets of Miranda.

Rights of criminal suspects remain intact. Requirements of public safety, meanwhile, receive a boost.

THE INDIANAPOLIS NEWS

Indianapolis, IN, June 15, 1984

Thanks to the Supreme Court, it will probably be even more difficult than before to be a criminal court judge in the coming months.

Earlier this week, the court eased the restrictions on evidence that could be used in criminal cases by providing a loophole to the "exclusionary rule." In a 7-2 decision, the justices ruled that illegally obtained evidence may be admitted in a trial if the prosecution can prove the evidence would eventually have been found through legal means.

The ruling pulled a 15-year-old Iowa murder case to a close. In that case, Robert Williams, the suspected murderer of a 10-year-old girl, incriminated himself by telling detectives where he had buried the girl's body during a long car ride across the state. What made the evidence illegal — until now — was the fact that the detectives had promised Williams' attorney that he wouldn't be questioned during the ride. In order to preserve the evidence, the prosecution argued for the "inevitable discovery exception to the exclusionary rule." That was the doctrine the Supreme Court endorsed.

The aim behind the ruling was to help end the spectacle of murderers being released for tiny technical violations of the law. There was clearly a need for such a ruling; the legal trend for several decades has been to support the criminal at the expense of the victim and law enforcement officers. The court was trying to even the scales of justice once again.

As Chief Justice Warren Burger wrote in the majority opinion: "Exclusion of physical evidence that would inevitably have been discovered adds nothing to either the integrity or fairness of a criminal trial."

However true that may be, the high court's ruling is still going to create a great deal of confusion. After all, it upends 70 years of Supreme Court "exclusionary rule" precedents.

The exclusionary rule, rooted in a 1914 Supreme Court decision, established the principle that prosecutors and police could not use evidence obtained through improper procedures in pursuing criminal cases.

The rule is not written in the U.S. Constitution, but is based on the Fourth Amendment: "The right of the people to be secure in their persons, houses, papers, and effects, against unreasonable searches and seizures, shall not be violated, nor warrants shall issue, but upon probable cause, supported by oath or affirmation, and particularly describing the place to be searched, and the persons or things to be seized."

The Miranda decision in 1964 etched the "exclusionary rule" in stone. In the aftermath of that ruling, it was already difficult enough for a judge to decide what evidence should be used in court and what should be thrown out. Now, the guidelines are less clear than before.

In addition to deciding if a defendant's rights have been violated during a criminal investigation, judges will now have to decide if those violations would ultimately change the outcome of the trial. Many constitutional questions are bound to occur.

And there is an obvious danger. Since the ruling reduces the chances that evidence obtained through a less-than-by-the-book method will be thrown out, it does offer criminal investigators some encouragement to take legal shortcuts. It is a discouraging possibility. No one wants to see the guilty go free, but no one wants to see innocent people harassed, either.

Some of this confusion may be ended with another Supreme Court ruling. The justices are now pondering whether to tack on a "good faith" exception to their ruling that would allow illegally obtained evidence to be used only as long as the police had a reasonable belief that they were acting lawfully.

Until the Supreme Court does rule again, however, criminal courts will be faced with some confusing days.

THE MILWAUKEE JOURNAL

Milwaukee, WI, June 14, 1984

The US Supreme Court hasn't completely torn down the constitutional barrier to the use of improperly obtained evidence in criminal trials, but clearly has chipped away part of that essential safeguard against police misconduct.

At issue is the exclusionary rule, which has been around for 70 years. No concoction of bleeding hearts, its roots are deep in the Anglo-American legal tradition. Its purpose is to prevent the use in trials of evidence obtained illegally by police.

Some observers say that the court's latest decision sanctioning an "inevitable discovery exception" to the exclusionary rule is not, in itself, a new threat. The exception already had been adopted by all federal appellate courts. Even Justices Thurgood Marshall and William Brennan, the most liberal of the justices, find the doctrine consistent with constitutional requirements.

Concern arises when the decision is coupled with earlier rulings, such as last year's decision permitting search warrants based on anonymous tips to officers. And the high court apparently plans to rule further on cases involving the exclusionary rule. That is worrisome.

In its latest decision, the high court affirmed a concept it introduced in a footnote in a 1977 review of the same case — the doctrine that illegally obtained evidence *is* admissible in a trial if the prosecution can demonstrate that the evidence would have "inevitably" have been obtained by lawful means.

The ruling came in the case of Robert Williams, who twice has been convicted of the murder of a 10-year-old Iowa girl. Williams' first conviction was overturned when the high court held in 1977 that a detective who persuaded Williams to lead police to the body violated the suspect's right to counsel and induced Williams to incriminate himself. However, the court suggested then that evidence about the body might have been admitted, even had Williams remained silent, if a lawful search "inevitably" would have disclosed the body. It is that concept that has now been reaffirmed.

Meanwhile, there is support in the Reagan administration and elsewhere for a broader exception to the exclusionary rule. It would admit illegally obtained evidence if police acted in the "good faith" belief that their conduct in evidence-gathering was constitutional.

Citizens understandably are concerned when criminal convictions are overturned seemingly on "technicalities." However, a just and lawful society *must* have a means to check misconduct by police. The high court's shrinking of exclusionary-rule safeguards inevitably threatens a just and lawful society.

Birmingham Post-Herald

*Birmingham, AL,
June 14, 1984*

The U.S. Supreme Court has chipped away part of the controversial "exclusionary rule" that some people believe lets guilty defendants walk away free.

The exclusionary rule heretofore has barred introduction during a trial of any evidence that police obtained by violating a suspect's constitutional rights. It didn't matter whether the evidence proved guilt beyond any doubt.

The actual impact of the rule on criminal prosecutions is debatable. A few studies have purported to show that significant numbers of criminals have escaped punishment because evidence was suppressed under the rule. But other studies indicate that only a very small number of cases have been affected by the rule. In at least one case the same study has been interpreted to support both sides of the debate.

The Supreme Court loosened the rule in an Iowa murder case that has dragged through the courts for 15 years.

The case involved the Christmas eve 1968 kidnapping and murder of a 10-year-old girl in Iowa. A suspect, Robert Williams, was arrested before the body was found and a detective suggested to him, without a lawyer being present, that the girl deserved a "Christian burial." Williams then led police to the culvert where he had placed the body.

Williams was convicted, but the verdict was overturned on the grounds that the detective violated the defendant's constitutional rights by beginning to question him outside his lawyer's presence.

The Supreme Court upheld reversal of the verdict in 1977 but changed its mind this week in an appeal of Williams' second conviction. This time the court ruled that courts may accept illegally obtained evidence — in this case the child's body — if that evidence would inevitably have been discovered by lawful means.

How far the court intends to go in relaxing the exclusionary rule remains unclear. Another case that should be decided before the current term ends may provide better answers. In that case, the court must decide whether evidence obtained illegally by police acting in good faith can be used in court. Adoption of a "good faith" standard could open a major loophole in the exclusionary rule, depending on how the court defines it.

In contrast, the "inevitable discovery" exception established in the Iowa case is limited in scope. It appears reasonable and unlikely to apply to many cases. It would have been a gross miscarriage of justice to let Williams off simply because a lawyer wasn't present when a detective persuaded him to lead police to a body that would have been found anyway.

The San Diego Union

San Diego, CA, June 15, 1984

In two separate decisions this week, the U.S. Supreme Court reaffirmed the sometimes-forgotten principle that the *raison d'etre* of a criminal trial is to determine the guilt or innocence of the accused.

On consecutive days, the court modified two important judicial doctrines that were originally designed to reduce police misconduct but which have become shields for the guilty to hide behind. The first decision amended what is called the exclusionary rule, which prohibits the use of illegally obtained evidence in criminal trials. The second ruling involved the well-known Miranda warning, which requires police to inform suspects of their constitutional right against self-incrimination.

Although the court still must rule in an even more important case involving the exclusionary rule, this week's decision should gladden the hearts of police, prosecutors, and a public grown weary of watching obviously guilty criminals freed on legal technicalities that have nothing to do with guilt or innocence.

The 70-year-old exclusionary rule was the result of a 1912 case in which federal marshals, without attempting to get a search warrant, broke down the door of a Missouri man's home, rummaged through his belongings, and seized every document they could find. In 1914, the Supreme Court, justly appalled by the marshals' misconduct, threw out the man's conviction for possession of lottery tickets, ruling that the evidence was seized illegally and could not be used in his trial. This original decision applied only to federal courts; it was not until 1961 that the Supreme Court extended its scope to state courts.

Unfortunately, since that time, many state courts, including the California Supreme Court, have made such strict interpretations of search-and-seizure requirements that persons proven to

have committed heinous crimes have been freed because police haven't dotted every "i" and crossed every "t" in obtaining search warrants or warning suspects of their rights.

Under the exclusionary rule as it now exists, if a warrant was improperly prepared or a suspect not adequately informed of his or her rights, any evidence obtained as a result cannot be used in the suspect's trial, even if there was no intentional wrongdoing by police and the evidence proved conclusively that the suspect was guilty.

In this week's decison, the Supreme Court upheld lower court rulings that had created an "inevitable discovery exemption to the exclusionary rule." In other words, illegally obtained evidence can be admitted in trials if it is obvious that the evidence would have been discovered without the police error or misconduct.

As Chief Justice Warren Burger aptly put it, "Exclusion of physical evidence that would inevitably have been discovered adds nothing to either the integrity or the fairness of a criminal trial."

This ruling came in an Iowa murder case that already had been before the court once before. A murder suspect led police to the body of his young victim after a detective asked the killer to "think about" the fact that "the parents of this little girl should be entitled to a Christian burial" for their child. Because police had promised the suspect's attorney they would not question the man during the long drive to jail, the Supreme Court in 1977 ruled that they had violated the man's constitutional right to counsel by inducing him to incriminate himself in the absence of his lawyer.

In this week's decision, the court ruled that the discovery of the girl's body was "inevitable," because 200 volunteers already were combing the area and were nearing the burial site before the

killer led police to the exact location. Therefore, seven of the Supreme Court's nine justices logically concluded that the discovery of the body should be allowed as evidence.

The ruling in the Iowa case could be a precursor to a badly needed and more sweeping change in the exclusionary rule that its opponents have sought for years — a "good faith" exemption. That is, a determination that evidence obtained illegally can be used in trials if police had a "reasonable and good-faith belief" that their conduct was legal. Such an exemption should be made, and it could come soon, as a result of another case now before the court.

In this week's Miranda case, the Supreme Court split 5-4 on whether there are times when a police officer's concern for public safety can take precedence over the Fifth Amendment rights of a suspect. In a case involving a fleeing rape suspect who had tossed a loaded gun into some cartons in a busy supermarket, Justice William H. Rehnquist and the court majority correctly concluded that indeed there are such occasions. Therefore, although a police officer asked, "Where's the gun?" before he warned the suspect of his rights, the court ruled that the "overriding considerations of public safety justify the officer's failure to provide Miranda warnings" and the gun still could be admitted as evidence in the trial.

Criminal defense attorneys undoubtedly will decry these rulings, and charge they tip the scales of justice toward the prosecution. Nothing could be further from the truth. What the court has done is to help restore balance to the criminal justice system and make the most important issue in criminal trials the guilt or innocence of the accused, not the ability of defense attorneys to find the right technicalities to free their clients.

Rockford Register Star

Rockford, IL, July 9, 1984

Don't expect the effects, good or bad, of the U.S. Supreme Court's landmark decision on the exclusionary rule to show up in criminal justice statistics.

The bad effects, which will outweigh the good, will be suffered by the innocent. The good effects, if good can come from such a wrong-headed decision, won't amount to much because the exclusionary rule, which has barred tainted evidence from criminal trials, has figured in only a tiny percentage of criminal cases.

The court now has ruled that evidence obtained under a defective warrant may still be used against a criminal defendant if police reasonably believe they were acting legally. The ruling creates a "good faith" exception to an exclusionary rule that has prevailed in American for 70 years.

It also creates, as Justice William Brennan argued in his bitter dissent, a climate in which police will tend to be vague in their applications for warrants, and judges might be less demanding in requiring probable cause before issuing warrants.

Heretofore, warrants were issued presumably only when reasonable cause to suspect wrongdoing was established. The purpose of this requirement was to deter police misconduct and to respect the constitutional rights of Americans to be secure in their homes against unreasonable search and seizure.

Those rights have been diminished by this latest ruling.

Justice Brennan may be premature in saying that "the court's victory over the Fourth Amendment is complete." The court has yet to create a "good faith" exception to privacy rights in cases where no warrant was issued.

But, alas, there is every indication in the latest ruling that this court eventually will apply the same specious logic to cases in which warrants aren't involved.

That questionable logic, in a nutshell, holds that catching and convicting crooks is more important than respect for constitutional guarantees of the sanctity of our homes.

The Seattle Times

Seattle, WA, July 6, 1984

THE headlines on a number of articles about recent Supreme Court rulings have referred to "illegal evidence" obtained by police that will be allowed at trials. The implication is that this evidence was stolen from a suspect's locked house, beaten out of him in a basement dungeon, or revealed through some unconscionable trickery by law-enforcement officials.

Nothing could be further from the truth. What's happening is that the Supreme Court is finally beginning to require that the controversial "exclusionary rule" meet the test of reason. Step by step, the court is reducing the scope of the exclusionary rule, which too often has helped criminals go free on legal technicalities.

The court's latest decision is a case in point: Acting on a tip, Burbank, Calif., police conducted a month-long surveillance of the home of a person suspected of dealing cocaine. They obtained a search warrant and seized more than four pounds of cocaine and 1,165 Quaalude tablets. But a federal judge ordered some of the evidence excluded from the trial because police hadn't established sufficient "probable cause" and shouldn't have obtained the warrant.

Such decisions have led many rational citizens in recent years to wonder which side is really being handcuffed — the police or the criminals?

Wisely, the high court reversed the lower-court ruling by a 6-3 vote. Henceforth, we hope, the exclusionary rule will not be used to exclude common sense along with criminal evidence.

The Houston Post

Houston, TX, July 8, 1984

Reaction to the U.S. Supreme Court's ruling last week creating a "good-faith exception" to the 70-year-old exclusionary rule was predictable. It was cheered by police, prosecutors and law-and-order advocates who believe the rule, which bars the use of illegally obtained evidence against a defendant, has thwarted justice. And it was condemned by civil libertarians and defense attorneys, who consider the rule an indispensable bulwark against unreasonable searches and seizures by authorities.

The high court unquestionably put a kink in the exclusionary rule with its 6-3 decision that some evidence obtained with a defective search warrant can be admitted in a trial if the officer using the warrant believed it was valid. But even the justices don't agree on the ruling's eventual impact on the criminal justice system.

Associate Justice Byron R. White, who wrote the court's majority opinion, warned that a police officer's belief in the validity of a warrant must be "objectively reasonable." But Associate Justice William J. Brennan predicted, in a scathing dissent, that the ruling "will prove in time to have been a grave mistake."

The fact is that the exclusionary rule affects only a minuscule number of criminal proceedings, freeing an estimated 2.35 percent of all defendants in felony cases. What galls opponents of the rule is its use in behalf of defendants who are guilty beyond any reasonable doubt but whose convictions are voided because the police have committed technical mistakes in gathering evidence.

Civil libertarians argue that the courts must not let public opinion influence their interpretation of the Constitution. They contend that upholding individual rights, such as the Fourth Amendment safeguards against unreasonable search and seizure, is essential in a free society, even if it means occasionally freeing the guilty.

But for the second time in a month, the Supreme Court has carved a narrow common-sense exception to the exclusionary doctrine. The first held that illegally obtained evidence can be used if the prosecution can prove that it would inevitably have been discovered by legal means. But the "good faith exception" carries us much closer to the thin line dividing the rights of the individual and society. The court must take care not to stray over that line in future decisions involving the controversial exclusionary rule.

Lexington Herald-Leader

Lexington, KY, July 8, 1984

The Fourth Amendment to the Constitution took a beating during the recent session of the Supreme Court. That's good news to the Reagan administration and others who want to get tough with criminals, but it's bad news for those who cherish the freedoms that the Fourth Amendment was designed to protect.

Here is the Fourth Amendment in its entirety: "The right of the people to be secure in their persons, houses, papers, and effects, against unreasonable searches and seizures, shall not be violated, and no warrants shall issue, but upon probable cause, supported by oath or affirmation, and particularly describing the place to be searched, and the persons or things to be seized."

In those few words, the Constitution establishes the basic rights of Americans with regard to police officers: that there shall be no unreasonable searches and that searches must be conducted on the basis of a warrant.

Since 1914, when the court drafted what became known as the "exclusionary rule," the Fourth Amendment has been interpreted to mean that evidence obtained under a faulty warrant was not admissible in court. Police and prosecutors have long complained about the rule, which they claim hampers law enforcement efforts.

But the basic reasoning behind the exclusionary rule is sound: If courts can accept evidence taken in unlawful searches, then there is no real distinction between searches that are lawful and ones that are not.

The court has now stood that reasoning on its head with a ruling that evidence obtained with a faulty warrant can be used as evidence so long as police were acting with an "objectively reasonable reliance" in the validity of the warrant.

The Fourth Amendment's standard of reasonableness is intended as a protection for individual liberties. Under the court's new doctrine, though, it becomes an excuse for illegal searches.

This ruling is only one in a series through which the court has reduced the scope of the Fourth Amendment's protections. In earlier cases, it has used such nebulous criteria as "good faith" by police officers and the "inevitability" of the discovery of evidence seized illegally.

These allowances are no doubt useful to law enforcement officials, but they run counter to the spirit and intent of the Fourth Amendment. The majority of the Supreme Court apparently feels that the benefits of the decision outweigh its costs, but that is a dangerous standard to apply to the constitutional protection of a basic liberty. Justice William J. Brennan was right when he wrote in his dissenting opinion that the court's decision "ignores the fundamental constitutional importance of what is at stake here."

Senate Passes Sweeping Anticrime Bills

Between Feb. 2 and Feb. 22, 1984 the Senate passed four major anticrime bills. If enacted into law, the bills would effect major changes in the federal criminal code. That code, however, applied to a very small percentage of criminal acts, because most criminal activity fell under state jurisdiction. The primary provisions of the anticrime bills would reintroduce the death penalty for several types of crimes, set stiffer federal standards, reduce the right of state prisoners to file habeas corpus petitions, allow some illegally seized evidence to be used in federal trials, increase penalties against convicted drug traffickers and members of organized crime, change federal law on the insanity defense and allow for pretrial detention of dangerous criminals. Some provisions of the bills had support in the House of Representatives. But Rep. Peter W. Rodino Jr. (D, N.J.), chairman of the House Judiciary Committee, was quoted in the Feb. 11 issue of *Congressional Quarterly* as saying the controversial Senate proposals on pretrial detention, evidence rules and habeas corpus were unlikely to gain the support of his committee.

The crime package was included in the omnibus spending bill passed by Congress Oct. 11, 1984 was legislation described as "the most important crime package passed by any Congress at any time." The legislation, similar to measures passed by the Senate in February, was signed into law by President Ronald Reagan Oct. 12. Among the major aims of the crime package were restricting bail for "dangerous suspects," standardizing prison sentences, ending parole, increasing penalties for drug convictions and limiting the use of the insanity defense. The bill did not include two particularly controversial provisions contained in the earlier Senate legislation: the establishment of a federal death penalty and the allowance of the admission at federal trials of illegally obtained evidence. The legislation applied only to federal crimes. According to the *New York Times*, only 5% of all criminal prosecutions took place on the federal level. Since the Senate had passed its crime package in February, President Reagan had persistently criticized House Democratic leaders for blocking passage of anticrime bills. The House had passed some of its own anticrime legislation but had balked over some provisions of the Senate package that had been viewed as infringing on civil liberites. The Reagan administration had often taken credit for the anticrime package, but many of the proposals had been made before the president assumed office.

THE BLADE

Toledo, OH, October 23, 1984

SOMETHING of a blow has been struck on behalf of more stringent federal crime laws. But despite the success that conservative lawmakers finally had in pushing the measure through Congress, there is little assurance that new laws will be miracle cures.

For months a series of steps to toughen crime laws has been bottled up in the House. Provisions that would make the insanity defense less available, do away with parole and allow judges to deny bail to a wider range of accused persons had been stalled, just as comparable measures in previous sessions were.

But thanks to parliamentary maneuvering and a perception that lawmakers seeking re-election must vote for anti-crime measures, the various bills finally won House approval and were signed into law by President Reagan. One reason for approval may have been that several especially controversial provisions — reinstatement of the death penalty in federal cases and relaxation of the exclusionary rule, to name two — were dropped.

More punitive and restrictive laws are welcome. Judging from the fact that at least some defendants commit crimes while free on bail awaiting trial, there is a need to give judges the power to deny bail in certain instances. Similarly, making the insanity defense less available to accused individuals could lead to prison terms for persons who were clear-headed when they committed a crime but claim insanity when brought to trial.

But new laws will not lead inexorably to a drop in the crime rate. Most persons are prosecuted under state and local laws. Although the new statutes may prove helpful in some instances, one cannot assume that the number of crimes will be substantially reduced.

Nonetheless, the new measures are about the best that can be done on the federal level. It is to be hoped that the U.S. Supreme Court will eventually view them as constitutional.

the Charleston Gazette

Charleston, WV, April 12, 1984

THE U.S. Senate, Republican majority, has enacted a federal anti-crime measure that the House of Representatives, Democrats in control, is having difficulty digesting.

Politics, says the *Charleston Daily Mail*, is at the root of the House resistance. That Democrats are reluctant during a presidential election year to enact a bill enthusiastically endorsed by President Reagan and his allies in Congress should surprise nobody.

On the other hand, no doubt about it, some sections of the anti-crime bill cause many people to gag. Death penalty provisions are controversial. Also changes in the exclusionary rule attributable to Supreme Court decisions trouble Americans who applaud constitutional barriers against highhanded police conduct.

Police everywhere criticize the exclusionary rule, insisting that too many scoundrels benefit because of it. Police argue that persons who commit serious crimes shouldn't be freed on technicalities which prevent clear evidence of guilt from being presented during a trial.

The Senate bill addresses this problem — or, perhaps it may be more appropriate to say, the bill tries to address the problem. The bill permits introduction of evidence that today couldn't be introduced, if the evidence was obtained by police acting in the good faith conviction that what they did was legal.

One nagging query: How does a jury, or a judge, determine that this officer acted in good faith while that one did not? What magic litmus test is provided in the Senate bill? If senators approving the bill were ever accused of a crime, would they in the subsequent trial want all t's crossed and all i's dotted by investigators? Or would senators be content to be tried under so elusive and so slippery a standard as acting in good faith?

Recognizing the penchant of some police to knock the whey out of victims, it is not beyond the realm of reason to think that unscrupulous police, of which the United States has too many, would exploit changes in the exclusionary rule and make America's system of justice even more unjust than it already is.

The *Mail* urges House passage of the bill. Maybe the *Mail* is correct. But one of its implied arguments is hogwash. The *Mail* intimates that if the bill becomes law, a welcome reduction in crime will occur. Anti-crime bills have scant impact on crime. What influences crime, especially serious crime, is the age of the population. Thus, in the next few years crime will decrease as the total of 16- to 27-year-olds in the population drops.

The Dallas Morning News

Dallas, TX, August 6, 1984

Three years and four months after he shot the president of the United States, John W. Hinckley Jr. has made a formal request to be released from the mental hospital where he has been confined.

Given the enormous public outrage when Hinckley was found not guilty by reason of insanity, and his three suicide attempts since he shot the president, his release isn't likely. But his request highlights the need for reform of the insanity defense.

As things stand, it is the prosecution's burden to prove sanity. The U.S. Senate's Comprehensive Crime Control Act, passed 91-1 but bottled up in the House Judiciary Committee, sensibly advocates shifting the burden of proof to the defense. To establish that the defendant was insane, the defense would have to show that he lacked the capacity to see the wrongness of his crime.

The present policy has perpetuated injustice and courtroom chaos, and the problems don't stop there. If mental-health professionals can determine insanity, it follows that they can also determine when a patient has regained sanity, and of course a free society cannot justly confine someone both sane and innocent.

The present process plainly makes a mockery of moral accountability. Reformers, keep pushing.

THE TENNESSEAN

Nashville, TN, February 12, 1984

NO matter how eager the U.S. Senate may be to appear tougher on crime, it ought to have been more thoughtful in its approach to legislation that it has approved

There were some relatively good aspects to the legislation, such as efforts to make sentencing more uniform and fair, to increase penalties for drug offenders, and to provide financial assistance for local law-enforcement programs, but there are some bad parts that seem to run headlong into constitutional guarantees.

For example it would approve "preventive detention" of unconvicted felons, if they are thought dangerous, on the flimsy basis of little more than their inability to prove they won't commit a crime if released. The principle has been such defendants be detained only when there is strong reason to believe that, if released, they would promptly flee.

Sometimes that has been accomplished by setting bail at a high figure, although the Eighth Amendment says that excessive bail shall not be required.

And, having thrown constitutional caution to the wind, the Senate then proceeded to turn around the "insanity defense." That defense now requires the prosecution to prove sanity on the part of the defendant. That can be, as some cases have proved, a tedious and difficult undertaking for the prosecution. So the Senate measure has simply reversed the burden to make the defense prove insanity.

It didn't stop there, but voted to limit the insanity defense to those unable to appreciate the nature or wrongfulness of their acts, which is a far more restrictive standard than under current law. That fails to recognize that there are mentally ill people who do comprehend right from wrong but may be driven by irresistible impulse to commit a murder or some other crime. What the bill would do is to remove distinctions about mental illness when crime is involved.

In a separate measure, the Senate has approved modification of the "exclusionary rule," which bars admission of evidence seized illegally. That rule was adopted by the Supreme Court in the early 1900s, so the courts could enforce Fourth Amendment protections against unreasonable searches and seizures. Originally that applied to federal criminal cases only, but the high court extended it to state and local courts in 1961.

The Senate bill would allow admission of improperly obtained evidence in federal criminal cases if law enforcement officials had a "reasonably good faith belief" they acted properly. That is opening the gate on opportunities for law enforcement to all but ignore the Fourth Amendment guarantees. Once a seizure of evidence is made, no matter under what circumstances, few if any law enforcement officers are going to admit they did not have a reasonably good faith belief they acted properly.

There was no reason for the Senate to act so hurriedly on the exclusionary rule in any case. The issue is likely to be decided by the Supreme Court, which has before it two pending cases where the "good faith" exception is the major issue.

The Senate has simply acted hastily amid its perception that the general public wants strengthened laws against crime. That may be a fairly accurate judgment, but that deliberative body should be the last to want laws that erode the constitutional guarantees that apply to all. The Senate-passed measures must now go to the House, where it is hoped lawmakers will take a more balanced view of the law and the Constitution.

The Salt Lake Tribune

Salt Lake City, UT, February 9, 1984

When the Senate votes 91-1 in favor of a tough new crime control statute it is easy to assume that the legislation is well on the way to swift enactment. But a key member of the House Judiciary Committee told the Associated Press this particular bill will be "dead on arrival" at the House.

That doesn't mean that everything in the Senate bill, including provisions for preventive detention of "dangerous" criminal suspects and abolishment of the federal parole system, will be lost. The House, it seems, doesn't like omnibus bills, which is what the Senate offering is despite the fact many of its more controversial original provisions were shaved off for individual treatment later.

There was a time not long ago when this newspaper denounced any tinkering with the Constitution's bail guarantees. We wonder still about the constitutionality of the proposed legislation's denial of bail to persons who may constitute a danger to the community but pose no danger of failing to appear for court proceedings.

Proponents of this practice say the crime control bill contains sufficient safeguards and that detention of dangerous suspects during the pretrial period will reduce the incidence of crime by suspects out on bail. We are not convinced it will work this way but the wisdom of denying bail to certain potentially dangerous individuals is difficult to deny.

It is much the same with other provisions of this still controversial — despite the 91-1 Senate approval — legislation. Creation of a commission to standardize sentencing by federal judges can be seen as an unnecessary restriction of the courts or as a more equitable and effective administration of justice.

Abolishing parole, it can be argued, is only getting the executive branch, which controls the federal parole procedure, out of the judges' wigs and giving the court final say in how long a prisoner serves.

We have never been attracted to any of these propositions in the past. But the inability of the judicial and corrections systems to stem crime under the more liberal existing concepts argues for trying sterner measures. The crime control bill passed by the Senate seems laced with sufficient safeguards against abuse. It offers an acceptable option to the flawed regulations now in place.

Minneapolis Star and Tribune

Minneapolis, MN, November 6, 1984

For more than a decade, lawmakers have strived to overhaul the federal criminal code. Last month they succeeded: A Senate eager to make an election-year display of fighting crime attached the Reagan administration's anticrime program to an emergency spending bill. The 365-page package includes some useful crime-fighting tools. But its utility is outweighed by repressive provisions.

The law overlooks some basic traditions in American justice. It prevents the parole of anyone jailed for committing a federal crime, thus denying the possibility of rehabilitation and ensuring further pressure in overcrowded prisons. It creates a new system of pretrial preventive detention that would punish without trial and violate the constitutional presumption of innocence before conviction. And the law allows the government to appeal some sentences it considers too lenient, thus contradicting the Fifth Amendment's protection against double jeopardy.

Some parts of the law give federal investigators broad new powers that could be used for political ends. One provision promises stiff penalties to any citizen who advises others to commit a violent crime — even if the advice is not followed. That provision could inhibit citizens' freedom to speak. Another part of the law expands federal authority for wiretapping without a warrant, conflicting with the Fourth Amendment prohibition against unreasonable search.

Use of the insanity defense is also curtailed. That change was apparently prompted by concern over the insanity acquittal of John Hinckley, the president's assailant. The insanity defense was flawed by the requirement that the prosecution prove a defendant sane — sometimes a nearly impossible task. That flaw could have been corrected by shifting the burden of proof and requiring the defense to prove insanity. Instead, the new law embraces the notion that a defendant should be judged insane only when he cannot distinguish right from wrong. But many mentally ill people who know right from wrong are nevertheless unable to control their actions. The law should not treat as criminals wrongdoers who suffer such severe disability.

The new law has the potential to do much good: It will help combat illegal drug traffic, spur a crackdown on computer theft, set useful sentencing guidelines and enable easier prosecution of money-laundering and kidnapping cases. But many short-sighted provisions restrict citizens' rights without doing much to stop crime. When the 99th Congress convenes, it should repeal the harmful elements of the new anticrime law.

THE DAILY OKLAHOMAN

Oklahoma City, OK, October 8, 1984

NO matter which party deserves the credit, the American public can be gratified that Congress finally has approved a package of legislation that should advance the war on crime in this country.

It will take time to sort out the details of what emerged in a compromise of House and Senate anti-crime measures. As far as can be determined, however, most of the provisions constitute a positive approach to correcting some long-standing deficiencies in law enforcement. While only federal statutes are involved, states often follow the government's lead.

One of the more important provisions authorizes a judge to hold without bail a defendant awaiting trial if the latter is determined to be a danger to the public. This is known as "preventive detention," and it has been bitterly opposed by liberals, who contend it is impossible to predict dangerousness. But cases are legion of criminals committing new crimes while free on bail from a previous charge.

Another desirable feature of the package calls for a new commission to establish guidelines that would ensure similar prison terms for people convicted of similar crimes. The objective is to reduce disparities among sentences handed down by federal judges in different parts of the country.

A significant change in the insanity defense is included. It would shift the burden of proof from the prosecution to the defense in cases such as that of John W. Hinckley Jr., who used the insanity plea successfully in his trial for the attempted assassination of President Reagan.

Stiffer penalties for convicted drug dealers and mandatory penalties for using firearms in a crime were also voted. Left out of the package were re-institution of the federal death penalty and modification of the exclusionary rule, but these omissions can be addressed in future legislation.

If both Ted Kennedy and Strom Thurmond can praise the package, it must be a good one.

The Union Leader

Manchester, NH, August 29, 1984

President Reagan has scored Congress repeatedly and justifiably for its failure to pass tough anti-crime legislation.

Last year, Congress approved a meagre $25 million for new prison construction — at a time when statistics clearly show ultimately $10 billion is needed to provide prison facilities to house more than 200,000 career criminals nationwide. The cost of incarcerating those criminals is, realistically, cheap at $10 billion, given the alternatives.

There is no question that prison construction is expensive, but crime is substantially more costly, particularly the crime perpetrated by career criminals.

But prisons alone are not the answer.

Congress also must enact measures like the Armed Career Criminal bill, mandating 15-year prison sentences for certain categories of repeat criminal offenders, the justice assistance bill to provide matching funds for anti-crime programs, the drug czar bill to coordinate federal drug enforcement efforts and the insanity defense reform bill, shifting the burden of proving insanity to the defendant.

The failure of Congress — and to an equal extent, state legislatures — to get tough on crime, to show criminals the public means business, insures those making a career of breaking the law and endangering law-abiding citizens they stand a better than average chance of getting away with it.

The criminal, today, clearly gets a better break than the victim. And that is a sorry commentary on American society.

The fault rests nowhere more than on Congress and elected state officials: If the public cannot have its lawmakers crack down on rampant crime with tough laws providing swift, certain punishment, then where can people turn? And why, pray tell, are legislators so reluctant to crack down on criminals?

With judges bending over backwards to protect criminals' rights, the least taxpayers can demand is that legislators compensate somewhat by providing tougher sentencing and more explicit statutes restraining judicial discretion.

President Reagan is correct to campaign hard against legislative laxity in cracking down on crime — and it is distressing he isn't getting more support, more activism instead of simple lip-service, from the rank-and-file citizens, whose rights he seeks to protect.

The Philadelphia Inquirer
Philadelphia, PA, October 27, 1984

Massive revisions in federal criminal statutes became law on Oct. 12 when President Reagan signed perhaps the most far-reaching overhaul of those laws in American history.

The package is diverse, including such matters as aircraft terrorism, missing children, victims' compensation, trademark counterfeiting, contract murders, computer theft and the use of firearms in federal offenses.

It includes measures that limit the insanity defense, make it easier to seize assets of organized crime and drug operators and increase penalties for drug dealers, repeat offenders and others.

Whether the legislation will reduce crime, as its adherents hope, or trample defendants' rights and increase prison overcrowding, as some critics assert, remains an unanswered question. There are more than 50 components in the package — far too many to clearly foresee all their long-range consequences, particularly since amendments were added in an 11th-hour compromise as the bill rushed toward passage in the hectic windup before Congress adjourned for the election.

It is the breadth of its sweep that causes concern. At the heart of the 635-page bill is the intent to make it easier for judges to imprison convicted criminals and dangerous defendants facing trial.

While few Americans argue the need for legislation that will control criminal behavior, some believe the new measure goes too far and poses a threat to individual liberties.

"It is fraudulent to claim that these measures which undermine fundamental constitutional liberties will reduce violent crime or make this a safer society," said Ira Glasser, executive director of the American Civil Liberties Union.

For the first time in peacetime history federal law explicitly authorizes detention without bail of allegedly dangerous defendants in cases other than murder and a few other crimes punishable by death.

This direction is a part of a trend that has led nearly two dozen states within the past decade to authorize judges to consider whether a defendant is a threat to others in deciding whether to release him or her on bail. The new law gives federal judges much broader powers to imprison defendants considered dangerous than do most state laws.

The preventive detention portion of the law is designed to reduce the number of crimes committed by repeat offenders free on bail. Civil libertarians insist, however, it will put innocent people behind bars without any significant reduction in crime.

Critics of the crime package further argue that the new system of preventive detenion should be unconstitutional. However, eyeing the growing conservatism of the Supreme Court, few would agree that inevitable constitutional challenges will be won.

There are, however, many positive laws contained in the package and overall it appears desirable. But as the complex measure is implemented, it needs to be examined carefully — plank by plank. Lawmakers and those whose responsibility it is to protect freedom and to increase community safety must determine with certainty that the new laws are prudent as well as protective of the nation's best and most enduring interests.

Birmingham Post-Herald
Birmingham, AL, September 29, 1984

There's nothing like an election to turn congressmen into crime fighters.

For months, an anti-crime package had been languishing in the House of Representatives. Then suddenly this week, the chamber approved it.

Why the switch? A major reason is that President Reagan made it a campaign issue.

In a July press conference, he accused the Democrat-controlled House of bottling up several pieces of legislation "that would benefit all Americans," including a crime-control bill approved 91-1 by the Senate last February. Since then, the president has returned to the subject several times.

The bill would make significant changes in federal criminal laws.

It would require defendants using the insanity defense to prove they were insane rather than requiring the prosecution to prove them sane.

It would allow federal courts to deny bail to criminal defendants if there is clear and convincing evidence that they pose a danger to society.

The measure would make it easier to confiscate the assets of persons convicted of racketeering or drug trafficking and would make it harder to move large amounts of cash out of the United States.

It would strengthen child pornography laws, and would create a commission to establish sentencing guidelines to make punishment more uniform for the same crimes.

All told, there are 46 provisions aimed at tilting the scales of justice more in favor of law-abiding citizens than of criminals.

There's one hooker in the House action. It attached the anti-crime package to a massive catchall spending bill, several provisions of which the White House opposes.

In addition to fearing political fallout if they voted against the crime-control amendment, some of those who supported it probably thought it would make the spending measure more veto-proof.

Senate-House conferees ought to eliminate the objectionable spending provisions before sending the final legislation to the president. It would be unfortunate if unnecessary spending was responsible for killing needed steps against crime.

THE MILWAUKEE JOURNAL
Milwaukee, WI, November 10, 1984

In its waning days, the 98th Congress passed a comprehensive crime-control act, which President Reagan signed. On balance, the new law is sensible, but there are some worrisome spots.

The act properly seeks to bring some uniformity to sentences for federal offenses. Hence, the measure establishes a commission to prepare sentencing guidelines. Once the guidelines are established, judges who depart from them would have to state in writing their reasons. We have urged similar provisions in Wisconsin law.

Also welcome are changes in bail procedures to permit pretrial detention of people deemed a danger to others or to the community. This is similar to Wisconsin's constitutional and statutory scheme, which has sought to replace the sub rosa pretrial detention system of high-money bail with a straightforward consideration of the critical issue of dangerousness.

The new law also significantly reforms the insanity defense in criminal cases. The burden of proving insanity is appropriately shifted to the defendant who raises the defense, and the defense is limited to those who are unable to appreciate the nature or wrongfulness of their acts. Trial courts will have to give careful guidance in applying the law, so that the defense can be used in proper cases.

In other key provisions, the legislation increases penalties for drug trafficking and labor racketeering. It sets up federal jurisdiction over murder-for-hire and solicitation to commit a crime of violence. It provides for criminal forfeitures in all drug felony cases and buttresses governmental authority to seize the profits from organized crime operations. The law also establishes a crime-victims' fund and sets a minimum mandatory prison sentence for use of a firearm in a federal crime of violence.

All of these initiatives are welcome. However, we question the law's reliance on determinate sentences (sometimes referred to as fixed or flat-time sentences), with foreclosure of the parole option. In some cases, such as particularly heinous crimes committed with firearms, mandatory minimum sentences can have a valid place. However, we fear that determinate sentencing will bring to the federal penal system the same problems of overcrowding and revolving-door stays that plague prisons in many states.

Of course, only time will tell whether the law will adequately meet the grave problem it addresses. On balance, however, Congress appears to have produced the best obtainable bill and has faced up to citizens' deep concern about crime. And the bipartisan support for the legislation may have reduced the potential for politicians to use the troubling issue of crime in demagogic appeals.

Legal Services Corp. Targeted in Reagan's Budget Proposals

President Ronald Reagan Dec. 5, 1984 gave his cabinet a fiscal 1986 budget draft that featured drastic spending cuts and even elimination of many politically popular programs. The president's preliminary plan would pare $34 billion from the 1986 budget. A further reduction of $8 billion would be sought, presumably from the defense budget, to reach a goal of reducing prospective massive federal deficits to about $100 billion by fiscal 1988. Among the popular programs the president proposed to eliminate was the Legal Services Corporation, the agency that provided legal assistance for poor people.

In a related move, Reagan had made 11 recess appointments Nov. 23 to the Legal Service Corporation's board of directors. The appointments were the same persons named previously to the board by the President but never confirmed by the Senate. By making recess appointments, when Congress was not in session, Reagan avoided the normal Senate confirmation process and the appointees could serve without such approval through the congressional session in 1985. Reagan had sought repeatedly to abolish the agency itself, but Congress had resisted the effort and his appointees were thought to share his philosophy to reduce or negate the agency's role. The current board had lacked enough directors to conduct business since October 1985, when previous recess appointments by Reagan of some of its members expired.

The latest appointments included Michael B. Wallace, a lawyer and former aide to Rep. Trent Lott (R, Miss.), whose name was sent to the full Senate without recommendation by the Senate Labor and Human Resources Committee. The committee had approved the other 10 nominees. The Senate, however, failed to act on any of the nominations.

Goaded by Reagan to put his fiscal 1986 budget to a vote, the Republican-controlled Senate Budget Committee did so March 13, 1985 and rejected the Reagan budget decisively, 17-4. The panel then struggled to round out its own budget plan, which would achieve savings of $55.1 billion in fiscal 1986—greater than those sought by the President—by slashing both military spending and a wide variety of domestic programs including the Legal Services Corp.

By 1988, Reagan had abandoned his effort to abolish the Legal Services Corp. In the $1.09 trillion budget he submitted Feb. 18, 1988 to Congress for the 1989 fiscal year, the President accepted the continued existence of the agency he had repeatedly attempted to delete earlier. But he called for an 18% reduction in its budget, to $250 million.

The Washington Post
Washington, DC, May 18, 1984

IF YOU'RE convicted of a crime because your attorney failed to call the one witness who could prove that you were 20 miles away when the dirty deed was done, can you win an appeal on grounds that your counsel was incompetent? Of course, said the Supreme Court this week, because there is a reasonable probability that if counsel had been on the ball you would have been acquitted. But if there were six eyewitnesses to the crime and you confessed as soon as the police came—but later changed your mind—will an appeals court reverse because your attorney was a recent law school graduate and you believe Edward Bennett Williams would have done a better job for you? Certainly not under the standard established by the court this week.

Two cases were decided dealing with the question of incompetence of counsel. The common question presented was whether an attorney's performance was so inadequate that the defendant was, for practical purposes, denied the effective assistance of counsel guaranteed by the Sixth Amendment. In an Oklahoma case, the appeals court had found that the circumstances surrounding the lawyer's representation—not enough time to prepare, inadequate trial experience and the complexity of the case—had made it impossible for him to present a competent defense. The Supreme Court reversed because there was no showing that the attorney made specific serious errors that would have changed the outcome of the trial.

A Florida case decided on the same day was more difficult because it resulted in a death penalty. Here, an experienced criminal lawyer was appointed to represent the defendant. Against the advice of his lawyer, the accused pleaded guilty to three aggravated murders, torture, kidnapping, severe assaults, attempted murders, attempted extortion and theft. Again, against the advice of his attorney, the defendant waived his right to an advisory jury at his sentencing hearing. After being sentenced to death, he sought reversal on the grounds that the lawyer did not provide adequate representation at the sentencing hearing. The justices found that the attorney's strategy was reasonable and that the facts were so overwhelmingly against the defendant that no attorney error was responsible for the outcome.

The standard established in these cases for reviewing attorney competence is a reasonable one. Cases will not be overturned if an advocate has provided "reasonably effective assistance" and if any errors would not have changed the outcome of the case. In capital cases, where incompetence of counsel is often alleged when other grounds for reversal have been rejected, there is a special obligation to review counsel's performance carefully. But this can be done, as even Justice Brennan, a firm opponent of the death penalty, found in the Florida case. The new guidelines, he wrote, "will go far toward assisting lower federal courts and state courts in discharging their constitutional duty to ensure that every criminal defendant receives the effective assistance of counsel guaranteed by the Sixth Amendment."

THE INDIANAPOLIS NEWS
Indianapolis, IN, November 6, 1984

Since its inception nearly two decades ago, the Legal Services Corp. and its affiliated agencies have repeatedly come under fire for straying into the area of social activism.

Most of the criticism has come from the political right. That was when local legal services organizations were waging class-action lawsuits against various government agencies, intervening in school desegregation suits and lobbying in the political arena.

Times have changed and the chickens have come home to roost.

Now the Legal Services Corp. is in the hands of Reaganite conservatives. It is the liberals' turn to squawk.

What they are squawking about are grants recently made by the corporation to aid causes or groups that are not so dear to the leftists.

One grant of $337,000 went to an organization known as the Constitutional Law Center, headed by James McClellan, a conservative legal scholar who has criticized federal court decisions expanding civil liberties in a number of areas.

McClellan, who recently complained that President Reagan had yet to abolish the Legal Services Corp., has been awarded the grant to provide advice on protecting the constitutional rights of the poor, according to LSC President Donald P. Bogard.

Another grant of $337,000 has been awarded to an Indianapolis group, the National Center for the Medically Dependent and Disabled, Inc., to assist in lawsuits on behalf of the rights of severely handicapped infants.

Two Democratic congressmen, Rep. Barney Frank, D-Mass., and Rep. Bruce A. Morrison, D-Conn., have called for a congressional review of the grants. They say Bogard failed to follow proper procedures in awarding the grants, but their main criticism seems to be that LSC is granting money "to organizations that do not serve poor people."

One is tempted to trot out the adage: "What is good for the goose is good for the gander."

But, this nation is faced with a ruinous federal deficit.

The LSC should stick to its original mission of providing legal counsel for those who genuinely do not have access to private sector attorneys. It should cease funding social activism, whether of the left or the right.

The Hartford Courant

Hartford, CT, November 27, 1984

U.S. Sen. Thomas F. Eagleton of Missouri once observed that there are three ways available to a president to kill a program, and that President Reagan had tried them all to phase out the Legal Services Corporation.

The president tried to abolish the program outright, but was stopped by Congress. He tried to fund it at such a low level that it would be inoperative, but Congress only cut the program by 25 percent in 1981 and has since restored some of the money. And he tried to put the management of the program into unfriendly hands, but Congress legislatively tied those hands to limit the damage they could do.

The president, frustrated by Congress' lack of full cooperation, last week appointed 11 people to the corporation's board of directors who had previously failed to obtain Senate confirmation. Since the appointments came during a congressional recess, the members can serve through most of the next session without confirmation.

The corporation provides money and oversight to more than 300 locally administered legal aid programs and support groups; their job is to represent poor people only in civil cases. Anyone not committed to the idea of equal justice for poor people doesn't belong on its board of directors.

The suitability of two of the appointees, in particular, is questionable.

One of them — opposed by Sen. Eagleton — is Michael B. Wallace, a former congressional aide who has advocated tax exemptions for segregated private schools and has worked against legislation to broaden the Voting Rights Act. The other is LeeAnne Bernstein, a corporation staff member whom Mr. Eagleton has accused of trying to dampen public participation in its meetings.

The timing of the appointments was indefensible, though one of the president's aides tried to defend it as necessary because "the board needs to be an active force to operate, and this is the most efficient way."

If the president wanted an "active force" on the board, he would have waited for Congress to convene in January and submit the names of 11 people for confirmation by the Republican-controlled Senate. The authority of unconfirmed "recess appointees" was sharply restricted by Congress, which was justifiably concerned that they would start dismantling legal aid programs out of favor with the administration.

Mr. Reagan has been fighting what he viewed as activist legal aid lawyers since his days as governor of California. A president is expected to implement all the laws, not only the ones he likes. If Mr. Reagan wants to undo Legal Aid, he can try again to persuade Congress to abolish it. If Congress isn't persuaded, the answer isn't sabotage by the executive branch, but compliance with what's required.

The News and Courier

Charleston, SC, November 30, 1984

It sticks in the craw of many advocates of federal help for the poor that President Reagan keeps filling the board of Legal Services' Corporation with interim appointees. What is happening is that the president submits names to the Senate for confirmation and the Senate refuses to act. Mr. Reagan then uses his lawful authority to make "recess appointments" good for a year, thus executing an end run that leaves enthusiasts for Legal Services angry and frustrated.

Though there has been much talk about this kind of behavior thwarting the intent of Congress with respect to Legal Services, the most that seems to us to have been proved is that Mr. Reagan's appointees don't have their hearts in the job.

No surprise there, we would think. Legal Services has had more than a fair chance to do what it was supposed to do and it has failed miserably. The Congress intended it as a government agency that could dispatch lawyers to the aid of those too poor to hire their own. That went down pretty well with the country, though there were those like us, who feared that it was a mission wide open to abuse.

In due time the abuse materialized. Lawyers employed by Legal Services got bored with the prosaic work of helping the poor They looked for new worlds to conquer. First thing anybody knew, some of the biggest thorns in the side of government were government-paid lawyers from Legal Services. It was the way that Legal Services actually operated — suing the taxpayers at the drop of a hat — rather than how it was supposed to operate — assisting the poor — that got it in trouble with Mr. Reagan and other people.

So the situation which has Mr. Reagan loading up Legal Services' board with people he can count on to restrain all those maverick lawyers, is pretty much of Legal Services' own making. And the situation in which the president uses his powers to appoint people Congress might not want for longer than Congress might like to see them around is of Congress' own making. The power of appointment offers a constitutional balance. Mr. Reagan has done his part to strike a balance by submitting names to the Senate. When the Senate fails to act, it neglects its part. For the resulting imbalance, if any, don't blame the president.

The Philadelphia Inquirer

Philadelphia, PA, August 14, 1984

Providing free legal service to the poor is not a well-known characteristic of the proverbial Philadelphia lawyer. But the Philadelphia Bar Association established one of the first volunteer pro bono programs in the nation.

Now it is dismaying to learn that bar association officials have reduced efforts to get lawyers to take on indigent clients at a time when the need is the greatest and while many other bar associations in the nation are increasing their involvement.

The need for the legal profession to provide more pro bono service has come as a direct result of the Reagan administration's drastic cuts in federal funding of legal service agencies for the poor. Community Legal Services, the primary agency that provides legal aid for the poor in Philadelphia, has had to close three offices and cut its staff in half because of a 25-percent reduction in federal support.

The bar association might have been counted upon to pick up the slack, but as Inquirer staff writer Henry Goldman reported last week, the number of cases referred to lawyers under the association's volunteer program has dropped from 701 last year to 145 for the first six months of this year. Thus, literally hundreds of indigent Philadelphians are being denied legal aid, particularly in such matters as divorce, custody, child support, unemployment compensation and mortgage foreclosures.

The reduction in pro bono work, according to Kenneth Shear, executive director of the bar association, is due to a number of factors, including the attitude of lawyers. Many lawyers provide pro bono work to segments of the community other than poor people. Mr. Shear also cited the fact that the Philadelphia Bar Association has less leverage on lawyers than do associations in other states where membership is a prerequisite for licensing.

Mr. Shear and other bar officials contend that the other local bar associations, some of which are just beginning volunteer programs will soon find that such efforts, no matter how successful, will not meet the need. They are correct. Nonetheless, that is no reason for the Philadelphia Bar Association not to try harder. It is not an either-or situation. Both private sector efforts like the pro bono volunteer programs and increased federal spending are needed.

In any case, the Pennsylvania Supreme Court has the power to raise funds from the legal profession and establish programs targeted for legal aid for the indigent. It should use it.

ST. LOUIS POST-DISPATCH

St. Louis, MO,
November 30, 1984

Despite rebuffs from Congress and the courts, President Reagan is still trying to undermine the Legal Services Corp., the agency that dispenses federal funds for legal aid to the poor in noncriminal cases. Again bypassing the Senate, Mr. Reagan the other day used recess appointments to put people on the LSC board who are known to be hostile to LSC cases. Only once (in 1983) during his tenure has Mr. Reagan submitted to the Senate a full slate of 11 nominees for the LSC board. The LSC has been overseen during the Reagan term by unconfirmed directors unsympathetic to its mission but able to hold office because they were recess appointees, most of them named while Congress was not in session and thus not subject to Senate confirmation.

This year a federal judge blocked an attempt by Reagan LSC nominees to shut down four legal services training centers. And the Senate, reflecting dissatisfaction with the 1983 nominees, never acted on them. Now Mr. Reagan has given recess appointments to some of the same people. One is Michael Wallace, a former aide to Republican Rep. Trent Lott of Mississippi. He was criticized for organizing opposition to extension of the Voting Rights Act and for devising the administration's scheme to confer tax-exempt status on private segregated schools. He was also criticized for helping to bar federal safety inspectors from Mississippi jails, in one of which 27 inmates later died in a fire fed by flammable material that didn't meet safety standards. LSC lawyers have brought voting rights and prisoners' rights suits.

Another of the renominated directors is Robert Valois, a lawyer reported to be involved in keeping poorly paid textile workers out of unions; a third is LeAnne Bernstein, criticized for her efforts as board secretary to keep LSC business as non-public as possible. The Senate should call on Mr. Reagan to carry out the law by putting the LSC under people who believe in its mission of helping the poor.

THE ATLANTA CONSTITUTION

Atlanta, GA, May 11, 1984

Frustrated so far in its attempts to kill the Legal Services Corp. outright — through dollar cutbacks and the stacking of its board with conservatives — the Reagan administration is now trying the silent treatment.

This is perhaps the most insidious attack of all on the federal agency that was established to provide legal help for the poor

Many of the agency's decisions could be made in secret, under proposed changes in its bylaws — changes that were themselves cloaked in secrecy until their publication in a recent Federal Register.

And no wonder. Had these changes been aired at a public meeting, as required by law, they would have brought down the immediate fury of anti-poverty watchdog groups. As it is, the Coalition for Legal Services, the National Legal Aid and Defender Association and other groups are scurrying to lodge their protests before the May 18 deadline for public comments.

In its zeal to disarm poor people of their access to the courts, those groups complain, the administration not only violates the sunshine law (which requires that all official government business be conducted in public); it broadcasts its intention to keep on doing so with impunity.

That would be the effect of the bylaw changes restricting access to its meetings.

One would require individuals who want to address a meeting to make a written request in advance, with no assurance that they will be recognized. Others would allow the board to hold meetings by telephone, and to act without meeting, if the members agree in writing. The board could even adjourn a public meeting and reconvene elsewhere, limiting the number of people at the second meeting, if in its judgment the first was hampered "by the acts or conduct of any members of the public."

These would seem dangerously evasive tactics even if the agency had an unblemished record under Reagan. It does not. On the contrary, it has displayed a rare eagerness for conducting its dirty work in private.

The five interim appointees who make up the Legal Services board, some of them outspoken foes of the program they oversee, have too often held controversial meetings in out-of-the-way spots. Last month, for example, they moved such a meeting from Washington, D.C., to remote Window Rock, Ariz. — on only eight days' notice; then they adjourned without recognizing seven of the eight people who asked to be heard.

It was precisely to avoid such chicanery that sunshine laws were established — and to safeguard the public interest that the proposed changes should be withdrawn.

Atlanta, GA, November 28, 1984

While President Reagan relaxed by burning brush on his ranch last week, his aides made a quiet announcement: The administration has appointed 11 people to the board of directors of the Legal Services Corp. With that, the president has reaffirmed one of the enduring travesties of his administration.

He wants to abolish federal legal help for the poor and throw such agencies as Legal Services Corp. into a bureaucratic brushfire. He hasn't had his way yet, but he has managed to create a thick smoke screen.

The administration would have us believe that government has no business in legal aid. That is plain wrong. The Legal Services Corp. — which typically represents the poor in disputes with landlords, creditors and the like — ensures that our legal system works for all. If the corporation were abolished, civil-court clout would be politely returned to the wealthy. Issues of right and wrong would be mooted.

The Reaganites protest that legal aid stirs up the poor with political agitation. Perhaps it *can* be said that government should not use tax dollars to whip up political froth. Perhaps there have been abuses.

But that is no reason to abolish the program. (Does anyone want to abolish the military for its legendary excesses?) And just what does the administration call political agitation? Does that include inmate lawsuits to require jails and prisons to meet constitutional standards? If so, we need more.

Part of the fuss now is because Reagan made his appointments while Congress is out of session. Recess appointments allow nominees to sidestep Senate confirmation. Indignation over this device is misplaced. It has been used since the time of George Washington on behalf of causes good and evil.

For indignation, consider some of the nominees. Michael B. Wallace is reported to have engineered that reprehensible plan to give tax advantages to segregated private schools. He is also rumored to have opposed extension of the Voting Rights Act. LeaAnne Bernstein, a lawyer who formerly served as secretary to the board, is said to have kept the board's business as secret as possible.

They're swell choices. In a now-familiar pattern, they will play Carrie Nation as the Legal Services Corp. stands in as the saloon. While this act grinds on, the nation's poor might be forgiven for wondering why government has turned against them.

The Des Moines Register

Des Moines, IA, December 4, 1984

The standoff between President Reagan and Congress over the Legal Services Corp. continues. Reagan last week gave recess appointments to a full board of directors of 11 members, because the appointments he made earlier this year were not acted upon by the Senate, so their nominations died. The recess appointees may serve, unconfirmed, until Congress acts on the nominations.

Among the 11 was — for the second time — Michael B. Wallace, who was instrumental in getting tax exemptions for racially discriminatory private schools, an effort shot down by the Supreme Court. Wallace never will be confirmed, so by renominating him Reagan is simply thumbing his nose at Congress.

The president wants to eliminate Legal Services — his critics say because it helped California migrant workers in their struggle against fruit and vegetable growers who were supporters of Reagan when he was governor. Reagan says LSC has gone beyond its proper function of providing legal aid to needy people and has done improper lobbying.

Congress has had some misgivings on this point, too, and when it approved the fiscal 1984 LSC appropriation it included restrictions on lobbying. However, it has refused to kill the agency, as Reagan wishes it would; and since 1981 it has refused to confirm any of his appointees to the board, believing them — with good reason — to be people who would undermine LSC programs.

For that reason, Reagan has continued to circumvent the nomination process by making recess appointments. This is a dreadful way to run an agency.

The president ought to recognize that Congress is not going to kill LSC, so he should nominate people who would administer it properly, people he has reason to believe would be confirmed. If he does that, the Senate also ought to bury the hatchet and confirm a board to serve a full term. This foolishness has gone on too long.

THE KANSAS CITY STAR

Kansas City, MO, November 30, 1984

The persistence of the administration in trying to immobilize the Legal Services Corporation is demonstrated again in President Reagan's appointment of an interim board to oversee the legal assistance program for the poor. Left to his own design, the president would have abolished the congressionally created organization long ago.

In recent days the president used his authority to make so-called recess appointments to provide the directors with a quorum. That had been impossible to have since the terms of four previous recess appointees expired in October. The president, by naming board members while Congress is not in session, avoids having to have them confirmed by the Senate. One of 11 of his recess appointments was rejected by a Senate committee this year. His recent appointees may serve without Senate confirmation until Congress quits work next year.

Thus Mr. Reagan uses this otherwise legitimate procedure in a Machiavellian way to circumvent rejection of his nominees by the Senate. Several have been previously rejected because some senators contended they appeared unqualified.

Most of the 11 recently named recess appointees either have demonstrated hostility to the program or have shown little or no prior interest in legal help for the poor. This is a potentially destructive combination because the activists are free to pursue damaging actions while other members would appear to lack knowledge sufficient to stop them, even if they were so inclined.

Congressional supporters of legal aid became so alarmed by the president's attempts to eradicate the program that Congress adopted a rider to prevent the board from cutting off funds for its various segments. That hasn't stopped board members from trying, however, though the amendment has prohibited great harm.

The administration's attack, while not always successful, nonetheless has set back legal counsel for the poor. Before Mr. Reagan became president this nation had reached what was considered to be a minimum service level with two legal aid lawyers for every 10,000 poor persons. The ratio in the private sector is far fewer clients for each lawyer. Since then the funding has been slashed.

By now advocates of the concept that poor people deserve a fair day in court should be under no illusions. The administration of President Reagan is out to eliminate the Legal Services Corporation, in every way, at every turn. If successful, it could have devastating consequences for the poor and our system of justice.

Newsday

Long Island, NY, February 20, 1984

Of all the agencies President Reagan marked for budget cuts when he took office, none has been in greater jeopardy than the Legal Services Corp., which provides lawyers for poor people. The President wants nothing short of its total extinction.

Three times Congress has refused to oblige, but funding for the corporation has dropped steadily since 1981. Now Reagan proposes to reduce it from this year's $275 million to $20 million in fiscal 1985 — a 92 per cent cut that would barely leave enough for Legal Services to phase itself out of existence.

By packing the corporation's board with directors hostile to its programs, Reagan has already succeeded in restricting the kinds of help local legal-aid offices may provide and the clients they may serve.

The corporation is now run by a board of recess appointees. The latest two were named just before Congress returned from its Christmas recess, to avoid the necessity for Senate confirmation. This practice mocks the spirit of the constitutional provision that high-level presidential appointments are to be made with the Senate's advice and consent.

A survey by the Washington Council of Lawyers last November found that the quality of legal assistance for the poor had dropped dramatically in the previous two years. Most local programs had failed to replace lost federal funds from private, state or local sources. By now, more than one-fourth of all legal-aid lawyers have been laid off.

There's no way the private bar can pick up the slack. And it's neither feasible nor fair to assign law students to represent the poor, as Edwin Meese, presidential counselor and Reagan's nominee for attorney general, has proposed.

Congress will surely refuse again to kill the program. But it should also reassert itself in confirming board members and establishing policies.

Justice Dept. Report Claims '84 Drop;

The Justice Department April 7, 1985 said the number of all U.S. crimes together had fallen by 4.5% in 1984, but that violent crime had not shared in the decline. The statements came in a report, based on a sample of some 125,000 people, issued by the department's Bureau of Justice Statistics. The report said that in all there had been 35.3 million crime "victimizations" in 1984, compared with 37 million in 1983. The bureau's director, Steven R. Schlesinger, said the fall had several explanations, including changes in criminal sentencing and the dwindling population aged 14 to 24, considered the age group most likely to commit crimes.

Among the report's findings:

■ The violent crime rate was 31 per 1,000 people, roughly the same as that for 1983.

■ One person out of every 1,000 was raped, a 19.9% rise over 1983.

■ Household burglaries dropped 11.3% while household larcenies fell 7.1%. Larcenies did not require illegal entry.

■ Personal larceny took place at a rate of 72.8 per 1,000, down from 76.9 per 1,000 the year before.

Serious crime across the nation had dropped by 2% in 1984 according to the FBI's annual survey, "Crime in the United States," released July 28, 1985. The decline was the third in three years, with 11.8 million crimes reported. The last time that figure had fallen below 12 million was in 1978. But violent crime had still risen by 1% in 1984 and rape by 7%. The Justice Department criticized the bureau figures as inaccurate.

The Eisenhower Foundation March 3, 1985 issued a report calling the U.S. crime rate "astronomical." It characterized street crime as "a form of slow rioting" brought on by economic suffering. The report claimed that crime "deterrence during the 1970s through more efficient police, courts and prisons did not work, in part because these agencies can merely react to crime, not prevent it." The foundation, a nongovernment body, had been established to continue the work of the late President Lyndon B. Johnson's National Commission on the Causes and Prevention of Violence, which had been headed by Milton Eisenhower. The Ford Foundation paid for the new study.

DESERET NEWS

Salt Lake City, UT, March 5-6, 1985

Crime rates are down slightly in the past two years, but the public fear of crime remains high — and with good reason. Consider these statistics:

● One in three U.S. households is touched by major crime in any year.

● Violence by youthful offenders in urban areas appears to be more frequent and serious than in the 1960s.

● The level of crime in the U.S. is astronomical when compared with that of other industrialized democracies.

● A survey of prison inmates showed that 28 percent commit new crimes while out on probation or parole for earlier lawbreaking.

Such figures seem to argue for tougher treatment of criminals and for harsher and longer sentences. But the Eisenhower Foundation, which this week released a comprehensive study on crime, indicated the U.S. already has moved far in that direction.

American imprisonment rates already "are higher than those of all other industrial countries, with the possible exception of . . . South Africa and the Soviet Union."

That's not exactly the most admirable company for the world's biggest democracy to be keeping. What is wrong with American society?

If putting more people behind bars longer isn't the answer, yet many crimes are committed while lawbreakers are free on parole, what is to be done? Obviously the problem has to be attacked on a broad front, including more than the criminal justice system.

As the Eisenhower Foundation report noted, there must be a strengthening of family ties, although just how that is to be accomplished in a society that seems to be trying to pull the family apart was not suggested. Other needs cited in the report included stronger neighborhoods and more jobs for young people.

One difficulty in dealing with crime is the fact that many questions remain unanswered. For example, the foundation study found that about half of those who are imprisoned and then released don't commit more crimes. Why don't they return? There simply hasn't been much research on that.

Certainly, the drug problem is one of the root causes of crime, but attacking drug smuggling and dealing is going to take more effort and resources than have been given so far.

If coping with crime is to be effective — and not just degenerate into an armed struggle between victims and lawbreakers — the nation has to be galvinized into action.

What is needed is a stirring call like the one the National Commission on Excellence in Education provided for schools. The response to that study has been little short of revolutionary.

President Reagan should move quickly to appoint such a commission — one that can rouse the nation into head-on confrontation with crime and punishment.

TULSA WORLD

Tulsa, OK, March 5, 1985

A NEW study from the Eisenhower Foundation says public fear of crime is as great as it was in the 1960s, the modern apex of violence in the U. S.

Why more public anxiety at a time when the number of serious crimes seems to be declining? Well, for one thing the U.S. crime rate is still "astronomical" compared to that of other industrialized democracies, says the Foundation report.

The report might have added that the public perception is that crime often goes unpunished. Even when criminals go to prison, they are often released after brief confinement to return to crime.

The Bureau of Justice Statistics reports that 61 percent of criminals admitted to prisons in 1979 had already served time for previous convictions.

And, 28 percent entering prison in 1979 would never have been on the streets to commit subsequent crimes had they served the maximum sentence imposed on the first offense.

But all over the nation the public is reluctant to vote tax dollars to build ever larger prisons.

Putting the cost of more prisons aside, there is a move toward less reliance on paroles. The Comprehensive Crime Control Act of 1984 will lead to an end of parole for federal offenders by 1986.

That reflects the desires of the public, which other surveys show is in favor of longer terms and less parole.

"There is a growing body of knowledge about criminal careers and the likelihood that many offenders will continue to commit crimes after they are released from prison," said the Justice study.

The dilemma for the public is growing very clear. Either bear the huge costs of imprisoning offenders for longer periods of time or be prepared to suffer more crime at the hands of those released before their sentences expire.

CHARLESTON EVENING POST
Charleston, SC, August 6, 1985

In 1984 overall crime in America decreased for the third consecutive year, according to the FBI's annual report. Violent crime, as a whole, rose 1 percent, however. The specific crime said to have increased most in incidence was forcible rape — up 7 percent. The statistic conveys encouraging news as well as disturbing news.

It is encouraging that officials in such organizations as People Against Rape attribute the increase to more reporting of sexual assaults, rather than to more offenses. Two factors apparently contribute to the growing willingness of victims to report rapes. One is the establishment of more crisis centers (South Carolina alone now has 15), which provide not only treatment for rape victims, but support by professionals and trained volunteers who understand the traumatic effects of the crime. The other factor is that today's criminal justice system is viewed as more receptive to rape victims than yesterday's system — thanks in part to enactment in several states of victims' rights laws.

Such progressive actions have served to remove the stigma once wrongly attached to so many victims of criminal sexual assault. Victims no longer feel impelled to remain silent. Their readiness to report rape and provide information for police investigations increases the likelihood of arrests and convictions. FBI figures support that conclusion: Arrests for forcible rape increased 8 percent nationwide in 1984.

Even so, the total number of forcible rapes reported in 1984 — more than 84,000 — is disturbing. It should send women a warning. It should remind those statistically more at risk — singles in the 16-to-25 age group — to take sensible precautions, day and night.

The Miami Herald
Miami, FL, August 14, 1985

MORALE is a primary weapon in fighting crime, and the Miami area's arsenal seemed depleted last week: FBI crime statistics for 1984 revealed that Dade County suffered the nation's worst murder rate and the nation's second-worst rate of general serious crime. Highway robbers on Interstate 95 added to the community's sense of siege and abandonment. That feeling of isolation is especially corrosive in Dade because the community has been so mistreated by the Federal Government in the Mariel affair.

Folks who have pulled their wagons in a circle need to hear the bugles of the cavalry from across the hill, and on Saturday Gov. Bob Graham provided that needed reassurance. "We simply cannot and should not and will not accept living in fear in this great paradise of ours," he said. The governor also brought welcome reinforcements in the form of 40 additional Florida Highway Patrol troopers to police I-95. That number should drive the thieves and thugs down onto city streets, where Miami and Metro police should be waiting with their own decoy patrols.

Permanent security on I-95 requires proper fencing and lighting in addition to police presence, of course. It's wasteful to let a handful of thieves indefinitely tie down 40 patrolmen, but the governor must keep the troopers in place until the highway is under control.

Similarly, the state must continue its pressure on the Government with respect to Mariel criminals. Over the weekend the Administration announced, then quickly rescinded, a new policy of releasing some Mariel offenders who have completed their terms in state prison. The stalemate over these undesirable entrants thus continues.

Neither state nor Federal government Constitutionally may hold prisoners simply because they are foreigners: If they've served their sentences and would be released if they were U.S. citizens, they cannot be held indefinitely. But the Reagan Administration's lame excuse that it "can't" deport convicted felons to Cuba is shameful. Foreign criminals who are ordered by U.S. courts to be deported must be sent back — by whatever means necessary, and with or without Fidel Castro's consent.

Fidel Castro isn't solely responsible for Dade crime, however. Local residents buy the handguns that escalate so many domestic quarrels to homicide. And local neighborhoods produce the unsupervised children who become the petty thieves, then the drug-using muggers, burglars, and armed robbers that plague the community. And South Floridians themselves tolerate the drug use and easy money that cause so much of their crime.

All these factors must be addressed in order for Dade to recapture momentum toward normal life. The heartening effect of the state response, visible on the interstate, now must be capitalized into a broad-spectrum community commitment to make Dade County once again a safe, secure place in which to live and conduct business.

THE CHRISTIAN SCIENCE MONITOR
Boston, MA, August 28, 1985

CONCERNS continue to grow about the reliability of statistics on serious crime across the United States. The shadows do not eclipse the good news — in 1984 serious crime declined for the third straight year, according to figures collected by the Federal Bureau of Investigation. Yet considerable improvement is required in the reliability of these statistics so that Americans can know the accurate nationwide crime picture.

Further, more accuracy in other areas by police departments across the United States could be expected to increase the percentage of crimes actually solved.

This, then, is no time for complacency. The US can do better still in its struggle against serious crime.

The 1984 figures should be viewed in perspective. Never before in the 25-year collection of such statistics had serious crime fallen three straight years. Yet it was falling from its historic high, and the US figures are considerably above those of other developed Western nations.

Disagreement exists as to why serious US crime has turned down. Some say it is because fewer Americans now are in their so-called crime-prone years, the late teens and early 20s. Others argue that the downturn stems from the more forceful ways that law-enforcement and judicial systems deal with offenders today. Very likely a combination is responsible.

The FBI's nationwide figures are a compilation of statistics provided by local law-enforcement agencies. A US Justice Department study group recently noted that the accuracy of statistics provided the FBI is believed to vary widely. In addition to the mistakes that derive from sloppy procedures, some communities are believed to deliberately report fewer crimes than occurred in order to improve their own images.

The Justice Department is in the process of proposing that these figures be made more accurate by requiring local agencies, especially in sizable cities, to provide more detailed reports of crimes. It also would require stricter auditing procedures of these agencies in an effort to make their reports more accurate. The aim of the changes is laudable.

The FBI finds major deficiencies in the accuracy of other information furnished by some local and state law-enforcement agencies. The FBI estimates that these agencies file at least 12,000 incorrect reports every day about criminal suspects whose arrests are sought. In addition, the FBI says, on an average day there are inaccuracies with some 7,000 reports of stolen vehicles or license plates.

Americans need not accept the inevitability of such a large number of errors. In recent years the level of professionalism in law-enforcement agencies has risen substantially, but many communities have yet a way to go. State and local agencies can meet higher standards of accuracy and should be expected to. As they succeed in meeting higher standards, they will also be solving an increased percentage of crimes; further, the potential for invading the privacy and freedom of the innocent will decline.

Individuals, too, have responsibilities for dealing with the concept of crime, beyond the ethical requirement that as citizens they cooperate with law-enforcement agencies and notify them of suspicious activities. Whereas it is wise to be prudent, it is not helpful to be fearful. Individuals must deal with the crime issue in their own thinking and realize that their protection ultimately lies in a higher power than the police.

The Miami Herald

Miami, FL, July 31, 1985

NO MATTER which way you slice the FBI's 1984 crime statistics, the news is devastating. The city of Miami has the third-highest murder rate of any U.S. municipality for the second year in a row, down from first in 1981. Dade County overall, meanwhile, posted the worst homicide rate of any metropolitan area in the nation, with 23.7 murders per 100,000 residents — three times the national average. Within Miami's city boundaries the rate was 42.2 per 100,000.

Perhaps even more frightening than the murder rate was the incidence of general violent crime. Dade was exceeded only by metropolitan Atlantic City, N.J., in its combined rate of murder, rape, robbery, aggravated assault, burglary, larceny, and auto theft.

No quick fix is evident. The 1984 numbers come in spite of the addition of hundreds of police officers and hundreds of detention beds since the crime-wave panic of 1981. They come in spite of minimum-mandatory sentencing laws, in spite of the resumption in 1979 of state executions, in spite of unprecedented investment in security systems and defensive weapons.

A few high-visibility crimes are amenable to quick action. The resumed banditry on Interstate 95 is one. Police presence and the building of proper barriers can and should stop that particular outrage.

But the I-95 jackals will simply move to other streets. That may be better than having them on the interstate, but it is hardly a solution. Solutions require a far more sophisticated analysis of the problem than the community yet has made. That analysis is essential to the tailoring of an effective, long-range community response to the disheartening statistics.

More police officers on the street might help in some areas and for some kinds of crime, but they cannot constitute the entire remedy.

To forge a comprehensive anti-crime package the community must know:

● Exactly how many crimes are related to drug trafficking.

● How much of the crime is domestic, and how that violence relates to family breakdown, unemployment, and other social factors.

● What crimes stem from local consumption of drugs and alcohol.

● Which crimes are specialties of youthful offenders and which are the province of older career professionals.

● The role of repeat offenders and probation violators.

● To what extent Dade crime still reflects the Mariel boatlift of 1980.

● How crime is apportioned among the community's various ethnic and racial groups, with respect both to victims and to perpetrators.

● Whether a proliferation of firearms, especially handguns, correlates to the increase in murder and other firearms crimes.

Other valid questions abound, but these few are among the most obvious.

All violent crimes are serious. But not all respond equally to the same official reaction. The Dade County Commission, the several city commissions, and the entire civic and social force of the community must be brought into the fight against crime. But before they can be effective, they must know the enemy. For that they need detailed and local information that can form the basis of specific and appropriate local responses.

Herald News

Fall River, MA, July 19, 1985

Statistics about crime can be somewhat depressing.

The Bureau of Justice Statistics used 1982 as a sample year to find out what is happening to criminals in our penal system

The Bureau learned, for instance, that about half of the nation's convicted murderers are paroled after serving an average of five years and nine months of their sentences.

A majority of the convicted rapists are paroled after serving three years or less.

In themselves, these figures are disturbing, but they become even more so when the Bureau also points out that 84 percent of the persons jailed in 1979 were repeat offenders.

Just as striking is the fact that one-fifth of the crimes of violence committed in any one year are committed by recidivists.

All these figures suggest that there has been widespread abuse of the parole system, not in any sense of personal corruption by parole boards, but simply because the system is weighted in favor of the criminal.

There must be a way of keeping persons convicted of crimes of violence behind bars for longer periods of time than is the habit at present.

Many states including this one are tightening up the procedures leading to the granting of parole.

No one can dispute that some convicts who are seriously repentant will be the losers when parole becomes harder to get, but at the same time many others who are simply waiting for an opportunity to return to a life of crime will be out of harm's way for a longer period of time.

Exploiters of the parole system have done immeasurable harm over the years.

They are the recidivists who are shipped back to prison after each fresh eruption of criminal activity.

In reality, they are sociopaths who take out their indifference or hostility to the world at large in acts of violence committed on helpless individuals.

Society deserves more protection against them than it has been receiving.

The Bureau of Justice Statistics has done us all a service by publishing the facts about the way in which persons who have been convicted of acts of violence are paroled after relatively brief periods of imprisonment.

Equally revealing are the figures about the number of persons who go on committing serious crimes all their life long and whose normal habitat is really a prison.

Finally society must face the implications of having a small but deadly mimority in its midst of people who are habitually criminal.

They should not be eligible for release by the ordinary processes of parole.

They should only be released on completion of their full sentences, and then only with the understanding on the part of penal authorities that they will be back again behind bars in a relatively short time.

The Dispatch

Columbus, OH, August 5, 1985

The ups and downs of the U.S. crime rate suggest the proverbial good-news, bad-news scenario: Crime in the nation is down 2 percent, but in Columbus it's up 4.2 percent. All this is according to Uniform Crime Report figures for 1984 released by the FBI.

Crime index offenses reported by 16,000 law enforcement agencies covering 96 percent of the nation's population totaled 11,881,800, the first time since 1978 that the number was less than 12 million.

Last year was the third straight for which a decline in the overall crime rate was reported.

But two important qualifiers ought to be noted:

● These data reflect *reported* crimes only. The actual level usually is higher and can be affected by a number of variables. In some jurisdictions, where victims of lesser crimes are required to file reports at the precinct houses, some decline to do so. Fear of police, particularly among immigrant populations, sometimes discourages the reporting of crime. Other crime victims doubt the effectiveness of the criminal justice system and consider filing a report a waste of time. In a few cases, police departments have overused the "unfounded" label in closing legitimate cases in order to protect their image and the political perception of their effectiveness.

● While the national crime rate is down, specific categories of offenses have shown increases.

And what about Columbus?

The 4.2 percent rise in local crime was in large part due to increases in the number of rapes (21.6 percent or 394 incidents compared with 324 the previous year) and aggravated assaults (14.8 percent). Non-vehicle thefts and vehicle thefts also were up about 7 percent each.

At the same time, the murder rate declined 16.2 percent from 74 homicides in 1983 to 62 last year, the number of arsons was down 27.9 percent, robberies were down 4.5 percent and burglaries were down very slightly.

Columbus Safety Director Alphonso C. Montgomery assures that figures so far this year suggest there will be "a downward trend" in local crime.

While the FBI figures show crime is down 2 percent nationally, regional figures show declines of 5 percent in the Northeast, 3 percent in the Midwest, 1 percent in the West and an *increase* of 1 percent in the South.

Relating actual crime reports to population shows 5,031 offenses per 100,000 citizens or a drop of 3 percent from 1983, but 539 violent crime offenses per 100,000, an increase of less than 1 percent.

On the whole, violent crime rose 1 percent last year. Murder and robbery declined 3 percent and 4 percent, respectively. Aggravated assault increased 5 percent and rape, 7 percent.

Property crimes were down 2 percent overall. Larceny-theft dropped 2 percent and burglary 5 percent, while motor vehicle thefts and arson each increased 2 percent.

The 18,692 estimated murders during 1984 was a 3 percent drop from the previous year, but rapes increased 7 percent, victimizing a reported 69 of every 100,000 females. Arrests on rape charges increased 8 percent over the previous year.

There were 485,008 reported robberies (down 4 percent), 685,349 aggravated assaults (up 5 percent) and 3 million burglary offenses (down 5 percent), which accounted for 25 percent of all crime index offenses.

Statistically, Americans are doing better in securing their homes and other structures against burglary, but this is still the largest single area of vulnerability to the criminal. Fewer citizens are being robbed and murdered, but more are the victims of aggravated assault and rape.

The 1 million motor vehicle thefts reported nationwide during 1984 (up 2 percent) accentuate the regional increase of 8 percent in the Midwest. Losses due to vehicle thefts hit $4.6 billion, or $4,418 per vehicle, a staggering testimony to increased insurance rates and the inability of Americans to effectively secure their cars and trucks.

The 101,836 reported arsons cost $10,378 per incident and $855 million overall.

Americans are doing consistently better — at least so far as these statistics reflect the number of actual offenses — in avoiding the label: crime victim. But there is still a lot of room for improvement.

The Times-Picayune
The States-Item

New Orleans, LA, October 16, 1985

The nation's two crime-measuring surveys have reported again, a week apart, and the public can be excused for being somewhat more confused than enlightened. The National Crime Survey reports an overall drop in crime of 4.1 percent in 1984 to a 12-year low. The FBI's Uniform Crime Report reports an overall increase of 3 percent in the first six months of 1985, the first such since 1981.

The problem with the figures is more than that they report on different timeframes; it is unlikely that a sudden upward swing in criminal activity would begin on Jan. 1. They actually measure different things, and it is encouraging that the drop in incidence of crime is found in the report considered the more reliable index: the National Crime Survey, informally called the victimization survey.

The FBI's annual Uniform Crime Report adds up crimes reported to local police departments. The Justice Department National Crime Survey adds up crimes reported by victims to the surveyors, though not necessarily to the police.

The Uniform Crime Report figures suffer from several defects. Not all crimes are reported to the police — the current estimate is that only about 35 percent are. More crimes can be reported, though more crimes are not being committed, if police departments have good relations with the public and do a good job of catching criminals. Thus, paradoxically, a city's crime rate may seem to increase because the police are doing a better job.

Police departments follow different procedures in listing crimes, and can even fine-tune the local crime rate for their own purposes. Changes in reporting methods can produce apparently large shifts in crime rates that do not reflect reality. Reforms of this system are being studied.

The victimization survey interviews about 130,000 members of 66,000 randomly selected households every six months. For last year, the survey found 35.5 million "victimizations," 14 percent below the peak crime year 1981 since the survey began in 1973.

The number of violent crimes within this lower total, however, increased moderately — 0.9 percent over 1983. The survey does not cover murder, since it is assumed that virtually all murders are either reported to or discovered by the police.

The FBI report does not necessarily conflict with this. Its finding of a 4 percent increase in violent crime and a 3 percent increase in property crime is a nationwide averaging. It reflects a 6 percent increase in the South and West, a 1 percent drop in the Midwest and no change in the Northeast.

Even so, according to an FBI spokesman, "the victimization rate for every major crime we measure with the exception of rape has declined significantly during the past three years." He attributed much of the decline as "most likely the result of increased citizen involvement in crime prevention activities" as well as greater police success in putting away repeat offenders.

Citizen-police cooperation is in fact considered the key to fighting "crime" — more precisely, "criminals." An alert and determined public, supported by an efficient police force, is its own best defense.

Attorney General Meese Attacks 'Miranda' Ruling

Attorney General Edwin Meese 3rd, in an interview, criticized the right of criminal defendants to have a lawyer present before questioning by the police. The interview was published in the Oct. 14, 1985 issue of *U.S. News & World Report*. "The Miranda decision was wrong," Meese declared, referring to the 1966 Supreme Court decision in the case of *Miranda v. Arizona*. The court ruled in this famous decision that a suspect must be informed of his right to have a counsel present during interrogation and must be warned that anything he says may be held against him.

Meese argued that the ruling did not protect innocent people, saying: "If a person is innocent of a crime, then he is not a suspect." He added: "Miranda only helps guilty defendants. Most innocent people are glad to speak to the police. They want to establish their innocence so that they're no longer a suspect." Meese said "coercive or abusive police tactics" had been "outlawed by other cases. So it [the Miranda decision] only has to do with the normal questioning of suspects, the people who have information about a crime."

Post-Tribune

Gary, IN, October 12, 1985

Maybe Ed Meese is maligned so often because he is just misunderstood so often; more likely it's because he is so clearly understood so often. His newest pronouncement on justice and the treatment of suspects is right to the point: the Miranda rule on the rights of suspects is an abomination. He's said that before, so it's an established Meeseism.

The Miranda ruling gives suspects the right to have a lawyer present before police questioning. Shouldn't people who may be innocent have such protection?

Yes, says the attorney general, but if a person is innocent of a crime he is not a suspect. What that means is that the police arrest only guilty people. That's dangerous nonsense. But anybody is innocent until proved guilty in court. Police are not supposed to be judges.

Meese is thrashing about in a thicket of ramblings when he argues that the Miranda rule "helps only guilty defendants." That view is as narrow as a string tie. And he declares that the country got along just fine for 175 years without the Miranda rule, handed down by the Supreme Court in 1966. Wrong again.

The need for that rule is what created it, making protection against self-incrimination universally available. The only people the rule hampers are those who believe that abusing some rights is admirable in the pursuit of convictions.

Chicago Tribune

Chicago, IL, October 14, 1985

For a person who has been accused and cleared of a crime, Atty. Gen. Edwin Meese shows a remarkable disinterest in the law's traditional presumption of innocence.

In a recent interview with U.S. News and World Report, Mr. Meese was asked whether he thought criminal suspects should continue to have the right to have their lawyer present during police questioning. "Suspects who are innocent of a crime should," he replied. "But the thing is, you don't have many suspects who are innocent of a crime. That's contradictory. If a person is innocent of a crime, then he is not a suspect."

Mr. Meese, you'll recall, underwent investigation by a special federal prosecutor after he was accused of a dozen charges of illegal conduct in connection with financial dealings during his service as counselor to President Reagan. The special prosecutor found that there was no basis for bringing a prosecution.

Did Mr. Meese have a lawyer? He sure did, and the lawyers submitted to the government a bill for more than $720,000.

If there is a contradiction here, it isn't in the law that requires police to inform criminal suspects of their right to an attorney. It is in Mr. Meese's position.

But then no one has ever accused Mr. Meese of being a legal scholar.

The fact is, Mr. Meese deserved to be considered innocent until proven guilty. And so does every other person who becomes a suspect. This is the individual's greatest protection against government tyranny, and as a conservative—if not as a former suspect—he ought to appreciate that.

There is plenty of room for disagreement about the legal rule requiring police to read a suspect his rights or lose the chance to use a confession against him. A lot of people are uncomfortable with letting defendants go free simply because the police fouled up an interrogation or a search.

On balance, this newspaper has not been persuaded that any other device can deter police misconduct; it has supported the so-called Miranda rule, despite misgivings about its consequences in certain cases. But in the interview, Mr. Meese went way beyond an argument about how best to discipline police. He made it sound as if he believed in the Red Queen's system of justice, in which an accusation is proof of guilt.

The spokesman for the Justice Department says that Mr. Meese unsuccessfully tried to get U.S. News to delete the passage. It was an accurate statement, said the spokesman, but "not very clear."

Unfortunately, Mr. Meese's point was quite clear. And quite wrong.

The San Diego Union

San Diego, CA, October 14, 1985

Both critics and supporters of U.S. Attorney General Edwin Meese III are stunned by his recent comments to the editors of *U.S. News & World Report.*

Mr. Meese was asked about his reservations on the Miranda warning, a U.S. Supreme Court ruling that gives arrested suspects the right to remain silent and warns that anything they say "can and will be used against them in a court of law." The Miranda ruling is familiar to many Americans — reading someone his rights is the stuff of countless television police shows.

"Shouldn't people," asked the editors, "who may be innocent, have such protection?" Mr. Meese replied, "Suspects who are innocent of a crime should. But the thing is, you don't have many suspects who are innocent of a crime. That's contradictory. If a person is innocent of a crime, then he is not a suspect."

Granted an interview can yield a misspoken word or an out-of-context phrase. Yet, Mr. Meese's remarkable answer is complete and direct. It is also an affront to the American justice system. Because, in effect, Mr. Meese is saying that a suspect is guilty until proved innocent. One need not possess a legal background to conclude that this contradicts a basic tenet of American justice — that a person who is a suspect is presumed to be innocent until proved guilty.

There is no question that technical court decisions on Miranda have liberated numerous criminals and long frustrated law enforcement officials. That's what the Attorney General was trying to say according to a Justice Department spokesman — that "Miranda is used in a way as to release (criminals) . . . on a technicality."

But that's not what the nation's top law enforcement officer said.

THE ARIZONA REPUBLIC
Phoenix, AZ, October 14, 1985

WE have a few questions we would like to ask you, Attorney General Ed Meese, but first please be informed of your rights:

"You have the right to remain silent. Anything you say can be used against you ... You have the right to an attorney prior to questioning and to be with you during questioning by *U.S. News & World Report*. If you cannot afford an attorney, a Republican banker will provide you with an interest-free loan.

"Do you understand these rights? Do you understand your responsibilities as the highest law enforcement officer in the United States?

"Now then, Attorney General Meese, did you, or did you not, on or about the Oct. 14 issue of *U.S. News & World Report*, state: 'You don't have many suspects who are innocent of a crime. That's contradictory. If a person is innocent of a crime, then he is not a suspect?'

"Mr. Meese, do you understand that the presumption of innocence is the foundational principle of the American system of justice?

"Surely, Mr. Meese, you, who so recently enjoyed the benefits of the presumption of innocence, are not suggesting that a mere police accusation is *prima facie* evidence of criminality?

"You are aware, are you not, that in despotic nations suspicion is the equivalent of guilt?

"While there are ample grounds for criticizing the present application of the Miranda ruling, why are you unable to articulate intelligibly those legal issues?

"Have you ever heard of the Fifth Amendment to the U.S. Constitution? Would you like to invoke it now?

"Are you now or have you ever been an officer of the court pledged to defend the Constitution of the United States?

"Are you aware, Mr. Meese, that the Constitution protects you from self-incrimination, that you do not *have* to say these foolish things for the record?

"Is it not also true that you attempted to suppress your dangerously uninformed opinions in the free press? Of course, we can hardly blame you for trying, Mr. Meese.

"Do you know that the best legal minds in the country are shocked and astounded at your bizarre declarations?

"Do you regret, Mr. Meese, having embarrassed yourself and your president? And if not, why not, Mr. Meese?

"Are you not aware this line of questioning is aimed at protecting you from yourself, not to mention the country?

"That will be all, Mr. Meese. You may, if you wish, step down as attorney general. We have no further questions."

The Grand Rapids Press
Grand Rapids, MI, October 15, 1985

Perhaps U.S. Attorney General Edwin Meese was dozing on that day in law school when the difference between a suspect and a criminal was defined. If so, Congress should spend a few bucks on a refresher course for him.

In a recent issue of U.S. News and World Report, Mr. Meese repeated his criticism of the 1966 Miranda rule, which requires police to inform a suspect of his or her right to an attorney and of the right to remain silent. When asked if people shouldn't have such protection, Mr. Meese said: "Suspects who are innocent of a crime should. But the thing is, you don't have many suspects who are innocent of a crime. That's contradictory. If a person is innocent of a crime, then he is not a suspect."

It's hard to believe the country's top law-enforcement officer said such a thing. Even a person of Mr. Meese's ideological zeal should be able to admit that thousands of innocent people have been criminal suspects, and that, in the pre-Miranda days, many of those succumbed to police pressure and confessed to crimes they did not commit. More often than not, those railroaded are the poor, who often don't know their rights.

But these are not the sorts of people Mr. Meese understands or cares to protect. In his pristine world, good people stay clear of the police and the police do not make mistakes. At no time in history, and in no place in the real world, has this held true. But Mr. Meese would have us, and the Supreme Court, believe that this fantasy is the norm.

Mr. Meese has not said if he will seek to bring a case challenging the Miranda rule before the Supreme Court. In the recent past, the court has diluted the rule in a variety of cases. However, the justices have not denied suspects and defendants fundamental protections, of which the Miranda notice is but one.

The real danger with Mr. Meese's overreaching is the effect on the public and on the general understanding of the Constitution. Without public officials to defend its precepts, the law of the land is in real danger of being undermined. In a recent poll, 25 percent of those questioned said they didn't support the Constitution's separation of church and state. There is a serious movement afoot to convene a national constitutional convention, at which these misgivings about the Constitution might take the form of crippling amendments.

The Miranda rule grew logically from the Constitution and a system of laws that presupposes innocence. To invalidate Miranda now would weaken the Constitution as a protector of the individual from government and society. Mr. Meese would have us believe that we have nothing to fear from our institutions. The founding fathers did not believe that, and history has borne them out.

The war against crime is vital and the police are a force for good. But the Miranda rule and the Constitution protect us from the excesses of authority. There may come a time when all of us, Mr. Meese included, better appreciate these safeguards.

The Des Moines Register
Des Moines, IA, October 11, 1985

When the president submits a nomination to the Senate, we believe that Congress should confirm, unless something comes up that shows the appointee to be clearly unacceptable.

Attorney General Edwin Meese III is an exception: It was clear from the beginning that he was unfit for the job after an independent investigation concluded that, while no crime was committed, Meese's ethics were seriously in doubt because of the way he got government jobs for friends who helped him out financially.

Since then he has proved his incompetence time and again. The latest evidence came in an interview with U.S. News and World Report in which he showed a total lack of respect for a bedrock principle of American criminal law: the presumption of innocence.

Asked why he opposed the Supreme Court's Miranda decision, which protects suspects against police questioning without legal counsel, he said: "Suspects who are innocent of a crime should [be protected]. But ... you don't have many suspects who are innocent of a crime. That's contradictory. If a person is innocent of a crime, then he is not a suspect...."

Not only does Meese not believe in presumption of innocence; he seems to think a guilty person has no right to a fair trial.

Meese later said he did not make himself clear, and asked the magazine to omit the question and answer. Meese's meaning, alas, is all too clear.

A review of the record of his public statements since taking over at Justice is a sad commentary on the man charged with defending the Constitution.

In the text of a speech for the American Bar Association, he made the remarkable assertion that the Bill of Rights does not apply to the states. Somehow, in his law-school studies, Meese must have failed to read the Fourteenth Amendment, which brings the states under constitutional jurisdiction.

It was a mistake to make Meese attorney general; it is a mistake to keep him on the job.

THE ATLANTA CONSTITUTION
Atlanta, GA, October 14, 1985

A right answer to the question required neither a law degree nor a particularly keen grasp of civics. Astonishingly, Edwin Meese, U.S. attorney general, missed it by a mile.

U.S. News & World Report magazine lobbed this question to the nation's top law enforcer: "You criticize the Miranda ruling, which gives suspects the right to have a lawyer present before police questioning. Shouldn't people, who may be innocent, have such protection?"

Edwin Meese III

Meese answered this way: "Suspects who are innocent of a crime should. But the thing is, you don't have many suspects who are innocent of a crime. That's contradictory. If a person is innocent of a crime, then he is not a suspect."

Hold everything. By this reasoning, the Miranda rule is fine, and trials are the real fly in the criminal-justice ointment. If innocent folks are rarely suspects, as Meese insists, why do states take such pains to prove guilt beyond a reasonable doubt? Why don't they adopt a Meese doctrine: If police think someone is guilty, he probably is. The billions saved in court costs could be plowed into prison construction.

Well, yes, the U.S. Constitution would never permit such a thing. There may be a more basic reason, too. Few other officials are known to have inherent, extralegal abilities to sort the innocent from the guilty. Among Meese's criteria: "Most innocent people are glad to talk to the police. They want to establish their innocence so they're no longer a suspect." Hmmm. Such standards could take a while to teach.

What deflates any humor is the fact of Meese's office. We are not talking about Deputy Barney Fife of Mayberry here. Ed Meese has even been touted as a candidate for the U.S. Supreme Court. Ironically, his chances likely died when he was suspected — yes, *suspected* — of financial and ethical improprieties.

Something else makes this not so funny — the consistently fine performance of the much-maligned Miranda rule. It has done a Herculean job of cleaning up abusive police practices. No longer do suspects routinely confess under rubber-hose duress.

Delaware Sen. Joseph Biden perhaps put it best: "My God, Ed Meese's answer is overwhelming proof of why we need Miranda . . . because there are people like Ed Meese who believe that anyone who's a suspect is guilty until proven innocent. My God, this guy is beginning to worry me."

Here's today's trivia question: In the following exchange, who is being interviewed?

Q. You criticize the Miranda ruling, which gives suspects the right to have a lawyer present before police questioning. Shouldn't people, who may be innocent, have such protection?

A. Suspects who are innocent of crime should. But the thing is, you don't have many suspects who are innocent of a crime . . . If a person is innocent of a crime, then he is not a suspect.

The choices:
1. Former Philadelphia Mayor Frank L. Rizzo
2. "Dirty Harry" Callahan
3. Attorney General Edwin Meese III

The answer is C—Meese gives just that response in the current issue of U.S. News & World Report.

It is bad enough that the nation's top law enforcement officer would have so little sensitivity to constitutional protections against self-incrimination. But it is simply astonishing that he would suggest that any *suspect* in a crime is, by definition, guilty.

This view overturns the whole tradition of American justice—that those accused of a crime are presumed innocent until *proven* guilty.

Under the Meese theory, guilt can be assumed at the point of arrest. Let the police adjudicate. Why bother with the formality of a court trial?

All the Miranda ruling does is require police to warn arrested suspects of their constitutional rights.

The attorney general of the United States thinks that suspects—being guilty, you see—shouldn't have that knowledge. Astonishing.

FORT WORTH STAR-TELEGRAM
Fort Worth, TX, October 13, 1985

Attorney General Edwin Meese shares the frustration felt by most Americans about crime and what sometimes seems to be the tilting of justice in favor of the criminals.

It is a frustration that is easy to understand. But it is also a frustration that must not be carried to extremes.

Meese, as his mindset is revealed through a question-and-answer interview in the current issue of *U.S. News & World Report*, may be carrying it beyond the limits of the Constitution.

Asked if suspects in a criminal investigation should not have the Miranda Rule protection of having a lawyer present when questioned by police, Meese said, "Suspects who are innocent of a crime should. But the thing is, you don't have many suspects who are innocent of a crime. That's contradictory. If a person is innocent of a crime, then he is not a suspect."

Huh?

A spokeman for Meese said that the attorney general felt his answer to the Miranda question was unclear and wanted the magazine to omit it.

Legal scholars and civil libertarians are afraid the answer is altogether too clear.

Meese went on to amplify his statement in the interview, saying, "We managed very well in this country for 175 years without it (the Miranda Rule). Its practical effect is to prevent the police from talking to the person who knows the most about the crime — namely, the perpetrator . . . Most innocent people are glad to talk to the police. They want to establish their innocence so that they're no longer a suspect."

What Meese seems to say is that any suspect is guilty until he establishes his innocence and that he should be able to do this without the aid of counsel.

That is scary.

He seems to question the entire tradition of presumed innocence.

What is at stake is not the Miranda ruling, which has not in itself been an excessive burden for law enforcement officers, or even the courts' sometimes baffling use of technicalities that seem to obstruct justice.

What is at stake is respect and confidence in the law, which in a free society is fashioned as much to protect individuals from the power of the state as it is to punish those who break the law. If the nation's No. 1 legal officer seems to question the basic presumption of innocence and to be saying that the police should be judge and jury, then who is to protect the innocent?

"If a person is innocent of a crime, then he is not a suspect."

It then follows that if a person is suspected — not tried, not even charged — that person is guilty.

This is wrong. Obviously others in the Justice Department know it is wrong. Surely Meese knows it is wrong. On this, even the American Civil Liberties Union and the attorney general should see eye to eye.

Surely Meese misspoke himself.

Surely.

Otherwise the Bill of Rights, the nation and all its people are in deep trouble.

ALBUQUERQUE JOURNAL

Albuquerque, NM, October 13, 1985

Attorney General Edwin Meese has once again demonstrated a severe lack of understanding of criminal defendants' rights and of the Constitution. The principle of innocent until proven guilty would appear to be foreign to this man.

Meese's latest attack on the Constitution is found in the current edition of U.S. News & World Report. Responding to a question regarding his past criticisms of the Miranda ruling, which gives persons accused of a crime the right to have an attorney present during police interrogations, the nation's highest-ranking lawyer said: "Suspects who are innocent of a crime should (be entitled to an attorney). But the thing is, you don't have many suspects who are innocent of a crime. That's contradictory. If a person is innocent of a crime, then he is not a suspect. ..."

Meese said Miranda prevents police interrogations of criminals and "only helps guilty defendants. Most innocent people are glad to talk to police."

Understandably, civil libertarians and constitutional scholars across the country have criticized these comments. They demonstrate a disdain for constitutional rights and for the presumption of innocence. Meese shows an extreme misunderstanding of Miranda — which is intended to protect the rights of all citizens, including those who later may be found guilty but who are nonetheless entitled to constitutional protections. An unfortunate byproduct of such constitutional guarantees is that sometimes an obvious criminal is released as a result, often because of poor police work. But that is not too large a price to maintain constitutional integrity. Also, Meese is guilty of plain stupidity if he actually believes that innocent people are not sometimes accused of crimes.

But such demonstrations are not new to Meese. Last spring, he told a group of prosecuting attorneys that the exclusionary rule, which bars the use in court of illegally obtained evidence, should be eliminated. And he termed the Miranda and exclusionary rules "tragedies ... in our system of jurisprudence, where valid ... evidence, the truth in other words, is excluded from a trial."

Meese's philosophy is that guilty people have everything to hide and the innocent have nothing to hide, so therefore we don't need laws protecting the civil rights of individuals. It might be excusable for a layman. But for a lawyer, who heads this nation's Justice Department and who has been mentioned as a candidate for the Supreme Court, it is indefensible and dangerous.

It becomes even more difficult to understand when one considers that Meese himself has benefited from the presumption of innocence during an investigation involving certain of his own past dealings. The tab Meese submitted to the government for his legal expenses during that episode indicates he certainly took advantage of the sort of legal counsel he would deny other accused persons.

Supreme Court Curbs 'Shoot-to-Kill Laws

The Supreme Court ruled, 6-3, March 27 that police did not have the right to shoot fleeing criminal suspects who were not armed or dangerous. "The use of force to prevent the escape of all felony suspects, whatever the circumstances, is constitutionally unreasonable," Justice Byron R. White said in his majority opinion.

The case, *Tennessee v. Garner*, concerned the shooting and killing by a Memphis officer of a youth fleeing unarmed from a house burglary. He had stolen two $5 bills and a purse. "It is not better that all felony suspects die rather than escape," White said.

The dissent, by Justice Sandra Day O'Connor, could not "accept the majority's creation of a constitutional right to flight for burglary suspects seeking to avoid capture at the scene of the crime." Burglary was "a serious and dangerous felony," O'Connor said, and the "public interest in the prevention and detection of the crime is of compelling importance." She considered the police action in the case reasonable. To avoid the risk to his life, she said, "the suspect need merely obey the valid order to halt." Her dissent was joined by Chief Justice Warren E. Burger and Justice William H. Rehnquist.

Arkansas Gazette
Little Rock, AR, April 1, 1985

It's a striking thing — and reassuring —that local police officers seem less disturbed by the Supreme Court decision on deadly force than some politicians. And some Supreme Court justices, for that matter.

In a 6 to 3 decision, the court said that the police cannot use deadly force to prevent the escape of an unarmed suspect if the escape poses no apparent threat to police officers or others. Justice Byron R. White wrote for the majority: "It is not better that all felony suspects die than that they escape."

The court struck down a Tennessee law that authorized policemen to use deadly force (that usually means "shooting") against fleeing felons. A number of other states, including Arkansas, have similar statutes.

Attorney General Steve Clark said that the court decision invalidated a provision of Arkansas law that authorizes a law enforcement officer to use deadly force "when he reasonably believes that it is necessary to effect an arrest or to prevent the escape from custody of an arrested person whom he reasonably believes has committed or attempted to commit a felony." Clark said the decision wouldn't affect another part of the Arkansas law, which says that deadly force may be used by an officer "to defend himself or a third person from what he reasonably believes to be the use or imminent use of deadly physical force."

There were the predictable cries of outrage from certain quarters, encouraged by a harsh dissent from Justice Sandra Day O'Connor, who said that the court majority had created a new constitutional right — the right of a suspected criminal to flee with impunity.

But law enforcement officers in Arkansas remained calm. Both Little Rock Police Chief Walter E. (Sonny) Simpson and Col. Tommy Goodwin, director of the State Police, said that their agencies' "deadly force" policies already were in line with the Supreme Court ruling — which means the policies were more restrictive than the state law. Simpson's comments may be particularly noteworthy. The Little Rock Police Department has been accused, justly or unjustly, of excessive use of deadly force. If Simpson doesn't see the court's decision as a burden, how heavy can it be for others? Even United States Representative Tommy Robinson of Jacksonville, a former tall-walking and tough-talking sheriff of Pulaski County, said that the provision of Arkansas law invalidated by the court was too generous in its allowance for deadly force. So, not only is the decision humane, it appears to be practical as well.

We suspect that one reason these local lawmen aren't as upset by the decision as are some civilians is because they recognize that the vast majority of suspected criminals go along quietly when the police come for them. The need for chasing and shooting is much more common on television than in real life.

The taking of human life is just about the most serious business there is; if errors are made, better they be made on the side of mercy. That philosophy is part of what this country is about. The court's decision affirms it.

BUFFALO EVENING NEWS
Buffalo, NY, April 1, 1985

SHOULD POLICE shoot to stop a fleeing criminal or suspected criminal? The Supreme Court had this issue before them in a case brought by the family of a 15-year-old Memphis boy who was shot dead while fleeing from a house where he had stolen $10.

The police officer had not violated Tennessee law, which allowed police the "use of all the necessary means to effect the arrest." But the youth of this boy and his tragic death made starkly clear that the Tennessee law was too broad. Now the Supreme Court has made the proper distinction, ruling 6-3 that it is unconstitutional for police to use deadly force against suspects who are not armed or believed dangerous.

The majority opinion, written by Associate Justice Byron R. White, made the vital distinction between criminal suspects who pose a danger and those who do not.

Thus the court ruled that states may still authorize police to use deadly force to prevent escape "if the suspect threatens the officer with a weapon or there is probable cause to believe that he has committed a crime involving the infliction or threatened infliction of serious physical harm."

But in other cases, the court said, "the fact that the police arrive late or are a little slower afoot does not always justify killing the suspect."

This important distinction should not pose great problems for law enforcement authorities. Indeed, the ruling was endorsed by the International Association of Police Chiefs. Police departments today have a vast array of electronic devices, autos and helicopters to track down suspects. While the laws of about half the states have in the past allowed police to shoot to prevent the escape of suspected felons, local police regulations have been much more in line with the new high court ruling. New York State law meets certain aspects of the Supreme Court standard. The Memphis police in 1983 adopted a policy of not shooting unless the lives of officers or citizens were in danger.

Several Supreme Court rulings recently have made the work of police easier by expanding their powers in the investigation of crimes. This latest ruling may hamper them slightly, but the use of deadly force is a power that should be closely circumscribed, and the high court was right to find the use of such force "unreasonable" in the shooting of the Memphis boy.

The Hartford Courant

Hartford, CT, March 30, 1985

The U.S. Supreme Court's declaration that police can't use bullets to stop fleeing criminal suspects who don't seem dangerous isn't a surprise. Although a persistent minority, and sometimes a majority, of the justices has narrowed the rights of criminal suspects and defendants in recent years, what the court would say on this question wasn't in much doubt.

What is surprising is that such a sizable minority — one-third of the court, including the chief justice — would consider such use of deadly force permissible, and that almost half the states have for so long neglected to amend their laws authorizing it.

Connecticut is one of them. Its deadly force statutes let a police officer or correction official shoot to kill when he thinks it necessary in order to "effect an arrest or to prevent the escape from custody of a person whom he reasonably believes has committed or attempted to commit a felony."

This and similar provisions in at least 20 other state codes will have to be rewritten because of the Supreme Court's assertion that, under the Constitution, no public interest in catching felons justifies killing them regardless of circumstances. "A police officer may not seize an unarmed, non-dangerous suspect by shooting him dead," wrote Justice Byron R. White for the court.

The case before the court shows why such a decision was predictable, and why it came decades late.

In 1974, a Memphis, Tenn., police officer responding to a report of a prowler saw a 15-year-old boy running away from a house. He later said he was "reasonably sure" and "figured" that the boy wasn't armed. Although the officer shouted "Police! Halt!," the boy began climbing a 6-foot fence.

Rather than give chase or summon help, the officer fired, fatally wounding the boy in the back of the head. If he hadn't shot, the officer explained, the boy would have escaped. So the cop got his man, or boy, and recovered the fruits of the crime: $10 and a purse.

The Fourth Amendment guarantees freedom from unreasonable search and seizure. What form of seizure could be less reasonable — to put it mildly — than killing a suspect who isn't dangerous? What judge *couldn't* have found that such a killing was unsanctioned by the Constitution?

Justice Sandra Day O'Connor, for one, and she also spoke for Chief Justice Warren E. Burger and Justice William H. Rehnquist. The dissenters thought the boy's killing, while "tragic and unfortunate," was perfectly all right from a legal viewpoint.

The dissent reflects a disturbing belief that escaping felons, even escaping *suspected* felons, who may be innocent, have forfeited their right to live.

Since many big-city police departments, including Hartford's, tell their officers to use deadly force only in dangerous situations, the risk of overreaction has been small despite the overbroad state laws. State legislators thus have some excuse for not altering the laws before this, although their duty now, of course, is clear.

FORT WORTH STAR-TELEGRAM

Fort Worth, TX, April 1, 1985

Seldom have the two opposing viewpoints on an issue been better expressed than they were in the U.S. Supreme Court's majority opinion and minority dissent after a 6-3 decision against unrestrained use of police deadly force to halt fleeing suspects.

Justice Byron White wrote for the court, "It is not better that all felony suspects die than that they escape."

And Justice Sandra Day O'Connor, dissenting, wrote that the decision "allows burglary suspects to flee unimpeded from a police officer who has no means short of firing his weapon to prevent escape."

The court's decision will not settle the debate, but it does put constitutional interpretation in line with guidelines and procedures already adopted by most law enforcement agencies in an effort to reduce the number of shootings by police officers.

The national trend is toward rules such as the Fort Worth police department's under which officers may fire their weapons only at suspects who present a danger to the officers or other citizens.

And that is basically what the Supreme Court endorses.

Critics from the ranks of law enforcement are correct that such guidelines force officers to make quick decisions as to whether the situation allows them to shoot.

But that is nothing new. It is a decision the police always have had to make, and make instantly. It has always been an important decision, because a lethal gunshot leaves no room for error. A dead suspect has no opportunity to defend himself against criminal charges.

Despite well-publicized cases, it is a credit to American police officers' judgment that more innocent suspects have not been victims of instantaneous decisions to fire.

It is also true that strict adherence to the court's rule may allow some suspects to escape, as O'Connor indicates.

What is left is the continuing question for Americans — ordinary citizens as well as justices and police officers — of how serious we are about cracking down on crime and how far we are willing to go to protect the rights, as well as the lives, of suspects.

The operative word is "suspects," used in both justices' opinions. Most Americans, while seeking better law enforcement and supporting the idea of getting the felons off the streets, also adhere to the principal of innocent until proven guilty. We recognize the danger of six-gun justice.

The nation is bound by law and tradition to seek both enforcement and protection of rights, and the court's decision is entirely proper in that context.

The Des Moines Register

Des Moines, IA, April 3, 1985

The Supreme Court these days is accused of curtailing criminal suspects' rights in order to ease the work of police. Now even the police are applauding a ruling that clearly protects the rights of suspects.

A substantial majority of six justices — substantial for this court — held that it is wrong for a peace officer to shoot at a fleeing suspect who is not armed or who does not present a threat to the officer or others.

Given the court's movement in recent years to grant more power to the state in police matters, this decision is reassuring. Police groups also see the ruling as good for law enforcement, which has long struggled with the question of using deadly force.

The ruling invalidates statutes in about half the states that allow the use of deadly force to stop fleeing suspects.

Iowa's law seems not to be affected, because it permits deadly force only when the suspect has "used or threatened to use deadly force in committing a felony" or when the officer "reasonably believes the person would use deadly force against any person unless immediately apprehended."

The court ruled in a case in which a Memphis police officer killed a fleeing prowler who refused an order to halt. The suspect was 15 years old, 5 feet 4 inches tall and weighed about 100 pounds; he was unarmed and had stolen $10 and a purse.

Writing for the court, Justice Byron White said Tennessee's statute, which permits "all use necessary" to make an arrest, violates the Fourth Amendment prohibition of unreasonable seizure because it does not distinguish between suspects who pose a danger and those who do not.

The most powerful law-enforcement tool a police officer carries is a handgun. It should not be fired to warn, to frighten or to wound. When necessary, deadly force should be swift and sure, but for one reason only: to stop a clearly dangerous person.

When to use deadly force is the toughest decision an officer will make; all law-enforcement officers should join the International Association of Chiefs of Police in applauding this ruling, which gives officers clear direction.

The Evening Gazette

Worcester, MA, April 1, 1985

The U.S. Supreme Court acted wisely in spelling out when police officers may shoot fleeing suspects.

The ruling allows officers to use deadly force if they have "probable cause" to believe a suspect is dangerous. Otherwise, officers "should wait and see if a person is innocent or guilty" instead of killing him. The justices said attempted escape was not a sufficient reason to shoot.

The ruling stemmed from a Tennessee case in which a Memphis police officer shot and killed a 15-year-old youth near the scene of a night burglary. The youth was climbing over a fence and ignored the officer's order to halt. The officer, who was "reasonably sure" the boy was unarmed, said he also thought he would not be able to scale the fence and catch the suspect in the darkness.

The court split 6-3 on the ruling. The dissenting justices said it disregarded the dangers involved in residential break-ins and effectively created a "constitutional right" for burglary suspects to flee the scene of the crime.

That opinion was echoed by some lawmakers, who said it is impossible for an officer to be sure whether a suspect is armed. Some critics of the ruling said it made law enforcement a foot race between young thugs and old police officers. Others said it was a signal to felons that if they run from the police, their chances of getting away will be pretty good.

But the court ruling was supported by the American Civil Liberties Union and by the International Association of Chiefs of Police, whose guidelines are almost identical to the ruling.

Many states already have deadly force guidelines that conform to the Supreme Court ruling, the justices noted. Some law enforcement agencies, including the FBI, have guidelines more restrictive than the ruling. Court rulings have prohibited deadly force in California. In some states where officers are allowed to shoot fleeing felons, local police departments have for years banned the practice when the suspects are not considered dangerous.

The justices cited a trend away from the centuries-old English common law rule allowing police to pursue and, as a last resort, kill all fleeing felons. They noted that times have changed since virtually all felonies were punishable by death. Now only murder is punishable by death in this country, they observed, and sophisticated techniques of apprehending suspects and swift and far-ranging communication among police have made it easier to catch escapees.

The justices found no evidence that, in states with restrictions on officers, there has been a "rash of litigation" against officers who used their guns.

The ruling should not be viewed as an impediment to law enforcement, but as a reasonable guideline for use of deadly force. It stakes out a sensible middle ground, protecting suspects' rights without tying the hands of police officers.

The Dispatch

Columbus, OH, April 5, 1985

The U.S. Supreme Court's decision that police officers may not shoot at fleeing felony suspects who are unarmed represents a cautious approach to a difficult problem. Fortunately, it will not pose much of a problem for local police departments — including the Columbus Division of Police — which already have regulations restricting the use of deadly force.

The court decided that the U.S. Constitution bars the police from shooting to kill fleeing, unarmed criminal suspects. Writing for the majority, Justice Byron White declared, "It is no doubt unfortunate when a suspect who is in sight escapes, but the fact that the police arrive a little late or are a little slower afoot does not always justify killing the suspect."

That makes sense to us. No one doubts that the police officer's job is a difficult one and that he or she faces dangerous, even life-threatening crises at the turn of every corner. In the emotion of a moment, however, good judgment can be eclipsed and deadly force could be used under circumstances that may not fully justify it. It could be that the fleeing suspect is unarmed or that the person leaving the scene of a crime had nothing to do with the crime. But the effects of deadly force, later determined to be unneeded, cannot be undone.

The restrictions on the use of deadly force against unarmed fleeing suspects may result in the escape of persons who have committed crimes. But in our determination to get tough with criminals, the nation must be guided by the same Constitution that the criminal violates when he or she commits illegal acts. Justice will be done, but it must be done carefully.

The TENNESSEAN

Nashville, TN, March 30, 1985

THE U.S. Supreme Court has ruled by a 6-3 vote that police may not shoot unarmed fleeing felony suspects when there is no apparent threat of harm to police officers or others.

"It is not better that all felony suspects die than that they escape," Justice Byron R. White wrote in the majority opinion.

The ruling, coming in a case from Memphis, declared Tennessee's "fleeing felon" law unconstitutional insofar as it authorized deadly force against apparently unarmed, non-dangerous fleeing suspects.

The high court upheld a decision of the 6th U.S. Circuit Court of Appeals in Cincinnati which was written by Judge Gilbert Merritt of Nashville. That decision in 1983, which overturned a district court ruling, found that Tennessee's law was unconstitutional because it did not differentiate between violent felonies such as rape or murder and non-violent offenses such as tax evasion. The Supreme Court's affirmation of this view is a credit to the Appeals Court and Judge Merritt.

Justice White wrote that the Tennessee law is constitutional only in authorizing police to shoot to kill "if the suspect threatens the officer with a weapon or there is probable cause to believe that he has committed a crime involving the infliction or threatened infliction of serious physical harm."

The Appeals Court and Supreme Court decisions uphold traditional American principles of justice. Some police officers argue that they need the power to shoot fleeing felony suspects because they may have committed a violent crime. But this is execution on suspicion and violates the principle that every accused person is entitled to a trial.

The Memphis case involved the slaying by the police of a 15-year-old boy allegedly fleeing from a home burglary. The boy failed to heed police orders to halt and was shot once in the head as he tried to climb over a fence. Police found $10 worth of money and jewelry on the boy's person after the shooting, according to the court record.

It has always been an American judicial principle that it is better to let a guilty person go free than to punish an innocent one. Now the Supreme Court has strengthened this doctrine by declaring that it is better to let some fleeing felons escape than it is to kill them when they pose no physical threat. Certainly no reasonable person would argue that a 15-year-old boy should give up his life for the theft of $10.

The Supreme Court's decision should not interfere with the enforcement of the law or endanger the life of any officer. The police still have adequate authority under the ruling to use necessary force in self defense and to prevent the escape of felons when there is reasonable cause to believe they have committed a violent crime or may do so. The Metro police say they have already been operating in compliance with the Supreme Court's ruling, and this apparently has not hindered the apprehension of felons here.

The high court's ruling is a reaffirmation of constitutional guarantees. There is no reason why the criminal laws cannot be properly enforced without eroding these safeguards.

The Knickerbocker News
Albany, NY, April 3, 1985

The new Supreme Court ruling on police use of deadly force is as notable for what is says about the justices who wrote it as it is for the reasonable restraint it imposes on law-enforcement authorities nationwide.

By ruling that police may not open fire on a fleeing suspect if they believe him to be neither armed nor dangerous, the court reinforces a basic principle of today's civilization — one that places a higher value on human life than on private property.

The case on which the justices ruled testifies to the need for such a principle: Eleven years ago, a Tennessee teen-ager was suprised by a police officer outside a house he had just burglarized. The police ordered him to halt, but the 15-year-old burglar, who was unarmed, tried to flee on foot. The officer shot and killed the boy, whose "haul" consisted of $10 and a purse.

By imposing restraint on police power to "shoot to kill," the court acknowledges that some felons probably will escape capture and punishment for their crimes.

But as the majority of the court agreed, for a society that places a high value on human life, there is no other choice. "The use of deadly force to prevent the escape of all felony suspects, whatever the circumstances, is constitutionally unreasonable," wrote Justice Byron White. "It is not better that all felony suspects die than that they escape."

Just as important, the ruling helps to dispel growing concerns that the court is resolutely conservative on all issues of law and order. In recent years, the court has seemed callously disinterested in granting last-minute stays of execution. Other rulings — granting police more latitude to detain suspects, while weakening Miranda protection for suspects — have furthered the court's hard-line image.

While the latest ruling can't be construed as a change in the court's temperament, it does signal a capacity for moderation and an appreciation for the rights of both police and suspects.

Even so, the court's ruling leaves other troubling questions unanswered. For example, what are the guidelines when police are confronted by a mentally or emotionally disturbed suspect, as they were recently in both Albany and New York City?

In the Albany case, the suspect, Jessie Davis, was shot by police after he lunged at the officers with a knife and fork. In New York, Eleanor Bumpurs was killed after she resisted police attempts to evict her from her welfare apartment.

Police in both cities have been criticized for overreacting. Police, in turn, have maintained their right to defend themselves against suspects who appear intent on inflicting serious harm.

In the Tennessee case, the high court only hints at how it might view such cases. On the one hand, the majority said police should issue warnings to suspects whenever feasible. On the other, they upheld police use of deadly force "if the suspect threatens the officer with a weapon or there is probable cause to believe that he has committed a crime involving the infliction or threatened infliction of serious physical harm."

A future ruling that specifies how these guidelines apply when the suspect is disturbed seems both necessary and overdue.

The Atlanta Journal AND THE ATLANTA CONSTITUTION
Atlanta, GA, March 30, 1985

The U.S. Supreme Court has ruled, 6-3, that a Memphis policeman was wrong to kill an unarmed 15-year-old boy who fled the scene of a $10 burglary. From now on, police may use deadly force only if a suspect poses a threat of serious injury to others.

The decision is a welcome burst of enlightenment from a court too often given to retrenchment on civil-liberties issues. (Let us forget for now that three justices thought the officer was within his rights as he shot the boy dead.) The ruling creates a salubrious effect that will quickly extend to the public and to the police themselves.

It will require police departments to be more efficient. The Memphis officer testified he fired at the boy in part because his partner was late getting to the scene. Lethal force thus was used to compensate for a logistical problem. Now police agencies must prevent such problems from the outset.

The restriction will make officers more careful about their own safety. If they can't always rely on their service revolvers, they will take fewer chances. It is no coincidence that injuries and deaths to officers dropped in many cities (examples: Atlanta and New York) when they limited the use of force.

Moreover, the court thundered to the rescue of some mayors engaged in strident local battles on the issue. While almost half the states (like Georgia) let police kill fleeing felons, the policy long has been an urban sore spot. Victims of police shootings are disproportionately poor and minorities. More than a few mayors won office pledging to end such abuses.

In other ways, too, the decision will prevent community dissension. Police shootings frequently rip a city's social bonds. By outlawing the most dubious of these shootings, the court has spared communities countless wrenching squabbles.

It did not end such agonies, of course. "Where the officer has probable cause to believe that the suspect poses a threat of serious physical harm ... it is not constitutionally unreasonable to prevent escape by using deadly force," cautioned Justice Byron White in the majority opinion.

What constitutes probable cause? What threat of physical harm is considered serious enough for lethal force? Specific answers are impossible. Those questions will confront courts and police review commissions, case by case, as long as there are police officers and criminals.

But for many communities, the court has done something crucial: It has shown where the balance lies between effective law enforcement and proper treatment of felony suspects. That is no small favor.

F.B.I. Finds Increase in Crimes; Justice Dept. Finds Crime Drop

Reported crimes had risen 4.6% in 1985, the F.B.I said July 26, 1986. The figure appeared in the FBI's annual summary of findings by its Uniform Crime Reporting Program. The increase followed three years of decline, but the FBI and private crime experts cautioned that the findings could not be used to predict future trends. Among other factors, an estimated two-thirds of the nation's crimes went unreported. The FBI said 12.4 million crimes had been reported to U.S. law enforcement officials during 1985, for an average rate of 5,207 reported crimes per 100,000 U.S. residents. Murder, rape, aggravated assault and all categories of property crimes were said to have increased. Since 1976, the report said, violent crimes as a whole had risen 32%, while property crimes had gone up 7%. It also found that in 1985 there had been 11.9 million arrests, an increase of 3%. About 2.8 million of these had been for intoxication or drunken driving.

Georgia had posted a 16% rise over the previous year's crime figures, giving it the largest increase of any state. Florida, Arizona and Texas were close behind. Detroit replaced Gary, Indiana as the city with the highest murder rate. Detroit's rate was 58 murders per 100,000 inhabitants, compared with Gary's 43.

Crime had affected members of 600,000 fewer households in 1985 than it had in 1984, the Justice Department's Bureau of Justice Statistics had reported June 29, 1986. The bureau based its findings on Census surveys rather than on individuals' complaints to law enforcement officials. According to the bureau, 22.2 million households had been touched by crime in 1985. That was about 25% of national households, a small drop from 1984. The bureau held a household to have been touched by crime when a household member had been victimized by burglary, personal theft, auto theft, rape or assault. A household was counted once, without regard to how many times it might have been victimized.

The Boston Herald

Boston, MA, July 7, 1986

WHILE certainly indicative of movement in the right direction, crime statistics recently released by the Justice Department are hardly a cause for celebration. If anything, they stress the desperation of the situation confronting us, and the need to redouble our efforts to combat the criminal menace.

According to the department's Bureau of Justice Statistics, one in every four American households was touched by crime last year. A household is affected by crime, under this definition, when it is burgled or when a family member is robbed, raped or assaulted, wherever the offense occurs.

In 1985, 22.2 million families were victimized, compared to 22.8 million in 1984. This decline is part of an ongoing trend. In 1975, one-third of U.S. homes were hit by crime.

In part, this reduction is attributable to the drop in that portion of the population in the 15-to-19 age group, those individuals statistically most prone to engage in criminal activities. There are two million fewer Americans in this group today than there were five years ago.

The picture is far from rosy, however, when one contemplates the fact that since 1960 violent crimes have increased an estimated 250 percent. Clearly, Americans are much less secure at home or abroad today than they were a quarter of a century ago, despite a massive increase in spending on law enforcement and criminal justice services.

Fortunately, public opinion has shifted drastically away from the position, which held sway in the '60s and early '70s, that criminals are society's victims, that the key to crime control is understanding and helping these unfortunates.

The public is correct. It's time to get tough with those who prey on the people of this nation. Giving police the procedural tools they need to do the job, in addition to presumptive sentencing and lengthy prison terms for the worst offenders all can make important contributions to this effort.

The Star-Ledger

Newark, NJ, May 5, 1986

After three welcome years of decreases, crime changed direction and went bad again in 1985, heading worrisomely upward.

The change in direction is all the more disturbing because law enforcement officials are at a loss to explain the return to crime and because the increase has affected all categories of crime and all sections of the country.

Well, not quite all regions. It seems that the FBI's Uniform Crime Report found that crime in the Midwest was unchanged for the year. But that better-than-average performance was offset by that region's 9 percent increase in murder—the biggest increase in that category in the nation.

The Northeast showed a modest 2 percent increase in crime, which compared favorably with the 4 percent rise overall, a 5 percent increase in the West and an alarming 8 percent rise in the South. Still, the upswing was no cause for complacency.

Law enforcement officials will have to review the data to find out what went wrong last year. They had been patting themselves on the backs for the encouraging reduction in crime which had been recorded in the three previous years, generally crediting the favorable trend to tougher enforcement and stiffer sentences for convicted offenders.

Traditionally, this one-two punch of intensified enforcement followed by harsher sentences becomes a strong deterrent force as word of the no-nonsense brand of justice filters down to the street.

The formula seems to have worked for three consecutive years, and it is important to learn whether the magic is gone from the tough enforcement-sentencing approach, or if the backsliding 1985 results were an aberration and 1986 will see the nation return to the happier days of reduced crime.

Officials would be making a big mistake if they were to ignore the distressing 1985 data. They must face up to the unpleasant statistics and develop fresh campaigns to contain criminality. Crime must not pay—and it must not be allowed to increase.

Detroit Free Press

Detroit, MI, July 5, 1986

AS GRIEVOUS as the crime problem remains for many Americans, it is helpful to know that progress — a lot of progress — is being made on **reducing** the number of American households affected by crime. In 1985, 25 percent of American households were affected by crime. That's a lot, but back in 1975 **almost one-third** of households were touched by crime.

With the aging of the population and the decline in the number of people in the crime-prone age groups, the country **ought** to be making headway against crime now. Young men commit a disproportionate percentage of the crimes in this country; the explosion of crime in the '60s and '70s reflected, in part, the growth of the population groups most likely to commit crimes. Shifts in the population have more to do with why we're making headway than do changes in public policy.

The natural decline, though, does provide an opportunity such as we have not seen in several decades to iron out some of the wrinkles in the way we police cities, the way we handle juvenile crime, the way our criminal justice system works. If we will keep our heads, if we can strengthen the systems for combating crime, we can make the society a good bit safer and more orderly without making it repressive.

What is worrisome is the temptation to look for symbolic, quick fixes in combating crime. Especially in urban areas, where crime remains far too serious, the temptation to opt for draconian measures, such as capital punishment or harsher sentences, diverts attention from the effort to make the system respond more effectively or to get at some of the root causes of crime. Crime is a hateful cancer, and it remains far too prevalent. We are making progress, though, and we can make even more if we look for real answers rather than easy answers.

Herald News

Fall River, MA, March 12, 1986

More American families are taking self-protective measures to increase their security at home.

The Bureau of Justice Statistics says that a third of all American families now participate in at least one of three major crime prevention programs.

Either they have placed identifying marks on their valuables, or they have installed a burglar alarm or they have enrolled in a neighborhood crime watch program.

Some have done all three.

The important thing is that more Americans all the time are not simply leaving the protection of their homes up to luck. They are taking measures to help themselves.

The Bureau of Justice Statistics points out that there is a distinct correlation between the economic level of a household and the steps taken to ensure its security.

The number of homes protected is at its maximum in suburban communities, at its minimum in low-income urban areas.

Nevertheless, there has been a generalized increase in the number of households taking steps to improve their own security, and this, the bureau believes, is a step in the right direction.

For one thing, it reflects an awareness that although there has been a decline in the number of crimes committed in recent years, the decline has by no means meant an elimination.

Crimes are being committed all the time, and presumably they will continue to be.

Furthermore, many of those crimes involve breaking into homes and the theft of personal property.

It is the public's awareness of this that has led so many households to take private measures to protect themselves.

It has also led neighborhoods to band together and constitute themselves as informal guuardians of their own security.

This by no means reflects on the quality of police protection, but what it does mean is that the police need public cooperation in order to function efficiently.

In effect, this is what the public now realizes.

Protection now is a cooperative function shared by the police and the public.

Security is also cooperative, and households can help themselves and one another in this respect.

After so many years of confusion over how to cope with the spread of crime, the public and the police seem finally to have settled into a pattern of shared responsibility that suggests a period of improved security for us all.

What has apparently been outgrown is the obsolete notion that the public can stand aside and leave its protection to the police alone.

The security of our homes is at least in part our own responsibility.

ST. LOUIS POST-DISPATCH

St. Louis, MO, April 27, 1986

Perhaps some of the more misleading figures that come out of Washington are those contained in the Uniform Crime Report, released annually by the Federal Bureau of Investigation. This report can instill either comfort or fear and outrage, depending on whether we're told that our city streets are safer or that we've earned the dubious distinction of being the murder capital of the nation. Fortunately, St. Louis doesn't qualify for the latter dishonor in the latest batch of federal crime statistics.

But that is not to say we should find comfort in the FBI's finding that St. Louis' crime rate fell by almost 1 percent in 1985. The reason is that the figure represents only an average for the entire city and averages can be misleading. The Police Department was asked for a breakdown of the crime figure so as to shed some light on the nearly 1 percent drop.

You may be surprised to learn — as we were — that crimes in some districts were shockingly higher than the FBI's comforting numbers. For example, in the Central District, which covers downtown St. Louis, crime was up by 22.5 percent last year. In the Lucas District, which covers the Central West End and the midtown area, crime was up 12.4 percent. It also was at least 6 percent higher in the three districts on the North Side — Ruskin, Union and Deer — and was up by 3.5 percent in the Penrose District. So where's the decrease? In two districts in South St. Louis — Carondelet (down 11 percent) and Hampton (down 9 percent) — and in the Lynch District (down 0.8 percent) on the Near South Side.

Thus, the report of an overall crime drop conceals a disturbing increase in several parts of the city. Obviously, then, FBI statistics require elaboration and analysis before citizens can draw any useful conclusions about crime in their city.

The Birmingham News

Birmingham, AL, July 5, 1986

In 1975, 32 percent of American homes were hit by serious crime. That seems to have been the climax of a 20-year crime spree in the United States. The rate eased to 30 percent in 1980-81.

Last year, the rate had dropped to 25 percent of U.S. households. In other words, one in every four American households was touched by crimes of violence or theft in 1985.

As tragic as those figures may be, they still are the lowest level in 11 years, according to the Bureau of Justice Statistics.

The drop in crimes committed against households is not yet cause for celebration. Some 22 million households still experienced rape, robbery, assault, burglary or theft last year, down only 1 million households compared to the record in 1975.

The decrease occurred, the bureau said, despite an increase of about 16 million households in the nation during the same period.

While these figures look promising on their face, they may not be a real indicator of the true dimensions of criminal activity. The bureau says much of the credit for the decline must go to the 10-year trend of households moving from urban areas to suburban and rural sections.

Despite more promising statistics, the truth is that the war against crime still must go on. With illegal drug traffic and drug addiction claiming a larger number of Americans each year, the number and seriousness of crimes may rise sharply in the next few years.

We have heard few optimistic predictions that the wave of criminal activity will recede in the near future. Some of this pessimism is based on the nation's inability to stop drug smuggling from foreign countries such as Colombia and Mexico.

While reasons for hope are not completely absent — societies in the past have been known to change directions when they saw the precipice ahead — we would do well to face up to the probabilities that overall the crime rate will increase during this decade, unless drug abuse diminishes.

THE INDIANAPOLIS STAR

Indianapolis, IN, July 13, 1986

Crimes of violence or theft "only" touched one in four American households in 1985 — the lowest level in 11 years, according to the Bureau of Justice Statistics.

But that is nothing to shout about.

In 1975 such crimes hit 32 percent of U.S. households. Last year they affected 25 percent of the nation's 88.8 million households.

Even though 11 million fewer households experienced rape, robbery, assault, burglary or theft last year compared to 1975, the figure is still far too high.

The 1985 report was not sweetened by the information that a decline in thefts accounted for most of last year's decrease. The percentage of households affected by rape, robbery, assault and burglary "did not change significantly," the report said.

In fact, the 1985 report takes on an edge when you realize the drop is traceable not to a mellowing of the criminal population but primarily to a 10-year trend of households moving from urban to suburban districts.

Once this fact sinks into criminal minds, what is to keep rapists, robbers, strongarm hoodlums, burglars and thieves from pulling hit-run crimes in the suburbs? In some suburban areas, for that matter, crime is rising.

One potent strategy against neighborhood crime is alertness. There is widespread evidence that the right kind of nosy neighbors are far more effective weapons than guns. Obviously they are much less dangerous.

People who keep a sharp lookout and quickly call police when they spot criminal activity are strong forces against crime in urban as well as suburban neighborhoods.

A tested strategy always open to police, prosecutors and courts is to take chronic criminals out of circulation — the relatively small percentage of repeaters who account for most serious crimes.

A nation in which one of four households is hit by a major crime in a year has an unacceptably high crime rate.

TULSA WORLD

Tulsa, OK, July 2, 1986

SOME 600,000 fewer American households were touched by crime last year than during the year before, the Department of Justice reported Monday. Only one in four families was victimized by a crime of violence or theft in 1985, the lowest rate in a decade.

That's good news, but it doesn't necessarily mean that law enforcement is working any better. And there is a notable catch or two in the statistics.

It would be comforting to know that improved police work, crime-prevention and social programs aimed at improving American life were all working to reduce violence and theft. But the evidence is that the levelling off is mainly the result of changing age statistics, notably a smaller ratio of young people in the age bracket most likely to be involved in crime.

A significant factor, says Professor Alfred Blumstein of Carnegie-Mellon Institute in Pittsburgh, is a drop of nearly 2 million over the past five years in the size of the 15- to 19-year-old age group.

Further, the statistics count each household only once. So no matter how many times a single household may have been victimized by crime, it shows up only one time in the statistics.

What the statistics tell us is that Americans are not growing less criminally inclined, only older.

Getting old and raising fewer teen-agers is not the perfect crime prevention program; it's merely the only one that works.

The Dispatch

Columbus, OH, July 28, 1986

Proving you can do whatever you want with statistics, final crime data for 1985 just released by the FBI show we are either winning or losing the war on crime, depending on how one interprets the figures.

What we mean is the number of criminal offenses in 1985 was 5 percent above the 1984 figure, which is not very good. But last year's figures were a 7 percent improvement over 1981, which sounds like progress.

Crime went up 4 percent in the cities and 6 percent in the suburbs, which can be taken to mean that as more people move to the suburbs, those with criminal intentions are right on their heels.

The particular crime that rose the most last year was the non-violent one of motor vehicle theft. As crimes go, most people would choose car theft over getting bopped on the head in a robbery assault. But car theft is expensive and inconvenient for the victims. Motor vehicle theft was an astounding $5.1 billion business last year. Those figures argue for police to put more effort into breaking up organized chop-shop rings that are responsible for so much motor vehicle theft.

Excluding simple traffic arrests, 25 percent of all arrests were for drunken driving — a statistic which underlines sharply how pervasive this potentially deadly crime is. Fortunately, the spotlight has been turned more brightly on drunken drivers in the past couple of years. Perhaps that fact, along with tough sentences by judges, will start turning the tide in this area.

Murders were up by 2 percent over 1984, and it should come as no surprise that the weapon of choice among those intent on homicide was a firearm. In a nation that lets handguns proliferate so freely, what else would one expect?

Last year rape grew by 4 percent in the cities and suburbs, and a startling 9 percent in rural areas. This is another crime that has seen stepped-up consciousness lately, and rightly so. That might mean that the crime is being reported more widely than before, but such a supposition is only speculation. The figure for conviction in rape cases was 54 percent, which leaves much room for improvement.

And one more chilling note — 78 law enforcement officers were killed in the line of duty last year. We ought to reflect that those who are sworn to protect us sometimes are called upon to make the ultimate sacrifice.

Are there any conclusions to be drawn from this mish-mash of statistics? First, this country has not made much progress in dealing with the abject poverty that is the breeding ground for so much crime. Second, if crime statistics continue to grow, law enforcement authorities should be thinking about ways to reverse the tide and citizens ought to give police all the help they can when called on.

Considering the crime reported in every nook and cranny of our society, all those who came out of 1985 unscathed must consider that they had a very good year indeed.

The Dispatch

Columbus, OH, March 15, 1986

It was surprising to read the statistics in a recent report on the number of criminal offenders on probation and parole, and it was even more surprising to read about the number of adults on probation, under parole supervision or in prison. The numbers say a lot about American society.

The numbers were compiled by the Bureau of Justice Statistics of the U.S. Justice Department. The report stated that criminal offenders who are on probation and parole outnumber those who are in jail by a 3-to-1 margin. It concluded that one of every 65 adults in the United States was on probation, under parole supervision or imprisoned, and that one of every 35 adult men was under some kind of corrections supervision in 1984, the most recent year for which figures are available.

The numbers suggest that prisons in the nation are overcrowded and that judges are opting for alternative penalties because there is little room left to lock criminals up. The statistics indicate that punishing criminals is a national priority but that taxpayer interest in building prisons is not as great.

The numbers also suggest that many adults — particularly adult males — have gotten involved with law enforcement agencies.

The numbers do no more than reflect reality, but the reality they reflect is surprising and a bit unsettling.

Supreme Court Restricts Juror Exclusion

The Supreme Court ruled, 7-2, April 30, 1986 that exclusion of blacks and other minorities from juries on the basis of race violated the 14th Amendment guarantee of "equal protection of the laws." The decision, in *Boston v. Kentucky*, overturned a 1965 ruling by the court, *Swain v. Alabama*, written by Justice Byron R. White, who agreed with the reversal. "It appears," White said, "that the practice of...eliminating blacks from...juries in cases with black defendants remains widespread...so much so that I agree that an opportunity [to protest such actions] should be afforded when this occurs." The 1965 decision barred such exclusion if the defendant showed that the prosecution did it "in case after case."

Under the latest ruling, written for the majority by Justice Lewis F. Powell Jr., minority defendants would be permitted to object if a prosecutor used peremptory challenges to exclude minorities from juries. Such challenges did not require a reason and constituted automatic exclusion. Normally, prosecutors had power to remove a limited number of potential jurors from a trial without question. The power often had been used by prosecutors to exclude blacks from juries when the defendant was black, on the theory that black jurors would be sympathetic to black defendants. Powell ruled out the court's sanction of an "intuitive judgment" by the prosecutor that the juror in question "would be partial to the defendant because of their shared race."

"Purposeful racial discrimination violates a defendant's right to equal protection because it denies him the protection that a trial by jury is intended to secure," namely, a jury of his peers. Under the ruling, if the minority defendant objected to the peremptory challenge the prosecutor would be required to convince the court that his reasons were not racially motivated.

Justice Thurgood Marshall, the court's only black member, joined Powell's "eloquent opinion" as "a historic step toward eliminating the shameful practice of racial discrimination in the selection of juries." The Reagan administration took sides with Kentucky to support the continued use of the accustomed prosecutorial powers. But Powell rejected their arguments. "Selection procedures that purposefully exclude black persons from juries undermine public confidence in the fairness of our system of justice," he said.

Justice William H. Rehnquist dissented, joined by Chief Justice Warren E. Burger. In Rehnquist's view, there was "nothing unequal" about the use of peremptory challenges to exclude blacks from juries so long as they were also used to exclude whites "in cases involving white defendants, Hispanics in cases involving Hispanic defendants, and Asians in cases involving Asian defendants, and so on."

In a related development, the Supreme Court ruled, 6-3, May 5, 1986 that staunch opponents of the death penalty could be barred from juries in capital punishment. The ruling, written by Justice Rehnquist left unchanged the convictions of 1,714 inmates on death row. The practice of removing death-penalty opponents from juries in capital cases was followed in virtually all of the 37 states that used the death penalty.

THE BLADE

Toledo, OH, May 15, 1986

ONE CAN hardly disagree with the proposition that the trial of a black defendant by a jury from which blacks have been excluded may well violate the equal-protection guarantee of the U.S. Constitution. But the question is not quite as simple as that.

The U.S. Supreme Court has decided by a 7-2 vote to limit the ability of prosecutors to exclude black jurors simply on grounds that they might show undue favoritism to a black defendant. Practically speaking, the decision shifts the burden of proof to the prosecutor to show that he has other valid reasons than race to exclude a black juror. Before that decision, it was up to the defendant to show a systematic pattern of racial discrimination — virtually an impossible task.

All well and good so far. But as the two dissenters pointed out, the peremptory challenge is a well-established part of the common law. It enables opposing lawyers to dismiss a prospective juror without tipping his hand and possibly angering other jurors.

But it can be used for many reasons, including dismissal of jurors who are deemed to be too intelligent or too well-informed, and thus likely to dominate jury deliberations, or those who are a bit too belligerent for the lawyer's taste.

Undoubtedly, peremptory challenges are made against a disproportionate number of blacks, if only because, as compared with other minorities, larger numbers of blacks wind up in court as defendants. A peremptory challenge is far easier to exercise than a challenge for cause. The decision will force prosecutors to work harder to get a jury biased in the direction he wishes it to be. The defense lawyers, of course, exercise their peremptory challenges for the same reason.

One wonders, though, if there will be other suits against the peremptory challenge, say, on the basis of sex, intelligence, education, or occupation. It could well be that the high court has opened a Pandora's box by its decision.

THE DAILY OKLAHOMAN
Oklahoma City, OK, May 2, 1986

IN its continuing concern for the rights of defendants in criminal trials, the Supreme Court has also opened to convicted murderers a way to escape the death penalty simply by watching their p's and q's.

Setting aside the death sentence of a convicted South Carolina murderer, the court ruled he was wrongfully denied a chance to assert "all mitigating circumstances." He had tried to introduce testimony from three witnesses at his sentencing trial that he had made a good adjustment to jail during the seven months before his trial.

The court decided this exclusion deprived the man of his right to place before the sentencing judge relevant evidence in mitigation of punishment.

Oklahoma law specifies eight aggravating circumstances to guide the court in determining whether a defendant should receive the death sentence or life imprisonment. At least one must be found to warrant death.

Mitigating circumstances that would point to a life term rather than death are not spelled out. But if any aggravating circumstances are outweighed by a finding of one or more mitigating circumstances, a death sentence cannot be imposed.

Thus, no matter how vicious a killer was before he was caught, by deliberately playing the good guy while in jail awaiting trial, conceivably he could beat the death penalty that he really deserved.

The Atlanta Journal
THE ATLANTA AND CONSTITUTION
Atlanta, GA, May 3, 1986

All-white juries in racially charged cases have long represented an unsubtle thumb on the scales of justice. Until now, though, prosecutors have had broad leeway to keep blacks off juries of black defendants. Finally, the U.S. Supreme Court has acted to stop this fundamental unfairness.

Across the nation — but especially in the South — the ploy against black defendants is painfully familiar. It works this way: As potential jurors are called, the prosecution uses its peremptory strikes, one by one, against blacks in the jury pool.

In the past, defense objections usually failed. To succeed, defense attorneys were required to show a pattern of exclusion by the prosecutor's office. The standard was well-nigh impossible. No more. The court's decision shifts the burden of proof to the prosecution. Now, when a prosecutor strikes blacks from a jury, a defense objection will bring a hearing. The prosecution must prove its actions were not racially motivated.

The decision is a nice piece of work for today's court, which is not known for its concern about defendants' rights. The edict serves notice that even in these times of retrenchment, blunt racism won't be tolerated.

Nevertheless, it is not clear precisely how momentous the ruling will be. As Justice Byron White put it: "Much litigation will be required to spell out the contours of the court's ... holding today."

For example, the court didn't say if its decision should be made retroactive. If it does become retroactive — and by all rights it should — the impact could be dramatic.

No one knows how many blacks have been tried, convicted and (often) sentenced to death by juries from which blacks were pointedly excluded, but such cases are thought to number in the hundreds. Provided the jury issue was raised at trial, each case presumably could be retried.

Given that possibility, the courts should automatically stay executions of blacks who were convicted by all-white juries until the matter is resolved.

There will be other questions as the new rules are implemented. What happens, for instance, when a prosecutor seats one black on a jury, then strikes all others? Will trial judges and their appellate brethren see that 11-to-1 ratio as possibly unfair? Or will the practice of racism in jury selection only trade bluntness for a subtler approach?

Whatever happens, the court has ruled wisely. If the scales of justice continue to sway sometimes with the prevailing breezes, at least an odious burden of unconcealed racism has been removed.

THE ARIZONA REPUBLIC
Phoenix, AZ, May 13, 1986

IN a decision widely hailed as "a historic step" toward eliminating racism in trial juries, a case can be made to add the word "backward" to complete the description of the U.S. Supreme Court's recent ruling.

The high court, ostensibly to end racial discrimination in jury selection, ruled the other day that prosecutors trying black defendants and, presumably, other minorities, no longer are able to exclude jurors because of concern they will favor a defendant of the same race.

Striking a blow at the racial impact of the courtroom practice of "peremptory challenge," the justices ruled 7-2 that prosecutors may be required to defend the exclusion of a black juror from a panel selected to try a black defendant. In jury selection procedures, called *voir dire*, both the defense and the prosecution can exclude jurors for "cause" — a particular knowledge of, or relationship to, the case — and are allotted a number of "peremptory challenges," whereby they can eliminate potential jurors without any articulated reason, based upon suspicions, perceptions or mere whims.

Overturning part of a 1965 landmark ruling which held that a defendant needed to show a pattern of cases in which minority jurors were excluded, the burden now rests on the prosecution to prove that peremptory striking of minority jurors is not racially motivated.

No doubt the court's "step" was justified — nothing should jeopardize a fair and impartial trial, particularly the despicable practice of racism — but it appears to be in the wrong direction. By attempting to eliminate racial bias, the court's majority decision has introduced racial selection into the courtroom. Defendants now must show that they are members of a cognizable racial group, and potential jurors must be questioned about, and identify, their race.

The court also fell short in attempting to balance the Equal Protection Clause of the 14th Amendment with the Sixth Amendment right to a fair and impartial jury.

To ensure a fair and impartial jury coupled with equal protection, it would seem only logical that protection from other biases, such as sex and religion, be afforded a defendant. For instance, in a rape case, a defense attorney may use peremptory challenges to exclude all potential female jurors, hoping males would be more inclined to support the defendant.

Additionally, the decision sets no limits on the defense counsel, who could exclude all whites or all minorities or all whatevers from a jury panel to attain whatever perceived advantage. Instead, the court ruled narrowly on the matter of racial construction, in effect according preferential, unequal and color-specific constraints into a judicial process that is supposed to be colorblind.

If peremptory challenges are viewed by the court as aiding and abetting discrimination, should not all peremptory challenges, not just those relating to minorities, be eliminated to ensure that fairness and, above all, equality remain at the cornerstones of our justice system?

The pernicious "venire" of racism must never be allowed to stain the judicial process, but "justice for *all*" demands nothing less than the equal application of the rules of law.

The Des Moines Register
Des Moines, IA, May 23, 1986

Does a juror's position on capital punishment color the ability to render a fair judgment?

The Supreme Court, which has struggled with the question before, reconsidered it recently in a case in which a defendant sought to show that jurors without substantial qualms about the death penalty are more likely to convict. The court was unmoved.

At issue was its 1968 Witherspoon vs. Illinois decision, which set the standard for excluding from juries opponents to the death penalty: Those who (1) would never consider imposing the death penalty or (2) whose strong opposition to the death penalty would make it impossible for them to be impartial.

In his lower-court appeal, Ardie McCree, convicted of murder, produced studies purporting to show that jurors who either favor or do not strongly oppose the death penalty are more likely to vote for conviction.

Writing for the majority, Justice William Rehnquist dismissed the studies as seriously flawed. But, even if they are valid, he said it would make no difference because, in capital cases, juries needn't be "balanced" with pro- and anti-death-penalty jurors.

He said the Constitution demands only that jurors chosen from a cross-section of the community be able to "conscientiously and properly carry out their sworn duty to apply the law to the facts and particulars of the case."

But the decision reveals an inconsistency on the part of the court: The majority accepts the notion that opposition to capital punishment could render a juror predisposed to acquit, but not the logical opposite case, that a pro-death-penalty juror might be predisposed to convict.

If jurors' death-penalty views predisposed them toward conviction, as seems likely, that should be cause for removal. The tough question is determining how seriously their capital-punishment views affect their impartiality.

Unfortunately, this decision does not move any closer to answering that question. Thus, because a number of pending appeals were based on similar arguments, the ruling will result in a spate of executions in states that permit capital punishment.

Pretrial Detention of Suspects Upheld by Supreme Court

The Supreme Court May 26, 1987 upheld the practice of "preventative detention" before trial if a federal court determined the suspect was a danger to the public. In a 6-3 decision written by Chief Justice William Rehnquist, the court affirmed the constitutionality of the Bail Reform Act of 1984, which provided for the government to request preventative detention and for a court to hold a hearing to determine whether the accused posed a threat to others or to the community. Before 1984, bail traditionally had been denied primarily as a guarantee that the accused would show up for trial or to prevent suspects them from intimidating judges, jurors, witnesses or prosecutors.

Rehnquist, in *U.S. v. Salerno*, noted that "in our society liberty is the norm, and detention prior to trial or without trial is the carefully limited exception. The provision for pretrial detention prior to trial or without trial is the carefully limited exception," he said. Justice Thurgood Marshall, in sharp dissent, called the law an "abhorrent limitation on the presumption of innocence." The federal appeals court in New York had ruled in July 1986 that detention in this case, under the Bail Reform Act, was unconstitutional. It was "repugnant to the concept of substantive due process, which we believe prohibits the total deprivation of liberty" in order to prevent future crimes, the court said. The case involved alleged Mafia leader Anthony (Fat Tony) Salerno, head of the Genovese crime family, and Vincent (Fish) Cafaro, an alleged captain in the organization. Salerno, 76, was already in jail from another case. Cafaro was released on bail in October 1986.

The court's decision on the controversial issue was seen as a victory for the Reagan administration, which defended the 1984 law, and as a blow to civil libertarians. Terry Eastland, spokesman for the Justice Department, said "the decision means that our society will be a safer one." David Goldstein, an attorney for the American Civil Liberties Union, said, "What the court has done is to reverse the 200-year assumption of innocence and replace it with this vague notion of dangerousness."

THE ARIZONA REPUBLIC
Phoenix, AZ, May 27, 1987

IN a key test weighing constitutional protections of individual rights vs. the rights of society to be protected against criminal dangers, the U.S. Supreme Court has logically and prudently tipped the scales of justice toward the greater good.

By a 6-3 vote in a case involving the disputed concept of preventive detention, the majority of the high court Tuesday upheld a provision of the Bail Reform Act of 1984 allowing suspects to be held without a right to bail if they are found to present a clear and present danger to the rest of society.

Overturning a decision by the 2nd U.S. Circuit Court of Appeals that preventive detention violated the "due-process clause" of the Constitution embodied in the Fifth Amendment and in Eighth Amendment prohibitions against excessive bail, the high court said the compelling interests of society can sometimes outweigh the rights of the individual.

The test case involved two reputed Mafia leaders in New York City who had been arrested and charged with a variety of offenses ranging from racketeering and bid-rigging to murder conspiracies. The government, arguing the defendants were "lethally dangerous" to society, requested the pair be held in custody without bail to prevent their return to "business as usual" — threats, beatings, intimidation and murder.

After hearing evidence linking one of the defendants to plans to kill four mob figures, three of whom were killed, a federal judge granted the government's motion. The order was overturned by the appeals court on the grounds that a prediction of future criminal activity should not abrogate constitutional protections.

Writing for the high court's majority, Chief Justice William Rehnquist disagreed, saying: "Congress did not formulate the pretrial detention provisions as punishment for dangerous individuals. Congress instead perceived pretrial detention as a potential solution to a pressing societal problem. There is no doubt that preventing danger to the community is a legitimate regulatory goal."

When applied prudently, judiciously and with inherent safeguards, preventive detention — far from establishing a precedent for police-state action, as some critics have charged — is a logical extension of the long-held concept that individual freedoms do not guarantee the right to interfere with or abrogate the rights of others. In this case, and in other such cases containing a demonstrative threat to society, the fundamental rights of the majority — to life, liberty and the pursuit of happiness — demand equal protection under law.

Omaha World-Herald
Omaha, NE, May 28, 1987

The U.S. Supreme Court, by upholding preventive detention, has given law enforcement officers a tool that can enhance public safety without unduly restricting the rights of people accused of a crime.

Preventive detention is a difficult concept for some Americans to swallow, and understandably so. One of the foundations of the U.S. legal system is the presumption of innocence — a person accused of a crime is innocent until proved guilty.

Denying a defendant the right to be released on bond between arrest and trial seems to some people to contradict the presumption of innocence. Justice Thurgood Marshall, who dissented in the 6-3 decision, accused the majority of sacrificing the presumption of innocence in the interests of expediency.

Situations sometimes arise, however, in which the defendant, while entitled to the presumption of innocence, is also demonstrably dangerous. Twenty-four states, including Nebraska, have passed laws permitting a judge to hold a defendant without bond in specific kinds of cases, such as murder and rape, if the judge is convinced that the public's safety requires it. The federal government passed such a law in 1984.

Congressional supporters of the no-bail provision gave the example of a schoolyard drug pusher who could ruin countless young lives if permitted to keep his business afloat between arrest and trial. The case before the Supreme Court involved two accused crime syndicate bosses who, prosecutors convinced the judge, would be likely to resume their loan-sharking, gambling and extortion if set free.

The Supreme Court decision doesn't mean that judges will be able to jail just anyone before trial. Defendants will still have their rights and the presumption of innocence. Before a judge can hold a person without bond, strong evidence must be presented concerning the threat to the public's safety.

Not everyone who is arrested and held in jail is guilty. On the other hand, criminals sometimes go free because the evidence isn't sufficient to convince the jury. The system isn't perfect. But it has a number of safeguards to minimize the chances of a defendant's being denied his right to be presumed innocent.

As Chief Justice William Rehnquist noted in the majority opinion, the courts have previously held that the government's interest in public safety, in appropriate circumstances, outweighs an individual interest in personal liberty. One of those circumstances, obviously, is when the evidence strongly indicates that the defendant, if released on bond, would endanger the public.

The Register-Guard

Eugene, OR, May 31, 1987

When the Chief Justice of the United States writes an opinion stating that two amendments to the Constitution don't mean what they say, Americans should tremble for their rights. William Rehnquist did just that last Tuesday when he issued an opinion on behalf of a six-member U.S. Supreme Court majority upholding a law that allows preventive detention of criminal suspects.

Congress passed the law in 1984 as part of an anti-crime bill. Its purpose is to allow the government to deny bail to accused criminals who might pose a danger to society if released. The law specifies the types of crimes for which a suspect can be detained and establishes procedures for evaluating the risk that they might commit further crimes if released.

A challenge to the law came from lawyers representing Anthony "Fat Tony" Salerno, the head of an organized crime family who is accused of various violent crimes. He has been held without bail since March of 1986. Federal officials worried that if bail were set, Salerno would have no trouble raising the money and would resume his criminal activities.

The challenge was destined to fail. The plaintiffs claimed the preventive detention law was unconstitutional on its face, which meant they had to prove that it could not be valid under any circumstances. The government's power to hold suspects without bail in certain situations is well established.

But Rehnquist's reasoning in his opinion upholding the law is troubling. He swept aside arguments that preventive detention violates the Fifth Amendment, which states that no person shall be deprived of liberty without due process of law. "The mere fact that a person is detained does not inexorably lead to the conclusion that the government has imposed punishment . . . ," he wrote. Preventive detention, he reasoned, is not a substantive punishment, but a procedural method of regulating suspects' behavior.

Rehnquist then offered a novel interpretation of the Eighth Amendment, which states that excessive bail shall not be required. "This clause, of course, says nothing about whether bail shall be available at all," Rehnquist wrote.

Justice Thurgood Marshall expressed his alarm at Rehnquist's logic in a sharp dissent. "The majority proceeds as though the only substantive right protected by the due process clause is a right to be free from punishment before conviction" of a crime, Marshall wrote. "The majority's technique for infringing on this right is simple: merely redefine any measure which is claimed to be punishment as 'regulation,' and, magically, the Constitution no longer prohibits its imposition."

Marshall was equally unpersuaded by Rehnquist's reading of the Eighth Amendment. Judges could skirt the prohibition against excessive bail, he wrote, by refusing to set bail at any amount. Marshall asked whether Congress would ever need to pass a preventive detention law, since under Rehnquist's interpretation nothing prevents judges from denying bail even when there is no evidence that the suspect poses a danger to society or would fail to appear for trial.

People should be less concerned about the law itself than with the court majority's reasoning in its favor. The law is narrow, providing specific limitations for preventive detention and allowing adversarial hearings when bail is denied. But the decision is broad, casting doubts on the protections provided by the basic rights to due process and reasonable bail.

Even people such as Anthony Salerno deserve to have those rights preserved. Marshall explained why Rehnquist's reinterpretation should be greeted with dismay: "Honoring the presumption of innocence is often difficult; sometimes we must pay substantial social costs as a result of our commitment to the values we espouse. But at the end of the day the presumption of innocence protects the innocent; the shortcuts we take with those whom we believe to be guilty injure only those wrongfully accused and, ultimately, ourselves."

Los Angeles Times

Los Angeles, CA, May 28, 1987

The majority opinion by Chief Justice William H. Rehnquist that it is constitutional to hold dangerous criminals without bail turns logic and the Constitution on their heads. The chief justice and five of his colleagues reached this conclusion only by the most tortured twisting of the English language and in spite of the plain meaning of the Fifth and Eighth Amendments. There should be no mistake about it: The majority of the Supreme Court does not believe that accused persons are innocent until proven guilty.

To be sure, there are conflicting rights here, namely, society's right to protect itself from murder and mayhem and an individual's right not to be incarcerated without trial. When rights conflict, as Rehnquist noted in his opinion, judges must balance one against the other in deciding where justice lies. Reasonable people can disagree about how to strike the balance. In the case before the court (United States vs. Salerno, 86-87), six justices favored society's right to protect itself, while three justices—Thurgood Marshall, William J. Brennan Jr. and John Paul Stevens—would have balanced on behalf of an individual's right to due process of law.

We are more comfortable with the view of Brennan, Stevens and Marshall, who correctly called the majority's opinion an "abhorrent limitation on the presumption of innocence." The Constitution is designed to protect any such limitation and to make it impossible for the authorities to keep someone in jail merely by labeling him "dangerous." Rehnquist and the majority neatly skirt the problem of punishment without trial by declaring that pretrial detention is "regulation" rather than incarceration.

And in the most tortured reasoning of all, Rehnquist opined that even though the Eighth Amendment forbids "excessive bail," it "says nothing about whether bail shall be available at all."

The purpose of bail is to make sure that an accused person will appear at trial while not keeping him in jail before he is convicted. It is a perversion of the system to use bail to keep people in jail without trial. If there is a case to be made against someone, let the government make it. If not, "preventive detention" should not be used as a substitute.

In the case of the Mafia leader Anthony Salerno, there is a strong social desire to keep him locked up, but the nation's legal system should not go down that slippery slope of keeping people in jail because we don't like them.

MILWAUKEE SENTINEL

Milwaukee, WI, May 29, 1987

A US Supreme Court ruling upholding so-called preventive detention laws should encourage their use by state courts.

Here in Wisconsin, legislation permitting denial of bail to accused persons deemed dangerous to the community was enacted in 1982 as the result of a landmark constitutional amendment approved overwhelmingly by state voters.

Under Wisconsin law, those accused of serious crimes such as first-degree murder and first-degree sexual assault can be held without bail for up to 70 days.

Preventive detention is seen as a threat to civil rights by some and caution must be taken against its abuse. But the law can and should be used as a tool for assuring public safety if imposed under procedures that require a formal request by the prosecutor and a finding of need by a judge.

In the absence of such legislation, bail generally has been denied only if a judge determined a defendant was likely to flee. Chief Justice William H. Rehnquist, writing for the six-member majority in the case before the high court, said the Constitution did not require that judicial decisions be tied exclusively to preventing a defendant from fleeing.

Cases involving people out on bail who have caused harm or death to others have occurred frequently enough to show that having the accused skip town is not the worst thing that can happen before he comes to trial.

In opposing the majority, Justice Thurgood Marshall argued that preventive detention was consistent with tyranny and a police state. His is a valid concern.

But the defendants involved in the case that the court considered are reputed New York bosses of crime syndicates that routinely employ tyranny and disdain law enforcement. Evidence against one of the men indicated he was involved in ordering murders.

While preventive detention may temporarily deprive them of their liberty, they still retain the right to a speedy trial. Preventive detention should encourage them to press for that opportunity while easing fears of a concerned public.

Birmingham Post-Herald

Birmingham, AL, May 29, 1987

While acknowledging the "importance and fundamental nature" of the right of suspects to remain free pending trial, the Supreme Court has ruled, correctly in our opinion, that there are times when this right can be circumscribed in the public interest.

In a 6 to 3 decision, the court settled the decades-old argument over whether defendants may be held in custody before their trials if their release would present a danger to the community. It upheld the constitutionality of a 1984 law that allows such "preventive detention" under certain conditions.

When the measure was before Congress, it was supported by President Reagan, law enforcement officials and a bipartisan coalition that included such liberal Democrats as Sen. Edward Kennedy and Sen. Joseph Biden of Delaware, now a presidential candidate.

Not everyone is happy with the law. A spokesman for the American Civil Liberties Union said that what the Supreme Court has done is "to reverse the 200-year assumption of innocence and replace it with this vague notion of dangerousness." And Justice Thurgood Marshall, writing a dissenting opinion, likened the "preventive detention" statute to the tactics of a "police state."

The court's majority ruled, however, that despite "the individual's strong interest in liberty," the right to remain free under a presumption of innocence until proven guilty may in some situations be "subordinated to the greater needs of society."

The opinion, written by Chief Justice William Rehnquist dismissed the argument that preventive detention constitutes "punishment," saying instead that it falls under the description of government "regulation." The chief justice wrote: "There is no doubt that preventing danger to the community is a legitimate regulatory goal."

He also pointed out that the 1984 law has substantial safeguards against abuse. It requires that a federal judge hold a hearing to decide whether an accused person poses a threat to others. It entitles the accused to have a lawyer present. The evidence must be "clear and convincing" to obtain a detention order, the accused must be given written reasons for being held, and the detention may be appealed to a higher court.

The Supreme Court's action has been described as among its most important criminal rulings of recent years. The public will be safer for it.

The Times-Picayune
The States-Item

New Orleans, LA, May 30, 1987

The U.S. Supreme Court's ruling on what is not quite accurately being called "preventive detention" brings common sense to the application of constitutional principles to providing for the common welfare. The court, 6-3, ruled that a judge can deny bail to a person if there is "clear and convincing" evidence that he would be a danger to the community if freed on bail.

"Preventive detention" is usually used to mean detaining someone who has done nothing criminal to prevent him from doing something criminal. Its most benign use is in rounding up potential threats in a specific situation — a visit by a president, pope or controversial public figure. Its malign use is in tyrannies to jail indefinitely and without charge opponents of the regime.

But such cases were not before the Supreme Court. It was considering people arrested on specific crimes against whom an additional case could be made that they might commit other crimes if allowed freedom before trial on the original charges.

The specific case involved two Mafia chiefs, but less dramatic applications come easily to mind: career criminals with uninterrupted and violent pre-arrest records of robbery, rape or whatever. Many instances also spring to mind of arrestees who rob or steal to pay the bondsman who stood their bail.

The court minority and, predictably, the American Civil Liberties Union, argued that denying bail for such a reason unconstitutionally presumes guilt before a trial verdict. Bail has traditionally been a right to be denied only when the judge believes the arrestee might flee or be a threat to witnesses in his case.

It hardly seems an unconstitutional extension of bail-denial to include the probable threat the arrestee would pose to the community among the accepted reasons for denying bail.

"We have repeatedly held," wrote Chief Justice William Rehnquist for the majority, "that the government's regulatory interest in community safety can, in appropriate circumstances, outweigh an individual's liberty interest. The government's interest in preventing crime by arrestees is both legitimate and compelling."

The qualifications of "in appropriate circumstances" and "clear and convincing" evidence makes it unlikely that "this is going to force some innocent people to spend a great deal of time in jail that they didn't deserve," as David Whitmore of the Louisiana ACLU argues.

We do not suggest that only the guilty are arrested or that no one can argue a right to bail. As to the federal statute upheld by the court, a Justice Department spokesman said that in the last year and a half federal prosecutors have successfully petitioned for denying bail 2,500 times, generally in organized crime and drug cases.

"The ultimate impact of the court's decision," he said, "will be on the streets of our nation." State laws tracking the federal law should increase public safety without interfering with constitutional due process in criminal cases.

FORT WORTH STAR-TELEGRAM

Fort Worth, TX, May 29, 1987

Once again this week, the U.S. Supreme Court addressed the balance between the protection of society and the rights of the individual within that society.

The court's 6-3 decision to uphold the preventive detention clause of the 1984 anti-crime bill falls on the side of society in this continuing battle, but it also should focus our attention on the need for vigilance in the application of all our laws.

Under this law — enacted in response to what Congress saw as a problem of crimes being committed by persons granted bail — approximately 2,500 indicted criminal defendants have been denied pretrial bail because prosecutors argued, and judges agreed, that the defendants would pose a danger to the community if freed.

In a passionate dissenting opinion, Justice Thurgood Marshall sees pretrial detention as a threat to liberty and a denial of every American's right to presumption of innocence.

His deep-felt concern should be shared by all Americans. Indeed, it must be shared by the court's majority.

But Chief Justice William Rehnquist, writing for that majority, points to the specific restrictions Congress placed on preventive detention.

"In our society," said Rehnquist, "liberty is the norm and detention prior to trial or without trial is the carefully limited exception."

There is no evidence that pretrial detention has been, or will be, employed in an abusive or capricious manner. Provision for adversary hearing and appeal help guard against this. There is protection against Marshall's concern about a "police state."

Rehnquist recognizes the fears raised by Marshall but says, "The fact that an act might operate unconstitutionally under a conceivable set of circumstances is insufficent to render it wholly invalid."

There is, in most laws, a possibility of abuse or misuse. That's why we have courts. They hold the reins to society's justice and the individual's liberties.

Preventive detention, as spelled out by Congress and upheld by the highest court, is a tool that must be used carefully and sparingly, even against organized crime bosses and drug traffickers. It can never be a substitute for efficient police work, speedy trial or a smoothly functioning system of criminal justice.

But it is part of the law, meeting the legislative and judicial tests prescribed by the nation. Like most laws, its usefulness depends on officers' and judges' intelligent and honest application. Only in that way can society be protected while individual liberty remains, in Rehnquist's words, "the norm."

ST. LOUIS POST-DISPATCH
St. Louis, MO, May 28, 1987

The cherished American tradition of innocent until proven guilty was dealt a damaging rebuff this week by the Supreme Court. In a 6-to-3 ruling, the court upheld a law allowing federal judges to deny bail to defendants on the ground that, if freed, they would commit a serious crime. Thus, the court has countenanced the spectacle of a person being regarded as innocent of the crime with which he is charged but in effect found guilty of a crime that has not occurred.

In upholding preventive detention, Chief Justice William Rehnquist, writing for the majority, swept aside the Eighth Amendment's prohibition against unreasonable bail. It doesn't apply, he said, because preventive detention does not seek to prevent flight, which is the purpose of requiring bail. Instead, it seeks to prevent a person from committing a crime. That being so, one would think the practice would violate the Constitution's due process clause. Not so, Mr. Rehnquist said. Society's interest in safety outweighs the individual's interest in liberty, he argued.

That line of reasoning can be used to suppress virtually every right Americans thought was guaranteed by the Constitution. It can justify silencing the press, preventing citizens from holding protest meetings, forcing individuals to testify against themselves, confiscating property or conducting secret trials. This is not to suggest that Mr. Rehnquist favors such actions in the name of safety. Rather, it is to say that his rationale for imprisoning a person for a crime that has not been committed can provide the underpinning for even more drastic deprivations of liberty.

It is important to point out that the law at issue in the case, enacted in 1984, does not limit preventive detention to defendants thought to pose a threat of violence. It also includes those charged with drug offenses and certain repeat offenders. At least five states now have preventive detention laws similar to the federal government's, and the Supreme Court ruling is certain to encourage many others to follow suit.

In his dissent, Justice Thurgood Marshall drove home just how thoroughly incompatible preventive detention is with the principle of presumed innocence: "Let us suppose that a defendant is indicted and the government shows by clear and convincing evidence that he is dangerous and should be detained pending a trial, at which trial the defendant is acquitted. May the government continue to hold the defendant in detention based upon its showing that he is dangerous?" Of course not, but the logic of preventive detention requires that it should be able to. After all, the man is just as dangerous, presumably, after his acquittal as he was before he went on trial.

What the preventive detention decision means, as Justice Marshall observed, is that America lacks the courage of the convictions set out in the Constitution about due process. What other constitutional protections will we lose faith in next?

Newsday
Long Island, NY, May 28, 1987

Backed by the Constitution's due-process requirements, the presumption of a criminal defendant's innocence until guilt has been proved is a formidable barrier to the abuse of police power. That barrier was seriously undermined by the Supreme Court this week.

In a 6-3 ruling Tuesday, the court upheld a 1984 federal law that permits preventive detention before trial if a judge decides the defendant threatens "the safety of any other person and the community." So judges may deny bail to competent, adult Americans not only to guarantee their appearance for trial or to prevent them from threatening jurors or witnesses, but to forestall the possibility that they *might* commit some hypothetical crime.

The defendants in this case do not evoke sympathy. They are Anthony Salerno, an organized-crime boss serving a 102-year sentence after conviction in another case, and Vincent Cafaro, now an informer testifying for the government.

But while the issue of preventive detention is moot for the two who brought the appeal, it's very much alive for thousands of others. Since the law was enacted, about 2,500 federal defendants have been held without bail. What's more, several states have passed similar laws. But prison overcrowding — or the expense of building and staffing more prisons — is not the critical issue here. The abandonment of the presumption of innocence is.

Chief Justice William Rehnquist argued for the majority that preventive detention is "regulatory" rather than punitive in nature, and that society's need to protect itself takes precedence over an individual's right to liberty. But jail is jail, whether you're there because a judge thinks you may pose a threat or because you're being punished for committing a crime.

Rehnquist also contended that even though the Eighth Amendment prohibits "excessive" bail, it "says nothing about whether bail shall be available at all." But as Justice Thurgood Marshall noted in a stinging dissent, "Whether the magistrate sets bail at $1 billion or refuses to set bail at all, the consequences are indistinguishable."

Americans have no doubt paid a price for presuming innocence and guaranteeing due process; some criminals do commit more crimes while awaiting trial or go free because of procedural errors. But the price of weakening those restrictions is potentially far greater. Marshall recognized that when he wrote:

"Throughout the world today there are men, women and children interned indefinitely awaiting trials which may never come and which may be a mockery of the word, because their governments believe them to be 'dangerous.' Our Constitution . . . can shelter us forever from the evils of such unchecked power."

Not if the Supreme Court continues down this path.

PEOPLE ACCUSED OF CRIMES MAY BE DENIED BAIL BEFORE TRIAL IF DEEMED DANGEROUS TO THE COMMUNITY. —U.S. SUPREME COURT

Federal Sentencing Guidelines Offered

A federal commission April 13, 1987 released guidelines for federal judges to follow in sentencing criminals. The panel asked Congress to delay imposition of the system until August 1988 so it could be tested first. Under the law establishing the U.S. Sentencing Commission in 1984, its proposals were due by April 13 and were to take effect in six months unless Congress blocked or amended them. But the panel asked Congress for an additional delay of nine months to allow judges to continue current practices while compiling reports for the commission on what the sentences would be on the same cases under the new system.

The new system was constructed with 43 levels of sentences, from no imprisonment to a life term. Each crime was assigned a level, such as a level-six sentence, up to six months in prison, for a first offender convicted of fraud. If the amount of the fraud was between $50,000 and $100,000, the sentence level would be raised to 11, which meant eight to 14 months. If more than one person was defrauded, the sentence rose two levels to a prison term of 12 to 18 months. Repeat offenders faced higher levels and additional jail time.

Early release through parole would be abolished under the new system, which focused instead on "real-time" prison terms. "The number of individuals who will be required to serve some period of incarceration has increased" under the new system, said U.S. Court of Appeals Judge William Wilkins, chairman of the commission. Probation was retained and would be permitted for some part of the prison term. But the commission warned Congress that, "Under present sentencing practice, courts sentence to probation an inappropriately high percentage of offenders guilty of certain economic crimes, such as theft, tax evasion, antitrust offenders, insider trading, fraud and embezzlement..."

Under the new code, a first offender for securities fraud, such as insider trading, would get two to eight months in prison. If the gain was between $1 million and $2 million, the sentence would be two years to 30 months. Prior convictions could add an additional three to six months, etc. Judges would be required to follow the code whenever possible. If the situation varied from the guidelines, however, the judges could depart from the rules, so long as they presented their reasons in writing. The departures would be subject to appeal.

ST. LOUIS POST-DISPATCH
St. Louis, MO, April 24, 1987

The chairman of a commission proposing sensible new guidelines on sentencing criminals to federal prison says the rules would eliminate wide disparities between what he calls "the hanging judge and the Baby Ruth judge." The proposals, said commission chairman William Wilkins, a federal appellate judge, would see to it that "similar defendants who commit similar crimes will receive similar sentences."

The proposals are not without their problems, however. Federal prisons are already 53 percent above capacity, and critics of the guidelines say an estimate that the new rules would lead to a 10 percent increase in prison population over the next 10 years is much too low.

Still, a criminal justice system that administers punishment evenhandedly is essential. Under the guidelines, each federal crime would fall into one of 43 categories and each category would carry a range of possible sentences. The proposals would eliminate the parole system, which often makes original sentences meaningless by allowing prisoners to spend far less time in custody than the judge intended. Time earned for good behavior would still be allowed.

To safeguard against unduly rigid sentencing requirements, the guidelines have a provision allowing a judge to hand down a sentence outside the allowable range if he details what factors influenced him to make an exception. Both the prosecution and the defense could appeal such a sentence.

The new guidelines could go a long way toward answering frequent complaints about the current system, complaints such as a lenient stance toward white-collar criminals and unequal treatment by the federal parole system. The new guidelines need careful study by Congress, but they appear to be a major step toward equal justice under the law.

THE ATLANTA CONSTITUTION
Atlanta, GA, April 16, 1987

Don't be misled. The guidelines issued by the U.S. Sentencing Commission are not a reform. Nor do they represent a bold stroke for honesty in the criminal-justice system. Rather, they are evidence of a nation that is tired of facts and reason — a nation ready to fool itself into thinking that it has taken a decisive stand against crime and criminals.

It hasn't. At best, it has cut its losses from a program it never learned to manage: the "rehabilitation model" of penology. At worst, it has established a system that will perpetuate, rather than curb, criminality.

Parts of the rehabilitation model date back 200 years, to a meeting of Quakers in the home of Benjamin Franklin. The group outlined a need for indeterminate sentences and programs of individualized treatment for wrongdoers. As implemented much later, parole boards were created to decide when inmates were ready to rejoin society.

And yet, notions of rehabilitation have always clashed with an ever-popular clamor for punishment. So for all our advancements in psychiatry, education, criminology and other social sciences over two centuries, clear-cut success stories among inmates have been few. To this day, prisons are good at degradation and inept at most else.

In 1984, Congress decided to "reform" the mess. It abandoned the rehabilitation model (as if it had ever really embraced it), abolished parole and told the Sentencing Commission to establish a system of less flexible terms. Under the circumstances, the panel did as well as anyone could expect.

Its guidelines, if ratified by Congress, would increase the likelihood of hard-time for white-collar criminals. Fine. If prison does little to deter ordinary criminals, its specter can deter more sophisticated folks. While judges, alas, will find it tougher to tailor specific sentences to specific convicts, the task will not be impossible. A judge may impose a sentence outside the guidelines by citing, in writing, mitigating or aggravating circumstances that led to the decision.

Nevertheless, the changes are a dead cinch ultimately to do more harm than good. By the conservative reckoning of the commission chairman, they will boost the federal prison population by 10 percent. But according to Alvin Bronstein of the American Civil Liberties Union's National Prison Project: "I would project that in five years, you could be 200 percent over capacity, unless there was a massive prison-building campaign."

Even a 10 percent increase would mean big trouble. The reason: The federal prison system is 53 percent over capacity already. Without intervention from Congress, the rest of this dismal script is obvious: Crowding will worsen. Violence will rise. Educational, vocational and psychological programs will get short shrift. Men will emerge from their confinement all the more brutalized for the experience — and society will pay dearly.

Strangely, though, we are doing little to protect ourselves. Juvenile-justice programs get scant attention in Washington nowadays. Nobody wants to consider rehabilitation. The fashion is punishment, just as it was in the days before that 1787 meeting at Ben Franklin's house in Philadelphia.

Sentencing reform? The nation is still waiting. Congress could start by scrapping the commission's plan and starting over again. It probably won't, but it should.

DAYTON DAILY NEWS
Dayton, OH, February 18, 1987

This should be an easy one for the U.S. Supreme Court.

The justices recently heard arguments on the constitutionality of a 1984 federal law that allows defendants to be jailed while they are waiting to go to trial if there is evidence that the accused might do something violent in the interim.

Some lawyers think this is a thorny question because the practice amounts to punishing someone before he has been convicted. The system is supposed to treat people as if they're innocent until proven guilty.

There are exceptions, however, to this rule. Courts throw defendants in jail when there's reason to believe that they will flee or that they'll harm anyone who will be participating in the case against them, such as the judge, prosecutor or a witness. These precautions are considered constitutional.

Chief Justice William Rehnquist captured the crucial issue in this case when he asked the defense attorney arguing against detention of his clients this question: "Why is the sanctity of the judicial system so much greater than the sanctity of the life of someone who is not involved in the judicial system?"

The defense attorney probably had a hard time with that one.

The defendants in this case aren't nice people, according to the prosecutor. He said they are "lethally dangerous" and that they likely would engage in "murder and mayhem" if they were released pending their trial. The trial judge also had agreed with this contention, ruling that there would be people at risk if these men were allowed on the streets.

The point is that somebody didn't just decide arbitrarily to send a couple of defendants to jail early. Evidence was presented, arguments were heard and an objective third party decided that there was a good chance the fellows he was hearing about weren't just bad-check passers. Ample procedural precautions were taken.

Judges ought to be able to make these kinds of judgments, as a protection for society. Innocent people don't deserve to be hurt or die because the system can't make exceptions and recognize obviously violent people.

THE LINCOLN STAR
Lincoln, NE, April 15, 1987

Change always involves a certain risk, and such is the case with the proposed new criteria for criminal sentencing in the federal courts.

Now, federal judges pass sentence much as their state court counterparts within the broad outlines of what the law prescribes. Parole or probation is always a possibility after sentencing.

On Monday, the U.S. Sentencing Commission submitted to Congress a sweeping revision of procedure. In a sense, judicial latitude in sentencing will be expanded but the criteria involved will be more specific.

As briefly explained in press reports, the change would be something similar to Nebraska law governing application of the death penalty. Nebraska law in such cases allows the death penalty when certain conditions are found to have existed, including commission of the crime in an especially heinous manner and exhibiting unusual depravity in the process.

Criteria in the Nebraska situation are few; in all criminal cases at the federal level they will be many. The commission might have been well advised to consider Nebraska's experience in drafting its new program.

A sentencing procedure that establishes more definitive standards of measure offers the possibility of more equality of justice, but it also offers the possibility of greater inequality. Nebraskans are not so sure that use of the death penalty is any more equitable here than it has ever been.

In nearly every case in which Nebraska applies the death penalty, there is at least some public perception that the judges made a poor decision. The reason for this is that you cannot write a process for sentencing that does not allow for some subjectivity. Total objectivity cannot be achieved because people simply do not agree on the precise meanings of words.

Under newly proposed federal procedure, each federal crime would fall into one of 43 categories for sentencing. That may contribute to more equal administration of justice or it may broaden the margin for error.

Better sentencing decisions will be more important because the new process eliminates the opportunity of parole. If an individual is sentenced to five years in a federal prison, he will serve the full term, with time off for good behavior.

Parole would be mandatory for a prescribed period of time following completion of the sentence. Parole was never intended as a means of mitigating wrongful judicial sentencing, but it will be missed as one tool in the rehabilitation arsenal.

The commission recommendations will become law Nov. 1 unless Congress objects. Congress may not object, but the changes will not be made without some misgivings.

The Washington Post
Washington, DC, February 16, 1987

LEGISLATORS WRITE a criminal code setting out a range of sentences for each offense. Judges impose those sentences and the executive branch of the government is responsible for carrying them out, whether this means providing supervision for those on probation or parole, or comprehensive care for those in prison. Because officials in each of these three branches of government look at the criminal justice system from a different perspective, there is never complete cooperation among them.

In this city, for example, some members of the city council, responding to the electorate, promote legislation requiring mandatory minimum sentences for certain offenses. The judges object that these penalties are simplistic, and the executive complains that its resources for handling prisoners are strained. Or the judges, shocked by overcrowding and inhumane conditions in prison, order reforms that the council must find the money to pay for and the mayor must put into effect, often over the objections of neighborhoods that don't want new prisons in the area.

None of this is unusual—it goes on all over the United States—but it provides the context in which disagreements over criminal sentencing should be considered.

For three years, the D.C. Superior Court Sentencing Guidelines Commission has been working on a plan to reform felony sentencing. The 19-member commission is composed of judges, other government officials, lawyers and plain citizens. It is led by Chief Judge Fred Ugast of Superior Court, and the majority can fairly be said to represent the point of view of the judges. The commission's objective is to encourage both consistency and certainty in sentencing in order to avoid the injustice that occurs when two offenders with similar backgrounds who are convicted of the same crime are sentenced to widely disparate terms.

Last week, the commission released a report that accomplishes this objective by categorizing offenses in terms of seriousness, and offenders in terms of a number of characteristics, while using a point system to determine suggested sentences. It is a thoughtful and welcome report, but according to a minority of the commission members—none of them judges—it is flawed because, in the aggregate, the sentences recommended will result in slightly longer prison terms and, eventually, add to significant prison overcrowding.

City council president David Clarke, who wrote the minority report, suggests that all sentences be reduced by a fraction—about 6 percent—to avoid the problem of overcrowding. While it would be wrong to tell a judge he couldn't sentence an individual offender to prison because of overcrowding, it would not be unreasonable to cut back all minimum sentences slightly for the same reason. But perhaps Mr. Clarke was unable to sell his fellow commissioners—and particularly the judges—on this approach because only a few months ago the council passed a law that greatly expanded good-time provisions in order to encourage early release of prisoners, and this was done without any serious effort to involve the judges whose decisions were thus eroded.

The praiseworthy objectives of sentence guidelines and the admirable work of the commission need not be at odds with the very practical considerations that must be faced by the council and the mayor. But continuing cooperation is needed. The commission's proposals have been set out for a period of public review. The views of the other branches of government deserve consideration and so do the comments of citizens organizations, attorneys, criminal justice experts and court reform groups. The new guidelines present a good opportunity to explore the problems and prerogatives of the diverse elements of the criminal justice system.

The Star-Ledger

Newark, NJ, May 18, 1987

Few people are happy with the disparities in sentences meted out to persons convicted of crime. Sentences can range from a wrist slap to a long prison term for the same offense, contributing to public dismay and encouraging would-be felons to see if they can make crime pay.

General dissatisfaction with this situation prompted a thorough review by the U.S. Sentencing Commission. Members spent 18 months sifting through disparities in sentences and formulating recommendations to achieve more uniformity.

The guidelines which emerged from the study, however, will not be adopted out of hand. Instead, the commissioners have wisely decided to give the guidelines a trial by fire—an actual testing by federal judges to determine their suitability and effectiveness. Feedback from the judges will be used to evaluate the recommendations and help to determine whether they should be made permanent.

Surely, the most revolutionary change—and a welcome one—will introduce a new get-tough attitude towards white-collar crime. Under the guidelines, persons convicted of white-collar offenses can expect to serve time behind bars.

Judges will no longer be allowed to respond to leniency pleas based on themes that have become all too familiar—that the offender has been disgraced and has already been punished enough. Instead, the judges will be expected to sentence the white-collar criminal to at least some period in prison.

Perhaps the best reason for a trial run of the guidelines was provided by one of the seven commissioners, Paul Robinson, a professor at the Rutgers University School of Law. He rejected the recommendations and suggested the commission be given more time to conduct empirical studies. In effect, the nine months of field testing will provide an opportunity for such studies.

U.S. Circuit Court Judge William W. Wilkins Jr., the commission chairman, says the guidelines "will provide certainty of punishment, and that translates into deterrence." If actual experience during the trial run produces certainty of punishment and deterrence, the recommendations would bring substantial improvement in sentencing practices.

But it also will bring a significant increase in prison population—10 percent or more over the next decade. Given its explosive potential, prison overcrowding is a problem that should be given a concurrent priority with the sentencing reforms.

The Dispatch

Columbus, OH, April 16, 1987

Newly prepared guidelines for sentencing persons convicted of federal crimes should do a better job of protecting the public, deterring crime and punishing offenders. They also will cost more.

The U.S. Sentencing Commission spent a year and a half drafting a system that would abolish parole boards and lessen, slightly, the sentencing discretion of federal judges. Congressional review of the sentencing guidelines is required, but may be delayed nine months while comment from judges is sought and refinements made. The guidelines otherwise become effective Nov. 1, unless vetoed by both houses of Congress.

Commission chairman William Wilkins, himself a federal appeals court judge, concedes the new approach will increase prison populations, but says it will not be substantial.

He said setting sentencing standards to conform with the available number of prison beds is a "dangerous case of the tail wagging the dog."

Federal prisons are currently home for 42,000 convicts, an incredible 75 percent increase since 1980. Public sentiments increasingly are toward tougher sentencing and a more equitable balance so that no one receives what amounts to preferential treatment.

These new sentencing practices, if implemented as written, should better protect the public and provide a standard of fairness so sentences for the same crime will not differ dramatically from one area to the next.

In brief, convicts will serve the full sentence for the crime of which they are convicted less some time for good behavior while in prison. Judges have the total burden in sentencing but retain discretion and may depart from the guidelines for any "aggravating or mitigating circumstance."

Where convicts in the past could turn to the parole board to reduce what might seem too severe a sentence, they will under these guidelines be required to serve the time required less whatever consideration they might receive for their in-prison conduct.

The commission's guidelines seem to strike a proper balance between toughness and fairness. As taxpayers, we can't have it both ways. If convicts are going to pay the piper, we will have to be willing to pay the freight.

ATTEMPTED MURDERER, MUTILATOR, RAPIST TO BE PAROLED. -NEWS ITEM

The Register

Santa Ana, CA, May 22, 1987

Few things raise the public's hackles faster or higher than revelations of the early release of criminals sentenced to California prisons for heinous crimes.

The Lawrence Singleton case, much in the news recently, is but the most recent instance of public outrage. Singleton was released after serving 8½ years of a 14-year sentence for raping a 15-year-old girl, leaving her for dead in a ditch after hacking off her arms with an ax.

A number of other instances have involved release of criminals — after sharply abbreviated prison sentences — which brought the public mood to boil. William Archie Fain. Dan White. Morris Solomon.

It may be, as some sociologists contend, that the public wants to punish, and re-punish beastly felons forever, refusing to forgive their extreme violations of civil decency, and declining to accept the theory of prison-inculcated remorse and rehabilitation.

It well could be, on the other hand, that the public is entitled to become especially livid when it feels duped by a judicial-penal system that appears to work with elastic rules in the sentencing and incarceration of murderers, rapists, child molesters, and others with extreme anti-social attitudes.

Much of the public does not understand, for example, why Singleton is on the streets now, with police babysitters, after serving only 60 percent of his imposed sentence. They believe a 14-year-sentence should last 14 years, and, in Singleton's case, even 114 years.

If fully informed, the public would be little impressed, more likely disgusted, by the internal — often arcane — procedures that really determine the length of prison stays.

For example, inmates' sentences are automatically cut by one-third when they enter prison (subject to revision for poor behavior) and they can reduce their time in half if they work at prison jobs because they get a day off their sentence for each day worked.

Surely, there must be room for mercy and flexibility in our penal system; it is no mere canard that prisons often amount to "graduate schools in crime." But the public never knows what the length of sentence really is for felons in California.

The sentences decreed in courts and printed in newspapers have little relation to reality. Our legislators don't know either, although they vote into existence the sentencing laws.

Since 1977, California has operated under provisions of the determinate sentencing law. Prior to that the sentences were "indeterminate," or left to the discretion of prison, probation, and parole officials.

The state changed from the latter system to the former when some legislators, primarily liberal of philosophic persuasion, felt some inmates were being unduly penalized regarding timely release from prison and held too long.

Now, other legislators and elected officials have become convinced that the determinate sentencing system has equal — if not greater — flaws and want to return to the indeterminate sentencing method. These officials say the average length of sentence has been reduced from 40 months to 23 months under the determinate system, that we are beginning to operate the kind of penal revolving door that becomes so apparent in cases such as Singleton's.

No matter which system is employed in California's judicial-penal system, the public has a right to expect that, in general, a sentence handed down in a courtroom will be the sentence to be served, not the starting point for negotiated lesser incarceration.

Let us have some "truth-in-sentencing" from our judges and our penal authorities. We really don't need passage of new laws. Our courts should simply tell the public the truth about the real length of time likely to be served by a man like Singleton, even if it must be given in ranges such as 10 to 20 years.

To do less is a disservice to the public as well as the judicial and penal systems, which, under existing conditions, are seeing an erosion of public confidence and support.

Another thing that really riles the public is to learn that our public officials, elected and appointed, don't believe we're intelligent enough to understand their deliberations and decisions and, therefore, should be kept unaware of the fine points involved.

We are often told that justice delayed is not justice. Is justice stayed or justice waylaid any better?

The Washington Times

Washington, DC, March 9, 1987

In the era of the spy — Pollard, Pelton, the Walkers — it is interesting to recall that, 15 years ago, the Supreme Court essentially wiped out the federal death penalty, once the punishment for treason and espionage. But now the U.S. Sentencing Commission is flirting with the idea of meeting the court's standards, and some congressmen are having conniptions.

Sen. Joseph Biden, for example, argues that Congress deliberately excluded the death penalty from the 1984 Sentencing Reform Act, the law that created the Sentencing Commission. He's wrong. The law says that the commission's guidelines shall apply to "any federal statute," except where "otherwise specifically provided," and nowhere is the death penalty excluded.

For good reason. According to a recent poll by Media General and the Associated Press, 85 percent of the people support the death penalty. Those who want to finish off the death penalty must have it quietly asphyxiated. If brought to a vote, the death penalty almost certainly would be affirmed.

Yet the Sentencing Commission seems to be getting cold feet. As chairman of the Judiciary Committee, Sen. Biden is capable of making trouble, and he has powerful allies, including Sen. Edward Kennedy, who accuses the slippery old Reagan administration of "trying to slip the death penalty into the back door." Even Commission member Paul H. Robinson, who favors the death penalty, says he would vote against reviving it because "it is not clear Congress intended the commission to have this authority."

Let's see if we have it right. The death penalty is on the books, put there by a majority vote of Congress, but the sentencing procedures are 15 years out of step. The 1984 Sentencing Reform Act gives the commission authority to bring the procedures up to date, effectively restoring the death penalty, but congressional opponents say this would be underhanded.

Or to put it another way, restoring the death penalty, which the people favor, would be slipping something over on them, whereas abolishing the death penalty without ever voting on it is representative government. Got it.

Washington, DC, April 13, 1987

The U.S. Sentencing Commission is to recommend today elimination of that curious process whereby juries convict and judges hand down tough sentences, only to have the sentences abbreviated by federal parole boards. The commission wants parole boards done away with, and its recommendations become law unless Congress aborts them within six months.

Stand by to repel boarders. A move so sensible is bound to stir hostility among those who blame societal shortcomings for crime and feel that criminals, being no more than artifacts, should be rehabilitated (how is unclear), not punished.

Such people naturally gravitate to parole boards, where they have contributed greatly to galloping recidivism and nationwide cynicism about criminal justice. But if the Sentencing Commission has its way, they will have to devise new ways to further their well-intended mischief.

Under the commission's proposals, parole boards would be abolished and prisoners required to serve out their sentences — all their sentences, and no time off for disdaining to knife one's jailer or for singing in the glee club. Since criminals prefer being on the street to being in stir, stiff sentences with no prospect of parole are likely to get their attention.

As for federal judges, they would be required to adhere to sentencing guidelines, which the commission spells out in detail, or explain in writing their failure to do so. Since federal trial judges like to be well thought of — good reputations help move them up the ladder to more important appellate courts — they are likely to treat the guidelines with respect.

One initial result will be more criminals in prison — appalling in the view of some "social scientists and civil libertarians," as The New York Times describes them. Fret not. When criminals realize that parole boards can no longer be bamboozled because there are no boards to bamboozle, the zeal to be locked up will diminish.

Part II:
Organized, White-Collar &
Government Crime

Everyone knows about organized crime. We read about the elaborate criminal organizations in the daily press, books and magazines. Law enforcement officials declare that huge amounts of money are illegally obtained by organized crime and used to gain more untaxed money and wield more power. Movies such as *The Godfather* graphically portray the brutality, power and wealth of organized crime. In previous decades the question of whether a "Mafia" truly existed was hotly debated and the drive to deny the existence not only of the Mafia, but also, in some cases, of organized crime continued. Italian-American groups, scholars and even FBI chief J. Edgar Hoover denied its existence. The mafiosa, naturally, gladly went along with the official denials.

Attitudes have since changed across the board. Federal law enforcement agencies, ethnic Italian-Americans and others have changed their position. Instead, they argue that organized crime is bigger than the Mafia and that by focusing on the Mafia alone, the government perpetuates anti-Italian sentiment. Of course racism and bigotry has been a motive in the exposure of the Mafia. But there can be little doubt that not only an ethnic Italian Mafia has existed but other ethnic organized crime groups, such as Jewish and now Asian, as well.

Aside from white-collar crime, most crime springs from ethnic, inner-city situations, generally determined by which groups occupy the ghetto, which itself is sub-divided into smaller ethnic areas. There is an ethnic succession in the American ghetto and, correspondingly, an ethnic succession in crime. The infamous criminals of 19th century America, for instance, were Irish as were the most feared street gangs. As the Irish vacated the ghettos, their criminal legacy was repeated by other ethnic newcomers, first by Jews and Italians and then, later, by blacks, Hispanics and Asians. In turn, crime statistics take on new ethnic flavors, determined by society's new have-nots.

This, however, has little to do with the Mafia, organized crime or why the United States is the only industrialized country in the world with such a pervasive organized crime establishment. It is generally agreed that it was the combination of three vital forces that allowed organized crime to develop and achieve its power. Before 1920 organized crime, at least in its current sense, did not exist in the U.S. Indeed, there were bands of criminals but crime itself was not organized. It did not involve the vast interplay of a network of gangs with certain territorial rights. The advent of Prohibition created something very new in criminal history and catapulted crime bosses to new heights of power. They accumulated such wealth that they were no longer the puppets of the political bosses and their police lackeys. Sicilian-born Lucky Luciano and a Polish-born Jew, Meyer Lansky, emerged as the two most powerful and important criminals of the day and successfully unified the great criminal gangs into a national crime syndicate.

Though the end of Prohibition could have spelled the end to organized crime in America, the syndicate had become so rich it could suffer the Depression and move into other operations. In addition, because the Depression froze the Italian and Jewish populations in the ghetto, organized crime had a steady supply of new recruits from its ethnic ranks.

An ironic and little-known chapter in the history of organized crime's solidification of power involves the cooperation of some elements of law enforcement. The national syndicate had little difficulty corrupting the criminal justice system on a local and often statewide basis. But as its tentacles lengthened and strengthened nationally, it felt little resistance from the federal government partially because the various law enforcement agencies tended to remain separate and focused their energy on their particular sphere of interest. What was needed was the strategic employment of the FBI to battle organized crime. But the FBI, under the ironfisted rule of J. Edgar Hoover, was nowhere to be found and would remain outside the fray until the late 1950s. The FBI, in fact struck a deal with the mob during World War II. In exchange for releasing the then-imprisoned Luciano, the mafia would patrol the Brooklyn waterfront for enemy subversion and attack for the government. This astonishing period of malfeasance in leadership resulted in the tragic consequences of organized crime's entry into the narcotics trade.

The 1980s have brought the continued official claim that organized crime and the Mafia is, at last, on the run. But politicians for half a century have made similar claims, sounding the death knell of organized crime with massive convictions. Similar police and judicial actions have been undertaken in the 1980s. Though organized crime seems to continue in a "business as ususal" manner, law enforcement officials and politicians say that if we maintain pressure, the Mafia will be gone with a decade. Perhaps Meyer Lansky said it best years ago when he bragged about the syndicate: "We're bigger than U.S. Steel." Apparently little has changed except the players.

Crimes committed by wealthy, educated and influential people are called white-collar or economic crimes. The U.S. Department of Justice defines white collar crime as an offense that is nonviolent and involves deceit, corruption or breach of trust. Offenses such as voter fraud, consumer fraud committed by small businesses, shakedowns and kickbacks by public employees as well as multi-million dollar frauds and breaches of trust by public officials are included in this definition.

Typically, the white-collar criminal is a white, middle-aged and well-educated business or professional man. Hard facts about white-collar criminals are few as we still do not know the full extent of such offenses but the white-collar crime rate does rise proportionately to the efforts and funds made available to uncover and prosecute such wrongdoing.

White-collar criminals make a conscious choice to disobey the law, acting with forethought and deliberation. A recent American Bar Association report and federal statistics substantiate the public perception that white-collar crime does pay and that the poor and non-white offender will go to prison for small crimes while the rich who steal millions will get probation.

Italy, U.S. Cooperate in Mafia Crackdown

The confessions of an important Sicilian Mafia figure, Tommaso Buscetta, sparked a wave of arrests in both Italy and the United States of suspected organized crime figures. The U.S. Justice Department Oct. 1, 1984 ordered the arrest of 28 U.S. citizens and Italian nationals on charges of murder, drug trafficking and racketeering. The 28 were among 366 people named in Italian arrest warrants in a large-scale operation intended to strike at the heart of the Sicilian Mafia. Buscetta had broken organized crime's traditional code of silence, giving Italian officials not only the names of particular individuals but also providing details about the structure of organized crime in Italy and the U.S. Because of Buscetta's revelations, prosecutors in the U.S. became aware of a separate Sicilian Mafia operating independently of older organized crime structures. Most of the 28 suspects were arrested in connection with an organized crime ring responsible for bringing $1.65 billion worth of heroin into the U.S. since 1979, operating under the cover of pizza parlor operations.

Officials of both nations hailed the cooperation between the U.S. and Italy as a signal event in the war against organzied crime. One element in this cooperation was a new extradition treaty that allows charges against suspects to be forwarded to the U.S. Justice Deptartment by Italian authorities. Suspects could now also be tried in the U.S. on charges brought in the U.S. before being extradited to Italy to face charges there.

The Dispatch

Columbus, OH, October 8, 1984

The arrests of hundreds of persons in the United States and Italy on charges of involvement in illegal Mafia-related activities will greatly disrupt the repugnant activities supported by organized crime. The arrests will not, however, bring to an end organized crime activities and there should be no letdown in law enforcement efforts to combat these activities.

The arrests began 10 days ago after Tommaso Buscetta, a Mafia figure jailed in Italy, broke the organization's code of silence and began implicating persons in crimes. What's more, Buscetta has described in detail to police the organizational superstructure of the Mafia in Italy and the United States, giving law enforcement officials a better idea of how organized crime operates.

Buscetta is reported to have broken the code of silence to avenge the slayings of several of his family members and close associates.

Italian police issued warrants for 366 persons and, so far, 28 of them are being sought in the United States. These people are believed to be involved with illegal drug trafficking between Italy and the United States. Some have also been implicated in murders, prostitution and extortion. "This is an historic case, making it possible to rip apart the Sicilian Mafia," commented Rudolph Giuliani, the U.S. attorney for the Southern District of New York.

Indeed it is. The U.S. government has stepped up its own anti-drug trafficking crusade in recent years and it has focused primarily on contraband from Central America. It has been difficult for the government to crack the Italian connection, although arrests in connection with the so-called "pizza connection" — in which drugs were smuggled into this country in pizza supplies — was a significant breakthrough earlier this year.

But rarely before have law enforcement officials gotten such a good look inside the operation of the Mafia. This knowledge will be a useful tool in future activities.

The arrests by no means, however, signal an end to the Mafia, an organization that has proved to be a durable conspiracy over the years. The Buscetta revelations are being compared with those made by organized crime boss Joseph Valachi in 1963 in terms of damage to the Mafia. It is instructive to note — when talking about the Mafia's durability — that it survived the Valachi disclosures and apparently has flourished in spite of them. The Buscetta disclosures will hurt, but they are unlikely to eliminate the Mafia.

Law enforcement officials in Italy and their associates in the United States can be justifiably proud of the breakthrough. But they must not let down now. The Mafia is on the run. Law enforcement officials should keep it that way.

THE SACRAMENTO BEE

Sacramento, CA, October 6, 1984

Not for the first time, the Justice Department is claiming to have launched a "devastating assault" on organized crime, in this case against the Italian Mafia and its American counterpart. Italian authorities also are pleased about the roundup of dozens of suspected Mafiosi in this country and in Italy that was triggered by the detailed revelations of two informants. But, having had a couple of centuries' experience dealing with the phenomenon, the Italians' joy is a little more restrained, with reason.

It's not yet clear how much the two major narcotics traffickers, arrested in Spain and Brazil and now in Spanish and Italian custody, know about the workings of the Mafia and of its American counterpart, La Cosa Nostra. It is known, though, that neither was a "godfather" privy to the innermost secrets of one of the most pervasive criminal organizations in the world. The wave of arrests in Italy and in the New York area may in time lead to the kind of devastating blow of which Attorney General William French Smith spoke the other day, but that remains to be seen.

Among other things, it's been learned already that an American branch of the Sicilian-based Mafia exists, separate from the Cosa Nostra organization. The fact that this was never before known to law enforcement organizations is testimony to how successfully organized crime is capable of functioning. There remains, therefore, a major task ahead.

In Italy, recent years have seen a dramatic increase in public support for going after the Mafia, and the Italian government has matched this with serious efforts that have resulted in many arrests and convictions, albeit at the price of the lives of a number of courageous public servants, including prosecutors, judges and police officers. Even so, the Mafia is far from being at the edge of extinction, so deep and broad are its roots.

Similar gains have been made in this country, but if anything, organized crime in the United States is even more elusive than in Italy, partly because it seems almost invisible to most people. Moreover, it is so finely interwoven with legitimate institutions — business, labor and government — that unraveling it would entail disturbing a number of important centers of power and influence. In short, there is a great deal of vested interest to contend with.

In light of these realities, the breakthrough made recently by Italian and American authorities must be seen as important and encouraging, but not by any means decisive in the war against organized crime. Victory on a major scale would require a degree of public commitment rarely seen in this or any other society plagued by crime and its chief lubricant, corruption.

THE ATLANTA CONSTITUTION
Atlanta, GA, October 5, 1984

Those who scoff at Attorney General William French Smith's pronouncement that the recent U.S.-Italian crime crackdown is "the single most devastating assault on the Mafia in its entire history" should be pardoned for their cynicism.

In the 30-plus years since the Kefauver Commission first exposed the outlines of a Sicilian-controlled empire of nearly mythical proportions, federal law-enforcement offensives against the mob have been uniformly overblown and underaccomplished.

But there is a combination of factors that sets this latest attack on The Outfit apart from its predecessors, suggesting that if the Mafia isn't on the ropes, it's beginning to be backed into a corner.

First, there's an unprecedented level of cooperation between the United States and Italy, in no small part a result of the efforts of Smith and the year-old government of Premier Bettino Craxi, which seems determined to uproot the Mafia cancer.

Italian-U.S. meetings this past year have produced two salutary agreements: a ratified treaty that streamlines extradition procedures and a pending accord that would enable lawmen in both countries to deal directly with one another outside the routine diplomatic and bureaucratic channels.

Next, there are the explosive disclosures of Tommaso Buscetta, which have led to nearly 400 arrest warrants being issued in Italy and the United States in the past week. Unlike Joe Valachi and Jimmy Fratianno, notorious Cosa Nostra canaries of the recent past, Buscetta is no ordinary syndicate soldier, or even a lieutenant. A highly placed drug trafficker connected to crime hierarchies on three continents, Buscetta may prove far more damaging to the Mafia than any previous informer.

Buscetta's willingness to break his fraternity's vow of silence is symptomatic of another problem nagging at the Mafia: a general breakdown in discipline. Years ago, the *capos* of the old school resisted the idea of moving into drug-dealing as a dirty business, one that might tear at the fabric of their time-honored structural restraints. They were right.

Competition for control of the "narcodollar" largesse has been bloody, especially so in Sicily in the last two years. Buscetta was touched personally, losing seven relatives, including two sons, in the gang war — the prime reason, lawmen think, for his informing on his hoodlum cohorts.

It would be sweet irony, indeed, if the Mafia crumbled under the weight of its own excessive corruption. Alas, like other malevolent creatures that have assumed near-bogeyman proportions in our culture, the Mafia has remarkable recuperative powers. All the more reason for Attorney General Smith and his Italian justice allies to walk softly and carry a big wooden stake.

THE LINCOLN STAR
Lincoln, NE, October 8, 1984

Someone talked, finally, and more than 300 alleged Mafia gangsters are being sought for arrest here and in Italy. The hallowed code of silence has long protected criminals from the petty purse snatcher to the organized crime boss who deals in drugs, gambling or prostitution.

The arrests in Italy and the United States have been called variously "without precedent" and the "largest anti-Mafia operation since World War II."

U.S. Attorney General William French Smith lauded it as "the single most devastating assault on the Mafia in its entire history."

Perhaps this is a bit of hyperbole. Organized crime exists today largely because of its tenacious hold on survival, bolstered by the complicity with or infiltration of local governments. It is, often, a family business, odd as that sounds, with a history and culture that help it thrive.

YET DAMAGE has been done. And all it took was the confession of one man, Tommaso Buscetta, arrested last week by Italian police, to strike a severe blow to a worldwide criminal organization that has defied law for decades. Some of Buscetta's testimony has concerned the code of silence that has shielded the lawless from prosecution. He has revealed the extent to which the old codes and traditions within crime families are being broken or abandoned. These revelations could be used in future anti-Mafia operations.

As many as 30 people implicated by Buscetta, reputed to be one of the most wanted underworld narcotics traffickers, may be arrested in the United States, testimony to the cooperation between U.S. authorities and the Italians.

Governments working together to stem lawlessness will increasingly reap the benefits of this cooperation. Technology that brings the world together in a global market also enables a criminal network to function with extreme sophistication.

In fact, much of the information Buscetta has supplied to authorities concerns the international links between crime organizations. The degree to which the American La Cosa Nostra takes orders from crime bosses in Palermo and Sicily, Italy, should be of particular interest here to law enforcement authorities.

INDEED, THE cooperation has led American officials to the discovery of a previously unknown arm of the Sicilian Mafia operating in the Untied States. It was set up by Sicilian crime families, completely bypassing the old American families.

Last year, U.S. and Italian authorities cracked a drug connection between an Italian crime boss and a string of pizza parlors he operated as drug fronts in the United States. The ring leader in that operation also turned informant, providing information which Buscetta has built upon. Continued stabbing thrusts such as this into the heart of organized crime and some official some day might actually be able to declare it mortally wounded, no hyperbole. It is certain a sustained assault, an all-out war if you will, is the only way to bring organized crime to its knees. The grisly business of organized crime certainly warrants this declaration.

The Pittsburgh PRESS
Pittsburgh, PA, October 6, 1984

Possibly the greatest chance ever to make a worldwide assault on organized crime has been presented by a Sicilian Mafia leader who has broken the "code of silence" — one of the biggest defense weapons used for decades by the organization.

Already, the crack in the Mafia armor has led Italian authorities to start rounding up nearly 400 underworld figures, 28 of them in the United States.

Tommaso Buscetta, who was arrested in Brazil and extradited to Italy in July to face murder and drug charges, is reported to have given Italian investigators information on about 100 specific crimes. He also supplied Italian and American investigators with a detailed picture of the Mafia structure in Sicily, Naples and this country.

Those named in 366 arrest warrants issued in Italy are suspects in the multibillion-dollar international heroin trade. The 28 Americans and Italian nationals arrested or being sought in the United States were described as high-level intermediaries with the Sicilian Mafia.

A federal prosecutor in New York, Rudolph Giuliani, called it a "historic case, making it possible to rip apart the Sicilian Mafia." U.S. Attorney General William French Smith was even more jubilant. He described the Italian-American operation against organized crime as the "single most devastating assault on the Mafia in its entire history."

There are, however, caveats. Italy has been criticized for years as lacking the will to fight organized crime, and there have been reports of links between the Mafia and the Christian Democrats, the party that has dominated Italian politics for four decades.

In addition, Mafia strains, even through their own civil wars, traditionally have been able to close ranks to present a solid phalanx against the common foe, justice.

One Italian newspaper wondered whether the Buscetta revelations will hold up in the courts "or if, as often happens, everything will come to an end like a soap bubble."

In any event, Buscetta's confessions came at an opportune time to boost a joint anti-organized crime drive agreed to last October by President Reagan and Italian Prime Minister Bettino Craxi.

Part of that agreement was a new treaty to streamline extradition of suspects in each country's criminal cases. The 28 U.S. suspects will face hearings and possible removal to Italy under the treaty approved by the Senate July 3.

An FBI spokesman said agents "debriefed" Buscetta in Italy and "there will be related investigations started here, based on the information that he provided."

The break the United States, Italy and the rest of the world needed has been provided.

The governments of countries into which Mafia tentacles reach have been handed an opportunity to control what once was thought uncontrollable, to conquer what once was thought impregnable and unconquerable.

Not to provide the offensive weapons — determination, cooperation and financing — to complement the information, and wage the battle would be unthinkable.

The Virginian-Pilot

Norfolk, VA, March 3, 1984

The FBI is busy tearing into the Mafia and other hoodlum gangs. Nothing spectacular: No staccato bursts from Thompson submachine guns in half-deserted warehouses. No careening cars of hoods pursued by daredevil agents. No bloody shootout at the OK Restaurant. Just patient eavesdropping on mobster chieftains' sinister conversations. And painstaking tracing of the route taken by "laundered" dirty money. And the tedious accumulation of testimony about kickbacks here and extortion there and murder contracts now and then.

The Mafia is getting a hard time, these days, in Italy and in the United States. It couldn't have happened to a nicer bunch of guys. The Mafia's game is making megabucks in outlawed ways — illicit-drug trafficking, loan-sharking, trading in stolen or phony securities, prostitution and other sexploitation, taking over and looting legitimate businesses and labor unions, skimming cash at casinos.... Breaking up the game has defied the best efforts of even dedicated law-enforcement officers, until recently.

Former FBI Director J. Edgar Hoover shied from the challenge, for several reasons, including the Mafia's code of silence — since broken — which made collecting evidence extremely difficult; arresting and convicting Mafia dons when real insiders refused to talk was nearly impossible.

The Racketeer-Influenced and Corrupt Organization Act of 1970 handed federal prosecutors a weapon strong enough to reach the kingpins of crime. But more than a decade passed before the feds learned to wield the weapon — as it is now being wielded against the nine members of the Mafia ruling council indicted in New York this week.

The Mafia crew arrested last week is said to compose the commission that authorities describe as the guiding force behind organized crime in New York and other major American cities. If that is accurate, then the Mafia has been dealt a severe blow that could throw its operations into disarray, at least in the short term. If the FBI, in concert with local law-enforcement agencies, continues to allocate extensive resources against organized crime, the heat on the Mafia will not let up for years.

That's an encouraging prospect. The leaders and aides of the New York Mafia "families" are charged with conspiracy and conducting the affairs of the commission "through a pattern of racketeering activity." According to the indictment, the commission established rules governing the families, extended formal recognition to newly elected bosses, approved initiation of new members and controlled relations with the Mafia in Sicily. The racketeering-conspiracy charge said that the commission had resolved a dispute within the Bonanno group by authorizing five murders, all of which made headlines.

The Mafia isn't the whole of organized crime in the United States. The Syndicate — headed for years by the late Meyer Lansky — presumably survives. Investigating congressmen have lately learned of Chinese-American and Korean-American gangs. And in the week before it netted the Mafia chieftains in New York, the FBI arrested members of motorcycle gangs engaged in interstate drug trafficking.

Arrests and indictments of mobsters are but the beginning of long battles through the courts. But the beginning is welcome.

THE INDIANAPOLIS NEWS

Indianapolis, IN, July 4, 1984

The U.S. Supreme Court recently made the right ruling with the wrong result.

Its ruling concerned the federal Racketeer Influence and Corrupt Organization Act, better known as the RICO statute. Enacted in 1970 to combat organized crime, the law was designed to allow prosecutors to go after the financial assets of crime syndicates which engaged in repeated conduct of illegal activity.

Civil provisions of the law allow for triple damages and lawyer fees to be collected in successful actions against a defendant found to have engaged in two or more acts from a long list of underlying crimes, which include violating various state laws, federal securities provisions and federal mail fraud and wire fraud statutes — the latter being extremely broad statutes in and of themselves.

Recently, civil portions of the RICO statute have been used in numerous actions not to combat organized crime or even illegal drug rings, but in connection with lawsuits against business organizations such as American Express Co., E.F. Hutton & Co. and Lloyd's of London.

The 2nd Circuit Court of Appeals, however, ruled that the RICO statute was being stretched too far in connection with a lawsuit against a New York firm accused of fraud in a venture to provide electronic component parts for a North Atlantic Treaty Organization subcontractor. In its ruling the appeals court said that no RICO civil suit could be filed against someone who was not convicted of criminal charges. It also required that parties suing under the RICO civil provision prove a "racketeering injury" in addition to showing they were victims of specific crimes, such as fraud.

In a 5-4 decision, the Supreme Court upheld the existing broad use of the RICO statute. It properly refused to second-guess the motives of Congress in enacting the law.

As Justice Byron R. White suggested in the court's majority opinion, if the effect of the law was not what Congress intended, "its correction must lie with Congress."

But Congress should act quickly to narrow the scope of the RICO statute so it applies more exclusively to its intended target — organized crime. It should not be allowed to continue as a catch-all statute allowing excessive fines and unfair labeling of otherwise legitimate businesses.

The 2nd Circuit Court of Appeals was philosophically correct when it held, "The uses to which private civil RICO has been put have been extraordinary, if not outrageous."

The Miami Herald

Miami, FL, March 27, 1985

IN THE WAR between organized crime and law enforcement, the bad guys enjoy one important advantage: They aren't constrained by county lines. One loan-sharking operation may span a dozen counties, but no single state attorney enjoys such wide jurisdiction. When prosecutors in one county crack down, the well-managed criminal enterprise simply moves elsewhere.

The Florida Department of Law Enforcement has statewide responsibility for investigating organized criminal activity, but no corresponding agency is empowered to prosecute criminals who operate throughout the state. The few criminals indicted by the Statewide Grand Jury customarily have been prosecuted by local state attorneys appointed *ad hoc* by the governor.

The inadequacy of this catch-as-catch-can approach is apparent to law-enforcement officials throughout Florida. That's why Gov. Bob Graham and Attorney General Jim Smith have asked legislators to endorse a constitutional amendment creating a statewide prosecutor's office. If lawmakers approve, the amendment would be submitted to voters in November 1986.

The statewide-prosecutor proposal is the brainchild of a blue-ribbon panel led by Alan Sundberg, former chief justice of the Florida Supreme Court. Florida's 20 state attorneys have received it coolly. Some prosecutors' reservations reflect nothing more than territorial jealousy. Others have legitimate fears that the proposed statewide prosecutor's office would divert already-scarce resources from local prosecutorial efforts.

Parochial turf disputes shouldn't be permitted to block creation of a statewide prosecutor's office, but any realistic proposal will have to address both of the state attorneys' concerns.

Dade State Attorney Janet Reno and others have proposed that the statewide prosecutor be barred from taking jurisdiction over any case without the consent of the appropriate county prosecutors. That may be the political price of the interoffice cooperation that any statewide attack on organized crime must have in order to succeed.

At the same time, legislators must be prepared to arm the statewide prosecutor with adequate resources *in addition* to providing proper funding for local state attorneys. Another layer of enforcement won't help unless it's given the means, not merely the authority, to pursue criminals wherever they go.

Those provisos aside, there's simply no excuse for Florida to continue fighting big-time criminals with small-time tactics. South Florida legislators should lead the effort to enact this proposal.

THE DENVER POST
Denver, CO, December 14, 1984

MARIO CUOMO, governor of New York state and professional Italian, Tuesday attacked the news media for using the term "Mafia" to describe the organized crime syndicate which police believe is responsible for Monday's assassination of one of its ring leaders, Paul Castellano.

Cuomo claimed that journalists using Mafia to report on the activities of the syndicate imported into this country from Sicily were actually trying to stereotype all Italians as criminals.

Well, we learned during the tax-reform debate that trying to educate Mario Cuomo is a well-nigh impossible task. But here we go again:

The Mafia is an unfortunate historical fact, the mention of which no more stereotypes all Italian Americans as criminals than calling Cuomo governor typecasts them all as politicians.

Actually, as defector Joe Vala-chi testified, the syndicate describes itself by the more intimate term: "Cosa Nostra," which means "our thing" in Italian.

Still, we were intrigued enough by Cuomo's outburst to wonder what history might look like if information in the files of the New York City police department were rewritten to placate Cuomo's commissars. According to those files, there are five chief groups of the Maf . . . err, the Cosa Nostra . . . in New York city, organized into five "families." They are:

- ✔ The Gambino family.
- ✔ The Genovese family.
- ✔ The Colombo family.
- ✔ The Lucchese family.
- ✔ The Bonanno family.

In the world, according to Cuomo, these are all direct descendants of a nice clan in Scotland.

And if you believe that, you believe Fettuccine is an opera.

The Washington Post
Washington, DC, December 6, 1984

MEMBERS of Congregation Beth Yetzhok in New York had a dispute over succession to the leadership of their Hasidic congregation, and one faction sued the other in federal court. In another case a citizen, annoyed about the way Democratic Party funds were distributed in the last election, sued Walter Mondale and the Democratic National Committee using the same federal statute. A woman displeased by her divorce settlement, a writer with a gripe against the American Broadcasting Company and a group of tenants protesting their landlord's utility charges all used the same law to bring a civil suit. What's the common thread? It is, believe it or not, racketeering.

Fifteen years ago, Congress passed the Racketeering Influenced and Corrupt Organizations Act, known as RICO. It was essentially a criminal statute aimed at mobsters, but in the House a provision was added allowing persons hurt by organized crime to bring civil suit against the wrongdoers. Plaintiffs could simply allege that they had been harmed by the kind of activity usually associated with organized crime—murder, arson, kidnapping, extortion and various kinds of fraud—and bring their complaints in federal court, instead of overcrowded state courts. In addition, they could win triple damages if their suits were successful.

For about 10 years there was little civil RICO litigation, but since 1981 the number of cases has skyrocketed as all sorts of people began to realize the potential of the statute. The Justice Department estimates that now only about 7 percent of RICO civil suits involve racketeers of any kind. Most defendants are businesses, brokerage houses, bankers, unions and occasional unlikely parties such as those described above. In most cases the "racketeering" alleged is mail fraud ("he sent the contract through the mail"), wire fraud ("she promised me on the phone") or securities fraud ("they sold me an interest in a business deal that didn't work out").

The Supreme Court has ruled that the RICO statute does in fact authorize all these suits, but even the justices expressed skepticism that Congress intended this result. Dozens of organizations as diverse as the American Bar Association and the United Auto Workers have called for amending legislation and the House subcommittee on criminal justice is now considering a bill introduced by Rep. Frederick Boucher (D-Va.). It would allow civil RICO suits only against persons who already have a criminal conviction for a racketeering offense.

The current law crowds federal courts with run-of-the-mill commercial disputes and allows citizens such as the Brooklyn rabbi and the Democratic nominee—not to mention countless honest businesses—to be smeared with the label "racketeer." Congress should end these abuses and clarify its original intention by passing Mr. Boucher's bill.

THE CHRISTIAN SCIENCE MONITOR
Bostn, MA, December 20, 1984

FOR much of this century, the public has shown ambivalence about the role of organized crime in America. Films, from "Little Caesar" in the early 1930s to "The Godfather" in more recent years, have gained large audiences. Accounts of crime incidents — such as this week's shooting of mob chieftain Paul C. Castellano in New York — are given prominence on television and in newspapers.

It would be unfortunate, however, if the fascination — one might almost say the perverse fascination — that some people may unwittingly have with the sense of "order" based on criminal activity and intimidation were to overshadow the genuine gains that have been made against organized crime in the United States and the world community.

Indeed, if the written record of the war against crime says anything at all about what is now happening, it is that significant players within the international community are bringing organized-crime figures to the bar of justice in a systematic — and relentless — way. These international efforts deserve the continued support of the world community.

- In the US, federal, state, and local anticrime task forces have won indictments or convictions against the top hierarchy of every major organized-crime family. Equally important, the prosecutors and law enforcement officers who are targeting these crime families, such as the FBI and Rudolph Giuliani, the United States attorney in Manhattan, have built up a considerable case log of knowledge about the way organized crime operates within the business sector.

- In Europe, officials in such nations as Italy and France have stepped up their assaults on crime networks. Italy's performance has been especially important. Recently, for example, magistrates indicted 475 Mafia suspects in Sicily.

Much more remains to be done. Curbing criminal groups that have a cultural basis for their existence, such as La Cosa Nostra or the Japanese Yakuza and Chinese Triads, will not be easy. Organized crime, after all, operates in a larger public setting. It is especially important that the new groups now attempting to gain a foothold in the US, the Asian and South American groups, for example, be quickly brought to justice.

The key factor is that organized crime cannot exist without the help of others — including, in far too many instances, the inadvertent complicity of the public itself. Organized crime costs Americans hundreds of millions of dollars. In some communities it has links to construction work, garbage collection, and food service companies, as well as labor unions.

Could organized crime endure if the public were to take a strong moral stand against activities that allow criminals to flourish — gambling, loan sharking, prostitution, drugs? It is essential that government agencies continue their increasingly successful assaults on organized crime. At the same time, as individuals gain a clearer sense of integrity in society, they will be fostering a moral climate that precludes the inroads of crime.

Rev. Sun Myung Moon Tax Conviction Appeal Refused

The Supreme Court May 14, 1984 refused to review an appeal by the Rev. Sun Myung Moon of his 1982 federal conviction for tax fraud and obstruction of justice. In that decision, a New York federal court jury found Moon guilty of conspiring to evade personal income taxes and filing false returns for 1973 through 1975. Moon, who became a permanent U.S. resident in 1973, is a controversial South Korean evangelist who had founded the Unification Church. He had been fined $25,000 and sentenced to 18 months in prison for failure to pay income taxes on over $1.7 million income. Moon had argued unsuccessfully that the money belonged to his church and was therefore exempt from taxes. Solictor General Rex E. Lee, representing the Reagan administration, had filed a brief in April 1984 asking the high court not to hear Moon's appeal. The Unification Church and dozens of religious and civil liberties groups had urged the court to review the case and overturn the conviction.

Pittsburgh Post-Gazette

Pittsburgh, PA, May 16, 1984

It is often said that the First Amendment erects a "wall of separation" between church and state. If so, the wall is a porous one, since one measure of the vitality of religion is the involvement of churches in a wide array of activities, some of which will necessarily come under governmental oversight.

That point is worth remembering in the aftermath of the U.S. Supreme Court's refusal to disturb the tax-evasion conviction of the Rev. Sun Myung Moon, the Korean-born leader of the Unification Church.

Mr. Moon's followers were not the only ones who denounced the high court's action, which cleared the way for Mr. Moon to be sent to a federal prison. Some "mainstream" clergymen were quick to point out that less constitutional protection for the "Moonies" — a derisive name that speaks volumes about the Unification Church's unpopularity — would also threaten their religious liberty.

Their general point is correct, but the question remains: Were Mr. Moon's First Amendment rights violated when a jury convicted him for failing to pay taxes on interest from a bank account in his name?

Mr. Moon's defenders insist that a central tenet of the Unification Church's faith is that its leader — Mr. Moon — should be entrusted with the disposition of church funds; thus the fact that the funds involved in the case were deposited in his name. In treating that account as personal income, they argue further, the government unconstitutionally substituted its preferences in church discipline for those of the Unification faithful.

But a little reflection suggests that even religious organizations must make some accommodation to regulations that govern society as a whole, especially since churches enjoy tax-exempt status. To take an obvious example, priests and rabbis must pay tax on their income, and religious institutions are obligated to maintain records on how much tax is withheld from the paychecks of their employees, lay and clerical.

Questions about the accuracy of such records, and whether church employees actually perform the duties for which they are compensated, cannot be declared off-limits for federal investigators. (The Post-Gazette made the same point at the time of a federal investigation of the financial affairs of the late Cardinal John P. Cody of Chicago).

If a religious institution decides to pay its leader $100,000 — or $1 million, for that matter — for his stewardship, it is not for the Internal Revenue Service to question that valuation. But the IRS does have the right to demand that the beneficiary of such trust pay his fair share of taxes. Granted, the line between income for a religious leader and church funds placed under his discretion can be a subtle one; but to deny the existence of the distinction would be to exempt religious figures from civic obligations that must be borne by every citizen.

To the extent that Mr. Moon's defenders argue that religious figures should be immune to reasonable criminal investigations, they are mistaken. A harder question is whether the jury in the Moon case was unfairly influenced by unfavorable publicity about the Unification Church and its proselytizing tactics. Doubts about jury prejudice might be a reason for the judge in the case to reduce Mr. Moon's sentence from 16 months in prison to a shorter term.

But on the larger issue raised by Mr. Moon's defenders, the principle is a clear one: The First Amendment is not a license for violation of the tax laws.

THE INDIANAPOLIS STAR

Indianapolis, IN, May 21, 1984

The U.S. Supreme Court's rejection of the Rev. Sun Myung Moon tax evasion case appeal leaves controversies and doubts seething over the constitutional question of state-church relations.

By failing to review the Moon case, the high court compounded the error it made in the Bob Jones University case. Then it let stand the Internal Revenue Service's sharply-criticized administrative tampering with tax law, which enabled the IRS to revoke the university's tax-exempt status.

Moon, the 62-year-old Korean evangelist and founder of the Unification Church, was sentenced in July 1982 to 18 months in prison and fined $25,000 and costs for income tax evasion. He was convicted in May 1982 of concealing $162,000 in interest on bank deposits.

His defense attorneys contended that the funds in question were not personal but church funds, to be used for church purposes.

Laurence Tribe, a Harvard University law professor representing Moon in his appeal, said the evangelist was the victim of "widespread hostility" among "millions who believe he has built an empire on brainwashed flower children."

Moon's church has a financial-industrial empire claiming worldwide assets of more than $15 million. The church claims 3 million followers, including 40,000 in the United States, where its recruits are mostly clean-cut middle-class young people who preach on street corners and peddle flowers, trinkets and candy to raise funds.

Moon preaches anti-communism and requires his followers to refrain from liquor, drugs, smoking and extramarital sex. He said the charges against him stem from religious bigotry and racism.

After the rejection, Tribe said: "The sad fact is that the court acted against the urging of a unique coalition of dozens of *amicus curiae* groups running from nearly all the mainstream churches in America."

The American Baptist Churches had filed a friend of the court brief on behalf of organizations, including the National Council of Churches, representing dozens of religious groups who fear Moon's prosecution opens the way for government intrusion into church affairs.

The American Civil Liberties Union and the American Jewish Congress expressed disappointment at the outcome of the case.

Churches and church organizations and their clergy and officials are not and should not be exempt from law or from criminal action or investigation by due process when circumstances call for it.

Yet both law and governmental regulations are potent weapons that can be abused. In the climate of aggressive anti-religious feeling that exists in some segments of society today, those weapons are liable to be abused.

And the power to tax does involve, as Supreme Court Justice John Marshall warned in 1819, the power to destroy.

With shrewd manipulation, enemies of religion could convert the machinery of government into tools to harass, intimidate, weaken and even destroy religious organizations.

Under such circumstances, the role of governmental authority with respect to churches should be far more clearly and precisely defined than it is at present. That is a proper task for the Supreme Court.

THE BLADE
Toledo, OH, May 20, 1984

THIS nation has had a history of constitutional tolerance for the activities of religious groups, and thus the Government should be sensitive in applying the tax code to them. But that is no reason to permit religious groups or their leaders to evade the law, even if it means some of them must pay criminal penalties for disobedience.

The case in point is that of Rev. Sun Myung Moon, leader of the Unification Church, who has lost what may be the final round in his federal income tax evasion case. The U.S. Supreme Court's refusal to consider his appeal means that, unless Moon can find another avenue to challenge a lower court's rulings, he must serve a maximum of 18 months in prison and pay a $25,000 fine.

The primary issue was the Korean-born religious leader's failure to pay taxes on $162,000 in income from stocks and a bank account. The Government contended the money was part of Moon's personal assets; the defendant argued that the funds, while in his name, really belonged to the church, which he has said he personifies.

Young adherents of the Unification Church, sometimes called Moonies, have worked street corners and other public places seeking converts and cash, and widespread concern has been voiced about the church's recruiting and use of "brainwashing" techniques, as well as the sizable worldwide financial empire it has created for itself.

But other church organizations have rallied to Moon's defense. Religious leaders do have reason to be fearful that their wealth, if not defined to the satisfaction of the tax collectors, might become the target of Internal Revenue Service scrutiny. In a broader sense churchmen also fear a blurring of the traditional line of separation between church and state in this country. They are wary of a government that might consider trying to do away with the immunities that churches have always enjoyed.

At bottom, though, even the churchmen rushing to Moon's defense should not forget that the Federal Government has an obligation to enforce the tax laws in connection with everybody who is under this country's legal jurisdiction.

This decision is a judgment call that may leave some churches nervous about long-range implications of the case. But Moon had every opportunity to make certain his finances were in line with the prevailing view of federal law. If he failed to do so, he deserves to be treated as any other tax evader.

EVENING EXPRESS
Portland, ME, May 16, 1984

By declining to review the Rev. Sun Myung Moon's conviction for federal income tax fraud, the U.S. Supreme Court has affirmed that the Constitution's guarantee of religious freedom does not give anyone the right to break the law.

In the 1982 trial that led to his conviction, Moon argued that income taxes should not be imposed upon $162,000 he earned from stocks and bank interest. He claimed the assets, while in his name, belonged to the church that he "personified." A jury disagreed, and relevant court decisions suggest the jury was right.

In Maine. U.S. District Judge Edward T. Gignoux ruled only last year that the Constitution protects religious beliefs but not religious practices, particularly when those practices violate the law.

Gignoux's ruling came in the marijuana smuggling trial of an Ethiopian Zion Coptic Church member who claimed marijuana is a religious sacrament of the Coptics and that church members should be immune from prosecution for importing, growing or using the drug.

The Coptics, Gignoux said, are free to believe as they please, but their practices are accountable to the nation's drug laws.

The finding was sensible then. The same approach is sensible now. Nothing suggests the sound legal distinction between religious belief and practice changes when the issue is money, not marijuana.

Several church groups are concerned that the ruling against Moon—which carries an 18-month prison sentence and $25,000 fine—could jeopardize some of their informal financial arrangements. The government has denied it.

Churches have it in their power to make the denial stick simply by paying their legally obligated taxes.

Arkansas Gazette.
Little Rock, AR, May 24, 1984

The Supreme Court has refused, without comment, to review the income tax fraud conviction of Rev. Sun Myung Moon, founder of the Unification Church. A lower court had decided, after a six-week jury trial, that Mr. Moon was guilty of refusing to "render unto" the Internal Revenue Service the tribute that belonged to Uncle Sam.

The defense based its arguments on the tenet that churches are not subject to the payment of income taxes. Mr. Moon "personified" the Unification Church; ergo, he should not be taxed.

The argument apparently did not track or the judges failed to make the connection. Perhaps they were not sufficiently schooled in the mystic theology of the Korean evangelist. Devout disciples of the spiritual leader obviously would have no difficulty in accepting the proposition that Mr. Moon really is the incarnation of all that is good and pure in the 3-million-member fellowship.

The jury and the judges, being secular in their orientation, remembered their obligation to consider the case on the basis of law and testimony. They saw a little old man hovering over a portfolio and a bank account that earned, in a specific period, sufficient income to generate a tax obligation of $162,000. Furthermore, he refused to pay the tribute on the grounds that he "personified" an organization that was exempt from taxes. The defense could not explain away the fact that the money was in Mr. Moon's name and the income accrued to his assets.

Dozens of religious and civil liberties groups filed briefs seeking to persuade the Supreme Court to consider the case but the arguments did not bring a rise from a single judge. Some of the supporters may have needed a precedent.

The First Amendment to the U.S. Constitution provides essential guarantees protecting the freedom of religion. So far as can be determined from a casual reading, it does not allow for a claim of "personification" that exempts an individual from the obligation to pay income taxes, regardless of the measure of holiness with which the spiritual leader may be endowed. If a precedent were set in this area, we could expect that society would be flooded with embodiments and incarnations of spiritual movements that have not even been invented.

Come to think of it, the ecclesiastical equipment is already in place for the exploitation of such a tax dodge. The Supreme Court made a wise decision when it refused to hear the appeal.

THE SAGINAW NEWS

Saginaw, MI, May 17, 1984

Few will mourn for the Rev. Sun Myung Moon. A fair number who have lost loved ones to his "Moonie" persuasion will take comfort, actually, that the Supreme Court refused to hear his appeal of a conviction for tax evasion.

Since when, though, was popular approval required for any religion, sect or cult or whatever, to enjoy religious freedom?

In the wake of Mr. Moon's conviction — pending a plea for a new trial — that question was asked by many "main-line" denominations. They supported Mr. Moon, while making it clear they did not sanction the tenets of his Unification Church.

Despite its clean-cut, patriotic veneer, the Moon movement is a disturbing phenomenon. Yet adherents seem to join up voluntarily. They are not slaves. Whatever many may think of it, the Unification Church is indeed a church — and other churches consider this case a general threat to their own liberties.

The prosecution argued that Mr. Moon personally controlled a large amount of church funds, and therefore should pay taxes on that income. He countered that he was only a trustee of the money. What bothers many denominations is that they, too, give pastors or bishops sole control over church funds and investments. They envision the government deciding what constitutes a "religious" use of their resources — and therefore, what "legitimate" religious belief is.

Perhaps Howard Simon of Michigan's Civil Liberties Union is right that it's all a matter of proper bookkeeping. It isn't likely, either, that prosecutors will now crusade against the collection plates of Methodists and Catholics.

But that's just the point. Unlike those denominations, Mr. Moon's is, in the public eye, on the fringe — despite its 3 million members worldwide. Yet they should not be judged differently under the Constitution.

The impression is strong that Mr. Moon was singled out for prosecution because of the controversial nature of his ministry. The pleasure some may take in his troubles is no solace for the hole being torn in the fabric of religious freedom — a cloak that either covers all, or, eventually, none.

San Francisco Chronicle

San Francisco, CA, May 18, 1984

WE HAVE NEVER understood the Rev. Sun Myung Moon's claim to be God's chief agent on earth, or in the words of Dr. Mose Durst, Moon's top American vicar, "the central figure through whom God will work in this age."

Consequently, we do not fear that the Rev. Moon's conviction and sentence for evading $160,000 in income taxes payable on interest earned on $1.7 million in personal funds will endanger his or any other religion's freedom.

Two years ago, a federal jury found Moon guilty of working a fraud on the Internal Revenue Service by fabricating and back-dating documents. People who dodge paying their lawfully due taxes are entitled to justify themselves as best they can, but their claim to be considered martyrs, especially religious martyrs, when they are caught does not, we think, enjoy wide popularity. So we are rather astonished that Moon's fellow clergy in the National Council of Churches and the National Association of Evangelicals have expressed their alarm about the government's intruding on religion by prosecuting this self-nominated deity of the Unification Church. When a member of the clergy is found pinching money from the collection plate, the ACLU does not ordinarily rush to his defense under the First Amendment.

WE GRANT THAT the ACLU may have had a point in coming in with a charge that Moon's constitutional rights had been violated when the trial judge refused his plea to take his case away from the jury and hear it himself. However, the Supreme Court has never held that it is a constitutional right to be tried without a jury, and evidently it continues to feel the same way.

THE KANSAS CITY STAR

Kansas City, MO, May 18, 1984

The income tax case of the Rev. Sun Myung Moon has raised concern of American church and civil liberties people who feel no allegiance whatever to the Unification Church. This disquietude centers on the extent to which internal church matters are subject to federal tax law; specifically, whether assets are the property of the congregation, even though they are held in the name of the spiritual leader. Thus the issue touches the relationship between clergy and flock.

These informal arrangements, rather common in this country, are not in danger of federal prosecution, officials say, if they are maintained in good faith. That brings little comfort to religionists who are not sure about the government's definition of "good faith."

Churches and their clergy comingle funds on presumptions rooted in English common law, including doctrines established by John Wesley (1703-1791), founder of Methodism. Under these rules, assets controlled by a religious leader that have been acquired by a church, and are to be used by a church, are the property of that organization, even though it is held in a leader's name.

This issue and one regarding the corporate status of a Moon organization prompted some religious groups, including the National Council of Churches, to file friend-of-the court briefs in support of the Moon arguments. The facts were not in dispute. The federal government, pursuing the case as a secular violation, charged Mr. Moon did not pay taxes on income from what it considered to be his property. The minister countered that he was not liable because the assets, though in his name, were church property and exempt from tax. He was found guilty by a jury in U.S. District Court.

In his unsuccessful appeal to the 2nd U.S. Circuit Court of Appeals, Mr. Moon's arguments contended the jury was not directed to consider church doctrine related to ecclesiastically owned property. The government maintained that once it was determined the property in question was owned by Mr. Moon, guilt was evident.

The Supreme Court's rejection, without comment, of Mr. Moon's appeal was not based on the merits of the case. It indicates that the court, for whatever reasons, was not ready to review the matter at this time. That means the appeals court decision stands and that Mr. Moon is likely to serve a prison sentence.

This may not be a purposeful, frontal attack on church doctrine but it is likely to cause more careful treatment of church funds as a way to meet the government's "good faith" requirement. And it is unlikely to be a final answer.

St. Louis ♞ Review

St. Louis, MO, May 18, 1984

Firm adherence to our constitutional guarantee of religious liberty has been one of the stellar accomplishments of the American experience. By and large our legislative institutions have refrained from trying to define religion, or to set standards for legally acceptable religious practice.

Because church and state necessarily interact, there have been occasions on which our civic institutions have acted, presumably for the common good, to limit the completely free exercise of religion. For example, courts have overruled the religiously oriented decision of parents to withhold certain forms of medical treatment for their minor children. Again, our laws prohibit polygamy, which is in accord with the tenets of Moslems and some elements of the Latter Day Saints.

During the past week, the U.S. Supreme Court refused to review a request by the Rev. Sun Myung Moon to hear his appeal against a 1982 conviction for tax evasion. Many respected church leaders and legal experts are convinced that Rev. Moon's case has serious implications for all hierarchically organized churches.

Many churches hold the property and funds in the name of their religious leader or bishop. It is quite right, as the appeal court declared, that there is a distinction between the functions of a religious leader and his actions as a private taxpayer. The jury in Rev. Moon's case determined, at least implicitly, that assets of the Unification Church were used for personal rather than religious purposes. This determination was made with very few clear standards and was at variance with the Unification Church's position.

We do not suggest that religious leaders are not accountable for their actions as private taxpayers. Nevertheless, it has not been a recognized prerogative of the courts or our legislative bodies to determine what is acceptable in church structure and operations. There is widespread popular suspicion and some hostility toward Rev. Moon and his followers. Under the circumstances, it would be wise to provide every avenue for Rev. Moon and his church to present their case. A somewhat unpopular church and its leader must not become the objects of a legal religious persecution.

The News and Courier

Charleston, SC, May 16, 1984

The Supreme Court's decision to reject the appeal of Sun Myung Moon against an 18-month sentence for tax evasion was wise, just and suitably exemplary.

Mr. Moon, who believes that he is the son of God and says that he intends to rule the world, is an extremely dangerous charlatan. The Supreme Court was shrewd enough to see through Mr. Moon's pseudo religiosity. Mr. Moon, a former agent of the South Korean CIA — and we are talking here about a murderous organization which has not been used for national security so much as to torture and assassinate democratic political dissidents — has built an enormously powerful business organization by exploiting the thirst for religion among many people, particularly the young. Instead of working for the glory of God, Moonie minions work for the enrichment of Mr. Moon.

He has built up a massive industrial empire, which ranges from armament factories in South Korea to a newspaper — a Trojan Horse disguised as a conservative response to The Washington Post — in the nation's capital. But along with seemingly legitimate business enterprises, Mr. Moon has a number of extremely shady operations.

The misleading title, Unification Church, enables Mr. Moon's manipulators to recruit many well-intentioned young people who are brain-washed into a blind belief in the Korean shyster by exploiting their innocence. By claiming that The Washington Times will always enjoy editorial independence, The Moonies have managed to lure highly experienced, conservative-minded journalists to the newspaper. The appeal — apart from a continued livelihood for newsmen who found themselves out of a job when the Washington Star closed — is that the Times is a right wing alternative to the liberal Post.

Mr. Moon, however, goes even further than that in political chicanery. In Latin America,

his henchmen have established close working relationships with the most unsavory dictatorships in the hemisphere. The Unification Church was cuddling up to the Argentine military at the height of murder and torture of thousands of people by the regime's security forces. Mr. Moon's men were with the Bolivian military when they savagely overthrew a civilian government, killing hundreds of people. Today the Moon empire's strongest outpost in Latin America is in Uruguay, where the "church" runs a newspaper, owns the biggest hotel and works hand in hand with the dictatorship. Mr. Moon discovered long ago that he could win both power and money by preaching religion and anti-communism. It is fortunate for the United States that the courts, right up to the highest tribunal in the land, have seen through Mr. Moon. Yet Mr. Moon had the money to hire one of the leading civil rights lawyers in the United States to fight his case for him and appears to have been persuasive enough to dupe a group of clerics into supporting his appeal to the Supreme Court.

The church and civil rights leaders who have given their support to Mr. Moon fear that the tax evasion conviction against Mr. Moon could lead to similar action against them. It is hard to see how the Supreme Court's decision to uphold the conviction against Mr. Moon can fail to set anything other than a good precedent. Mr. Moon claims he is a religious leader and that the organization he runs is a church. These are both dubious claims. Mr. Moon is a highly ambitious power seeker who has successfully exploited religious feelings to secure cheap labor and build a vast business empire. It is surprising that respectable religious leaders — who are not paid for their services like Mr. Moon's lawyers — should wish to identify themselves with him.

DAYTON DAILY NEWS

Dayton, OH, May 21, 1984

Leaders of some church groups, ranging from the Unitarian-Universalists to the Southern Christian Leadership Conference, are alarmed that the U.S. Supreme Court unanimously upheld Rev. Sun Myung Moon's conviction on tax evasion charges. The leaders are worried that, with this precedent, the government might strongarm its way into the financial books of other religious leaders.

Their fear is that Rev. Moon was pursued because he is unpopular. But there is just as much evidence that the Rev. Moon's finances were looked into because he is unusually rich and there was evidence of some hanky-panky. The results bore that out. There are plenty of precedents for investigating such matters, and some of those investigated have been right in the middle of the mainstream of religion and business. Pardon the irony, but some of this nation's most upstanding politicians, citizens and businessmen have been sent to prison.

The findings against Rev. Moon were very specific. He took a lot of money that he didn't pay taxes on. To top it off, he cooperated in a scheme to forge documents to support his claim. That's wrong, and it's illegal. A person shouldn't expect to be exempt from the law because he might be popular or unpopular.

Nine Indicted as Mafia Leaders in New York City

A New York City federal grand jury Feb. 26, 1984 indicted nine men as the leaders of "the five La Cosa Nostra families" headquartered in New York City. F.B.I. Director William H. Webster announced: "The ruling body of the most powerful organized crime elements in the United States...has now been brought to the bar of justice." Webster was one of 17 law enforcement officials to appear at a press conference to announce the 15-count indictment. The men were accused of racketeering and conspiracy, because of their alleged participation in a "commission" that regulated the affairs of the city's organized crime families. Two of the defendants were accused of conspiring to murder Carmine Galente in 1979. The commission was accused of having approved the killing in order to settle a power struggle between two of the city's crime families. Eight of the defendants were also indicted on 10 charges of extortion, and three of labor bribery, in connection with "the club," an alleged operation to rig the awarding of contracts to concrete construction contractors in the New York metropolitan area.

The Pittsburgh PRESS

Pittsburgh, PA, March 2, 1985

The arrest of nine reputed underworld leaders on charges of criminal conspiracy indicates that law-enforcement authorities may finally have figured out an effective way to attack organized crime.

The nine, who were said to represent five crime "families," were accused of a pattern of "racketeering" that involved control of the New York cement industry.

They also were charged with conspiracy to commit six murders to resolve a leadership dispute in one of the gangs.

Those indicted were not minor underworld figures. They included five who were identified as the heads of the Gambino, Columbo, Colombo, Lucchese and Bonanno Mafia families.

What sets these apart from the usual run of indictments is that this was the first attempt by federal authorities to prosecute members of the Mafia governing body as a group of racketeers. They were accused of taking part in a "commission" that controls Mafia crime.

The indictments were brought under a federal law called the Racketeer-Influenced and Corrupt-Organization Act (RICO). This measure provides a broad basis for bringing conspiracy charges against underworld leaders who usually keep their distance from the crimes that they order carried out.

Although RICO has been on the books since 1970, it has only lately become an important tool in fighting organized crime.

"We had RICO for almost 10 years before we knew what to do with it," said FBI Director William Webster, who was present when the nine indictments were announced. Mr. Webster said that last year there were 3,118 indictments and 2,494 convictions of organized crime figures in the United States.

If authorities can make the nine indictments stick — and that's a big "if" — the Mafia will have been dealt a severe blow.

The Wichita Eagle-Beacon

Wichita, KS, February 28, 1985

THE Reagan administration's vigorous war against crime — particularly organized crime — seems to be paying off. The recent arrests of reputed top Mafia leaders is the latest sign that war can be won.

The arrests of the Gambino, Genovese, Colombo, Bonanno, and Lucchese family bosses and underbosses — nine of the reputedly most powerful gangsters in America — was the result of an 18-month FBI investigation. The families allegedly cooperated in Mafia activities, including an extortion ring that manipulated construction bidding. This is a perfect example of how the Mafia infiltrates and bullies legitimate business operations. And it's good to see Mafia bigwigs on the hot seat for a change.

The Mafia's power is perpetuated by a number of myths: that organized crime is too pervasive and powerful to crack, that the Mafia "code of silence" and threats of retaliation would prevent victims from testifying against mobsters.

All of that's changing now, thanks to aggressive investigative work. Top Mafia leaders are speaking out, the code of silence has been shattered — and as more of these mobsters are brought to justice, the more victims will be emboldened to testify against them. It's important the FBI, together with local and state authorities, follows up on these arrests, and works to put lower-echelon mobsters behind bars — those who would move up to fill the power void.

Above all, the FBI's growing success against organized crime shows that — with patience, hard work, and cooperation among law enforcement officials and the public — this criminal scourge can be removed from society.

BUFFALO EVENING NEWS

Buffalo, NY, March 5, 1985

THE INDICTMENT of nine reputed top mobsters on racketeering charges strikes at the pinnacle of what federal prosecutors describe as a secret high commission formed in 1931 to govern organized criminal activities in the New York City area and beyond.

Allegedly, several of those indicted are bosses of separate criminal groups, or families, in New York. All nine are accused of participating in racketeering patterns linking them to conspiracies to commit six murders and the extortion of $1.4 million from concrete contractors in New York.

Calling the indictments "historic," FBI Director William Webster said the action "exposes the structure and leadership of organized crime on a scale never done before. It alleges not only the activities regulated and authorized by the commission but also a 54-year history of the commission's role in facilitating the illegal activities of la Cosa Nostra."

It has been claimed that hitting top crime figures means little because others will quickly move in to fill the vacancies. But that is an oversimplification. "To run a (crime) family requires expertise," Mr. Webster said. Sophisticated legal assaults by law enforcement against top mobsters expose complex operations to the light. They disrupt settled relationships, creating uncertainty and stripping away reputations for invincibility and immunity from prosecution by those in command.

The indictments flow from the 1970 federal Racketeer-Influenced and Corrupt Organization Act, or RICO. This statute equipped law enforcement with strong anti-crime weapons it had lacked before, especially those directed at criminal conspiracies in racketeering areas like gambling, narcotics and extortion, and broadened opportunities for prosecutors to seize illegal assets realized from criminal gains. One key provision of this law makes illegal the operation of any "enterprise" by a pattern of racketeering.

Federal agencies did not make energetic use of the RICO statute in the years immediately following its enactment. But that has changed. In the past two years federal prosecutors have indicted more than 2,000 suspects, many under the RICO provisions.

Regrettably, efforts to enact a New York State law modeled after the federal statute have not yet succeeded. The issue should be pushed again in the current Legislature. It is inexcusable that state prosecutors should not have the modernized legal weapons available to their federal counterparts for combatting organized crime.

The News and Courier

Charleston, SC, March 6, 1985

As a result of Hollywood romanticizing, the American public has regarded the Mafia as a spicy part of our folklore. Marlon Brando, cast as Don Corleone in the movie "The Godfather," portrayed the don as an eloquent, badly misunderstood yet almost noble arbiter and defender of Italian immigrants. And Brando's cardinal rule for Mafia business was to stay away from drug trafficking. So much for folklore.

Last week, the leaders of five Mafia families were indicted in New York City charged with conspiracy to murder and other racketeering charges including the marketing of hard drugs. The fat, graying old men filmed while being arrested and then released on bail, showed little of the Brando image. The FBI and other cooperating law enforcement agencies deserve credit for going after the dons and not just their consigliere.

The Mafia capitalizes on human fear, savagely using it to capture power. As an organization, it takes advantage of American freedoms to corrupt America. It's about time the government issued a "contract" for their execution — legally, of course.

THE INDIANAPOLIS STAR

Indianapolis, IN, March 1, 1985

Federal indictment of the reputed godfathers of the nation's most powerful Mafia families in New York is good news to law-abiding Americans.

There was a time when the word went out to the underworld: "You don't mess around with Uncle Sam." That was after Eliot Ness and the famed "Untouchables" came down hard on the Chicago bootlegging mob in a sweep in 1931 that sent its leader, Al Capone, to federal prison for 11 years.

Later the pressure let up and organized crime spread its tentacles throughout the nation, extending its power with terror and murder. The result was a a multibillion-dollar empire that controlled drug trafficking, labor racketeering, gambling, prostitution, loan sharking and other lucrative mob activities.

It appeared that the mob had put "the fix" in high places even though from time to time lesser figures in the crime brotherhood were caught and put behind bars. The big shots seemed to be beyond the law.

Some crime researchers voiced suspicion that organized crime had grown too big to smash and even suggested a mob conspiracy arranged the assassination of President John F. Kennedy.

Whatever the reason for slackening the drive against the syndicate, a crackdown on the Mafia was announced in 1982 by President Reagan.

In the last year investigations paid off with the indictment of more than 300 accused organized crime figures in New York.

"Historic" is the word FBI Director William Webster applied to this week's action, saying: "The major muscle of organized crime has now been brought to the bar of justice."

The arrests climax a 19-month investigation by federal, state and New York City investigators during which agents who planted listening devices in a boss's chauffeured car and other rendezvous points taped "thousands of hours" of conversations of mob figures discussing Mafia activities. Interrogators questioned 30 witnesses who broke the Mafia's code of silence.

The racketeering charges on which the bosses of the Gambino, Bonanno, Genovese, Colombo and Luchese crime families were indicted carry maximum penalties of 20 years in prison.

An America where Uncle Sam proves beyond anybody's doubt he is tough enough to smash organized crime will be a healthier America.

The Dallas Morning News

Dallas, TX, February 28, 1985

THE everlasting war against organized crime is one that must be massively discouraging for the good guys. But as the headlines this week demonstrate, they keep on fighting. The rest of us should be proud and happy that the professionals of American law enforcement have that kind of dedication.

The crime empire is immensely wealthy. Able to afford the best lawyers, it has been successful in using every legal technicality to hobble and divert the police, state and federal agencies that are trying to defeat it and bring its leaders to justice. In addition to money, the crime barons have no hesitation in using murder or any other violence to keep insiders or citizens from going to the police with information about their activities.

Worst of all, the lawmen know that the revenues that fuel all of this come from the supposedly "law-abiding" citizens. Gambling and other services offered by mob fronts are well patronized by the very people in whose behalf the law-enforcement officers serve. For all of these reasons, a big victory is as welcome as it is rare. And this week, with the roundup of five reputed leaders of Mafia families, the lawmen scored a huge victory.

It has been called by the Justice Department "a bad day, probably the worst ever, for the Mafia."

And William Webster, FBI director, had plenty of praise for the men and women whose hard work and cooperation made it happen: "Never have I seen the law-enforcement community better mobilized."

The bad day for the Mafia is a correspondingly good day for the country. Let us salute those whose outstanding performance of their duty brought it to pass.

The Miami Herald

Miami, FL, March 3, 1985

HEREWITH, a tale of two commissions, a snazzy black Jaguar, some nervous mobsters, and unprecedented cooperation between law-enforcement agencies. While members of the President's Commission on Organized Crime heard horror stories from Mafia informants during meetings in Miami last week, a Federal indictment was in the works against some of the very subjects of the hearings. They're Mafia chieftains who form a "commission" that rules much of organized crime in the United States.

The 15-count indictment charges the "commission" members, five Mafia-family bosses, and four other persons with authorizing Mob executions and directing several criminal enterprises. Seven of the executions were connected to a war for control of the drug trade in South Florida. Broward County sheriff's investigators worked with the FBI and New York law-enforcement agencies during the 19-month investigation, which resulted in the grand-jury indictments. The united efforts of state and Federal lawmen paid off handsomely, says FBI Director William Webster, who called the indictment historic in scope.

Two legal tools aided the investigation. The first is a small radio transmitter hidden in 1983 behind the dashboard of a Jaguar owned by one Mob boss's chauffeur. Two lawmen stealthily installed the court-approved bug while the car sat outside a Long Island restaurant. The bug provided five months of eavesdropping and 75 hours of incriminating tapes.

The second assist is a 1970 Federal statute that holds leaders of an organization liable if its members commit racketeering crimes repeatedly. Like some of its targets, the law has a nickname: RICO, for "racketeer-influenced corrupt organization." Federal prosecutors are finding it very useful in breaking up the old gangs.

No one is naive enough to think that these indictments, major though they are, will eradicate the Mob. Yet there is good reason to believe that the power structure of the "commissioners" has been badly shaken. Mafia members gathered in Fort Lauderdale this week to stave off disarray, redistribute the illegal pie, and worry a lot.

The Mob's worst fear is of informants. As the bloody ties that bind start to fray beneath good detective work, the instinct for survival may override many mobsters' loyalty. Nothing could please lawmen more, for this is one group they'd just love to put out of commission for good.

Chicago Tribune

Chicago, IL, February 28, 1985

Law enforcement officials deserve applause for winning indictments against reputed leaders of New York City's five underworld crime families. Their success shows how such controversial crime-fighting techniques as wiretapping can be effectively used against the highest level of organized criminal activity.

Too often, investigators waste their best technology on two-bit hoods. This time 175 federal agents and 25 city detectives cooperated in a three-year investigation using undercover agents and 171 court-authorized telephone taps and "bugs"—the biggest federal assault on the mob since Al Capone was nailed for income tax evasion in the 1930s.

He was imprisoned as a tax cheat because federal agents were unable to prosecute him for any of his more serious crimes. These new indictments are backed with such dramatic evidence as recorded conversations of mob business conducted in the chauffeur-driven car of a major crime boss.

Although these indictments are not likely to deal the lethal blow to organized crime that some jubilant legal officials say they will, they do put mobsters on notice that federal authorities are serious. They have the technology and they will use it.

The Washington Post

Washington, DC, March 11, 1985

A FEDERAL GRAND JURY in New York has indicted nine mafia figures, charging them with multiple crimes such as extortion, labor racketeering and complicity in murder. Last year, there were more than 3,000 indictments of organized crime figures nationwide, but this case is different. Prosecutors say they have, in this one sweep, moved to reach the top leaders of the mafia, an organization which, according to the indictment, has been an ongoing criminal operation in this country since 1900. The investigation was a cooperative effort involving the Justice Department, the FBI, state and city police, the New York State Organized Crime Task Force and the Brooklyn district attorney. Officials here have also received assistance from their counterparts in Italy. Crucial evidence was obtained by state officers who were able to plant a bug in a mafia car. Leadership and determination were provided by FBI Director William Webster, whose decision to make the mafia a top bureau priority is a welcome departure from the policies of his predecessors and deserves praise.

Forget about that nice Marlon Brando worrying about his tomatoes and his grandchildren. Don't be misled by the cutsie names—"Tony Ducks," "Joe Bananas." These people are charged not only with specific acts of violence and crime; they also run a tightly organized crime empire. More than gambling, drugs, loan-sharking and prostitution are involved. Legitimate industries are nearly captured through the use of force, threats and sabotage, and forced to pay tribute. The New York indictment, for example, charges that the mafia decided which companies would get large concrete-pouring contracts in New York. They designated the contractor who would make the successful bid, took large kickbacks on the contracts and punished businessmen who wouldn't cooperate by stopping their access to supplies or by creating "labor problems" with the cooperation of corrupt union leaders. The indictment charges mafia leaders with ordering murders of both outsiders and competing bosses within the organization.

The mafia doesn't run all the organized crime in this country. A Florida law-enforcement official appearing on "Face the Nation" a week ago warned that Colombian crime families now controlling cocaine traffic and counterfeiting are, in his opinion, "totally psychopathic . . . cold-blooded killers" who make the mafia look good by comparison. Justice Department lawyers have no illusions about the difficulty of combatting these syndicates. But they are very optimistic about breaking the mafia. U.S. Attorney Rudolph Guiliani says that four or five years of indictments like the ones handed down last week, and prosecutions of successive waves of leaders, will destroy the organization. The department is off to a good start.

The San Diego Union

San Diego, CA, March 1, 1985

The historic, 15-count indictment brought this week against the heads of five Mafia families in New York City marks the most ambitious federal assault yet on the high command of organized crime. Two vital aids to law enforcement made it possible: The 1970 federal racketeering statute and the extensive use of wiretapping and other forms of electronic eavesdropping.

The Racketeer-Influenced and Corrupt-Organization Act of 1970, commonly dubbed RICO, provided the Justice Department much broader grounds on which to pursue conspiracy charges against those participating in organized crime. And, of course, electronic monitoring offers one of the few ways to overcome the traditional, and heretofore hightly effective, secrecy of Mafia-style organizations.

Significantly, both RICO and the use of wiretaps raise constitutional questions and are accordingly viewed suspiciously if not opposed outright by some civil libertarians. The debate over what role wiretaps, with their inherent invasions of privacy and potential for abuse, should have in law enforcement was particularly fierce during the 1970s when the Justice Department's present tactics against organized crime and white-collar conspiracies were being devised.

The New York indictments were a measure of just how critical that debate was. Without electronic eavesdropping, including the use of telephone taps and surreptitious cameras, much if not most of the evidence against the nine men indicted this week could not have been obtained. And the RICO statute has been the principal weapon used by federal prosecutors in indicting more than 2,000 organized-crime suspects during the last two years.

Every police power in a free society is a two-edged sword. The greater its capacity to protect society, the greater its potential for misuse, intentional or otherwise. But if Americans want effective prosecution of an organized crime syndicate whose command structure has remained almost immune from law enforcement for nearly half a century, broadly drawn racketeering statutes and considerable electronic eavesdropping will continue to be essential.

The Kansas City Times

Kansas City, MO, March 1, 1985

For years the reputed top leaders of organized crime were seemingly immune from the law. No more, as the federal indictment of nine individuals in New York this week dramatically indicates. Or, for that matter, the deep inroads that have been made by a special task force into the criminal element here. It now appears the scales are tipping away from the Mafia in favor of law enforcement.

Of course, no convictions have been obtained in New York, as of now. However, the United States Attorney's office in Manhattan has an outstanding record in prosecuting such cases. The arrests represent, one official noted, "probably the worst day for the Mafia."

To understand the indictment of some 2,000 individuals in recent years, many of them presumably tied to organized crime, it is necessary to know two basic factors. One is the Racketeer Influenced and Corrupt Organizations Act (RICO), a federal law enacted by Congress in the last decade. The other is recent presidential administrations, including that of Ronald Reagan, which have placed high priority on uprooting the underworld from highly lucrative, illegal ventures such as gambling, prostitution, drug trafficking, loan sharking and labor racketeering.

RICO differs from other criminal laws. Instead of restricting prosecutions to a specific crime, it offers more grounds on which to base conspiracy charges. An important section outlaws an "enterprise" developed from a pattern of wrongdoing. Thus evidence can be presented purporting to show the accused conspired to commit any two of more than 30 violations.

The big nine were accused of taking part in a "commission" dating to the early 1930s that allegedly rules five organized crime "families" in New York, as well as those in other places. They were charged with what one report called a pattern of crime tied to conspiracies involving murder and extortion of $1.4 million from the concrete industry in New York.

It is plain that law enforcement officials are now using RICO and technology, including electronics, to good advantage in a laudable effort against an insidious and dangerous public enemy. It would be premature to suggest this spells the beginning of the end of the Mafia in the United States. But if the nine are found guilty, it would place a huge dent in that evil operation.

The Star-Ledger

Newark, NJ, March 3, 1985

Breaking up the mob—the tightly knit national consortium of organized crime "families"—has been an unrelenting top priority of the FBI, a legacy of its founding director, J. Edgar Hoover. His long career as a vigilant overseer of federal law enforcement was focused in large measure on a commitment to wipe out the Cosa Nostra, the underworld syndicate that controls various highly profitable illicit operations in the United States and Europe.

As a crime fighter, Mr. Hoover had some notable successes, but he was never able to achieve his lifelong objective of permanently destabilizing organized crime elements. Years after his death, the crime syndicate is still functioning—and flourishing better than ever because of its lucrative drug trafficking.

But that could change appreciably with the sweeping federal indictment of nine "dons" who head the five most powerful Mafia families in the metropolitan New Jersey-New York region. The indictments could have a deep, long-range impact on mob activities, such illicit operations as narcotics, loansharking, labor racketeering, gambling and extortion.

A dramatic series of raids by federal agents that led to the arrests and indictments of the crime bosses was characterized by FBI Director William Webster as a "historic" assault on the Mafia's inner council, the nerve center of mob operations.

The information gathered by electronic surveillance was the basis for the indictments. The charges, authorities said, "expose the structure and leadership of organized crime," and the operations of an underworld "commission" that controls Mafia activities in this country and abroad.

The New York investigation of racket operations also turned up information that could be extremely useful for New Jersey law enforcement officials in a similar sweeping crackdown on high-level members of the New York mob who are operating in this state. If the information developed from wiretaps in the New York probe results, as expected, in indictments of New Jersey figures, it would mean that a fortuitous double blow has been dealt to massive racketeering in both states.

The indictments of organized crime kingpins are of particular importance to New Jersey because of the highly vulnerable presence of Atlantic City casinos. This state has been acutely conscious of the disruptive potential of mob infiltration in the South Jersey resort.

Exposing the clandestine operations of the major crime families should be invaluable for the state's law enforcement agencies in neutralizing these nefarious criminal elements in the Garden State—making them persona non grata everywhere in the state.

THE ARIZONA REPUBLIC

Phoenix, AZ, March 5, 1985

A S of now, the score stands at Feds 9, Mob 0.

But it's only the first inning, and in the immortal words of baseball great Yogi Berra, the game isn't over until it's over.

Still, it's a good beginning.

A federal grand jury's 15-count indictment charging nine reputed top leaders of New York City's five organized-crime families with participating in a "commission" that governs mob operations should put a crimp in the underworld.

The indictment describes the fabled commission as the "ruling body" of a criminal enterprise that deals in murder, labor racketeering and extortion.

The commission reputedly has served as organized crime's board of directors since the days of Prohibition.

"The commission promoted and encouraged a climate of fear" to keep Mafia factions from warring among themselves, from breaking the traditional code of silence and from infringing on each other's territory, the indictment read.

The crime sweep that snared the alleged Mafia chiefs was the result of months of diligent police work that relied heavily on electronic wiretaps and bugging devices.

In the end, a bug planted in a car used by one of the suspects proved their undoing.

In the opinion of FBI Director William Webster, the arrests strike a blow at "the symbol of power" by exposing "the structure and leadership of organized crime on a scale never done before."

Other lawmen are equally encouraged.

Information provided by the surveillance, it is noted, is like money in the bank because it will help develop cases against mobsters in the future.

There is some concern that, just as nature hates a vacuum, the void created by the racketeering indictment will be quickly filled by a younger and more belligerent breed of gangsters.

However, the fear of a tougher mob is partially offset by the feeling that the so-called new Mafia will be easier to track because of a lack of internal discipline.

All that is speculation, of course.

In the meantime, the "commissioners," who have pleaded innocent, face lengthy trials that could go into extra innings.

As for the demise of the mob and organized crime if they're convicted, don't bet on it.

Hutton Guilty in Check Scam

The giant brokerage firm of E.F. Hutton and Co. Inc. May 2, 1985 pleaded guilty to federal charges stemming from the fraudulent manipulation of its checking accounts. The firm entered its plea in federal court in Scranton, Pa. At the heart of the scheme were check-writing practices by regional and branch offices that gave Hutton the interest-free use of as much as $250 million per day that the company did not actually possess. Some 400 banks and other financial institutions had been affected. The scheme had first been discovered in Pennsylvania. Hutton pleaded guilty to 2,000 charges of mail fraud. The New York City brokerage house agreed to pay $2 million in fines, to assume the $750,000 spent by the government in its investigation and to pay back as much as $8 million to the defrauded banks. No individuals were charged, a decision that stirred controversy. A companion civil suit enjoined Hutton from several practices not mentioned by the criminal charges. These included "criss-crossing" checks by writing checks for the same sum from two different accounts and then criss-crossing them. Hutton did not contest the injunction.

Prosecutors said the Hutton scheme had lasted from July 1980 through February 1982 (a period of near-record high interest rates) and had involved checks totaling about $4 billion. Prosecutors claimed the scheme had helped boost Hutton's earnings by about $8 million. Hutton said that the deception had been launched by regional and branch officers, who could increase their compensation by cutting their interest costs and thereby boost their profits. According to prosecutors, a Hutton regional or branch officer would write a check for more money than the office had on account with a particular bank. The difference would be covered within the next few days with a check from an account in a different bank of another Hutton office. For the next few days before the checks cleared, Hutton would be able to use the overdrawn check's supposed value without paying interest.

Hutton also pleaded guilty to trying to lengthen the check-clearing delay, known as a "float." In this variation of the scheme, branch offices would pool the funds they were supposed to send to a regional office. Instead of sending several small checks they would send a single large one, which frequently would take longer to clear. Hutton on occasion was able to use as much as $250 million per day without paying interest by using the scheme, prosecutors claimed. Many of the victimized banks were small and in rural areas. They had fewer resources to detect the fraud and took longer to process large checks. Hutton officials also reportedly used the company's good reputation to bully bankers who questioned Hutton's actions.

Attorney General Edwin Meese 3rd hailed the Hutton prosecution as a signal "to the business world that so-called white-collar crime will not be tolerated." But the Justice Deptartment came in for criticism from Democrats over its decision not to charge individual Hutton employees. According to prosecutors, hundreds of Hutton employees were involved in the scheme, either wittingly or not. About 25 persons were identified as the organizers of the plot. Some 50 of the employees had been given immunity in order to spur the investigation. These included about half of the supposed ringleaders. Robert Fomon, the chairman of E.F. Hutton Group Inc., the brokerage's parent, maintained that none of the employee's involved apparently knew the scheme was illegal or contrary to the firm's policy.

E.F. Hutton & Co., Inc. Sept. 5, 1985 released a report by former Attorney General Griffen Bell on the company's illegal check-overdrafting scheme. The report faulted many of Hutton's highest officials for poor management but cleared them for taking part or in condoning any violations. Hutton Chairman Fomon said the company backed Bell's findings. "We accept his conclusions and will implement all his remedies," Fomon declared. Hutton said three of its top-ranking officials had agreed to leave their posts while 11 others would be disciplined. All had been among the 16 Hutton officials Bell's report had named in connection with the scheme.

WORCESTER TELEGRAM

*Worcester, MA,
July 11, 1985*

Until last spring, most Americans probably regarded General Electric Co. as a model corporation. That was before it pleaded guilty to 108 counts of defrauding the government on defense contracts in 1980. Following that, the government suspended GE's eligibility to bid on new government contracts.

GE had been convicted of price fixing and bribery years ago, but it had since won a reputation as a well-run, respectable company that manufactures high-grade products.

The indictment and the guilty plea came as a shock. The investment committee of a major insurance company discussed whether it should continue to invest in GE. In response, GE expressed its determination to root out all wrongdoing.

According to an article in The Wall Street Journal last week, GE was genuinely shocked and chagrined by the disclosures that some of its officials condoned and encouraged phony time card figures on government contracts. GE Chairman Jack Welch has made a videotape for GE employees in which he warns that such conniving will not be tolerated. But the Journal article raised doubts that Welch can enforce his strict standards in a company that employs more than 330,000 people and sells billions of dollars of merchandise every month.

The problem is not confined to GE by any means. The government reportedly is investigating several dozen major defense contractors suspected of fraud and other crimes. But at least, the top management of GE has the decency to show remorse and to express a determination to straighten things out. In that respect, at least, GE's performance is far preferable to that of General Dynamics, which has arrogantly tried to justify its exorbitant billing practices.

the Charleston Gazette

Charleston, WV, May 18, 1985

ONE of the meaner anomalies of American justice is that white-collar criminals rarely are awarded the punishment they deserve, even when they're apprehended, which, as is true of most criminals, is too seldom.

In a commendable attempt to correct this egregious defect the Justice Department wants to develop a computerized system through which thousands of police agencies can exchange information about white-collar criminals and crime, much as they do today about other criminals and crimes of a more violent variety.

The proposal contemplates a new exchange of data: information that would include unverified rumors.

And that has certain libertarians in the U.S. Congress upset — understandably.

Notwithstanding this agitation and concern, it's about time the nation's police agencies undertook the difficult task of bringing to justice those individuals occupying corporate board rooms across the nation who are responsible for a multi-multi-multibillion dollar drain on the American economy.

White-collar crime covers a wide assortment of criminal activities: embezzlement, conspiracy, price-fixing, antitrust and fraud by individuals in government, commerce, industry, business and the various professions.

Such crime is being combated, reports David Burnham in *The New York Times*, on an ad hoc basis with none of the routine efficiency that is required to expose and to prosecute entrenched and sophisticated wrongdoing.

The recommendation of the Justice Department to develop a computerized system has been approved by the National Advisory Panel to the National Crime Information Center, which is the Federal Bureau of Investigation's computer network.

Bringing to justice more white-collar criminals won't be easily achieved. Yet it is an objective that must be pursued, if this society is to tackle equitably and fully all crime.

From an economic standpoint white-collar crime costs the nation far more than do all types of violent crime added together. The most recent comparisons we have encountered touching upon the subject estimate the annual bill for corporate crime at $44 billion and for all property crime at $4 billion, a tenfold bulge.

The fears of congressional civil libertarians must be taken into account. At the same time these fears can and must be dealt with in such a way that the rights of citizens are upheld, as they always have been, and white-collar criminals brought to justice and punished, as their crimes so richly deserve.

Coddling white-collar criminals is no less reprehensible than coddling any criminal.

The Wichita Eagle-Beacon

Wichita, KS, July 10, 1985

HOUSE scrutiny of the Justice Department's questionable fraud settlement with the E.F. Hutton brokerage firm in May appears to be having positive results. Investigators for the House Judiciary Committee's subcommittee on crime have turned up memos suggesting the Hutton leadership may have known about — and condoned — the routine illegal overdrawing of checking accounts by Hutton branches.

Those memos, including two sent in 1982 to Hutton's then-president, George L. Ball, weren't among the evidence that Justice's white-collar crime unit used to force the company to concede it was guilty of more than 2,000 counts of fraud, and to extract a $10 million fine. Now, a lot of folks in Congress and the securities industry have good reason to suspect that Justice didn't drive as hard a bargain with Hutton as it could have.

At the time Justice's settlement with Hutton was made public, it seemed incredible that 2,000 individual crimes — willfully writing checks on accounts with insufficient funds, to deprive the victim banks of interest earnings — were admitted to, but that no specific Hutton employees were guilty of committing them. Instead, Justice said, only the company itself was guilty. Such settlements in major crime cases contribute to the popular conception that when it comes to prosecuting crimes, the Department of Justice has two standards, a tough one for poorly connected individuals and a lesser one for the "big boys" on Wall Street.

To be fair, Justice well may not consciously have applied the lesser standard to Hutton. It's possible white-collar crime unit investigators didn't know of the memos' existence while the Hutton investigation was in progress. And word that Attorney General Edwin Meese may have ordered the investigation reopened suggests that current and former Hutton executives, who deliberately may have withheld key documents from the unit, eventually will be held accountable.

It's important now that the House subcommittee and the Senate subcommittee scheduled to open parallel hearings later this month hold Justice's feet to the fire — either to demonstrate that the May settlement was fair, or to bring any new charges warranted. The American people, who need to believe their prosecutors are uniformly tough with lawbreakers, deserve that much.

The Courier-Journal

Louisville, KY, July 18, 1985

EDWIN MEESE has a reputation as a hard-nosed law-and-order man when it comes to street crime. But the U.S. Attorney General seems to have a soft spot for outlaws who wear pin-stripe suits and spend their office hours running prestigious corporations.

That has been especially evident in the case of E.F. Hutton & Company. The big brokerage firm pleaded guilty last May to 2,000 counts of mail and wire fraud in connection with a complicated check-kiting scheme. The company promised to pay more than $2 million in fines, as well as $8 million in restitution to the banks it bilked. But not a single Hutton executive was indicted.

In other words, crimes clearly had been committed, yet the Justice Department somehow couldn't spare the time and energy to find the criminals.

This laid-back approach to the case may now have to be scrapped. It turns out that Hutton has discovered, and turned over to the feds, 18 additional documents related to the check-kiting scheme — documents that may implicate top company executives, including a former E.F. Hutton president who has since resigned.

In light of this development, Mr. Meese says the Justice Department's "attention to the case continues . . . . we are keeping our eyes open to any new information." Meanwhile, congressional committees, the Securities and Exchange Commission and a host of state banking regulators also are looking into the Hutton affair.

All of this is reassuring. But in the case of Mr. Meese, one would suppose that the nation's top law enforcement officer could do more than just keep his eyes open, ready to spot any fresh evidence that's slipped under his door or tossed through the transom. The prosecutor who originally made the case against Hutton — a 35-year-old assistant U.S. attorney in Scranton, Pennsylvania — followed up a tip and spent three years poring over truckloads of Hutton documents.

That's the kind of hustle and tenacity needed to nail powerful, well-connected corporations. Too bad his bosses back in Washington haven't displayed the same zeal in trying to pierce the corporate veil and put the actual culprits behind bars. As *Los Angeles Times* columnist Ernest Conine argued the other day, a spell in jail for law-breaking executives is a far more powerful deterrent to white collar crime than fines that are mere chickenfeed to multi-billion-dollar corporations.

THE LINCOLN STAR

Lincoln, NE, May 8, 1985

The best measure of a society's justice system is how it treats its privileged.

The case in point is E.F. Hutton, the country's fifth largest brokerage firm. Last week after protracted negotiations with federal prosecutors, Hutton pleaded guilty to fraud. The firm shifted billions of dollars among banks throughout the country to earn interest on more money than it actually had on deposit. From July 1980 to February 1982 this float scheme illegally earned Hutton $8 million in additional interest.

Hutton agreed to pay criminal fines of $2 million, $750,000 for the cost of the investigations and to repay the $8 million to banks it defrauded.

None of the 25 individuals who were identified as knowing participants were charged.

Is that justice?

IF AN INDIVIDUAL in a position of trust stole $8,000, would he pay a fine of 34 percent on the principle, return the money and continue his career?

At a minimum, a convicted individual would be on probation looking for a new line of work with a record of dishonesty following. A stretch in jail or many hours of mandatory unpaid community service would be likely.

The slogan "When E.F. Hutton talks, people listen" probably will need a replacement, there will be a round of jokes for Hutton employees to endure, the stock will waffle for a bit. But does our justice system punish the officers, stockholders and upper managers responsible for insuring and maintaining ethical corporate standards? Are those privileged individuals held accountable in this judgment for the check kiting example their company set? For the degradation to our social fabric? For the ugly money-grubbing American image they sent abroad?

The bedrock standards of Western jurisprudence are that individuals will be treated equally under the law and that punishment will fit the crime. When we try to apply the standards of individual penalties to corporations, the punishment ceases to fit. It's time to find a new scale.

AS OF 1983 Hutton had estimated total assets of $13.2 billion. A $2.75 million fine is the equivalent of $20.80 to an individual with a net worth of $100,000.

That's peanuts and a sham.

Worse, Attorney General Edwin Meese defended the bargain basement justice by saying the settlement sent "a clear message to the business world that so-called white-collar crime will not be tolerated."

If the United States is interested in sending a message about justice in our society, it's time that it dock corporate outlaws on the order of six months' earnings for misdemeanors such as the Hutton case, and a significant percent of a company's net worth in cases of criminal negligence leading to many deaths or injuries.

The mere possibility of such punishments would quickly refocus stockholder and boardroom attention from the next dividend check to a company's ethical behavior, and in turn assure compliance with our society's laws and value system.

THE SACRAMENTO BEE

Sacramento, CA, July 26, 1985

When a corporate chief commends a branch office for aggressive practices that earn an extra $30,000 a month, that's business. When the practice involved is overdrafting at the bank, that could be a crime. And when the corporate chief doing the commending is George L. Ball, former president of the brokerage house E.F. Hutton & Co., that raises troubling questions about how and why the Justice Department let the whole company plead guilty to 2,000 counts of fraud without prosecuting individual Hutton officials.

In recent weeks, there has been a steady flow of leaked documents and newspaper interviews with Hutton employees that suggest the Justice Department was less than diligent, and Hutton less than forthcoming, in the investigation of the overdraft scheme. Documents released the other day by Hutton — internal memorandums that Hutton admits were denied to a grand jury even though they were well within the scope of a subpoena — suggest that top managers were aware of and encouraged the practice of overdrafting accounts at banks around the nation to earn interest for the firm. The documents reveal that among those urging on the troops in their overdrafting was Ball, now president of Prudential-Bache Securities. Ball denies the activities he encouraged were those for which the firm was prosecuted.

Nonetheless, it is more difficult than ever to credit the Justice Department's original assertion that the overdrafting scheme was the work of a few middle-level managers. Even Robert Fomon, chairman of Hutton, is disbelieving. "The Justice Department's description seems incredible to me," he says.

He's right. It is time for the Justice Department to investigate whether Hutton withheld evidence from prosecutors, thereby sheltering officials, and for Congress to take a deeper look, both at Hutton's practices and at the Justice Department's shoddy performance in this case.

The Hutchinson News

Hutchinson, KS, July 13, 1985

The words coming out of E.F. Hutton & Co. these days are certainly worth listening to.

Even more words should be expected. And demanded.

More words should also be demanded from the U.S. Justice Department. It should be forced to explain further the administration's earlier decision to let every human being connected with the huge fraud off the hook.

A congressional panel investigating the Justice Department's incredible decision has uncovered new evidence that should surprise no one over the age of 8. The new evidence suggests the huge E.F. Hutton fraud was not the work of only several third-rank clerks in the middle of nowhere (as the Justice Department had tried to pretend).

The new evidence suggests that high brass did, indeed, know about it. Even the chairman of Hutton now admits that.

When 400 banks were victimized in a longstanding corporate effort at overdrafting between 1980 and 1982, only the Justice Department under an establishment-protecting Ed Meese could really believe that real-life executives could be ignorant of the source of so much corporate profit.

Forthcoming committee hearings probing both Hutton and the Justice Department should be a provocative forum about ethics in business and equity in law enforcement.

Pittsburgh Post-Gazette

Pittsburgh, PA, June 17, 1985

When companies with once-venerable names such as General Electric, General Dynamics, E. F. Hutton and the Bank of Boston have been accused of criminal practices, does it mean that white-collar crime is booming again?

The Sunday New York Times Business section raised that question in a recent article, contending, "A corporate crime wave appears to be exploding across the nation. Not since the mid-1970s, when a series of corporate bribes and illegal political contributions shocked the body politic, have there been so many deep gashes in corporate America's moral armor."

The Times reported that the prestigious Business Roundtable hasn't done anything on the subject since issuing a major pronouncement on business ethics a decade ago. And one corporate executive dismissed the business crime with the comment, "Ever since Watergate people have been looking under the bed for something."

But, the Times reported, many businessmen interviewed as individuals expressed concern. Some cite a breakdown in moral values throughout society; others say that new pressures on managers for constantly rising earnings in an increasingly competitive environment prompt shady dealings. And still others say that the Reagan administration's laissez-faire attitude toward business has been interpreted by some as a green light to ignore regulations.

Ralph Nader, the consumer advocate, contends that there is a double standard — one for crime in the streets and one for crime in the suites. He says that dozens of corporations have been caught illegally dumping toxic wastes; yet small fines are assessed. And the FBI has no corporate-crime equivalent in its Uniform Crime Reporting System for street offenses. "As a result," Mr. Nader charges, "corporate apologists for years have downplayed the seriousness of corporate crime — where there are no official counters, crimes don't count."

Nevertheless, a message adverse to business seems to be getting through — one that the business world should not ignore. A recent New York Times-CBS News poll asked: "Do you think American corporate executives are honest, or not?" The answer: 32 percent of those polled said they are honest, 55 percent said they aren't.

This should be of concern to executives, especially those who run honest businesses. In contrast to, say, the Depression era, business now is rather highly regarded, with men such as Lee Iacocca of Chrysler folk heroes and many of the brightest young people going to work for large corporations. It would be too bad if this favorable picture increasingly were undercut by the villainy of a few.

Ethical leadership from the top of corporations on down is one answer. Another is that sentences for white-collar crime have been too lenient. "Perhaps the only point of unanimity among businessmen, consumer advocates and government officials these days is that more harsh sentences are needed to stem the wave of corporate crime," the Business page article said.

Fortunately, corporate Pittsburgh has not been touched by the current wave of misdoing. All the more reason, therefore, for some leadership on the issue to emanate from here, including reaffirming for employees and the public the ethical positions numerous local firms announced a decade ago when Gulf Oil Corp.'s bribery problems were in the limelight.

The Miami Herald

Miami, FL, September 22, 1985

SOMETIMES an effect is so salutary that it is pointless to continue arguing about its cause. That verity applies to the Justice Department's newfound determination to seek better tools with which to prosecute white-collar crime. It doesn't really matter whether Attorney General Edwin Meese is merely reacting to congressional criticism of Justice's "prosecution" in the E.F. Hutton and other cases, or whether Mr. Meese would have shown this toughened attitude without Congress baying at his heels.

Mr. Meese this week accused the press of distorting Justice's efforts in prosecuting white-collar crime. He welcomed a Senate Judiciary Committee investigation, particularly of the way Justice handled the Hutton check-kiting case. And he trotted out eight anti-fraud bills and urged their adoption to help in prosecuting these economic crimes.

Considering Justice's record of fining corporations guilty of criminal conduct but letting their executives escape prosecution, Mr. Meese's allegations of distortion ring hollow. Nonetheless, his announced determination to crack down on white-collar crime is welcome. Without the Attorney General's active leadership, prosecution of companies and executives will never receive its due priority.

Congress should continue looking into the E.F. Hutton prosecution, in which the firm pleaded guilty to 2,000 felony counts while none of its executives was charged individually. Mr. Meese insists that his prosecutors couldn't have obtained evidence sufficient to convict E.F. Hutton without granting immunity to executives who detailed how the check-kiting scheme worked. That explanation simply won't wash, but there's little gain in dwelling excessively on this and other Justice Department bobbles.

Rather, there's more profit in looking forward and in strengthening the law to make it less difficult for the Justice Department to obtain the evidence that it says it cannot obtain now. Mr. Meese is asking for bills to permit Federal prosecutors to obtain for civil prosecutions evidence turned up by Federal grand juries. He wants to empower Pentagon auditors to subpoena books and records of defense contractors. And he wants a law that would permit a penalty of up to 10 times any bribe paid in connection with a Federal contract.

These deterrents, if adopted, should give Mr. Meese some of the key tools that he says he needs to improve his Department's prosecutorial record against white-collar criminals. Even then, unless Mr. Meese is willing to prosecute culpable executives as vigorously as corporations, white-collar crime will remain unconscionably immune from punishment.

The Washington Post

Washington, DC, September 19, 1985

"THE JUSTICE Department," charges Sen. Howard Metzenbaum, "seems to think that all the poor people ought to go to jail while the rich people go to their country clubs." That off-the-wall statement accompanied last week's announcement that the Senate Judiciary Committee would undertake an investigation of the department's handling of certain white-collar crime cases involving large corporations. The attorney general quickly countered in defense of the department, professing nevertheless that he welcomed the investigation as the "ideal forum" in which to examine the record. We don't take at face value either Mr. Metzenbaum's hyperbole or Mr. Meese's professed enthusiasm for the hearing, but we do think it's a good idea. There are serious matters to be considered.

The common thread that unites the cases at issue —E. F Hutton, SmithKline, Eli Lilly, General Dynamics and General Electric, to name a few—is the allegation that corporate officers are not being vigorously prosecuted individually for wrongdoing by their companies. Some of the cases are still in progress, but others have been settled, usually with the corporation's paying a large fine and the officers' being penalized lightly, if at all. The Judiciary committees in both houses—the House subcommittee on crime began its investigation last spring—are the right forums for these inquiries, since they have oversight responsibility for the Justice Department.

If political influence has been brought to bear in these criminal cases, that would be a major scandal. It is more likely that investigations will focus on less spectacular but important questions of general policy and on specific decisions. Justice Department officials say, for example, that they could not prosecute individuals in the Hutton case because, in an effort get evidence about participation of the company's top executives, they granted immunity to regional and branch managers who turned out to be the real culprits. The best to be said about that is that it was a mistake. Or was it worse than that? Congress should satisfy itself on the answers.

Prosecutors, it is true, necessarily exercise a great deal of discretion. Every potential case must be evaluated in terms of the importance of the offense, the evidence available and the wisdom of granting immunity in return for testimony. Government attorneys also have to consider the alternative benefits of accepting a plea to avoid a costly, time-consuming and possibly unsuccessful trial. Even if there is no conspiracy in the Justice Department to leave wealthy wrongdoers to their country clubs—this department, after all, prosecuted Paul Thayer, a corporate mogul and administration big shot, and sent him to prison on securities charges—what remains is the essential question of how that discretion was exercised. For everyone's peace of mind, the Judiciary committees should find out.

General Dynamics Accused of Fraud; NASA Chief, 3 Others Indicted

A federal grand jury in Los Angeles Dec. 2, 1985 indicted General Dynamics Corp. and four current or former executives of the company on charges of conspiring to defraud the U.S. Army on a weapons contract. The weapon in question was the DIVAD (division air defense) Sergeant York mobile antiaircraft gun. Defense Secretary Caspar W. Weinberger had canceled the DIVAD production program in August, citing cost overruns and poor test results.

The alleged wrongdoing had occurred between July 1, 1978 and August 31, 1981, when General Dynamics was developing a prototype of the DIVAD in competition with Ford Aerospace & Communication Co. (a division of Ford Motor Co.). At the time all four indicted individuals had been executives at General Dynamics' Pomona (Calif.) Division, which developed the prototype. The most prominent of the four was James M. Beggs, then the administrator of the National Aeronautics and Space Administration. Beggs had been a General Dynamics executive vice president and a director. He had left the company in 1981.

If convicted, General Dynamics faced a maximum fine of $70,000. The individuals faced a maximum penalty of five years in prison on each count. General Dynamics issued a statement Dec. 2, saying that "the company and the individuals intend to contest these charges vigorously. General Dynamics knows that the individuals were honest in their judgment and acted in complete good faith." The individuals Dec. 2 all denied wrongdoing.

A federal judge in Los Angeles June 19, 1987 dismissed criminal fraud charges against General Dynamics Corp. related to the defunct Army DIVAD Seargent York mobile antiaircraft weapon. U.S. District Judge Ferdinand Fernandez dismissed the case June 19 at the request of U.S. Attorney J. Stephen Czuleger. The prosecutor informed the judge that the "allegations of the indictment" were "not supported by sufficient evidence."

LOS ANGELES HERALD EXAMINER

Los Angeles, CA, December 6, 1985

Back in 1961, President Eisenhower coined the phrase "military-industrial complex" to describe the close ties between government and business in America — a symbiotic relationship that can lead to the kind of dangerous mutual dependency that seems to have developed between the Navy and General Dynamics.

The defense contractor, cited for bilking the U.S. out of millions, has been barred twice in the last year from competing  for government contracts. Yet the Navy is inclined to see that General Dynamics has a crack at defense dollars.

The Navy's position is defensible: If General Dynamics were out of the running for building certain weapons-systems, there might be no competition at all. Take, for example, the planned construction of four more nuclear-powered attack submarines, on which bids are due this week. With General Dynamics under an indefinite suspension, only one other company, Newport News Shipbuilding, is prepared to bid for the contract. Thus, chances are that the Navy will postpone the bidding until the expiration of General Dynamics' suspension.

The government has gotten itself in a bind. It can't live with dishonest defense contractors and it can't live without them. After all, nuclear-powered submarines can hardly be manufactured in the local tool and die shop. Neither can anti-aircraft guns or computerized tanks. Indeed, General Dynamics, a huge conglomerate involved in defense research and manufacture, is one of the few contractors, and is sometimes the only one, able to provide the military with the weapons it needs and wants. Suspending a company from bidding for government contracts may therefore affect not only the company but the nation's defense capabilities.

In Southern California, a suspension of government business could also have a negative effect on the economy. General Dynamics employs more than 11,000 people in the Los Angeles area, and, at the company's Pomona plant, virtually all the business comes from government contracts.

One way of solving these problems would be for the government, instead of suspending an entire company, to focus on the individuals responsible. In this case, a federal grand jury has already charged four General Dynamics executives. So why the suspension? Our hunch is that zealous criminal prosecutions alone will deter greedy contractors who are tempted to defraud American taxpayers.

The Miami Herald

Miami, FL, December 5, 1985

THE INDICTMENT charging the administrator of the National Aeronautics and Space Administration and three former colleagues at General Dynamics with fraud in the handling of a weapons contract is a welcome reassertion of the principle of individual accountability.

For months the nation has listened to Government accountants detail the outrageous billing and pricing policies of military contractors. The $435 hammer, $640 toilet seat, and $7,600 coffee pot are products not just of greed. They occur because of a system that never asks how much something *should* cost, encourages contractors to load expenses onto their Government contracts, and rarely holds anyone personally accountable as the bills pile up.

Indicted on Monday along with General Dynamics itself were NASA Administrator James M. Beggs, a former General Dynamics executive vice president and director; Ralph Hawes, Jr., currently vice president and general manager of the firm's Valley Systems Division; David McPherson, vice president for research; and James Hansen, director of the Stinger missile program. The seven-count indictment accuses them of illegally shifting $7.5 million in expenses on a $39-million contract to build two prototypes of the Army's Sergeant York anti-aircraft gun. As a result, General Dynamics was reimbursed $3.2 million. If convicted, the men face five-year prison sentences and $10,000 fines on each count; the corporation a maximum fine of $70,000. The Sergeant York gun never worked, and Defense Secretary Caspar Weinberger canceled the development program in August after $1.8 billion had been spent.

Mr. Beggs says that he's innocent, but he has taken a leave of absence from NASA until this matter is resolved. A General Dynamics spokesman asserts that what is at issue is "a highly sophisticated regulatory and accounting matter which should be resolved in a civil forum."

No, that's not the issue. The history of Government prosecution of white-collar crime shows that dragging amorphous corporations through civil proceedings is not sufficient to impose any sense of corporate responsibility. General Dynamics, the nation's third-largest defense contractor, has been called on the Pentagon carpet so many times as a corporation that the rug is threadbare.

Corporations don't make decisions; individuals do. There's no hope of curbing "corporate" abuses unless *individuals* are held personally responsible for their corporate actions. May these indictments signal the beginning of a Government policy of doing just that.

Richmond Times-Dispatch

Richmond, VA, December 9, 1985

DIVAD, the anti-aircraft gun infamous for missing its targets and ultimately abandoned by the Pentagon, seems finally to have hit an unintended one: The nation's third-largest defense contractor is accused of having defrauded the Defense Department in the course of developing two DIVAD prototypes. General Dynamics has been indicted, and suspended, temporarily at least, from new federal contracts. Three current executives, and a former vice president who recently became administrator of NASA, have also been indicted.

All deny any wrongdoing. Said James Beggs, in taking a leave of absence from NASA: "There is nothing that I did in the case involved that I would not do again ... We acted in an entirely ethical, legal and moral manner."

Maybe. Forty million in tax money was budgeted for those two prototypes. After $40 million, the DIVAD account was essentially closed. But, according to the indictment, General Dynamics spent $7.5 million more, which it included in Pentagon billings for R&D on new weapons and preparations to sell them. A federal grand jury saw possible fraud in that. General Dynamics sees "a highly sophisticated regulatory and accounting matter which should be resolved in a civil forum, not in a criminal case."

We see two matters to be resolved, in whatever suitable forum. First, the governing regulations. Are they so "sophisticated" that a giant corporation's accountants can't tell whether it's OK to shift billings at will from one account to another? Are the rules so "sophisticated" as to allow shifting the cost of a contractor's every miscalculation to the taxpayer? Are they so

"sophisticated" as to provide a handy niche in which to stash any unanticipated expense?

The argument that defense contractors must be free of the worst vicissitudes of the marketplace has merit. That hardly means they must be freed of all customary costs and risks of doing business. It hardly means that the usual and useful connection between decisions taken and profits made or lost must be severed. And it doesn't mean that the bounds of ethical conduct must be elasticized. To the contrary: Defense contractors are *more* bound by them precisely because they are largely protected and subsidized — and because they are dealing with not only the nation's money but the security it must buy.

If contracting regulations are so "sophisticated" that defense contractors can get confused as to right and wrong, and the Pentagon can't enlighten them, then the regulations are in dire need of de-sophistication.

The second matter to be resolved is the guilt of actual persons. The four indicted in this case say they did nothing criminal, and they may well have not. General Dynamics says nothing criminal was done, and that may be. But if something criminal was done, somebody did it. Prosecuting him, or them, may help pierce the notion that the "defense industry" is an amorphous entity, in which everyone — therefore no one — is responsible when that other amorphous entity, the "taxpaying public," is ripped off.

A matter of "cost-accounting judgments," says General Dynamics of this case. Indeed, it is one of many cases suggesting a pattern in defense contracting: too much left to the judgment of too many people without the guidance or ethics to exercise it well.

The Washington Post

Washington, DC, December 4, 1985

A FEDERAL grand jury on Monday indicted General Dynamics Corp., three of its current executives and its former executive vice president, James Beggs, now administrator of NASA, for allegedly seeking to defraud the Defense Department in connection with a celebrated anti-aircraft contract from 1978 to 1981 and making false statements in the matter. Mr. Beggs, the others named, and the company promptly declared that they are innocent and may well prove to be; the perils of prejudging cases like this are well known. The incident as reported is still instructive, at the least a metaphor for the badly blurred relationship between buyer and seller in defense.

It is probably useful to remember that you go back to the Carter administration in this case, a lean time for defense contractors, not a boom. Two companies, General Dynamics and Ford Aerospace and Communications Corp., a subsidiary of Ford Motor, were competing for what then seemed likely to be the lucrative right to build a new forward anti-aircraft gun for the Army, the DIVAD, which this year was dropped from the budget. General Dynamics had been given $40 million to build two prototypes of its proposed version.

The models turned out to cost more than that. Instead of absorbing the excess, the company, according to the indictment, charged it to two other Defense Department accounts. One was to pay for

research and development, the other to compensate the company for the costs of preparing bids and proposals; in effect, these accounts were paying the part of General Dynamics' overhead given over to thinking up and selling the services on new weapons. The prosecutor said $7.5 million was fraudulently billed to these sustaining accounts, of which $3.2 million was paid. The company lives in a different world. The dispute, it said, involves not fraud but "cost-accounting judgments" and "a highly sophisticated regulatory and accounting matter which should be resolved in a civil forum, not in a criminal case."

The fiction is maintained that defense contractors are private firms dealing at arm's length with their public customer. Yet often they are little more than jobbers. The government provides them with plant and equipment. There are subsidies for interest when the companies have to borrow and, as the General Dynamics indictment shows, for what in the private world would be normal costs of doing business—items such as research. As a study commissioned by Navy Secretary John Lehman shows, profits are high as well. It is a cosseted, semi-public, cost-plus industry—and perhaps it has to be. In the U.S. economy that may be the only way for it to exist. But one price of this, as other recent cases have suggested, and as this new case now suggests, is a diminished sense of public responsibility.

THE BLADE

Toledo, OH,
December 11, 1985

THE Justice Department in one major instance has proved itself up to the task of searching out fraud among defense contractors. It has indicted James M. Beggs, former executive vice president of General Dynamics Corp., on charges of defrauding the U.S. Army.

The Administration could have tried to ignore the transgressions of General Dynamics and Mr. Beggs, whose is also administrator of the National Aeronautics and Space Administration. But given widespread concern about fraud and waste among defense contractors, in particular General Dynamics which has had a troubled history, the problems could not have been swept easily under the rug.

What led to the indictments was one of the most glaring boondoggles in recent defense-contracting history, the Sergeant York air-defense gun. After seven years and $1.8 billion worth of testing and limited production, the Reagan administration last August abandoned the weapon, which had never worked right. Now the Justice Department is alleging that Mr. Beggs and his former associates were illegally billing the army for millions of dollars in cost overruns on the project.

The fact that General Dynamics is in trouble again is hardly surprising. It has been involved in a seemingly never-ending string of incidents of questionable conduct. In the wake of the Beggs indictment the Pentagon has suspended the firm from obtaining new federal contracts, an obvious and necessary step.

Mr. Beggs also has agreed to take an indefinite leave of absence from his NASA post until his guilt or innocence can be determined. That is appropriate; it would be difficult for a man under such a cloud of suspicion to function effectively in office while he prepares for a trial.

There has been growing pressure in Congress to attack the fraud and waste that characterize much of the expanded defense-contracting program. Perhaps the General Dynamics indictments will send a message to contractors to clean up their acts.

The Morning News

Wilmington, DE, December 6, 1985

THERE'S no way to sternly punish a huge defense company whose dealing with the government, and taxpayers' money, is found, let's say, irregular.

Consider barring General Dynamics Corp. this week, from getting new defense contracts. Within days the Navy extended the bidding process on four submarines, apparently keeping General Dynamics in the running for the job.

The suspension apparently will have only a token effect on the company. One analyst was quoted as saying the submarine bid extension means the Pentagon action is less "toothy" than first thought. A company spokesman almost shrugged off the effect of charges of defrauding the Army. Nobody, he remarked, has "found anything wrong with our products, just the execution of some contracts."

Just? But that was the point of the investigation and charges.

The company has vowed to do better, even to instituting a new "ethics code."

But in the name of accountability, government must act against individuals if there are signs of wrongdoing. A federal grand jury found reason enough to indict four present and former company officials. One was James M. Beggs.

Mr. Beggs, former senior executive vice president of General Dynamics, is now administrator of the National Aeronautics and Space Administration.

After first stating that he'd stay at his NASA post despite the indictment, he said Wednesday he would take an unpaid leave while defending himself against the charges.

President Reagan has praised Mr. Beggs' performance at NASA, where he is a fervent advocate of plans for a U.S. space station, and defended his former actions. Nonetheless Mr. Beggs would be disabled as administrator.

Some members of Congress, indeed, insist that the only proper recourse is Mr. Beggs' outright resignation.

Unpaid leave, as he undergoes his defense, is correct enough for now. His post will be manned by his deputy, William R. Graham, who joined NASA only last week.

Mr. Beggs says he'll "be around to assist Bill Graham in any way I can." That's all right, especially in view of the acting administrator's lack of direct experience with NASA.

But carrying out NASA's $8 billion program is a job for one not disabled and distracted by a cloud of indictment.

The Boston Herald

Boston, MA, December 5, 1985

THERE are several things about the latest General Dynamics scandal more shocking than the fact that the nation's largest defense contractor and four of its executives — including former executive and current NASA Administrator James M. Beggs — have been accused of cheating the government.

One is that its indictment for submitting phony bills to cover cost overruns was the second time in less than a year that it has been caught at this kind of thing.

Another is the revelation that many corporations engaged in defense-related work reportedly do pretty much the same thing General Dynamics has been charged with doing on its $40 million contract to build two prototypes of the totally-useless, and now abandoned, "Sgt. York" anti-aircraft gun. (You might recall that the only thing this weapon, designed to be deadly to enemy helicopters, destroyed in its test firings was a portable powder room near the test site.)

The third, perhaps worst, facet is what seems to be an air of resignation that this sort of thing is almost impossible to detect and control.

Not for a minute should the American people accept that defeatist reaction. General Dynamic's shifting of a $7.5 million over-run on the job from a fixed-price contract under which the com-

pany would have had to swallow the loss, to another, cost-plus contract under which the government paid it, was uncovered by federal auditors.

If nothing else, this proves it's possible to detect this kind of juggling. And the fact that the Pentagon is currently engaged in probing more than 40 contractors suspected of various forms of cheating demonstrates that there is a will in the Defense Department to root it out.

It figured that the feds would put the arm on General Dynamics a second time. A gang that would bill Uncle Sam for country club memberships for the big brass or kennel fees for the big brass' pups was sure to stir the interest of government probers.

The $7.5 million the corporation is accused of clipping through fraudulent billing on the Sgt. York might be considered small change. But when one considers that the Pentagon spends about $2 billion on research and development of military hardware annually — and 45 defense contractors such as General Dynamics are engaged in this activity — small change becomes big bucks. The spending of this money, the work it buys, and the bills for it must be monitored every step of the way.

Its purpose is to make the nation strong, not to keep fat cats comfortable.

The Kansas City Times

Kansas City, MO, March 1, 1985

For years the reputed top leaders of organized crime were seemingly immune from the law. No more, as the federal indictment of nine individuals in New York this week dramatically indicates. Or, for that matter, the deep inroads that have been made by a special task force into the criminal element here. It now appears the scales are tipping away from the Mafia in favor of law enforcement.

Of course, no convictions have been obtained in New York, as of now. However, the United States Attorney's office in Manhattan has an outstanding record in prosecuting such cases. The arrests represent, one official noted, "probably the worst day for the Mafia."

To understand the indictment of some 2,000 individuals in recent years, many of them presumably tied to organized crime, it is necessary to know two basic factors. One is the Racketeer Influenced and Corrupt Organizations Act (RICO), a federal law enacted by Congress in the last decade. The other is recent presidential administrations, including that of Ronald Reagan, which have placed high priority on uprooting the underworld from highly lucrative, illegal ventures such as gambling, prostitution, drug trafficking, loan sharking and labor racketeering.

RICO differs from other criminal laws. Instead of restricting prosecutions to a specific crime, it offers more grounds on which to base conspiracy charges. An important section outlaws an "enterprise" developed from a pattern of wrongdoing. Thus evidence can be presented purporting to show the accused conspired to commit any two of more than 30 violations.

The big nine were accused of taking part in a "commission" dating to the early 1930s that allegedly rules five organized crime "families" in New York, as well as those in other places. They were charged with what one report called a pattern of crime tied to conspiracies involving murder and extortion of $1.4 million from the concrete industry in New York.

It is plain that law enforcement officials are now using RICO and technology, including electronics, to good advantage in a laudable effort against an insidious and dangerous public enemy. It would be premature to suggest this spells the beginning of the end of the Mafia in the United States. But if the nine are found guilty, it would place a huge dent in that evil operation.

The Star-Ledger

Newark, NJ, March 3, 1985

Breaking up the mob—the tightly knit national consortium of organized crime "families"—has been an unrelenting top priority of the FBI, a legacy of its founding director, J. Edgar Hoover. His long career as a vigilant overseer of federal law enforcement was focused in large measure on a commitment to wipe out the Cosa Nostra, the underworld syndicate that controls various highly profitable illicit operations in the United States and Europe.

As a crime fighter, Mr. Hoover had some notable successes, but he was never able to achieve his lifelong objective of permanently destabilizing organized crime elements. Years after his death, the crime syndicate is still functioning—and flourishing better than ever because of its lucrative drug trafficking.

But that could change appreciably with the sweeping federal indictment of nine "dons" who head the five most powerful Mafia families in the metropolitan New Jersey-New York region. The indictments could have a deep, long-range impact on mob activities, such illicit operations as narcotics, loansharking, labor racketeering, gambling and extortion.

A dramatic series of raids by federal agents that led to the arrests and indictments of the crime bosses was characterized by FBI Director William Webster as a "historic" assault on the Mafia's inner council, the nerve center of mob operations.

The information gathered by electronic surveillance was the basis for the indictments. The charges, authorities said, "expose the structure and leadership of organized crime," and the operations of an underworld "commission" that controls Mafia activities in this country and abroad.

The New York investigation of racket operations also turned up information that could be extremely useful for New Jersey law enforcement officials in a similar sweeping crackdown on high-level members of the New York mob who are operating in this state. If the information developed from wiretaps in the New York probe results, as expected, in indictments of New Jersey figures, it would mean that a fortuitous double blow has been dealt to massive racketeering in both states.

The indictments of organized crime kingpins are of particular importance to New Jersey because of the highly vulnerable presence of Atlantic City casinos. This state has been acutely conscious of the disruptive potential of mob infiltration in the South Jersey resort.

Exposing the clandestine operations of the major crime families should be invaluable for the state's law enforcement agencies in neutralizing these nefarious criminal elements in the Garden State—making them persona non grata everywhere in the state.

THE ARIZONA REPUBLIC

Phoenix, AZ, March 5, 1985

A S of now, the score stands at Feds 9, Mob 0.

But it's only the first inning, and in the immortal words of baseball great Yogi Berra, the game isn't over until it's over.

Still, it's a good beginning.

A federal grand jury's 15-count indictment charging nine reputed top leaders of New York City's five organized-crime families with participating in a "commission" that governs mob operations should put a crimp in the underworld.

The indictment describes the fabled commission as the "ruling body" of a criminal enterprise that deals in murder, labor racketeering and extortion.

The commission reputedly has served as organized crime's board of directors since the days of Prohibition.

"The commission promoted and encouraged a climate of fear" to keep Mafia factions from warring among themselves, from breaking the traditional code of silence and from infringing on each other's territory, the indictment read.

The crime sweep that snared the alleged Mafia chiefs was the result of months of diligent police work that relied heavily on electronic wiretaps and bugging devices.

In the end, a bug planted in a car used by one of the suspects proved their undoing.

In the opinion of FBI Director William Webster, the arrests strike a blow at "the symbol of power" by exposing "the structure and leadership of organized crime on a scale never done before."

Other lawmen are equally encouraged.

Information provided by the surveillance, it is noted, is like money in the bank because it will help develop cases against mobsters in the future.

There is some concern that, just as nature hates a vacuum, the void created by the racketeering indictment will be quickly filled by a younger and more belligerent breed of gangsters.

However, the fear of a tougher mob is partially offset by the feeling that the so-called new Mafia will be easier to track because of a lack of internal discipline.

All that is speculation, of course.

In the meantime, the "commissioners," who have pleaded innocent, face lengthy trials that could go into extra innings.

As for the demise of the mob and organized crime if they're convicted, don't bet on it.

President's Panel Issues Final Mob Report

The President's Commission on Organized Crime April 1, 1986 detailed racketeering's cost to the U.S. in the third and last of an ambitious series of reports. But nine of the panel's 18 members charged that commission missteps made its record "a saga of missed opportunities." The final paper, called "The Impact: Organized Crime Today," gave statistics on the nationwide economic damage caused by mob crime: the loss of 414,000 jobs, an increase in consumer prices of 0.3%, an annual reduction of the gross national product by $18.2 billion and an estimated $6.5 billion in lost tax revenues for 1986. The panel said the result of this drain on the economy would be the loss in 1986 of $77 from every American's personal income. The figures came from a report prepared by Wharton Econometric Forecasting Associates Inc. The study estimated organized crime's annual revenues at $41.6 billion to $106 billion.

The commission also called attention to groups emerging to share the stage with the Mafia. Four or more motorcycle gangs had evolved into "full organized crime groups," the report said, while U.S. prisons had spawned at least five secret societies that could make the same claim. Chinese, Vietnamese, Japanese, Russian, Cuban, Colombian and Irish ethnic organized crime groups were all said to be flourishing.

The report urged countermeasures. It called for the states to follow the federal government's lead in permitting electronic surveillance, immunity for witnesses and the forfeiture of criminal proceeds. It also urged an assault upon corrupt allies of the mob in business, politics and the law. Of the three, mob-linked lawyers received the lengthiest treatment. The panel urged stricter policing by bar associations and judges, as well as in some cases of electronic surveillance. The National Association of Criminal Lawyers attacked the proposals.

A report supplement signed by nine commission members took to task the entire series of commission papers. "We have not done an adequate job in assessing the effectiveness of the federal government's response to organized crime," the statement said. "Poor management of time, money and staff has resulted in the commission's leaving important issues unexamined."

The Dispatch

Columbus, OH,
April 7, 1986

The President's Commission on Organized Crime has concluded its work by estimating that organized crime figures in this country reap $100 billion a year in profits — and that higher profits will be realized in the years ahead unless action is taken to combat organized crime.

The panel, concluding 2½ years of work, estimates that the illegal activities cost the economy more than 400,000 jobs annually and rob the average American of $80 in yearly income.

It recommends that state and local government officials be given greater powers to fight organized crime activities and that the success of the anti-crime effort depends more on local officials that federal officials.

Also, the commission called upon the legal profession to rid itself of lawyers who aid and abet organized crime figures in their illegal activities. The commission recommended that the legal profession change its rules of professional conduct to require an attorney to report serious misconduct by another attorney. Disciplinary bodies should more aggressively investigate lawyer misconduct cases, and law enforcement agencies should use wiretaps and informants to investigate lawyers and rid the profession of attorneys suspected of organized crime activity, it added.

These recommendations deserve serious consideration and implementation, where appropriate. The fight against crime — especially organized crime — must be vigorous, creative and effective. Law-abiding citizens cannot afford to be complacent about this problem.

Herald News

Fall River, MA, April 4, 1986

The President's Special Commission on Crime has concluded its long period of investigation and deliberation. It has now published its report, based on the testimony it heard.

Commissions of this kind are seldom effective in the long run. They submit their reports and recommendations which tend to repose unread and unheeded in filing cabinets forever after.

It is to be hoped this is not the case with the Crime Commission's report.

In the first place the Commission points out that this year alone organized crime will cost the country 400,000 jobs and each person in the country $80. The revenue of organized crime this year alone it estimates at more than $100 billion.

The structure of organized crime, the Commission claims, is changing rapidly, and for this reason the range of law enforcement efforts must be broadened.

What the commission means by crime's changing structure is that it has become a major industry, larger than the rubber and tire industry, for instance.

It cannot be treated in the old-time cops and robbers fashion. It has outgrown that and become too dangerous.

Several members of the Commission have criticized its procedures and findings, claiming it was so large as to be unwieldy and that it lacked the funds to do the job it was intended to do.

Perhaps it should have done more, but still it accomplished a great deal, exposing criminal activities that had gone hidden for years.

Again, the report does not confine itself to generalities. It names names.

Among them were alleged crime bosses. Boston police say the information the Commission received and published was out of date.

Perhaps so, but at least names were used. The Commission did not hide behind verbiage.

The Commission may not have done all it could, but what it did accomplish is by no means negligible.

The Times-Picayune
The States-Item

New Orleans, LA, April 5, 1986

The third and final report of the President's Commission on Organized Crime has not added significantly to knowledge of the subject, but it has put a new price tag on the public cost of organized crime and stirred a mini-tempest or two.

The commission, which spent $5 million and 36 months on its task, concludes that organized criminal operations are continuing and expanding and constitute "an entrenched and pervasive phenomenon that is not easily attacked or readily eliminated." The commission went beyond the usual concentration on old-line Mafia families to list among criminal organizations outlaw motorcycle gangs and a "united nations" of new ethnic gangs — Mexicans, Chinese, Vietnamese, Japanese, Colombian and Cuban.

The economic impact study of organized crime was done for the commission by the prestigious Wharton Econometric Forecasting Associates of Philadelphia. The Wharton report says organized crime cuts U.S. economic output by $18.2 billion a year, reducing employment by 414,000 jobs and raising consumer prices by 0.3 percent. It estimates that the collective mob's annual gross income, much of it derived from control of or interest in legitimate business, exceeds $100 billion.

Consumers, say Wharton Associates, pay higher prices when the mob can suppress competition, that workers are paid less when the mob controls labor unions and that the mob evades taxes on most of its income.

There is nothing much new in this, nor in the commission's recommendations for action. The federal anti-organized crime campaign has had some signal successes in recent years. One problem the commission notes, which is also nothing new, is that the mob has "protectors" in corrupt public officials, lawyers and businessmen.

The report calls for stepped up action by state and local law enforcement agencies. It urges all states to adopt electronic surveillance laws, statewide grand juries and racketeering statutes modeled after the federal Racketeer Influenced Corrupt Organizations law, which is now the chief federal weapon against mobsters.

Nine members of the 18-member commission criticized the final report and the commission itself as a "saga of missed opportunity." The commission, they charged, mishandled some areas and left many important issues unexamined.

The report's mention of crooked lawyers, elaborated by five case studies, has raised some hackles in the legal profession. The commission urges going after lawyer criminals the same way police go after other criminals, including wiretapping. That has drawn charges that such actions could interfere with an accused's right to legal counsel. But mobsters' "mouthpieces" have long been standard characters in gangsterdom, and one can pursue a reasonable cause for believing someone's attorney is trying to evade a grand jury or tamper with a trial jury, for example, without denying his suspect employer his own rights.

THE SUN

Baltimore, MD, April 11, 1986

It is unfortunate that the President's Commission on Organized Crime was so disorganized. The impact of criminal organizations on the United States is enormous. It is clear from every study of the subject that more and different weapons and strategies are needed in the fight against crime. And the public needs to be informed and enlisted. When a commission like this one ends its tenure with its members and staff bickering among themselves, that becomes as much news as the findings and recommendations, and the public's attention is diverted.

Nine of the 18 commission members criticized the panel's work habits and final report. Part of their complaint about the *modus operandi* seems based on personality conflicts. It is hard for outsiders to assess this part of the dispute. But the dissenters are persuasive when they argue that the commission failed in a basic way by choosing not to examine in detail federal and state efforts to fight organized crime. It is difficult to know what must be done without first knowing what already is — and is not — being done.

The commission's handling of the question of illegal drug traffic was unfortunate. It correctly noted that "the user is a part of the trafficking." But by commenting approvingly on a testing program so massive as to be unachievable even if constitutional, it appeared to be giving up on the idea of containing the traffic by prosecuting suppliers and dealers.

Organized crime's influence on the legitimate economy is great. The commission did some good work here. It gave the public a better idea of how and where criminals move in on honest enterprises — and came up with an estimate that organized crime costs the average American $77 a year. When Americans come to understand the true costs of crime, they will be willing to pay the price to cut it down to size. We trust the budget cutters at the Department of Justice and the Office of Management and Budget will be willing, too.

Finally, to its credit the commission has painted an up-to-date picture of organized crime that is much different from the image much of the general public still entertains. There is more to big-time criminal enterprise in this country than the romanticized Italian-American organizations of the largest cities. There are several other groups organized along ethnic or cultural lines that are growing in size and power. If the infamous Mafia were "disabled" tomorrow, the commission concluded that several of these newer groups are "able and eager" to take over for it.

The San Diego Union

San Diego, CA, April 12, 1986

The final report of the President's Commission on Organized Crime is a shocker. It dissects a top U.S. growth industry that could turn a $75 billion profit this year.

The report describes organized crime as a $106 billion-a-year business that robs the United States of 414,000 jobs, $6.5 billion in lost taxes, and costs every American $77.20.

Although the 24 La Cosa Nostra families that constitute the Mafia leadership remain the best-known and most-powerful organized crime groups, the commission report warns of growing criminal activity by motorcycle gangs, Asian crime rings, and other ethnic gangs. Several of these groups are active in California.

The bulk of organized crime's illegal earnings come from drugs, illegal gambling, loansharking, and prostitution, but the Mafia also has made inroads into almost every major U.S. industry. These gains have come despite the passage of tougher anti-racketeering laws and increased federal prosecutions of organized crime figures during recent years.

Another real problem addressed by the report deals with mob-connected attorneys. State bar associations and law enforcement agencies are urged to crack down on unethical members of the bar who cooperate with criminals. Moreover, states are urged to combat organized crime through greater use of undercover tactics, electronic surveillance, and grand jury investigations.

One area the commission failed to address is the significant contribution ordinary citizens can make toward better law enforcement. Many otherwise law-abiding Americans support organized crime by buying illicit drugs or placing illegal bets with their neighborhood bookies. Nationwide, this amounts to substantial revenues for the illegal economy.

Law enforcement can't bring down organized crime by itself. There must be active support from an aroused citizenry.

The Star-Ledger

Newark, NJ, April 12, 1986

A presidential commission has confirmed a widely held belief by law enforcement agencies that organized crime has become an institutionalized, clandestine form of Big Business. Despite government efforts to inhibit these criminal elements, they have continued to prosper, grossing more than $100 billion a year in illicit revenues.

In its final report, the President's Commission on Organized Crime included a study that showed crime organizations are larger than some major industries, including paper and rubber industries, and comparable in size to textile and metal industries.

Another unsettling aspect, the panel found, is that while the Cosa Nostra is still a "dominant factor in organized crime," there are other emerging major crime groups operating throughout the country and routinely engaging in illegal activities and violence.

In winding up its comprehensive examination of organized crime, the commission underscored a sense of enforcement futility in trying to curb the pervasive presence of crime groups who reap huge profits from drug trafficking, labor racketeering, embezzlement, fraud, extortion and infiltration into legitimate businesses.

Nevertheless, it is imperative, as the commission's chairman, Federal Judge Irving Kaufman, warned, that the public must "overcome its inertia in tolerating organized crime as a necessary evil." What the panel's wide-ranging findings conclusively reveal is the inherent difficulty in apprehending and successfully prosecuting organized crime figures.

The Justice Department has intensified efforts in recent years to curb racketeering, but it has become so firmly entrenched in our social fabric that it has continued to flourish despite the expanded federal effort.

The analysis by the presidential panel of the problem as a national phenomenon should be useful in updating and redefining the nature of organized crime. It could serve as a basis for a redeployment of enforcement efforts, channeling them into specific areas of clandestine mob operations. There may well be a need to formulate new strategies in attacking these burgeoning criminal activities.

It is important, moreover, to maintain vigilant federal and state enforcement pressure on organized crime as an ongoing, unrelenting institutionalized commitment. Otherwise, organized crime will become even more pervasive and engrained in our society.

THE KANSAS CITY STAR

Kansas City, MO, April 5, 1986

President Reagan's Commission on Organized Crime has rightfully focused attention on the economic loss inflicted by illegal syndicate activities. Construction prices are inflated by payoffs. Organized crime drives up prices in industries where it suppresses competition. Invasion of labor unions has been a major scandal. Illegal drug trafficking imposes a particularly heavy price. It promotes robbery and burglary as users attempt to meet the cost of their habit. It results in absenteeism, individuals displaced by drug problems and huge expenditures for rehabilitation.

The commission placed the loss of economic output at $18.2 billion a year. That may be light. The report does not delve into killings and intimidation brought about by criminals.

Just now, after a special federal government drive dating to the early 1970s, deep inroads are being made into mobster groups. The result, in Kansas City and elsewhere, is the imprisonment of top leaders, and often their underlings. This nation is the better for this effort.

The Seattle Times

Seattle, WA, April 3, 1986

EVERY American administration for at least the past quarter-century has — with great fanfare — declared war on organized crime. Although there have been some spectacular victories, the United States continues to lose this war.

That much was clear from the final report issued this week by the President's Commission on Organized Crime. What was not clear was whether the commission had really done its job.

Fully half of the 18-person panel named by President Reagan nearly three years ago issued a blistering separate statement asserting that the commission had done some good work but mishandled certain areas and left many important issues unexamined.

"Poor management of time, money ($5 million), and staff has resulted in the commission's leaving important issues unexamined, most notably the questions of the effectiveness of federal and state anti-organized-crime efforts," the dissenters charged.

It appears that organized crime has so pervasive a grip on the economy that its scope defies adequate study, let alone control.

The nine dissenters said poor management denied panel members the opportunity to review many of the official findings and recommendations. That much was apparent last month when two of the commissioners said they had not even seen an interim report that recommended controversial drug testing for federal workers.

The commission did perform useful service in making clear the amazing variety of ethnic-based U.S. crime groups, of which the Mafia — or La Cosa Nostra — is but one.

The official report strongly recommended that states enact a number of specific laws to combat mob activity. That's all very well, and yet the scope of organized crime obviously is so vast that only the federal government is big and powerful enough to strike decisive blows.

By far the most financially rewarding of organized criminal enterprises is the sale of illegal drugs. Prostitution and gambling are the next most lucrative activities.

The big money lies in simply catering to human weaknesses. Thus it is beyond argument that those chiefly responsible for the entrenched position of organized crime in our society are millions of ordinary Americans.

The Evening Gazette

Worcester, MA, April 10, 1986

One of the tasks of the President's Commission on Organized Crime was to calculate the financial impact of crime in the United States. The figures are shocking.

In its final report, issued last week, the panel estimates that racketeers will take in $75 billion — that's $75 *billion* — during this year alone. It also estimates reduced competition in several industries resulting from mob activities will will cost the country some 400,000 jobs.

Closer to home, the commission estimates that the annual income of each law-abiding American, all 240 million of us, will be reduced by nearly $80 because of the activities of organized crime.

The commission places part of the blame for the problem on the lack of adequate action by state and local law enforcement agencies. Its report urges states to adopt legislation modeled after the federal anti-rackets laws. It also says the legal profession shares the blame for not purging itself of corrupt lawyers who further the interests of racketeers.

Some commission members were critical of the final report, with more than half of them saying too many facets of the crime problem were not covered. One group of commissioners said poor management of time, money and staff resulted in the commission leaving important issues unexamined.

One of them may have been the part of ordinary citizens in fighting organized crime. In its fight against international drug trafficking, federal agencies now emphasize that the battle cannot be won simply by burning coca fields in Latin America nor by intercepting drug smugglers at our borders; only an end to the demand for illegal drugs among ordinary citizens will bring a permanent solution.

That lesson applies to the fight against organized crime within our borders as well. A seemingly harmless action by an ordinary citizen — buying an illegal sports-betting card, for instance — becomes part of the problem. Every dollar helps fuel the organized-crime juggernaut.

FORT WORTH STAR-TELEGRAM

Fort Worth, TX, April 8, 1986

Income tax time provides an appropriate juncture for taking a long, hard look at the impact organized crime has on the average, law-abiding American's personal finances.

A report released by the President's Commission on Organized Crime contains some startling statistics: Organized crime is reducing U.S. economic output by an estimated $18.2 billion annually, cutting employment by 41,000 jobs, lifting consumer prices by 0.3 percent and reducing per-capita income in this country by $77.22.

That damage results from underpayment of taxes by crime figures and from higher consumer prices generated by mob involvement in industry. "The effects of organized crime on the legitimate economy show up in higher prices for consumers when competition is suppressed, lower wages for workers when labor unions are controlled and less safety when corners are cut," the report said.

Organized crime's impact on the average American is felt at tax time because, the study said, taxes on ordinary citizens must be higher by the amount of taxes not paid by criminals in order to provide the government with needed revenue.

In other words, because of big-time crime, your taxes are higher, the prices you pay for goods and services are higher and your community, wherever it may be, is a more dangerous place in which to live.

Perhaps, when we all grow sufficiently tired of that situation, we will work actively to strengthen the national resolve against crime. Until that happens, of course, we're doomed to remain victims of criminals who use our own system against us.

The State

Columbia, SC,
April 13, 1986

A RECENT report on organized crime underlines the enormous price that illegal acts exact from the economy and the problems police face in adjusting to the changing structure of criminal activity.

The President's Commission on Organized Crime, making its last report before disbanding, summed up the cost to society: $100 billion and 414,000 jobs, cutting a typical person's income by $77.

Furthermore, noted the chairman of the panel, the power of the Mafia and other illicit groups is "an entrenched and pervasive phenomenon that is not easily attacked or readily eliminated." But La Cosa Nostra is not the only factor. The commission pointed to newer crime organizations: outlaw motorcycle gangs, Chinese and other ethnic gangs.

The new look in crime challenges American law enforcement to adjust to the changing elements by broadening the scope of its efforts, as well as adopting appropriate training for officers.

THE BLADE

Toledo, OH, April 11, 1986

IF A politician has a tricky issue that he would just as soon duck, one way to do it is to appoint a commission to study it to death. By the time the group has presented its assessment of the problem, the public may have turned its attention to other matters.

This approach, however, can fail when half of a commission, such as nine members of the President's Commission on Organized Crime, disagrees emphatically with the other half as to the nature of a problem and how to address it. This in turn may serve to focus more attention on the issue at hand than the usual dry-as-dust report.

At the heart of their complaint is a view that the Justice Department is too inflexible in pursuing certain aspects of organized crime. "The true history of the commission . . . is a saga of missed opportunity," the nine dissidents reported recently. They placed blame on poor management of time, money, and staff which left some key problems unexamined.

Because commissions wield no real power — one view is that they are merely there to reaffirm the prevailing views of policy makers — perhaps "bomb-throwing" of this kind will serve a higher purpose: to challenge the Government to more thoroughly and creatively attack society's problems.

Teamsters Union President Indicted for Racketeering

Jackie Presser, President of the Teamsters union, was indicted on federal racketeering charges May 16, 1986. On May 21, he was overwhelmingly elected to continue for five more years as president of the union. Presser had been appointed to his post in April 1983 by the union's executive board to replace Roy L. Williams, who resigned after conviction on federal bribery conspiracy charges. The Justice Department had dropped an investigation of Presser then without filing charges, after being told by F.B.I. agents in Cleveland, Ohio that Presser was playing an undercover role for the F.B.I. and that the activities on which a potential indictment was being sought had been performed at the F.B.I.'s behest.

The Presser case was reopened, reportedly after questions arose about the validity of the reports by agents in Presser's F.B.I. connection. Presser was indicted by a federal grand jury in Cleveland. The racketeering and embezzlement charges, and charges of filing false union reports with the government, involved a payroll-padding scheme to pay three so-called "ghost employees," people who did not work but received salaries, on the Teamsters Local 507 in Cleveland, Presser's home local. Presser was listed as secretary-treasurer of the local in addition to being president of the international union. The payments to the "ghost employees" totaled more than $700,000 between 1972 and 1981, according to the indictment. Presser's election to a five-year term took place amid much hoopla at the union's convention in Las Vegas May 21. The vote was 1,729 to 24 against the token opposition of C. Sam Theodus, secretary-treasurer of Cleveland Local 407.

Labor Secretary William E. Brock, in a blunt speech to the convention May 19, urged the Teamster membership to "clean house" and rid the union of the criminal influences. "As a national organization, you've lost a great deal of public trust," Brock told the delegates. "As secretary of labor, it isn't easy to hear about mobbed-up locals, or pension-fund abuse—misuse of members' blood and sweat," he said. "It's impossible for me to ignore that. It is necessary for you to address it."

THE ARIZONA REPUBLIC

Phoenix, AZ, May 23, 1986

THERE was a sense of *deja vu* in Las Vegas when delegates to the convention of the 1.6 million-member International Brotherhood of Teamsters again elected to the union's presidency a man under indictment.

Jackie Presser, charged with embezzlement and racketeering in an alleged payroll-padding scheme involving $700,000 paid to employees who did no work, was elected overwhelmingly by the puppet delegates to the convention.

A reform movement favoring rank-and-file election of the union's boss never had a chance against the machine-picked delegates. In a *Politburo*-style election, the reformist candidate received only 24 of the 2,000 ballots cast.

The undemocratic and probably illegal system under which the national leadership is elected by incumbent union bosses stifles opposition movements and guarantees organized crime's grip on the union. The convention defeated all reform measures, but did amend the union constitution making it even more difficult for dissidents to become delegates.

There are, however, still two dozen courageous and honorable leaders in the free world's largest and richest trade union.

Presser is the fourth of the last five Teamsters presidents to be charged with a crime. All three previous union leaders who stood trial were convicted. It's an open secret that the union's huge pension fund and extensive financial assests have been virtually an open bank vault for organized crime.

The Teamsters were the only major union to endorse Ronald Reagan in both 1980 and 1984, and the leadership views Presser's indictment as a betrayal by the administration that had received their loyalties.

Presser calls the indictment "persecution," and the head of the AFL-CIO-affiliated American Postal Workers Union told the cheering Teamsters that the federal prosecution represents an attack on all of organized labor.

A Chinese proverb says a fish rots from the head. Well, the Teamsters union stinks of criminal corruption, and it begins at the top.

Secretary of Labor William Brock told convention delegates they need to clean house. That is a little like the attorney general telling organized crime bosses to start being nice guys and decent law-abiding citizens.

Authorities on the mob's influence on the Teamsters allege Presser owes his 34-year union career to mob patrons who promoted him through the ranks to the top levels of leadership.

One longtime observer of the union said neither Presser nor any other president can cut out the organized crime cancer. If they tried, they would, in Damon Runyon's words, "wake up dead." The lesson of Jimmy Hoffa's disappearance hasn't been lost.

The only way the Teamsters will be reformed is for the federal government to step in, take control of the union, appoint an interim conservator, and install democratic structures to return control of the union to the membership.

DESERET NEWS

Salt Lake City, UT, May 21-22, 1986

In speaking to delegates at a Teamsters Union convention this week, Labor Secretary William Brock was blunt and outspoken. He said the Teamsters had "lost a great deal of public trust," to put it mildly, and asked if it wasn't "time to clean house?"

That was obviously a rhetorical question, since it not only is time for the Teamsters to clean house — it's way past time.

The powerful union has been linked to corruption, violence, and intimidation. A White House commission recently concluded the union has been under the influence of organized crime since the 1950s."

Leadership of the union has shared a depressingly monotonous history. Dave Beck, Teamster president from 1952 to 1958, was sent to prison while still in office. James R. Hoffa, president from 1958 to 1971, also went to prison while in office. Frank Fitzsimmons, president from 1971 until his death in 1981, was being investigated at the time of his death for possible federal crimes. Roy Williams, president from 1981 to 1983, resigned after being convicted of federal crimes.

Now the current Teamster president, Jackie Presser, has been indicted on federal racketeering and embezzlement charges.

Cleaning up the Teamsters Union is not going to be done by edicts from Washington officials. It will have to be carried out by the union members themselves. But the chances of that happening appear discouragingly slim.

Brock's speech was greeted with stony silence by the 2,000 delegates. By contrast, when Presser addressed the audience he was received with a cheering, standing ovation.

Presser's election to a new five-year term is considered a foregone conclusion. If he is convicted of the federal charges, he'll have to resign. But as noted above, that kind of ending to Teamsters' leadership isn't new.

For some time to come, the Teamsters Union apparently is going to continue to be characterized by its seedy image of corruption and organized crime — and to be an embarrassment to the rest of the labor movement.

The Burlington Free Press

Burlington, VT, May 22, 1986

The nation's labor movement has traveled some distance from its lean days when down at the heels organizers tried to persuade American workers to band together in an effort to improve their lot.

Editorials

During the trench warfare of the 1930s and 1940s, strikers could expect little or nothing in the way of income to replace their wages while they walked to picket lines. Organizers were a scruffy group who often were paid scant salaries for their work. And union offices were sought more for the prestige than for the money.

By contrast, the current Teamsters convention in a plush setting in Las Vegas can only be described as an abomination. That Jackie Presser, Teamsters president and reportedly a sometime companion of the patriarchs of organized crime, was carried into Monday night's party in the convention hall in a sedan chair in Roman splendor was a spectacle that insulted the memory of the founders of the union movement. The 5,000 delegates cheered wildly as Presser was brought to the dais. During the business meeting Tuesday, some proposed that he should be given a $1 million raise, an offer he magnanimously rejected. His annual salary is estimated at $550,000. And there is little doubt that he will be elected to a full five-year term as head of the union even though his tenure has been riddled with scandal.

Not only has he been accused of being a crony of organized crime figures but he also is said to be an FBI informant. In fact, an FBI agent has been indicted for covering up for Presser who is is under indictment on federal racketeering charges in connection with the alleged embezzlement of $700,000 in union funds.

Which raises questions about Labor Secretary William Brock's warning to the delegates to "clean house" whenever criminal influence is found in the union. Knowing that Presser has been charged with corruption, Brock could have told the delegates that the government will conduct vigorous investigations of all union leaders and will do everything possible to put the crooked officials in jail. He could have urged the delegates to support efforts by dissidents to change the union's constitution to provide for direct election of officers by the membership. As it stands now, only convention delegates, most of them officers of locals, are allowed to vote.

If corruption in the Teamsters union and other labor organizations is to be cleaned up, the government cannot continue to play a dual role in union affairs, using officials of Presser's stripe as informants, on the one hand, while condemning their shady activities on the other.

The Oregonian

Portland, OR, May 28, 1986

Teamsters union President Jackie Presser was lavishly feted last week at the union's national convention in Las Vegas. Presser received repeated ovations from the delegates, and one delegate from New Jersey called him "a Moses ... a Martin Luther King." He was overwhelmingly elected to a new five-year term as union president.

All of this comes on the heels of Presser's recent federal indictment in Cleveland on racketeering charges involving the alleged embezzlement of $700,000 in union funds.

To be sure, Presser is considered innocent until proven guilty. And, of course, criminal allegations are nothing new for the Teamsters union. Four of its last five presidents have been indicted. Still, the sheer adulation delegates have lavished on Presser is astonishing, especially considering that it is their money he is accused of misusing.

One explanation is that the delegates to the national convention do not represent rank-and-file Teamsters, since the selection of delegates is strongly influenced by the national union leadership. Dissident union members have argued for new, more democratic selection procedures, and the Department of Labor is considering making recommendations along those lines.

But there seems to be no clear evidence that Presser lacks support among the rank-and-file. Indeed, some argue that under Presser's leadership the union has been especially successful in securing favorable contracts and freezing dues. From the standpoint of the individual member, this may be all that counts.

Delegates, however, would have improved their union's standing in the public eye by giving less praise to Presser and more attention to Labor Secretary William Brock. He delivered a tough speech saying the union needed to "clean house" wherever it finds criminal elements, although he emphasized that he was not making a judgment on Presser's guilt or innocence.

That was sound, though unwelcome, advice.

LAS VEGAS REVIEW-JOURNAL

Las Vegas, NV, May 21, 1986

The Teamsters are down but not out. As the big Teamster convention this week in Las Vegas demonstrates, the Teamsters have plenty of clout in reserve. They can still draw out the big political guns — even those from the same administration which sought and got an indictment against Jackie Presser, head of the international.

Yes, the Reagan administration broke the back of the air traffic controllers. Yes, the Reagan administration is attempting to nail Presser on racketeering charges. But, nonetheless, who shows up at the Teamsters convention? Why Secretary of Labor William Brock. And GOP Chairman Frank Fahrenkopf. And former Secretary of State Alexander Haig, a possible presidential candidate. And there were video messages from U.S. Sen. Paul Laxalt, Reagan's best friend and a man who's being talked up as a presidential contender himself. And Vice President George Bush, another possible presidential candidate.

The Republicans, after all, owe Presser and the Teamsters a big debt of gratitude. The Teamsters were the only major labor union to endorse Reagan in both the 1980 and 1984 elections. That endorsement had to have delighted the GOP, which worked hard to shed its "rich-man's- party" image and needed that blue-collar vote of confidence to round out its appeal.

Racketeering charges against Presser aside, the Republicans — especially three of their potential contenders in 1988 — cannot afford to snub the Teamsters. There are 1.6 million of them out there. Throw in their families, and the Teamsters almost represent a state with the voting power of Michigan.

It is clear, however, that the power of the mighty Teamsters is in decline.

The Teamsters may have lost fully half a million of their number since membership peaked in the mid-1970s.

Deregulation of the trucking industry hurt the Teamsters on their traditional turf, the freight-hauling industry. Deregulation may have cost the union 100,000 members. Those losses have reportedly prompted the union to increase its organizing activities elsewhere in the labor force, and the Teamsters have made some headway among health care workers and government employees. In Las Vegas, the Teamsters have been trying, with notable lack of success, to organize casino dealers. But then, following the massive hotel-casino strike of 1984, which was widely viewed as a victory for management and a defeat for the Culinary Local 226, the climate along the Strip and Glitter Gulch is viewed as decidedly anti-union.

Indeed, the Las Vegas Teamster Local 631 has experienced problems of its own in recent years. Many members of the local were chagrined to learn that former Secretary-Treasurer Jim Rice was paid nearly a quarter million dollars in severance pay when he left his post. Rice was targeted in a federal racketeering investigation but no indictment ever emerged.

The indictment of Presser may hurt the union's organizing efforts nationwide. But, given the fact that the Teamsters' top leadership seems always to be either under indictment or targeted in some federal probe, it is doubtful that Presser's situation will affect the union severely.

Secretary of Labor Brock had some good advice for the Teamsters when he addressed the Las Vegas convention on Monday. Brock drew a parallel between the current Teamsters situation and the problems the Republicans confronted following the Watergate scandal and the resignation of Richard Nixon.

Brock suggested the Teamsters be vigilant for situations where institutional processes make it easy for members to be exploited and to be on the watch for the influence of crime interests. "Are there areas where good people have been silent for too long — where it's just plain time to clean house?" Brock asked the delegates.

The Teamsters should ask themselves the questions Brock suggested. The long-term survival of the union may depend on periodic housecleaning.

THE PLAIN DEALER
Cleveland, OH, May 17, 1986

Nearly four years after federal investigators began their probe, Teamsters' President Jackie Presser has been indicted on charges of embezzling money from his Cleveland local. The case has distinguished itself as one of the more bizarre incidents in U.S. law enforcement history, proving to be an embarrassment to the FBI, the Justice Department and the Labor Department. Needless to say, it is another embarrassment to organized labor as well.

Many cases are thwarted by miscues; few involve so many of them. In this one, federal investigators and prosecutors have worked in opposition to one another. One agency blocked the criminal investigations of another. The government initially backed off the criminal prosecution of Presser months after federal prosecutors had recommended an indictment.

Convictions against two persons, including Presser's uncle, Allen Friedman, had to be overturned when the initial case against Presser was dropped. There also is the matter of a Labor Department memo charging that the FBI attempted to defame Labor Department agents and "neutralize a key government witness . . . ." These are the kind of shenanigans on which best-selling crime novels are based.

The Presser case evolved from allegations that he had authorized more than $700,000 in payments to Friedman and to John Nardi Jr., the son of a slain Teamsters' official. The two did nothing to earn the money. A report to Senate investigators maintains that the Justice Department decided not to indict Presser when told that the payments were sanctioned by the FBI. But that assertion by FBI agents, it now has been charged, was not true. The Washington grand jury yesterday indicted agent Robert Frederick, of the Cleveland office, on criminal charges of lying to Justice Department investigators probing the Presser case.

Presser's lawyer, John Climaco, repeatedly has denied the allegations, though federal officials talk so matter-of-factly about Presser's role as an informant that many people have accepted it as fact. There is a keen interest among many people, including Teamsters' union officials, in what or who the labor leader may have informed the agency about. And union members certainly ought to have an interest in finding out whether their union dues were used to pay ghost employees.

Many questions surround the Presser affair, and now that indictments have been handed down, answers may be provided in court. But it is clear that the public interest has not been served by the manner in which the case has been handled by federal agencies. Such bungling cannot help but erode public confidence in the accountability of the federal law enforcement community. Regardless of what happens to Presser, some action must be taken by federal officials to ensure against the mishandling of similar investigations in the future.

Birmingham Post-Herald
Birmingham, AL, May 24, 1986

The spectacle of Teamsters president Jackie Presser being carried around the Caesars Palace ballroom on a sedan chair like a Roman emperor was exceeded in grossness only by the union's later election of yet another president under criminal indictment.

But it was par for the course for the scandal-scarred International Brotherhood of Teamsters. After two earlier presidents were elected while facing criminal charges, it's hardly surprising that a third would be.

And it's appropriate that the union holds its conventions in Las Vegas, a city noted for gambling and mob connections. The federal President's Commission on Organized Crime recently said that Teamsters leaders "have been firmly under the influence of organized crime since the 1950s."

Presser was appointed union president in 1983 after his predecessor, Roy Williams, was convicted and jailed for trying to bribe a U.S. senator. Two other presidents, Dave Beck and Jimmy Hoffa, also were sent to prison.

The 1986 convention was all Presser's. He was greeted as a hero by delegates when he arrived after being indicted in Cleveland on racketeering and embezzlement charges. Delegates elected him president by a vote of 1,729 to 24.

The only rain on Presser's parade was Labor Secretary William Brock's admonition to the union to clean up its act.

In truth, the union needs help in cleansing itself. Brock could provide it.

The Landrum-Griffin Act, passed by Congress in the 1950s to reduce corruption in unions, says that their presidents must be elected by secret ballot among members or at a convention whose delegates have been chosen by secret ballot. The Teamsters do not follow such a procedure.

Delegates to Teamsters conventions are handpicked by about 5,000 union officials across the nation, who have an interest in maintaining the status quo. They are the ones who collect handsome salaries, and they send themselves to conventions to protect what they've got.

Brock could challenge the Teamsters election procedure, but so far he hasn't.

Crime commissioners said the government should consider removing Teamsters officers and placing union activities under court supervision. The Labor Department has made no move in that direction, either.

Unless internal rules changes are forced on the union, the Teamsters hierarchy is going to keep on truckin' just the way it has for 40 years.

Post-Tribune

Gary, IN, May 23, 1986

Jackie Presser thinks he's being persecuted. A delegate to the Teamsters convention in Las Vegas shouted, "We should be paying him a million." Presser already makes at least $750,000, so what's a few thousand more? The issue that counts is the integrity of the big, tough union.

Presser, indicted this week on racketeering and embezzling charges, has not raised the integrity level nor has he erased the perception that it's business as usual in that union.

Our opinions

Four of the last five Teamsters presidents have been indicted and three went to prison. Some record. Union officials have had resounding support, but that does not mean the rank and file members endorse corruption and abuse of power. Dissidents have not been heard much, though, and they have not been listened to at this convention.

The peculiar thing about the Presser indictment is the way the Reagan administration has handled the long investigation into his operations. Last year, administration officials said that Presser's work as an informer in several investigations was an obstacle to his indictment. The indictment's timing, coinciding with the convention, may be a coincidence, but it enraged Presser loyalists.

Presser has been one of President Reagan's few friends among labor leaders, and he supports Reagan's policies. Maybe that's why the indictment smarts so much.

The appearance by Labor Secretary Bill Brock at the convention was significant. The reaction of delegates was mixed. They were apprehensive. The secretary could have canceled his speech, as some political advisers wanted him to. But he went on, saying nobody is guilty until it is proved in court. Brock's real mission, though, seemed to be telling the union it should clean house.

He's right. The Teamsters Union has "lost a great deal of public trust."

He made sense in advising the delegates to see that "the good, honorable decent people run every local."

Unless some election rules are changed and the historical practice of arrogant power at the top is changed, the good, decent, honorable members of that union will continue to be ignored.

Union solidarity is fine, and standing behind a leader in trouble is admirable. But a union that for decades has elected presidents who were symbols of corruption and abuse of power has indeed eroded its credibility. Why the membership tolerates such behavior is a puzzle.

Jackie Presser has not been convicted of anything. But anyone who buys his charge that "this smells like persecution" has blinders on.

He has visited the White House several times. Since Donald Regan became White House chief of staff, those contacts have become very rare. If Regan caused that turnaround, it is one of the better things he's done.

The Honolulu Advertiser

*Honolulu, HI,
May 21, 1986*

Both the Teamsters Union and the Federal Bureau of Investigation have problems in the current situation centering around Jackie Presser, the union's controversial, hard-driving boss.

Presser last week became the fourth president of the Teamsters to face federal charges in the last 30 years. He was indicted by a grand jury in Cleveland and accused of participating in a scheme to embezzle more than $700,000 in union funds in a payroll scam.

THAT HAD little effect this week in Las Vegas as Teamster delegates overwhelmingly rejected reform proposals, including for direct election of top union officers.

Despite the charges — indeed in defiance of them — Presser was expected to be elected without serious challenge to a new five-year term by the delegates, who are now mostly selected by incumbent Teamster officials. Dissidents control only about 20 votes among the 2,000 delegates.

But if there is little doubt of his continuing grip on the troubled Teamsters, Presser's future in court could be far darker. And some of the shadows extend to agents of the FBI.

In fact, one FBI agent was indicted for allegedly aiding the Presser payroll scheme. Two other FBI agents involved in the case are still under investigation and may face charges.

ALL THIS reportedly involves the way in which previous charges against Presser were dropped amid reports he had been cooperating with the FBI in cases concerning other union officials.

Further complicating that picture is the fact Presser was the only leader of a major union to endorse President Reagan in both his campaigns, and he has high-level political contacts.

In any event, the indictments are coming down, and it can be hoped trials will clear the air for the FBI and Justice Department. The reputation and reality of the Teamsters seems likely to remain the same.

The Record

Hackensack, NJ, May 22, 1986

The tradition is so hoary it has whiskers. The mighty International Brotherhood of Teamsters holds its convention, and the secretary of labor — political party doesn't matter — pours praise on the thousands of delegates. The beaming secretary is then photographed in a bear hug with the Teamster president of the moment, despite the fact that the august official is probably under federal indictment.

Never mind that the delegates are not democratically elected. Never mind that the workers' pension funds have been looted by corrupt union officers from coast to coast. Never mind that four Teamster presidents (out of five) have been indicted in the last 30 years. The most recent was the incumbent, Jackie Presser, indicted last week on charges of labor racketeering. Never mind that drivers are cheated of contract wages and benefits and deprived of the right of honest union representation. Never mind that the Mafia runs scores of Teamster locals, selling sweetheart contracts to crooked employers and running the gamut of criminality — loansharking, drug-peddling, hijacking, extortion, and murder. Forget all that, the labor secretaries have told themselves, and remember instead the big political contributions and the union's enormous ballot-box power.

That's the creaking, two-faced tradition that Labor Secretary William Brock trashed this week when he went before the convention in Las Vegas and said, "It isn't easy to hear about mobbed-up locals or pension-fund abuse — misuses of members' blood and sweat. As secretary of labor, it is impossible for me to ignore that."

Mr. Brock was the first labor secretary to speak the truth at a Teamster convention in many years. But more than that, he also forced a housecleaning in the Justice Department. Labor investigators had been pursuing Mr. Presser for five years and were ready to indict him in 1984 when they learned to their dismay that the FBI was using him as a confidential informant. Some of the acts for which he was to be charged were allegedly performed under FBI supervision. Mr. Brock's dogged pursuit of this issue has resulted in the indictment of one FBI agent and the investigation of several others on charges that they deliberately obstructed the Labor Department's investigation of Mr. Presser.

Mr. Brock was appointed to rescue the reputation of the Labor Department after the departure of Raymond Donovan. He had already won public trust in his earlier government service — especially as President Reagan's top trade official. He has redeemed his agency's good name and earned high marks and public gratitude for candor and courage.

Attorney General Meese Asks Probe of Wedtech

Attorney General Edwin Meese 3rd May 11, 1987 requested that an independent counsel undertake a criminal investigation of his ties to the Wedtech Corp., a New York-based defense contractor that was already the subject of a number of federal and state inquiries. Deputy Attorney General Arnold Burns May 11 relayed Meese's request to independent counsel James McKay, who later that day accepted the assignment. Since Feb. 2, McKay had been examining actions taken on behalf of Wedtech by Lyn Nofziger, a former White House aide. McKay, in effect, agreed to expand that investigation to include Meese. Burns had been the final authority over all Wedtech-related federal criminal investigations since April 8, when Meese decided to disqualify himself from any role in such investigations. In November 1986 Meese had disqualified himself from any role in the investigation of Nofziger's lobbying on behalf of Wedtech and other clients. Meese had, however, remained, at least nominally in charge of other Wedtech-related investigations. McKay's agreement to expand his investigations to include Meese followed escalating demands in recent days for an independent probe of Meese's involvement with Wedtech.

Congressional concern had been fueled by disclosures that San Francisco lawyer E. Robert Wallach, a longtime Meese friend, had become a target of a Wedtech grand jury along with W. Franklin Chinn, a San Francisco financial consultant with whom Meese had invested money in a "limited blind trust." Meese April 6 acknowledged that while serving as counselor to President Reagan, he received a number of memos from Wallach, whom Wedtech had hired as lawyer early in 1982, about Wedtech's efforts to get a no-bid contract to build generator engines for the Army under the government's minority business program. In response to Wallach's memos, Meese said he had interceded on Wedtech's behalf to make sure that the company, which had run into stiff resistance at the Pentagon, got "a fair hearing."

Buffalo Evening News

Buffalo, NY, May 13, 1987

ATTORNEY GENERAL Edwin Meese III did the right thing in asking a special federal prosecutor to take over the Justice Department's investigation of Meese's connection with the Wedtech Corp., a South Bronx minority business that has won large military contracts.

As attorney general, Meese heads the Justice Department. Thus, it is appropriate that this investigation, whatever its ultimate findings, be conducted by a special counsel independent of that department.

Moreover, an independent counsel, James C. McKay, is already probing the relationship of Lyn Nofziger, a former Reagan administration aide, to Wedtech. Expanding the investigation to include Meese is thus logical, and McKay immediately agreed to the attorney general's request.

The question to be resolved is whether Meese broke any laws in his activities concerning Wedtech. Meese has acknowledged that in 1982 he interceded in support of Wedtech's eventually successful efforts to win a $32 million Army contract.

The number of former and present members of the Reagan administration who are or have been subject to scrutiny by court-appointed independent counsel, informally called special prosecutors, has multiplied to embarrassing proportions.

This is the third such probe into activities by Meese, who was cleared of any wrongdoing in the only one completed so far. That investigation, which preceded his confirmation as attorney general, looked into allegations that he had illegally rewarded friends with federal jobs. Meese is also included in the investigation of the Iran-contra arms affair being conducted by Lawrence E. Walsh.

Earlier, Raymond J. Donovan, former secretary of labor in the Reagan administration, was the subject of an independent counsel's inquiry.

Still another investigation, conducted by Whitney North Seymour Jr., has led to the indictment of Michael K. Deaver on perjury charges related to his lobbying activities after he left the White House as a top Reagan aide.

These inquiries all arise from the 1978 Ethics in Government Act. Similar investigations, conducted by independent counsel chosen by a special panel of federal judges, occurred during the Carter administration, though not in such disturbing abundance.

The 1978 law is a good one. It provides a sturdy legal mechanism for independent investigations of allegations against high-ranking executive agency officials. Meese's proper decision to substitute this kind of outside inquiry for an internal probe by the department that he heads will add credibility to its conclusions.

But if many more of these independent investigations are launched any time soon, the public will require a legal score card just to keep them all straight.

Fort Worth Star-Telegram

Fort Worth, TX, May 14, 1987

Edwin Meese is the Cabinet officer equivalent of the police lineup regular who is frequently arrested but never quite convicted.

He is by now surely the most-investigated sitting attorney general in American history, even allowing for such predecessors as Harry Daugherty (of Harding administration fame) and John Mitchell (of Watergate fame). For the second time in his Washington career, Meese is the subject of an investigation by an independent counsel (formerly known as a special prosecutor).

Meese also is further evidence that the weakest facet of Ronald Reagan's presidency has been his choice of appointees and underlings. So many have had to be investigated or have left under an ethical cloud or have even faced criminal charges — Raymond Donovan, Michael Deaver, Lyn Nofziger, Rita Lavelle, Ann Gorsuch Burford, Richard Allen, Oliver North, and on and on.

Meese's current difficulties over his role as a "friend" of the Wedtech Corp. in its efforts to gain defense contracts is not the first time he has been suspected of peddling influence. There were similar allegations when Meese was White House counsel. Obviously, he always has been cleared, or at least the allegations have gone unproven.

But enough should be enough.

It is the pattern of recurring suspicions that is troubling and diminishes the respect, trust and confidence that the American public must have in its top lawman.

It is possible for an attorney general to do his job and remain free of such problems. Griffin Bell, Jimmy Carter's attorney general, is an example, and, despite all-too-frequent use of the attorney general's office as a handy repository for presidents' personal and political cronies, there have been other attorneys general who were models of deportment.

Meese has been controversial for his ideological bent as attorney general, but, like it or not, that alone doesn't disqualify him. His political philosophy is close to Reagan's, and no one expects a president to appoint aides who disagree with him.

However, his penchant for walking a thin line along the ethics of private use of high public office makes Meese a liability not only to an already-beleaguered president but to the confident administration of the Justice Department. We don't need an attorney general who has to recuse himself from his department's business because of his own involvement in matters being investigated.

It is time for the president to talk resignation with Meese. It is time for Reagan to begin making a list of attorney general candidates who can be expected to run the Justice Department the next 19 months without further embarrassment.

THE SACRAMENTO BEE
Sacramento, CA, May 13, 1987

Where there's Meese, it seems, there's muck. The attorney general, whose confirmation was delayed for a year in 1984 by a special criminal investigation of sweetheart loans from individuals who later received government jobs, is once again the target of a special prosecutor. This time the probe concerns his role in promoting Wedtech, a New York company under investigation by federal, state and local prosecutors for bribery. How often can the nation's top law enforcement official stray into the ethical swamps without some of the mud sticking, both to him and the president he serves?

In asking for the special probe, Meese said he wanted "this matter be resolved as promptly as possible and in a forum that will prevent partisan political exploitation." Certainly, a criminal investigation should go forward if there is a possibility Meese has broken the law. But the key question of the moment is not legal, but ethical and political; not whether Meese broke the law, but whether what he did was right and proper for a high official. And the answer is no.

Meese's admitted involvement in the Wedtech business is of a piece with the pattern of conduct brought out three years ago, when it was revealed that Meese had received financial benefits and cut-rate loans from people whom he later promoted for federal jobs. In 1982, Meese, then counselor in the White House, directed subordinates to see that Wedtech, which was seeking an Army contract to build engines, was given "a fair hearing" by the Pentagon. Meese had been alerted to the firm by E. Robert Wallach, a close friend and personal adviser, in a series of memos. Despite objections from the White House counsel and Cabinet secretary that it was improper for White House officials to interfere in contract letting, James Jenkins, Meese's top deputy, held a meeting in the White House with the Army and the Small Business Administration to promote the company's proposal. The company later received a no-bid contract.

Wallach, who represented Meese during the 1984 special prosecutor's probe, was later retained by Wedtech and received stock worth $600,000. Jenkins was hired last year as Wedtech's Washington marketing director. In 1985, Wallach introduced Meese to Franklyn Chinn, a Wedtech director, with whom the attorney general then invested $60,000 in a "limited blind partnership."

A New York grand jury investigating Wedtech is currently deciding whether any of these individuals was involved in the company's efforts to win contracts by fraud and bribes. But it doesn't take a grand jury to decide that Meese's White House intervention on behalf of the company gave an appearance of improper favoritism. Nor does it take an investigation to wonder why the attorney general waited until a month ago to remove himself from a criminal investigation involving close associates and, potentially, himself.

Meese and the president may believe that it's enough that the nation's highest law enforcement official not sink in the legal goo. But citizens have the right to expect an attorney general who has an ethical compass with which to know where the muck is and stay away from it. Meese, though not indicted, failed that test in 1984, and whatever the outcome of the current criminal probe, has flunked it once again.

ST. LOUIS POST-DISPATCH
St. Louis, MO, May 7, 1987

With the public and press attention fixed on the congressional Iran-Contra hearings and the blowup over Democratic presidential candidate Gary Hart's possible involvement with a young woman, the Wedtech scandal has fired very little interest. But all of that could change now that the Justice Department has begun an inquiry into possible illegalities by its own boss, Attorney General Edwin Meese.

The Wedtech affair is no minor indiscretion. Even by the lax standards of the scandal-marked Reagan administration, the Wedtech affair could well be in a class by itself. Conservative political columnist William Safire has already characterized this scandal as the "Teapot Dome" of the Reagan administration — "our era's top-dollar corruption."

Wedtech Corp. was a small, minority-owned tool and die company in New York City that landed some $250 million in no-bid contracts from the Army in the early and mid-1980s. The firm is now bankrupt and is the subject of an intensive criminal investigation. Several of the company's top officials have been charged and are now cooperating with federal authorities. It is alleged that Wedtech was awarded military contracts, despite the Army's strong objections, because of high-level lobbying and bribery.

Special Prosecutor James McKay, who is already investigating former top Reagan adviser Lyn Nofziger's role in the affair, is reportedly sharing with the Justice Department's Public Integrity Section evidence that could establish illegal ties between Wedtech and Attorney General Meese.

It has been reported that in 1982, while he was a presidential adviser — and over objections by the White House counsel of possible charges of favoritism — Mr. Meese interceded on Wedtech's behalf on a $32 million Army contract. Three years later, the attorney general took a $60,000 share of a so-called "limited blind partnership" with a Wedtech official. In addition, Mr. Meese's former chief White House deputy, James Jenkins, became Wedtech's "director of Washington marketing."

The Justice Department is currently conducting a so-called threshold inquiry to see if a preliminary investigation is necessary. Only after the second investigation will a decision be made on giving the Meese case to a special prosecutor, formally known as an independent counsel.

The evidence — as circumstantial as it may be — and the involvement of such a high-ranking administration official as Mr. Meese would argue for appointing a special prosecutor without procedural delays. Accusations that the man who is now the nation's top law enforcement official was involved in influence peddling must not be allowed to languish unresolved — or worse, to be whitewashed.

The Wichita
Eagle-Beacon
Witchita, KS, May 13, 1987

From a minor irritant, Attorney General Edwin Meese's relationship with a small scandal-beseiged defense contractor, Wedtech Corp., has grown into something much more. In asking the Justice Department Monday to appoint an independent counsel to look into his ties to Wedtech, Mr. Meese accepts the seriousness of the charge.

Mr. Meese has survived similar charges of influence-peddling before. In 1984, before he became attorney general, an independent counsel investigation cleared him of charges he'd arranged federal jobs for two savings and loan officials who'd allowed him to fall behind on mortgage payments on his California home.

In the case at hand, Mr. Meese has acknowledged that in 1982, while he was White House counselor, he successfully interceded with the Pentagon to give Wedtech a $32 million contract to build engines for the Army. Then it was learned Mr. Meese's investment manager was on Wedtech's board of directors in 1985, and that Mr. Meese had invested $60,000 in a "limited blind partnership" with him. Whether any of that money went into Wedtech isn't known.

It appears, in short, Mr. Meese got a payoff from Wedtech, which federal investigators alleges paid off dozens of federal, state and local public officials in return for public contracts. The fact the company's president and four other former company executives in January pleaded guilty to paying members of Congress and federal employees "for services rendered" makes Mr. Meese's involvement with Wedtech all the more questionable.

Mr. Meese acceded to the inevitable in requesting the independent counsel investigation. Though the Justice Department once more is in the ethically precarious position of having to investigate its boss, the truth — whatever it is — will come out. Mr. Meese will survive or perish accordingly.

The Chattanooga Times
Chattannoga, TN, May 13, 1987

In the context of Gary Hart's withdrawal last week from the 1988 presidential campaign and the beginning of congressional hearings on the Iran-Contra affair, the possibility of a scandal involving Attorney General Edwin Meese and the Wedtech Corp. looms for the moment as a shadow no bigger than a man's hand. But last week the Justice Department announced it has begun an inquiry to determine whether Mr. Meese committed possible illegalities in his relationship with Wedtech. And on Monday, Mr. Meese himself, through a Justice Department statement, asked that an independent counsel conduct an investigation of that relationship. Both steps are welcome.

From 1981 through 1985, Wedtech, a small New York City tool-and-die company that is minority-owned, received approximately $250 million in Army contracts on a no-bid basis. Wedtech has since declared bankruptcy and its practices are the subject of a criminal investigation. That investigation is being helped along by several company officials who, having been charged, are cooperating with federal authorities to bring the issues to light. Essentially, the investigation hinges on allegations that intensive lobbying and bribery combined to produce the contracts, despite the Army's objections.

Actually, independent counsel Jim McKay has been investigating the Wedtech matter for several months, focusing primarily on the role of former White House adviser Lyn Nofziger's involvement. From that investigation, Mr. McKay reportedly has been supplying information to the Justice Department's Public Integrity Section that could provide an illegal link between the company and Mr. Meese.

For instance, there have been reports that in 1982, Mr. Meese, then an adviser to President Reagan, interceded on behalf of Wedtech to help it obtain a $32 million Army contract. This was done, according to reports, despite the White House counsel's objection that the intercession could lead to charges of favoritism. Apparently the objection fell on deaf ears.

Worse, it was revealed last month that beginning in 1985, Mr. Meese's investment manager, W. Franklin Chinn, became a member of the Wedtech board. At about that time, Mr. Meese entered into a $60,000 share of a "limited blind partnership" with Mr. Chinn. The Justice Department statement issued Monday said also that Mr. Meese has taken action to terminate his relationship with Mr. Chinn.

Until the action by Mr. Meese on Monday, the Justice Department was conducting what it calls a threshold inquiry, which is undertaken to determine whether a preliminary investigation is warranted. The procedure is that a case goes to an independent counsel only after completion of the second phase. Granted, the case so far is circumstantial. But given the prominence of the people involved, it would be wiser to take the case directly to an independent counsel without delays. It would be hard to think of anything worse in this regard than delay. Keep in mind that the issue here involves possible influence-peddling by the nation's chief law enforcement official. The sooner this matter is resolved, the better for all concerned.

The Seattle Times
Seattle, WA, May 14, 1987

ATTORNEY General Edwin Meese did the right thing when he asked that an independent prosecutor probe Meese's connections with Wedtech Corp., the New York firm being investigated for possible fraud in obtaining no-bid federal defense contracts reserved for minority enterprises.

Now, Meese should do one more thing: He should step aside — a long vacation or leave of absence, for example — until the investigation is completed. Meese has not been accused of wrongdoing. But his personal and financial ties to Wedtech raise ethics-in-government questions that impair Meese's capacity to serve as the nation's chief law-enforcement officer as long as they remain unanswered.

Meese never has been a strong symbol of high ethical standards. This is, in fact, his second time around as a target for investigation by a special prosecutor, the process for weighing questions about unethical conduct by high-ranking administration officials.

In 1984, Meese asked an independent counsel to look into allegations he'd helped get federal jobs for people who'd given him financial assistance in the days before he joined the government.

Edwin Meese   —Bill Plympton

While the investigation found no basis for prosecuting Meese, the prosecutor took pains to note he was making "no comment on Mr. Meese's ethics and the propriety of his conduct."

The 1984 controversy caused a 13-month delay in Senate confirmation of Meese's appointment by President Reagan — longer than any other Cabinet nominee in modern times.

LOS ANGELES HERALD
Los Angeles, CA, May 12, 1987

As if the Iranscam hearings weren't trying enough for the White House, an investigation in New York has uncovered evidence that could lead to an indictment of Attorney General Edwin Meese for illegally helping a defense contractor gain government business. Meese agreed Monday to appoint a special prosecutor. But even if the attorney general isn't indicted, the case raises an issue

that many in the administration keep forgetting: Government service requires officials to avoid even the appearance of impropriety.

The company, Wedtech Corp., used to be just a big machine shop in the South Bronx. Then its owners decided to enter the federal program that permits minority firms to obtain government work without bidding. By 1986, Wedtech had $250 million in contracts.

In fact, its business acumen was aided by a bribery campaign that four of its former executives say involved 200 government officials, including three who have already been indicted. Wedtech also was helped by then-presidential aide Lyn Nofziger and Meese's former deputy, James Jenkins. Nofziger got Wedtech stock and Jenkins later went to work for Wedtech. Meese's close friend, E. Robert Wallach, and his financial adviser, W. Franklin Chinn, worked for or received stock from Wedtech.

Last November, Meese said he didn't remember ever discussing Wedtech with Wallach, and at a news conference in December, he said he had heard of the company only vaguely. In February he denied having any financial interest in Wedtech.

But on April 6, he admitted that he had received "a half dozen memos" about Wedtech from Wallach asking him to help the company get a fair hearing at the Pentagon. And investigators have uncovered 1981 memos from White House counsel warning Meese's aides not to intervene on behalf of Wedtech contracts.

Moreover, in 1985, when Meese put his investments in a blind trust, the trustee he chose was Chinn, who had just joined Wedtech as an adviser.

It remains to be seen whether the special prosecutor will be able to improve the attorney general's faulty memory still further. For the sake of reducing the number of national scandals, we certainly hope so.

UH OH! IF ANYONE ASKS, YOU'RE MY NIECE.'

THE CHRISTIAN SCIENCE MONITOR

Boston, MA, May 13, 1987

ATTORNEY GENERAL Edwin Meese did just the right thing in calling for an inquiry by a court-appointed independent counsel into his dealings with a South Bronx firm that is now the subject of a federal legal probe. As Mr. Meese obviously recognizes, there can be no gain for him in continuing congressional unease over his links with Wedtech Corporation.

For Mr. Meese, who is also a subject in another probe – that of the Iran-contra affair – it is better to have the Wedtech matter looked into as expeditiously as possible in a nonpartisan forum. The alternative, it might be noted, would have been a full-scale congressional probe, marked by all the television cameras, microphones, and publicity on evening newscasts that such undertakings inevitably produce. And, of course, Congress could yet include Mr. Meese in an open hearing.

Wedtech is a minority-owned defense contractor. In 1982, Mr. Meese sought to ensure that the firm would be considered for a $32 million contract from the Army. Meese was then presidential counselor. He subsequently invested $60,000 with a partnership established by a San Francisco investment manager who was a director and consultant for Wedtech. Mr. Meese announced this week that he was pulling his funds out of the partnership.

The independent counsel's office is also expected to look at Meese's connections, if any, with former White House aide Lyn Nofziger's lobbying efforts on behalf of Fairchild Industries, another defense contractor, after Nofziger left the White House.

Mr. Meese maintains that the record will show that he did nothing wrong in connection with the two defense contractors. Key congressional Democrats have praised him for calling for the inquiry by the independent counsel. Precisely because of the important position of Mr. Meese within the government, it is to be hoped that the investigation will be wrapped up as quickly, but thoroughly, as possible.

THE PLAIN DEALER

Cleveland, OH, May 13, 1987

Even by the remarkable (to say nothing of casual) ethical standards demonstrated by members of the Reagan administration, Edwin Meese III is a standout. The present attorney general has just become the first government official to be the focus of not one, not two, but three—count 'em—probes by special prosecutors. In the latest go-round, independent counsel James McKay, who is investigating White House links with Wedtech, a minority defense contractor, has been asked to expand his inquiry to include Meese. The request came from Meese through his lawyer and Deputy Attorney General Arnold Burns. It narrowly stole the thunder of the Justice Department's Public Integrity Section, which had concluded that allegations against Meese were credible enough to deserve McKay's attention.

According to Burns, Meese interceded to help Wedtech win a no-bid Army contract in 1982. At the time, Meese was presidential counselor. Since then, Meese also has invested $60,000 in a blind trust through financial consultant W. Franklin Chinn. Chinn, a one-time Wedtech adviser, also served as a Wedtech director. Meese also is linked to E. Robert Wallach, the San Francisco lawyer who recruited Meese's assistance for Wedtech. Reports say that Wallach received more than $600,000 in Wedtech stock and $360,000 in legal fees for his work. McKay already was probing Lynn Nofziger, a for-

mer Reagan aide who also interceded for Wedtech while working in the White House. McKay says that after leaving government, Nofziger and his associates received $700,000 in Wedtech stock in addition to an undisclosed retainer.

Meese's financial arrangement with Chinn is a "limited blind trust"; there is no evidence that he had invested in Wedtech. The probe into Meese's relationship with Wedtech is only that—a probe. There has been no finding of criminal actions. Yet, the truth remains that Meese is no stranger to ethical/criminal inquiries. His confirmation as attorney general was delayed for six months while a special prosecutor examined the way in which friends of Meese, including some who made him advantageous loans, subsequently found high government positions. Meese also is a figure in the Iran-contra investigation.

The nation's chief law enforcement officer must always be above suspicion. For that reason alone, probing Meese's relationship with Wedtech is warranted and welcome. Voters should be less content, however, with the fact that Meese remains active as attorney general. He might be completely innocent, but such a verdict would nevertheless be tainted by the conflict of interest that is possible by his continued stewardship at Justice. If Meese wants to do what's right, he will step aside while the inquiries are completed.

The Miami Herald

Miami, FL, May 14, 1987

HE WHO DIVES into dark waters when common sense and the lifeguard both shout "Don't!" should hardly be surprised if he hurts himself, perhaps badly. Witness Attorney General Edwin Meese III. He now faces a special prosecutor's inquiry into his dealings with Wedtech, a tainted company that he would have shunned had he heeded those warnings.

In 1981 while he was White House counsel, and in 1982 after he became Attorney General, Mr. Meese intervened to help Wedtech, then known as Welbilt, win a $32-million no-bid Army contract for generator engines. The Army, which had denied Welbilt the contract because it thought the unit costs unjustified, reversed itself after Mr. Meese intervened. Mr. Meese says that he simply sought a fair review, not favoritism, for the company. Even so, the White House's ethics counsel advised against his efforts. And his personal lawyer, who also represented the company, had written him several memos on its behalf.

Then, in 1985, Mr. Meese invested $60,000 with a financial consultant who worked for, then became a director of, Wedtech. Although he insists that he doesn't know whether any of his blind trust was invested in Wedtech, Mr.

Meese at the very least acted unwisely and in disregard of ethical appearances.

Wedtech, now in Chapter 11 bankruptcy, is under five separate state and Federal investigations for alleged bribery, fraud, and misrepresentation in obtaining contracts. Former White House aide and Meese associate Lyn Nofziger is being investigated for his lobbying on Wedtech's behalf. In part because of these Administration ties, Wedtech in four years won $250 million in Federal contracts under a program designed to help minority owned firms.

It remains to be seen whether Mr. Meese overstepped the bounds of the law in his relationship with Wedtech. It should be evident to all but the blind, however, that he dove into waters whose rocks he knew not.

Because he dove, the nation's chief law-enforcement officer is now under investigation by a special prosecutor for the third time. How many investigations will it take to teach Mr. Meese to avoid not just the obvious conflict of interest, but the appearance of it?

Deaver Found Guilty of Lying About Lobbying

A federal jury in Washington, D.C. Dec. 16, 1987 found former top White House aide Michael K. Deaver guilty on three of five counts of perjury for lying under oath about his lobbying activities. Deaver was the highest-ranking member of the Reagan administration to be convicted of a crime. His conviction was the first arising from the 1978 Ethics in Government Act, which provided for the appointment of special prosecutors in cases of suspected wrongdoing by high government officials. Deaver had been deputy chief of staff at the White House from 1981 until May 1985, when he left to establish a private lobbying and public relations business, Michael K. Deaver & Associates Inc. He was a 20-year associate and personal friend of the Reagans and during Reagan's first term had, along with Edwin Meese 3rd and James A. Baker 3rd, been regarded as one of the "troika" that governed the White House agenda.

The perjury charges stemmed from the testimony Deaver had given to a federal grand jury and a congressional subcommittee. Both were investigating whether Deaver had illegally used his influence in the White House and his long personal relationship with the Reagans in his lobbying business to advance his clients' interests. Testimony depicted a behind-the-scenes world of influence and access to power.

Deaver was convicted of lying to the House Energy and Commerce Committee's oversight subcommittee about his role in setting up a personal meeting between a trade representative of the South Korean government and President Reagan.

The Washington Post

Washington, DC, December 19, 1987

THE FOOTNOTES in the Deaver case are threatening to overwhelm the text. The latter is simple and well known. Michael Deaver was an old and valued friend as well as aide to President and Mrs. Reagan who spent the first Reagan term as deputy White House chief of staff, then left to set up a lobbying and public relations firm. He sought in that to capitalize on his closeness to both Reagans as well as his former service high in the administration.

His access and purported influence enabled him to charge his clients, which included importuning foreign governments, enormous fees. The brazenness, not to say compulsiveness, with which he went about this brought investigations down upon his head, first by a House subcommittee, finally by an independent counsel, Whitney North Seymour Jr. Mr. Seymour ultimately had Mr. Deaver indicted not for having lobbied but for having lied about it, both to the subcommittee and to a grand jury. Mr. Deaver was tried on five counts of perjury and this week convicted of three. He should neither have lied nor put himself in a position where he felt he had to. He got what he deserved. The creaky old system worked, above all in the sense of demonstrating that not even the most powerful can flout the law.

Now for the footnotes. They are more complicated; they have to do with sanctimony. What Michael Deaver did—not the lying, but the influence-peddling—is done every day in this town. At a certain level you could argue that our system of government both presumes and even depends a little on this constant plucking at its sleeve. Some of the people professing to be most aghast at Mr. Deaver's behavior either do the same things themselves (and would do more if they could) or well know others who do, whom they greatly admire.

Mr. Deaver's sins, if sins they were, were less in kind than in degree. He went too far, but the lines in this swamp are blurry. Even as you look, they move. The preachily titled Ethics in Government Act, whose strictures on lobbying are what got him into trouble—though he was never officially accused of having violated them—is feel-good legislation. It tries to bottle air. The lines it draws as to where a former high official can lobby and how long he must wait are as arbitrary as they are golden in intent. Like so many other such rules, in the cutesy evasions to which they lead they spawn as much corruption as they cure.

The Ethics in Government Act also provides the authority for the appointment of independent counsels. These are meant to avoid the impossible damned-if-they-do and damned-if-they-don't situations where an administration would otherwise be required, at the highest levels, to investigate and prosecute itself. The device is a good one, which Congress and a reluctant president have now sensibly extended. Critics complain that the counsels are not properly accountable so that the power in their offices can be abused. In fact the opposite has happened. Those appointed over the years have been respected members of the bar who have acted with restraint. Far from running wild, they have uniformly said—until this case—that they could find no grounds for prosecution.

Mr. Seymour has now broken with that good tradition twice. The first was in the creditable work he did in confounding a not inconsiderable number of skeptics and critics and winning Mr. Deaver's conviction. The second was in the lamentable and unprofessional way in which he then sermonized about it all afterward. He attacked George Shultz for having had the temerity to say some good things about Mr. Deaver from the witness stand. He favored us with the observation, well within his competence of course, that there is "too much 'loose money' " in this town, and "Washington money men will continue to undermine public confidence in government until lawmakers, business and community leaders and individual citizens decide to cry 'Enough.' "

That's what we cry right now: "Enough." Some people do indeed try to get ahead by corrupting the government . . . and others by moralizing about it. It's not always clear which does the most harm. The prosecution's over, Mr. Seymour. You did a good job. Take the day off.

Omaha World-Herald

Omaha, NE, December 20, 1987

Former White House aide Michael Deaver got what he deserved in his Washington perjury trial. Deaver, who exploited his access to the president and then "forgot" when investigators asked about his activities, was convicted of three counts of lying under oath and faces a possible fine and prison sentence.

Deaver was accused of lying twice to a federal grand jury and once to a Senate subcommittee. He had testified on those occasions that he couldn't recall making improper contacts for clients in the months after he quit his White House job to become a public relations consultant.

Deaver's lawyers speculated after the trial that their decision not to present a defense was a mistake. Maybe so, but the defense they had considered wasn't guaranteed to produce results, either. The lawyers didn't plan to challenge the allegation that Deaver had engaged in illegal influence-peddling. Instead, they planned to explain Deaver's memory lapse before the Senate panel and the grand jury as a consequence of his acknowledged alcoholism.

Would the jury have bought the story that a person can be in sufficient control of himself to arrange high-level meetings between clients and government officials and be so stupified by alcohol that he can't remember having done so? It's possible. Anything can happen in a jury trial. Jury verdicts don't always make sense.

In the Deaver trial, the verdict did make sense. The evidence showed that Deaver said he couldn't remember things that anyone should have been able to remember. The jury came down on the side of the prosecution, which had accused Deaver of lying when he said he didn't remember arranging meetings between his clients and high government officials in violation of the Ethics in Government Act.

Among the things Deaver said he didn't remember was a meeting he arranged between President Reagan and a South Korean trade official with whom Deaver was trying to cut a business deal. It wouldn't require alcoholism to blot out the memory of such a thing. For some people who had so grossly abused a friendship, just the shame would make it hard to talk about.

THE ATLANTA CONSTITUTION
Atlanta, GA, December 29, 1987

Remember John Mitchell's admonition? President Nixon's attorney general once told Americans to "watch what we do, not what we say." As it turns out, this advice still comes in handy. President Reagan has mastered the art of unabashedly clinging to old rhetoric while abruptly shifting to new policies. It is necessary to watch his actions carefully. Consider the strange case of the independent-counsel bill.

The president signed the measure into law on Dec. 15, and for that the nation should rejoice. It extends for five years the procedure that authorizes independent counsel (also known as special prosecutors) to investigate allegations of wrongdoing in the executive branch of government. It makes sure that nobody — including top White House officials — is above the law.

But if the president acted admirably, one thing takes an edge off his assent: He has consistently denounced the bill. In fact, as he signed it, he reiterated his belief that it is unconstitutional. Why did he sign it? "In order to ensure that public confidence in government not be eroded," he said.

The real reason is probably less lofty. One day after Reagan signed the extension, his friend and former adviser, Michael Deaver, was convicted under the law. Other Reaganites such as Attorney General Edwin Meese are the targets of special-prosecutor investigations. The White House probably worried that opposition to the bill might be perceived as retaliation.

So the president did the right thing, if for selfish reasons. As for the claim the law is unconstitutional, Deaver's conviction hands the Supreme Court a fine opportunity for review. Don't expect the law to crumble, though. Congress has taken care to see that it complies with the separation-of-powers provisions of the Constitution.

In ways admirable and not-so-admirable, the administration has advanced this statute nicely. The president has put his name to it — while the actions of his associates have reminded us of why it is necessary.

AKRON BEACON JOURNAL
Little Rock, AR
December 19, 1987

ALL ALONG in his ordeal, Michael Deaver suggested that the perjury charges against him were dubious, that if he had done something wrong in his lobbying business, he would've been indicted for violations of the Ethics in Government Act. His conviction this week on three perjury counts should end those protests.

The ethics law regulates the lobbying activities of former federal officials, limiting their ability to influence former associates in government. In court, Deaver, one of President Reagan's closest and longest political associates, might have prevailed if he had been charged with violating the ethics law. But that says little about the right and wrong of his work as a lobbyist. It says much more about the law, which suffers from loopholes and ambiguity.

Indeed, in view of a 1983 White House interpretation of the law, Deaver could have argued that he had gotten approval for lobbying his former associates. But that trial didn't take place. Deaver was indicted for perjury, and it wasn't a matter of pinning a lesser charge on him.

A jury found that the former presidential aide lied to Congress and a grand jury about his lobbying activities. In short, he conducted a cover-up. He obviously sought to avoid charges that he had violated the ethics act. Moreover, he was concerned such charges would harm his lobbying firm and likely embarrass the President and Nancy Reagan, for it would become clear that he had exploited his access to the Reagans for his own gain.

The most troubling aspect of the Deaver affair is that the former aide's conviction, in the words of Whitney North Seymour Jr., the independent counsel, is only a "thumb in the dike" against the flood of influence peddling in Washington. During the Reagan years, ethical standards have plunged to the point where if an act is not illegal, it's considered acceptable. As Seymour pointed out, the ethics law has "served only to breed cynicism by making lawful what otherwise would plainly be improper."

The Ethics in Government Act should be strengthened to provide the Deavers less room to maneuver. But beyond any changes in the law, there must be a change in attitude in Washington. Public service has taken on an unfortunate and sleazy taint. It has become not only a noble endeavor but also a tool for personal profit.

Deaver attempted to turn his post in the White House into a gold mine. That's not what public service is about, and we suspect Michael Deaver knew that. Otherwise, he wouldn't have lied to cover up his lobbying.

Arkansas Gazette
Akron, OH, December 18, 1987

Government service can be a hazardous profession, particularly for people with thin skins, a weakness of moral character, or a taste for high living. Public employes bask in the spotlight where the media and ordinary citizens monitor their moves. Their opportunities for misbehavior are abundant, and their modest salaries are inadequate for the lifestyles to which they would like to become accustomed. Michael K. Deaver, the former White House aide who has been convicted of perjury, may have possessed the political skill and tough skin needed for public service; he apparently could not resist the temptation to exploit his White House connections in a game of influence peddling.

President Reagan sometimes described Mr. Deaver as "almost a son" but the prodigal departed, presumably to peddle the influence he had accumulated during 20 years of close association with the man who served as governor of California and as president of the United States. Mr. Deaver's credentials as a lobbyist were well established; his use of the connections raised serious questions.

The Ethics in Government Act, passed in the aftermath of the Watergate scandal, prohibits a former official from using his connections for lobbying purposes for a specified period after he leaves government service. Mr. Deaver explained when he left the White House that he could not afford to stay with a low-paying job and needed to make a great deal of money in a hurry. He apparently was doing rather well before his activities came under suspicion. He booked about $3 million worth of business in seven months, which suggests the connections indeed were valuable.

Mr. Deaver was not tried for violating the Ethics in Government Act. Instead, he was found guilty of lying under oath to a grand jury and to a House subcommittee.

Even though this was the first conviction stemming from an investigation under the Ethics in Government Act, more than 100 Reagan appointees have been accused of various crimes. Some have been convicted of schemes involving such things as kickbacks, special treatment, and tax matters. The Iran-contra scandal is still under an investigation by a special prosecutor and could produce a flock of convictions. One cabinet secretary is the subject of a couple of investigations.

None of these people enjoyed Mr. Deaver's close relationship with the First Family. Mr. Reagan cited Lt. Col. Oliver L. North as a national "hero" and praised some of the other suspects for their outstanding service to the government and the administration but only Mr. Deaver was "almost like a son," albeit a prodigal.

If the conviction stands, Mr. Reagan will be faced with a difficult decision. He could permit Mr. Deaver to pay the price for his sins, perhaps by feeding the swine or engaging in some other menial task at a federal prison, or he could grant a pardon and kill the fatted calf to celebrate the prodigal's return to open society.

Since the matter will be settled during his last year in office, Mr. Reagan would suffer no political penalty if he brought out the finest robe. The precedent, however, might be dangerous. He could spend his last months in office granting pardons to people who, at one time or another, have been praised as heroes or dedicated public servants.

THE INDIANAPOLIS STAR
Indianapolis, IN, December 20, 1987

Except perhaps to those of saintly compassion, Michael K. Deaver is not a sympathetic character. Big time operators, inside dopesters and influence peddlers seldom are.

Like hucksters and hustlers, they serve a purpose. As to lovableness and purity, the less said, the better.

A U.S. District Court jury in Washington found Deaver guilty of three counts of perjury, deciding that he had lied twice to a grand jury and once to a House subcommittee investigating allegations that his lobbying violated federal ethics laws.

Another way of looking at it is that Deaver was found guilty of being a longtime friend and former top aide to President Ronald Reagan and of irritating members of the Washington liberal establishment, among others.

Federal ethics laws were cunningly spun, but mostly they were spun by Democratic spiders to catch Republican flies that sinned by cashing in on juicy Washington opportunities just as liberal establishment insiders have been doing for generations.

They were designed to catch upstarts like Mike Deaver, who make the silk-stocking establishment regulars' blood boil.

Deaver is no Goody Two-Shoes. But he is no Machiavelli either. His blunders as a presidential aide were incredibly indiscreet, with a zaniness reminiscent of a Woody Allen comedy.

As advance man, he OK'd the misbegotten presidential Bitburg Cemetery visit while scouting Germany for discount BMWs for himself and friends. He steered Nancy Reagan to a Katharine Graham (the *Washington Post* publisher) party to rope the first lady into a new detente. He tried to get the president to cave in on Canada's controversial acid rain reduction program, which would have been an economic disaster for the Midwest.

These actions were rash but hardly criminal.

At first Whitney North Seymour Jr., the special prosecutor assigned to get Deaver, tried to nail him on ethics charges involving his lobbying activities. Next to government, influence peddling is the biggest industry in Washington. If it is a crime, much of the population belongs in jail. Seymour's attempt failed. So he scratched about for some other way to cook Deaver's goose and settled on a perjury rap.

In view of the outcome it was a good idea.

But before it is engraved in bronze that justice was done, consider that it takes pure guesswork to conclude that someone is lying when, in answering hostile questions about far-from-recent activities, he gives inconsistent answers or says that he does not remember.

Having a poor memory is no crime. The only sure way the jury could have discovered what was going on inside Deaver's head would have been to read his mind. There were no mind-readers on the jury. Deaver is appealing. He wants a new trial.

Under the circumstances, who can blame him?

The Seattle Times
Seattle, WA, December 17, 1987

THE man who sat at the door of the Oval Office and managed President Reagan's image could not in a court of law erase his own image as a big-bucks wheeler-dealer who cashed in on his closeness to the First Family.

That is the human side of yesterday's conviction of Michael Deaver on three of five charges that he had lied under oath in denying allegations of improper influence-peddling.

What is most important about the verdict, however, is not its my-how-the-mighty-have-fallen aspect. The verdict gives heart to that rare breed of idealistic thinkers who, in the face of massive evidence to the contrary, hold out hope that there is a way to get a handle on runaway influence-peddling in government at any level.

Deaver is the first White House official to be accused by a court-appointed independent counsel under the Ethics in Government Act. His conviction is the first obtained by a prosecutor appointed under that Watergate-era law.

Deaver, however, was not charged with violating the act — but with lying to a grand jury and a congressional subcommittee that were looking into possible violations of the act, which limits government contacts with former top officials.

That and the fact that the defense was so confident of victory that it called no witnesses are perhaps illustrative of the difficulties facing attempts to control influence-peddling by law.

A constitutional challenge to the ethics law pending in a federal appeals court could result in Deaver's conviction being set aside.

In 1852, James Buchanan complained in a letter to Franklin Pierce: "The host of contractors, speculators, stock-jobbers and lobby members which haunt the halls of Congress, all desirous . . . on any and every pretext to get their arms into the public treasury, are sufficient to alarm every friend of this country. Their progress must be arrested."

Buchanan would still be wringing his hands if he could view the Washington scene today. Still, the conviction of Michael Deaver, master contact man, is a signal that limits do after all prevail.

BUFFALO EVENING NEWS
Buffalo, NY, December 18, 1987

WHEN PRESIDENT REAGAN reluctantly signed a five-year extension of the special prosecutor law this week, he said he did it to preserve "public confidence" in the law while the administration appeals its constitutionality.

The perjury conviction of former Reagan aide Michael K. Deaver a day later shows that such public confidence is well-placed.

Deaver, a long-time Reagan associate, was convicted of three counts of lying under oath about using influence garnered during his White House years to benefit high-paying clients of a consulting firm he set up after leaving government. He now faces penalties of up to 15 years in prison and $22,000 in fines, although his lawyers plan to appeal.

Deaver was the first White House aide indicted and the first person ever convicted under the special prosecutor provisions of the 1978 Ethics in Government Act, which restricts the lobbying activities of former high-ranking government officials.

The special prosecutor provision — technically called the independent counsel law — calls for court-appointed independent counsels to investigate alleged wrongdoing by senior administration officials. The measure is intended to prevent the conflict of interest that would result from having the Justice Department, an arm of the executive branch, investigating executive branch officers.

There is nothing to suggest that the Justice Department would not have prosecuted the Deaver matter just as vigorously and been just as successful in winning a conviction. However, in matters of governmental ethics, an already skeptical public can logically conclude that justice is being pursued in a more even-handed manner when the competing players are not former teammates.

Whitney North Seymour Jr., the special prosecutor in the Deaver case, alluded to that when he noted the verdict "reconfirmed the constitutional tradition of equal justice under law."

Deaver, who served as deputy White House chief of staff, was one of Reagan's closest advisers before leaving the administration in 1985. His firm then did more than $3 million worth of business in its seven months of operation. He was convicted of lying when he told a congressional committee and a grand jury that he didn't assist or couldn't recall assisting company clients who were lobbying the government for help.

While lauding the first conviction under the independent counsel law, Seymour nevertheless pointed to technical loopholes in the Ethics in Government Act that he said allowed many of the contacts Deaver made and that "serve only to breed cynicism by making 'lawful' what otherwise would plainly be improper."

That cynicism is what the law is supposed to prevent. If these loopholes do indeed exist, officials should act quickly to close them.

But in the Deaver case, at least, the statutes seem to have worked well to help preserve public confidence in government.

LOS ANGELES HERALD

Los Angeles, CA, December 18, 1987

Federal conflict-of-interest laws impose what amounts to a "decent interval" between employment in federal agencies and representing clients before the same agencies. But former White House chief of staff Michael Deaver, in the "greed is good" spirit of the age, just couldn't wait. Upon resigning, he immediately began hustling accounts to build his firm into the financial wonder of Washington. Now he's been convicted of perjury for lying about it to a House subcommittee and a federal grand jury.

The charges stemmed from his efforts upon leaving the government to launch a political consulting — read "lobbying" — firm by trading on contacts in the executive branch, including President Reagan himself.

His attorneys didn't bother to deny the charges, planning a defense based not on exoneration, but mitigation: To wit, he was too drunk to know to know what he was doing. Deaver, they said, was an alcoholic suffering impaired judgment and loss of memory. But in a calculated gamble, they chose to call none of some 200 potential witnesses, including experts on the effects of alcoholism. Without them, said the judge, the jury couldn't consider that argument, leaving Deaver without a case.

He's the first high-level federal official bagged by a special prosecutor, but only one of many under investigation. Independent counsels, as they're formally known, are appointed by a panel of federal appeals court judges to avoid having Justice Department political appointees investigating other executive-branch officials.

Because President Reagan's own ethics are above reproach and have never been seriously questioned, he seems unable to understand and unwilling to enforce a similar code for others, which has contributed to the perception of a "sleaze factor" in his administration. For instance, he only grudgingly signed a bill this week extending the special-prosecutor law.

But the conviction of his old friend Deaver makes the best possible argument for an Ethics in Government Act. It was no doubt a painful lesson, and one that future presidents should remember well.

the Charleston Gazette

Charleston, WVA, December 18, 1987

AT THIS TIME of the year, there's a tendency to feel forgiveness for people who suffer crushing defeats, even if the defeat stems from their own crookedness.

But former White House aide Michael Deaver deserves no sympathy. His perjury conviction Wednesday proves that he used his connections with government officials to enrich himself. Worse, when caught, Deaver sought to hide behind a phony excuse of alcoholism.

Deaver resigned as deputy White House chief of staff in 1985 to set up a Washington consulting firm. All the while, he denied any intention of lobbying former co-workers on behalf of his new clients. But why else would giant corporations such as TWA and the governments of South Korea and Canada choose Deaver to represent them?

From the moment he left Reagan's side, Deaver planned to make a fortune trading on his 20-year relationship with the president and Nancy Reagan, and his connections with those remaining in the administration.

That's against the law.

When Congress asked Deaver about his involvement in arranging a meeting between Reagan and South Korea's trade representative, concerning a contract worth $475,000 a year, Deaver lied.

When a grand jury asked him about a TWA request that he intercede on its behalf with then Transportation Secretary Elizabeth Dole, Deaver lied.

When a grand jury inquired into talks he held with Secretary of State George Shultz and former National Security Adviser Robert McFarlane, this time on behalf of Puerto Rico, Deaver again lied.

Those are the three charges for which the jury found him guilty. With a string of other administration officials under investigation, indictment or conviction, the Reagan White House easily will go down as the most corrupt since Watergate.

We think anyone abusing such positions of influence — whether in the White House, the statehouse, the courthouse or city hall — ought to bear the full weight of the law. More than many, they have benefited from all this country has to offer, making their greed even more offensive.

Michael Deaver should go to jail, not only as an example to others contemplating influence peddling, but because that's what he deserves.

Ivan Boesky Fined $100 Million & Sentenced for Insider Trading

Shortly after the stock market closed Nov. 14, 1986, the Securities & Exchange Commission (SEC) announced that arbitrager Ivan Boesky had agreed to pay $100 million in fines in connection with illicit profits from stock trading based on inside information about corporate takeovers. Boesky also agreed to plead guilty to one unspecified criminal charge and would be barred for life from securities trading. The penalty, which was by far the largest ever imposed for insider trading, grew out of the SEC's investigation of Dennis Levine, an investment banker who June 5 had pleaded guilty to trading based on nonpublic information about pending takeovers.

According to the SEC complaint Nov. 14, Levine had furnished Boesky with information obtained from his work at Shearson Lehman Brothers Inc. and Drexel Burnham Lambert Inc. The complaint alleged that in the spring of 1985 Boesky had agreed to pay Levine 5% of the profit from any stock purchase made on Levine's recommendation, and 1% of the profit from stocks that Boesky already owned but Levine provided information on. Levine had himself agreed to pay $11.6 million in fines, illicit profits and back taxes, which had been a record penalty at the time. Boesky's $100 million penalty comprised a $50 million fine and $50 million in returned illegal profits obtained during seven corporate takeovers and restructurings. The SEC had imposed a total of just $3.7 million in insider trading fines in the entire fiscal year that ended in September. Boesky was to be allowed 19 months to close out his business before his lifetime ban from Wall Street would begin. A 1986 estimate by *Forbes* magazine had put Boesky's wealth at $200 million. Although other estimates suggested that he was even wealthier, his lawyer, Harvey Pitt of Fried, Frank, Harris, Silver & Jacobsen, said that "very, very little" of his fortune would remain after he paid the penalty.

Boesky was well known for his lack of interest in sleep or other activities besides work, and most of his working time was reportedly spent on one of the 160 or more phone lines in his office or one of three phones in his car. Boesky reportedly obtained information from countless Wall Street contacts besides Levine. Most analysts suspected that Levine was not the only banker who provided arbitragers with confidential information, although he might have been the only one with whom Boesky had an explicit agreement. Following the SEC announcement, reports swept Wall Street that other investors would be caught up in the growing scandal. The rumors were fueled Nov. 17 by reports that for several weeks before the announcement of the fine, Boesky had tape recorded all of his telephone conversations as part of an earlier agreement with the SEC to gather evidence against others in exchange for leniency. At the center of the rumors was Drexel, Burnham the fast-growing firm that had participated in most recent takeovers by raising money through high-risk, high-yield "junk bonds."

A federal judge in New York City Dec. 18, 1987 sentenced Boesky to three years in prison for conspiring to file false stock trading records. Boesky had pleaded guilty in April 1987 to a single felony count that carried a maximum of five years in prison and a $250,000 fine. In sentencing Boesky, Judge Morris Lasker indicated that the sentence took into account the "unprecedented" extent of his cooperation with federal prosecutors, as outlined in a presentencing memo submitted by the government that had been released—with many deletions to protect ongoing probes—Dec. 14. A prison sentence, however was necessary, the judge said, because "the public has come to regard this proceeding as the ultimate representation of the insider trading scandal." The judge imposed no fine, saying Boesky's assets should be available to the many people who had sued him. The 50-year-old former arbitrager was said to be on the verge of bankruptcy. He was to surrender for jailing March 24, 1988, and would be eligible for parole in a year.

DESERET·NEWS
Salt Lake City, UT
November 20/21, 1986

In a stock market that reacts almost instantly to a missed beat in the presidential heart, it's easy to imagine the impact of the scandal that has rocked Wall Street for the past few days. The Dow Jones industrial average fell 43.31 points Tuesday — fourth largest loss in history.

The Securities and Exchange Commission last Friday nailed one of the biggest and most influential traders on Wall Street — Ivan Boesky — for "insider trading." In other words, Boesky conspired to take the risk out of his huge market deals by promising substantial profits to market specialist Dennis Levine for passing on inside tips on pending mergers.

Where others could only guess if and when a merger offer would take place — which quickly affects stock prices of target companies — Boesky knew when those offers would take place and what chance they had. No wonder he became known as "Ivan the Terrible" for his correct "hunches," running up a fortune of more than $200 million.

SEC regulations forbid trading on inside tips. The reason: it gives a very few traders information the public doesn't have access to. The potential for rigging the market is that much greater. And such trading quickly erodes public confidence in stocks.

What to do? The SEC's record $100 million negotiated settlement with Boesky — $50 million of which goes to the Treasury — should strike fear into the hearts of others who try to deal with inside tips.

More heads ought to roll. Boesky helped the SEC gain information on others who are similarly implicated. But how long this case exerts a deterrent effect depends a great deal on how much money there is to be made by using such questionable practices.

While loopholes can be found in any formal deterrents, at least the present law can be tightened. One drawback is that the law is fuzzy in defining insider trading. Is a market professional infringing the law when he analyzes companies, interviews executives, and tries to gain other material information not available to the public? That's all part of trying to predict what a stock's future price might be.

Whatever new laws are written should clarify those issues, as well as get tougher on insider trading.

The Washington Post

Washington, DC, December 21, 1987

THE MAN who boasted, "Greed is healthy. You can be greedy and still feel good about yourself" will have three years to think about that proposition. Ivan Boesky, the leading figure in the Wall Street insider trading scandal, was sentenced to prison Friday for his crime. U.S. District Judge Morris Lasker said, "Some kind of message must be sent to the business community that such activities cannot be wholly repaired simply by repaying people after the fact." Was the penalty for this white-collar first offender too harsh? We don't think so. In fact, a good argument can be made that he worked out a very sweet deal with prosecutors, considering the magnitude of his scandalous operations.

Mr. Boesky was well known on Wall Street as an aggressive trader and self-described expert on risk arbitrage. He even wrote a book describing his economic theories and game plans for the market. It turns out, though, that he wasn't so much a scholar as a schemer who used inside information—not scientific analysis or brains—to build a personal fortune in the hundreds of millions of dollars. His greedy deals hurt thousands of other investors and rocked the public's confidence in the stock market. Implicated early in the scandal by one of his confederates, Dennis Levine, Mr. Boesky initially faced charges on at least seven felonies involving insider trading.

Within days of receiving an SEC subpoena, however, his lawyers arranged a plea bargain. Mr. Boesky admitted his guilt with respect to one charge, and the government dropped the others and promised not to prosecute him for any other crimes uncovered subsequently. He paid $100 million to the government. Half was put in what is called a disgorgement fund—a return of illegal profits—to indemnify some of his creditors. The rest was a fine. The fine, however, was paid in stock, which has lost 40 percent of its value since it was transferred.

In exchange for being allowed to plead to a single felony—with a maximum sentence of five years—Mr. Boesky has been cooperating with the government in the broader investigation of Wall Street. His lawyer told Judge Lasker that he had implicated 14 additional suspects and five major brokerage houses, so perhaps the hastily arranged plea bargain paid off. Before you shed too many tears for Mr. Boesky, remember that his family still has millions of dollars in assets, and he will be eligible for parole in 12 months. This, of course, could change dramatically when those who were cheated by him prosecute their lawsuits.

The San Diego Union

San Diego, CA, December 23, 1987

Ivan Boesky is luckier than he deserves to be. The once feared and powerful Wall Street speculator in takeover stocks received a much lighter sentence than was expected for his monstrous white-color crimes. He was sentenced to three years in prison for conspiring to violate securities law. He could have received five years and been fined $250,000. But U.S. District Judge Milton Lasker waived a fine.

Boesky had already paid the U.S. government $50 million in fines, and returned another $50 million in illegal profits. He pleaded guilty last April to one count of criminal conspiracy after amassing a fortune of nearly $150 million from illegally trading on insider information.

Boesky's empire began to unravel in the spring of 1986 when Dennis Levine, an associate, was charged by the Securities and Exchange Commission with pocketing $12.6 million in profits from illegal stock deals.

Levine, who was given a two-year prison sentence last February and fined $362,000, testified against Boesky after agreeing to cooperate with the feds. Boesky in turn cut a deal with the government. As part of a plea bargain arrangement, he surreptitiously recorded telephone conversations with his alleged accomplices and wore a tape recorder when meeting with them in person.

The government netted some high rollers in Boesky's trap. The indictments and guilty pleas that resulted were a bonanza for law-enforcement officials. Indeed, without Boesky's help the vast illegal underworld of insider trading, which the SEC described as "staggering" in its size, might never have been exposed.

If Boesky hoped that spilling his guts and much of his bank accounts in fines and restitution would get him off lightly, he was right. Judge Lasker, in pronouncing sentence, said he was giving Boesky the three-year term not to deter him from committing such crimes again, but so he could serve as an example to others. Is it an example for others, or an example of judicial leniency?

The capital markets, composed of the stock exchanges and bond trading firms that are euphemistically known as Wall Street, are extremely important public institutions. They rely to a great extent on the confidence of individual investors. Undermine that confidence, as Boesky and others did, and the need for stern punishment becomes all the more apparent.

Boesky escaped the full wrath of the law, and that underscores another aspect of this case: Boesky was ruled upon by a judge of his own choosing.

Judge Lasker is a man with what The New York Times calls "a well-deserved reputation for leniency." Barely two months after Boesky pleaded guilty to violating securities law, plea-bargaining by "judge shopping" was severely curbed. Boesky got in under the wire, and his lawyers cut a deal with the government in return for having Judge Lasker preside over the case. Future white-color criminals will not be as lucky.

In a sense, Boesky himself has become almost secondary in this sordid drama. The government sees him as a means of delivering a message — come clean and cooperate — to those under investigation. He serves as an example for others considering stock scams. The message would have had more effect had Boesky received a stiffer sentence.

LEXINGTON HERALD-LEADER

Lexington, KY
December 22, 1987

When he gave Ivan Boesky three years in prison for breaking federal securities laws, U.S. District Judge Morris E. Lasker said he wanted to send a message to the nation's business community.

Perhaps the judge succeeded. Most observers seem to have been surprised at the stiffness of the sentence, even though the judge could have given Boesky five years and a $250,000 fine. Apparently, Boesky avoided the maximum sentence by cooperating with federal investigators and leading them to other inside traders near the top of Wall Street's hierarchy.

To those outside those rarefied circles, however, Boesky's sentence is bound to send a different message: If you're going to rob people, do it with the big boys.

Boesky is, after all, a man who systematically broke federal laws to make at least $80 million dollars. Boesky has paid a record civil fine of $100 million. But giving back the proceeds of a robbery wouldn't be enough reason for a light sentence. And Boesky's fine hardly makes it seem just that he will be out of prison in two years.

That time in the slammer won't be too tough, if Boesky's lawyers succeed in having him sent to the minimum-security federal penitentiary in Lompoc, Calif. There, Boesky will have plenty of liesure to contemplate how lucky he is to have chosen to lead his life of crime on Wall Street. If he had tried to pick up a few bucks by knocking over a convenience store, he might now be facing a longer sentence in a much tougher place.

The Boston Globe

Boston, MA, December 19, 1987

The sentencing of Ivan Boesky to three years in prison for his confessed part in the insider-trading scandal will certainly concentrate the minds of his former Wall Street colleagues as they ply their way through the shoal waters of merger finance. If Boesky can go to prison for his misdeeds, so could they – and probably faster.

Boesky, after all, played the manipulator all the way. He was able to limit the charge against him to a single count; he chose his court; he selected those of his assets subject to disposal to meet preliminary penalties by the Securities and Exchange Commission, together with the timing of their sale; he chose to open his activities to the authorities in an attempt to stave off prison, if not monetary loss.

He came close to succeeding – but had to play without the advantages he enjoyed on the street from his deft handling of prior knowledge about merger activities in the highly leveraged arbitrage markets. He paid money as penalties in unprecedented amounts, perhaps figuring that money, after all, can be made again. Freedom is another matter. Whether

three years (probably reduced by good behavior) is the right amount is less important than the fact that freedom lost is gone forever – a point that will weigh on the minds of everyone in the financial world.

One need not expect that Boesky's case will eliminate the problem of insider trading to believe that it will seriously affect the practices of many people in the business. The reality of potential prison terms for being found to have traded on insider information changes the risk-reward ratio for everyone tempted to take advantage of special knowledge for personal gain in marketplaces that must remain as open as humanly possible.

Some will continue to be drawn by the allure of fast winnings involving very large amounts of money. They will undoubtedly now be even more circumspect in how they go about it; they will certainly make every effort to cover their tracks better than Boesky was able to cover his. In doing so, however, they will create trails that, if found, will probably point even more incriminatingly at their guilt – and at the prison door.

The Hutchinson News

Hutchinson, KS
December 22, 1987

Don't call Ivan Boesky a stock manipulator. He's a looting pig who got off far easier (don't they all? than he should have.

A federal judge in New York

acted as if he were really socking it to Boesky Friday. Declaring that Boesky's thefts of upwards of $100 million were "too substantial merely to forgive and forget," the judge ordered the looter to jail for 3 years.

Boesky

Boesky will be eligible for parole after 1 year in jail.

That's getting tough.

A few years back in Reno County, a poor wretch was sentenced to 1 to 5 for breaking and entering. He stole a TV set and 180 pounds of meat.

Another guy got 2 to 10 in Hutchinson. He stole a motorcycle.

About a year ago, a local thief got a 5 to 20 stretch. But he used a gun to get a few paltry dollars in Reno County. Boesky used a pen to loot his hundreds of millions.

The Boesky sentence is vulgar.

If it's socially desirable to throw a poor thief in jail for 5 years for stealing 180 pounds of meat in Reno County, you certainly should throw a rich thief in jail for more than 3 years for stealing upwards of $100 million in cash. cash.

News-Tribune & Herald

Duluth, MN, December 20, 1987

This has not been a good autumn (fall?) for Wall Street. October's Black Monday is now called a stock market "crash" by even the most enthusiastic investors, what with about a third of just about everybody's equity gone.

And while the Ivan Boesky case predates Black Monday, his sentencing Friday to three years in prison for stock manipulation sent a chill through Wall Street that will be felt through a long winter of discontent.

Boesky was at the center of an insider trading scandal that is considered the biggest in the history of the nation. His sentence of three years of incarceration was shortened from the maximum five and no fine was imposed when $250,000 could have been levied because he agreed to cooperate with investigators and also paid a $100 million penalty to the Securi-

ties and Exchange Commission to settle an insider-trading complaint.

Insider trading is to the stock market what illegally drugging horses is to racing or loading dice to craps. Investors might wince at the comparisons with gambling, but that is always present in "playing" the stock market, as they say. And how nice if a person has some way of knowing in advance how a security will "behave" while others are investing in good faith.

Good faith is getting hard to find these days, in Wall Street and in politics. Boesky, it is said, once made a speech to graduates of a business school in which he extolled greed as a virtue.

What is the flip side of the old bromide? Time wounds all heels? Boesky's fate no doubt has plenty of other heels looking over their shoulders.

Newsday

Long Island, NY, December 21, 1987

It's hard to quarrel with U.S. District Judge Morris Lasker's sentencing decision in the matter of the notorious Mr. Ivan Boesky. The confessed inside-trader-turned-government-songbird was given three years in prison, out of a maximum of five, on his guilty plea to a single count of conspiring to lie to federal investigators. All things considered, that seems just about right.

Consider the fact that Boesky cooperated with the Justice Department's investigations of Wall Street wrongdoing. How fruitful his cooperation will prove to be in the end cannot yet be assessed. But there's no doubt that Boesky has been a necessary help to U.S. At-

torney Rudolph Giuliani, who said Friday that he agreed with the penalty Lasker imposed.

For the man who put together the biggest inside-trading scheme in Wall Street history was also in the best position to help the government unravel the myriad conspiracies and stop the rot. And even though Boesky turned himself in, his knowledge and his files over to the government back in April when it became clear to him that the heat in his kitchen had suddenly gotten truly alarming, he still received the longest prison term handed out so far in the widening securities-industry probe.

Lasker was quite right, too, when he said at the sentencing: "The time has come when it is

totally unacceptable for courts to act as if prison is unthinkable for white-collar defendants but a matter of routine in other cases. Breaking the law is breaking the law. Some kind of message must be sent to the business community that such activities cannot be wholly repaired simply by repaying people after the fact. The signal must go out, loud and clear, to those tempted to skirt, fudge or deliberately break the law that to preserve and nourish moral values . . . and to preserve not only the actual integrity of the financial markets but the appearance of integrity in those markets, criminal behavior such as Boesky's cannot go unchecked." Amen.

ALBUQUERQUE JOURNAL

Albuquerque, NM, November 21, 1986

The story seems to have all the classic elements of an American tragedy: immigrant parents, humble origins, ambition — and greed.

Wall Street arbitrager Ivan Boesky became successful by mastering the intelligence gathering and analyzing that is necessary to anticipate the ever-changing tides of the stock market. But mere success, apparently, was not enough.

Boesky made a deal — information for a share of the profits — with a man in a Wall Street firm that has provided much of the financial horsepower for corporate takeover efforts. Tipped off to imminent takeovers and the bidding up of stock, Boesky could make the stock market equivalent of a sure bet and rake in winnings that federal investigators allege have exceeded $50 million.

And, in the ultimate "insider" move, one of Boesky's investment funds sold at least $440 million in securities a week ago — just before the announcement of another kind of deal for Boesky.

He agreed to provide information that could lead to the prosecution of other Wall Street figures who profit illicitly from insider trading, to pay $100 million in restitution and penalties and to plead guilty to one felony count that carries a prison term of from one to five years.

Boesky likely will end up providing "insider" information to the Senate Banking Committee which, under the new Democratic chairmanship of Wisconsin Sen. William Proxmire, can be expected to pursue reform of regulatory practices. Certainly one aspect that merits examination is the annual budget of the Security and Exchange Commission, which is not much more than the $100 million Boesky will forfeit.

But more immediately, the moral of the Boesky story should have a chastening effect on a marketplace that rests upon a foundation of investor confidence: Integrity is one commodity that ought never be sold short.

TULSA WORLD

Tulsa, OK, November 20, 1986

REVELATIONS of a mammoth insider-trading scandal Tuesday sent the stock market tumbling 43 points on the Dow Jones industrial average, one of its worst daily losses in history.

The reaction was partly predictable. The market usually reacts negatively to bad news. But part of the problem is that the market is now computer programmed in a way that seems to exaggerate any kind of negative influence.

The trouble began with news that Ivan Boesky, a well-known short-term trader, had agreed to settle charges of dealing on insider information involving stocks of companies involved in real or rumored takeovers.

Stocks of the affected companies were affected, and the uncertainty spread through the rest of the market. Then, as has occurred before, a number of things began to happen automatically. Many big stockholders have computer-programmed "sell" orders that are activated when an issue reaches a certain level. These pre-programmed sales then triggered other pre-programmed sales until the market had lost billions.

It is doubtful much can be done about computers. They are here to stay.

But the Securities Exchange Commission and the major markets can do something about gross violations of insider trading and other non-computerized, human activity that lowers confidence in the market.

The need for confidence is greater than ever before, because the market is now computer programmed to self-destruct when confidence is lost.

The Grand Rapids Press

Grang Rapids, MI, November 20, 1986

For several years now, we've enjoyed the Wall Street bull. Last week, we saw, with less enjoyment, the china shop the bull has been trashing.

Ivan Boesky, a high-stakes stock speculator, last week admitted to an unprecedented run of insider trading, meaning the use of corporate information to make stock-market killings. His greed upsets the delicate balance of trust and fairness that sustains the market. If unfettered lust for money is allowed to overwhelm all else, destroying the public's willingness to invest, then the game on Wall Street is ruined.

Some fear that this federal crackdown on avarice will depress the stock market, but in fact the market and the financial world are in need of a little purifying. Capitalist legends like Mr. Boesky might make good copy but the underpinnings of the stock market, and all of corporate America, are the small investors, those who don't know an arbitrageur from a used-car salesman. The gambling spirit doesn't come easily to such investors. If they become convinced the market is a rigged game, the bull will become a bear in a twinkling.

Congress, which has looked askance on the takeover fever of the past few years, now might resurrect some reform bills. In general, a tightening of securities laws to insure a fair stock exchange would be welcome. A bill that sounds promising would discourage secret takeover bids by requiring speedy public disclosure once five percent of a company has been obtained.

Another tack might be to stiffen the penalty for violations. Why a thief of the magnitude of Mr. Boesky is still rich and free after his confessions while small-timers of all stripes sit in jail is difficult to understand. The moral of Mr. Boesky's sentence is that it's good to accumulate all the wealth you can, so you can pay the big fine when you're caught. Better for Mr Boesky would be a slice of another kind of life — a prison farm, for example, where he migh develop calluses and a new perspective.

Of benefit, too, might be a spate of congressional hearings on the mores and morals of today's Wall Street. It would be instructive to explore, along with stockbrokers and investment bankers, the thin line they walk between competitive business practices and immoral, unethical or illegal acts. Young people enthralled with high finance often seem poorly schooled in the fundmamentals of human social behavior, and misbehavior.

Without a grounding in ethical values, a person breathing the heady air of Wall Street will run after profits without a thought to whom or what is trampled upon in the process. The stock market is people loosely bound by a common interest. If individuals like Mr. Boesky are permitted to redesign the concept — exchanging common or shared interest for utter self-interest — the structure of corporate America will lose its foundation.

The Boesky case accentuates a problem of values and principles that has lain dormant too long. Wall Street, like most institutions, is susceptible to disease spread from within. Unfortunately, there are no vaccinations for greed.

The Birmingham News

Birmingham, AL, November 28, 1986

The stock market went on an uneasy roller-coaster ride recently while professional analysts tried to sort out what the insider trading scandal involving stock speculator Ivan F. Boesky would mean for the market at large.

Although stock prices have since recovered, it is just this kind of market volatility in response to a matter that has nothing to do with the state of the economy or the health of individual companies that makes the stock market so scary for individual investors. The regulators should not make it scarier.

The Securities and Exchange Commission, which is supposed to protect investors, could best do so by keeping its interference in the workings of the stock market to a clear-cut enforcement of the rules. If someone breaks the law, as Boesky apparently did in his alleged scheme to steal news of intended stock tender offers, it should act quickly and decisively to punish the wrongdoer and aid his victims.

But the behind-the-scenes investigation growing up around the Boesky case may have hurt investors more than did the insider trading it hopes to curtail. The market dropped more than 40 points in one day last week because of news of the widening probe. That represented a $34 billion drop in stock values, *The Wall Street Journal* said, far more than the $203 million in trading profits Boesky is said to have reaped.

The Wall Street debate over what should be allowed in the realm of insider trading and who has been doing what to whom may seem far removed from the interests of most Alabamians, but its effects on the stock market are not. Thousands of Alabamians own stock, and many thousands more participate in pension plans in which benefits depend to some degree on the performance of stock market investments.

These people are not privy to the rumors and rumblings that the big traders follow. They are best served by a fair and orderly market.

The big SEC investigation seems intended to make the market fairer, but the regulators should also be sensitive to what their poking around means to the small investor.

Now that everyone knows a big probe is under way, the SEC should wrap it up quickly and publicly. Public trust in the market requires not only enforcement of the rules, but also removal of the shadow cast by investor uncertainty about what the regulators have in mind.

DAILY NEWS

New York, NY, November 18, 1986

MOST PEOPLE CAN'T IMAGINE what $100 million means. It's like one of those old Ripley's Believe-It-or-Nots: "If you converted $100 million into Mason jar caps and put them edge to edge, they'd stretch from Mars to the second moon of Uranus."

But just about everybody who can read knows there's at least one guy who knows *exactly* what $100 million is. He's Ivan Boesky, terror of Wall Street, the Attila of arbitrageurs (whatever *they* are), a wheeler's dealer or dealer's wheeler, depending on which side of the trade you're looking from. Boesky's latest deal was made with the U.S. government. It was made public Friday, after the markets closed.

And boy-oh-Boesky, what a deal!

On the face of it, it looks like punishment: a $50 million fine and another $50 mil in nonreturnable settlement costs to help make whole the people he cheated. And, down the road, there's the possibility of a five-year federal prison term: Boesky entered a guilty plea to a single criminal count of illegal stock trading. Presumably, *if* he should fail to go on cooperating with the federal authorities, he *could* be sentenced.

But that's clearly *not* the deal he—and the feds—have in mind. And, in turn, that's a shocker.

However many other criminal "inside traders" Boesky leads the feds to, he's likely to remain the grand champion of all white-collar criminals. The $100 million leaves him, by informed, conservative estimates, with $150 million in personal net worth. And for all this deal's seemingly impressive restrictions against returning to manipulate the market, he's still free to make zillions in overseas stock markets, where he's already hyperactive.

If the government is to emerge from this mess with *any* credibility, Boesky *must* go to prison—and not for one of those approximations of a long weekend. Anything less than long, hard time—counted in years actually behind bars, not months—will send one message to the street and the market: Massive securities crimes are no more than a social indiscretion—and "proper" punishment is a moderately priced retroactive fee for a license to steal.

INSIDER TRADING.

AKRON BEACON JOURNAL
Akron, OH, December 22, 1987

"BREAKING THE law is breaking the law."

That's how Judge Morris Lasker succinctly explained the logic of his decision to sentence Ivan Boesky, the disgraced stock-market speculator, to three years in prison for illegal insider trading. Too often in the past, white-collar criminals have received comparatively light sentences — despite studies indicating that potential white-collar criminal are more likely to be deterred by the prospect of a jail term than violent criminals.

Boesky

The judge wanted to set an example with Boesky. "Some kind of message," he said, "must be sent to the business community that such activities cannot be wholly repaired simply by repaying people after the fact."

Rudolph Giuliani, the U.S. attorney who headed the Boesky prosecution, called the sentence "well-reasoned." That sounds about right, especially when the jail time is combined with the record $100 million fine Boesky agreed to pay as a result of an earlier plea-bargain. He still faces a slew of civil suits, which could cost him even more money in the future. The combination nicely offsets the estimated $80 million Boesky illegally earned as a result of his scam.

The justice system rarely operates outside the gray area. The Boesky case is the norm, not the exception. While many, including ourselves, agree that the crime justified a stiffer sentence, it must be taken into account that Boesky cooperated greatly with the government investigation. His information pushed matters ahead by years. He opened the door to widespread corruption that might not have been discovered.

There's wisdom in encouraging people to come forward and expose the full extent of criminal networks. And the only credible incentive is more favorable treatment in the courts. Boesky did not receive the maximum sentence of five years; he will probably serve scarcely more than one year of his three-year term. But in the wake of his disclosures, more indictments are expected in the Wall Street scandal.

What Ivan Boesky did is reprehensible. In effect, he profited hugely at the expense of all honest investors in the stock market, and then flaunted his success as if it were all his own. He contributed greatly to the speculative mania that helped lead to Black Monday. The prosecution asked Judge Lasker to "fashion a sentence to instruct the financial community that power and position create no immunity from punishment." That should be the signal. Boesky will be behind bars, and the prosecutions will proceed.

THE TENNESSEAN
Nashville, TN, December 26, 1987

STOCK speculator Mr. Ivan Boesky has been sentenced to three years in prison but not fined on his guilty plea in the Wall Street insider trading case, and that is too lenient.

His criminal conduct was outrageous. He is responsible, in effect, for stealing millions from investors. He could have been sentenced to a maximum of five years and given a $250,000 fine on his plea of guilty to one count of conspiracy to make false statements to the Securities and Exchange Commission.

U.S. District Judge Morris Lasker said he was not imposing a fine because of the record $100 million civil penalty Mr. Boesky paid the SEC, adding that "it is appropriate that your legitimate creditors be given a claim to your assets prior to that of the government." The former stock speculator faces a score of civil lawsuits.

"Breaking the law is breaking the law. Some kind of message must be sent to the business community that such activities cannot be repaired simply by repaying people after the fact," said Judge Lasker. He added, "The signal must go out loud and clear, to those tempted to skirt, fudge or de-

liberately break the law ...and to preserve not only the actual integrity of the financial markets, but the appearance of integrity in those markets, criminal behavior such as Boesky's cannot go unchecked."

Judge Lasker would have sent a louder, clearer signal if he had imposed the maximum penalty of five years in prison. The lesser sentence may have taken into account that Mr. Boesky has been cooperating with U.S. attorneys and will testify against others.

Both the prosecutors and the defense attorney have told Judge Lasker in lengthy pre-sentencing memos that Mr. Boesky revealed his involvement in far more widespread illegal activity, including manipulating stock prices, unlawful takeover activity, undercapitalized broker-dealers and false record keeping.

If Mr. Boesky had robbed a liquor store with a gun and took $100 he could have gotten 20 years in prison. He pulled off his robberies with a pen and a computer and robbed others of millions. In the sense of equal justice it doesn't seem fair that he gets three years and probably won't serve half of that. ■

DAILY ❦ NEWS
New York, NY, December 19, 1987

IVAN BOESKY, A CANCER ON THE HEART of capitalism, got sent up for three years yesterday. At worst for him, he'll spend a portion of that on a federal rest farm like Allenwood, designed by politicians to make absolutely sure that neither prosecutors nor judges can be really rude to corrupt pols or other hoodlums with good connections.

Three years and no fine. No fine! He could have been nicked for $250,000. But U.S. District Judge Morris E. Lasker noted Boesky already had forfeited $100 million to the federal government in his plea bargain on a single count of conspiring to make false statements to the Securities and Exchange Commission. Actually, it doesn't matter much anyway. A quarter mil to Boesky is equivalent to what most honest, truthful Americans pay for a shoeshine.

Lasker should have gone for the whole five years—all he was allowed. Petty change though it would have been to Ivan Megabucks, the whole fine would at least have offered the healthy symbolism of saying max, max, max.

WITH HIS REPUTATION FOR SOFT sentencing, Lasker did well to note that "the time has come when it is totally unacceptable for courts to act as if prison is unthinkable for white-collar defendants but a matter of routine in other cases."

Right on! But then he said he was convinced Boesky would not repeat his illegal insider trading or commit other crimes. And that's just plain naive.

Boesky is one of the most cynical, amoral, brilliant economic sociopaths in the long and ugly annals of crime.

Today, he is worth untold hundreds of millions of dollars. There is deep doubt that a single dime of that was gained honestly. In a land and on an Earth where poverty still is rampant and a mass thirst for fairness and justice rages unslaked, the very idea of a Boesky putting in a few months with a reduced staff of servants is obscene.

More important, though, is the message, the deterrent effect, or lack of it, of the Boesky disposition.

Who are his victims? Every man, woman or child, living or dead, who owns or has owned a single share of corporate stock or a single bond. Everybody who's part of a pension plan, owns insurance, deals with a bank. Or works for a company whose stock is on the market. Everybody, thus, who depends on the mechanisms and devices of U.S. capitalism for security, nourishment or hope.

ISN'T THAT A BIT HEAVY? Not for a minute. What *was* Boesky's crime? Well, technically it was to have lied to some federal bureaucrats. But in truth it was to have made rollicking mockery—worth hundreds of millions of dollars—of the economic structure of this nation. It was to have danced to the very pinnacle of wealth, influence, privilege and prominence on a stairway of lies and crime.

It was to turn into dirty jokes the words "trust," "fidelity," "surety," "guarantee," "equity," "obligation," and the other terms that suggest reliability in financial institutions.

It is absurd to think that, left with vast wealth, Boesky will not go on doing exactly what he got away with for decades, if a wee trifle more carefully. It is equally absurd to think that that very same message is not being absorbed and digested by millions of Americans, no small number of them working on or near Wall Street.

The decent among them will shy from trust in the market, from brokers, banks—from anything but cash. The weak and sordid will seek, with new vigor, to emulate Boesky. Who among them wouldn't trade a couple of dozen months on reduced rations for a life of wealth beyond counting?

FOR INVESTIGATING AND PROSECUTING Boesky, a good deal of credit should go to U.S. Attorney Rudolph Giuliani, along with his staff and a lot of usually obscure, diligent professionals in the SEC, the FBI and elsewhere. But even if, as is claimed, civil suits drain from Boesky a significant part of his vast ill-gotten wealth, he has been given far too easy a ride.

Whatever the effects on other cases—none of which could equal his in importance—he should have gone down on enough counts and years to have kept him locked up until he is too old to rise again. Long, long years enough to discourage those who now see him as a glittering role model.

That he was not prosecuted with proper force is a failing of Giuliani and others in the federal establishment.

Finally, Boesky's most deeply wounded victim is the concept of free enterprise. For who, looking at the man, his crimes and his rewards, can escape wondering? Wondering whether capitalism's mortal enemy, socialism, for all its simplism, its gross inefficiency, its tyranny over the human spirit, does not offer something more dignified, more decent, than the vulgarity of Ivan Boesky walking free and filthy, filthy rich.

Post-Tribune

Gary, IN, November 19, 1986

Wisconsin ⛪ State Journal

Madison, WI
November 21, 1986

Wisconsin Sen. William Proxmire, the new Democratic chairman of the Senate Banking Committee, has let it be known that he plans to hold extensive oversight hearings into the Ivan F. Boesky "insider trading" scandal and other stock-market problems. Proxmire's House counterpart is waxing his gavel, too.

If those hearings shed more light on how Boesky — who has pleaded guilty to a felony charge of securities fraud, agreed to pay a record $100 million penalty and may go to prison — ripped off the system, then so much the better.

But if the idea is to smear all stock arbitrage with a broad brush dipped in the paint of suspicion and thus bring down new congressional regulation of the markets, then Proxmire and Co. must tread carefully.

Corporate raider Boesky has admitted to offering a commission to Dennis Levine, a former Drexel Burnham Lambert merger specialist, for passing on confidential information. Levine would give Boesky valuable tips about companies targeted for takeover; Boesky would then buy huge amounts of stock in those companies and wait. Once the information he had already illegally obtained became public, the stock price would rise in anticipation of a takeover bid and Boesky would sell his stock.

Boesky got rich, Levine got a cut and the unfortunate investment bank that had counted on confidentiality got burned.

This was a blatant violation of laws policed by the Securities and Exchange Commission (SEC). But should the Boesky-Levine affair become an excuse to foist new regulations on the markets?

For the most part, stock arbitrage is an honorable (but high-risk) business that serves a useful purpose. The system helps to restructure poorly managed or undervalued companies and, yes, occasionally makes a smart player rich. Many also lose their shirts.

Arbitragers create a "liquid market" for investors who don't care to gamble on the outcome of the takeover bid, and are willing to settle for only a portion of the profit. If honestly performed, arbitrage helps make Wall Street more efficient while channeling private money into productive enterprise.

It is worth asking the SEC why took so long to halt the Boesky-Levine scheme, which began in February 1985, and whether existing rules need tightening or clarifying. There is also some value at examining the use of "junk bonds" as a means of financing takeovers.

But Congress should not get carried away by proposing laws that could hamper the *legal* flow of information that is the life's blood of a healthy market.

Ivan Boesky is a predator, a shark, a vulture, a thief in a white collar.

So are others who connive and deal in the fantasy world called the stock market. They feed on inside information and make big, obscene profits.

Americans, from the president on down, who lament the decline of the country's morality, should study this one carefully. It should make them sick.

Boesky has been known as a brilliant fellow with a golden touch. Finally, he got caught. He used inside information to profit on takeover bids. He is linked to Dennis

Our opinions

Levine, a former investment banker arrested last spring and charged with insider-trading violations. Levine pleaded guilty and that took down several other Wall Street operators.

That was just the tip of a very rotten iceberg. Boesky has been recording conversations with investment people and stock speculators — he did it so the government would consider leniency. One Wall Street fellow said the revelations would have a "sobering effect."

Another said, "There is a lot of fear out there." That's good news. Let the predators worry and squirm.

Boesky will pay a $100 million fine to settle charges by the Securities and Exchange Commission, a figure most of us cannot comprehend. He is barred from the security business forever. Bringing him down is a major victory for the SEC. There may be none bigger than Boesky in this scheming orgy of greed on Wall Street.

Before this is over, many other major figures may be tainted. Nobody caught in this kind of operation deserves more than a passing thought of sympathy. The incongruous aspect is that bank robbers go to prison. So do burglars. But the white-collar thieves usually do not. Yet they are more threatening to the moral fabric of the country than the robbers. No, they do not shoot anybody or do people bodily harm, but they rob. Prison is where they belong.

They damage the credibility of the stock market. Small investors should be frightened and very careful.

One of Boesky's deals involved Texaco's takeover of Getty Oil. He made about $120 million on the shares he had bought in anticipation of the takeover. Having inside information helped. That's slick, but is it ethical?

Calls for social justice cannot ignore the manipulations of Boesky and others like him. The hostile takeover practice is suspect, because it hurts so many people. Insider cheating is malignant. America's business schools should consider emphasizing ethics as much as skill in the business world. There are some excellent case studies that document that need.

Chicago Tribune

Chicago, IL, November 20, 1986

Exactly what constitutes illegal insider trading has at times been hard to define. But there are no gray areas in the charges against arbitrager Ivan F. Boesky. This one was open and shut.

But because of Mr. Boesky's fame as a corporate raider, the growing rumors that there will be charges against others and the size of the $100 million penalty—which is nearly as much as the entire Securities and Exchange Commission annual budget—this case is getting a lot of attention. And it should. But not for the reasons that already have some congressional committees warming up their witness chairs.

The downfall of Mr. Boesky, and any others who may have been a part of this insider trading ring, was precipitated by the downfall in May of Dennis B. Levine, an investment banker with Drexel Burnham Lambert Inc. No new laws against insider trading would have stopped this illegal scheme. Mr. Boesky and Mr. Levine broke laws already on the books. They were found out and they are being punished.

It took some time, but the SEC was able to build such a strong case against Mr. Boesky that he agreed to plead guilty to one felony count—for which he should go to prison—to return $100 million and to be forever barred from trading securities in this country. That the SEC could topple one of the towering figures in the risky but highly lucrative arbitrage field should send a sufficiently chilling signal to others considering breaking the law regarding the illegal use of inside information.

But this flagrant conspiracy should not be used to turn risk arbitrage or hostile takeovers into the whipping boys of Wall Street. Both are useful mechanisms for restructuring undervalued or poorly managed companies. That point should not get lost in the panic of Tuesday's sharp drop in the markets, prompted by a scandal-related selloff of stocks rumored to be takeover targets and exacerbated by computer-triggered trading.

The problem with policing insider trading is that it usually isn't nearly so clear-cut or blatant as it was in these cases. In its simplest form, the conspiracy worked this way: Mr. Levine gave Mr. Boesky inside information—important facts that had not been publicly disclosed—about companies targeted for takeover. Mr. Boesky then used this knowledge to buy up stock of those companies. When the information became public, the price of the stock generally rose, at which time Mr. Boesky would sell his stock. He agreed to give Mr. Levine a percentage of the profits.

The gray areas in the SEC regulations regarding insider trading should be clarified so there is no confusion in anyone's mind about what is and what is not legal. And perhaps particular attention should be paid to detailing the proper relationship among arbitragers, corporate raiders and investment banking firms using junk bonds as a mechanism for takeovers. Junk bonds are not new but their use in this manner is.

But beyond that, any efforts to hinder the legal and essential flow of information among buyers, sellers, market makers, managers, raiders and arbitragers should be resisted. The financial markets of America are vibrant and healthy and capable of making people rich. That is their fascination and their appeal.

Their strength is that they are efficient and there are rules against the few taking advantage of the many. Many in the securities business are applauding the fall of Mr. Boesky. There was a growing suspicion that his magic touch was too good to be true. It was indeed too good to be legal. All of this suggests that illegal insider trading is not pervasive on Wall Street, nor are the laws against it unenforceable.

Birmingham Post-Herald

Birmingham, AL, November 21, 1986

Move over, Black Thursday (the October 1929 day the stock market collapsed, ushering in the Great Depression). Wall Street now has Black Friday, the day last week the feds got Ivan Boesky, and many traders are sick with fear.

For years Boesky posed as the steel-nerved speculator in takeover stocks, the gambler who took huge positions, usually guessed right and ran up a fortune of $200 million.

Trouble was that Boesky was not a gambler but a cheat. He dealt from a stacked deck, betting on sure things. Boesky had an illegal advantage: Dennis Levine, a mergers specialist at Drexel Burnham Lambert, the investment bankers.

Because Drexel invented the method of financing takeovers with high-yield, high-risk "junk bonds," it got much acquisitions business. Levine got loads of inside information, and "Ivan the Terrible" became a financial-district legend.

Last May the Securities and Exchange Commission nailed Levine for $12.6 million in illegal profits. It again proved there's no honor among thieves. To lighten his sentence, Levine gave the SEC his co-conspirators at other investment houses and a big fish: Boesky.

To limit his own stay in the pokey, Boesky paid a record $100 million penalty and let securities cops listen in as he discussed insider deals with top investment bankers, takeover specialists and financial lawyers, who now are receiving subpoenas and bad cases of heartburn.

Boesky's fall and his turning in of his peers are bound to be healthy. The SEC likely will send some big names to jail for illegally profiting from privileged information, and markets should be fairer and more honest than they were before Friday.

With Democrats in charge of both houses of Congress, Wall Street can expect unfriendly hearings and tougher regulations. If the resulting legislation discourages insider trading and helps the SEC enforce legality, it will be welcomed.

However, the pro-regulators in Congress plan to use the Boesky scandal as an excuse to curb hostile takeovers and corporate "raiders." That could be harmful, because there is a key difference between Boesky-like operators and raiders.

The latter, much maligned by corporate fat cats, can be useful. They often identify poorly run companies whose stock sells below its potential. By forcing entrenched management to shape up or by taking over themselves, they benefit shareholders and make firms more efficient.

It is a painful, messy process that sometimes produces undesirable results. But it is the essence of free enterprise and Congress should take great care before hobbling it.

Newsday

Long Island, NY, November 18, 1986

Three observations on the dramatic Ivan Boesky case:

• First, the Securities and Exchange Commission deserves credit for mounting what appears to be the first sustained assault against insider trading on Wall Street. Unchecked, this practice will erode the public's confidence in the integrity of the securities industry. Insider trading is the buying and selling of stocks on the basis of confidential information not available to the investing public. Huge profits have been made using such illegal tactics.

The SEC began its crackdown on insider trading last summer when it moved against the young and brilliant Dennis Levine, then a Drexel Burnham Lambert merger specialist. Levine now is assisting the SEC in the widening probe whose trail led to Boesky, a celebrated arbitrager and one of the richest men in world. Boesky, 49, has agreed to pay $100 million in fines and restitution, plead guilty to one felony count of securities fraud and cooperate with federal investigators.

• Second, for now at least the SEC must be taken at its word when it says it accepted the plea-bargain deal with Boesky in return for his help in nailing other insider traders and illicit networks. But at some point the public might begin to wonder why so few people are jailed for a crime that is surely as corrosive to society as any number of so-called blue-collar crimes, such as burglary or car theft. And the public may also start entertaining the notion that while Boesky's penalty is more than a slap on the wrist — even for him, $100 million is real money — no financial assessment will ever prove as awesome a deterrent against insider trading as a prison sentence.

• Third, even with the threat of imprisonment, insider trading will not cease to be a viable road to riches until the institutions of Wall Street — the stock firms, investment banking houses and law firms — add to their working environment an ethos that rejects cheating the public.

Insider trading is a product not only of opportunity — in recent years the proliferation of mergers and acquisitions has created all sorts of windfall possibilities for white-collar criminals — but also of moral malaise. The Street must make it clear to its employees that not being square with the public is an unacceptable way of doing business. There are more methods of committing serious violence against society than hitting someone over the head with a blackjack. Insider trading amounts to mugging the system.

The TENNESSEAN

Nashville, TN, November 24, 1986

THE public image of Wall Street could only improve with the removal of Mr. Ivan Boesky, who built a fortune on raw, unscrupulous greed.

Mr. Boesky has admitted he had made $50 million in one year by the use of illegal insider information. He agreed to return the profits, and pay another $50 million as a civil penalty. He is in the process of settling criminal charges against him, and is barred for life from the securities business.

Mr. Boesky was Wall Street's dean of arbitrage, which is the practice of buying big chunks of stock in companies that are ripe for a takeover, and then selling them at a higher price after the takeover.

The risk of arbitrage is that the takeover may fall through. But Mr. Boesky had so much capital that his participation in a deal virtually erased the gamble. With a bankroll that often hit $900 million, Mr. Boesky could buy so much stock that he could force a company either to restructure or to sell out. And the word that Mr. Boesky was buying a certain stock was enough to make other arbitragers go for it.

It is important to understand that arbitrage itself is not illegal. It becomes illegal when the players cheat by using information not available to the public.

Mr. Boesky crossed the line from businessman to criminal in 1985 when he entered an agreement with Mr. David Levine, a former Wall Street merger specialist. Mr. Levine provided Mr. Boesky with private information about deals his company was working on, and Mr. Boesky paid Mr. Levine a percentage of the profits he made using that information. Mr. Levine pleaded guilty in June to four felony counts on insider trading.

Mr. Boesky's great personal wealth, which was estimated last year to be $200 million, and the fact that his fine is the largest of its kind in history have piqued the public's curiosity. But Mr. Boesky's case has significance far beyond personality and profits.

The securities industry is, for the most part, honest. But the very nature of insider trading has made it extremely difficult for the government to nab the few who cheat.

Mr. Boesky's apprehension is a huge feather in the cap of the Securities and Exchange Commission. He was generally considered to be the most successful and skillful in his profession. If the government can corner him, then it can corner any of them.

■

Attorney General Meese Tied to Iraqi Pipeline Affair

U.S. Attorney General Edwin Meese 3rd had received a memo from a friend in 1985 suggesting that a plan for building a $1 billion Iraqi pipeline would involve bribing Israeli officials to assure that Israel would not attack it, the *Los Angeles Times* reported Jan. 29, 1988. The pipeline was never built, but Meese's role in discussions about it was being probed by a special prosecutor, and the latest example of alleged misconduct by the attorney general immediately became a subject of heavy press coverage. Meese Feb. 1 denied any wrongdoing and said he had not been aware of the bribery scheme. He also said he was the victim of distorted and sensational news stories. Officials in the White House and Justice Department discounted rumors that Meese might resign over the latest scandal, unless he was eventually indicted. President Ronald Reagan Jan. 29 publicly reaffirmed his faith in Meese, a longtime friend.

Independent counsel James C. McKay Jan. 29 met with senior White House aides and warned them that his inquiry was very serious and that Meese had become its focal point. The pipeline probe was an outgrowth of McKay's investigation into Meese's role in the Wedtech Corp. scandal. McKay himself did not make any public statements. But sources familiar with his inquiry said the pipeline memo was being regarded as the most serious issue so far in the Meese investigation. In particular, McKay was said to be examining possible violations of the 1977 Foreign Corrupt Practices Act, which made the attorney general responsible for prosecuting U.S. citizens or companies that tried to bribe foreign officials.

After the *Los Angeles Times* disclosed the existence of the memo, the *New York Times* and the *Washington Post* Jan. 30-Feb. 4 followed up with in-depth examinations of the tangled pipeline deal. According to a variety of sources, the plan had its origins in 1982, when Syria—an ally of Iran in its war with Iraq, shut down a pipeline that carried Iraqi oil to the Mediterranean. Iraq's own oil imports had been destroyed at the outset of the war, so Baghdad became desperate to develop new overland export routes.

The Honolulu Advertiser

Honolulu, HI, February 3, 1988

Calls for Attorney General Edwin Meese to resign or be fired are regular as the seasons. Because of his high office he is a special embarrassment, even to an administration which has had at least 110 officials accused or convicted of illegal or unethical conduct.

The last go-round was in November when Meese gave the president such horrible advice on choosing a new Supreme Court justice. Before that were the questions about his slow response in the Iran-Contra scandal, questions still under investigation by an independent counsel. And there have been allegations in the Wedtech case, another on-going investigation.

The latest charges have to do with Meese's possible knowledge (from a close personal friend) and inaction on plans to bribe high Israeli officials as part of an Iraqi pipeline deal that never got off the ground.

As before, Meese is presumed innocent until proved otherwise. But he is having to spend more time defending himself in a lengthening list of cases than prosecuting cases as head of the Justice Department.

Although he should do so in this case, President Reagan hates to fire anyone, especially a close friend who is the last prominent aide who came with him from California.

And although he should do so, Meese is equally unlikely to resign. It's been clear for years that he has a very elastic view of propriety in government service and professes to see no wrong in his own actions.

Since Reagan won't fire him and Meese won't quit, the only hope would be to find him some lower-profile post for the remainder of the administration. Unfortunately for the nation, this probably won't happen either.

THE SUN

Baltimore, MD, February 2, 1988

The latest Ed Meese flap is the most disturbing yet in the seven-year-long soap opera that his insensitivity to propriety in public affairs has become. This story involves potential compromise of national security interests to the benefit of an influence-peddling friend and his client.

In a nutshell: Iraq wanted the Bechtel Corp. to build it a billion-dollar oil pipeline through Jordan. Iraqi and Bechtel officials needed insurance against the possibility that hostile Israel might destroy the pipeline even before it was completed and paid for. They wanted Israeli and U.S. promises of support. Bechtel brought in as a partner in the deal a Swiss businessman, Bruce Rappaport, known to have friends in the Israeli government. He hired E. Robert Wallach, a California lawyer who had just helped his friend Edwin Meese III with some financial problems.

At Mr. Wallach's urging, Mr. Meese got the National Security Council to support what had been a dead project. The NSC and Justice Department sought ways to complete the deal, but ultimately, at the urging of former NSC chief William Clark, it was abandoned as hopelessly compromised by the conflicting public and private interests.

The privatized aspect of Iran-contra was bad enough, with vultures swooping in to make money off a policy that had to be carried out in secret. This appears to be much worse — with the vultures trying to set policy.

Some newspapers have reported that Mr. Wallach wrote Mr. Meese a memo in which he indicated U.S. citizens might be involved in paying bribes to Israeli officials. That would be a clear violation of the law. For the attorney general of the United States to read such a memo and not act, even against a friend and benefactor — in fact, especially against such a person — would be the rankest dereliction of duty.

Mr. Meese says the implication that his friend contemplated an illegal bribe is based on only 10 words in a long Wallach-to-Meese memo, words he does not recall reading. But a special prosecutor told White House officials that the memo might be a problem — and that Mr. Meese is now "the focal point" of its inquiry into this affair.

After the special prosecutor briefed him, White House Chief of Staff Howard Baker said, "I see no reason on earth for the president to take any action unless and until it is made to appear that Mr. Meese has done something wrong . . . A person is innocent until proven guilty." That statement is beneath Mr. Baker. The presumption of innocence has to do with criminal guilt. It is not a standard for determining fitness for cabinet-level office. Mr. Meese appears to have let friendship if not sense of obligation influence him in a matter upon which the prospect of millions of dollars in private gain was entwined with complicated issues of international security — and that is wrong.

THE PLAIN DEALER
Cleveland, OH, February 2, 1988

White House moderates should have begun lobbying for Attorney General Edwin Meese's resignation long ago. Now they should insist on it. Reports during the weekend indicate that Meese at least was aware of plans to bribe an Israeli official in exchange for promises that Israel would not bomb an Iraqi pipeline. Those plans, made by a Meese crony who currently is under indictment for racketeering in the Wedtech scandal, complete the veneer of smug ethical disdain on Meese's already lackluster and sometimes painfully ignorant tenure at Justice.

According to independent counsel James C. McKay, who is leading the Wedtech probe, Meese received documents in which the possibility of trying to bribe Foreign Minister Shimon Peres was mentioned. At the time, Peres was Israel's prime minister. He was being asked for assurances that Israel would not threaten the $1 billion project, which would carry oil from Iraq to the Jordanian port of Aqaba. The Bechtel Group, an American engineering firm that supplied many Reagan administration officials, was seeking the pipeline contract. Bechtel entered a partnership with Bruce Rappaport, an expatriate Israeli millionaire, who in turn hired E. Robert Wallach, a lawyer and close friend of Meese. Wallach has since been indicted in the Wedtech affair.

The web becomes much more complicated, but the allegations are simple enough. Wallach is thought to have used his close association with Meese to expedite American and Israeli support for the pipeline. In the process, he managed to involve officials at the highest levels of American government—in Justice, in the National Security Council, even, apparently, in the CIA. At one point, he prevailed on the Overseas Private Investment Corp., a government agency, to bypass normal channels and present a new pipeline deal directly to Meese for review. According to one report, the package ended up being reviewed by a Justice attorney who owed his job to Wallach.

Fortunately, the deal collapsed. Neither Jordan nor Iraq was satisfied with Israel's promises. But even in failure, the scandal presents a familiar pattern. It is one in which influential private citizens try to manipulate American foreign policy; in which American agencies are lured into positions of compromise and discredit; in which the president and his administration are subverted by the complicity of their greedy intimates. The effect has been twofold: to lower public expectations for administration ethics, and to paint the president as weak and exploited. On both counts, the worst offender is the attorney general.

Meese was investigated by a special prosecutor after allegations of questionable financial dealings with people who later received administration posts. He has been questioned several times by a special prosecutor about his involvement in the Iran-contra scandal and roundly criticized for his suspiciously lax handling of the initial investigation. He has been the target of the independent probe into the Wedtech scandal. That's three different investigations, which is only half the story. At various times, he has said that all suspects are guilty; that hunger in America is anecdotal; that the Supreme Court need not be taken too seriously. Further, he apparently has lied about his investment in telephone companies that were seeking relief through his office.

The short form is this: His consistent failure to recognize and abide by fundamental standards of ethical appearance discredits the presidency, the administration and the Justice Department. His reign at Justice has been demoralizing. His advocacy of ill-formed judicial doctrines has embarrassed the president and at least two Supreme Court nominees. His ability to stay one step away from indictment might be a talent, but his constant flirtation with ethical limits undermines the authority of his office and the managerial judgment of his president.

Does Meese represent the sort of judicial legacy that Reagan will leave behind? The attorney general has yet to be indicted of criminal wrongdoing, but with each day it becomes more difficult to rationalize the disdainful judgment of a man who demeans the Justice Department, humiliates the White House and embarrasses the nation.

The Washington Post
Washington, DC, February 1, 1988

THE IMMEDIATE interest of the latest tale of intrigue to unfold around the name of Edwin Meese III is what its impact may be on the standing and tenure of the much-investigated attorney general. Press disclosures of the past few days have only begun exploring a matter that a special prosecutor has been probing for some months. Any impulse to rush to judgment of Mr. Meese has to be checked by considerations of fairness and by a recognition that the whole story remains to be told. But the political effect of these new disclosures and allegations about the government's chief law enforcement officer is bound to be severe.

If it is too early to say what if any laws or proprieties Mr. Meese might have violated, however, it is not too early to express astonishment at two particular aspects of this affair. The first concerns the easy access to his presence and office that Mr. Meese seems to have been ready to extend to old friends. In this case, his former lawyer, E. Bob Wallach, evidently brought to him a matter of the utmost legal and international delicacy. It concerned a plan for an American firm, the Bechtel Group, to build a billion-dollar oil pipeline for Iraq (blockaded by Iran) through Jordan and for ensuring Israel's sufferance for the project. Some part of the plan that went across Mr. Meese's Justice Department desk, it seems, concerned a payoff to Israel's Labor Party. No part of the plan is known to have been consummated, but what concerns the investigators now is whether Mr. Meese, whose lawyer describes his involvement as "very limited . . . passive only," handled the project in the right way.

The other astonishing thing is confirmation of the pattern of out-of-channels foreign-policy-making seen to such dismal effect in the Iran-contra affair. Smack in the middle of this episode of big money and high policy were assorted unofficial actors such as Mr. Wallach and Bruce Rappaport, a Swiss businessman who apparently was helping smooth Bechtel's way with the Israelis. Quite out of the action, from available reports, was the agency that should have been in the center of it—the State Department, where former Bechtel official George Shultz had recused himself from any dealings with his old firm. This may help explain why, in 1985, two secret projects were moving through Washington. One, involving the arms sales, was meant to reach out to Iran; the other, involving the pipeline, was to assist Iraq. Not surprisingly, both failed, leaving behind an array of wreckage of which Mr. Meese's current embarrassment is but one part.

MILWAUKEE SENTINEL
Milwaukee, WI, February 3, 1988

In hot water because of bribery allegations involving a proposed pipeline in Iraq that was never built, Atty. Gen. Edwin Meese III Monday asserted that he did nothing wrong and didn't even remember reading a controversial passage in a key memo.

And some reports about the probe by independent counsel James McKay say there is not enough evidence to seek charges against Meese in the case.

But criminality aside, Meese's judgment in this matter and some others is highly questionable.

Meese is linked to the Iraqi pipeline controversy because the classified memo was written to him by Robert Wallach, a close friend, unofficial adviser and former personal attorney.

Allegations in published reports suggest Wallach sought administration support for the $1 billion pipeline in which Wallach had a financial interest, part of which involved pay-offs to Israel for not interfering with the project.

Wallach currently is under indictment on racketeering charges in a scandal involving no-bid contracts for government defense projects. Meese is under investigation in the same case.

Given their close relationship, Meese should have had an agreement with Wallach as soon as he became part of the Reagan administration that the two maintain an arms-length arrangement on any matters involving government policy.

Merely accepting a memo on this kind of issue can give the appearance of doing a favor for a friend, or at least of giving such treatment consideration.

While such conduct might be acceptable in private business, it gives rise to suspicion when one party is representing the public interest in a private matter.

It is noteworthy that Secretary of State George P. Shultz sent a handwritten letter to then-Israeli Prime Minister Shimon Peres saying that he, Shultz, was a former top executive of the firm that was to build the pipeline, and would not deal with Israel on the matter.

This is the kind of discretion that has too often been absent in the Reagan administration. The result has been the justified suspicion that the bonds of friendship involve special privilege, even when that may not be the case.

Telegraph Herald

Dubuque, IA, February 12, 1988

Edwin Meese III, attorney general of the United States, should resign.

That the nation's chief law enforcement officer himself has been in so many brushes with the law — never convicted, mind you — and again is being investigated for possible illegal activity became an embarrassment to President Reagan long ago. Though never convicted and never even indicted, Meese, investigations have shown, has conducted himself improperly.

The president, Meese's long-time friend and supporter, apparently has allowed loyalty and friendship to obscure his vision. Reagan can't see the black mark Meese has cast on his administration. Reagan can't see that his hopes for effectiveness in his last months in office will be hampered as long as Meese is in his cabinet. Since Reagan can't see that, Meese himself should recognize this reality, save the president the embarrassment and discomfort of firing a good friend, and step down.

Meese's defenders are correct when they say the attorney general is innocent until proven guilty. But in government and politics, being innocent and being a liability can be altogether different. The suggestion by some — including conservative columnist William Rusher, whose views appear on today' page — that this is a liberal-media witch hunt are ridiculous. Rather than addressing the facts and defending the propriety and legality of Meese's conduct, they try to cloud the issue by charging bias.

Meese has survived investigations concerning his use of office to intervene on behalf of a friend, Robert Wallach, on a number of matters, including federal defense contracts and appointment as ambassador to the U.N. Human Rights Commission.

Meese has survived investigations concerning receipt of loans from several people who obtained high-level federal jobs.

Meese, meanwhile, is under investigation for his actions involving telephone industry regulation while he held stock in regional phone companies, his investments and, most recently, his possible role in, or knowledge of, a possible payoff plan to win Israeli support for a proposed $1 billion Iraqi pipeline.

Even if he survives those investigations, too, Meese will have been of little service to the president. Indeed, he will have been a liability. Guilty or innocent, the attorney general should allow the president to complete his term without being encumbered by a Cabinet member on the hot seat.

The Burlington Free Press

Burlington, VT, February 3, 1988

Attorney General Edwin Meese III wants Americans to believe that his latest brush with the law is just another of those unfortunate situations in which he so often finds himself. He asks too much!

This time Meese says his memory failed him. It seems Meese doesn't remember reading the critical part of a lengthy classified memo in which longtime friend E. Robert Wallach is said to describe a payoff plan to assure a proposed $1 billion Iraqi pipeline was protected from Israeli bombing. As attorney general, Meese would have been obligated to prosecute any American involved in an attempt to bribe a foreign official.

The latest allegation against Meese comes even as an independent counsel is investigating Meese's involvement with Wedtech Inc., a New York defense contractor that is alleged to have secured government contracts by bribing numerous public officials.

Meese, of course, was censured by Congress for his handling of the early investigation involving the sale of weapons to Iran and the illegal transfer of money from the sale into secret accounts for use by the Contras.

It's impossible to understand how a public official who so often has come under investigation for supposedly unethical or illegal conduct can remain in office — especially when the office is that of the nation's top law enforcement official.

Meese's problems began before he was confirmed as attorney general by the Senate in early 1985. In fact, it was former President Gerald R. Ford who suggested in 1984 that Meese resign as White House counselor as a result of Meese's failure to report reimbursements he received for 30 trips he made as an aide to President Reagan.

Meese's supporters argue that Meese has never been indicted for any of his alleged offenses. But Americans really ought to judge public officials by a tougher standard than that. His supporters conveniently forget that a 1985 staff report by the Office of Government Ethics concluded that Meese violated federal conflict-of-interest rules. The ruling was subsequently overturned by the agency director.

They forget, too, that in June 1987, the Office of Government Ethics concluded that Meese violated financial disclosure requirements after investing $60,000 with a Wedtech Inc. officer. And the General Accounting Office on Aug. 4, 1987 charged that Meese failed to properly disclose the assets held, purchased and sold by a business partnership formed by Meese and his wife.

Equally disturbing is President Reagan's continued support for Meese. The question Americans should want answered by Reagan is not whether Meese will go, but "when?"

The Seattle Times

Seattle, WA, February 2, 1988

ATTORNEY General Edwin Meese called in reporters yesterday to deny any knowledge of possible illegalities in a 1985 Mideast oil-pipeline project, an issue that has rocked political and government circles in Washington, D.C., and Israel.

It was yet another instance of what presidential candidate Richard Gephardt, D-Mo., has called the "disconcerting" need for the nation's chief law-enforcement officer "to spend so much of his time trying to prove" he hasn't violated any laws. And, it raised fresh questions about Meese's capacity to serve as attorney general and the negative impacts of his tenure on the remaining days of the Reagan administration.

Isn't it past time, in fact, for Meese to step aside?

Meese felt compelled to speak publicly yesterday, he said, because of "a cascade of misinformation, false headlines, half-truths, innuendo and misunderstanding of the law." He was referring to newspaper reports that a special prosecutor, James McKay, has notified the White House he is continuing to investigate Meese's role in a never-consummated private pipeline venture pushed by E. Robert Wallach, a longtime Meese associate.

Edwin Meese   Bill Plympton

Because of his close ties to Meese, Wallach had been hired by private entrepreneurs promoting a pipeline to transport Iraqi oil via Jordan, to replace Persian Gulf oil facilities destroyed by Iran. Meese yesterday denied that a Wallach memo to him suggested Israeli officials be paid off in exchange for promises not to interfere with the project. (Israeli officials earlier dismissed talk of bribes as "complete nonsense.")

As he has in the past, Meese declared: "I am convinced a thorough inquiry conducted in a professional manner . . . inevitably will result in a conclusion favorable to me."

He expressed similar thoughts last May at the beginning of the independent prosecutor's probe of Meese's connections with Wedtech Corp., a New York firm being investigated for possible fraud in obtaining no-bid federal defense contracts reserved for minority enterprises.

In 1984, another special investigation found no legal basis for prosecuting Meese over allegations he'd helped get federal jobs for people who'd given Meese financial assistance in the past. But the prosecutor emphasized his investigation did not cover matters of propriety and ethics.

As White House chief of staff Howard Baker says, Meese has done nothing wrong from a technical standpoint. But Meese's penchant for political tackiness allows little room for the respect due the American system of laws or to the example-setting obligations of the nation's chief legal officer.

About the best that can be said for Meese is that he has been politically loyal to the president. He can best demonstrate that loyalty now by leaving his post.

"WHAT PIPELINE?"

THE ARIZONA REPUBLIC
Phoenix, AZ, February 7, 1988

ONCE upon a time the international construction giant, the Bechtel Group, had a wonderful idea: "Let us build an oil pipeline from Iraq's Kirkuk oil fields through Jordan to the Red Sea port of Aqaba."

All the engineers and bankers nodded their heads and agreed. It was a splendid notion. Then one gloomy consultant pointed out that Israel and Iraq didn't exactly get along, and who could forget what the Israeli Air Force did to that nasty Iraqi nuclear reactor. What to do?

Bechtel did what everybody in America does when they need to get something done: it hired a lobbyist, Robert Wallach, who was an old law-school chum of Attorney General Edwin Meese.

"Maybe," Wallach told Bechtel, "we can get the Reagan administration to twist Israel's arm into promising not to bomb our nice pipeline." So Wallach sent a letter to his old buddy asking for this very thing.

Now, Meese took no action on the request. Wallach was disappointed, as was Bechtel. Even though Israel did agree on its own not to bomb it because Jerusalem was dancing a diplomatic pas de deux with Jordan's King Hussein, the pipeline never got past the blueprint phase. And everyone lived not-so-happily ever after.

Well, not exactly. Enter independent counsel James McKay. He was investigating Wallach and the massive Wedtech fraud in the South Bronx. In December, McKay cleared Meese of any wrongdoing in that affair. Apparently disappointed that he couldn't get Meese on the Wedtech rap, McKay began poking into the defunct pipeline scheme.

Eureka! McKay found a pot of allegations: Wallach's letter to Meese, it was said, hinted that a bribe might be paid to then-Prime Minister Shimon Peres for an Israeli insurance policy against aerial bombardment.

Even if Meese didn't go along with the bribe idea, McKay harumphed, he nevertheless had violated the Federal Corrupt Practices Act by not acting against his old schoolmate.

Meese took umbrage, calling McKay's pipe dream a "cascade of misinformation, false headlines, half-truths, innuendo." Peres denies that any bribe was solicited, offered or paid. The White House has agreed to declassify the Wallach letter, insisting that it contains no mention of a bribe.

The noble concept of prosecutorial discretion apparently doesn't exist for such independent counsel as James McKay. They are footloose types, following their noses willy-nilly anywhere they lead, from the South Bronx to the Gulf of Aqaba, impugning the honesty of the leader of one of Washington's closest allies, meddling in sensitive foreign policy, hurling around unfounded allegations, and attacking Ed Meese because — well, because he's Ed Meese.

And that is why the Good Judge of the East, Federal Appeals Court Justice Laurence Silberman, pronounced the independent-counsel law unconstitutional.

The Salt Lake Tribune
*Salt Lake City, UT,
February 4, 1988*

As U.S. attorney general, Edwin Meese III has been more liability than asset for the Reagan administration. Unfortunately, neither he nor the president seem to see it that way.

The latest disclosure prompting Mr. Meese's defensive denials concerns evidence that he both helped a friend get government consideration for a private oil pipeline deal and neglected to see possible illegal proposals in a memorandum about the matter. Too typically, another Meese muddle.

In answering accusations from an ongoing independent counsel investigation of Meese transactions, the attorney general said Monday he didn't previously read the memo in question, but that on re-reading it, he gained no impression of "illegality." That's not the form in which the issue surfaced.

Rather, it's been reported that James E. McKay, the independent counsel probing Mr. Meese's past, found in a communication from E. Robert Wallach to the attorney general a suggestion that top Israeli officials might be encouraged, with financial donations, to prevent the pipeline, built from Iraq to Jordan's Red Sea port at Aqaba, from being attacked during Israeli-Arab warfare. At this point, Mr. Meese refuses to release the memo, claiming it is "classified."

The proposed pipeline, in fact, was never built, but apparently Mr. Meese somehow made it possible for Mr. Wallach, a Meese friend and attorney representing the project's promoters, to discuss the subject, while it still simmered, with National Security Council staff members. Also, legal questions about it submitted to the Justice Department were reportedly given approval by an attorney Mr. Wallach helped gain a Justice Department position, but were accorded an opposite interpretation by other department analysts.

It's one of those knotted webworks requiring patient untying, but it's fair to wonder why Mr. Meese is repeatedly the central figure in these entanglements. He became the subject of an independent counsel probe because previously discovered evidence implicated him in influence peddling for Defense Department contracts.

In 1984, Mr. Meese, prior to becoming attorney general, was investigated by another independent counsel after it was alleged he helped friends who loaned him money obtain federal jobs. That produced no indictments.

Next, his initial handling of the Iran-Contra discoveries was considered sloppy and unprofessional with critics claiming that, too, is traceable to an overweening concern for political acquaintances and allies.

A Ronald Reagan spear carrier since the president's days as California governor, Mr. Meese was effective as the chief executive's White House domestic adviser. However, as attorney general he's been consistently in so much hot water, calls for his resignation have reverberated like a constant echo.

He hasn't accommodated before and unless a criminal charge is actually filed against him, isn't apt to this time. But at least when Mr. Reagan departs the White House in 11 months, it's also, "Adios Mr. Meese," and, "How about taking your friends with you?"

Two Top Justice Dept. Aides Quit

Two top Justice Department officials abruptly quit their posts March 29, 1988 in protest of Attorney General Edwin Meese 3rd's continuing legal entanglements. Neither man, Deputy Attorney General Arnold I. Burns, holding the department's No. 2 post, nor Assistant Attorney General William F. Weld, head of the department's criminal division, publicly explained the reason behind their moves. But the two men were said to have informed White House Chief of Staff Howard Baker Jr. two weeks before of their concern that the protracted criminal investigations focusing on Meese had brought the department to a standstill and undermined its credibility. But the word from President Ronald Reagan was that removing Meese was out of the question, promoting the officials' resignations. Recurrent calls for Meese's resignation had been heard as independent prosecutor James C. McKay continued investigations of the attorney general's involvement with a proposed Mideast oil pipeline and Meese's efforts to help the Wedtech Corp., a bankrupt defense contractor enmeshed in a kickback scandal.

The Burns and Weld resignations were accompanied by those of their four top aides: Associate Deputy Attorneys General Randy Levine and B. Boykin Rose for Burns and Acting Deputy Assistant Attorney General Mark Robinson and Special Counsel Jane Serene for Weld.

The resignations evoked fresh calls from the Democrats for Meese's resignation. Republicans expressed concern that Meese's troubles could stain the party's campaign efforts in an election year. President Reagan conveyed continued confidence in his aide, responding to reporters' shouts at a Rose Garden ceremony March 30. "I have every confidence in him," Reagan told them. "He's been a friend for 20 years, and I'm not going to comment any further on what's going on." Meese saw "no reason to resign." "Business is operating as usual at the Justice Department," he said March 30.

The Honolulu Advertiser

Honolulu, HI, April 9, 1988

Attorney General Edwin Meese and former White House aide Lyn Nofziger are more than just a disgrace to the Reagan administration. They have come to typify what is bad about it.

Were he not so bad in one of the nation's most important jobs, Democrats might want to urge that Reagan stick by Meese to the bitter end. He promises to be one of the year's better election years with Vice President Bush running on the Reagan legacy.

Meese's latest blunder is almost, but not quite, beyond belief. His choice for the number two job in the embattled Justice Department is under fire for belonging to clubs that discriminate. The nominee also faces allegations — from a woman named Sinner, yet — that they had an affair and he let her write $120,000 in illegal checks to herself. Congress and Johnny Carson will have fun with that.

In turn, Meese is under fire for rushing to fill the spots vacated by protest resignations and not getting proper background checks.

The attorney general is innocent unless proven guilty of any criminal wrongdoing in various allegations against him. But other evidence indicates he's already guilty of monumental bad judgement, carelessness and cronyism in his dealings.

Nofziger, on the other hand, was found guilty by a jury of illegally lobbying administration officials (including Meese) after he left the White House. He got a light (90-day) sentence yesterday. It is suspended pending appeal.

But Nofziger has set a standard for public arrogance. He terms such influence peddling as "like running a stop sign" and labels as "lousy" a law that bans high-ranking executive branch officials from lobbying their former agencies within a year of leaving office.

President Reagan is famous for being loyal to his old friends. But in these cases it seems he is being loyal to incompetence and sleaze.

The Dallas Morning News

Dallas, Texas, April 1, 1988

Attorney General Edwin Meese still has the support of his boss and longtime friend, the president. But the unexpected resignations this week of two top Justice Department officials and four of their aides should make it abundantly clear that the nation's chief law enforcement officer has lost the confidence of many of those with whom he works.

Although it is possible that some of the criticism may be politically motivated, it still is disconcerting that seldom a month goes by that Meese is not accused of questionable dealings. A government special prosecutor has been investigating the attorney general for nearly a year because of his involvement with the scandal-plagued Wedtech Corp. and with a $1 billion Iraqi pipeline project and because of some personal financial affairs.

So far, Meese has avoided conviction, or even indictment, despite the barrage of criticism. And he certainly is entitled to every presumption of innocence that American justice affords. But one indisputable fact, made even more evident by the resignations, is that his legal problems have become too much of a distraction to the Justice Department.

Having the attorney general under investigation on so many different fronts severely tarnishes the image of a department whose integrity should be above reproach. And just as important, the heavy demands those investigations place on the man's time and attention deprive the department of a leader whose energy should be devoted entirely to the duties of his office.

President Reagan is standing firmly by his embattled attorney general. Such loyalty, however, only is making matters worse for the overall workings of the Justice Department. The president needs to see the untenable situation for what it is and ask for his friend's resignation. If he cannot, Meese should spare his boss the anguish of witnessing a Justice Department in disarray by quitting. Now is the time for the attorney general to return the loyalty the president has shown him.

The continued controversy surrounding Meese's tenure as attorney general ought to serve as an object lesson for those who aspire to become the next chief executive. Much too often during the past several decades, the Cabinet post has been used by Democratic and Republican presidents alike to reward old friends and allies for services rendered. Such cronyism has to stop.

A new president could demonstrate his sincere commitment to high ethical behavior in government no better way than to appoint an attorney general whose legal experience justifies the honor of being the country's top lawyer and whose personal credentials are as impeccable as Caesar's wife's.

Herald ⚜ News

Fall River, MA, April 1, 1988

The resignation of key aides in the Department of Justice has created fresh calls, especially from Congress, for the resignation of Attorney General Meese.

The attorney general's role in the Iran-Contra affair, the Wedtech scandal, the Iraqi pipeline and in the dealings of some telephone companies is being investigated by an independent counsel, and has been for over a year.

As one scandal after another broke, Meese himself, with the President's backing, has protested his innocence of any wrongdoing, and in fact, no indictments against him have been returned.

Now, however, some of his principal aides have resigned, and others are rumored on the verge of following suit.

As a result Elliott Richardson, no mean judge of federal departments and himself a lifetime Republican, now says he does not see how Meese can continue to direct the Department of Justice.

It should be stressed that Richardson's remark makes no reference to the attorney general's involvement in the various scandals being probed. All that he said was that he does not understand how he can continue to conduct the Justice Department whose business must be conducted day by day in the nation's interests.

Furthermore, the aides who re-signed gave no public reason for their action, but it is hard to construe it as anything but the equivalent of a vote of "no confidence" in the Attorney General.

President Reagan has reiterated his own confidence in Meese, but the attorney general himself might wonder whether he is best serving his faithful friend in the White House by continuing in office.

Understandably he may not wish to take any action that could be interpreted as an admission of wrongdoing.

But it should be possible for him to take what in effect would be a leave of absence until the investigation of the affairs in which he may have participated is complete.

A leave of absence would permit the appointment of someone who could take his place during whatever interim there may be, and it should be borne in mind that the entire administration will be going out of office at the end of the year.

The President will clearly refuse to take any action forcing Meese to resign, but the attorney general could act himself in the interests of the Department of Justice and indeed of the Reagan administration as a whole.

If he will not resign for fear of the inferences that would be drawn if he did, then at least he should stand aside until the current investigation is over.

Lincoln Journal

Lincoln, NE, April 4, 1988

Obviously, Edwin Meese III is innocent until he's proved guilty. In truth, he hasn't even been charged with anything, and a special prosecutor says at this point there isn't enough evidence to indict the attorney general.

But none of that offsets the fact that Meese continues to be under investigation and is an increasing embarrassment to President Reagan and a burden for the Justice Department.

His competence and ethics have been questioned repeatedly since the moment he was appointed. Scandal swirls about him. Things have reached the point where there is no way that Meese can deal with his personal legal problems and have enough time and energy left over to do a decent job of running the Justice Department.

To have political foes after your scalp is one thing. It's another matter entirely when friends tell you to leave. Some of Meese's closest associates in the Justice Department have quit — because, it is plain, Meese wouldn't. And Strom Thurmond, ranking Republican on the Senate Judiciary Committee, now regards the attorney general as a GOP albatross.

Reagan may be standing by Meese, but Vice President George Bush is understandably edging toward an "Ed who?" stance. As long as the attorney general remains in office, Democrats will be encouraged to cry "sleaze, sleaze" throughout this year's political campaign.

The president's loyalty to his friend is admirable in a way, one supposes. What would be more admirable would be for Reagan to show greater sensitivity to public opinion and respect for the reputation of the Justice Department and his administration. He should tell Meese it's time to leave.

As for Meese's loyalty, it's clearly not directed to the president. One doesn't put one's friends in the difficult position in which Meese has placed Reagan.

A special prosecutor's interim conclusion of insufficient evidence to indict is an inadequate standard for an attorney general. Nor will a hasty scramble to fill vacancies at the Justice Department solve all the problems there. The good of the president and the nation requires Meese's prompt departure.

Portland Press Herald

Pittsburgh, PA, March 31, 1988

The tangle of questionable financial deals and actions surrounding Attorney General Edwin Meese III has now spread to the Justice Department itself.

The resignations this week of the department's two ranking lawyers make it plain that Meese's effectiveness as the nation's top law enforcement officer is over. What's more, Meese's conduct strongly suggests that it should be.

At the heart of the deals enmeshing Meese is his longtime friend and former lawyer, E. Robert Wallach. In December, Wallach was indicted on federal charges of defrauding the Wedtech Corp and of accepting funds to influence Meese to benefit Wedtech. Despite that indictment — obtained by his own department — Meese persists in publicly affirming his friendship for Wallach.

For a year, special prosecutor James C. McKay has been investigating Meese's 1982 intervention with the Pentagon, at Wallach's repeated request, leading to award of a no-bid $32 million Army engine contract to Wedtech.

In addition, Wallach played a central role in financing an Iraqi pipeline project for Israel. That project, which was never built, has raised serious questions as to Meese's knowledge of activities in violation of the Foreign Corrupt Practices Act against which he, as attorney general, should have taken action.

The trail of dubious dealings, now including suggestions Meese used undue influence in obtaining a $40,000-a-year charity job for his wife, would be enough to cast doubt on the lowliest government official. But an attorney general must be held to a higher standard, one closer to Benjamin Disraeli's definition of justice as "truth in action."

It is a standard Meese fails. He should resign.

The Oregonian

Portland, OR, April 1, 1988

President Reagan's loyalty to beleaguered appointees is well-known and in many ways commendable. But with regard to Attorney General Edwin Meese III, president and appointee both should recognize that the immediate issue is not loyalty or guilt but failure to perform competently in an important and sensitive job.

The resignations of two high-ranking Justice Department officials and four of their subordinates should alarm the president and provoke serious scrutiny of the situation in the department. If scrutiny supports news reports that the resignations were prompted by low departmental morale and subordinates' perceptions that Meese's preoccupation with his own legal problems was harming the department, Meese should depart — not because he should be assumed guilty of any crime but because the nation needs a well-run Justice Department.

The holder of a Cabinet office should be willing to leave that office when he becomes a burden on it.

We were not convinced that Meese was the best choice for attorney general when he was nominated by Reagan in 1984. But we also have a deep aversion to persons being forced from office by allegations of impropriety unsubstantiated through a legal process. Fairness demands that the accused have his day in court before judgment is rendered.

The public interest, however, also demands something — that holders of public offices be able to meet the day-to-day obligations of the job. Public office is not a property right to be lost only by court action. Whether his problem — personal or professional — is of his own making or due to outside forces, the holder of a position of trust should recognize when the problem overwhelms effectiveness.

In the case of the attorney general, Reagan should take special note that the new calls for Meese's resignation were not provoked by opponents of his administration but by the resignations of his own appointees, including the second-ranking official in the Justice Department.

The implication that the Justice Department as a credible, functioning agency is in trouble puts obligations on the nation's chief executive that outweigh the admirable quality of loyalty. If Meese does not resign and cannot administer, Reagan should find another, less-critical job for his old friend.

THE SACRAMENTO BEE

Sacramento, CA, March 31, 1988

The resignation en masse of the deputy attorney general, the head of the Justice Department's criminal division and their four top aides is not, as the White House would have it, mere end-of-administration job shuffling. They resigned, according to everyone the six have spoken to, because of their conviction that the Justice Department couldn't function honorably under an attorney general who is currently the subject of four criminal investigations, whose friends are under indictment and who has had to excuse himself from participation in 20 of the department's most important cases because of his personal associations with those accused or, as in the case of the department's challenge of the special prosecutor law, because of his personal stake in the outcome.

"These are," as one department official said, "truly resignations of conscience." And they have made all the more conspicuous its absence in the one quarter where it's most needed.

The criminal division head, William F. Weld, apparently has been bucking Attorney General Edwin Meese for some time, protesting his handling of the early Iran-Contra investigations and arguing against his decision to attack the constitutionality of the special prosecutor law. Deputy Attorney General Arnold I. Burns had been considered more of a Meese loyalist. Yet both now agree that things have "gone too far," in the words of another associate. "Meese's troubles were so all-encompassing that something had to be done. The proud traditions of the Justice Department were being dragged down by this."

They took their concerns first to the White House, where the shared conclusion of these two very different men should have been compelling — as it was to the growing list of Republican and Democratic party leaders calling for Meese's resignation. But they were told that the president would not ask Meese to leave. So they left. It was the honorable thing to do. Meese is said to have been shocked by it.

Meanwhile, Meese himself continues to gamble on some kind of personal vindication — or anyway another non-indictment — as if his personal fate were the most important issue here. His incomprehension of the larger stakes, of the cloud of impropriety under which the entire Justice Department must operate as long as he stubbornly stands his ground, is of a piece with the ethical tunnel-vision that landed him in the middle of one after another of these scandals in the first place.

The San Diego Union

San Diego, CA, March 31, 1988

How much longer will Attorney General Edwin Meese continue to embarrass not only the Justice Department but also Ronald Reagan and the Republican Party by clinging to office despite the criminal investigations being conducted against him?

This President is well known for his loyalty to long-term friends and aides who have become caught up in investigations of wrongdoing. No matter how dire the circumstances, there is little reason to believe that Mr. Reagan ever would demand the resignation of Mr. Meese, whom he described yesterday as "a friend for 20 years."

So, as we have suggested before, it is up to the attorney general himself to ponder how much disgrace he is willing to heap on the President and his party by hanging tough while special prosecutor James C. McKay probes his financial dealings.

Mr. Meese's effectiveness as the nation's top law-enforcement officer was eviscerated long ago by the dismal litany of poor judg-

ment and ethically questionable activities uncovered by various inquiries into his conduct. The resignations of six senior Justice Department officials on Tuesday vividly illustrate the extent to which Mr. Meese's mounting legal problems are convulsing the department. The attorney general is, in fact, far too distracted now to manage the day-to-day workings of the Justice Department.

Meantime, the stain created by

Mr. Meese has begun to tarnish, by political extension, Vice President George Bush as well as Mr. Reagan. If the attorney general stubbornly holds onto his office until the fall, his record is almost certain to be an issue and a liability for the GOP nominee.

Mr. Meese is indeed entitled to a presumption of innocence in the criminal allegations being examined by the special prosecutor. But the office of attorney general imposes a higher ethical standard than simply being free of felony indictments. By his lack of judgment and a sustained pattern of skirting the laws he is sworn to uphold, Mr. Meese already has failed the test.

Integrity cannot be restored to the Justice Department with Mr. Meese at the helm. The longer he remains, the greater the damage will be to the administration, Ronald Reagan's standing, justice in this country, and the Republican cause. It is time for the attorney general to put these larger considerations ahead of personal pride.

The Evening Gazette

Worcester, MA, April 1, 1988

It's unfortunate that President Reagan continues to defend his attorney general and close friend, Edwin Meese. While Meese has not been found guilty of criminal activities, he has long since undermined the integrity of the Justice Department and become a burden on the judicial system.

For some time, Meese has lived and worked under a cloud of suspicion that has all but eroded his effectiveness. A special prosecutor is looking into his involvement in the notorious Iraqi oil-pipeline caper and a kickback scheme involving a New York military contractor. The scope of these matters is so serious that Meese should have resigned long ago.

Like anybody else under investigation, the attorney general is entitled to a fair and thorough review of the evidence. But it should be remembered that he is the highest law-enforcement officer in the land and must set a moral tone above reproach. The country looks to him to make sure the laws are obeyed, the Constitution protected.

The recent resignations of two top Justice Department officials, Deputy Attorney General Arnold Burns and Assistant Attorney General William Weld, and some of their aides indicate that Meese's problems are interfering with the department's work. Solicitor General Charles Fried urged Meese to resign.

The administration of justice in a democracy is more important than any person. No individual should be allowed to cast a shadow over it, and Meese should know that. It is regrettable that he continues to cling to his office.

Perhaps he is encouraged by President Reagan's stand: "I have every confidence in him." Unfortunately, that confidence is no longer shared by the public. Reagan makes a dreadful mistake by backing Meese to the hilt.

Meese must leave and rid the administration of a major embarrassment and the Justice Department of an interfering distraction. Doing otherwise is a disservice to both his president and the American people.

Post-Tribune

Gary, IN, April 1, 1988

Ed Meese is a political cartoonist's delight. From the beginning of his tenure as attorney general, it was easy to lampoon him. Some of it was lighthearted.

But there is nothing light or amusing these days about the man who heads the Justice Department. He is a pathetic figure who insists, like the emperor, that he has clothes on. That does not make it so.

The recent resignations of more top figures in the department, including its No. 2 man, show how far the morale of his staff has fallen. Two of those who quit told Meese he had "lost his moral authority" to lead the Justice Department. That is a strikingly compelling reason for him to leave.

Another solid reason is what he does to the Reagan administration's credibility. He is a political liability, as the president's chief of staff and the vice president have told him. It is also reported that Nancy Reagan agrees. Being a political liability is bad enough, but this involves not just a candidate or some minor official — it involves the president of the United States.

Meese apparently does not see that there is a problem, which suggests that picturing him as a bumbling, well-meaning fellow is being charitable. Reagan seems to be immobilized either by the bond of friendship or the inability to understand what the fuss is about.

The president deserves better from the head of the Justice Department. More important, the country deserves better.

Part III:
Gun Control & Vigilantism

The debate about gun control is revived with each publicized shooting incident. The deaths of John Lennon and Sen. Robert Kennedy, the attempted assassination of President Reagan and the Bernhard Goetz case stirred emotions but produced no consensus. There are three primary views in contention. One is to do nothing; guns do not kill, people do. A second is that a handgun exists only to kill and its production and possession should be tightly restricted. A third is that certain kinds of violent encounters are more likely to have lethal consequences if guns happen to be readily available and that society ought to devise ways of reducing that availability among people likely to be involved in such encounters.

Gun-control advocates argue that the first view is correct but misleading. Though people pull triggers and some triggers are pulled by people so determined that the gun is merely a tool, they argue that many crimes are committed by persons who are enraged, drunk or looking for trouble. People in such cases let the means at hand determine what kind of force they will employ and against whom. To substantiate their view, gun-control advocates point to the numerous studies that show that fights which occur in settings where guns are present are more likely to be fatal than those that occur where guns are absent.

The second view is widely considered to be wrong or at, least, unfeasible in that there are handguns in at least one-fifth of all American households. In addition, the vast majority of these weapons are never used to threaten or injure anyone. And, while banning the production of new handguns might prevent that stock from increasing, and the buying back existing guns might reduce that stock slightly, it would be enormously expensive and, without production controls, futile. Larger reductions would require confiscation and run afoul of the constitutional right to bare arms. Critics argue that even if all these policies were adopted, and the reductions of ownership substantial (say, by 50%) the remaining arsenal could easily support current rates of robbery at gunpoint for some time.

Neither of these policies is likely to be adopted because the average legislator simply cannot afford to come before his or her constituents with the following proposal: "Your government, having failed to protect you against crime, now proposes to strip from you what you regard as an effective means of self-defense."

A third view is one that policy-makers have begun to take more seriously, despite the strong lobbying power of the National Rifle Association. That is, the recognition that people have a right to own guns but do not have the right to use them criminally, such as shooting a tresspasser. A 1974 Massachusetts law, for instance, that severely penalizes people who are found in possession of guns while committing a crime or for participating in a violent dispute, has proven quite effective as such incidents have reduced in that state. Federal and state laws now make it unlawful for convicted felons, ex-addicts and mental defectives to possess a handgun. In addition, in many states and most big cities, it is illegal to carry a concealed handgun, except for a small number of people with police permits.

Vigilantism began in America in the 19th century as a response to the absence of law on the frontier. Vigilantism was initiated by the settlers who were inadequately protected by the law, but it gained support, and often leadership, from members of the American political, intellectual and business establishment. Governors, senators, judges, ministers, and even two presidents—Andrew Jackson and Theodore Rosevelt—were vigilantes or vigilante supporters.

Historically, vigilantes have found it difficult to distinguish between taking the law into their own hands when it could not function and taking the law into their hands when it did not function as they wanted it to. Therefore, in the 20th century, vigilante movements turned their attention away from horse thieves, cattle rustlers, counterfeiters and assorted criminals and outlaws, and toward street crime. Because of this, vigilante violence is often perceived to have a strong politically conservative bias.

The similarities between the wild west heroes and modern urban avengers are clearly identifiable. The concurrent social conditions are also similar. Violence abounded in the wild west because there was a lack of organized, effective justice. Many would argue that similar conditions exist in many of America's large cities. Sociologists describe these conditions in many different ways, but usually summarize them by the term "alienation." Average citizens can develop an acute feeling that justice is not being done while they search for and demand a solution. The lone urban avenger in the Charles Bronson film *Death Wish* is the product of this alienation and may have partially created the cultural environment by which Bernhard Goetz acted. However, the difference between Goetz and the wild west figures is that he represents the alienated middle class of urban America.

Senate Bans Armor-Piercing Bullets

The U.S. Senate March 6, 1986 voted to ban the manufacture and import of armor-piercing bullets. Ninety-seven senators voted against the so-called "cop-killer" bullets. The lone holdout was Sen. Steven D. Symms (R, Idaho). The House had voted a similar ban in 1985, 400-21. There was one difference, one that gun advocates complained of as a serious flaw: the House measure said bullets already in store inventories could not be sold, the Senate bill did not.

BUFFALO EVENING NEWS

Buffalo, NY, January 5, 1986

AFTER YEARS of effort, Congress at last seems ready to outlaw the "cop-killer bullet" — an armor-piercing projectile that easily penetrates the "bullet-proof" vests often worn by police officers. The House recently approved such a ban by an overwhelming 400-21 vote, and a similar measure is before the Senate.

Ordinary bullets, which are made from lead, flatten on impact, but the so-called cop-killer bullets are hardened through the use of such metals as tungsten, iron, brass or bronze. Sen. Daniel P. Moynihan, D-N.Y., who is sponsoring the legislation in the Senate, said: "These bullets serve no purpose but to kill and wound police officers."

The protective vests used by police will stop ordinary bullets, but they are useless against hardened, armor-piercing bullets. In an impressive California test, a cop-killer bullet penetrated four bullet-proof vests and five Los Angeles telephone books placed behind the vests.

Several states already have banned the use of such bullets, but the majority have not. Thus a federal ban on the importing, manufacturing or sale of the bullets will fill an important need.

The legislation is supported by law enforcement groups across the country, including the International Association of Chiefs of Police, the Fraternal Order of Police, the National Sheriffs' Association, the National Troopers' Coalition and the Federal Law Enforcement Officers Association.

The National Rifle Association and other sportsmen groups have objected to some aspects of the legislation in the past, fearing restrictions on legitimate sporting activities, but many of their objections have now been met through changes in the measures.

The cop-killer bullet legislation ought to receive top priority when the Senate session is resumed this month. Police officers often have to risk their lives in the performance of their duties. They deserve the added protection afforded by this overdue measure.

The Times-Picayune
The States-Item

New Orleans, LA, February 9, 1984

We find it hard to understand what the problem is with bills before Congress to ban the manufacture, import, sale and use of new-style armor-piercing handgun and rifle bullets. The chief opponent, predictably, is the gun lobby led by the National Rifle Association, but its complaint doesn't even have the stopping power of a popgun. The bills, an NRA official argues, "are nothing other than one more attempt to separate law-abiding gun owners and the nation's sportsmen from their firearms and ammunition."

The new bullets were designed for use by police, but they have been banned by most police departments because of the danger their power and range pose to bystanders. They are small-caliber, pointed bullets made of steel or hard brass sometimes coated with Teflon; they fly fast and keep their shape on impact. They can go through walls, but most particularly, they can go through police vests that are proof against ordinary bullets.

A spokesman for the International Association of Chiefs of Police says his group "can find no legitimate use, either in or out of law enforcement, for this type of ammunition." It seems to us it could be of use to SWAT teams in controlled situations, but we fail to see what better use it could be than ordinary ammunition to a sportsman or someone who keeps a gun for legitimate self-defense.

In any event, the general public has long been "separated" from certain types of arms and ammunition — "dum-dum" bullets, sawed-off shotguns, machine guns, for instance. The police as well have denied themselves certain weapons; many police forces ban .357 Magnums because of their ability to fire bullets through walls and thus endanger non-targets, and many require short loads of cartridges to reduce a bullet's range.

The point of the proposed ban, clearly, is to deny such ammunition to criminals who would use it against law-abiding citizens and the police whose job it is to catch criminals. The general public's right to bear arms, as regulated by law, would not be denied. Instead, the public's right to protection from the criminal element would be enhanced by denying criminals the means to "out-bullet" the enforcers of the law.

The Boston Herald

Boston, MA, March 10, 1984

THERE WOULD seem to be no sensible need or reason for anyone to oppose a bill to outlaw those armor-piercing bullets known as "cop killers" from use in handguns.

But the National Rifle Association does.

At a Senate hearing in Washington the other day their lobbyist, Warren Cassidy, said bills to ban the bullets were "nothing other than one more attempt to separate law-abiding gun owners and the nation's sportsmen from their firearms and ammunition."

These, mind you, are small-caliber missiles made of steel or hard brass that are able to penetrate "bullet-proof" vests police wear. The hearing was told that one type, coated with Teflon, is powerful enough to pierce four such vests — plus five Los Angeles County phone books placed directly behind them. We find it difficult to disagree with the position of the Fraternal Order of Police that "there are no legitimate or practical uses (for them)... by either law enforcement officers or sportsmen."

It is, admittedly, true that no law enforcement officer has yet been slain by one of these bullets — but that neither lessens the peril they pose nor refutes the reason for banning them.

"Do we wait until police officers are killed... do we wait for them to die before shedding crocodile tears?" asked U.S. Rep. Mario Biaggi of New York, who was shot no less than 10 times during his 23 years as a police officer and is, understandably, one of the sponsors of the bills.

Clearly, outlawing them would be a safety measure, not an impairment of the claimed rights of gun owners or fanciers — whose interest might, in the long run, be harmed more by the blind opposition of the NRA than by as reasonable and modest a prohibition as these bills seek.

ST. LOUIS POST-DISPATCH

St. Louis, MO, March 12, 1984

The U.S. Senate is considering a bill that would ban the manufacture, import, sale or use of armor-piercing ammunition, the so-called "cop-killer" bullets.

What is at issue here is the banning of a special type of bullet that has no legitimate function. Its primary purpose is to penetrate the lightweight synthetic fiber armor vests worn by police office. The National Rifle Association — in the wrong-headed belief that *any* firearm control legislation is harmful to the nation's gun owners — is opposing the new law on the ground that it is "too broadly drawn." (Apparently, there is a latent threat from armored deer.)

But others have more a rational view on the issue. Rep. Mario Biaggi — a New York Democrat and 23-year police veteran who was wounded 10 times on duty is sponsoring the bill. He states, "There's no legitimate use either in or out of law enforcement" for this type of ammunition. Furthermore, he explains, "My legislation is not some deviously contrived gun control measure. I'm not for gun control."

The proposed law would subject an importer, manufacturer or dealer who violates the measure to a maximum fine of $10,000 and 10 years in jail. Anyone who is caught and convicted of either possession of or firing these "cop-killer" rounds would also be subjected to a mandatory one- to 10-year sentence for a first offense. A second offense could result in a 25-year mandatory sentence.

It is a good basic law that will protect literally hundreds of thousands of law enforcement officers. Congress should pass this measure quickly.

The Hartford Courant

Hartford, CT, August 10, 1984

Although Defense Secretary Caspar W. Weinberger criticized the House defense appropriations subcommittee for releasing its report outlining U.S. military unpreparedness, the panel has provided a real service: It has made public facts and figures that could illuminate the debate over military spending.

National defense issues took center stage early in the current political season. Not only is the subject dear to politicians' hearts, but it deserves much public discussion — not least because military costs are a major factor in creating the massive federal deficits.

President Reagan might have won election four years ago because he campaigned so hard on a promise to strengthen America's military might. But despite record outlays for new weapons procurement, America's field commanders say they feel unprepared to fight a conventional war, complaining of unreadiness by air, land and sea.

In reports to Congress earlier this year, Adm. Wesley L. McDonald of the Atlantic Command cited munitions shortages; Adm. William J. Crowe Jr. of the Pacific Command said he was concerned about shortages; European commander Gen. Bernard W. Rogers admitted that his command would be unable to sustain its conventional forces in combat for long; and Gen. Wallace H. Nutting, who commands American forces within the United States, reported equipment and personnel shortages.

Chillingly, Dr. William Mayer, assistant secretary of defense for health affairs, estimated that armed forces medical units could care for only two of every 10 soldiers wounded in battle.

In their annual report to Congress in February, the Joint Chiefs of Staff complained of inadequate operations and maintenance and said "shortfalls in authorized end-strength, senior grade enlisted personnel, spare parts, munitions, training funds, chemical defense, survivable communications systems and intelligence-support capabilities continue to inhibit readiness."

The House panel's report implied that if war came, the United States would either have to surrender to a major adversary or resort to nuclear combat.

The Reagan administration asked Congress for $300 billion for defense for 1985, and House and Senate negotiators initially agreed to spend a record $297 billion. Although their compromise has broken down, the public still might ask how it could be that while the Pentagon spends more than ever, U.S. forces might have to choose between losing a war or using nuclear weapons.

Analysts answer that expensive new weapons favored by the administration are consuming ever more of the defense budget. This will be the first year in which spending for exotic weapons systems, including the MX missile, would so closely approach spending levels for military pay, operations and maintenance. And while weapons spending increases, the Pentagon has taken no significant steps to curb waste and fraud in its purchasing programs.

The prospects for a spending slowdown are not encouraging given the fact that, for the first time in 15 years, the United States has stopped arms control negotiations with the Soviet Union.

If the House subcommittee report is anywhere near accurate, it describes a national emergency caused by a badly misdirected military policy. Neither President Reagan nor Democratic presidential candidate Walter F. Mondale should be able to get away with election-year generalities about building the nation's defenses.

Something's gone wrong, and voters deserve to know what each candidate plans to do about it.

THE KANSAS CITY STAR

Kansas City, MO, April 30, 1984

The struggle in Congress to outlaw so-called cop-killer bullets has suffered a setback at the hands of the National Rifle Association and other opponents of gun control. The losers are mainly police officers and public officials who rely on protective vests that ordinary bullets cannot penetrate. Cop-killer bullets can.

The show of power was awesome. Recently Sen. Edward Kennedy, Massachusetts Democrat, proposed an amendment to a piece of legislation being prepared by the Senate Judiciary Committee. The rider would have prohibited the manufacture or importation of this type ammunition. A writer for Congressional Quarterly describes what happened next: "Before the committee could vote, Sen. Orrin G. Hatch, Utah Republican, offered a substitute that put no constraints on production of the bullets and instead required a mandatory sentence for crimes committed with them." The Hatch amendment won approval by a vote of 14 to 1.

An NRA official argues that measures to bar these bullets are an attempt to deprive law-abiding citizens and outdoorsmen of their ammunition. Opponents of the ban claim that it is impossible to define armor-piercing handgun bullets. One witness told the committee that many rifle cartridges used for sport would be banned because they could also be fired from handguns.

Supporters, including most major law enforcement professional organizations, attack these contentions. They say cop-killer bullets can and should be defined in the interests of police and others who must wear bullet-proof vests for their protection. Generally armor-piercing bullets contain hard metal, travel fast and retain their shape after they hit their target. Regular missiles tend to move slower and flatten after they strike because the metal is softer.

Plainly the gun lobby is putting its resistance to control ahead of police safety. That is a warped idea of what freedom is about in this country.

The Des Moines Register

*Des Moines, IA,
June 28, 1984*

A ban on cop-killer bullets, which quite recently appeared to be a lost cause, now seems certain of passage in Congress, thanks to a united effort by the nation's four major police organizations.

The gun-dealers' lobby and President Reagan, who opposed an earlier effort, now support a revised version. The switch followed a strongly worded message from the police to Congress.

The new bill prohibits the manufacture and importation of hardened bullets that can slice through a policeman's bullet-proof vest. Such bullets are usually coated with Teflon that protects gun barrels and adds 15 percent more penetrating power.

Unlike the earlier proposal, the bill does not ban the sale or possession of such bullets, on the unlikely theory that ammunition dealers might unknowingly carry the cop-killers in stock. This change gave the National Rifle Association a chance to save face.

Said the NRA: "We would be negligent in our duty to law enforcement ... if we did not state publicly, as we have in the past, that criminal behavior cannot be controlled by legislating against inanimate objects." (Should the public be allowed to buy hand grenades and land mines?)

"Equally as important, we have defeated the [earlier proposal to ban sale and possession] and reaffirmed our traditional support and friendship for the nation's law-enforcement community. We are therefore secure in the knowledge that our members and supporters will appreciate our position and unite against our common foe, the anti-gun organizations."

Good strategy. With the battle lost, the NRA contends that it was always on the winner's side; it's gunning for those other guys.

In any event, it is good legislation that should help protect police from the crazies. And with the NRA helping to assure that nothing is done to halt the insane proliferation of handguns, they need all the help they can get.

Arkansas Gazette

Little Rock, AR, March 9, 1984

Armor-piercing handgun bullets have no place in civilian life and Congress need not hesitate in outlawing them. They are useful only to penetrate protective vests worn by policemen and therefore have no socially redeeming value.

Bills to ban this "cop-killer" ammunition are in both houses of Congress and a Senate Judiciary subcommittee held a hearing on the issue just the other day. The legislation, as might be expected, attracted the opposition of the National Rifle Association, which said that it was just "one more attempt to separate law abiding gun owners and the nation's sportsmen from their firearms and ammunition." Think about that for awhile.

The bills are aimed at armor-piercing bullets for handguns, but the NRA apparently fears that such legislation also could be used to ban rifle-type ammunition that also can be fired from handguns. It has long been a mystery why legitimate hunters and target shooters have need for armor-piercing rifle bullets when conventional bullets can accomplish the same deadly conclusion anyway.

Congress' overriding concern should be the danger that armor-piercing handgun bullets pose to innocent persons, including police officers, and the evidence is overwhelming on this point.

Impetus for the bills comes from police or organizations, many of which favored the manufacture and even use of armor-piercing bullets by law enforcement when they came on the market a few years ago. Now, says a spokesman for the International Association of Chiefs of Police, the group "can find no legitimate use, either in or out of law enforcement, for this type of ammunition." Most police departments have banned the use of armor-piercing bullets by their own personnel because of the danger that ricochets pose to bystanders and police officers.

Armor-piercing bullets can penetrate the light-weight protective vests (in one test several vests were penetrated) that are worn by an estimated 250,000 policemen nationwide. These vests, however, can stop conventional bullets and it can be said that they have saved lives.

Whether Congress will push aside the proposed bills to ban such dangerous handgun bullets, which are freely available now through local gun shops, is by no means certain. The NRA enjoys extraordinary influence on Capitol Hill, which is as much the fault of timid members of Congress as anyone else. But no one in Congress can dismiss one cold fact: armor-piercing handgun bullets are, simply, "cop-killers" and therefore have no legitimate place in American society.

Roanoke Times & World-News

Roanoke, VA, May 20, 1984

THE DRAWN-OUT legislative effort to ban armor-piercing ammunition bogged down again the other day. It was another demonstration, if one were needed, of the power that organized gun-owners wield with Congress.

The Senate Judiciary Committee was marking up gun-related legislation. Sen. Edward M. Kennedy, D-Mass., offered an amendment to bar production and import of armor-piercing handgun bullets.

The fact that Ted Kennedy offers legislation doesn't make it automatically good or bad. Maybe his amendment was deficient in one or more ways. But the committee never voted on it. Sen. Orrin G. Hatch, R-Utah, offered a substitute amendment that put no limits on production of the bullets; all it did was require a mandatory sentence for crimes committed with them. The substitute was approved 14-1.

It seems almost reflexive, on the part of both the gun lobby and the legislators. This wasn't an attempt, like many others in recent years, to curb access to handguns. It would affect only a tiny segment of the ammunition market: tiny, but significant because of the threat that these specially coated bullets pose to police who wear soft body armor on duty.

But gun advocates see it as the tiny edge of the wedge: J. Warren Cassidy, executive director of the National Rifle Association's Institute for Legislative Action, calls efforts to ban armor-piercing bullets "nothing more than one more attempt to separate law-abiding gun owners and the nation's sportsmen from their firearms and ammunition." Hearing the NRA's call for help, key legislators snap to — even to the point of tacking on that favorite "deterrent," the mandatory-sentence clause. Better a pound of cure than an ounce of prevention.

The Reagan administration still can't get its act together on this question. Philosophically it opposes more gun controls. But it's also pro-police, and many police fraternal organizations would like to see armor-piercing ammo outlawed. The Justice Department has been working, at a glacial pace, on a legal definition that would cover these handgun bullets without banning other, legitimate ammunition. But an official of the Treasury Department — which enforces gun laws — testified against such legislation in March.

The NRA's position is that these bullets pose a negligible problem and that discussion only serves to alert criminals to their usefulness. However, word gets around in the underworld by other means; armor-piercing ammo has been turning up in criminals' possession for several years. Even if a ban were to affect bullets used by a few sportsmen, this would seem a small sacrifice if it helped protect police officers.

Craig Floyd, an aide to Rep. Mario Biaggi, D-N.Y., remains optimistic that a workable bill will emerge and be enacted. Treasury, he said, is looking at its own versions for defining the ammunition. Once consensus is reached within the administration, he thinks, it shouldn't take long to pass legislation.

Biaggi has sounded less patient. "Cop-killers don't wait for others to act," he has said, "so why should we? We should be trying to prevent police deaths instead of responding to them." His words come from the heart. Before going to Congress, he spent 23 years as a New York City policeman and was wounded 10 times.

THE ARIZONA REPUBLIC
Phoenix, AZ, March 11, 1984

THERE'S no conceivable reason why anyone should go out and buy armor-piercing handgun bullets unless he wants to kill a police officer.

Deer don't wear armor, nor do doves.

Police officers sometimes wear lightweight vests that can stop conventional handgun bullets. And many a cop owes his life to his vest.

Conventional handgun bullets flatten on impact because of their hollow-point or soft-metal composition. Armor-piercing bullets are something else. Usually made from brass or steel, they maintain their shape on impact.

The Senate Judiciary Committee is now considering a bill that would ban the sale of armor-piercing bullets. It has the backing of the International Association of Chiefs of Police and the Fraternal Order of Police.

In fact, it has the backing of just about everyone except the Mafia, assorted terrorist gangs — and the National Rifle Association.

A NRA official, Warren Cassidy, testified before the committee that his organization considered the bill as "nothing other than one more attempt to separate law-abiding gun owners and the nation's sportsmen from their firearms and ammunition."

Bosh.

What would a law-abiding citizen do with armor-piercing handgun bullets? It's useful only to criminals.

The NRA has the same kind of mentality as those civil-liberties groups that fight hanging the Ten Commandments on a classroom wall because, they say, it would be the first step to making the United States a theocracy. It simply has no sense of proportion.

If the bill would save one cop's life, Congress should pass it. And every member of the NRA, who isn't an extremist, should tell his congressman and senator so.

The Wichita Eagle-Beacon
Wichita, KS, March 13, 1984

The National Rifle Association, which is engaged in an expensive national image-enhancement campaign, is damaging its own credibility with its continued opposition to a measure that would ban armor-piercing handgun ammunition.

Kansas and Oklahoma are among nine states that already have done so, but armor-piercing ammunition — some of which has been made even more deadly by the addition of Teflon coating to enhance its penetration power — remains available for purchase by anyone in gun shops throughout much of the nation. As long as that's so, even wearers of bullet-proof vests of the type worn by about half the nation's police officers are vulnerable. A single Teflon-coated bullet can pierce four standard police vests and continue on through five 1,200-page telephone directories.

Representatives of the Fraternal Order of Police and the International Association of Chiefs of Police told the Senate Judiciary Committee last week such bullets have no legitimate use, either in or outside law enforcement, and their manufacture, sale, importation, use and possession should be banned.

Ironically, coated armor-piercing bullets (ordinary bullets flatten out on impact; these do not) originally were designed for police use. But most police departments have forbidden their use both because of their over-kill capabilities and because hard-nosed bullets tend to ricochet, endangering bystanders and passersby.

But the NRA contends that since some kinds of rifle-type ammunition also can be fired from handguns, the legislation is "nothing other than one more attempt to separate law abiding gun owners and the nation's sportsmen from their firearms and ammunitions." That is sophistry in the *n*th degree.

BUFFALO EVENING NEWS
Buffalo, NY,
February 20, 1984

In their war on crime, nearly half of the nation's 528,000 police officers wear bullet-proof vests at times to protect themselves against criminal attack. Such vests are credited with saving over 400 lives in just the past five years. Yet these vests are now being rendered useless by the increasing use by criminals of a vicious, deadly weapon — the "cop-killer bullet."

Ordinary lead bullets flatten on impact and lose their penetrating power. These new armor-piercing bullets are made of hard steel or brass and have five times the penetrating power of a lead bullet. In tests, they have penetrated several bullet-proof vests and kept going.

Law enforcement authorities across the nation are working to ban the manufacture, import and sale of these bullets, and 11 states and the District of Columbia — but not New York State — have outlawed them. Now Congress is considering a similar federal ban under a proposed Law Enforcement Officers Protection Act, and it deserves strong support.

Sen. Daniel P. Moynihan, D-N.Y., has introduced the measure in the Senate, and Rep. Mario Biaggi, D-N.Y., who as a New York City police officer was wounded 10 times in the line of duty, is sponsoring a companion bill in the House. Rep. John LaFalce, D-Town of Tonawanda, and Rep. Stanley Lundine, D-Jamestown, are co-sponsors of the measure, and support appears to be growing as the need for the measure becomes known.

The powerful National Rifle Association, which has generally refused to accept any hint of a limit on the "right to bear arms," remains staunchly opposed to the measure, in spite of an effort to placate it. The measure now before Congress would affect only ammunition for handguns, so that it is difficult to see how it would result in any adverse effects for hunters or sportsmen.

There is no reason why such dangerous handgun ammunition should be manufactured and sold. As a Miami police officer put it: "The only thing that bullet is designed for is to hurt police officers."

Los Angeles Times
Los Angeles, CA, February 16, 1984

Teflon-coated handgun bullets are deadly. Their penetrating power is awesome, and they pose a threat to the safety of all citizens. In the hands of criminals they make the police especially vulnerable. So-called bulletproof vests worn by police are no defense against these bullets, which can pierce four of the vests with ease.

Several states have banned the bullets, but they should be outlawed nationally. That is the purpose of legislation sponsored in the House by Rep. Mario Biaggi (D-N.Y.) and in the Senate by Sen. Daniel Patrick Moynihan (D-N.Y.). The Senate subcommittee on criminal law will begin hearings on March 7. Known as the Law Enforcement Officers Protection Act, the Biaggi-Moynihan bill would ban the manufacture, sale and possession of armor-piercing handgun bullets. The legislation also would require mandatory jail sentences for using the ammunition in a crime.

The bullets were developed for police use, but police departments reject them as too dangerous, and law-enforcement organizations throughout the country urge their elimination. Despite the solid support by police for the bill, the National Rifle Assn. is fighting it. The group argues that there is no "bad or good bullet." Biaggi disagrees. He believes that the bullets are "bad," but admittedly is prejudiced. A veteran of the New York City Police Department, he was wounded by gunfire 10 times in the line of duty, and wants to protect civilians and police from bullets that can penetrate a protective vest as easily as they can rip through a cotton shirt.

It would be nothing short of intolerable if Congress failed to enact this legislation.

New York Subway Shooting Sparks Vigilantism Debate

A white man shot and wounded four black youths, whom he evidently believed to be threatening him, on a New York City subway on December 22, 1984. All four of the youths had arrest records and three were carrying long sharpened screwdrivers at the time of the shooting, although it was unclear whether these were brandished or even visible. According to witnesses, the man shot the black youths after they asked him for $5. He then spoke briefly to the conductor of the train before jumping onto the subway tracks and disappearing into the tunnel to the next station.

A little over a week later, Bernhard H. Goetz surrendered to police in Concord, N.H., claiming he was the man who had shot the youths. In the meantime, a special telephone number set up by police to gain information about the case had received more calls backing the actions of the assailant and offering to pay his legal expenses than offering any new information about the incident. Three of the youths Goetz had shot were still in the hospital on the day he surrendered, and one was paralyzed from the waist down. Nevertheless, the shooting had won sympathy and approval nationwide. The unexpected popular support for Goetz was generally believed to reflect a widespread overwhelming frustration with the level of crime in U.S. cities, and anger over the plight of the individual when trapped in such a potentially dangerous situation. Goetz, 37, was described by the police as an electronics specialist. He had no criminal record but had been mugged three years before; his subsequent application for a license to carry firearms was denied.

New York City Mayor Ed Koch, responding to the outpouring of support, declared that "vigilantism will not be tolerated in this city." Goetz was returned to New York for arraignment Jan. 3, 1985.

THE INDIANAPOLIS STAR
Indianapolis, IN, January 5, 1984

The bizarre official reaction to the so-called "vigilante" shootings of four teen-age robbers is a key to the runaway crime that plagues New York City and much of the nation.

Official anger is focusing not on the youths armed with sharpened heavy-duty screwdrivers who admitted "hassling" the victim on a subway car and asking him for $5.

The indignation of authorities is concentrating upon their target, Bernhard Hugo Goetz, 37, Manhattan, who had the audacity to draw a .38 caliber revolver and shoot all four of them.

The attitude of some law enforcement officials seems to be: Who does he think he is, resisting a crime?

Goetz had been beaten and robbed in 1981. All four youths involved in the latest incident had arrest records. Three were armed with sharpened heavy-duty screwdrivers which make ideal stiletto weapons that can kill a victim in an instant.

It does not take a Sigmund Freud to analyze the situation that Goetz faced in the subway or the danger he was in. He could have been killed if he yielded or hesitated. Countless victims are.

More than 1,700 murders are among the 150,000 violent crimes a year reported in the New York metropolitan area. And among the more than 98,000 victims of reported robberies, hundreds are cut, battered, stomped and permanently maimed.

Countless New Yorkers are afraid to go out after dark. As the state's Association of Supreme Court Justices said in a report last year, civilization is at bay, criminals have the upper hand and law-abiding citizens live in a state of siege.

That explains why after the Dec. 22 shooting, when police set up a hotline for information about the shooting, 99.9 percent of callers favored the gunman, wanted to give him a medal, run him for mayor, buy him bullets and give to a defense fund if he wound up in the law's clutches, which he soon did by his own choice.

But Mayor Ed Koch said: "We will never tolerate vigilantism. Even if someone thinks he is in the right, he may not take the law into his own hands." The odd mindset of officialdom was revealing itself. The law was exhibiting a dog-in-the-manger attitude.

The law did not protect Goetz. Now its spokesman was denying him the right to protect himself. He was a vigilante, said the voice of the law, although he did not stalk the four to punish them but they stalked him to rob him.

So, incensed New York law officials prepared to lower the boom on the villainous Goetz: An arrest warrant was issued charging him with four counts of attempted murder and another charging him with criminal possession of a dangerous weapon.

New York robbers, street and subway muggers, rapists and killers could breathe a little more easily now. For a while there, they were worried.

Is it any wonder the New York metropolitan area has more than 778,000 reported crimes, including 150,000 violent crimes, 98,750 robberies and 1,749 murders a year?

Newsday
Long Island, NY, December 29, 1984

Given the pervasive climate of fear in New York City's subways, it's understandable — if no less deplorable — that many people have expressed admiration for the gunman who shot four teenagers aboard an IRT express train last Saturday.

Before fleeing, the man told a conductor the four had tried to rob him. What actually occurred is unclear. Three of the youths were armed with sharpened screwdrivers, but none of the witnesses questioned by police said they saw the teenagers threaten the gunman before the shooting.

The youths reportedly had harassed him by asking for a cigarette, a match and finally for $5. That may have been annoying — or even disturbing — but it was surely no justification for wounding four people with a handgun. Short of an overt threat to life or physical safety, there's no room in a civilized society for that kind of behavior.

It's clear, though, that many people feel differently. They're frightened by crime in the subways and on the streets,

they're angry because the police seem unable to curb it, and they're frustrated by their own feelings of helplessness. In short, they're mad as hell and don't want to take it any more. That's the message contained in hundreds of calls to a police hot line set up to gather information on the gunman. Some callers have even offered to contribute to his legal defense.

But surely they realize, on reflection, that the gunman was wrong, that his violent response simply breeds more violence, and that our entire social system is gravely threatened if it allows people to walk around carrying guns and taking the law into their own hands. Both Mayor Edward Koch and Gov. Mario Cuomo said as much in deploring the outpouring of praise for the gunman. "You are not going to have instant justice meted out by anybody because that is not justice," the mayor said.

He's absolutely right. But rhetoric alone won't discredit vigilante vengeance. More police — and more effective crime prevention — are needed to do that.

ST. LOUIS POST-DISPATCH
St. Louis, MO, January 12, 1985

How is a nation's character to be judged? One way is to look to those events that evoke public protest. By that standard, several recent and disquieting displays can be read as possible signs of an unwholesome trend.

Consider the public's response to Bernhard Goetz, who seriously wounded four youths who approached him on a New York subway car, asking for money. Mr. Goetz has become a folk hero, cast into the role of the little guy who stood up to the thugs, the patron saint, apparently, of crime victims. Does no one worry that revenge should be the stuff of dreams these days?

The spectacle of people rejoicing in the death of another human being is grotesque. But the execution of Robert Lee Willie, convicted of murdering a young woman, was the occasion for just such a ghoulish display. Minutes after witnessing the execution, the victim's mother and stepfather threw a party outside the prison gates for family members and friends.

Less publicized but even more disquieting was the reception given the Rev. Denis O'Mara, an American priest expelled from Chile. His offense: to have sent Christmas greetings bearing wishes for "a New Year without torturers." On landing in Miami, he was hounded by a crowd. "Communist," they shouted, "Viva Pinochet," and "Get out." His support for human rights — whether in Chile, Afghanistan or Cuba — apparently isn't welcome here, either.

Perhaps these celebrations are as aberrant as they are abominable. Other demonstrations, such as the protests against apartheid at South Africa's embassy, offer evidence that Americans are by no means of one mind on matters of conscience.

Still, if the ugly and mean-spirited manifestations of all that is worst in us are not answered in voices just as strong that well from our better selves, those protests that today seem so uncharacteristic and unseemly could well be tomorrow's norm.

Will we know then how that happened?

Chicago Tribune
Chicago, IL, January 6, 1985

When Kitty Genovese was killed in New York City, voices across the nation expressed shame. Twenty years later, in the same city, a man known in headlines as the "subway vigilante" and the "Death Wish gunman" shoots four teenage boys on a subway and a disturbing number of voices express delight.

When Miss Genovese screamed for more than a half-hour as she was being brutally stabbed, at least 38 of her neighbors witnessed her ordeal but did nothing. The episode became a shameful symbol of urban degeneracy. It is to this degeneracy that many Americans are reacting when they make a hero out of a man who says he took the law into his own hands because he thought he was being robbed.

It will be up to the courts to determine whether suspect Bernhard Hugo Goetz is guilty of the four counts of attempted murder with which he is charged. But the public reaction is disturbing in its display of disbelief that law enforcement authorities will protect people against street crime, and in its display of belief that the rule of force is all that is left.

When individuals feel they are not adequately protected, they will take steps to protect themselves. Public praise for the "subway vigilante" encourages others to carry—and use—illegal weapons in a society that already has too many weapons in irresponsible hands. Underscoring that point the very night after Mr. Goetz turned himself in, a 13-year-old boy became Chicago's first homicide of the year, thanks to a stray bullet apparently fired by a New Year's Eve reveler.

Some observers complain that reaction by whites would not have been as sympathetic if the races of the white shooter and his four black targets were reversed. Perhaps. But blacks are, by an overwhelming percentage, the most frequent victims of black criminals. Many share in this outcry of support for those who mimic the fictional crime victim who armed himself and stalked criminals in the movie "Death Wish."

The best way to fight crime without resorting to jungle justice is with effective enforcement of the law. Police protection must be adequate and visible. Punishment must be meted out uniformly in the courts. Parole and probation officials need the resources to prevent their cases from getting lost in a bureaucratic shuffle. With those remedies in place, communities can begin to work on the underlying social problems that lead some young people to become social problems for everyone else.

The Washington Post
Washington, DC, December 28, 1984

NEW YORK has a new folk hero, the slim, bespectacled young man who was reading a newspaper and minding his own business on a Manhattan subway train early last Saturday afternoon when four young men began to hassle him. According to witnesses, the four, armed with sharpened screwdrivers, approached the rider and "asked" him for money. He stood up, calmly drew a silver revolver from his belt and shot all four. Then he helped a few women to their feet, told the conductor he was not a policeman and disappeared into the subway tunnels. Of the four, all are in the hospital, one paralyzed by the gunman's bullet.

The event has provoked an enormous public response. A columnist speculates that the gunman had seen the current Charles Bronson movie "Death Wish." A hot line set up to receive tips about the man with the gun was deluged by thousands of calls supporting him. Mayor Koch has promised an all-out effort to solve the case, but the joke on the streets is that he just wants to find the gunman before the Republicans nominate him for mayor.

It's easy to understand why New Yorkers are responding in this spirit. Their subway, once a fast, efficient, cheap, 24-hour-a-day transit network that other American cities envied, has fallen on hard times. Much of the equipment is old and constantly breaking down. The cars and the stations are filthy, covered with graffiti and littered with trash. There are thousands of fires in the system each year, most started in refuse strewn on the tracks. But the most frightening element is the crime. The four young men involved in Saturday's incident all had arrest records and appeared to be typical of the toughs who roam the trains, even in midday, terrorizing and robbing passengers.

This is the heart of it. The mayor has put more than 3,000 uniformed police officers on the trains and stations, and Gov. Cuomo has counseled calm. "A very firm, even, tough criminal justice system," says the governor, is the way to fight crime. He's right, of course, but such a system is not in place. When people feel they are not adequately protected, the force of the argument that they should not take their defense into their own hands diminishes.

The subway riders of New York have been sorely provoked. An episode of do-it-yourself law enforcement has undeniable implications of spreading violence and chaos, but it reflects directly upon those in official positions, like the mayor and the governor, who have failed to provide the protection that the citizenry has every right to demand.

THE BLADE
Toledo, OH, January 6, 1985

LET'S do it to them before they do it to us," a police sergeant on TV's "Hill Street Blues" warns his troops during a roll call. That viewpoint has a growing number of adherents in urban America.

The latest expression of this vigilante attitude took place on a subway train in New York City on Dec. 22, when a man, asked for money by four teen-agers, pulled out a handgun, shot them, and walked off the train. One of the teen-agers is paralyzed below the waist because of the shooting.

The violent act — reflecting the mentality found in the film "Death Wish," in which actor Charles Bronson does much the same thing — stirred up New York. Many subway riders who live under the daily fear of robbery or assault agreed vociferously with the man's behavior, even though it was denounced by Mayor Koch and others.

Then, on Dec. 31 Bernhard Goetz of New York walked into a New Hampshire police station and said he was the gunman. Mr. Goetz will be returned to New York, where he will stand trial on four counts of attempted murder and one count of illegal possession of a weapon.

It is justifiable for people to take steps to protect themselves, their families, and their property from criminal attack. But there are unacceptable risks attached to using a gun, even in self-defense.

The presence of such a weapon might persuade an assailant to shoot first or an intended victim might wound or kill an innocent bystander. Or an edgy citizen might shoot or stab a person who looks suspicious but is only asking for the time of day or a handout.

It is difficult to persuade the victim of a robbery or an assault that there is any better response than planning a violent counterattack should it happen again. The obvious answer is that police — trained to handle violent confrontations — ought to be available in substantial enough numbers to discourage attacks on urban dwellers.

Crime is a much-discussed problem in New York subways. So why have police officials there failed to do more to get it under control? No city can blanket all buses and trains with police, but ways should have been found long ago to deal with the problem.

The presence of more police is certainly one way to head off the kind of vigilantism that took place in New York. It will not provide absolute reassurance to Americans who live under the threat of violence, but it is the most responsible and effective response.

The State

*Columbia, SC,
January 6, 1985*

LEGAL proceedings against Vernhard Hugo Goetz will likely shed light on why he shot four teenagers in a New York subway.

Goetz, a 37-year-old self-employed New York City engineer, was harassed by the youths on a Manhattan subway car on Dec. 22. Although he told police he didn't feel threatened, he reportedly told the youths, "I have $5 for each of you," then drew a gun and shot them.

The four victims, three of whom carried sharpened screwdrivers, were seriously wounded. Two remain hospitalized.

The highly publicized case has revealed a disturbing aspect in the psyche of New Yorkers — a vigilante mentality. Police seeking the suspect received hundreds of calls praising his act. Callers to radio talk shows hailed the gunman as a sort of folk hero.

The public reaction was reminiscent of the misguided support that Richard "Tony" Cimo of Murrells Inlet got when he hired a convict to kill the man who had murdered his parents.

Perhaps, too, an analogy can be drawn with those fanatics who condone the recent bombings of abortion clinics.

It is understandable that New Yorkers are concerned about safety in the subways where the shadow of violence has long hung, just as anti-abortionists are incensed by abortions.

But vigilante acts are just what New York Mayor Edward Koch labeled them: "Animal behavior ... If you allowed instant, self-meted out justice, we would have crimes committed against innocent people. That's the difference between civilized society and the Wild West."

Or as New York Gov. Mario Cuomo said, "... if we're talking about vindication, or impatience with using the judicial system, we're talking about attempted execution. The people supporting this guy should think of it that way — unilateral execution without trial. Does that really sound appealing?"

Indeed, it appears it does sound appealing to too many people, and that attitude is far more disturbing than the crime itself.

Too often, we find that people who decry crime in the streets are supporting it in cases like that of Mr. Goetz. In a vigilante society, the rights of all are jeopardized, and anarchy is the next step.

THE ARIZONA REPUBLIC

Phoenix, AZ, January 1, 1985

MAYOR Edward Koch of New York City is angry about the subway rider who shot four would-be robbers rather than submit to their threats.

But the mayor's stern warnings about citizens taking the law into their own hands seem to be falling on deaf ears.

The fact is, the subway vigilante has become something of a hero to other New Yorkers, who have tolerated the insulting behavior of street thugs and subway bandits for years without much hope of help.

So, when a subway rider pulls out a pistol and pumps bullets into four young punks trying to shake him down for $5, New Yorkers cheer for someone finally standing up.

A man identified as Bernhard Goetz, a 38-year-old electrical engineer, surrendered in New Hampshire and said he's the gunman.

Goetz surely will not lack for public support if he is brought to trial.

There is even reason to suspect that Goetz might not even be brought to trial on the shooting charges, since a reasonable police investigator might conclude that Goetz was acting to defend himself.

So that leaves the issue of whether he should be charged under New York's tough gun-control law with carrying a concealed weapon. Police may have no choice in that matter.

Then there is the question of the four youths whom Goetz shot.

Will police charge them with attempted robbery? Will they be convicted and sentenced?

That will be the acid test.

For, if the youths are in effect let off with little more than a slap on the wrist, it will be proof enough that the criminal-justice system deals more harshly with people defending themselves than with criminals.

The Grand Rapids Press

Grand Rapids, MI, January 10, 1985

A nation hungry for heroes in the shadowy struggle against crime has found an unlikely one in the gloom of a New York City subway tunnel.

How that came about says a lot about the hero, but even more about the crowd doing the cheering. We are revealed as a country bitterly angry at the thugs and thieves haunting our lives and fed up with a justice system that has failed to control them.

The peril there is plain: People sending praise and bail money to Bernhard Goetz in reward for his subway shooting are people ready to accept personal justice as a fitting remedy for the crime situation in general.

The subway episode is an understandable flashpoint for such emotional tinder.

Mr. Goetz is a quiet man, given to minding his own business. Five years ago, he was beaten and robbed by three youths in a subway station. One of them was nabbed and eventually served four months in jail.

After that, Mr. Goetz bought a .38-caliber revolver and on December 22 had it in his waistband when he was surrounded by four toughs working a subway car. They asked for a match, the time of day and for five dollars; but their real point — to frighten, humiliate and rob — was made by the sharpened screwdrivers carried in their pockets. Mr. Goetz's violent response came from the gut of every American ever in that circumstance or terrified of the possibility.

He also played out the imaginings of millions of people never directly touched by crime, but whose lives — where they can go, when, with whom — are nonetheless daily disfigured by the threat of violence and who are furious at the justice system's inability to turn things around.

The teen-age outlaws who harassed Mr. Goetz illustrate the problem. Each of the four has a criminal record; between them they have a total of 10 warrants for their arrests for failure to keep court dates. They represent a class of street types responsible for 38 felony crimes reported each day on the New York subways — and they mirror a culture of lawlessness that has Americans generally afraid to walk the streets at night.

The country's outrage at the situation is underscored by the outpouring of hurrahs for Mr. Goetz. That reaction is frightening, but potentially useful:

—*Frightening* because it signals approval of Mr. Goetz's brand of destructive individualism. Down that road is disintegration of social order as each of us jams a .38 into our belt before daily venturing out for shop or school. The prospect is of national retreat into the summary justice — and injustice — of the frontier a hundred years ago.

Yes, this country has always regarded citizen safety as fundamentally important, but it was also built around concepts of rights and deliberative processes in protecting every person's claim to fair judgment. Packing a six-gun betrays something very different: a readiness to declare guilt and deliver a sentence on the spot. Those willing to give up the Bill of Rights for such a hanging-tree society, please stand up.

—*Useful* if it pushes government to act more forcefully against crime. The alternative is to accept an increasing public cynicism about the country's system of law and a willingness to edge back to the idea of every man for himself. Those are attitudes poisonous to orderly community life.

One remedy is in more imaginative attempts at rebuilding inner city areas, including restoration of jobs — and hope.

But there can be no getting around the importance of a larger government investment in law enforcement — in Michigan, that means more prisons — and in more practical interpretations of criminal law by courts. Public confidence is inspired neither by prisons that don't hold violent criminals nor by judges who refuse to send them there.

The one thing government at all levels must not do is regard Bernhard Goetz as some sort of bizarre aberration. He was on his own on the subway car, but he's got lots of company now.

The Record

Hackensack, NJ, December 28, 1984

Last Saturday, on an IRT train in Manhattan, a neatly dressed man in wire-rimmed glasses opened fire on a quartet of youths who had allegedly tried to shake him down for five dollars. The horrifying thing about the shootings was not so much that they happened, though that was bad enough. Nor was it, exactly, that thousands of New Yorkers called a police hot line to express their approval of what the gunman had done. The horrifying thing was that those New Yorkers had a point.

We don't mean that anybody has a right to shoot anybody else — particularly, as in this case, over a matter of harassment and petty thievery — or that civilians should be taking the administration of justice into their own hands. That kind of behavior is stupid and dangerous. (What if one of the youths had had a gun? What if a shot had killed a bystander?) Regardless of the wishes of those citizens who have been calling the police hot line, this gunman must be hunted down and prosecuted, and the message must go out that — as Mayor Ed Koch put it — "vigilantism will not be tolerated in this city. . . . You are not going to have instant justice meted out by anybody, because that is not justice."

But that is only half an answer to the questions raised by this incident. We don't know what brought it about, though we suspect a degree of derangement — no matter how outwardly calm, a sane person doesn't carry a gun into the subway and start firing it in a crowded car. But we think we understand why so many people responded to it as if it were a heartwarming Christmas story.

They are enraged — enraged at what has happened to their city and to once-proud institutions like the subway system, enraged at the seemingly unimpeded proliferation of dangerous youths in places that used to be safe, enraged at the failure of the police and the courts to bring these youths to justice. Virtually every New Yorker has been mugged or burglarized, or knows somebody who has been; they are enraged by the need to triple-lock their doors and avoid certain blocks at night. They are enraged by subway graffiti and rooftop murders, enraged by their own sense of helplessness.

Of course, calling a police hot line and saying something like "Right on" or "It's about time" and hanging up is a cheap way of expressing that rage. It is even cheaper than going to the movie "Death Wish," with which the subway vigilante's behavior is being compared, and cheering as Charles Bronson blows away yet another gang of feral punks. We don't want to commend anybody for venting his anger in this fashion.

But it would be just as wrong to deny that the anger is real — real and well-founded. We don't blame New Yorkers for being angry at the punks who terrorize them. We only wish they'd learn to direct their anger not just at the punks but at the conditions that are producing them — the devastated ghettoes, the dead-end schools, the drugs and misery and squalor of the inner city. Thousands of angry people can be a powerful force for change — for the worse, or for the better.

Fort Worth Star-Telegram

Fort Worth, TX, January 4, 1985

New York City police were hunting for a man who gunned down four youths in a subway, when, lo and behold, he surrendered in Concord, N.H.

If the volume of telephone calls and other responses to the case is any indication, most New Yorkers were hoping he would get away. Some even wanted him to run for mayor.

According to witnesses, the gunman was accosted on the subway by one of the youths, who demanded $5. His answer was to pull a pistol and shoot all four of the young men. Then he calmly disappeared for 10 days.

Obviously, no city, not even New York, can afford to have gun-toting citizens blazing away on subway cars. Vigilante law is wrong, even if the vigilante feels he is being threatened, to say nothing of the danger posed to innocent bystanders. In this case, the other subway passengers were fortunate that the gunman was accurate and hit only what he was aiming at.

The city is right. He must be prosecuted. The law demands it.

On the other hand, even the police realize the underlying appeal to the public of the shooter's deed.

"People," said a police spokesman, "are just tired of being victims."

In this case, the gunman was white, the victims all black. Yet the Congress of Racial Equality, a civil rights group, has offered to pay for his defense.

There have been more than 12,000 reported robberies and other felonies committed on the New York City subways this year.

All races and all classes of society have been victimized. That is why the public has reacted as it has.

The conditions that exist are intolerable, and the police know it. The public knows it. Evidently, the gunman knew it. Indeed, he had apparently been hassled by other youths on the subway in 1981. Those youths were not prosecuted.

Unfortunately, if the city is not able to do more to protect citizens, it may find more fed-up citizens blazing away on their own at muggers and supposed muggers.

That's why this gunman must be prosecuted.

In the meantime, the way a lot of New Yorkers look at it, the four wounded youths won't accost any more subway passengers. And other would-be muggers may be a little less brazen about ripping off honest citizens. A new element of doubt, of risk, has been injected into the subway war.

The gunman is at fault. He acted illegally. His victims were also at fault. But the greatest fault may lie with a city whose citizens feel unsafe. There is a lesson there for all growing communities.

THE CHRONICLE-HERALD

*Halifax, N.S.,
January 2, 1985*

FOUR days before Christmas, a bespectacled man was accosted by four youths on a New York subway train. He pulled a gun from his waistband and shot the four of them, one seriously. The gunman then calmly explained to other passengers that he was tired of the hassling, left the subway train and disappeared.

Reactions to the episode have been about what one would expect. City officials are outraged over the outburst of vigilante-ism. To the citizens of New York, however, the fugitive appears as a hero. The sympathies of a long suffering public are very much on the side of the man who used a gun when confronted by hoodlums.

Mayor Edward Koch has condemned the shooting. He has been no less critical of the public mood of support for the gunman. He is right on both counts but, as head of the government of one of the world's largest cities, he surely should see that the entire episode is an effort to tell the authorities something.

That something is that the public is thoroughly fed up with the crime that has found a place on city streets. In lesser degree because the cities are smaller, the same mood is growing right across the continent. Vigilante-ism may not be the proper answer to crime in the streets but the public cannot be blamed for asking what other option it has.

It is a dreadful situation in which people no longer can walk the streets in safety. Not even Halifax is free of the situation, a fact attested by the muggings and rapes which occur from time to time.

Elected officials complain that the public cannot properly be protected because of a lack of funds to provide the necessary policing. That is not what those same elected officials were saying a few years ago when Ottawa moved to discourage Canadians from the possession of firearms.

Nobody wants to see vigilante-ism on the rampage. At the same time, however, people want to be able to leave their homes with an assurance that they will be safe in their wanderings and that their properties will not be rifled during their absence. The problem is one which should occupy a prime position on the agendas of civic councils.

Following the episode in New York, police assigned hundreds of patrolmen to the case. Had there been one on the subway car, the shooting might not have occurred.

There is a clear message to authorities everywhere and it affirms that the public is losing patience with crime on the streets and with the inability of the authorities to cope with the matter.

THE MILWAUKEE JOURNAL
Milwaukee, WI, January 2, 1985

It's troubling that a man who shot four youths in a New York subway is now a hero of sorts to New Yorkers weary of crime and the fear of crime.

Regrettably, it also is understandable.

Apparently the youths had been harassing the man and had asked him for $5. "Yes, I have $5 for each of you," he replied, whereupon he stood up, drew a gun and shot them, wounding all four.

Even before a suspect was captured, New Yorkers rallied to the man's defense. Some who called a police hot-line established to receive information about the gunman offered instead to help pay for his legal defense.

New York Mayor Edward Koch — who sometimes indulges in heated rhetoric about crime and criminals — sensibly said that New York wouldn't tolerate the vigilantism shown by the gunman. "We will not permit people to take the law into their own hands," Koch said. "You are not going to have instant justice meted out by anybody, because that is not justice."

The mayor is right about that. The gunman's attempt seemingly to mimic the avenger's role played by actor Charles Bronson in the film "Death Wish" must not go unpunished.

However, there also needs to be an understanding of New Yorkers' fear of crime. The rampant breakdown of discipline on the city's subways greatly feeds that fear. Little wonder that some citizens feel they must look to themselves for protection against serious assault.

Perhaps the subway incident unleashed some instincts that New Yorkers had repressed. A few days later, a hit-run driver who struck and killed a pedestrian was badly beaten by an enraged crowd.

Such vigilantism cannot be condoned, of course. But the authorities must recognize that their own failure to protect citizens itself breeds crime.

The Miami Herald
Miami, FL, January 4, 1985

ANYONE who ever has ridden on New York's subways can empathize. The express train from the Bronx was clattering along beneath Manhattan. Alone sat a middle-aged man, presumably minding his own business. Four teen-age punks gathered round him. They asked him the time. They asked for a match. They asked for $5.

They carried long-handled screwdrivers, though it is not known if they threatened him with them. Accounts vary as to precisely what happened next; eyewitnesses say that the man pursued the youths after an unspecified interval, and found them in another subway car. The youths say that they always were together with the man in one subway car.

"Yes, I have $5 for each of you," the man said as he stood, according to the teen-agers. He pulled a revolver from his waistband and methodically shot each of them, three in the chest, one in the back. A dozen other riders dove for cover. The gunman threatened no one else. He even paused to converse briefly with the halted train's conductor, then leaped into the dark tunnel and escaped.

The gunman immediately became a folk hero, precisely because so many people do empathize with his plight and even admire his response. He became the embodiment of the modern urban soul who, as the movie *Network* put it, is "mad as hell and I'm not going to take it any more."

On Monday, nine days after the shootings, Bernard Hugo Goetz, 37, surrendered to police in Concord, N.H. He asserts self-defense, that he "did nothing wrong," that "I'm sorry for what happened, but it had to be done."

Did it? Much depends on facts not now clear. Were the punks threatening him up to the moment of shooting, forcing him to defend himself, or had the hassling ended before he hunted down his tormentors? Such details could make the difference legally.

What about morally? The gunman took the law into his own hands, but many would argue that where he was, there is no law. Some 12,000 felonies were reported in New York's subways last year; fewer than 1,000 resulted in jail sentences. Those numbers add up to utter failure of the city's criminal-justice system.

The subway gunman dispensed vigilante justice. He appears to have gone beyond self-defense to immediate, severe retribution. One wounded teen-ager remains in critical condition, paralyzed from the waist down. Vigilantism cannot be condoned. The dangers of vigilante violence are as fearsome as those of unchecked predators in the streets. Innocent bystanders can be shot.

Similar episodes could happen in any big American city. People will defend themselves if they cannot reasonably rely upon government to protect them. The law-abiding would prefer civilized justice, but when individuals feel that their only real choice is between being a victim or being a vigilante, many will prefer the latter. That is the challenge to America's criminal-justice systems. If they do not provide better justice and protection to the law-abiding, then America's cities will descend further into anarchy.

Portland Press Herald

Portland, ME, January 3, 1985

The outpouring of public support for the man who, when confronted by four teen-agers on a New York City subway, pulled a gun and shot all four is understandable. Many New Yorkers and others who daily experience the torment of the possibility of mugging or robbery, or worse, doubtless feel an affinity for the person who stood up and fought back.

Moreover, there is the legitimate question of self-defense. Reportedly, the youths were shot after having asked or demanded that the man give them $5. Three of the teen-agers were carrying long screwdrivers in their pockets. All have criminal records.

In addition, the man who turned himself in to Concord, N. H.; police, saying he had shot the four, is believed to be the same man who was attacked by three men in 1981.

Taken together then, it's hardly surprising that the gunman has become a hero to many and that a defense fund is being raised in his behalf.

But to understand the phenomenon is not to applaud it. In fact, the episode raises as many as yet unanswered questions. Did he have to shoot? Did he endanger bystanders? Was it necessary that he flee?

And, fundamentally, is the message to be drawn from the affair that citizens should begin arming themselves when they take to the street? Is the solution to street crime vigilante justice? Will that, in the long run, make us safer and more secure?

The answer, to us at least, is to combat crime with increased law enforcement by well-trained officers who have the public's support. In that regard, it's worth noting that the shootings in New York have prompted an increase in transit police patrols.

Still, one nagging question remains: Would the police have beefed up subway manpower if the victims had been—not four teen-agers with criminal records—but, say, two innocent elderly women who had been slashed and robbed?

Boston Sunday Globe

Boston, MA, January 6, 1985

In 1921, when Charles Bunchinsky was born in Ehrenfield, Pa., the world was simpler. After working in coal mines and serving in World War II, he joined the Pasadena Playhouse and changed his name to Charles Bronson. Dialogue was seldom his forte; ordnance was. As one of "The Magnificent Seven" and "The Dirty Dozen," Bronson let bullets do the talking.

In 1974, he portrayed an architect avenging the murder of his wife and daughter in "Death Wish." He flushed the New York City subway system of muggers and rapists, then repeated his commercially successful performance in 1983, exterminating the sadistic vermin of Los Angeles in "Death Wish II."

As Hollywood fantasy, Charles Bronson has as much to do with the saga of Bernhard Goetz as Walt Disney. Yet the image of Bronson's impassive marksmanship has created the widespread impression of life imitating art.

The events that took place on a New York subway train Dec. 22 have engendered joy in the salivating tabloids and will probably fill learned journals of sociology with more somber folly. The issue remains simple: did he violate the law and under what circumstances? If guilty, what punishment?

The tragedy is that the apparent fantasies of pistol-packin' Bernhard Goetz are shared by so many so quickly. With no psychiatric evaluation yet made, he may resemble Richard Speck more than Wyatt Earp.

Even so, headline descriptions of Goetz are unfair to him. It is not proven that he is a "vigilante killer." A dictionary definition of vigilante implies summary punishment; Goetz has yet to make an argument in court, but if he acted in self-defense, he is no vigilante. The what-ifs of the Goetz case include a racial question. Had he been black and the four persons shot white, he might not be such a hero. But most crime in the subways or on the streets is not interracial.

What happened between Goetz and four teen-agers was one of 13,991 crimes reported last year on New York's subways. Those tunnels creeping through four boroughs are places of primordial fear for millions, especially at night. That is the crux of public anxiety.

The few potential victims able to defend themselves, and the many more who cannot, sympathize with Goetz. The rush to judgment and the eagerness to contribute to his defense fund are based in part on another widespread stereotype among Americans – Inspector Clouseau-ism, typified by another movie series, the Pink Panther comedies. "Do you have a lee-sawnce for your min-key?" the late Peter Sellers officiously asked an organ-grinder as armed robbers frolicked behind him.

On the New York subways, many riders wonder where the 700 transit police are when danger seems near. As a character says to police after Bronson saved his wife from would-be rapists, "Where were you guys? Out giving parking tickets?"

The "Death Wish gunman" has been condemned in New York by Mayor Koch – "the right of self-defense cannot be extended to cover the right of revenge" – and Governor Cuomo – "We are living in a time when there is decreasing respect for the subtle wisdom of the law. We can't ride along with that trend. We must seek to reverse it."

At Goetz's arraignment, Judge Leslie Snyder, a former prosecutor, said $50,000 bail was too low. "I'm surprised," she said. "If Western civilization has taught us anything, it is that we cannot tolerate individuals' taking law and justice into their own hands."

These reactions sound like dialogue for character actors in a Charles Bronson movie. But life is not a movie. The law and the courts have inferior scripts, but the law and the courts will determine the facts of what happened in the hands - and in the head - of Bernhard Hugo Goetz.

Pittsburgh Post-Gazette

Pittsburgh, PA,
January 4, 1985

This much is known: On Dec. 22, 1984, four youths confronted a subway passenger in lower Manhattan and asked for $5. He responded by shooting all four with a .38 caliber revolver.

In that real-life scene, which sounds like something out of the Charles Bronson movie "Death Wish," a number of people have discerned a noble epic. The man who shot the four (all had arrest records, three were found to be carrying screwdrivers apparently as weapons) has won wide praise as the "subway vigilante."

New York Mayor Ed Koch was among those to condemn this knee-jerk public reaction, but his voice has been drowned out by the chorus of approval. People, of course, say they are tired of being ripped off. If the police can't protect citizens, the popular sentiment goes, then they have the right to protect themselves. The punks got what they deserved; justice has been done.

But justice has not been done. No court this side of Iran would order petty criminals to be shot for trying to steal $5. While these were thugs generally undeserving of sympathy, that does not change a simple fact: This free-lance punishment did not fit the crime, not by any civilized standard anyway. Although all four of the would-be robbers will live, one will be paralyzed for life.

Self-defense, of course, might be a justification for this shooting. People do indeed have the right to protect themselves, but the question concerns the ways and means. More facts about the circumstances may be brought out when Bernhard Hugo Goetz, the man who surrendered himself to police in New Hampshire, is brought to trial in New York.

One common-sense question goes begging now: Why did the man have to shoot all four of his tormenters? Was this necessary in the interests of legitimate self-defense? Was this a controlled response? Or was this simply gross retribution for a robbery attempt? Of course, common-sense suggests the latter answer.

Another question arises: Would the shooting have been justified if an innocent bystander had been struck by a bullet? The risk is very real in such situations. It is why responsible police departments have guidelines on the use of deadly force. And it is why a scared amateur shooting with no restraints poses a general danger as he seeks his own individual justice.

But, the sympathetic will say, the man's action *worked*. Yet that is not the case in the long term. Here is the deadly myth of firearms: They seem to bring safety when, in fact, they often increase the danger.

Perhaps some muggers will be deterred initially by this episode, but people are still going to be robbed in big cities. If anything happens, it will be that the violence will ratchet up a notch or two. Muggers will not stop and ask, they will just hit and take. If people have guns, the thugs will carry them as a matter of course. Streets and subways do not become safer by being turned into free-fire zones.

Goetz Indicted for Attempted Murder

A New York City grand jury Jan. 25, 1985 indicted Bernhard H. Goetz for possession of unlicensed weapons. Goetz had shot and wounded four black youths on a subway train in December 1984. The grand jury rejected prosecution charges that included four counts of attempted murder and four of reckless endangerment. Instead Goetz was indicted only on the charge of criminal possession of a weapon in the third degree for the gun used in the shooting. The jury also indicted him on two counts of criminal possession in the fourth degree for two unlicensed pistols, which he kept at home. The Manhattan (New York County) district attorney, Robert M. Morganthau, said that the jurors had decided Goetz had been under likely attack, and so had been justified in using force. A lawyer for Goetz, Joseph Kelner, called the indictment "practically an exoneration for our client." Liberal activist lawyer William Kunstler, however, Jan. 29 filed a separate $50 million lawsuit against Goetz on behalf of one of the wounded youths, Darrel Cabey, who was paralyzed and had sunk into a coma.

The grand jury had met for three weeks and heard 12 witnesses. District Attorney Morganthau did not compel Goetz or the four youths to testify, since they would have won legal immunity for any crimes they testified about. The panel did watch a videotape confession in which Goetz said that, terrified, he had shot to kill and had kept on shooting until out of bullets.

Since the shooting, Goetz and his actions had become something of a symbol for dissatisfaction with the relative ineffectiveness of law enforcement agencies in controlling urban crime. A *New York Times* poll published Jan. 14, 1985 found that 52% of New York City residents were "generally supportive" of Goetz; only 28% said that they were not. About 49% of respondents called crime the city's worst problem, by far the largest percentage for any problem listed.

A New York City grand jury March 27, 1985 indicted Goetz on charges that included attempted murder. The decision capped weeks of controversy following Goetz's first indictment, in January, when his shooting of four black youths on a city subway train had resulted only in charges of unlawful possession of weapons. Under the March indictment, Goetz faced four charges of attempted murder, four of assault, one count of reckless endangerment and one of possessing a weapon with intent to use it.

District Attorney Morganthau said "new evidence had a substantial impact" upon the second grand jury, although the rules of grand jury secrecy did not allow him to specify this evidence. The March grand jury, unlike the first, had heard testimony from two of the youths Goetz had shot. For their testimony, the district attorney granted both youths immunity from prosecution. After the second indictment, Barry I. Slotnick, a lawyer for Goetz, called his client a "victim" of "political football." Goetz, he said, "faces 25 years for protecting himself."

The calling of a second grand jury was very unusual. Under state law, a case could be heard by a second grand jury only if the prosecutor has found evidence not heard by the first panel. The account of the shootings that Goetz had given police, revealed in newspaper reports Feb. 28, was widely believed to have had an impact upon the decision to seek a second indictment. Many observers felt the police summary of Goetz's statement shook the widespread popular belief that Goetz had acted in self-defense. Goetz had told police he felled the four youths and then "checked" their bodies. He saw no blood on one of them, he said, and placing his gun to the youth's ribs, fired a fifth shot. "You don't look so bad," Goetz recalled saying, "here's another." The youth, Darrel Cabey, the only one of the four to be wounded seriously, was paralyzed by one of the shots.

THE BISMARCK TRIBUNE

Bismarck, ND, January 22, 1985

Bernhard Goetz, New York's so-called subway vigilante, seems well on his way to becoming a genuine folk hero.

And all because he hauled out a gun and shot four youths who apparently wanted some of his money. Bang, bang, bang, bang.

That's all it took, and now offers pour in for movies, books, interviews, endorsements, "for many sorts of projects ... anything and everything you could mention," according to his lawyer.

But what's really fascinating about this social phenomenon is that Goetz was only a bit player.

The folks who played bigger roles and who really deserve the bows are the members of the criminal justice system, starting with police officers who would have us believe they can protect us and continuing right on through to the hospitals, the juvenile homes, the jails and the penitentiaries that do all too little to rehabilitate.

Goetz was only one of many people in high-crime areas who carry guns these days. Surprised? Don't be.

And why do they carry the guns? Because they doubt the ability of the police officers to protect them.

Oh sure, the cops can take reports in triplicate and put out bulletins and maybe, on a good day, apprehend a criminal or two. But they can't be at the scenes of most crimes, ready to prevent the robberies, the thefts, the murders or the rapes.

And yet, we have New York Police Commissioner Benjamin Ward saying that he "would not glorify this person (Goetz) under any circumstances. I can't imagine any circumstances under which a person would pull out a gun on a typical New York City subway and fire. ..."

It strikes us that the commissioner is spending too much time riding around in his official car, and not enough time riding on his city's subways. Many New Yorkers believe the subways are not safe, and judging by the public outpouring for Goetz, many people can, indeed, imagine circumstances in which somebody would pull out a gun and start blasting away.

We're not saying Goetz was right, mind you. In fact, in the heady world of criminal justice theory, he was wrong, because he took the law into his own hands and sat as judge and jury. Bang, bang, bang, bang. All on his own, without policemen, judges or juries.

Our system isn't supposed to work like that. But then again, our citizens aren't supposed to be such easy prey, either, in desolate parks or in crowded subways.

So Goetz' actions, while they may be wrong, are the result of a criminal justice system that has run amok — so far amok, in fact, that some ordinary, law-abiding citizens pack a gun to protect themselves.

Who is the real culprit in the Goetz case? Goetz? The four punks who tried to mug him?

Not really. The real culprits are the people charged with keeping the peace and ensuring our safety as we go about our business. They're not doing their jobs, and the crime statistics in New York City and elsewhere certainly support that.

The Goetz case has prompted serious discussion, and let's hope people such as our New York City police commissioner start re-evaluating their own performances and conclude that the law-abiding public has some rights, too.

Like the rights of life, liberty and the pursuit of happiness.

The Washington Times
Washington, DC, February 1, 1985

Not only is Bernie Goetz the most popular figure in law enforcement; in the eyes of the public, he seems to be something of a moderate. Americans increasingly dislike the idea of handling criminals with care, preferring to see them handled with pitchforks — perhaps not an altogether reasonable attitude, but understandable.

Attitudes are shifting perceptibly. Except for purists who go for the Black Hole of Calcutta approach, the idea that man, even in his most debased state, should live at least as well as a dog (which these days means three squares and psychological counseling) is still fairly popular. Even so, the limits of compassion seem to be shrinking.

The death penalty — the ultimate response to ultimate crimes — was supported by 45 percent of Americans in 1964, according to polls. By 1983, support had risen to 72 percent. Today, according to a Media General-Associated Press survey, 84 percent of Americans say it is right to kill criminals for certain crimes, even though half the respondents say the death sentence is imposed unfairly from case to case.

What causes decent people to discount their own sense of what is right? Most likely concern for fairness is superseded by the fear that crime is out of control (even while decreasing in some categories) and that the courts are incapable or unwilling to dispense justice. Feeling themselves at war with crime, Americans may be less and less inclined to show mercy.

Nothing is wrong with a society avenging the murder of its better citizens by its worst. Fairly applied in cases of grievous crimes, it is the only proper response, and justice sometimes can be served in no other way. But when those better citizens are willing to ignore those aspects of their character (such as a sense of fair play) that make them superior, the worst effect of coddling criminals is produced: society is dehumanized, making justice even harder to achieve.

Newsday
Long Island, NY, February 1, 1985

Given the widespread fear of street and subway crime, a Manhattan grand jury's refusal to indict Bernhard Goetz on a charge of assault or attempted murder wasn't entirely unexpected. But New Yorkers should be careful about the conclusions they draw from the panel's action last week.

By voting to indict Goetz on a felony gun-possession charge, the panel served notice that it didn't necessarily countenance an illegally armed citizenry even if it found extenuating circumstances in Goetz' use of his weapon.

Apparently the grand jurors concluded that Goetz — whether or not he should have been carrying a gun — was justified in shooting four teenagers on an IRT subway train after one of them asked him for money. The panel also implicitly expressed the rage and frustration of ordinary citizens over government's failure to provide what they consider adequate protection from street criminals.

That's what the immense public outcry in this case is all about: a perceived breakdown in the city's criminal justice system. But a violent response is not the answer to that kind of breakdown.

One of the four teenagers Goetz was accused of shooting suffered a severed spinal cord and is in a coma. The bullet that hit him could just as easily have struck an innocent bystander.

The mayor, the governor and the city's police commissioner say vigilantism shouldn't be tolerated — and they're right. Making the streets and subways safe is a job for a beefed-up police force, not for gun-toting amateurs.

The Des Moines Register
Des Moines, IA, January 29, 1985

Bernhard Goetz just won't go away. Although he apparently would like to fade back into obscurity, the public won't let him. His shooting of four youths who tried to hustle him for $5 in a New York subway car has made him very nearly a folk hero in a n... sick and tired of street crime.

From eyewitness accounts, this particular shooting was not in self-defense. As soon as Goetz pulled out his handgun, the youths gave up; he then — whether deliberately or irrationally — shot them in the back as they fled.

So there is no excusing what Goetz did, but a grand jury was willing to indict him for nothing more serious than illegal possession of a gun. The significance in this affair is the prevailing situation that caused Goetz to do what he did, and that has caused an apparent majority of the populace to at least sympathize with him.

Four ghetto youths with a record of petty crimes are a microcosm of the tens of thousands from all races who have been destroying civilized life in major American cities. People whose memories go back 30 or 35 years know that New York and Chicago and other cities were not, during the 1950s and earlier, the dangerous, disagreeable places to live in that they are today.

Whether you blame the decline on flawed character, disintegrated families, lower moral standards, racism, poverty, drugs — whatever — you can be sure that fear and violence, if unchecked, will lead to more vigilante actions and still more violence.

Unfortunately, the answer to the problem of urban disintegration and crime is almost no answer at all because of its immensity, complexity and cost.

It would require a major shifting of national priorities — a redistribution of resources — to rebuild the cities, create economic opportunities and require better education for the next generation of urban youth, as well as provide the police and correctional facilities needed to restrain the present destroyed generation.

What it does not require is for people like Bernhard Goetz to take the law into their own hands.

The Hartford Courant

Hartford, CT, February 21, 1985

Connecticut lawmakers, with grand jury reform on their agenda, may want to look at the famous case of Bernhard Hugo Goetz in New York.

Three days before Christmas, four teenagers surrounded Mr. Goetz in a New York City subway car. One of them demanded $5 from him. Mr. Goetz turned his gun on them, shot all four — two of them in the back. One of the wounded remains in a coma. Mr. Goetz, in a videotaped confession, said he intended to kill the youths.

Forget, for the sake of this argument, whether Mr. Goetz did the right thing. What's important is the grand jury proceeding that followed.

Twenty-three jurors, as prescribed by law, met to consider felony charges against Mr. Goetz. They decided that he was justified in using deadly force and declined to indict him for attempted murder. They indicted him on three gun possession charges.

As required by New York state, the names of the jurors were kept secret. Their deliberations were secret. No juror or prosecutor could disclose who the witnesses were, what they said or any other grand jury business. A judge was present, but only to answer questions and guide the proceedings.

In other words, the prosecutor was the key player.

The prosecutor, who presented the evidence, said later he did not try "to push" the panel in any specific direction. He merely presented the evidence and the law, he explained.

He may have done so, but there is no way to corroborate his version. The public knew what the prosecutor wished the public to know — no more, no less.

There was good reason for absolute secrecy of grand juries in colonial days when the intent was to protect ordinary citizens from the absolute power of the crown. But the United States hasn't been ruled by a colonial power for more than two centuries. The reasons for keeping all proceedings sealed have long faded.

Connecticut uses a one-person grand jury to investigate most allegations of criminal conduct.

The juror — a judge — and the prosecutor are the key players. The proceedings are kept in the dark. An effort to bring some sunshine into the system has been recommended by Chief Justice Ellen A. Peters, but some prosecutors aren't happy with it. A suggestion has been made to adopt the New York grand jury system.

But as the Goetz case shows, that system would not constitute reform. Let's stick with the Connecticut system and improve it.

The Virginian-Pilot

Norfolk, VA, January 13, 1985

Life is rarely as tidy as melodrama. In the popular film "Death Wish," actor Charles Bronson portrays an architect/vigilante who, bereaved and angered following the murder of his wife and the rape of his daughter by street criminals, roams Manhattan's asphalt jungle at night, calmly and competently shooting muggers who attack him. When the police in "Death Wish" finally track Bronson down, he is quietly freed because he is a popular hero, the summary justice he metes out to punks cheered by a public fed up with crime.

Bernhard Hugo Goetz, who shot four youths who apparently attempted to shake him down in a New York subway, seemed to be an equally cool customer. Publicity about his shooting of the menacing quartet prompted sympathetic New Yorkers to tie up a police hotline with expressions of approval and offers of financial aid for the gunman's legal defense.

The truth about the incident has yet to be established in a courtroom. But it appears that Mr. Goetz could have scared off the youths by drawing the gun on them and telling them to back off or by holding them at gunpoint for the police to arrest them. But he didn't. He shot them, without warning and seemingly before his own life was endangered. If that's what happened, what he did was wrong.

Freed last week on $50,000 bond, Mr. Goetz presumably will be tried for the shooting. That he will be punished isn't clear, however. Manhattan District Attorney Robert M. Morganthau has refused to grant immunity from prosecution to the wounded teen-agers, one of whom was crippled for life by a bullet from Mr. Goetz's gun and all of whom were already facing criminal charges before the subway confrontation. As a result, they balked at testifying before the grand jury that would have been called upon to consider indicting the "subway vigilante."

A 37-year-old electronics specialist who owns his own business, Mr. Goetz reportedly became emotionally involved in anti-crime efforts in his neighborhood and seems to have been traumatized by a mugging. He is said to have resolved not to become a victim again and to have begun carrying a pistol.

Permitting anyone and everyone to carry guns won't make streets safer, no more than it did in the Wild West of truth and fiction. But, then, neither is giving hoodlums something close to free rein — which seems to be the norm in many neighborhoods — the answer to crime. Deploring vigilantism without beefing up security or improving the efficiency of the judicial system isn't the answer either. In the case under discussion, New York City ought to assign more cops to its subways.

Millions of Americans live with varying degrees of fear of criminal attack on themselves or their dwelling places; many are virtual prisoners inside their houses and apartments after dark, their freedom effectively restricted by violent young men.

Yes, crime rates have been dropping. Home burglar-alarm systems, private security forces and sundry structural anti-crime devices in buildings and public areas are proliferating.

But Americans continue to be uneasy, and understandably so. Something close to the breakdown of law-and-order — to a diffused riot — prevails in many places. The shooting on the subway has brought to the surface grass-roots frustration and anger at failure to check the crime plague. No neat endings — neither for Mr. Goetz nor the crime plague — are in prospect.

The Evening Gazette

Worcester, MA, February 26, 1985

"Subway vigilante" Bernhard Goetz, who has maintained a low profile for most of the past two months, surfaced again over the weekend.

Goetz has said he shot four teen-agers in a New York subway in December when they asked him for $5, believing he was being robbed. Although two of the four were wounded while fleeing, a grand jury refused to indict him in the shootings, charging him only with illegal weapons possession. One of the youths remains hospitalized and semi-comatose.

Federal authorities decided against investigating whether Goetz may have violated the youths' civil rights. Black leaders, who charge the shootings were racially motivated, are attempting to have the federal prosecutor's decision reconsidered.

Goetz, lionized by some as an urban hero, now seems to be seeking the limelight. He appeared at an arraignment for Andy Frederick, 25, who was charged with the stabbing death of a man who allegedly stole candy bars from a subway newsstand. "I know how you feel. I was just like you, Andy. But remember, you have the support of the people," Goetz told him.

Goetz tried to attend the wake of a cab driver who was slain in a robbery last week, but was turned away by the funeral director. He succeeded in getting into the news, though, expounding in newspaper and television interviews on the moral and social problems of New York City.

It will come as no surprise if, soon, Goetz begins making the rounds of TV talk shows, making book and movie deals and even running for public office. Judges and politicians should take the Goetz phenomenon seriously: He has touched a responsive chord among urban Americans, who are increasingly doubtful about the judicial system's ability to cope with crime and who understandably are sick to desperation of living in fear behind triple-locked doors.

But the implications of the public's adulation of a man who chose to become judge, jury and executioner one night on a subway train are disturbing. As a candidate for the status of American hero, Goetz is a poor choice.

The Washington Post

Times Herald

Washington, DC, March 31, 1985

NEW YORKERS seem to be having a hard time deciding whether Bernhard Goetz is a hero or a villain. The 37-year-old electronics expert, who shot four young men in the New York subway in December, was first hailed as a Clark Kent figure, the unassuming, apparently mild-mannered passenger who struck with force when a marauding band of toughs tried to rob him. New Yorkers, long disgusted by the unsafe and crime-ridden transit system, cheered the avenger and expressed sympathy with his rage and his reaction. But, as is true of almost any action taken under stress, second thoughts have set in.

Mr. Goetz himself may have been the first to reconsider his actions. From the beginning, he protested that he was not a hero, that he did not seek praise. In a taped telephone conversation with a friend before he turned himself in, he admitted, "I responded viciously and savagely . . . just like a rat. I saw what was going to happen and I snapped." Still, there was sympathy from the public and from a grand jury, which indicted him for gun offenses but not for the shootings.

With each passing week, however, sympathy has diminished. One victim, it is clear, will suffer permanent serious disability. The public learned that Mr. Goetz did more than fire in self-defense. He sought to finish off one victim who appeared to be only wounded. His personality began to wear with frequent media appearances and staged sojourns to other criminal trials. Some of his early supporters began to ask whether Mr. Goetz was really acting as they would have in the circumstances, or whether his response was so extreme as to be indefensible.

Last week a second New York grand jury heard new evidence in the case and considered the testimony of two victims who had not been called before the earlier panel because the district attorney, at that time, would not give them immunity from prosecution. The second grand jury has indicted Mr. Goetz on four counts of attempted murder. Does this necessarily mean that public opinion has turned 180 degrees in a few months and that the accused is now a pariah?

Don't bet on it. A grand jury does not hear defense testimony. Mr. Goetz did not testify nor did any witnesses in his behalf. His version of the encounter, his fears and his state of mind were not considered by the panel. That will all come at his trial, where once again New Yorkers will be asking themselves not only what they think about what he did, but also what they themselves might have done in his place.

THE MILWAUKEE JOURNAL

Milwaukee, WI, March 28, 1985

The court of public opinion isn't the right forum to decide whether Bernhard Goetz acted in self-defense when he shot four young men on a New York subway. The issue belongs in a court of law, where the evidence can be methodically examined. At last, that's where it seems to be headed.

For a time it appeared that the question would just be left hanging. The first grand jury assigned to the case neglected to bring any serious charge against Goetz, even though he had said in a taped statement that he shot to kill and quit firing only after he ran out of ammunition. Now a second grand jury, after hearing testimony not available to the first, has indicted him for attempted murder.

Goetz recently said he wanted the opportunity of a trial to clear himself, and expressed confidence that his actions could be justified as self-defense. However, if one is to judge by Goetz's own public utterances and by the published remarks of others, neither he nor the prosecution has an open-and-shut case.

True, much of the public is inclined to excuse him entirely. Many people victimized or menaced by young hoodlums in New York and other cities are ready to praise Goetz as a hero championing their own cause. However, as President Reagan said in his initial comments on the Goetz case, "There's a breakdown in civilization when people start taking the law into their own hands."

Some would argue that the breakdown had already taken place in New York long before Goetz and the young men crossed paths. Sadly, there's some truth to that. Society surely has a right to expect better protection than it is getting in some cities. But that's not what's at issue in Goetz's case.

The issue for the court to decide is whether he faced peril sufficient to justify the force he used.

THE ARIZONA REPUBLIC

Phoenix, AZ, March 31, 1985

IF there's any emotion shared by most Americans regardless of race, economic and social standing or place of residence, it's the incurable fear of becoming a victim of crime.

Little wonder, then, that public opinion rallied so strongly to the side of Bernhard Goetz after he shot and wounded four youths on a New York City subway on Dec. 22, claiming they tried to shake him down for money.

Now, however, a second New York grand jury has done what another grand jury would not do — it has indicted Goetz for attempted murder, alleging that he showed "depraved indifference to human life" when he shot the four youths.

Goetz practically invited the indictment.

He has been popping off tirelessly since he was lifted from obscurity to national fame.

With his own words, Goetz seemed to suggest that the circumstances of the shooting were less than coincidental.

No matter.

The question now is whether any jury would convict Goetz, an otherwise undistinguished law-and-order citizen, on the testimony of the youths, who have been in and out of trouble.

Is there any New Yorker who has not endured the quiet, chilling fear of being mugged on a subway?

A betting person would wager that Goetz will get off on this one.

Which leads, inevitably, to a discussion of the U.S. Supreme Court's ruling that police may not use deadly force on fleeing suspects who are unarmed.

It is a ruling that literally invites crime.

The fear of being shot surely has been a deterrent to some crime, and surely one reason why criminals surrender at the scene of a crime.

With the court's ruling, why should any criminal obey a police officer's command to halt and surrender?

The time surely will come when criminals concealing firearms will turn and fire on police officers who were unaware the fleeing suspects were armed.

After a few police officers are killed by fleeing suspects, or disabled for life, the high court unquestionably will be asked to modify its ruling, just as it has slowly but surely modified the so-called exclusionary rule on evidence.

The high court majority — Chief Justice Warren Burger and Associate Justices Sandra O'Connor and William Rehnquist dissented — has given a boost to criminals.

The probability is, however, that any police officer who does use deadly force on an unarmed fleeing suspect probably would not be convicted by any thinking jury in this country.

The impulse among most Americans is to fear for their lives, defend themselves and then ask questions.

The first test of this mood among Americans will be when a jury must reach a verdict in the case of Goetz's use of deadly force.

THE PLAIN DEALER

Cleveland, OH, March 29, 1985

Now that Bernhard Goetz has been indicted on four charges of attempted murder (plus assorted lesser charges), the law has finally, fully, sloppily been served. It shouldn't have required two grand juries to return the indictments; and it probably wouldn't have if the nation hadn't been so susceptible to the crude appeal of vigilantism.

The initial outpouring of support for Goetz was so overwhelming that even the law could not remain unbowed. That was especially the case in New York City, where Mayor Ed Koch condemned Goetz' act with one statement and expressed understanding with another. And where the prosecutor obviously tiptoed into the grand jury when he should have strode through it.

Not even the White House was immune, in those first days, from being too careful. President Reagan condemned vigilantism, we recall, but allowed in the same breath as how crime was a problem. That's all the nation needed to hear.

Fortunately, that vast support has ebbed. Goetz began to pose as an authority on street crime and justice, his only credentials being that he shot four youths and managed to remain physically and legally unscathed. If the public was uncomfortable with his posturing, it was even less content with the news that, in his initial confession in New Hampshire, he all but admitted to premeditation.

He said he acted on the basis of "body language," and that after firing four shots, he approached one of his "assailants" and said: "You don't look too bad. Here's another." Not exactly Mr. Milquetoast, yet Goetz might have gotten away with it if he hadn't pushed his luck as a crimestopper.

Goetz' victims are not attractive, but that's not the point. The point is that there was use of deadly force, there are suggestions of premeditation and there are questions of self-defense. Those are legal issues and should be decided by the courts, not by the nation's vicarious sense of vengeance.

□

It is difficult to feel comfortable with the belated indictments against Goetz. Regardless of the law, the charges retain a hint of double jeopardy. And regardless of the trial's outcome, Goetz seems destined for some form of martyrdom. If found guilty, many will see him as a victim; if found innocent, his actions will be viewed as admirable.

Yet there is a hope in all this: That the Goetz affair will prompt the law and its managers to acknowledge that there is, throughout the nation, a growing cancer of fear and frustration. If our streets are not made safer, there might ultimately be more Goetzes, and more shootings . . . and, ultimately, less security for everyone.

THE ⬛ SUN

Baltimore, MD, March 29, 1985

When the first New York grand jury refused to indict Bernhard Goetz (except for possession of an illegal weapon) on charges of shooting four youths he said threatened him on a subway, it was natural to conclude that Mr. Goetz had been engaged in self-defense. Now that a second New York grand jury has indicted him for attempted murder in the case, the inclination is to assume that he was engaged in vigilantism. The proper thing to do at this point is to wait for the trial, assuming nothing about Mr. Goetz's guilt or innocence.

While waiting for justice to be done, however, the public can employ this case usefully to ponder the difference between self-defense and vigilantism. In one instance, you act to protect yourself from harm. In the other, you, in effect, punish those who you feel deserve punishment which they have escaped somehow. It is not always possible to determine the state of mind of someone who shoots and claims self-defense. But when juries are convinced that the motive was something other than that, they must mete out punishment. A civilized nation's justice system must never encourage in any way the use of violence by private individuals. This is particularly true when weapons such as handguns are involved, since their use in many instances threatens innocent bystanders.

Some defend the use of deadly force in a no-longer-threatening situation on the grounds that it is not *punishment* but *arrest*. You're not a vigilante, just a good citizen making a citizen's arrest. It is an interesting coincidence that on the day Mr. Goetz was re-indicted, the Supreme Court ruled that a police officer may not use deadly force to apprehend a fleeing suspect except when the suspect poses "a significat threat of death or serious physical injury to the officer or others." If police officers trained in protection and the skillful use of firearms may not use deadly force to apprehend (much less punish) criminals, obviously the man in the street must not.

Taking the law into one's own hands, particularly in a violent way, threatens society as well as the immediate target. It undermines the legitimate institutions of law enforcement and the administration of justice. The next step after vigilantism can be a form of terrorism.

No, we're not calling Mr. Goetz a terrorist, or even a vigilante. We're not calling him anything. He may have acted in the only sensible way in his situation. He may have overreacted, but in easy-to-understand panic. There may be other perfectly acceptable explanations for his action. But if not, if he was playing policeman, prosecutor, judge, juror and executioner on the subway that December night, then he, as much as the hoodlums who prowl the night streets, is dangerous and must be punished by the law.

Roanoke Times & World-News

Roanoke, VA, March 29, 1985

FROM THE MOMENT those four teen-agers approached Bernhard Goetz in a New York City subway train last Dec. 22, there was a tendency to react reflexively, to jump to conclusions, to make hasty judgments.

Goetz did it when he pulled his gun and started firing. Many members of the public did it when they enshrined Goetz as a folk hero, a man who would not stand still to be mugged, who would not trust to the uncertain workings of police and the courts. The criminal justice system fell in line when a grand jury let Goetz off with only a weapons charge.

A lot of people, in official positions and out, have had second thoughts in recent weeks. Other details of the incident became known, casting Goetz in a less heroic light. The implications of encouraging individuals to take the law into their own hands began to sink in.

Goetz himself, after shunning the public eye, began to bask in media attention: expounding on the big city's "sickness," offering counsel to other muggees to get the gun out quickly and not fumble around. The crowd that had gathered to cheer him began to melt away. The case was put again to a grand jury, and last Wednesday he was indicted on four counts of attempted murder.

This seems entirely fitting. To say so is not to defend the actions of the teen-agers; they may not have threatened Goetz directly, but — given the setting and his past experience — it is not hard to imagine that he felt menaced. Those four may have something to answer for in a court of law.

To approve the Goetz indictment is not to say, either, that he should be convicted of murder; that would be another kind of hasty judgment. It is the court's role to weigh the evidence and make a deliberate decision in Goetz's case.

Deliberation is the heart of the matter. The underworld element may act quickly, directly, cruelly, for selfish ends. Society should not, because its values are different. Unlike criminals, it prizes humanity and exalts due process because this is the best shield against emotion and desire run rampant. The big city may often seem sick and uncivilized, but it would soon destroy itself if every man and woman settled personal scores on the spot.

Bernhard Goetz had a right to protect himself against a perceived threat, so long as he used measures proportionate to the occasion. He seems to have gone far beyond that. What he is accused of doing is appointing himself judge, jury and hangman, and carrying out indictment, trial, sentencing and attempted execution all in a matter of seconds. Now he is to receive the due process that he apparently denied to others, and the public will have a better chance to ponder the rationale for and the fruits of vigilantism.

The Washington Times

Washington, DC, March 29, 1985

Manhattan DA Robert Morgenthau, crowing over the pliancy of the second Bernhard Goetz grand jury, says that in his town "we don't have summary justice." In a city where muggers and rapists are routinely released without bail, Mr. Morgenthau's remark is a bit of an understatement. The Big Apple doesn't punish violent criminals summarily. It scarcely punishes them at all.

Examples could be in multiples, but the case of Morris Lasker, a federal judge in New York, suffices. In 1983 Judge Lasker ordered 613 accused criminals freed on grounds of prison overcrowding, at the same time holding up construction of a prison because the design posed the possibility that inmates might fall over a railing. Within 24 hours of the release, one of the former detainees committed a rape. Further violence followed. A month later the City Bar Association held a conference on "The Criminal Justice System and the Public: Are They Communicating?"

New York is safe for those who live in good neighborhoods and take cabs. Judges and district attorneys are recruited from this class. Herein lies the racism of the "system": it ignores law-abiding black people, the vast majority of whom do not live in "good" neighborhoods, cannot take cabs, and support Bernhard Goetz.

Because of complex rules on immunity, Mr. Goetz chose not to testify; so the grand jury had little choice but to heed the testimony of James Ramseur, career criminal and admitted hoaxer, and Troy Canty, the drug abuser who was lured by the prospect of selling movie rights to his story.

The case will go to trial, and Mr. Goetz will finally testify under oath. Probably not many surprises will emerge in the testimony. Now unknown facts might come out, but there should be no difficulty apportioning credibility between criminals bought with immunity and a self-defender with no criminal record.

Senate Votes to Weaken Gun Control Curbs

The U.S. Senate July 9, 1985 voted 79-15, in favor of a bill relaxing an array of restrictions contained in the 1968 Gun Control Act. The National Rifle Association vigorously backed the new bill, while various law enforcement groups opposed it. Under the new bill, firearms could be bought outside the purchaser's home state, a practice that was then currently illegal. The bill did state that the sale would have to be made in a face-to-face meeting between seller and buyer, and that the sale would not be allowed if it violated any law of either the dealer's or purchaser's state.

Other provisions of the bill would: limit federal inspections of gun dealers' compliance with gun control laws to once a year, with a prior warning; allow firearms owners to transport their weapons through other states without abiding by those states' weapons laws, provided that the firearms were unloaded and relatively inaccessible; and protect individuals from prosecution under gun control laws unless they could be shown to have "willfully" broken the laws in question. To become law, the bill would need confirmation by the House of Representatives. But Rep. Peter W. Rodino Jr. (D, N.J.), chairman of the House Judiciary Committee, declared he would make sure the bill never reached the House floor.

St. Petersburg Times

St. Petersburg, FL, July 11, 1985

The case for controlling handguns is made by statistics that show the United States to be the most dangerous place in the civilized world. Each year, more than 10,000 Americans are murdered with handguns. Handguns figure in another 250,000 rapes, robberies and non-fatal assaults. In Florida alone in 1984 six law enforcement officers were killed with firearms at close range.

These are the facts the U.S. Senate disregarded Tuesday when it voted to weaken — not strengthen — the existing federal firearms laws. A plausible argument might have been made for relaxing some of the laws on interstate sales of rifles and shotguns, which are used primarily for sporting purposes and only incidentally for crime. Nothing but political cowardice explains the Senate's decision to relax the controls on handguns, too.

Opinion polls consistently show that most Americans want tougher handgun laws. But public opinion is rarely a match for the muscle and money of dedicated single-interest lobbies such as the National Rifle Association (NRA), which gave $1.4-million to federal candidates in the last two elections and delights in telling politicians that its members vote the gun issue and nothing else.

At least the Senate's bill faces stiff opposition in the House, where Rep. Peter W. Rodino Jr., D-N.J., declared it "dead on arrival." Rodino, chairman of the House Judiciary Committee, has made it clear he will work hard to keep the legislation off the House floor.

THE PERFORMANCE of Florida's senators contrasts with the courage Gov. Bob Graham displayed when he vetoed the bill that would have let just about anyone with the $100 price of a license carry a concealed weapon in public. Florida Sens. Lawton Chiles and Paula Hawkins voted to pass the NRA bill, after having voted to table Sen. Edward M. Kennedy's amendment to differentiate between sporting weapons and handguns. Chiles has long been a lost soul on this issue, but better might have been expected of Hawkins considering her tireless interest in the cause of missing and abused children. Children are handgun victims, too: Consider the tragic shooting in Seminole Wednesday.

As the Senate passed it, the bill makes only one constructive contribution to the war on crime. It would forbid the continued importation of the parts used to make cheap, small pistols such as the one John Hinckley Jr., used in his attempt to kill President Reagan. (It is already illegal to import the small guns themselves.) But this gain fails to reach the underlying problem with handguns, which has to do less with their cost than how easily they can be concealed. Cox Newspapers, which conducted thorough research on that subject, reported in 1981 that 10 of the 15 leading crime guns were made in America of U.S. parts, and most of them did not come cheap.

THE MOUNTING toll of handgun crimes argues for stronger federal legislation concerning the sale and possession of these weapons. The Senate's bill points the wrong way by making it legal to buy a gun outside the purchaser's home state. The bill purports to require that the sale be face-to-face and that it comply with the local laws in force in both states. That's unworkable to the point of being facetious, since by one estimate gun dealers would have to be familiar with 20,000 different local laws.

Another mischievous provision restricts federal officials to one annual inspection of a gun dealer's records. That's a severe handicap on law enforcement and a significant benefit to organized crime.

There's no doubting that the gun laws are a burden on legitimate dealers, target shooters and hunters, the vast majority of whom are law-abiding people. But that burden is justified by the great harm that comes from letting handguns fall into the wrong hands. In their selfish interest to be rid of federal regulation, the gun lobbyists and their Senate allies would make America an even more dangerous place to live.

BUFFALO EVENING NEWS

Buffalo, NY, July 12, 1985

EACH YEAR 10,000 Americans die by gunfire. Each year there are 500,000 violent crimes involving guns. Each year the nation piles another 2.5 million handguns into the private arsenals of its citizens. Yet the Senate has overwhelmingly passed a bill that would make it easier rather than more difficult to buy and sell these deadly weapons.

The Senate measure would significantly weaken the gun-control law passed in 1968 following the assassinations of the Rev. Dr. Martin Luther King and Sen. Robert F. Kennedy.

The bill would add a ban on the importation of parts of small pistols, such as the Saturday night specials so often used in crimes. But plugging this loophole in the 1968 law is almost the sole redeeming value of the Senate proposal.

Most interstate gun purchases are now illegal. The chief defect of the new measure is that it would cripple that responsible gun-control provision. It would allow a buyer from one state to purchase a gun in another state over-the-counter, provided the sale didn't violate the laws of either the seller's or the buyer's state.

Rejected by the Senate was an effort to impose a waiting period during which a dealer could check out a potential buyer or an emotionally upset buyer would cool down. Also rejected was a sensible compromise offered by Sen. Edward M. Kennedy that would have allowed the interstate sale of rifles and shotguns, thus accommodating the legitimate interests of sportsmen and hunters, but retained the ban on interstate sale of pistols—the weapons most often used in crimes.

Although weakening of the interstate gun-sale rules represents the gravest drawback of the Senate bill, it is not the only one. Enforcement standards would also decline. Prosecutions would be prohibited unless the alleged violator knew he violated the law. Law enforcement officials, many of whom oppose the Senate bill, would find it harder to keep weapons seized in criminal activities. Whereas the records of gun dealers may now be inspected by federal officials at any time, under the Senate bill inspections would be limited to once a year.

No wonder that Sen. Kennedy said the legislation "undermines the fundamental effort to protect citizens from violent crime."

That frames the perspective from which the House should look at the bill. No one should object to the possession of guns by sportsmen, hobbyists and those with a demonstrated need to protect themselves. But with so much public concern over crime, and with so much of it violent crime, why make it easier for everyone, including criminals, to secure concealable weapons?

The answer is that Congress shouldn't do that, and the House should assure that result.

The Hutchinson News

*Hutchinson, KS,
July 10, 1985*

The National Rifle Association wants greater freedom for the sale of guns in America.

What the gun lobby wants, it may very well get.

The Senate Tuesday passed changes that would further weaken the nation's already pathetically weak gun control laws.

The key change would remove an existing ban on interstate sales of guns. A buyer of a gun could leave his state, go across the state line and pick up a gun, so long as the sale didn't violate the laws of either the seller's state or the buyer's state.

Other technical changes would make life easier for the gun buyers and gun sellers.

The changes would not make life easier for the law enforcement officers who have to deal with the effects of guns in America.

Five national police organizations have vigorously opposed the changes. They're right in opposing these changes, though changes are needed.

The changes that are needed, however, would strengthen the regulations against handguns. Assembly, sale, manufacture and spread of handguns should be much more difficult, not much less difficult, in America.

Post-Tribune

Gary, IN, July 12, 1985

Hunting elk in Idaho is not the same as hunting people in Gary, Baltimore or Houston, but many U.S. senators apparently don't see the difference. The Senate has passed a bill that would allow interstate sale of handguns not now allowed under federal law. It's wrong.

Members of the House should correct this mistake. The bill sponsored by Sen.

**Our
opinions**

James McClure of Idaho is too broad. It would allow a hunter from New York to buy a replacement rifle in Idaho, for example, instead of having to return home for the purchase. This would be a convenience for the hunter, but it also would be an invitation for a nut to buy a handgun he can't get back in his home state.

True, the law in the gun buyer's home state must be obeyed under this new bill — that is, if New York had a waiting period between sale and possession of the weapon, the Idaho dealer would have to honor that rule. But opponents of the bill said this would give gun dealers a massive headache. Can they learn details of hundreds of laws across the country?

There was an answer to that, but the majority paid no attention. Sen. Daniel Inouye of Hawaii proposed a 14-day waiting period before a purchaser could take custody of a handgun. He lost, of course. Lack of a uniform federal waiting period makes a joke of attempts to keep handguns from people who shouldn't have them.

The bill has other provisions that make anti-gun control people happy. The revisions to the 1968 gun control act indicates the gun lobby is growing restive. Many leading police officials opposed the changes, because they see the loosening of restrictions on handgun sales. The vice president of the International Association of Police Chiefs predicted the Senate would pass the bill because most senators who want to be re-elected are impressed with the power of the National Rifle Association. He has a point.

Doing a favor for sportsmen is commendable. But surely there can be a compromise between making it easier to buy a rifle and opening the doors to more handgun sales. Easing needless red tape is commendable. Weakening the law that applies to handguns and "Saturday Night Specials" is foolish.

The title of the Senate bill is a masterpiece of diversion. It is called a measure "to protect firearm owners' constitutional rights, civil liberties and rights to privacy." But it does not fool police officials, nor does it ease the ache of people whose relatives have been shot down by nuts with handguns.

The Providence Journal

Providence, RI, July 9, 1985

When the Senate votes today on a bill to weaken the nation's already inadequate gun control law, the American public will be watching. The polls show that a majority of people in this country want some form of gun control. As far back as 1938, Gallup found 79 percent favored government registration of pistols and revolvers.

For the last decade the gun lobby, led by the National Rifle Association (NRA), has been trying to undermine the Gun Control Act of 1968, a law of feeble pretensions that seeks to set some limits on what gun dealers and owners can do to promote commerce in lethal weapons. It bans the importation of "non-sporting" handguns but not handgun parts. It requires a purchase form to be filled out with answers to certain questions but verification of the individual's identity is not required. And it bans interstate traffic in guns. In essence, however, it relies on the states to enact and enforce their own statutes.

When the NRA began its campaign, it referred to the McClure-Volkmer bill, scheduled for today's Senate floor vote, as "the first step toward repeal" of the 1968 law. It would alter the interstate commerce ban to allow the purchase of handguns across state lines, so long as laws in the buyer's and seller's states were not violated. It would also allow the interstate transport of guns, but this provision was modified when critics complained that it would invalidate some state laws. It now provides that only unloaded, inaccessible weapons can be so transported.

Other sops for the gun lobby include an end-run around record-keeping requirements by allowing dealers to maintain "personal" gun collections from which individual items could be sold without the usual paperwork. Further, surprise visits to gun dealers by law enforcement officers would be prohibited. Under the bill dealers would have to be warned in advance.

The only possible justification for this dangerous bill is a compromise change worked out on June 24. It would, finally, deal with the question of importing gun parts for small cheap handguns assembled in this country and sold by the millions — the so-called Saturday Night Special. It would ban imports of barrels, frames and receivers of handguns not intended for sporting use.

Perhaps someday Congress will get around to curbing sales of machineguns. The .45-caliber Ingram MAC-10, said to be popular among drug dealers and right-wing extremist groups, can be bought by anyone with no record of felony convictions who fills out a form and pays a $200 tax. The weapon fires 1,200 rounds a minute.

The McClure-Volkmer bill is a Trojan horse designed by its supporters to subvert the only federal gun control law the country has. The importation of handgun parts should have been ended years ago. This merits strong separate legislation. But McClure-Volkmer for the most part is a thinly disguised travesty to take the wraps off gun trading in America and get the Bureau of Alcohol, Tobacco and Firearms off the gun owner's back. It should be defeated.

The Kansas City Times

Kansas City, MO, July 11, 1985

The Senate ought to hang its head in shame for its retreat on gun control. How quickly are forgotten the agonies of public assassinations and private "accidents." How easily are put aside outraged determination to end such a barbaric way of life in America.

The loosened law the Senate likes comes from a muddled issue. It appears to clearly pit sportsmen against traditional gun control advocates. But in truth, that's a distraction. The gun lobby pursues the same old demands.

Sen. James A. McClure's bill is curiously called "a reform," usually taken to mean change for the better. This isn't. Its outstanding feature makes it easier to buy guns. The arsenal in the bosom of families and decent neighborhoods is already fatally swollen. More guns aren't needed. Trafficking is too easy.

Isn't anyone alarmed that law enforcement officials are opposed? They're not just benignly observing the bill as something of no value for controlling the astounding flow of weapons; they practically begged legislators at congressional hearings not to hinder their work.

The McClure bill would lift a ban on gun sales to out-of-state residents, provided they're qualified under local laws and their own state's. Imagine monitoring the nation's 250,000 gun dealers to see that they know all those laws and are abiding by them. Police say they can't. They say they have a hard enough time now enforcing the ban on selling guns to felons, addicts and mental patients.

And to make matters worse, the measure lacks a waiting period for background checks of purchasers. Sane voices urge a two-week interval before a weapon is handed over.

It's too bad Missouri and Kansas senators all jumped on the bandwagon. Moreover, the notion this is the only way to ensure that a vacationing Missouri hunter whose rifle is damaged in Colorado can buy a replacement immediately is ridiculous. A compromise to ease hunters' problems introduced last year by the Senate Judiciary Committee disproves it. Fortunately, amendments to plug the law's major holes loom ahead in the House. Maybe more courage in bucking the National Rifle Association and friends will be evident there.

Congress ought to listen to law enforcement protests. If professionals call this law wrong, they can't be dismissed as mere misguided sentimentalists.

Los Angeles, CA, July 11, 1985

The Senate has just approved an overhaul of federal gun-control laws. The new law retains many of the restraints of the old, including the requirements that buyer and seller transact their business face-to-face and that the sale not violate state regulations. So far, so good. But one major change was imprudent. The bill would permit a person from one state, say, California with its strict gun-control laws, to go to another state with less stringent regulations, say, Nevada, and buy a gun. That may be all right for shotguns or rifles, but the Senate should not have eased the interstate rules for the short-barrelled handgun, sometimes called the "snubbie."

The Gun Control Act of 1968 no doubt needed many of the changes made by the Senate. Its prohibition on citizens from one state buying, selling or transferring weapons to citizens from another prevented a gun owner from even giving a gun to an out-of-state relative as a gift. The law was never meant to be this sweeping. Moreover, according to the National Rifle Association, which flexed its lobbying muscles in the one-sided Senate victory, the record-keeping requirements in the existing law led to some gun dealers being prosecuted for honest mistakes.

We do have doubts about the upper house's refusal to require a 14-day waiting period before a buyer can take custody of a gun. The NRA argues that criminals don't buy their guns from legitimate gun dealers. That may be true much of the time, but some criminals doubtless obtain guns legitimately. And we suspect that some of the drug abusers, mentally ill and illegal immigrants who are legally barred from buying guns get their weapons the same way. A 14-day delay could only inhibit them.

Still, imposing that waiting period would have required a new restriction. The relaxed attitude toward "snubbies," by contrast, involved removing restrictions that have long been in force. We hope and expect that the House will balk at lifting existing restraints, and that in respecting the right to bear arms, it will recognize that not all arms are created equal.

LAS VEGAS REVIEW-JOURNAL

Las Vegas, NV, July 5, 1985

Each year 10,000 people are murdered with firearms. Each year firearms are involved in half a million crimes of violence.

In testimony before a Senate committee, it was estimated that a new handgun is sold every 13 seconds, and each year 2.5 million handguns are added to private arsenals. Some estimate that by the year 2000, Americans will own 100 million handguns.

But then, guns don't kill people, we are told. Only people kill people. That's true, as far as it goes. But if guns weren't so readily available, there would be more than a few people walking around who aren't now. If triggers were harder to come by, fewer would be pulled.

Clearly, guns can cause problems, and there should be laws governing them.

A bill changing the Gun Control Act of 1968 is scheduled to come to a Senate vote next Tuesday. It does several good things:

It allows the government to ban importation of barrels, frames and receivers for guns not intended for sporting purposes. It allows for licensees to sell guns at gun shows, which incorporates regulations already adopted by the Bureau of Alcohol, Tobacco and Firearms.

It would increase penalties for use of a firearm in commission of a felony under federal law, and strengthen existing law that now prohibits gun dealers from transferring weapons to forbidden categories of buyers. Under the bill, not only licensed dealers but also "any person" would be prohibited from transferring weapons to felony fugitives, drug abusers, illegal aliens, mental incompetents and others.

The bill, however, does several bad things.

It relieves gun dealers from some of their record-keeping requirements. Specifically, it would allow gun dealers to maintain "personal" gun collections from which they could sell handguns without keeping any records. And it abolishes the requirement that records be kept on the sale of ammunition.

This has raised concerns in the law enforcement community. In 1982, police were able to trace about 30,000 handguns used in crimes because of the record-keeping provisions of the 1968 act. In 81 percent of these traces, it helped authorities solve a crime, recover stolen property or convict a suspect. John Hinckley's handgun was traced in less than 15 minutes.

The bill also would overturn federal regulations on interstate sales by allowing them as long as the sales are lawful in the sellers' and buyers' jurisdictions. This would put a tremendous onus on gun dealers to be familiar with every state and local jurisdiction's gun laws. If gun dealers feel they can handle it, fine. But ignorance will be no excuse when it comes to prosecution.

And the bill does not go far enough in at least one other area. There should be a national waiting period for handgun buyers to allow for a criminal records check by local police.

The bill has its merits. There are other considerations, however, that the Senate and the full Congress must address before it becomes law.

The Houston Post

Houston, TX, July 13, 1985

Why the U.S. Senate wants to add new poundage to the already heavy burden on the back of U.S. law enforcment is beyond us. Yet that is the almost-certain effect of the gun bill passed 69-15 by the upper chamber on Tuesday if it becomes law.

The measure, sponsored by Sen. James McClure, R-Idaho, would override state laws regarding transportation of firearms and would permit sales of guns to out-of-state customers so long as the sale was legal in both states. This was touted by backers as a means to free hunters and gun collectors from excessive restrictions.

As with much political rhetoric, this is true as far as it goes. What it also would do is remove those same restrictions from every petty criminal and hit man in the nation. It's cliched but true: handguns aren't sportsmen's weapons. The Senate could have freed up just the long guns, but it would brook no compromise.

With 200,000 to 250,000 firearms dealers in the country, sales of handguns to people who are up to no good will surely skyrocket while the weapons themselves become as needles in the paperwork haystack. Too, there is that nagging question of whether local lawmakers may not know best what their people need and want.

The House should bury this bill — deep, cold and dead.

Albuquerque, NM, July 13, 1985

Once again the U.S. Senate has capitulated to the National Rifle Association, this time by gutting the already-weak 1968 Gun Control Act. It is now up to the House to exercise good judgment by killing S-49.

The Senate voted 79-15 to repeal federal laws that ban interstate and quickie sales of handguns and other firearms. The laws were adopted in 1968 in reaction to the assassinations of Sen. Robert F. Kennedy and the Rev. Martin Luther King.

The Senate bought arguments of the NRA that the laws imposed too much of a nuisance on dealers, sportsmen and others interested in prompt transactions. By rejecting a 14-day waiting period on handgun purchases, the Senate sold out to deranged killers, criminals in a hurry and impulse buyers.

By kowtowing to the gun lobby, 79 senators thumbed their noses at advice of the nation's top law enforcement officials and recommendations made in numerous crime study reports.

And to what end? So that even more Americans can be shot and the nation can continue to lead the world in the annual toll of deaths by gunshot.

Rep. Peter W. Rodino Jr., D-N.J., and the House Judiciary Committee he chairs, can do some killing of their own by burying the Senate bill quietly — or with the pomp and circumstance deserving such a victory for Americans concerned about their safety.

The Senate obviously has chosen to ignore widespread support for more — not fewer — controls on handguns. Let's hope the House acts more sensibly.

THE CHRISTIAN SCIENCE MONITOR

Boston, MA, July 12, 1985

AH, summer — a time for lounging and relaxation. Perhaps it's the fact that millions of Americans are now on vacations, or just "thinking summer" by focusing on such pastimes as baseball and the beach; perhaps it's the fact that the daily flow of news has been dominated of late by the hostage crisis. But whatever the reasons, the American public is apparently unaware that Congress is in the midst of making significant changes in what has been one of the most controversial laws ever enacted by the US government.

We are referring to the Gun Control Act of 1968, which was passed after the assassinations of the Rev. Dr. Martin Luther King Jr. and US Sen. Robert F. Kennedy. The measure was enacted to prevent, as much as possible, firearms from coming into the hands of dangerous persons.

Earlier this week, by a top-heavy 79-to-15 vote, the Senate startled much of official Washington by enacting a measure that would substantially loosen the 1968 act. The measure now goes to the House, where proponents expect a much tougher fight.

Proponents of change would seem best served in going through the regular committee process in the House. That would be better than bypassing the committee system and going directly to the House floor, as they were able to do in the Senate. The 1968 act has been on the books for almost two decades. That means that proponents of change would seem to have the burden of proof to show why reform is necessary, and why loosening the law would not lead to even more problems than exist under the current legal framework.

The committee process would also enable the public as a whole — rather than just interest groups ("pro-gun" or "anti-gun") — to take part in the debate. Several of the proposed changes warrant detailed analysis:

● The Senate measure would make it easier to buy a firearm outside the buyer's home state. Currently, most interstate gun purchases are prohibited. Would such a relaxation lead to an increase in the number of firearms held by Americans, already extraordinarily high?

● Collectors who occasionally sell firearms and people who sell ammunition would, in certain instances, no longer have to obtain a dealer's license. Also, normal federal inspections would be restricted. At present, federal agents can inspect records at any time. Under the Senate measure, there would be one inspection a year. Might such changes reduce useful monitoring of the firearms trade?

The House should examine the Senate measure with as much deliberation as possible.

House Vote Loosens Firearms Curbs; Strong NRA Lobbying Cited

The U.S. House of Representatives April 10, 1986 voted by a wide margin to ease firearms restrictions. The House measure, together with a similar bill passed by the Senate in 1985, would make the first significant changes in the landmark 1968 Gun Control Act. The vote, after intense lobbying by groups for and against the measure, was not close: 286 in favor, 136 opposed. Among Republicans, 158 favored the bill; 128 Democrats voted for passage.

Observers called the bill's passage a victory for the powerful National Rifle Association (NRA) and remarked that House debate had been largely confined to how much of the 1968 Gun Control Act ought to be changed. There had been little said on whether the measure should be kept intact. The House bill, drafted by Rep. Harold Volkmer (D, Mo.), corresponded closely to its Senate counterpart, the work of Sen. James McClure (R, Idaho). The House and Senate bills were officially known as the Firearms Owners Protection Act (FOPA). Among other things, FOPA would end the current ban on the transportation of firearms across state lines, ease the record-keeping requirements for gun dealers, require "willful" violations for felony prosecutions of dealers, allow more people to sell firearms without keeping records and permit the sale between states of rifles and shotguns. There were differences between the House and Senate measures. Unlike the Senate measure, the House bill would not allow handguns to be sold between states. And the House measure would ban the sale and possession of machine guns, although without requiring confiscation of those that had already been purchased.

Intense lobbying over FOPA had been marked by a split between traditional allies: the NRA and law enforcement groups that in the past had sided with the NRA to oppose gun control. Now almost a dozen police groups opposed FOPA as an aid to criminals. However, with about 3 million members and a sophisticated political apparatus, the NRA was widely credited with the ability to cause serious trouble at the polls for the officeholders it targeted. Following the April 10 vote the group estimated that it had spent some $1.6 million on advertising and lobbying. The police group's lobbying had cost about $15,000, according to the International Association of Chiefs of Police.

Lincoln Journal

Lincoln, NE, April 11, 1986

Let the gun lobby crow about its victory Thursday in the U.S. House, whose members voted to weaken the national gun law. It may have won the battle, but along the way it lost some important allies, and that will make future fights tougher to win.

Indeed, Thursday's triumph was far from clear-cut. Gun-control advocates could also claim victory on a crucial issue — interstate handgun sales. The House voted to retain a ban on such sales.

Still, as Hubert Williams, president of the Police Foundation, said, the Volkmer bill adopted by the House is bad legislation. It allows interstate sales and transportation of rifles and shotguns. It relaxes reporting requirements for gun dealers and limits unannounced inspections of dealers' records by U.S. agents to once a year. It permits dealers to transfer guns from inventories to their private collections.

In a society as concerned about crime as ours is — especially terrorism — how can Congress justify any softening of firearms regulations? But pressure from the gun lobby was intense. The National Rifle Association reportedly spent $1.5 million on advertising supporting the Volkmer bill.

To the credit of a number of representatives, they found elimination of the ban on interstate handgun sales too much to swallow and switched positions, reversing an earlier vote on that question. Ready availability of handguns contributes to the appalling record of murders, accidents and suicides that makes the United States the scandal of the civilized world.

Salvaging that ban, together with a prohibition on traffic in machine guns, is an achievement on which gun-control supporters can build.

They can also take heart from the fact that the traditional tie between the gun lobby and law enforcement officers appears ruptured beyond repair. Nearly a dozen police groups, many of whose members also belong to the NRA, saw the Volkmer bill as a way to put more guns in the hands of criminals. They are bitter about the gun lobby's stand.

The House bill goes to the Senate, which must accept it or seek its reconciliation with the Senate's own measure. In that and other gun-control struggles to come, police groups can recognize the forces behind sensible firearms laws as their true friends.

Arkansas Gazette.

Little Rock, AR, April 12, 1986

In the end, the gun lobby appears to have won most of what it wanted, with the help of most members of the Arkansas congressional delegation. The exceptions, within the legislation and within the delegation, are worth noting.

Over the objections of police officers from across the country, the House of Representatives voted 292 to 130 Thursday to weaken the federal gun control law, which was enacted 18 years ago in reaction to the murders of Dr. Martin Luther King Jr. and Senator Robert F. Kennedy. The bill approved Thursday makes it easier to buy and transport rifles and shotguns across state lines, and relaxes record-keeping rules for gun dealers. All four Arkansas representatives voted for the bill, as both Arkansas senators had voted for a similar bill previously.

The House bill now goes to the Senate, which can accept it as is or demand a conference to work out the differences between the two bills. The big difference is that on one key provision, the House sided with the police rather than the National Rifle Association, voting 233 to 184 to retain the present ban on interstate sales of handguns. Three of the Arkansas representatives went down the line with the NRA on this vote, too.

But Representative Beryl Anthony of El Dorado showed his mettle, voting to retain the ban. Anthony also voted for two other amendments, both defeated, that were backed by the police and opposed by the NRA.

So it was that Anthony alone among Arkansas congressmen stood up for law and order in the crunch, and deserves the credit. It is no coincidence, as Anthony himself noted, that he is a former prosecuting attorney and knows first-hand the need for restrictions on the arms traffic. Representative Tommy Robinson of Jacksonville, who also claims some law-enforcement experience, followed the NRA line docilely. But Robinson was always more showman than sheriff — and he got a timely $4,950 campaign gift from the NRA last year when he signed on the NRA's bill.

(Senators Bumpers and Pryor might have shown up better — we'll never know for sure — had the NRA not misled the Senate. At the time the Senate voted, the NRA was telling senators that the police supported removal of the ban on interstate handgun sales.)

Despite winning one fall, those who favor sensible laws on gun trafficking must consider this new legislation a setback, if the final House version becomes law, as it probably will. The names of the victims may not be as big as they were in 1968, but the slaughter continues. There is no good reason to weaken the existing gun control laws. We should be moving in the other direction.

St. Petersburg Times

St. Petersburg, FL, April 12, 1986

On Thursday, the House of Representatives rewarded the tireless efforts of the National Rifle Association by voting to make it easier to buy, sell and transport most firearms.

The next morning, as the NRA celebrated its victory, two FBI agents died and five others were wounded in an intense gun battle with suspected bank robbers at Miami.

"There must've been 100 rounds fired," said a witness. "They were shooting for 10 minutes."

To reprise the NRA position on such matters, criminals who want guns will always find a way to get them, so the solution is not to restrict guns but to prosecute criminals to the fullest extent of the law.

THE CRIMINALS in this case cannot be prosecuted because they are dead. The slain FBI agents cannot be brought back to life. And the NRA argument is garbage, as America's police tried so hard to tell Congress this week.

Police work is especially hazardous in the United States because the country is awash in all kinds of guns, including an estimated 60-million handguns as well as an undetermined number of machine guns, the legality of which defies all common sense. No one can say that gun control wouldn't work, because the NRA has never allowed real gun control to be attempted. But the federal law in force since 1968 at least has given the police and public more protection than they would have had without it, and it has given law enforcement another way to stop some criminals before they kill.

That's the law the House voted to gut despite the concerted opposition of 10 national police organizations, including the one that represents federal agents. The police — and the public — won one important concession when the House voted to retain the existing ban on the interstate sale of handguns. They won another forbidding the private purchase and sale of machine guns. A serendipitous result is that America's police now know the NRA for what it is — their enemy.

But the bill as passed would legalize the interstate transport of all firearms, including handguns, through states and communities that attempt to prohibit them. It requires gun dealers to keep fewer records and display them less often to federal agents and allows dealers to transfer guns from their commercial inventories to their private collections, from where they could be sold to others without any records.

IT TELLS all that there is to know about the NRA that it opposed the amendments to ban machine guns and prevent the interstate sale of handguns, and that it even lobbied against an amendment, not formally offered, to prevent the sale of silencers and the new plastic-component handguns that may be undetectable by some airport screening devices. Why should any law-abiding citizen need a silencer? To dispatch wounded game, says the NRA!

A much better compromise bill was on the floor, but the NRA wouldn't hear of it being taken up. So Thursday was a day of disgrace for the House of Representatives, which should have killed the NRA bill, and doubly so for those members, including most of Florida's, who rejected the police-backed amendments to continue the ban on the interstate transportation of handguns. Florida Reps. William Chappell, Connie Mack and Michael Bilirakis even voted to legalize the interstate sale of handguns.

After the votes, an otherwise unidentified "leading western Democrat" was quoted in the *Washington Post* as saying, "If we cast a secret ballot, the police chiefs would win today. It's the kind of issue that could defeat me when nothing else could." The message to the police is that they are expendable but congressional careers are not.

The NRA's officers, meanwhile, have only to decide whether to put the House bill through the Senate, which passed a worse version last year, or go to conference committee. Ronald Reagan's signature is assured.

Do you suppose they'll take time to send condolences to Miami?

The Washington Post

Washington, DC, April 11, 1986

THE CHIEF LOBBYISTS of the National Rifle Association may gloat over their success in getting their paid army of House members to soften up this country's gun laws. But there is more than a little evidence that members of Congress, law enforcement officers and people in general are fed up with the NRA's tactics as well as its narrow dogma. In one rare and important defeat of the NRA, the House did vote yesterday to retain a ban on the interstate sales of handguns. Though this is status quo and hardly progress, the NRA has been pressing long and hard for a lifting of any restrictions on interstate traffic in concealable weapons.

And it is precisely this NRA attitude that has infuriated police, sheriffs, state troopers, public safety protectors and widows and family members of law enforcement authorities all around the country. They are the people who suffer most in the battle to control crime—and they have been pleading with Congress for this provision and others that would help them do their jobs and live to tell about it. And while they were pleased to have cracked the NRA's hold for once, they are still angry at the organization and at the individual House members who ignored their pleas.

Officials of the D.C. chapter of the Fraternal Order of Police—the country's largest police organization—said yesterday they will ask local FOP members to drop their NRA memberships. Thomas Tague, president of the local FOP, which has about 6,100 members in various law enforcement agencies in this area, said he also will ask national officials for support in helping to persuade the estimated 180,000 members around the country to quit the NRA as well. "The NRA is no longer a friend of law enforcement," said Gary Hankins, labor committee chairman for the local group. "They have become a lobbyist organization for gun dealers, not sportsmen. . . . This bill is very dangerous to us and very dangerous to the community. . . . We will have more people to honor, more dead to mourn in the coming years."

That, and not the legitimate interests of law-abiding gun owners, is what the NRA and its heavy political contributions are about these days—and if public safety is threatened by it, give their lobbyists and those who do their bidding on the Hill full credit.

THE CHRISTIAN SCIENCE MONITOR

Boston, MA, April 11, 1986

DON'T imagine for a moment that the gun lobby has relaxed for an instant its pressure to reverse gun control legislation since it was passed 18 years ago. This week it almost succeeded in repealing prohibitions on the interstate sale and transport of handguns. But it did ease record-keeping rules for dealers, and it won House approval of transportation of rifles and shotguns in interstate commerce.

Much of the original law stays in place. But the House vote nonetheless takes a perplexing step backward.

The original law was passed after the assassinations — by guns — of three national leaders as the nation was watching its cities go up in smoke and there was widespread concern over maintaining the fabric of American society. What is different today?

Little that would seem to justify changing the law. There was no effort afoot to make more stringent the controls that would affect, say, sportsmen. The general public still approves of limitations on gun ownership. If the concerns about crime are genuine, the spread of more concealable weapons designed chiefly to kill human beings would not make sense. If there is worry that law enforcement officials should have greater support in their work, the appeals of such officials to maintain current curbs should be heeded. If terrorism in the skies and abroad merits the attention it is getting, it hardly follows that acquiring the instruments for private acts of terror in our communities should be made easier. Some of these concerns were met in the House compromise result.

Many Americans continue to resent any abridgment of their individual liberties, whether having to wear a seat belt when driving or having to follow prescribed rules in buying weapons. Others may feel that owning a gun offers them some measure of protection against crime in an era of violence — despite evidence that owners or their families are the chief victims of their own weapons.

There is no evidence that Americans want to return to vigilantism — although Washington's impatience to blast back at terrorists or their sponsors, or to introduce armed force in Central America, may tend to induce such feelings.

It was a mixed outcome. The House held the line against handguns, and it won another prohibition against ownership of machine guns. But it yielded on the long guns that are sportsmen's main concern.

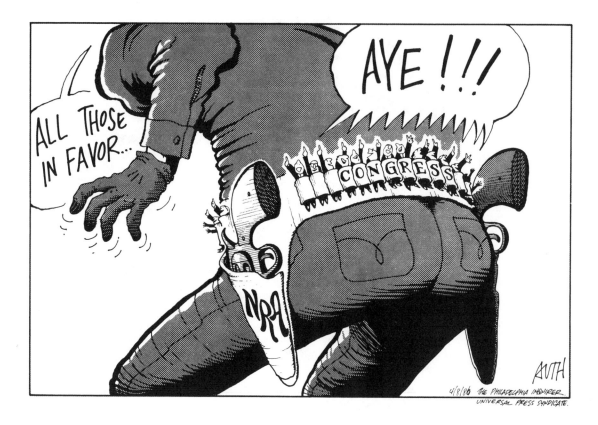

The Chattanooga Times

Chattanooga, TN, April 12, 1986

Although the House of Representatives approved on Thursday legislation which substantially weakens the Gun Control Act of 1968, the day was not a total loss. By a vote of 233 to 184, the House agreed to retain the prohibition on interstate sale of handguns. We were sorely disappointed to see that Rep. Marilyn Lloyd voted in favor of removing even that restriction. Her vote was cast against the interests of effective law enforcement in this country.

A coalition of national law-enforcement organizations lobbied the House against the Senate-passed legislation to weaken federal gun controls. Hundreds of uniformed officers were at the Capitol to plead their case that crime prevention would be hindered and the lives of police officers placed in greater danger if the bill were passed. Since handguns represent the greatest danger to public safety, maintaining the law against their sale across state lines was their top priority.

But the nation's law enforcement officers were outgunned, so to speak, by the National Rifle Association. The police coalition spent about $15,000 on its lobbying effort, compared to an NRA-financed, $1.6 million lobbying campaign in favor of emasculating gun controls. It's nothing to be proud of that the executive director of the International Association of Chiefs of Police can credibly say of the nation's capital, "As far as I can see, the NRA has a stranglehold on this city."

The legislation now returns to the Senate. We strongly urge the upper chamber to loosen the NRA stranglehold enough at least to accept the differences in the House-passed bill, most important among which is the ban on interstate sale of handguns.

BUFFALO EVENING NEWS

Buffalo, NY, April 14, 1986

IN THE WAKE of the murder of Sen. Robert F. Kennedy and the Rev. Dr. Martin Luther King Jr. in 1968, Congress passed the landmark Gun Control Act to curb criminal access to firearms. Congress is now acting to make the first major change in that law, and it is a change for the worse.

The House last week voted to ease the regulations of the 1968 law and make it easier to buy, sell and transport firearms.

Fortunately, however, the gun-control forces, including many police and law-enforcement agencies, did succeed in maintaining an essential ban on the interstate sale of handguns.

The Senate passed an even worse measure last year, opening up the interstate sale of all firearms, including handguns. In any House-Senate compromise, those fighting for responsible regulation of firearms must make sure that the House measure is not watered down any further.

The legislation was the focus of emotional appeals on Capitol Hill, where representatives of the powerful gun lobby were opposed by uniformed policemen and widows of slain officers. Some congressmen said privately they would have voted against the measure except for fear of the gun lobby in the coming congressional election.

The National Rifle Association achieved most of its objectives — the end of the ban on interstate sales of rifles and shotguns; the right to carry unloaded firearms, including handguns, across state lines; and a reduction in regulations concerning gun dealers: specifically, rules governing dealer record-keeping, reporting requirements and federal inspections.

Law-enforcement authorities rightly expressed concern over the weakening of firearms regulations. Jerald Vaughn of the International Association of Chiefs of Police said the House action would make it easier for criminals to obtain and carry firearms. This, he said, would impede law enforcement and make the work of police officers more dangerous.

The argument that "guns don't kill people — people do" falls flat in the face of statistics from other countries where there has not been the same enormous proliferation of firearms. In Britain, a country with strict gun controls, there were only four murders with handguns in all of 1983. In the United States, there were 10,000.

Sportsmen, hobbyists and those in need of protection should not be barred from obtaining firearms. But for the protection of all, the sale and possession of deadly weapons should be strictly controlled.

The 1968 law went a long way in this direction, although it should be strengthened to require a waiting period for prospective buyers of handguns so that their backgrounds can be checked prior to the final sale. This would not harm the interests of legitimate customers, and it could help prevent sales to criminals and others who might misuse the weapons.

Instead of bolstering the 1968 law, both houses of Congress have now acted to weaken it. The curb on handgun sales remains, however, and, since handguns are the weapons used in most crimes, it is most important to maintain this provision in the final version of the law.

THE COMMERCIAL APPEAL
Memphis, TN, April 15, 1986

THE National Rifle Association has won the battle in Congress to loosen federal gun controls, but it suffered a wound or two that may prove crippling in the long run.

The NRA and police organizations, allies in the past, developed a deep split. The police groups called the NRA-supported legislation a "cop-killer" bill. When the smoke had cleared after debate in the House of Representatives, some police organization spokesmen were urging officers to give up their memberships in the NRA.

The NRA may also have suffered a public image problem. The organization claims it looks out for the interests of sportsmen, but it came off as a lobbyist for gun manufacturers and dealers. It even successfully opposed a proposed ban on gun silencers, which are of no use to sportsmen but are of value to criminals.

When the legislation finally clears Congress — the House bill still has to be reconciled with a slightly different Senate version — it will be the first relaxation of federal gun controls in nearly 20 years. The current law, which is weak enough as it stands, was enacted during the national revulsion over the assassinations of Sen.

Robert Kennedy and the Rev. Martin Luther King.

The NRA, which rewards its friends in Congress with campaign contributions and works vigorously to defeat its opponents, reportedly spent about $1.6 million on lobbying and advertising to get its bill passed. The executive director of the International Association of Police Chiefs, Jerald Vaughn, complained after the House vote. "As far as I can see, the NRA has a stranglehold on this city."

The legislation will allow interstate sale of rifles and shotguns, ease record-keeping rules for gun dealers, restrict federal inspections of gun shops, lift a ban on transportation of guns across state lines, and otherwise weaken federal controls.

NRA opponents did manage to keep in the law a ban on interstate sale of handguns. Sarah Brady, wife of the White House press secretary who was severely wounded during the attempted assassination of President Reagan, saw that as a major victory.

Still, the NRA got most of what it wanted. But there were signs that the organization overplayed its hand in a way that may lessen its effectiveness in the future.

Los Angeles, CA, April 10, 1986

The national interest prevailed over the National Rifle Association today when the House of Representatives added a critical amendment to legislation revising the 1968 Gun Control Act. The addition maintained the ban on interstate handgun sales that was originally established by the '68 law. While the change didn't fix all that was wrong with the NRA-supported bill, introduced by Rep. Harold Volkmer, it made the legislation more palatable.

The House had an alternative, in a bill introduced by Rep. William Hughes, which it defeated yesterday. Both the Hughes and Volkmer proposals would revise the Gun Control Act to make it easier for sportsmen and collectors to pursue their hobbies lawfully. Both would lift restrictions on the interstate sale and shipment of rifles and shotguns. We support those changes.

But in lifting the '68 bill's ban on the interstate sale and transport of handguns, including the short-barreled "snubbies" that are the pre-

ferred weapon for many criminals, Volkmer's bill would go too far. Moreover, the legislation would allow these sales without requiring dealers to run a background check on purchasers. Thus, it created the possibility of a citizen from a state like California, which requires a 15-day waiting period before gun buyers can take possession of their purchases, traveling to a state like Arizona, which has no waiting period, and loading up legally.

Not surprisingly, many law enforcement organizations, including the International Association of Chiefs of Police, lobbied hard against Volkmer's bill. But the NRA framed the legislation in terms of the right to bear arms.

Volkmer's bill now goes to the Senate, which last year approved an NRA-backed measure which allows the interstate sale of handguns. Senators can accept the House bill, with its tougher limits on handguns, or send the issue to a House-Senate conference to work out differences. We suggest the former. Protecting the rights of gun owners is one thing. Increasing the profits of gun dealers is another. In supporting interstate handgun sales, the NRA has confused the two and has cheapened the values it purports to uphold.

THE ANN ARBOR NEWS
Ann Arbor, MI, April 8, 1986

There are few issues which put legislators more on the spot than gun control. It happens again this week.

On Wednesday in the House of Representatives, members are scheduled to debate and then vote on the first major revisions to the federal Gun Control Act since it was enacted in that year of violence and assassinations, 1968.

A bill sponsored by Rep. Harold Volkmer, D-Mo., and a similar bill passed by the Senate last year 79-15 would allow interstate sales of all firearms and eliminate some of the record-keeping requirements for weapons transactions. (Michigan's Democratic senators split on the Senate bill, Donald Riegle voting in favor and Carl Levin opposed).

The Volkmer legislation, heavily lobbied by (who else?) the National Rifle Association, also would eliminate any need for gun "collectors" to keep records of transactions and prohibit Bureau of Alcohol, Tobacco and Firearms agents from making more than one random inspection of dealer records per year.

Gun dealers and NRA members argue the current ban on interstate sales of firearms, except from one licensed dealer to another, infringes on the right of citizens to purchase guns in other states.

But citing restraint of trade doesn't carry weight with law enforcement groups which oppose the Volkmer legislation. They contend the proposed changes would pose an "immediate and unwarranted threat to the law enforcement community," as one joint statement said.

The 1968 law barred mail order or interstate shipment of firearms and ammunition and established licensing procedures for those who manufacture, import, sell or collect guns and ammunition.

The law required licensed dealers to keep records of all firearms transactions and authorized federal authorities to inspect a licensee's inventory and records at any "reasonable" time without advance notice.

Michigan law requires all prospective gun buyers to first get a permit from their local police department, which checks whether the individual has a history of mental illness or crime. If a purchase permit is approved, the buyer must record the gun's serial number on the form and a copy is retained by the policy agency.

The state's gun regulations and the federal statute have helped law enforcement agencies determine where guns which have been used illegally were bought or stolen. If anything, the traffic in handguns and the number of serious crimes involving a gun would argue for tougher, not liberalized, gun laws.

S 49, passed in the Senate last year, and HR 945 — the Volkmer bill — would in all likelihood make it harder to trace weapons and ammunition for those investigating crimes.

Who beside the NRA wants revisions in gun control legislation? Not police groups or the BATF, which already has too few (70) inspectors nationwide to monitor licensed gun dealers. In Michigan, there are only 13 BATF agents for the entire state.

Second District Rep. Carl Pursell, R-Plymouth, is receiving mail running 3-2 in favor of the Volkmer legislation, but the congressman's office reports most of that mail is of the postcard, cookie-cutter variety — strongly suggesting the NRA has cranked up its membership again. Pursell as of Monday was still undecided on the Volkmer bill.

This country is a long way from showing it is in control of handguns. The more available guns are, the more they are used for destructive purposes. No other progressive industrialized nation is so tolerant of guns and their proliferation in the general populace, yet seems so indifferent about the human toll that gun abuse takes.

There is no conceivable reason why the NRA and their thoroughly cowed allies in Congress, many of whom (including Volkmer) accept money from the NRA, should be allowed to carry the day on a vital public safety issue. Pursell and the rest of the Michigan congressional delegation should vote to reject any bill that in effect serves to put still more weapons in general circulation, where they are increasingly used to inflict injury and death.

AKRON BEACON JOURNAL
Akron, OH, April 8, 1986

THE U.S. HOUSE takes a crucial vote Wednesday on two pieces of legislation that will either keep the current, modest controls on handguns or seriously weaken them.

The most dangerous proposal is the Volkmer Substitute, an amended version of the McClure-Volkmer bill, which would make it easier for criminals to get handguns, thus endangering the public and police officers. Police officers know this and virtually every major police organization has lobbied hard against the bill.

The Volkmer bill is a shameless attempt to favor the gun lobby at the expense of public safety by legalizing the interstate sale of handguns, making it tougher to prosecute gun dealers who violate the law, allowing dealers to sell firearms from their "private collection" without keeping records of the sale, and loosening the definition of "dealer," which handgun-control groups say would make it easier for terrorists and other criminals to get untracable firearms.

The Volkmer measure is simply a bad bill and should be voted against by every House member who supports public safety and keeping guns out of the hands of criminals. Fortunately, there is an alternative — the Hughes-McCollum amendments which are being backed by law enforcement organizations after being unanimously passed by the Judiciary Committee.

The Hughes package, which owes much to some good work by Rep. Edward Feighan, D-Ohio, would keep the controls on handgun sales, ban the sale of many cheap handguns and impose a waiting period before a handgun is purchased to allow a criminal background check. These provisions are needed to protect citizens and law-enforcement personnel from handgun violence.

This is one case in which the goals of the gun lobby clearly are in opposition to law and order. House members should understand that when they vote Wednesday and should refuse to weaken the already too-weak national gun-control laws.

The Hartford Courant
Hartford, CT, April 14, 1986

The U.S. House last week passed a bill that would do less harm to the 1968 Gun Control Act than a measure approved in July by the Senate, but it's misleading to call such irresponsible legislation preferable and leave it at that.

What Congress should do about gun control — assuming that it can't bring itself to tighten the federal laws — is to leave well enough alone. That option, however, seems to have been eliminated by intense lobbying from the National Rifle Association and other pro-gun groups.

Yielding to the pressure, the House and Senate have adopted bills that would weaken the nation's firearms laws considerably.

The worst aspects of both measures are the provisions to relax controls on interstate sales and transportation of firearms.

The Senate bill would let a rifle, shotgun or handgun be bought outside a buyer's home state, provided the laws in both states were followed. Current law bans interstate sales, with a narrow exception for rifles and shotguns when adjoining states are involved. The House voted to keep the prohibition on interstate handgun sales, but to allow a rifle or shotgun to be sold anywhere regardless of the buyer's state.

Handguns are the most dangerous of small arms, as the House — under pressure from police organizations — evidently came to realize. It's to the credit of Rep. Nancy L. Johnson of Connecticut, the recipient of a sizable sum from the NRA's political action committee, that she voted to keep the handgun sales ban. Rep. John G. Rowland, the only other member of the state's House delegation who received financial support from the NRA, voted against the handgun ban.

But the House bill, though better than the Senate's on that point, stopped halfway. Allowing across-the-border sales of rifles and shotguns promotes their acquisition by people with criminal intent. A dealer in, say, Utah isn't going to be familiar with the firearms laws in, say, Connecticut.

Interstate transportation of guns is entirely regulated by state and local governments now, but the House and Senate bills would remove that authority. Owners of guns could freely carry them across all state lines, which would hamper the efforts of police to stop the flow of weapons used in crimes. One would have thought that we thought political conservatives — who are the bills' most enthusiastic supporters — believed in local control and law enforcement.

The House bill is preferable to the Senate's in several other ways, but even all of what makes it better isn't enough to make it good. Once again, Americans are being treated to the uninspiring spectacle of Congress knuckling under to the gun lobby.

Mrs. Johnson's misgivings about handguns, by the way, didn't keep her from joining Mr. Rowland in voting for the gun decontrol bill as a whole. Connecticut's other four House members had the good sense to say no.

THE SACRAMENTO BEE
Sacramento, CA, April 11, 1986

To cast their votes against preserving even the modest level of gun control that this country has had for 18 years, the members of the House of Representatives had to file past the silent phalanx of uniformed chiefs of police, officers and state troopers from around the country, who lined the Capitol hallways in commemoration of the 700 police officers killed by firearms in the last decade and the hundreds more sure to be killed when guns become even easier to buy and even harder to trace.

To cast their votes, they had to dismiss the poignant pleas of the handgun victims and their families. They had to ignore Sarah Brady, whose husband, presidential press secretary James Brady, is still physically and neurologically disabled five years after he was shot during the attempted assassination of President Reagan. Even with the old law in place, his assailant, a man with a record of mental illness, was able to buy a Saturday Night Special for $29 at a pawnshop.

The politicians had to vote, despite the states' rights rhetoric of most of them, to override the gun laws and ordinances of hundreds of states and local communities. They had to ignore public opinion, which remains overwhelmingly in favor of the gun-control law they were gutting.

And they did it anyway — did it under the gun of the National Rifle Association, which has proved itself such a formidable fund-raiser and re-election spoiler. It was a craven demonstration.

There were small victories for law enforcement and sanity: The House did impose restrictions on sales of machine-gun conversion kits and silencers, which no one could straightfacedly claim would violate the civil rights of sportsmen. And the legislators did agree to preserve the current legal ban on interstate sales of handguns — although not the gun-store record-keeping requirements, the interstate transportation restrictions or many of the other elements of the old law that had made it enforceable.

These amendments must be counted a figleaf of respectability, but they don't cover a lot. The cave-in to the gun lobbyists who are proclaiming this "only the beginning" could have been worse, but not much.

the Charleston Gazette

Charleston, WV, April 8, 1986

IN 1980 the United States again had the dubious distinction of being the world's No. 1 murder-by-pistol country.

A total of 11,522 Americans were murdered by pistol. That's a murder rate of 5.0624 per 100,000 population.

Here's the murder by pistol total and rate per 100,000 population of seven other nations:

▲ Australia, 4 pistol victims, .0274 per 100,000.

▲ Great Britain, 8 pistol victims, .0142 per 100,000.

▲ Canada, 8 pistol victims, .0335 per 100,000.

▲ Sweden, 18 pistol victims, .2168 per 100,000.

▲ Israel, 23 pistol victims, .5897 per 100,000.

▲ Switzerland, 24 pistol victims, .375 per 100,000.

▲ Japan, 77 pistol victims, .0659 per 100,000.

The pistol murder rate of the United States is 77 times greater than that of the seven other countries cited above combined.

Seventy-seven times greater.

Why?

The answer is that these other societies control the availability and proliferation of pistols.

These seven societies have tough laws on the books to prevent the sale of pistols to criminals and to certifiable loonies.

The United States has no similar laws, no similar prohibitions.

In far too many states across the nation criminals and psychopaths can walk into a retail store, buy a small, concealable pistol, sign a phony name to a piece of paper asserting buyer knows of no reason to bar ownership of a pistol, plunk down the necessary funds to complete the transaction and 10 minutes later walk out of the same store with the deadly purchase.

Interestingly, every state in the union demands accountability for motor vehicle owners. They must register their cars, trucks and motorcycles, new or used, and themselves with appropriate state authority. Yet in too many states no accountability is enforced upon pistol owners.

What an absurd contradiction.

And it exists because people who should know better — federal lawmakers like Sens. Robert C. Byrd and J.D. Rockefeller IV — are gutless wonders and won't face up to the National Rifle Association (NRA). They kowtow to this powerful lobby rather than do what they know in their heart of hearts is sensible and desirable.

What are a mere 11,522 pistol murders a year compared to the exaggerated fears about a communist takeover of the NRA, were U.S. federal authorities either to have or to have access to registration lists of pistol owners? The ridiculous presumption is that this country's pistol owners are all that stand between a foreign takeover and the preservation of American freedoms.

One West Virginia member of the Congress did regularly defy the NRA — former Rep. Ken Hechler — and it never prevented him from being elected to the House of Representatives. It's sad that Byrd and Rockefeller lack his courage on this issue and are willing to permit 11,-522 murders by pistol year in, year out for fear the NRA might be offended.

THE PLAIN DEALER

Cleveland, OH, April 11, 1986

The most rootin', tootin', sharpshootin' insti-toot'in east of the Pecos has brought what it reckons to be law'n'order to gun control. That is to say that the House of Representatives has adopted a new gun bill that it believes will be an improvement over the 1968 Gun Control Act. Smile when you say that, though, because if you don't, some law'n'order lobbyist from the National Rifle Association might transport his constitutional right to bear arms across state lines and make you.

You have to smile anyway, because if you don't you might cry. The McClure-Volkmer gun control bill passed by the House yesterday undeniably weakens gun controls. It creates the right to transport weapons across state lines. It doesn't extend that privilege to handguns, but so what? Neither did the old laws. It also eases record-keeping for gun dealers and allows them to transfer weapons from their commercial inventories to their private collections. That good idea will have the ultimate effect of deepening the reservoir of untraceable weapons that is flooding the nation.

In the bizarre spirit of the hour, both sides have claimed victory. Pro gun-control forces are satisfied because they managed to keep the law making it illegal to sell handguns across state lines; managed to make machine guns illegal; managed to bar the importation of parts for Saturday Night Specials; and managed to get a clause permitting spot inspections of gun dealers. The NRA, meanwhile, is satisfied because even though it lost the central handgun battle, it got the interstate sale clause for long guns, a transport clause for *all* guns, and eased the burden of record-keeping for gun dealers.

Well, maybe, but what's the point? Hunters who break their weapons on long trips or who are absent-minded enough to go hunting out-of-state without their rifles will be able to buy new ones. But that seems like a small gain, and the law won no meaningful new restraints in exchange. Making machine guns illegal isn't a concession, it's an essential. The same goes for the import restraints and spot checks. Thus, gun controls have been marginally weakened for the marginal benefit of a marginal number of people. What has not happened is that the laws have been strengthened. Even pro-control lobbyists, enthused by the bill's final amendments, admit as much.

Reps. Donald Pease and Dennis Eckart, both Democrats and both up for re-election, voted for the final bill. Pease says his mail was running 500 to 10 in favor of the Volkmer plan, and that the new measure only "relaxes" gun controls, presumably in some positive way. Eckart's spokesperson says the same thing, both about the pressure and the "fairness" to hunters. That's gunsmoke. It would have been "fairness" for Eckart and Pease to vote for a bill that balanced relaxed rifle controls and tighter handgun restrictions.

Every day, police blotters record the need for handgun controls. Yet too many lawmakers allow themselves to be dry-gulched by the NRA and its contorted, contagious logic. Rootin', tootin', sharp-shootin' Congress and its tenderfoots have slapped leather, and missed by a mile.

The Providence Journal

Providence, RI, April 12, 1986

Law enforcement groups led the fight this week against a House bill that would weaken the nation's only federal gun control law, but came away badly bruised by the powerful gun lobby — some say the most powerful lobby in Washington.

For the first time in 18 years, since the assassinations of the Rev. Martin Luther King Jr. and Sen. Robert Kennedy, Congress is on a fast track to hand the National Rifle Association almost all it asked for to ease the traffic in firearms. "As far as I can see, the NRA has a stranglehold on this city," said Jerald R. Vaughn, executive director of the International Association of Chiefs of Police.

Indeed, so it seems. The House -- on whose members, as well as senators, the NRA is said to have conferred $2.3 million in the 1984 campaign — virtually rolled over and played dead. It voted 286 to 136 for a bill that Mr. Vaughn says will impede law enforcement and make police work more dangerous. The influence of campaign contributions and lobbying is easily seen in Thursday's results, the NRA having spent about $1.6 million on an advertising and lobbying campaign for this bill alone, as opposed to $15,000 spent for lobbying by the police coalition.

The approved Volkmer bill, if passed by the Senate and signed by the President, would among other things lift the current ban on the transportation of handguns, rifles and shotguns across state lines, eliminate the ban on interstate sales of rifles and shotguns and reduce the record-keeping requirements of gun dealers.

Only two positive aspects of the House action helped to ease the defeat suffered by gun-control advocates, including Sarah Brady, wife of White House Press Secretary James S. Brady who was seriously wounded in the attempt to assassinate the President in 1981. On a 233-to-184 vote, the House retained a ban on interstate sales of handguns, and by voice vote added a ban on the sale and possession of machineguns.

If this outcome proves anything it is that average citizens along with law enforcement organizations must marshal their lobbying forces or learn to tolerate a private arsenal of unbelievable dimensions. Clearly the NRA will accept nothing less than unconditional surrender.

Black Dies Fleeing White Gang in New York City

A black man was hit by a car while fleeing a mob of white New York City teenagers Dec. 22, 1986. Described as a "racial lynching" by Mayor Ed Koch Dec. 22, the incident shocked the city and drew national attention.

The victim, Michael Griffith, had strayed into the predominately white neighborhood of Howard Beach with his stepfather and a friend after their car broke down. Police said a mob of from nine to 12 teenagers armed with a baseball bat and a thick tree branch and shouting, "Niggers, you don't belong here!" set upon the three black men shortly after 12:30 a.m., local time. One of the blacks, Timothy Grimes, 20, fled the scene without harm. But Griffith's stepfather, Cedric Sandiford, 36, was badly beaten twice. For his part, the fleeing Griffith was cornered before he ducked through a gap in a fence and dashed onto a highway, the Shore Parkway. There, at about 1 a.m., a car struck and killed him.

A team of 50 police investigators questioned community residents, and on Dec. 22 arrested three youths: Jon Lester, 17, Scott Kern, 17, and Jason Ladone, 16. A furor broke out Dec. 29, when Judge Ernest Bianchi of Queens Borough Criminal Court dismissed the charges of manslaughter and second-degree murder that the youths faced. This left only the lesser charge of reckless endangerment of human life. Explaining his decision, Bianchi cited the refusal of Sandiford to testify. It was the position of Sandiford and his lawyer, Alton Maddox Jr., that the driver who struck Griffith had been one of the pursuers, and that the prosecution wanted to conceal this because he was the son of a police officer. The driver, Dominick Blum, 24, had returned to the scene of Griffith's death about an hour after hitting him. He told police of what he had done, but had not been charged with any crime.

Twelve white teenagers were indicted Feb. 10, 1987 on charges ranging from second-degree murder to rioting in connection with the Howard Beach incident. Three of the twelve youths were charged with second-degree murder. Two of the three—Jon Lester and Scott Kern—had been previously had faced the same charge, but it had been reduced to reckless endangerment after one of the survivors of the attack, Sandiford, refused to aid in the probe. The third youth charged with second-degree murder was Robert D. Riley, 17. Riley had not previously been charged in the case. He was described as the only suspect who had cooperated with the special prosecutor's office. The youth originally arrested with Kern and Lester, Jason Ladone, was charged with attempted murder, manslaughter and other crimes.

To break a deadlock in the case, Gov. Mario Cuomo Jan. 13 had named a special prosecutor, Charles J. Hynes, to take over the case from Queens County District Attorney John Santucci. Cuomo had been under pressure for nearly three weeks, as black leaders continued to express little confidence in Santucci and called repeatedly for the governor to appoint a special prosecutor. Cuomo announced the appointment of Hynes after meeting for nearly six hours at his New York City office with a dozen black civic and religious leaders.

The Kansas City Times

Kansas City, MO, December 26, 1986

It is absolutely unthinkable that decades after civil rights laws and judicial remedies were enacted, three black men should have had to flee for their lives in Queens from an updated version of a lynch mob. Michael Griffith and his friends were chased through the streets by white teen-agers hurling racial slurs and clubs at them. The black men had stopped to use the phone in a pizzeria after their car had broken down. Griffith was killed when he was chased onto a beltway and struck down in traffic.

New York police charged three white teen-agers with second-degree murder. But at least a dozen assailants were involved, according to police and press accounts. That means there are many yet to come forward or be caught by the authorities. New York police would be wise to quickly solve this matter and not allow themselves to be swayed by arguments that arrests made now, during the Christmas season, would ruin the attackers' holiday. Queens is already sizzling and residents, black and white, are still reeling from the shock of the attack on the blacks. In addition, some blacks have not waited for authorities and have retaliated with violence.

Michael Griffith, 23, didn't have to die as he did. He and the others were told before their beatings that they didn't belong in the predominantly white, middle-class community of Howard Beach, where their horror began. Griffith and his friends were practically stranded there, not that that should have mattered. He and the others had just as much right to be there as the teen-agers who felt otherwise.

This entire ugly episode is evidence of a pervasive problem that exists not only in Howard Beach, but in all of America. No matter how much we try to deny it, racism still roams the nation in search of victims. Historically, these victims often are minorities.

The next time President Reagan, Clarence Pendleton and William Bradford Reynolds roll out their color-blind society argument, someone should remind them about Michael Griffith and his grieving family. The only reason he and his friends were bothered at all was because of their race and someone's territorial obsession.

THE ATLANTA CONSTITUTION

Atlanta, GA, December 31, 1986

The vicious attack by a dozen white teenagers on three black men in the mostly white Howard Beach section of New York recently, and the apparent retaliation by blacks in the mob-beating of a white teenager in a nearby black neighborhood, are disturbing in their own right, and the atmosphere has been made additionally tense by the uncertainty over just what charges will be brought in the death. But the incidents are all the more distressing because they fall into a growing pattern of racial harassment and violence nationwide.

Much of this racial hooliganism has manifested itself on college campuses: the harassment of a black cadet at the Citadel in Charleston, S.C.; a cross-burning outside a black sorority house at the University of Alabama; racial or anti-Semitic incidents at Harvard and the universities of Massachusetts, Texas and Rhode Island.

But such incidents have not been confined to the campus. In addition to the trouble in New York, Philadelphia experienced several days of racial tension when a black family tried to move into a white neighborhood. And there have been similar incidents in Cleveland and metro Atlanta.

What has gone wrong? Why is there an upsurge in overt bigotry now, when the bitter struggles of the 1960s over legal segregation and civil rights are far behind us?

Some civil-rights leaders charge that lax enforcement of civil-rights laws and a hostility toward affirmative action by the Reagan administration has created an atmosphere that encourages intolerance. There is certainly some truth to that. Others fear there is a kind of anti-anti-apartheid backlash at work, with whites tired of black demonstrations against the white minority government in South Africa. This supposedly explains much of the blatant bigotry at colleges.

Whatever the reasons, the nation must get a handle on the problem before it spreads further. That is going to require sober leadership from blacks and whites both, but especially from white leaders, whose silence or equivocation in such times can be deadly.

And maybe we need to revive an old idea as well. In recent years, most cities, including Atlanta, have scrapped the community-relations councils and other organizations that had been set up to soothe community tensions and build race relations. The thinking was that they had outlived their usefulness. Alas, the judgment may have been hasty.

WORCESTER TELEGRAM

Wocester, MA, December 26, 1986

Ours is not supposed to be an age of racial discord; the battle for civil rights was fought, and won, a quarter century ago. Still, the name of Michael Griffith will be counted with those who died in the struggle for racial equality.

The 23-year-old black construction worker from Brooklyn, badly beaten by a gang of white teenagers, was killed by a passing car in the Howard Beach neighborhood of Queens, N.Y., as he tried to escape his tormentors. His companions escaped with injuries as the three black men were attacked when their car became disabled in the all-white neighborhood and they walked to seek help.

New York Mayor Edward Koch rightly terms the harrowing incident a "racial lynching." Indeed, it is hard to understand, let alone explain, the hatred, ignorance and cynical attitudes this tragedy exposes. It points to the fact that some Americans have forgotten or never learned the lessons of the civil rights movement and the message of Dr. Martin Luther King.

Joseph Duffey, chancellor of the University of Massachusetts in Amherst, says that today there is "less inhibition of the kind of racial slur that a few years ago people would have been more sensitive about." Duffey's own campus was the scene of ugly racial incidents this year.

Residents of the Howard Beach neighborhood seemed remarkably unapologetic and remorseless. Several wondered if they wouldn't meet Michael Griffith's fate if they tried to walk through Harlem. Such a resignation to racial hate is dispiriting. It must be examined and confronted by community leaders, educators, the clergy and reasonable men and women everywhere.

The arrest of the young bullies of Howard Beach, while it was essential, will not remedy the situation. If the foundation of racial harmony, so painfully erected in the 1960s, shows signs of erosion, there is need for urgent reinforcement.

The Hartford Courant

Hartford, CT, December 26, 1986

The death in New York City of a young black man, Michael Griffith, tells a horrible story. He was one of three blacks beaten and chased by a group of white youths in the white, middle-class Howard Beach section of Queens. Michael was struck and killed by a car as he fled. It's clear the attack was racially motivated: Some of the whites hollered "Niggers, you don't belong here," as they chased the victims.

Mr. Griffith's death, for which three of the whites were charged with murder, was only one of several recent incidents spawned by racism. In another section of Queens Tuesday blacks punched and kicked a white teenager in retaliation for the death in Howard Beach. In San Diego a black man was arrested by a mounted police officer and led to the police station bound by a rope tied to the officer's saddle. A sheriff in Louisiana recently announced that blacks would be stopped on sight if found walking in a white neighborhood outside New Orleans. There have been racial incidents on campuses across the country this year.

What is happening to a nation that a few years ago made a tardy, but heartfelt commitment to civil rights? Has the veneer of civility been so thinly applied that within a generation the seeds of hate are able to sprout so vigorously?

There needn't be legal impediments to equality of the races as there are in South Africa for a nation to be dangerously divided on the grounds of race. Social barriers are every bit as real — and dangerous. In fact, those barriers are more insidious when they are ignored or treated as minor obstacles.

For six years the Reagan administration has softened enforcement of civil rights laws and attacked affirmative action, the tool used by government to afford equal opportunities for all. Its policies have earned it almost universal scorn from civil rights advocates. The administration's retreat on civil rights tends, as Rosalynn Carter said, "to make us comfortable with our prejudices." Is it any wonder that some have interpreted this lack of concern as a license to prey upon minorities?

But it'll take more than presidential leadership to address the rot within. It'll take courage, faith and a renewed commitment by all Americans to understanding between the races. Michael Griffith's death is an example of what can happen when we lack the nerve to conquer prejudice.

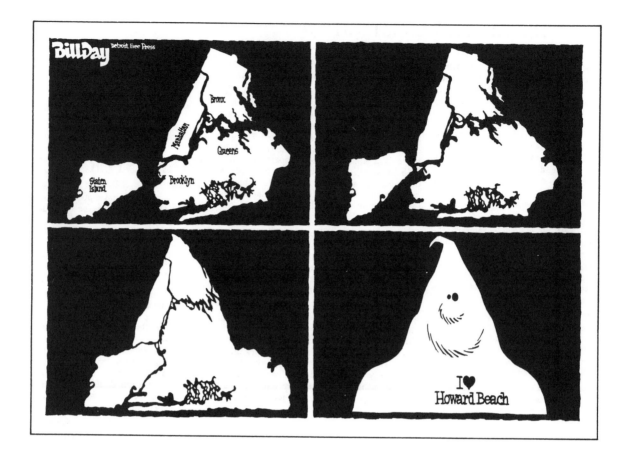

BUFFALO EVENING NEWS
Buffalo, NY, December 30, 1986

THE UGLY RACISM still existing in American life manifested itself recently in vicious incidents in New York City, where a young black man was chased by a cowardly gang of white youths onto a highway, where he was killed by a passing car. Three days later, a similar gang of black youths attacked a white teen-ager in retaliation, fortunately without causing serious injury.

The slain man and two other black men happened to be in the mostly white area of Queens because their car had broken down, and they had walked to the scene of the racial attack in search of telephone. Some white youths noticed them and, after reinforcing their numbers to about a dozen, attacked the three blacks with sticks and baseball bats.

Mayor Ed Koch took immediate, forthright action that resulted in arrests in both incidents, and he condemned the racist nature of the attacks, comparing the first incident to the lynchings that used to take place in the South years ago. He said that racism exists everywhere and that the best way of dealing with it was to acknowledge it and discuss it.

By simply stating the obvious, Koch himself became a target of mindless vituperation from some people in Queens who accused him of slandering the neighborhood.

The racial feeling that Koch referred to was well demonstrated when the three accused white men were cheered by a crowd of 50 youths as they were booked. And when 5,000 people — both black and white — marched in Queens in a demonstration against racism, they were met by a jeering crowd of some 200 whites.

Terrible as these incidents are, it would be wrong to see them as examples of a pervasive new wave of racism around the country. There have been several outrages recently, including cross-burnings on college campuses, and, in a recent survey, four out of five black students on predominantly white campuses reported personal experiences of racism.

Nevertheless, great progress has been made in the quarter century since Gov. George Wallace blocked the doorway of the University of Alabama to blacks and declared: "Segregation forever." Some 80 percent of American black students now attend predominantly white colleges or universities. Even the University of Alabama is 12 percent black. The successful integration of Buffalo's public schools is a tribute to mutual understanding and respect.

America has made great progress in advancing civil rights and reducing racism during the past generation, but no area of the nation can afford to take a holier-than-thou attitude toward such alarming racial incidents as have occurred in New York City or elsewhere in the nation. We as a people have come a long way, but there is a long way yet to go.

FORT WORTH STAR-TELEGRAM
Fort Worth, TX, December 26, 1986

New York Mayor Edward Koch recoiled with appropriate revulsion from the scene of the recent "lynching" at Howard Beach in Queens.

Koch called the incident "ghastly" and "unbelievable." And it was both. Such horrors seem totally out of place and out of time, not just in New York, but anywhere in today's America.

Although no one who is in touch with the social realities of this society believes racial prejudice has been expunged from the land, most Americans assume that lynchings are a thing of the past.

Certainly the three black men who fell prey to the wrath of a mob of race haters at Howard Beach would not have gone there had they dreamed that such a thing could happen.

Those three had walked to a pizzeria to use a telephone after their car broke down. After eating pizzas and leaving the restaurant, they were assaulted by a group of young men, some of them wielding baseball bats and tree limbs.

One of the black men was killed when he ran out into heavy traffic to escape the beating and was accidentally run down by an automobile.

Those responsible for the "ghastly" and "unbelievable" acts must be punished to the limit of the law to serve notice that such actions are, indeed, out of time and out of place in today's America.

Americans of all races and creeds must be free to come and go anywhere in this country without fear of being brutalized. This is not South Africa.

The Record

Hackensack, NJ, December 23, 1986

On Friday night, in Howard Beach, Queens — if the police accounts are correct — a lynch mob formed outside a pizza parlor and chased a 23-year-old black man named Michael Griffith to his death. They screamed racial epithets, they swung baseball bats, and they didn't stop until he was lying dead on the Shore Parkway, accidentally struck by a car as he staggered away from his pursuers.

As Mayor Edward Koch said in announcing a $10,000 reward for information leading to the arrests of these goons, "Crimes involving racial bigotry are the absolute worst." It goes without saying that they need to be hunted down and prosecuted without sympathy or reserve. But what do we do about those of their neighbors who think they did the right thing?

Over the weekend, reporters visited Howard Beach to gather community reactions to Friday night's incident. As you'd expect, many people were either ashamed or defensive; a priest said, "The reality of sin and evil has shown forth in our own neighborhood," and another resident asked, "Why blame the community?" But others delivered themselves of sentiments like these:

"Aw, the guy deserved it."

"It's very easy to spot a black person in this neighborhood, and whenever I see one I know he's up to no good. They come in the neighborhood and rob everybody. It's a known fact."

"You know how many houses they've broken into? . . . How come Koch doesn't make that a priority?"

"If you go into a black neighborhood, you're going to get it, too."

To the Howard Beach woman who asked, "Why blame the community?", there's a simple and painful answer: because some of your neighbors are guilty of a lynching, and others openly sympathize with them. What has life in Howard Beach been teaching these people, and what lessons are they teaching their own children? What are they teaching the black residents of South Ozone Park, the neighborhood that adjoins Howard Beach?

In the Forties, Billie Holiday sang about the "strange fruit" that grew on Southern trees — the bodies of black men, lynch-mob victims, swinging from branches. This Christmas week of 1986, the strange fruit that grows in Howard Beach, Queens, is the poison in the minds and hearts of those who think Michael Griffith got what was coming to him.

The Miami Herald

Miami, FL, December 26, 1986

THE RACIAL attack that left a black man dead in Howard Beach, N.Y., and other recent racially motivated attacks against blacks across the country impart an important lesson: Racial tolerance must be taught anew to every successive generation.

During the civil-rights movement's heyday, people *worked* at making desegregation work. Despite opposition from those who preferred segregation, there grew to be a national consensus, backed by laws, that all people *are* created equal.

Successive Presidents, save the current one, bolstered those laws. If tolerance didn't come naturally from within, it was thought that pressure from without could bring the desired result, which would be passed on, parent to child. By and large it has appeared to be working. That's why the Howard Beach attack and racial incidents in several cities and at about a dozen colleges this fall, including The Citadel and Harvard, are cause for alarm. Racism is on the rise again.

Why? Some civil-rights leaders cite "the laxity of civil-rights enforcement." Others cite anger from the perception that affirmative action has given blacks undeserved benefits. Still others point to the continuing existence in most cities of segregated communities, which perpetuate segregated schools, unequal opportunities, and widely disparate life styles.

In Howard Beach, 11 white teens beat three blacks whose car had broken down in "their" neighborhood. One victim, Michael Griffith, was killed by a car when he ran into its path to escape his attackers, three of whom have been charged with second-degree murder. A few days later, black youths beat a white teen in retaliation. And on Tuesday, in Ozone Park, N.Y., not far from Howard Beach, two Hispanic youths were beaten with baseball bats by white English-speaking attackers.

To stop further erosion of race relations, communities and individuals once again must *work* at practicing racial tolerance — and at teaching it anew to the young.

The News and Courier

Charleston, SC, December 31, 1986

New York Mayor Edward I. Koch enraged many people in Howard Beach, Queens, a New York suburb, when he described as a "lynching" the incident in which three black men, one of whom lost his life, were set upon and beaten by a crowd of white youths. When he visited their neighborhood last Sunday he was booed by white residents, who accused him of falsely labeling them as a racial community.

Mr. Koch, however, is not the only person who can be accused of pre-judging the case. According to the police, the young black man who was killed when he was trying to escape his attackers was the victim of a road accident. He was hit by a car as he was crossing a busy highway and police say that his death was accidental. Yet the Rev. Al Sharpton, a black minister in Brooklyn, does not believe the police report. "I guess what they're feeling is that to kill someone who's black is only assault at best. This is Johannesburg."

It is understandable that Mr. Koch and Mr. Sharpton, reacting to first reports, should make emotional remarks. It is lamentable, however, when lawyers allow their tongues to run away with them. As a consequence of the extraordinary attitude of the two attorneys representing the two young black victims of the white thugs, justice has suffered a tragic setback in New York.

The pretrial remarks of C. Vernon Mason, one of the attorneys, suggest that he is not interested in justice but is seeking a racial **cause celebre**. Mr. Mason has announced that, "We don't intend for people nationwide to think any longer New York is some kind of progressive place. It's as racist as Selma, Alabama, ever was ... "

The other attorney, Alton H. Maddox, has refused to allow his client, the other black victim and the key witness in the case, to give evidence. Without giving any evidence to support his contention, Mr. Maddox, claims that the driver of the car that hit Michael Griffth as he was fleeing was one of the original attackers. In doing so, Mr. Maddox revealed that he has a lynch-mob mentality. He demanded the arrest of the driver before he would allow his client to appear in court.

Mr. Mason is also on record as saying that, "In 14 years I've practiced law, not once has a white person been convicted of killing a black." That is also the kind of remark that reveals scant respect for due process.

As Richard Emery, the chief counsel of the New York Civil Liberties Union, remarked about the attitude of Mr. Maddox, "He has to answer for all of us — for not letting the justice system have a chance in this case." Because of his attitude, and the non-appearance of his client as a witnesses in the case against three men accused of being among the attackers, a judge on Monday dismissed the murder charges against them. The case will not end there, but as the water becomes muddier and muddier, the chances of justice being done, and being seen to be done, become fewer and fewer. It is bad enough that racism still lurks in the dark corners of American society. It is even worse that so many people, blacks and whites, seem to relish nothing more than exploiting it.

Three Convicted in N.Y.C. Racial Attack

Three white teenagers were convicted of manslaughter Dec. 21, 1987 in connection with the racial attack in the Howard Beach section of New York City that, a year and a day earlier, had left a 23-year-old black man, Michael Griffith, dead after he fled onto a highway and was struck by a car. After a three-month trial and 12 days of deliberations, a New York State Supreme Court jury found Jon Lester and Scott Kern, both 18, and Jason Ladone, 17, guilty of manslaughter in the death of Griffith. Lester and Kern were acquitted of second-degree murder. A fourth defendant, Michael Pirone, 18, was cleared of manslaughter and all other charges against him. The jury also found Lester, Kern and Ladone guilty of first-degree assault in the beating of one of two survivors of the attack, Cedric Sandiford, but rejected attempted murder charges in connection with the attack. Lester and Kern were also convicted of conspiracy. The trial was the first of two scheduled in the case. Seven defendants charged with lesser offenses would be tried separately in 1988. A 12th defendant, Robert Riley, 17, had originally been charged with second-degree murder, along with Lester and Kern. It was later revealed that, in return for aiding the prosecution, Riley would be allowed to plead guilty to assault.

Jury selection for the first Howard Beach trial began Sept. 8 and turned out to be a bitterly contested process, with special prosecutor Charles J. Hynes accusing the defendants' lawyers of trying to keep blacks off the jury and the defense countering that the prosecution was trying to exclude middle-class whites. In a ruling unprecedented in New York State, the presiding judge, Justice Thomas A. Demarkos, Sept. 21 backed Hynes and curtailed the defense lawyers' use of preemptory challenges, those for which no reason had to be given.

The verdict came after a day of protests against racism by hundreds of demonstrators, who, before the verdict was announced, snarled evening rush-hour traffic and subway service for a great many New Yorkers. Though some of the protesters later expressed disappointment or even outrage that none of the defendants had been convicted of murder, the black community at large reportedly reacted favorably to the verdict.

The Washington Post

Washington, DC, December 24, 1987

A QUEENS JURY, after 12 days of deliberations, has reached a verdict in the Howard Beach killing case. The panel, appropriately for New York City and necessarily in this racially charged case, was diverse: six whites, one black, two Puerto Ricans, two Asian Americans and a man from Guyana who is ethnically Asian. They were charged with deciding the hottest, most divisive and emotional case in New York since Bernard Goetz, and in spite of fireworks and outbursts in the courtroom and marches, civil disobedience and the threat of riots in the street, they managed to arrive at what looks to be a sensible verdict.

The case began just a year ago during Christmas week when a group of white teen-agers beat and chased three black men who had wandered into their white neighborhood. During the assault, one of the victims escaped and ran onto a busy parkway where he was struck by an automobile and killed. Was that racially motivated murder the act of a lynch mob, as Mayor Edward Koch described it, or was it a simple street fight that ended in a terrible accident? That is essentially the question that was before the jury at the trial of four teen-agers, two charged with second-degree murder and assault and two with second-degree manslaughter and assault.

Instead of capitulating to pressures on all sides, the jurors apparently went about their task with deliberation, making careful judgments about each of the four defendants based on the evidence presented in court. One young man was acquitted outright because the testimony did not tie him, beyond a reasonable doubt, to the event. As for the other three, the jury found that they had been aware of and consciously disregarded a substantial and unjustifiable risk that the victim, Michael Griffith, would be killed. But they did not find that the defendants had been, in the words the judge used to charge the jury, "so brutal, so callous, so completely dangerous and so inhuman" as to create a grave risk that caused the death of the victim. Thus, all three were found guilty of manslaughter, but not of murder. The former carries a penalty of five to 15 years in prison; the latter, 25 years to life.

But if this was not deliberate murder, it was not just a case of mischievous youngsters embarked on some kind of a prank that backfired either. A man died and those responsible should be punished. The jurors seem to us to have come out right.

An additional note: During the last days of the proceedings, reports were circulated that the forewoman of the jury had authorized an agent to negotiate with the media for the sale of her story. If the reports prove true, it would not be the first time a juror has entered into such a bargain, though others have done so after the trial was over. The general practice is odious: the potential for manipulating the jury process in the interest of creating high-priced drama is too great and represents a basic conflict of interest. Jurors deliberate in secrecy for a reason. If notes are being kept, if individual views are to be revealed and criticized publicly, juries will operate under a cloud of intimidation. Such arrangements should be strongly discouraged by the courts, and publicity-seeking jurors should not be allowed to profit from their indiscretion.

MILWAUKEE SENTINEL

Milwaukee, WI
December 26, 1987

The convictions for manslaughter of three white teenagers in the traffic death of a 23-year-old black construction worker last December in the Howard Beach area of New York did nothing to soothe strong emotions on either side of the racially divisive issues in the case.

But the evidence presented to the jury probably best fit this middle-ground between murder and accidental death. The victim, Michael Griffith, died when the three defendants chased him into traffic after his car had become disabled in the predominantly white area.

They may not have killed him if they had caught Griffith. But he wouldn't have died if they hadn't pursued him.

His death was the consequence of their ill-intent, whatever its limits.

But while Griffith's death was unfortunate, to say the least, the depth and scope of racial unrest that it unearthed in the New York area was disconcerting.

Black activists staged demonstrations before the verdict, shutting down the Brooklyn Bridge and three subway stations.

White area residents bombarded radio call-in shows complaining, in effect, that the guilty finding was reverse prejudice.

And New York Mayor Ed Koch touched off more ill-will by saying police statistics showed racial assaults by blacks on whites exceeded those by whites against blacks, even though there are fewer blacks in the city.

This sort of argument, even though not presented as a justification for the crimes in question, would have been better left unspoken. Indeed, while statistics of this kind may be of value, a public scorekeeping can only heighten the impulse to even the score.

All the city's resources obviously must be centered on a cooperative effort by leaders in the black and white communities to calm tensions and to caution against acts of violence in protest of the verdicts.

Instead, both communities should concentrate on an all-out assault on the problems that foster racism. These are easier to identify than to solve in a city such as New York. But that does not mean they can be ignored.

THE SACRAMENTO BEE

Sacramento, CA, December 23, 1987

A year ago last Sunday, Michael Griffith, a young black man whose car broke down outside the mostly white community of Howard Beach, N.Y., was attacked by a dozen neighborhood youths, all white, who screamed racial epithets at him, severely beat his two black companions and chased him out onto the highway, where he was hit by a car and killed. It was a violent and ominous death that quickly came to stand for all the lingering racism from which much of the nation still suffers.

Howard Beach thus became a symbol, and in that way the tragedy grew. For on such a rarified plane, nothing could have been healing — or, for that matter, satisfying — about the investigation or the trial that followed. Monday, after 12 days of deliberation, the jury found three of the white youths guilty of manslaughter; one was acquitted and several have not yet been tried. Although it was a just decision, in this case no verdict could have been sufficient.

The original incident was born of hatred, and nothing that followed transcended it. A special prosecutor had to be appointed because of the black community's distrust of the local, white district attorney; special jury selection rules had to be promulgated when defense attorneys tried to exclude all blacks from the jury and the prosecutor all whites. There were daily demonstrations in the courtroom and, on the last day of jury deliberations, throughout New York City. (Inevitably, there was also a side scandal about a participant — in this case the jury forewoman — who in the midst of it all allegedly tried to sell her story to the press.)

So, far from a catharsis, the trial, like Griffith's death itself, brought only a hardening of attitudes. The defendants came to see themselves as victims, and in some respects they were — victims of their own community, which brought them up with no understanding of what was wrong about what they did, and victims of the more affluent society outside their community, which ignored them until it was too late to make anything of them but an example. That symbolic condemnation of their symbolically so freighted crime was necessary, but it isn't and couldn't have been enough.

Los Angeles, CA
December 23, 1987

Last December's incident in the Howard Beach section of New York City quickly became something more than just another case of urban violence. The death of a black man fleeing a white mob symbolized something larger and more troubling — a simmering racial hatred that could turn a group of partying teenagers into a vengeful mob.

"This incident can only be described as rivaling the kind of lynching incidents which occurred in the Deep South," said New York City Mayor Edward I. Koch in the aftermath of Howard Beach.

Koch's remarks reflect a common conceit. Racism is easy to consider a distant threat. Deep South lynchings, now that's racism. But then comes an incident that forces us to face how close to home the problem really is.

All the portentous overtones of this sensational case were placed before 12 jurors. They deliberated for 11 days before convicting three of the defendants of manslaughter and assault. Two were convicted of conspiracy. One defendant was acquitted on all counts.

Those jurors faced the thankless task of "sending a message." Their verdict inevitably will be viewed not just as a judgment on the facts of the case, but as a judgment on racial intolerance. That is an unfair burden.

It might be more comfortable to think that this decision will quell the hatred displayed at Howard Beach. But prejudice is among the most durable of human emotions. People have always lashed out at those considered different.

The Howard Beach jurors couldn't change that. But they did help bring a just end to one particularly ugly case. Michael Griffith, 23, died when he was struck by a car when fleeing his pursuers at Howard Beach. Scott Kern and Jon Lester, both 18, and Jason Ladone, 17, face sentences of five to 15 years in prison on the manslaughter and assault charges. So, the incident took a particularly heavy toll — a life ended, other lives ruined.

Victim and victimizer — sometimes the lines can become blurry. Because in the end, prejudice victimizes us all.

The San Diego Union

San Diego, CA, December 23, 1987

Justice was served Monday in the verdict of a New York City jury that found three white teenagers guilty of manslaughter in the death of a black man in the Howard Beach section of Queens.

With no apparent motivation other than the color of his skin, the youths chased the man onto a busy highway where he was killed by a car. The case has become a symbol of the festering racial violence that seethes beneath the surface of some American cities.

Whether the youths had actually intended to kill their victim is impossible to tell, as the jury discovered while wrestling with the verdict for almost two weeks. But what was certainly evident was the awful malice in their hearts.

The trial touched a number of raw nerves, not least of which was the belief among some members of the black community that justice would not prevail in predominately white Howard Beach.

The trial touched a number of raw nerves, not least of which was the belief among some members of the black community that justice would not prevail in predominately white Howard Beach.

They charged that the Queens district attorney and police officials were trying to cover up aspects of the incident. In such a negative atmosphere, New York Gov. Mario Cuomo was well advised to appoint a special prosecutor to handle the case.

Although many Americans perceived the trial to be a search for justice, some considered it to be political theater on a grand scale. Hundreds of protesters took to the streets Monday even before the verdict came in.

Chanting dog-eared slogans and demanding police-state retribution, they poured onto subway platforms and blocked bridges over the East River.

When the Howard Beach assault gained national notoriety a year ago, Mayor Ed Koch correctly likened the suspects to the lynch mobs that roamed the Deep South early in this century. The mob that invaded the streets in New York Monday was also intent on a lynching, only this time the victim was justice.

Racial intolerance is a disease that turns ordinarily sensible people into apostles of hate, and communities into battlegrounds. There is no quick fix for the sickness. Years of painstaking work toward racial harmony by blacks and whites can be wiped away in a violent instant. The scars can remain for decades.

Certainly, one of the best antidotes to intolerance is justice. That is precisely what the jury delivered in Howard Beach.

DAILY ⬛ NEWS

New York, NY, December 30, 1987

The three young men convicted of manslaughter and assault in the Howard Beach murder trial deserved and received a fair verdict. Now they—Jon Lester, Jason Ladone and Scott Kern—should get the maximum sentence under the law.

By imposing the maximum, Queens Supreme Court Justice Thomas Demakos would be doing a couple of important things. First, he'd send out a clear, concise message: Racial violence will not be tolerated in New York. Second, he'd demonstrate to the naysayers of all races that justice, indeed, is color-blind.

While there have been other noteworthy incidents of racial violence in the city in recent years, few if any have stirred things up as Howard Beach has. It has become the focal point of a perceptible tension between black and white here. Thus, it is natural that the ultimate outcome of this case takes on special significance.

So now it behooves Justice Demakos to act decisively. If, as a result of such action just one act of racial violence is prevented, he will have performed a worthwhile service to the law-abiding people of the city. If just one potential victim is spared, New York will be a better place to live.

New York, NY, December 22, 1987

NO SINGLE SET OF VERDICTS could have pleased everybody. That's usually true. Trials have winners and losers. Nobody likes to lose.

Above all else, the Howard Beach verdicts left Scott Kern, Jon Lester and Jason Ladone losers, guilty of manslaughter and the toughest assault charge on the books. Some people, including the victims, may feel disappointed that Michael Pirone was acquitted, but the case against him was never strong. The three convicted defendants each face total potential prison terms of more than 15 years. It would be irrational to argue they got off easy.

Seldom has a criminal trial taken on so much emotional baggage from beyond the scene of the crime or the reach of the court. Even the Bernhard Goetz case, for all its notoriety, didn't carry the load of fear and resentment, the potential for mass outrage, that Howard Beach did.

Now the verdicts are in. Justice has been done. To the extent that participants or near observers yearned for total victory—convictions on all counts for all defendants, or exoneration of all—there may be frustration. There is ground for debate about details of the verdicts.

BUT THERE CAN BE LITTLE debate, and none of it responsible, that the jurors did a serious, deeply committed job of pursuing the truth. Racially and ethnically, it was a rainbow jury: white and black and Hispanic and Asian and West Indian. Time and again, the jurors reviewed testimony and other evidence. They deliberated more than 80 hours over 12 days, probably the all-time record for a Queens County court case.

Surrounded by tension, constantly under the glare of strong passions, the trial was conducted with impressive professionalism. Supreme Court Justice Thomas Demakos presided firmly and sensibly. The prosecution, though forceful, was properly restrained. The defense used every tactic available, as was its duty. The activists who often surrounded the courtroom did their witnessing and pleading, by and large, with dignity.

Because of the real, valid passions involved, the trial itself was put on trial. Seldom in New York has justice itself faced public judgment so squarely in the eye. And last night, justice was acquitted.

NOW IT'S OVER. ALMOST EVERYBODY in the entire City of New York, and decent, caring people from far away, have been drawn into the drama. It is in everybody's interest now to cool passions, to join in acceptance that justice—imperfect but convincingly fair—has been done.

The events of the Howard Beach drama were tragic for all involved—and for millions of others who have been driven to anger or empathy, to fear or sadness by the case.

The legacy of that tragedy, and now the trial that grew out of it, must be greater understanding. It must be a renewed and greater-than-ever resolve by all New Yorkers to live with each other in mutual respect.

That will take hard work and extraordinary moral force and leadership. It is impossible to imagine a more important time to tend to that than now: At the just end of this passion-filled prosecution, and on the eve of Christmas.

THE PLAIN DEALER

Cleveland, OH, December 26, 1987

The Howard Beach criminal trial, like the tragic incident that spurred it, has resulted in a deluge of divergent reaction, showing how severely polarized the nation remains along racial lines. The trial, which ended earlier this week, brought about a conviction of manslaughter for three white teen-agers who were involved in the death of Michael Griffith, who with two other black men, walked the streets of white, middle-class Howard Beach after their car had broken down. Griffith was killed by a car as he and his companions fled their attackers.

Even before the verdict was in, several hundred people in New York held a protest against racism and disrupted rush-hour traffic. At the conclusion of the trial, many of New York's black community believed the outcome only reinforced an unacceptable national climate of racism. They said a conviction other than murder for the teen-agers signals a need for blacks to revive the civil rights movement. On the other hand, some New York whites said that the manslaughter conviction was too serious. They said Griffith's death was purely accidental and that those who chased him did not actually kill him. The jury's decision, however, is about as justified as it could be.

Since the verdict, more protests have occurred in New York, including the assault of a white cab driver by several blacks. That incident, as was the Howard Beach assault, was an unfortunate return to the eye-for-an-eye, tooth-for-a-tooth mentality that has polarized blacks and whites for decades. The victims continue to be the innocents of both races.

St. Paul Pioneer Press & Dispatch

St. Paul, MN, December 23, 1987

Whether the manslaughter verdict in the Howard Beach affair was appropriate is difficult to tell from this distance.

The jury obviously felt there was not enough evidence to prove that the 12 white youths who harassed the three black men on the streets of Queens a year ago actually intended to kill them. One of the men, fleeing the attack, ran onto the freeway and was killed by a car.

The case has added to racial friction in New York. The verdict has generated additional stresses.

But another aspect of the case is very troubling.

Several hours before the verdict was announced, defense lawyers asked the judge to declare a mistrial because of reports that a television news producer, saying he was acting as the agent of the jury foreman, tried to sell publication rights of her daily trial diary to three New York newspapers.

The judge refused to conduct a hearing to determine if the allegations were true and denied the motion for the mistrial. He said he wouldn't hold a hearing based on hearsay.

That was a mistake. The judge should have made every effort to determine the truth of the allegation because, if it was true, the foreman could be in a position to influence the outcome of the case in a way that would be of economic benefit to her. And if the sale arrangements were made, the timing is important because the jury foreman was not supposed to communicate about the case with anyone prior to the verdict being handed down.

Unfortunately, the media are partly responsible for the problem. There are people in radio, television, magazines, books, movies and newspapers who often vie for the rights to print, broadcast or film the inside story told by participants in major news events. Like Watergate criminals.

It was only a matter of time before jurors decided to get into the act.

There is no way to prevent a juror from selling his or her trial memoirs once the case is closed. The free enterprise system and the First Amendment allow such transactions. But the material has to be interesting to sell. That raises the question of whether actions in the jury room will be designed more to create an audience than to ensure justice is done.

It is a dismaying thought.

THE ATLANTA CONSTITUTION
Atlanta, GA, December 23, 1987

After a three-month trial and 12 days of deliberation, a New York Supreme Court jury has finally spoken in the Howard Beach case, convicting three white youths of manslaughter and assault in connection with the vicious racial attack last December that culminated in the death of one black man and the severe beating of another.

Although many of New York City's blacks are angry that the jurors found the teenagers guilty of manslaughter rather than murder, the panel's decision is just. It is even courageous, considering the pressure cooker the jurors found themselves in as the result of a case that had focused wide attention on an isolated, predominately white neighborhood in Queens, making it a national symbol of urban racial violence.

The jury's message is unmistakable. Mindless intolerance will not be countenanced. Given other recent incidents that smack of bigotry and intolerence — the Bernhard Goetz shootings in New York and the disruption of a brotherhood march in Forsyth County, Ga., for example — the jury's message needs to be broadcast the length and breadth of this country.

In a nation as diverse as ours, those who practice or encourage racial violence and hooliganism must have no hiding place. Justice is the bond that holds us together. If it is diminished or threatened anywhere in America, it is diminished everywhere.

We cannot accept the proposition that there can be communities in this country that are closed to those of a different race or background, simply because of that difference. Otherwise, we are no longer a nation in any real sense, but merely a collection of clannish, warring camps, where your skin and ethnic characteristics are your uniform.

The ugly facts at the heart of the Howard Beach case were clear. Three black men were set upon, beaten with tree limbs, a baseball bat and an iron pipe after their car broke down in a predominately white Queens neighborhood. They were chased by white teenagers. One of them ran onto a busy highway where he was struck by a passing car and killed.

While the facts do not support murder charges against the white youths, they emphatically support second-degree manslaughter and assault charges. The youths' vicious conduct caused a death.

Many civil rights leaders viewed the incident as part of a nationwide pattern of rising racial violence and intolerance, nurtured at least in part by less than aggressive enforcement of civil rights and affirmative-action measures by the Reagan administration. Unwavering judgments like the one handed down by the jurors in the Howard Beach case should do much to put a halt to growing bigotry.

St. Petersburg Times
St. Petersbug, FL, December 24, 1987

The manslaughter convictions of three white teen-agers in the death of a black man in the Howard Beach neighborhood of Queens may not be as strong a punishment as some had hoped, but they send this hopeful signal: Black lives are not cheap.

As the three guilty verdicts and one acquittal were read in the Queens courtroom, one spectator shouted, "Murderers! Murderers!" Another tossed replicas of South African pass books into the air. Protesters arrested in a demonstration against racism that paralyzed rush hour traffic Monday said the verdict "does not end anything."

The case stemmed from the death of 23-year-old Michael Griffith, who was chased into the path of a car as he fled his teen-age attackers last December. Another man, Cedric Sandiford, 37, survived a beating that required 66 stitches to close his head.

Even though the defendants were cleared of murder charges, which would have required proof of "depraved indifference" to human life, and even though sentencing with a maximum 15-year penalty is yet to be determined, blacks and whites should take some heart in the outcome of this troubling case.

All too often, the judicial system has perplexingly worked against blacks who have died or been maimed at the hands of whites. Studies trumpet lower rates of convictions for white defendants when victims are black, and history bears countless shameful examples:

The white men charged with beating young Emmett Till to death for speaking to a white woman in 1955 Mississippi were set free. In 1980, six white former Dade County police were found innocent in the brutal beating death of Arthur McDuffie in Miami.

More recently, Bernhard Goetz was acquitted of attempted murder in the vigilante shooting of four black youths who asked him for money on a New York subway. One was left brain-damaged and paralyzed. The jury found Goetz, who some New Yorkers called "sick with racism," guilty only of illegal gun possession. He was sentenced to six months in jail and ordered to see a psychiatrist.

In the Howard Beach case, three white men were found guilty in the loss of a black human life. The victim's mother said she is "pleased with the verdict. God in the end did what was right."

There's no denying racism still abounds. There is still reason to demonstrate in the streets against discrimination, racial slurs and other insensitivities.

The Howard Beach verdicts are a start. They show there is a price for the ultimate racism. Americans should hope that price continues to rise.

THE KANSAS CITY STAR
December 24, 1987
Kansas City, MO

It's not macho to abduct and lynch a 19-year-old Alabama black man. Members of the United Klans of America did this to Beulah Mae Donald's son Michael in March 1981.

It's racist.

It's not macho for five white cadets at The Citadel to enter the room of a black cadet, shout racial epithets, burn paper crosses and wear white sheets emulating the Klan. This was done to Kevin L. Nesmith of Charleston, S.C., in October 1986.

It's racist.

It's not macho for hundreds of angry protesters to appear before the homes of black and biracial families in Philadelphia and shout about not wanting "their kind" there. This was done in the Elmwood community in November 1985. Marietta Bloxom, Charles Williams and their daughter eventually fled the neighborhood, leaving their possessions behind. Their home was torched.

It's racist.

It's not macho to fire pellets into the home of a black family who had moved from Alaska to a predominantly white neighborhood in Kansas City. This was done to Larry and Linda Collins who have since moved to another Missouri town.

It's racist.

It's not macho to paint slurs on the federal Immigration and Naturalization Service building near Kansas City International Airport. This was done in August 1987. References were made to Hispanic and Vietnamese peoples.

It's racist.

It's not macho to leave pamphlets on 150 cars in a parking lot of the Maple Woods Community College in Kansas City, North. Students, most of them white, were upset to find papers which read "love your own kind, fight for your own kind—or perish" last September. Gladstone police investigated the Missouri Knights who were believed to have been responsible.

It's racist.

It's not macho, as some hotshot New York attorneys maintain, for a white mob with sticks to chase black men exiting a New York pizzeria, shout racial slurs and frighten one so much that he did not see the car that struck him down. Michael Griffith, 23, died in Howard Beach on Dec. 20, 1986.

It's racist.

On Dec. 21, 1987, three of the Howard Beach youths, Scott Kern, Jon Lester and Jason Ladone, were found guilty of second-degree manslaughter. The jury, which deliberated for 12 days over the conviction, was composed of six whites, two Hispanics, two Asians, one black and a Guyanian of Indian descent.

It's justice!

Goetz Cleared of Attempted Murder

A New York State Supreme Court jury in New York City June 16, 1987 acquitted "subway vigilante" Bernhard Goetz of the attempted murder of four black youths on a New York City subway in December 1984. The verdict, after a seven-week trial and more than 30 hours of jury deliberations over four days, cleared Goetz of 12 of 13 criminal counts. Goetz was cleared of four counts of attempted murder, four counts of assault and one of reckless endangerment. He was also acquitted of three weapons-possession charges but was convicted of carrying a loaded, unlicensed weapon in a public place.

During the trial, which received enormous publicity, the jury heard more than 40 witnesses whose testimony filled thousands of pages of transcripts. But perhaps the most dramatic testimony came from Goetz himself, who never took the witness stand. Prosecutor Gregory Waples played two separate taped confessions—one on audio tape and one on videotape—that Goetz gave to police when he surrendered in Concord, N.H. nine days after the shootings. "I wanted to kill those guys," Goetz said on the videotape. "I wanted to maim those guys. I wanted to make them suffer in every way I could." The tapes provided the centerpiece of the prosecution's attempt to dispel the image of Goetz as a "perfectly normal New Yorker" acting in self-defense. Instead, said Waples, they showed him to be an obsessive, paranoid person who had a "score to settle" because he had been mugged and beaten in 1981 and felt justice had not been done.

Defense attorney Barry Slotnick told the jurors to disregard Goetz's taped accounts of the shootings as the unreliable perceptions of a "traumatized, sick and psychologically upset individual." Slotnick claimed that all four youths had surrounded Goetz before he began shooting.

An underlying but often unspoken element in the case was the issue of race. Although a possible racial motivation for the shootings was never charged in the trial, numerous demonstrations took place outside the courthouse, with conservative whites rallying to Goetz's cause and blacks and liberals portraying him as a symbol of a new resurgence of racism.

THE SACRAMENTO BEE
Sacramento, CA, June 19, 1987

"Mr. Goetz was not a vigilante; he was a sad frightened man. I ride the trains. I know what it is in New York."
—Michael Axelrod, a member of the Goetz jury

Bernhard Goetz was a victim himself, looking for his day in some court, and he posed nearly unanswerable questions about a place no longer certain it can call itself civilized. Other people who've been mugged, as Goetz had been, don't shoot black teenagers who ask them for money in the subway, but half of New York has had the fantasy about a lot less: the sullen kids on the train with their ghetto blasters daring you to complain; the eyes of fear avoiding the eyes of hate; the uncertainty that if anything happened anyone would look up from his newspaper, much less come to help.

Were they really threatening to mug him when he shot or were they just panhandling? Was Goetz, armed with a gun, looking for a confrontation or could he have moved away? Anyone who, as that juror says, "rides the trains" knows how thin the line can be between rage and fear, how narrow the scope for reason. Of course there was race in this crime and the contempt that a narrow righteousness feels for kids already written off as delinquents. But beyond that, there also is the inevitable sense that there is no community left, that between the people living behind their private security guards in their $3,000 a month apartments or in their $750,000 two-bedroom co-ops — people who do not have to descend into the subway — and the feral society of the tenements, there seems to be less and less.

Goetz did not need to shoot — certainly did not need to shoot again and again — to protect himself, any more than a kid brutalized every day by life in the ghetto needs to mug the old lady in the park. But somehow the jury sensed that in the context of the crimes, the corruption and the disregard that foster rage in a large city, the crime at issue in the courtroom, brutal as it was, becomes relatively unimportant, like the illegal possession of a gun. One side says that the decay is spread by such verdicts, the other that the decay justifies them. Sadly, they are both right.

▣ The Cincinnati Post
Cincinnati, OH, June 18, 1987

It isn't surprising that a jury absolved Bernhard Goetz of criminal responsibility in the New York subway shooting of four menacing young toughs. Six of the 12 jurors had been victims of crime themselves, three of them in the subway. And each of the four youths had a criminal record.

But the outcome of the trial raises the disturbing question of whether it will encourage others to react with blazing guns when similarly confronted.

Goetz is seen as a hero by some people who believe the four teen-agers, one of whom was partially paralyzed in the shooting, got what they deserved. But rational people surely will see the danger of armed citizens administering vigilante justice.

New York Mayor Edward Koch warned residents not to "misperceive the case" and said that authorities will not tolerate vigilantism.

But Koch and others in the government should not ignore an overriding message of the Goetz trial: New Yorkers are fed up with a system that allows muggers and murderers to terrorize the city.

Goetz was wrong to carry an unlicensed gun. He was wrong to shoot four people, one twice, because the "shine" he saw in one's eyes put him in fear of being attacked as the youths crowded around him and demanded $5. But clearly the jury sympathized with the defendant because its own members had experienced the fear that makes law-abiding citizens wary on subways, that makes them stay off city streets at night and avoid public parks.

The question for Koch is: What is the government going to do to make the city safe? There is only a one in 10 chance of a person being arrested after committing a serious crime in New York City. The chance of going to prison is one in 50.

And crime and the fear of it are not just New York problems. Many of the nation's metropolitan areas are similarly beset.

When governments find a way to deal effectively with robbers, rapists, murderers and assorted other miscreants who prey on the innocent, the Bernhard Goetzes of this world will no longer feel the need to carry guns.

St. Paul Pioneer Press & Dispatch
St. Paul, MN, June 19, 1987

One would like to believe that jurors in the Bernhard Goetz trial considered only legal questions, such as whether Mr. Goetz acted in justifiable self-defense when he shot four teen-agers on a New York subway in 1984. One hopes that they were interested only in examining the facts and applying the law rather than in sending some kind of signal or making some kind of statement. Courtrooms, after all, generally are dangerous places for second agendas.

Having said this, there is no reason to believe the 10 white and two black jurors overstepped their charge in acquitting Mr. Goetz on all but a comparatively minor weapons charge. They appear to have acted reasonably and fairly.

They appear to have done so despite the fact that the Goetz affair, from the start, has been loaded with symbols and statements. It is hard, in fact, to think of another recent case in which more suspect motives have been attributed to more people, be they near or far from the scene, and in which more claims have been made about race in the United States.

One claim is that if Mr. Goetz were black instead of white, and if the four teen-agers who were harassing him (and perhaps preparing to rob him) were white, then everything would have been different. A related fear is that the verdict endorses anti-black vigilantism, making innocent blacks no less vulnerable than not-so-innocent blacks.

None of this, of course, is easy to dismiss. Only bigots and naive fools can believe that race has been completely irrelevant. Still, there simply is no convincing reason to believe that the entire episode — if one is intent on inferring messages and meaning — has had more to do with racism than with profound public disgust with violent crime.

Note: *profound* disgust, particularly in high-crime communities.

In light of the way crime has absolutely contorted millions of lives in large urban centers (particularly black neighborhoods), it is remarkable that so little public voice usually is given to anger and frustration — entirely correct anger and frustration. Sure, there are regular denunciations. But they generally are more constrained than commensurate for several inadequate reasons, one of which is trepidation at being thought insensitive or racist.

Saying this in no way endorses vigilantism of any kind. In no way does it imply that law-abiding citizens and innocent third parties would be safer if more people packed handguns like Mr. Goetz did; the opposite is probably true. And neither does it suggest obliviousness to social and economic conditions that contribute to criminality.

What such an interpretation suggests, rather, is this: To the extent the case has given expression to deep and legitimate exasperation, unpoisoned by racial baggage and adoration of Rambo, then there is nothing inherently divisive about that expression or the verdict itself.

The Houston Post
Houston, TX, June 18, 1987

The jury that found Bernhard Goetz innocent of attempted murder decided it was illegal for him to carry a gun — but since he had it, it was all right to shoot four people. This defies logic.

The jurors apparently took into account the fact that Goetz — "the subway vigilante" to his supporters — had been viciously mugged three years before the now-famous 1984 incident. That attack led him to buy the gun this jury convicted him for carrying.

Anyone who has ever been attacked or threatened understands Goetz's resulting fear and rage. Also, the youths who confronted him are scum. Their legal and drug records and their admitted intention to rob video machines make this plain. But all this did not entitle Goetz to, in effect, make Barry Allen, Darrell Cabey, Troy Canty and James Ramseur pay for a three-year-old crime committed by others.

It is important to examine once more what Goetz did, and those reading these words should ask themselves if they would do the same in like circumstances. He drew the gun, and the youths backed away, turning to flee. A reasonable person would have been satisfied. The threat had been stopped. Yet Goetz, by his own admission, shot at least one of the four in the back and pumped another bullet into a victim lying wounded on the floor. This is overreaction in the extreme — the hysterical act of a coward.

Bernhard Goetz has been found innocent in the shootings. So be it. That is the way our system works. But the jurors who took this action cannot escape one fact: Intentionally or not, they have sent a message to New Yorkers that similar acts in the future will be looked on benignly. If it happens again, they will have to live with that

DAILY ☒ NEWS
New York, NY, June 18, 1987

IF YOU FIND EITHER JOY *OR* RAGE surging up when you think of the Goetz verdict, stop. Think hard. Then clear your head. Now, ask yourself a question: What kind of town do you want to live in? What kind of world?

Those questions should loom high in the minds of all New Yorkers today. The Goetz case became an international fascination and a New York preoccupation *because* of its deeper significances. It is time to examine them, with care and courage.

The case is closed. Guilty on a serious weapons charge. Not guilty on everything else. Anybody who wants to argue the verdict's merits is entitled to. The First Amendment lives. But the energy would be better spent debating the reasons behind the vacation habits of lemmings or the residency of Grant's Tomb.

The case was well tried. Good lawyers doing good jobs, a fine judge making difficult calls, a jury of intelligent, responsible citizens. Bernhard Hugo Goetz must be punished for the crime for which he was convicted. As to those for which he was acquitted, he deserves to be left in peace.

IT IS ONLY FAIR AND REASONABLE to conclude that justice was done and done well. The facts of the four shootings demanded testing in a court of law. To have failed to bring Goetz to trial would have been grossly irresponsible. That would have played into the hands of the most cynical demagogues of fear and hatred. It would have left richly nourished ground for the growth of theories of conspiracy, charges of fixes, allegations of arbitrary, casual—and corrupt—manipulation of justice.

So District Attorney Robert Morgenthau and his staff deserve respect and gratitude. They demonstrated courage, dignity and professionalism. No prosecutor ever loses when a jury acquits—*unless* there is incontrovertible guilt. There was clear guilt in the weapons charge. There was equally clear ground for doubt in the other charges. The integrity of the system of justice was at stake. It cried out to have the doubt settled by a jury, openly, in public.

So the Goetz case is closed. But the questions that it exposed, dramatized, amplified are now very much open.

What kind of town—world—do you want to live in?

The case's larger meaning casts two grim shadows:

✔ In New York, there is a deep fear of random, arbitrary crime, deep distrust of the justice system's ability to combat it. That accounts for a major piece of the celebration of Goetz' behavior.

✔ In New York, there is poisonous polarization of fear, resentment and other base emotions on racial lines. It comes from all sides, all hues, from many ethnic persuasions. Some of it is very subtle, hovering on the line of proper pride. Some of it is brazen, unapologetic, foul—the peddling of hate for the naked purposes of gaining political or economic power, or simply to hurt, to glory in conflict and bitterness.

THERE ARE TWO INESCAPABLE imperatives left today by the Goetz case.

One is to renew and redouble efforts to make the criminal justice system crack down on crime. To beef up, straighten up, speed up justice—from street cop to prison space. Tougher administration, more and better cops, prosecutors, judges, jailers—better managed and led.

The other imperative is more important, finally. It is more dangerous by a hundred times if it is neglected.

That is to bring together New Yorkers in common recognition of their common need for peace and order. To join in common acceptance of differences—and common commitment to respect those differences and to refuse to allow them to be used by the hounds of hate.

That imperative is the more immediate, demanding. Every leader in New York should rise to it, today—be they political, religious, academic, neighborhood, professional.

IDEALLY, EVERY AMPHITHEATER and meeting hall in the five boroughs should be filled to capacity this evening—with no two people of the same color or creed sitting next to each other. Ideally, every New Yorker this very night should be led to consider, long, deeply, openly, the questions of conflict and resentment. Made to think of the truths and consequences of racial polarization. Made to examine his or her heart—and the cold, practical realities of the dangers and costs of indulging fear and hatred.

That will not happen tonight. But how about tomorrow? And the next day? And the next?

Wisconsin ▲ State Journal

Madison, WI, June 19, 1987

The reactions (make that over-reactions) to a Manhattan jury's acquittal of Bernhard Goetz on attempted murder charges in the Dec. 22, 1984 subway shootings of four young men seem to be falling along two lines.

Line No. 1 — "This outrageous verdict means open season for whites on the lives of young black males," claimed Hazel Dukes, the head of New York City's NAACP.

Agree or disagree with the trial-court jury's verdict, it is hard to find evidence of racism there. The four-woman, eight-man jury included two blacks, and there were no hold-outs. The first grand jury to consider the Goetz case declined to even indict him for attempted murder — and that panel was predominantly black. The latest trial occured only after a second grand jury indicted Goetz on the basis of "new evidence."

Listen to what juror Michael Axelrod said after the trial ended this week: "We didn't consider it a black and white issue. We didn't bring it up in the jury room. We all live in Manhattan. We are 12 intelligent people. It was a man (Goetz) who found himself in an untenable position."

And juror Mark Lesly: "If Goetz were black and the four guys were white, it would have been the exact same situation."

The idea that whites will start hunting down black males because one guy defended himself against four thugs on a New York subway stretches the limits of imagination. Blacks who subscribe to that kind of thinking are ignoring a larger threat to young black males — other young black males.

Line No. 2 — Some people would have you believe the Goetz verdict is prima facie evidence of a change in American attitudes toward street crime; even changes in the the law itself. They see his acquittal on 12 of 13 counts (he was convicted of illegal gun possession) as a triumph for urban vigilantism.

The verdict did uphold a person's right to defend himself or his property if either is threatened — but it does not condone random violence or self-protective behavior radically out of line with the demonstrable threat.

The Goetz case was decided on specific facts, circumstances and community standards as reflected by the jury. Most important, it plowed no new legal ground. What was the law pre-Goetz is the law post-Goetz; vigilante justice has not displaced civil rights and due process.

In retrospect, the Goetz case is a tragic example of how violence and crime hurts everyone in our society. Four street toughs, all with police records, two who were admitted cocaine addicts, made the mistake of trying to rob a guy with a loaded gun and were injured. One is paralyzed for life. Goetz has already paid some consequences for using that gun in the form of 2½ years of expensive legal troubles. Now he's facing up to seven years in jail, and he's flat broke.

If there must be an overreaction to the Goetz case, let it be sadness.

the Charleston Gazette

Charleston, WVA, June 25, 1987

THE ACQUITTAL of Bernhard Goetz last week produced an immediate — and predictable — outcry of racism by many black leaders. Too predictable.

For blacks, and other racial minorities in New York, the acquittal may seem part of an unsettling pattern. At the same time of the Goetz trial, a white police officer was absolved from shotgunning an elderly black woman during an eviction dispute. In yet another case, transit officers were acquitted of mistreating a young black man who died in a coma after his arrest.

Consider one more case: In Brooklyn, one man shot another to death believing, like Goetz, that he was doing so in self-defense. Similarly, he was found not guilty. However, the defendant in this case was a young black — the man killed was a white priest.

As Russell Baker points out in the column at right, the Goetz case isn't so much a story about racism as it is an example of the failure of government. We would go further: It demonstrates, glaringly, the breakdown of America's social contract.

Too often, black leaders use the charge of racism where it is not warranted. Bernhard Goetz was paranoid about muggers. Had the four men who threatened him been Hispanic, Oriental or white, he probably would have responded just as violently.

Nor can these leaders fob off as racist the very real statistics showing that blacks commit robbery at a rate 10 times greater than whites.

What is discriminatory is the use of statistics such as these by whites to stereotype all blacks — especially young men — as potential criminals.

There is a continuing scourge of racial discrimination in this country. Blacks are denied housing; their unemployment rate is two and three times higher than it is for whites; too little has changed over too long a time. But that doesn't excuse crime rates such as the one mentioned above, especially as the victims often are blacks, too. Had Goetz been a black man, like his assailants, would he be accused of vigilantism? Somehow, we find it hard to imagine.

Judging Bernhard Goetz innocent was an indictment of the criminal justice system. Having abdicated much of their city to thugs, New York's movers and shakers shouldn't have been surprised at the Goetz shootings.

On yet another level, reaction to the verdict is a further example of the meaningless cacophony that passes for discussion of this nation's social and political ills.

WORCESTER TELEGRAM

Worcester, MA, June 18, 1987

Anyone who has ever been mugged, burglarized, threatened by street thugs or even ridden the New York subways knows what Bernhard Goetz must have experienced when four youths confronted him demanding money.

It took nearly two and a half years to settle this celebrated case, but in the end, justice prevailed. By acquitting him of all but gun-possession charges, a Manhattan jury recognized Goetz's right to self-defense and decided that he did not use unreasonable force.

The facts more than justify the verdict. Goetz, who was assaulted three times before, faced four men who, at the time of the encounter, had 20 arrests among them. The only member of the gang who is not in jail now for vicious crimes is the man who was paralyzed in the shooting. Given the background, Goetz had every reason to believe that his safety was in danger.

He chose to defend himself at a time when criminal justice in New York City was all but broken down. It still is. Perpetrators of felonies in the Big Apple face a 1 in 10 chance

of arrest; the chance for imprisonment is 1 in 50. New York police routinely advise the victims of violent crime to put stronger locks on their doors and stay away from dark alleys — that's all.

The unprecedented attention paid to the Goetz trial makes it a landmark case. Most people agree with the verdict. However, it would be unfortunate if the outcome were to be interpreted as an unrestricted license for vigilante justice. Upholding law and order remains the responsibility of police and the courts, and America's cities must not be turned into shooting galleries.

Goetz may still have to go to jail on the weapons-possession conviction. It seems, however, that throughout his long ordeal he has already paid the penalty for his offense.

Making Goetz into some kind of national hero would be a mistake. He is an ordinary man who, beleaguered by abuse, decided that he was not going to take it anymore and fought back. It's comforting that, in this particular case, a jury of his peers agreed with that decision.

The Salt Lake Tribune

Salt Lake City, UT, June 24, 1987

It didn't take long for the wrong conclusions to be drawn from last week's Bernhard Goetz verdict in New York City. Gun advocates are pacing the field with hastily derived, inaccurate advice.

In a "press release" from the Gun Owners of America, its president, one Lawrence Pratt, is pleased to embrace Mr. Goetz's non-guilt as an opportunity to foster the notion that personal handguns are an effective crime deterrent. His is not a conclusion sanctioned either by laws or official understanding of the outcome in the Goetz case.

In fact, although the celebrated New York City trial exonerated Mr. Goetz of shooting young men in a subway who he claimed were about to mug him, the jury found him guilty of carrying an unlicensed handgun. Moreover, in commenting on the matter, New York Mayor Edward Koch emphasized that his city's law enforcement people will take a grim view of any increase in guns being carried and used as a "vigilante" method of self-protection.

Utah residents who pack sidearms for personal defense, without first getting permission to do so, would themselves be risking possible prosecution. The state holds that toting unauthorized concealed weapons is, itself, a crime, a felony if such a gun is loaded.

Film fantasy to the contrary, pistolas are notoriously unreliable. At

close range, they may hit a motionless target, but as distance and movement increase, they are dangerously inexact, more capable of hitting anything in the vicinity — an assailant or an innocent bystander, a burglar or an heirloom umbrella stand. The inaccuracy factor accrues especially to untrained hands, the type most likely to possess these weapons if advice such as Mr. Pratt's is followed.

The Gun Owners of America honcho, citing evidence the source of which is not identified, claims "almost 600,000 crimes are prevented each year by people who use handguns to thwart criminals." If so, a sizable number comprising these statistics who are not police officers can expect to answer heavy questioning.

They would in Utah, where only certain circumstances are approved for firearms self-defense and all handgun incidents must be thoroughly investigated, with either or both shootee and shooter liable for conviction and punishment.

The Goetz verdict applies solely to one particular case and the specific facts defining it. No new precedent was set nor was any cockeyed view confirmed that the war against crime now can be augmented by every self-proclaimed enlistee shoving a revolver or automatic in purse, belt, briefcase or shoulder holster. Those who ignore or defy this understanding are as much cause as they are would-be eradicator of violent lawlessness.

The Chattanooga Times

Chattanooga, TN, June 22, 1987

In the wake of Bernhard Goetz's acquittal in the subway shootings of four black teen-agers, New York Mayor Edward Koch pledged to "come down as hard as we can" on anyone engaging in vigilantism. The mayor's response reflects widespread concern that the jury verdict will embolden those who would take the law into their own hands.

In December, 1984, Mr. Goetz was riding the subway in New York when he was approached by four black men who asked him for $5. The young men did not brandish weapons or make other threatening moves or statements. Mr. Goetz, however, claimed to have been frightened by the looks on the faces of the young men and by their "body language." He pulled out a pistol and shot them. When one of them appeared to be only slightly injured, he shot him again. Mr. Goetz acknowledged in a confession to police that his intention had been to "murder them, to hurt them, to make them suffer as much as possible."

Those are not the words, and his were not the actions, of a reasonable individual acting in simple self-defense. They are the words of a man driven to irrational violence by a generalized hatred of the "punks" of this world. Yet, the jury accepted Mr. Goetz's contention that the shootings were in self-defense. He was convicted only of illegally carrying a pistol.

We have no doubt that Mr. Goetz, a victim of a mugging some years ago, did feel threatened. As it turns out, the four men who approached him were unsavory characters — two of them are in prison for unrelated crimes. But it is frightening to think that a mere feeling of fear, engendered by no more than "body language," can be judged reasonable cause for use of deadly force in self-defense.

One can sympathize with Bernard Goetz's fear and with his anger at the inability of police authorities to effectively combat crime, but we cannot accept the idea of pre-emptive self-defense, the proposition that fear alone justifies the shooting of individuals who have not presented an overt threat, much less committed a crime. Even in the Wild West, a man had to be drawn upon before he could be justified in shooting another.

Mr. Goetz has become a hero to some who bemoan what they see as a lack of law and order in this country. But he is no hero and his actions did not advance the concept of law and order at all. Rather, resort to vigilante justice invites lawlessness and chaos.

There are also concerns about the racial implications of the Goetz case. It is reasonable to question whether Mr. Goetz would have been acquitted had he been white and the four young men black.

"The climate in which this decision was made," Dr. Roscoe C. Brown Jr., president of Bronx Community College, said after the verdict, "is one of racism and fear of black young men." Other black leaders spoke too of the widespread belief that young black men are by definition dangerous, a racial stereotype that unfairly burdens the vast majority of blacks, who are law-abiding. These leaders raised legitimate worry that the Goetz verdict will reinforce that perception and transform it into something truly threatening by fostering the idea that fear based on racial stereotype may be used to justify unprovoked violence.

The Goetz jury decided a single case. But the potential implications of that decision are ominous. We dare not become a society in which citizens fearful of crime shoot first and ask questions later.

The Providence Journal

Providence, RI, June 19, 1987

A jury found "subway vigilante" Bernhard Goetz innocent Tuesday of attempting to murder four alleged muggers under New York's streets two years ago. The verdict was based on a careful reading of state laws on self-defense. If further tragedy is to be avoided, public debate on the verdict must proceed with equal care.

Mr. Goetz's peers — six of the jury were victims of crime — agreed that the accused used reasonable force in defending himself. What constitutes "reasonable" force was the central question at the trial. As for the jury, it reportedly entered its deliberations already convinced by the facts of the trial that Mr. Goetz had been, as he described it, a "cornered mouse" at the mercy of the four young thugs.

Prosecutors failed to convince the jurors that Mr. Goetz should have spent more time reflecting upon how to defend himself in the most humane way possible. The jury did not believe Mr. Goetz acted like a vigilante: He did not go out looking for someone to punish, did not take the law into his own hands — and should not be punished for defending himself.

Yet, if Mr. Goetz was a cornered mouse, he was a mouse with a difference. He had a gun. The odd verdict from the 13-count indictment found him guilty of carrying his gun without a license. That the jury did not exonerate him for this argues powerfully that the verdict *cannot* be read as a "license" to carry weapons onto the New York City subways, as some critics contend. That this jury was composed of blacks as well as whites argues also that the verdict *cannot* be read as a "license" to use those guns in an "open season" on blacks.

But the message society takes from the verdict will not necessarily be tempered by the fine gradations of the law as determined by a jury. The words of influential public figures will influence public attitudes about its meaning. That the Goetz verdict is not a license to carry guns on the subway and open fire on blacks has not stopped some public figures from insisting — in what could become a self-fulfilling prophesy — that it *will* be perceived that way by many.

No evidence suggests that such fears are reasonable. To suggest that they are is irresponsible. In fact, the public reaction to the Goetz affair from beginning to end has been much

more responsible than portrayed by such wrongheaded critics. Mr. Goetz and his ordeal have been correctly interpreted by the public as reflecting the law enforcement system's failure to protect the public, even as the criminal justice system is perceived by many as going out of its way to protect those who commit crimes.

The public can be trusted not to descend en masse and in arms to police the New York City subway system. But individuals are a different matter. And the reaction of individuals to the Goetz tragedy cannot be made more responsible by irresponsible rhetoric. If society hopes to avoid further tragedy, Americans must use greater caution in judging what the Goetz verdict has to say about crime and justice in America.

Newsday

Long Island, NY, June 17, 1987

The jury verdict on Bernhard Goetz came in yesterday with all the finality that could have been expected in this case after two and a half years.

Except for third-degree gun possession, the 39-year-old electrical engineer was found innocent on all counts — including second-degree attempted murder and first-degree assault. With this verdict, a jury of eight men and four women brought to a dramatic conclusion a tangled and sometimes ugly criminal case that began in December, 1984, when Goetz, the "subway vigilante," shot and wounded four young black men on a D-train.

Some New Yorkers — and not only blacks — will question whether the verdict was just. They may wonder anew whether the criminal justice system accords equal justice under the law to black and white alike.

Others may take the verdict to mean that vigilante justice is permitted, even condoned — that they are free to carry unlicensed guns and mete out justice on their own terms.

But it would be an error to answer the question solely on the basis of this case — and an even greater error to conclude that it justifies vigilantism.

For that would place too heavy a burden of meaning on a single criminal trial. Twelve men and women cannot be asked to do more than assess the facts of a single case at hand. It's too much to ask that their verdict support some overarching conclusion about the city's indisputably troubled race relations.

Nor can the deliberations of a mere dozen jurors uphold a judgment final and firm on the state of society's undoubtedly flawed criminal justice system.

In this case the jury's verdict was that Goetz was innocent of all but the most minor charge. But in many far less publicized cases every day, defendants — white and black — are found guilty and sentenced to jail.

Yes, there is too much crime in New York's subways. And yes, much more must be done to assure public safety.

But no one needed the Goetz trial to prove that. Those charges were true long before Goetz came along — and they seem all too likely to remain true long after his name fades from easy memory.

Long Island, NY, June 22, 1987

Much of last week's reaction to the Bernhard Goetz verdict was overwrought. That would have been true no matter what the jury decided; the fascination of this case lay partly in the fact that everyone had strong opinions about it long before it was tried. But maybe now — almost a week after the verdict was rendered — the case can be put into some sort of perspective.

Goetz's acquittal Tuesday on all major counts unleashed a lot of second-guessing of the jury — and some soul-searching about New York City's future.

Many people sincerely see the verdict as a racist commentary that will polarize the city — demoralizing blacks, encouraging white racists, emboldening closet vigilantes and firing up the racial Bunsen burner for the long summer ahead.

But if the verdict was motivated solely or even primarily by racism, how to explain that two blacks were among the jurors who voted for acquittal on 12 of 13 counts? And since blacks as well as whites use a subway system

that can subject any and all riders to indignities, intimidation and crime, how to factor in the importance of that experience in the jurors' deliberations?

Would an all-black jury — weighing the same evidence and sharing the common experience of New York subway riders — have voted the other way? There's obviously no way of knowing, and it's entirely conceivable that any jury, no matter what its racial composition, would have reached the same basic conclusion.

Undoubtedly some politicians and community leaders saw (and still see) the verdict as a political gift horse to ride for all it's worth. But it's by no means clear that they can ride it very far in any community.

How truly stunned were New Yorkers by the verdict? The case took two and a half years to come to trial. There may be many — most notably Manhattan District Attorney Robert Morgenthau — who disagree with the jury's findings. But given the intricacy of the law that governs the use of

deadly force in New York, there are probably very few who were totally surprised by the trial's outcome.

Nonetheless, some of last week's commentary seemed to regard the city as a disturbed adolescent in need of calming down. No doubt Police Commissioner Benjamin Ward spoke for a lot of people when he blew up at the glib pontificating about the frightening "message" the verdict allegedly sent: "No one in New York City has a license to go out and hunt anyone — black, green, yellow or whatever — and nothing that came out of this case has given anyone the license to do anything." That may have been about the most sensible thing anyone in authority had to say all week.

Perhaps the Goetz case will further divide the city. But only a deranged person could regard this "subway vigilante" as a model to be emulated. If watching his taped account of the shooting evokes some pity for his terror, it certainly arouses no admiration. Whatever the justice of the jury's verdict, this man is an example for no one.

ALBUQUERQUE JOURNAL

Albuquerque, NM, June 18, 1987

No matter which side you were on in this highly emotional case, there is little to cheer about in Tuesday's acquittal of Bernhard Goetz.

A Manhattan jury found the 39-year-old electrical engineer blameless in 12 of 13 counts, including attempted murder, assault and reckless endangerment, in the shootings 2½ years ago of four teen-agers in a New York City subway car. Goetz claimed that the four were trying to rob him; the teen-agers maintained they were panhandling.

Goetz's shots reverberated across the nation. Some hailed him as a hero. Others deplored him as a vigilante. But most of us, perhaps, regarded his actions — and now his acquittal — with feelings far less settled.

Certainly it is easy to sympathize with those who are weary of being victimized by crime and frustrated by a criminal justice system that seems helpless to protect them. Have we no choice but to submit to being mugged and robbed?

But is Goetz's acquittal so clearly a victory for victims? The 2½ years spent in waiting and uncertainty were hardly easy. Goetz's only comment after the acquittal was a plaintive question to his attorney: "Can I go home now?"

Did Goetz's actions make subways safer? One could argue subways are less safe if nervous passengers take to packing pistols, and fellow riders risk being caught by a stray bullet intended for a rowdy teen-ager, a panhandler or someone who *looks* suspicious.

Did Goetz's action cause would-be criminals to think again? Goetz himself was not robbed that day, if that is indeed what the four young men had in mind. We have no way of knowing whether other potential criminals were deterred by the possibility of commuters toting guns. We do know that Goetz's action didn't deter those most directly involved: Two of the four teen-agers were convicted of other crimes committed in the months following the shooting.

But then, to assume that Goetz's acquittal will inspire vigilantism or deter criminals probably gives the case more significance than it merits. Goetz commanded our attention because of our concern with crime. But in the end, it comes down to one jury's ruling on one individual case, not a promotion — or an indictment — of taking the law into one's own hands.

Better to take the attention generated by the Goetz case and focus it in more constructive ways.

Tougher gun control laws — not more guns — are needed to stymie both criminals and trigger-happy vigilantes. Goetz does stand convicted of illegal weapons possession; the New York judge can emphasize the importance of gun control laws by sentencing Goetz to some time in jail for this serious offense.

A second step is better treatment of victims of crime. Three years prior to the subway shooting, Goetz was mugged. Furious at what he considered cavalier treatment by the police, Goetz decided then to protect himself. He did.

Taxpayers must be willing to pay for more police protection, particularly in such high-crime areas as the New York subways.

And all citizens need to address the problems of a growing underclass, where school dropout rates, unemployment and violence — particularly among black teen-agers like the four involved in the shooting — sentence a segment of our American society to a future without hope or direction, a future where they are likely to be victimizers and victims.

Part IV:
Drugs & Crime

The national preoccupation with drugs has reached a fever pitch. Hardly a day passes when some mention of drugs does not appear in the media. Countless lives have been lost, careers wrecked, heroes toppled, homes broken, businesses crippled, and policemen and politicians corrupted. Almost every aspect of public and private life has been tainted and billions bled from the economy. Since the late 1950s when drugs were found strictly in the domain of the underground, the drug scourge has escalated into a national scandal. Small-time drug runners have been replaced by ruthless, nontraditional modes of organized crime that continue to flourish. As a result, drugs are implicated in more than half the crime in the U.S. and our government's relationships with foreign powers have been compromised by drug traffickers and their millions.

The National Institute on Drug Abuse (NIDA) reported in 1986 that as many as 80% of "today's young adults" had "tried an illicit drug" by their mid-20s. More than half of those had used a drug besides marijuana. According to the report, America's "high school students and other young adults show a level of involvement with illicit drugs which is greater than can be found in any other industrialized nation in the world." The President's Commission on Organized Crime reported in 1986 that marijuana "was firmly entrenched" in American society, heroin had half a million steady customers and cocaine had as many as five million regular users. The so-called 'crack' epidemic, the government's self-declared "War on Drugs" and the growing prospect of employee drug testing have fueled the national controversy.

The first law in the U.S. to regulate narcotics was the Harrison Narcotics Act. Passed in 1914, it was designed primarily to channel the flow of opium and coca leaves and their derivitives and to make their transfer a matter of record. The Comprehensive Drug Abuse Prevention and Control Act of 1970, familiarly known as the Controlled Substances Act, is the modern legal foundation of a federal strategy aimed at reducing the consumption of illicit drugs. The Controlled Substances Act brought up to date and consolidated all federal drug laws since the Harrison Narcotics Act of 1914. The Drug Enforcement Administration (DEA), established in 1973 to replace the Bureau of Narcotics and Dangerous Drugs, is now primarily responsible for enforcing the provisions of the act. To this end, the DEA investigates individuals involved in the growing, manufacture or distribution of controlled substances destined for illicit traffic.

But the relation between drugs and crime runs deeper than the laws that regulate their use. Since drug users needs a vast amount of money to support a habit they usually obtain the necessary funds by illegal methods. The typical categories of crime indulged in by drug users to support their habits include theft, prostitution, gambling, forgery and drug dealing. Studies conducted by the NIDA have found that many drug users commit more than one type of crime to maintain their habits, although they tend to focus on a particular activity. It has also been found that those addicted to drugs at an early age tend to commit crimes frequently later on. The seriousness of crimes involved grows greater with age. Among youthful addicts there are more muggings and purse snatchings while older addicts commit robberies.

Everyone is a victim in crimes that involve drug abuse: the business community, the addict and the non-addict are all hurt. While it cannot be generalized that all addicts are criminals, there is an undeniable connection between crime and addiction. Additionally, there is a massive involvement of organized crime in drug trafficking largely because it is extremely lucrative. Illicit drug sales in 1986 were estimated by the U.S. government to be $70 billion, a figure nearly equal to the combined profits of the 500 largest industrial corporations in America. Drug money is often "laundered" or passed through legitimate businesses, some of which are fronts in major enterprises, before it is put back into the drug trade.

To combat organized crime and drug trafficking, the Reagan administration has reorganized the DEA and brought the FBI into the fight. To expand its facilities and become more efficient, the DEA began working with the FBI in 1982 when then-Attorney General William French Smith announced the groups would have concurrent jurisdiction of the federal drug laws. In addition, the Coast Guard are cooperating in interdicitng smuggling operations.

The Reagan administration's battle against drugs does not stop with law enforcement mobilization. President Reagan himself has sounded a massive publicity since his second press conference 1981 when he said, "It is my firm belief that the answer to the drug problem comes through winning over the users to the point that we take the customers away from the drugs." To that end, First Lady Nancy Reagan has made the drug issue her pet project, pushing the point with her "Just Say No" anti-drug crusade in the schools and pressing the entertainment industry to deglamorize the treatment of drugs in films, television and music.

However, despite the attention focused on the drug issue, the situation does not seem to be improving. Crack can be found in abundance on the streets on inner-city America and even heroin is said to be gaining renewed popularity. To make matters more confusing are the recent developments in Central America, particularly involving Panama'a de facto ruler, Gen. Manual Antonio Noriega, and his alleged cooperation with Colombian drug lords with the apparent knowledge of the U.S. government. The drug crisis has frustrated politicians and law enforcement to the point where the possibility of drug legalization has now entered the national debate.

'Crack' Explosion Alarms Nation; Cocaine Deaths Found on the Rise

About one million Americans had tried "crack," a cheap and potent form of cocaine that some experts ranked above heroin in danger, according to an estimate by the federal National Institute of Drug Abuse (NIDA), was reported June 13, 1986. Crack had been known in parts of the United States for as long as three years. But in the last months of 1985 and the first half of 1986, its use was said to have exploded. By one count, the drug could be bought and sold with relative ease in Los Angeles, Detroit, New York and 14 other major American cities. U.S. Attorney Rudolph Giuliani said crack accounted for up to half of all drug cases the federal government had prosecuted in New York since October 1985. Crack's sudden explosion in use met an outburst of public fear and anger. Newspapers, magazines and television have graphically painted its dangers. Churches and community groups mounted grass-roots campaigns to harass dealers and warn away potential users. The deaths of basketball star Len Bias and football star Don Rogers from cocaine overdoses at the time focused national attention on the issue. The widespread alarm also stoked growing public anxiety over cocaine itself.

Figures on who used crack were sketchy. Many in the public were most concerned for teenagers and even younger schoolchildren reported to have fallen victim to the drug. But preliminary findings suggested that most users were men aged 20-35, most often with incomes that were comfortable or better. About half were said to be black, and the majority lived in cities. But police reported that the drug was already spreading to suburbs.

While cocaine is sold as a powder, crack is available as solid chips and lumps, making it easier to smoke, with a more powerful effect. Crack is stronger than cocaine. The process by which it is created gives it a degree of purity that outstrips cocaine by 70% or more. A crack dealer boils down a mixture of cocaine, water and baking soda and allows it to harden. It is then sold off a few milligrams at a time for $10-25. While inducing a comparable effect, crack is more economical to use than cocaine. Yet crack's strength also means than an addiction could ultimately cost more than a dependency on cocaine or even heroin. Regular users of either cocaine or crack become ensnared in a cycle of chemical highs and lows. But crack's cycle is faster and, because of that, its grip is stronger. Addiction is quick. Experts estimated that cocaine dependency requires three to four years of use. Crack addiction is said to take six to 10 weeks.

The number of Americans killed each year by cocaine had risen to at least 563 in 1985 from as low as 185 in 1981, the NIDA reported July 10, 1986. But the number of cocaine users was thought to be stable. The figures, part of the findings of the NIDA survey, were unveiled by federal health officials at a Washington, D.C. news conference. "We're in a terrible situation with cocaine," said Dr. Donald Macdonald, administrator of the Alcohol, Drug Abuse and Mental Health Adminisration. The institute's survey of 700 hospitals found that emergency-room admissions for cocaine victims had gone up to 9,946 in 1985 from 3,296 in 1981. The figures were not intended as a total count, but merely to indicate national trends.

Use of crack had been exaggerated by the media, the federal Drug Enforcement Administration (DEA) said Sept. 24. The powerful cocaine derivative, and narcotics in general, had been the subject of a recent burst of attention from politicians and journalists. DEA spokesman Robert Feldkamp said crack was "the drug of choice in New York City," but that it was on a "secondary, not a primary drug problem, in most cities." Feldkamp was commenting on a new intelligence report by the DEA's Office of Intelligence, "The Crack Situation in the United States." This said 80% of U.S. crack was thought to originate in the New York area.

Thirteen percent of those surveyed believed that narcotics was the country's most important problem, according to results of a *New York Times/CBS* poll that the newspaper reported Sept. 2, 1986. Neither war nor any economic problem was cited by as many respondents. In April 1986, an earlier *New York Times/CBS* poll had found that just 2% of respondents considered drugs to be the nation's top problem. Crack was known to five out of six respondents in the September poll. More than 50% of respondents could provide some description of the drug.

The Star-Ledger

Newark, NJ, July 3, 1986

Last month, a 22-year-old college basketball star who had just signed a contract with the Boston Celtics that would have made him an instant millionaire overdosed on cocaine and died of cardiac arrest. Over the past weekend, a 23-year-old pro football player died from a lethal dose of cocaine that induced a fatal heart attack—24 hours before he was to be married.

These two drug-related deaths have attracted national publicity because they involved sports celebrities—and no doubt there will be more from that sector. But there will be a lot more deaths from cocaine overdosing that will remain virtually anonymous—mere statistics on police blotters—because the victims are ordinary citizens.

Nevertheless, they share a common mortal link: They are—or they will be—victims of the sharply rising addiction to cocaine, the "in" narcotic that not too long ago was widely accepted as a recreational drug, along with marijuana. Statistics now starkly reveal that cocaine has become a killer drug.

The deadly implications of cocaine use were clearly evident in the deaths of two well-conditioned athletes, Len Bias, University of Maryland basketball star drafted by the Celtics, and Don Rogers, who played for the Cleveland Browns. Their tragic fates should serve as a chilling social commentary on the mortal ravages of the Drug Age that had its insidious origins in the 1960s.

There is more than enough grim evidence to sustain the morbid finding that cocaine no longer can be casually regarded as a "recreational drug." The New Jersey medical examiner, Dr. Robert Goode, aptly noted that it should be viewed in a more ominous, contemporary vein as "recreational poison." Deaths related to cocaine use are expected to double or even triple because of the escalating use of the drug in all its forms.

Cocaine—and more recently, its more potent form, crack—has been taking a sharply increasing share of the illicit drug market. It is up to 30 percent, with half representing crack. A key reason for the rapidly expanding sale of cocaine is that it has become more available—and cheaper.

The illicit trade in cocaine has become big business, a multibillion-dollar industry, which has been wryly characterized by Peruvian President Alan Garcia as "Latin America's only successful multinational." And it is purely a matter of supply and demand.

Even the most vigilant law enforcement will not appreciably stanch the floodtide of illegal drugs moving across our borders. Drug pushers only thrive because there is a market for their illicit product. For drug abusers, the increased number of drug-related deaths could be a forbidding preview of their future.

Herald SYRACUSE American

Syracuse, NY, July 13, 1986

Federal officials this past week released statistics that should surprise no one who has read a newspaper lately: Compared to five years ago, three times as many people are dying as a result of using cocaine.

The evidence is all around us. In the last month, we have seen University of Maryland basketball star Len Bias and Cleveland Browns football standout Don Rogers added to the gruesome tally. Their cases are of the type that makes national news, but every city has its casualties. The drug is everywhere. Estimates vary, but virtually everyone with an informed opinion pegs the number of regular cocaine users in this country well into the millions.

Yet no one openly encourages it. On the contrary, everyone who speaks out voices' emphatic opposition to it. In just the last week, National Football League Commissioner Pete Rozelle unveiled a plan to have every player routinely tested for drug use. And Education Secretary William Bennett has threatened to cut off federal aid to colleges that fail to combat drug use on campus (as if it weren't already proscribed).

▽

First lady Nancy Reagan has made it a personal crusade, and the White House says the president has plans for a campaign of his own. Our own U.S. Sen. Alfonse D'Amato this past week demonstrated how easy it is to buy "crack," a variety of cocaine, on the streets of New York. And former Syracuse University basketball star Tony Bruin, after being sentenced to five years probation on a cocaine charge, vowed Thursday to spread the word to the community's youth about the dangers of the drug.

It's not as if this deadly peril is being kept a secret. The message is clear — cocaine is a killer.

So what is it that inspires people to use cocaine? If there were one, simple answer to that one, there would be no cocaine problem.

For many, it's an escape from the torment in their lives, a few moments of euphoria to mitigate the pain — or the monotony — of their day-to-day existence. But that doesn't apply to someone like Len Bias, who had the world by the metaphorical tail — success, money, fame — yet risked it all and lost it in an uncautious moment.

Why would Bias do it?

Why do millionaires crave more and more money? Why do happily married men cheat on their wives? Perhaps the answer is to be found in the title of the old song, "Is That All There Is?" — the fundamental human urge to seek the next plateau. And off the edge of that last plateau so often lies disaster.

▽   ▽

Given the opportunity — and in the case of cocaine, that opportunity is all around us — people will engage in self-destructive behavior for the smallest of reasons, or for no reason at all. The solution — if there is to be a solution — would seem to lie in minimizing the opportunity.

Authorities tell us that cocaine is cheaper, more potent and more available than ever before. Despite doubled and redoubled efforts by law enforcement at every level, every community is inundated with this garbage. No amount of official effort is able to put a dent in the trade, it's just too lucrative for those engaged in it. It's merely a handy target for candidates' righteous outrage at election time.

The cocaine business is flourishing for two reasons: 1) People want it; and 2) the people who don't want it, tolerate it. Too many people are simply looking the other way when they encounter the use of cocaine and other illegal drugs. Nothing, it seems, can stir them out of their lethargic attitude.

▽   ▽

There are no quick fixes to this problem. No amount of urine testing, police stings, political posturing, celebrity deaths will change anything as long as the public mindset is largely apathetic. If the same kind of public energy could be mustered in the fight against drugs as, for example, the anti-abortion movement, or the anti-Vietnam war crusade, some slow progress might be realized.

But despite all the recent publicity, no popular groundswell on such a scale is apparent. Drugs, for the most part, remain "somebody else's problem." Until they are perceived as the national scourge they are, drugs are likely to remain tucked conveniently away in the back of the public consciousness.

And the death toll will continue to climb.

Wisconsin ▲ State Journal

Madison, WI, August 1, 1986

The deaths of Len Bias, a young basketball star, and Don Rogers, a promising professional football player, brought home in shocking terms the message that cocaine can kill.

Medical professionals and others familiar with the drug were already painfully aware of its deadly effects. Sadly, it took the sacrifice of two healthy athletes to galvanize public attention.

Until the Bias-Rogers incidents, how many people were aware that cocaine has claimed more than a score of lives in Wisconsin? (Twenty-one deaths between 1980 and 1985 were related to cocaine, state figures show.)

So far as we know, most of the people who supplied those 21 fatal fixes are alive and well. Some probably remain in the cocaine supply "business," not really caring that their illegal actions could lead to even more deaths.

The Legislature recently toughened state laws dealing with cocaine possession and sales, but those changes did not address the question, "How should society deal with someone who supplies an illegal drug that kills someone else?"

Two state legislators, Republican John Merkt of Mequon and Democrat John Medinger of La Crosse, think they have the answer: treat them like killers.

They have proposed broadening the definition of second-degree murder to include deaths from cocaine and other drugs. Such cases probably would be tough to prosecute under Wisconsin's current second-degree murder law, which defines "conduct imminently dangerous to another" but also requires evidence of "a depraved mind" for a finding of guilt.

The state manslaughter law does not fit the bill, either, because it applies to killings in the heat of passion, in self-defense or in defense of another person.

Merkt and Medinger will present their proposal today at a meeting of the state Council on Alcohol and Drug Abuse. While rewriting a criminal statute is no minor undertaking, it is an idea the council should endorse.

If drug dealers know they are facing the possibility of a lengthy prison sentence every time they sell a gram of cocaine, the chilling effects on this despicable market could be significant.

The News and Courier

Charleston, SC, July 14, 1986

It was just a matter of time before the cheap and highly addictive form of cocaine called "crack" would show up locally. The question was how quickly police would act.

Now we have the answer. Following up on a tip last week, the police sent an undercover agent to a migrant camp on John's Island. By time the bust was over, nine farm workers had been charged and crack with an estimated street value of $15,000 had been seized.

County police Capt. Ronald R. Perry explained that the police are "sending a message to dealers that crack is dangerous, and

we're doing everything in our power to see that they go to jail." Magistrate Randell McIntosh, who set a total bond of $150,000 on the first suspect, sent the same message when he said that crack "is too potent for me to extend any kind of charity ... "

All but three of the eight who were arrested in the bust are being held in lieu of bonds ranging from $100,000 to $5,000.

The message from local police, judges and juries should be clear: Charleston county is not the place for dealers in crack. Their crimes will not be tolerated.

The Union Leader

Manchester, NH
August 10, 1986

A woman, the mother of two grade-schoolers, was watching a TV report on the deadly "crack" cocaine and those who push it to young and old alike.

Turning to a companion, the woman said, "I think they should kill the drug-pushers."

She is not alone. President Reagan said the same thing last week. It's a sentiment shared, we think, by millions of Americans.

There's a force alive in this country today that, if harnessed and correctly channeled, can put a huge dent in our drug problems.

It is the force of rage felt by reasonable, responsible Americans as they watch criminals literally getting away with murder and their friends and children destroying themselves and, in the process, tearing at the very fabric of society.

Surely, it is a time to shout, "Stop!"

But this must be a unified effort, led by elected officials and community leaders at all levels. It must be done by example and by deed. It must be led by officials unafraid of the criticism of the social tinkerers and self-proclaimed civil libertarians who don't care to protect the rights of the law-abiding majority.

Surely these leaders must sense

that the majority is on their side, that common sense dictates a fair, clear and firm approach to those who are wreaking destruction through drugs.

That common sense was evident in a random Union Leader poll of New Hampshire teens one day last week. Dozens of teens were asked what they thought of drug testing in schools, along with the seizure of automobiles used by teen drunks. The response seemed overwhelmingly favorable.

Colleen Mahoney, a 16-year-old junior at Merrimack High School, gave a typical response.

"As far as testing, if you don't have anything to hide, you don't have anything to worry about. Those who are using drugs are interfering with the learning process."

The death penalty for drug pushers? Yes, indeed. And for the mob kingpins who finance them, too.

Suspension from school for students on drugs? Again, yes. Offer help, of course. In fact, demand rehabilitation before re-admitting the student. But let all know that drug use can't and won't be tolerated.

It's time to act. The people demand it.

CRACK

The Evening Gazette

Worcester, MA, June 18, 1986

Crack: A highly addictive cocaine derivative that renders many users violent and paranoid.

Crack, sometimes called rock, was little used on the East Coast 18 months ago. But it has hit New York City and Boston, creating psychotic reactions in users that haven't been seen since the heyday of LSD. The Worcester Police Department has made its first seizure of what appears to be a small amount of the substance. Something must be done to rid the streets of the narcotic.

Crack is one of the deadliest forms of illegal drugs in use. A 16-year-old New York City youth calmly walked into a police station and told the lieutenant at the desk: "I want to report that I killed my mother." Two days before, the mother had caught him smoking crack and during the fight that erupted, the youth stabbed her to death in a drug frenzy. It was only after his supply was gone that he turned himself in. It was the eighth violent crime blamed on crack in the New York City in the past four months.

Police Chief Thomas Leahy says that Worcester doesn't yet have crack houses, spots that

serve high school students and young adults in New York. They're similar to opium dens that once catered to wealthy Chinese addicts. But crack houses have been found as close as Boston. A young man carrying 1,051 vials of crack in a duffel bag — worth about $26,000 — was arrested in Boston as well. The state police laboratory first pronounced that crack had been found in Massachusetts last December.

Heroin users who switched to crack say it is far more addictive and more dangerous to the user. Unfortunately, it is attractive to young people, affluent or poor. Victims as young as eight years old have been reported. In a recent sweep of street dealers in New York City, 18 of the 44 arrested were selling crack within a half block of a school. One expert on addiction calls it "the fast food of drugs."

In an age where parents worry constantly about what lies in wait for their children, crack is just one more monster to contend with. Drug Enforcement Administration officials are clearly worried that it will become the "drug of choice." The effect will be devastating to society should that occur.

The Pittsburgh PRESS

Pittsburgh, PA, August 10, 1986

Local and federal law enforcement officials in New York City have come up with a new wrinkle in the battle against "crack," the potent cocaine derivative.

They began confiscating cars driven by persons coming into town to buy the illegal drug.

A 16-year-old federal law allows the confiscation of property used in drug transactions. Heretofore, the measure has been used mostly against drug dealers. But officials decided to start using it against buyers as well.

During a four-day period, 30 cars were taken in Manhattan, mostly from young persons living in middle-class suburban communities. Police Commissioner Benjamin Ward issued a warning:

"If you come to New York to buy crack, bring carfare and be prepared to take the bus back."

Other areas would do well to follow New York City's lead. If a person stands to lose his wheels, he might think twice about running out to buy a dangerous drug for a momentary high.

The Afro American

Baltimore, MD, July 19, 1986

All too often, it takes a tragedy to spark action, and the recent deaths, by overdose of cocaine, of two top athletes brings to the fore, action in the war against drugs.

The myth has been promulgated for years, that cocaine use was non-addictive. Reports from the U.S. Public Health Service indicate that not only is the drug addictive, but it can kill — even on first use.

First Lady Nancy Reagan joined the war against drugs quite some time ago, and now President Reagan plans to join in, and give a series of anti-drug speeches in the crusade.

The new menace on the street, the drug "crack,"has alerted anti-drug officials, and brought into focus a concerted attack on this new threat.

There are about 300 bills pending in Congress to tighten drug controls. The tragedy has struck, and hopefully now, we will begin to see more action. Meanwhile, the toll-free Cocaine Hotline, 1-800-662-HELP, is there for those who need help.

THE ATLANTA CONSTITUTION

Atlanta, GA, June 20, 1986

Sen. Lawton Chiles (D-Fla.) thinks Congress should act immediately to give law-enforcement agencies help in combating the wildfire spread of the dangerous new drug known alternately as "crack" and "rock." He is right. The problem is serious. Crack, a highly refined form of cocaine that offers the intense high of free-basing without the potentially explosive distilling process free-basing requires, is almost instantly addictive. It can cause severe depression and paranoia. And doctors say frequent use can cause serious brain damage.

It's mind-altering effects have been blamed for at least five homicides in New York City in which users, apparently suffering extreme paranoia after coming down from a crack high, killed relatives or friends. It has contributed to a sharp rise in violent crimes in that city, and has led to a 48-percent increase in the number of people seeking help for cocaine addiction.

To make matters worse, it is also cheap. A fix sells for as little as $10. That has made it popular with teenagers and even schoolchildren.

Chiles has proposed legislation that would elevate crack to "Schedule I" status among illicit narcotics, putting it in a class with those drugs considered by the federal government to be the most dangerous. It deserves the honor. The change would allow for stiffer penalties against those found guilty of possessing or distributing it. Under current law, crack dealers get an undeserved break. They face relatively small fines and must be arrested several times before stiffer penalties can be imposed.

Chiles would also make it a felony to employ minors in the manufacture or distribution of the drug. That would double the current penalties for such offenses, which would mean that first offenders could face up to 20 years in prison. That may be excessive, but Chiles' point is important: Crack dealers routinely use minors in their operations to hustle customers on the street, to sell to other youngsters and to act as lookouts.

Again, Chiles sounds an important alarm: A rapidly growing national problem needs sustained national attention. His colleagues should be all ears.

Chicago Defender

Chicago, IL, July 30, 1986

There's a new group joining the army against the illicit use of cocaine and we think the organization is greatly needed. It is called the Cocaine Prevention/Advisory Group. Its formation was recently announced by Chicago Department of Health commissioner, Lonnie C. Edwards.

One of the great things about this new effort is that the group will be made up of representatives from treatment and prevention programs which are already in place. It will also have members from various Chicago community organizations as well as adolescents recruited from the schools and numerous youth establishments.

There are several positives to this. First of all, the group can act as an umbrella coalition where members regularly share anti-drug information in quick and effective ways. Such knowledge can then be disseminated by the members of CPAG among their own particular groups. It can then be used to increase the anti-narcotics educational awareness of users and potential abusers.

The group also will be able to make positive contributions to the residential adolescent substance abuse treatment program which will be opening in September at the Department of Health's Chicago Alcoholic Treatment Center (CATC).

New types of drugs are hitting the streets. Currently the average city may have designer drugs, crack (a new and deadly type of cocaine), and numerous other forms of illegal drugs pushed on its residents. These new narcotics demand the use of new anti-drug strategies by authorities.

Old ways and methods may prove ineffective in fighting against the current threat of these new and deadly drugs.

Crack is a particularly bad health threat. It is reported that: it can addict the consumer after two or three tries; the "high" from it is more intense than the average cocaine high, lasts for five or 10 minutes but is usually followed by severe depression, guilt, and feelings of worthlessness and; when the user tries to relieve the negative feelings by smoking more crack, the short high returns, followed by the long nightmare of bad feelings. It's a vicious, crippling and deadly cycle. Some people, not knowing the potency of the drug, have had strokes and heart attacks as a result of using it.

There's no doubt about the fact that drugs and the industry which distributes them are serious blights on society. It's also a fact that the major method of dispensing drugs in the United States comes from organized crime. To reduce its effectiveness, anti-drug elements have to be better organized. Their flows of information, methods of counseling and preventing the dispersal of drugs must be well-formed and functional. This is necessary whether the anti-drug organization is a medical, law-enforcement or advisory group.

"I firmly believe that in working together we can provide our young people with the help and support they need to resist the pressures they experience to use drugs," said Doctor Edwards. We agree. In fact, such action may be the best chance our young people have.

Reagans Declare National War on Drugs; Urge Anti-Drug Crusade

President Ronald Reagan Aug. 4, 1986 declared a "national mobilization" against illegal drugs, a problem that in the previous few months had become a top national concern. In a bow to his wife's highly publicized campaign against drug abuse, Reagan said that "starting today, Nancy's crusade to deprive drug peddlers and suppliers of their customers becomes America's crusade." The president listed goals ranging from stopping smugglers to treating abusers, but he laid most emphasis on using both government and private groups "to pressure the user at school and in the workplace to straighten up, get clean." Reagan offered no details on how he would accomplish his goals or how much money it would take. Questioned by reporters, he answered that details would wait until "the near future." "This is chapter one," the president said, "more to come."

A rival assault on the drug problem had already been proposed by Rep. Thomas (Tip) O'Neil Jr. (D, Mass.), the speaker of the House of Representatives. O'Neill July 23 had called for a bipartisan effort to draw up a comprehensive drug law that would address all aspects of drug trafficking and abuse. Despite the House's overburdened schedule, the speaker wanted the bill ready for a floor vote by September 10. Republican legislators were reportedly pressing the White House to come with detailed legislation before the Democrats could seize the drug issue for fall elections. But the administration was said to have already spent nine weeks debating the matter internally. Many drug experts and clinics were reported to be skeptical of the chances that substantial concrete action would follow Reagan's Aug. 4 announcement. Cutbacks in the federal budget under his administration were widely blamed for the overburdening of treatment centers.

One move Reagan set out in his announcement was mandatory drug testing of federal employees who held sensitive posts in law enforcement, national security, safety and public health. To show the way, Reagan underwent urinalysis Aug. 9. Vice President George Bush followed Aug. 11, and an undisclosed number of presidential aides and cabinet members also agreed to take part. Some critics objected that participants had been warned too far in advance. Notification had been issued Aug. 7, and many drugs required just four days or less for all traces to leave the system.

Reagan and his wife Sept. 14, 1986 broadcast a television and radio appeal for "a national crusade" against drug abuse. It was the first time Reagan and his wife had delivered a joint television address during Reagan's presidency. The talk came a day before Reagan unveiled a legislative package of antidrug proposals. The president said the government would "continue to act aggressively" against the narcotics problem, but that "nothing would be more effective than for Americans simply to quit using illegal drugs." He called for "a massive change in national attitudes" toward drugs. Mrs Reagan said: "There is no moral ground. Indifference is not an option. We want you to help create an outspoken intolerance for drug use." Adding a personal appeal to young people, she declared: "Say 'yes' to life. And when it comes to drugs and alcohol, just say 'no.'" "Just say no" was the slogan of the antidrug publicity campaign Mrs. Reagan launched after coming to the White House. The drive is aimed at preventing future drug abuse by appealing to children aged seven to 14. By one count, the drive had spurred the establishment of 10,000 clubs, in which at least 200,000 children had pledged not to use drugs. However, government spending for antidrug education and other prevention programs had fallen by 5% under the Reagan administration, the New York Times reported Sept. 14, 1986. Time magazine reported in its Sept. 15 issue that the Department of Education spent so little on the matter that there was no record of the funds.

Reagan Sept. 15 unveiled his package of proposed legislation for fighting the narcotics problem. The Reagan administration package was one of several to be prepared after a recent increase in public anger and concern over narcotics. The House of Representatives had passed a sweeping and far more expensive antinarcotics bill a few days before Reagan presented his package. Administration officials said they did not know how many people would be tested under the president's new executive order. The order instructed all heads of executive agencies to set up testing under guidelines to be issued by the Department of Health and Human Services.

SYRACUSE
HERALD·JOURNAL
Syracuse, NY, August 5, 1986

President Reagan's proposal that members of his Cabinet be tested for drug use ranks right up there with Sen. Alfonse D'Amato's much-publicized drug "buy" in New York City.

In other words, it promises to be a huge public relations spectacle with no meaning whatsoever. Set an example? What does he take us for? Does the president really believe that if this squeaky-clean collection of stuffed shirts allows their blood to be tested for the presence of foreign materials (we'll guarantee they won't do you-know-what in a bottle), that the dealers are going to close down operations in the Bronx?

And that malarkey about the death sentence for dealing drugs. Now seriously, folks. Even if he could get a majority of Americans to accept the death penalty for anything (for all we know, maybe he could), we New Yorkers could give him an earful about how tough penalties — remember the Rockefeller drug laws? — take drugs, druggies and dealers off the streets.

◇   ◇

Think about it for a minute: If you're a cop and you catch some small-time dealer — for instance those two Australians who were hanged in Malaysia a couple of weeks ago for possession of a couple of ounces — would you think twice about making the bust, knowing he was going to get the chair?

We're not saying anybody should go easy on drugs and dealing, particularly on those who are raking in millions at the top end of the delivery system, but we seriously question whether tougher laws are more appropriate than proper enforcement of the laws we have now and better interdiction of the drug supplies coming into this country.

You know, the president talks a good game against drugs, and he seems prepared to go for the headline-grabbers, such as testing his Cabinet — even sending troops to Bolivia (a move we applauded, by the way, as better than no action at all) — but he has not shown any inclination to beef up the U.S. Drug Enforcement Agency, the federal agency with the authority and responsibility to stop drugs from coming across our borders.

◇   ◇

In fact, he has done just the opposite; he has cut the DEA's funding to the point where it hasn't a prayer of doing the job entrusted to it. Does that sound like a president with a determination to put an end to the drug problem in this country? To us, it doesn't.

It sounds more like a politician who is willing to turn the spotlight on glamorous, perhaps even politically popular moves, while at the same time gutting the front-line agency, the agency that does the work while he grabs the headlines with meaningless gestures.

The Boston Herald

Boston, MA, August 10, 1986

EVEN the raw statistics are alarming. According to federal figures, there are some 5 million regular cocaine users in this country and as many as 24 million Americans have tried the stuff.

Some 30 percent of all college students have tried cocaine and 42 percent admit to having tried marijuana.

Another 500,000 Americans are heroin addicts.

It's a problem for schools, right down to the grade school level. It's a problem in the workplace — whether that be the assembly line or Silicon Valley or Wall Street. It's a problem in the sports world, which has lost too many of its promising young stars, and in the entertainment world, where too many careers and lives have been put on the line by drug abuse.

And now there's the growing realization that drug raids, even those that hit at the coca crop itself, only address half the problem — the supply side — but never really touch the other half — the demand side.

There's no doubt about the good intentions which drive both the White House and Capitol Hill in their truly national effort to combat the menace which narcotics have become to all Americans.

Our own war, the Alliance Against Drugs, was declared by Gov. Michael Dukakis some 20 months ago — and since that time upwards of 220 cities and towns have *voluntarily* enlisted in it.

The Alliance brings parents, police, educators, athletes, the media, medical personnel, other professions, and young people together in a cooperative effort to cut the trafficking in dope by reducing the demand for it. The federal Drug Enforcement Administration has become sufficiently impressed by the concept to offer to spread information about it to other states trying to launch their own attack on drugs. The DEA doesn't back dud ideas.

That's not to say the war has been won here. Far from it. Only two years ago a survey of 5,000 high school students found that 90 percent had taken drugs and/or liquor; 60 percent had used hard drugs; and 30 percent started using them when they were 12 — or younger. The same survey also showed that the traffic cut across all levels and neighborhoods of society; its victims came from cities and suburbs alike, from wealthy families as well as poor ones, from private as well as public schools.

But we are making progress. One reason for that has been the acceptance by the state of what the kids told them — that if young people were to be saved from drugs they had to be taught about its dangers in every grade from kindergarten on. Waiting until high school to educate them was too late — because by that time most of them had already flirted with narcotics and many had become hooked.

Out of all this has developed a statewide effort in which The Herald, WBZ-TV, and the Bank of Boston have enlisted as working partners with those who drafted and/or joined the Alliance. Briefly, the Alliance is doing these five things in cities and towns which volunteer to be part of it:

● Establishing a K through 12 anti-drug curriculum in the schools.

● Re-evaluating school discipline codes to deal effectively with students who use drugs and/or liquor, or who supply them to their classmates.

● Influencing local superintendents of schools and police chiefs to sign written memos of understanding spelling out exactly what each must do in proceeding against offenders. (This is intended to head off possible "turf wars" between educators and police.)

● Identifying treatment programs and centers in each city or town where kids who need help can receive it without difficulty or delay.

● Setting up community advisory groups of adults and youths alike, as well as all the professions cited above, in all communities to guide the Alliance and help reach its goals.

All this is aimed at teaching our children from their earliest years not only about the danger of drugs but the wisdom and necessity of avoiding them throughout their lives. That should, and we believe will, cut the demand for drugs. We believe all this is excellent, and are proud to be part of it. We urge other private interests and businesses to enlist in it too, in whatever way they can assist it most. And we wholeheartedly endorse its adoption by other states.

This war can't be fought to a stalemate; it's got to be waged by all until a complete and lasting victory is achieved. That will take a while, to be sure. But it's worth every ounce of sweat, effort, persistence, and dedication we possess. Enlist in it, please.

Edmonton Journal

Edmonton, Alta., August 7, 1986

Ronald Reagan has finally shifted the emphasis on his war on drugs from the supplier to the user, where it belongs.

But just how he plans to purge the U.S. of this "deeply disruptive and corrosive evil" is not clear.

In fact, Reagan's call for a major offensive against drug abuse is long on rhetoric and short on detail. Apart from his predilection for nationwide mandatory drug testing — a scary proposal that conjures up Orwellian nightmares — Reagan is vague on the programs and financing needed to fight drugs such as heroin, cocaine and crack.

His challenge is to address the reasons Americans take drugs; to treat the problem and not just the symptom.

That's not an easy task. Drug abuse affects every segment of society — from the unemployed, poverty-stricken junkie to the trendy yuppie. One person may take drugs to escape the reality of poverty; another for entertainment. Yet drug addiction has a way of making all its victims equal.

The U.S. government has a role to play in promoting public awareness and discussion of the dangers of drug abuse. But a lasting solution lies in changing society's attitudes, in dispelling the atmosphere of "public acquiescence" which Reagan says sustains drug abuse.

CHARLESTON EVENING POST

Charleston, SC, August 12, 1986

Secretary of State George Shultz said last year he would quit his job rather than take a government lie-detector test. Fortunately, it never came to that. But Mr. Shultz has agreed to participate in a voluntary White House drug program which involves a urinalysis. His sensibilities aren't as offended. Neither are ours.

A spokesman for Mr. Shultz explained that the secretary views drug testing as a much more reliable scientific tool than a lie-detector. What's more, the spokesman noted, the process is relatively non-intrusive. Let's even concede the possibility that mistakes will be made. The results will be kept confidential. Certainly there will be an opportunity to check and double-check. The goal is to provide help, not to send staffers packing.

The skeptics doubtless will point to a few well-publicized horror stories from the military side as evidence of how the test results can be skewed. We'll agree a case doubtless can be made for the proposition that there is no perfect system. But not even the most ardent civil libertarians would argue that the occasional error justifies abandoning all drug detection programs. There seems to be a consensus that those in certain critical jobs — including private, government-regulated industries such as the airlines — have to expect checks on whether they are operating with impaired judgment.

But more and more private employers — newspapers included — have become alarmed by the danger posed by drug-using employees. More and more are making drug-free test results a condition of employment. Certainly both private and public employers have every right to establish such a condition as long as it is administered uniformly. The tougher question is how and when to require tests of employees who were hired before such programs were initiated.

There was a time when testing of all employees wasn't even worth considering. The number of abusers simply didn't justify unnecessarily irritating good employees and kicking up the privacy issue. But no more. Drugs are being used in grade schools and on Wall Street. The odds are that if society had taken a tougher stand sooner, or a president had gotten at the head of the parade earlier, there'd be less need for such drastic steps now.

Military schools are tough on drugs not only because of their disciplined regimen but because an officer with a drug problem isn't going to escape detection long. Liberal arts colleges doubtless would be far less permissive on the subject if their graduates increasingly failed to pass the drug-free entrance tests in the marketplace.

Wisconsin ⛪ State Journal

Madison, WI, September 17, 1986

It seems that everyone — yes, even the news media — has declared War on Drugs.

Unfortunately, one of the early casualties in this war has been the U.S. Constitution, wounded first by the House of Representatives and now by President Reagan.

That lawmakers should be appalled, even frightened, by drug abuse in our society is righteous. Drug use is indeed epidemic and is extracting a terrible toll in wasted lives, economic malaise, criminal activity and social disintegration.

Likewise, the president and first lady Nancy Reagan are correct to use their powers of persuasion in hopes of making drug use unacceptable in our society. Only when Americans say "no" to drug use will true progress be made.

It is also proper for Congress and the president to authorize new spending for drug interdiction, primarily on our southern borders; for drug education, mainly for our youth; for drug-abuse treatment centers; and for drug enforcement efforts by federal, state and local agents and police.

We have no qualms, either, about handing out tough sentences for those convicted of profiting from this evil trade — whether they be "drug kingpins" or schoolyard pushers. Not 15 years with parole on the horizon, but harsh, determinate sentences.

There is also ample justification for allowing the military to "deploy equipment and personnel . . . sufficient to halt the unlawful penetration of U.S. borders by aircraft and vessels carrying narcotics," the language contained in the House bill. While we cannot blame other nations for our drug craving, we can certainly act to defend our borders against those who would pierce the front line in our defense — our national will.

Besides, U.S. troops are constantly training in this hemisphere and around the world. What's wrong with a "training exercise" in the Caribbean to intercept drug traffic from Mexico, Colombia and Bolivia? If cocaine-by-the-ton is not an invader to be feared, then what is?

Yet there is reason to worry about a crossfire in this War on Drugs, one which may catch our 200-year-old tradition of equal protection under the law.

Consider the House bill, passed 392-16, amid a flood of anti-drug sentiment. In addition to giving the armed forces powers to pursue suspected drug smugglers outside our borders, it allows the military to enforce civilian laws within the United States. No, there won't be "tanks coming down the streets, like in Chile," as one lawmaker warned, but a dangerous precedent is set if the sharp line between civilian and military law enforcement is blurred.

The House bill also provides a new exception to the so-called "exclusionary rule," which prohibits evidence obtained illegally from being offered in court. Such evidence would be allowed if "the search or seizure was undertaken in a reasonable, good-faith belief that it was in conformity with the Fourth Amendment to the Constitution," which prohibits unreasonable search and seizure.

The Supreme Court two years ago said the exclusionary rule could be suspended if officers had acted under warrants later found to be defective, but the House bill would permit "good faith" *warrantless* searches. That, it seems, is a difference worth pondering.

Now the president has ordered mandatory drug testing for federal employees in the fields of public health and security, law enforcement and other "sensitive positions." After a 60-day "grace period," federal agency heads will have discretion over whom to test and when to conduct their own testing programs. Employees will be given one chance to stop using drugs and they will be fired if caught a second time.

How many of the government's 2.8 million civilian employees would be tested? Well, no one seems to know, although about 1.1 million federal workers have various security clearances. To complicate matters, the order covers executive branch workers but not employees of Congress or the judicial branch. Are all of the government's "sensitive positions" confined to the executive branch?

By issuing such a broad testing order, the White House has glossed over three basic rights: No person shall be required to testify against himself; each of us is protected against unlawful searches; and every person is innocent until proven guilty.

It is one thing to test people who show signs of drug abuse, but quite another to test an entire class that presumably has no more nor less of a problem with illegal substances than any other segment of society.

The drive to control our national craving will fall short if ordinary citizens perceive that Washington, in its understandable zeal to snare the guilty, threatens the innocent.

Chicago Tribune

Chicago, IL, September 16, 1986

Ronald Reagan has made the First Lady's crusade against drugs his own. Together, they have asked the country to say no to the illegal, self-destructive habits that are swamping it.

This is a righteous cause. And by enlisting so prominently in it, he has marshaled the powers of the presidency and his own personal persuasiveness in a way that could very well begin to turn things around.

What Mr. Reagan is doing has two aspects. One involves specific new legal measures. For example, he has endorsed a proposal to impose the death penalty on drug dealers who intentionally kill someone while engaging in large scale drug transactions. He also proposes significantly increasing penalties for drug trafficking upon a second conviction. Drug dealing is a cold, calculating business, and these measures should raise the stakes enough to make some people think twice about what they are getting into.

The President also has proposed spending almost $1 billion more than previously planned on federal drug programs. He is more frugal than the House of Representatives in this regard, and that is where the posturing will take place as the politicians jockey with one another to be the toughest opponent of drugs.

But as important as anything else is Mr. Reagan's escalation of attention to this problem and his appeal to the country to start taking it more seriously. This is the beginning of a process of fundamental re-education, and it is about time.

Drug use is epidemic; the teenagers' traditional plea that "everybody else is doing it" this time seems to approach truth. The pervasive drug culture is rotting minds, infecting lives, forcing up crime rates, corrupting society. If reversing all this begins to seem like an obsession, that's good—it should be.

But what counts is not simply the degree of concern. More important is what Congress, state and local law enforcement officials and the public are prepared to do, and in that respect the news is not so encouraging. Americans still seem to have a divided mind about this challenge. We are like a squeamish patient who wants everything possible done to save him as long as it doesn't hurt.

The kinds of measures most in demand are sternly punitive—for someone else. We want drug profiteers jailed or executed, from the big international supplier down to the street-corner pusher. We want constitutional protections overhauled to make that easier. We want Mexico and Colombia and Turkey and Southeast Asia to crack down mercilessly on farmers who grow poppies or coca, on processors who turn them into heroin and cocaine, on suppliers who bring them into this country.

But when it comes to those who make this whole industry profitable, the American citizens who buy and use illegal drugs—well, that's different. They might be friends, neighbors, even sons and daughters. Maybe police can jail the teenaged addict from Robert Taylor Homes, but they'd better assign Officer Friendly to explain to little Tiffany, the North Shore high school cheerleader, why she shouldn't keep cocaine in her locker.

As important as it is to try to interdict drug smugglers before they reach the U.S. market and to punish dealers who are making extraordinary amounts of money satisfying this country's self-destructive impulses, it is at least as important to find ways to deal with users and to persuade nonusers not to start.

In this regard, President Reagan has embarked on a major program of drug testing among federal employees. The point, whatever else might be said about this program, is to show that the government takes illegal drug use seriously. This is the first step toward stigmatizing the conduct again.

It is not up to the federal government to enforce laws against possession of narcotics, but state and local officials ought to think about going after this kind of conduct in a concerted way. The purpose should not be to exact severe punishment but to get people into rehabilitation programs and to show everyone that this dangerous, illegal conduct will not be countenanced. Enforcement against possession of drugs could prove to be painful, and it could cause a lot of people an awful lot of embarrassment. But until the demand for drugs is brought under control, no amount of attention to the smugglers will keep the stuff out.

Public education is also a promising approach, but it will have to be planned with foresight. Students often may have more direct and detailed knowledge about the effects of drugs than the teachers explaining them, and unskilled teaching could only convince many that the warnings and laws don't make sense—at least not for them.

Congress may see this as a wonderful pre-election issue, but it won't be a joyride. Whatever laws it enacts will either be tough enough to hurt some of the people now demanding them, or be patent-medicine fakes that will make a real cure even harder.

San Francisco Chronicle

San Francisco, CA, August 6, 1986

WITH INCREASING public concern about narcotics, it is no surprise that the political word war against drugs is being stepped up. Words may be no substitute for tough, hard-nosed police action and effective rehabilitation programs. But, with proper focus, they can serve in subtle ways to alter the temper of our times, and discourage demand for these body-ravaging chemicals.

President Reagan is now taking a leadership role in this increased national effort. His status and popularity will mean more than most of the accompanying posturing. Promising a "Pearl Harbor" for drug traffickers, as the president did, and offering to take a urinalysis test, constitute gestures that hardly move beyond the veneer of public relations.

But his vows to continue to speak out against the drug threat and to marshal a six-point crusade carry more weight. As the president noted quite simply and directly: "Drugs are in one way or another victimizing all of us."

CONGRESS is in the process of drawing up its own battle plan against drugs, and the president has yet to spell out the specifics of his program. Money will be needed to beef up law-enforcement and prosecutions. But words still help: Words to convince prospective users they are indeed, dealing with death.

The Houston Post

Houston, TX, August 6, 1986

The president's declaration of war against illicit drugs was heartening — a call for going beyond the short-term campaigns of limited success that have characterized federal efforts in the past. The goals stated are worthy. Action should follow promptly.

The speech is, so far, just a declaration. There has been too much rhetoric and too little long-term substance in previous anti-drug measures. The president, encouragingly, seemed to acknowledge as much, saying he realized money would have to be found. And he enumerated the broad goals around which a long-term strategy (something previously lacking) can and should take shape.

Countries criticized by U.S. officials as suppliers of — or routes for — drugs like cocaine destined for North America have long replied that the problem would cease to exist if there were no demand. The goals outlined seemed to concentrate at least as much on drug users, on limiting demand, as on the supply. That is appropriate — those users among us are more accessible than laboratories or fields in remote areas of Latin America or Asia.

The battle, ultimately, is to dry up that demand. Everyone — our youth, our affluent, our poor — must be made aware that the consequences of using drugs far outweigh whatever purported benefits there may be. If drugs simply aren't a consideration, that would go a long way toward winning the war.

So Nancy Reagan's crusade against drugs is to become a national crusade. It has broad support in Congress — the main criticism seemed to be that it is late in coming. But it is here now. Let's hope we are about to begin the battle to overcome the plague that has brought tragedy to so many of our people and strained relations with countries who should be our friends.

DESERET·NEWS

Salt Lake City, UT
September 16/17, 1986

No one wants to see this nation's youth ravaged by drugs. The nation joins President and Mrs. Reagan in calling for a comprehensive effort to limit drug abuse by reducing both supply and demand.

White House backing for a reasoned, determined anti-drug push is welcome and comes as no surprise to those who have seen Mrs. Reagan's dedication to the issue over the past five years. President Reagan's ordering of mandatory drug tests for federal employees in sensitive jobs is a dramatic demonstration that he means business.

But voters are not naive. They recognize that drugs are not the nation's only problem. They know that hastily thrown together, election-year legislation, such as the House passed last week, that threaten constitutional guarantees are not the answer to a vicious, deeply ingrained national problem.

They're not ready to jettison carefully worked-out rules of evidence and let police use any illegal methods they please to convict someone, as long as the suspected crime involves drugs.

They're not ready to send soldiers rushing to the borders to start arresting suspected smugglers without some consideration of the implications of this blurring of military and police functions. Wisely, the administration has strongly opposed this measure in its present form.

They're not averse to using the death penalty in certain cases, but they want the gravity of the offenses and the standards of proof involved to be commensurate with those in other capital cases.

They're not aware that handing out life sentences without parole to every person convicted twice of selling drugs to minors would require a mind-boggling increase in prison cells.

In Utah, for example, voters haven't forgotten that the state prison is already filled to overflowing, and that new laws giving all drug users inflexible, mandatory punishments would mean more pressure on a system that is already turning prisoners out early.

Drug offenders are not the only dangers to society: Sex offenders released from prison without treatment because of lack of money for programs are also a cause to get up in arms about. Crime-fighting dollars must be allocated with a view to the entire problem.

Politicians say they're often pressured by special interest groups to cast votes based on emotions without consideration of the larger context and the general public good. In this case, it appears to be the public that is maintaining some perspective and the lawmakers who need to get their emotions under control.

"RELUCTANT? GOOD LORD, MAN, DON'T YOU THINK IT'S ABOUT TIME WE STARTED DEALING WITH THE DRUG PROBLEM REALISTICALLY?"

The Kansas City Times

Kansas City, MO, September 18, 1986

One plain truth about President Reagan's drug initiative is that no one knows if it will make much difference. Right now, that seems to be about the only thing anyone knows for sure about America's latest crisis.

Mr. Reagan, after wrestling about a campaign to counter the ones developed in Congress and launching his effort in a television performance, proposes nearly $900 million in additional federal funds to deal with the problem. The largest part, $500 million, will go for enforcement. Treatment and education also are to get new money.

Cynicism abounds because the initiatives are smack in the middle of fierce partisan politics. There are differences in the congressional and presidential proposals, but people are confused about what's real and what's illusion. This one won't work because there's not enough money, some critics proclaim. Another proposal won't because emphasis is on users rather than sellers, or sellers instead of producers, or Americans rather than foreign suppliers.

Nonetheless, on this issue the administration has taken the first step of leadership although it has made two major mistakes. The first is taking money to pay for it away from other programs. There's no excess.

Making mandatory testing of certain federal employees the centerpiece is another. It's a spot of drama that would at best barely dent the drug epidemic. But in light of the unreliability of testing now, it's a futile exercise. Damage to the innocent and the issue of invasion of privacy will spawn a whole new layer of litigation.

The only hope for resuming control in the streets is statesmanship. Elected officials and government specialists should know that concentrated attacks must be made on the many faces of the enemy. Throwing everything against one would be a waste. Round up drug smugglers at the borders, but let addicts suffer unto death? Imprison pushers for long terms; but do nothing to strengthen children against drugs? It is a circle of demon tails with no one part uglier than the one before.

Mr. and Mrs. Reagan know this. Now the country waits for leadership with a generosity of spirit on multiple fronts.

THE ARIZONA REPUBLIC
Phoenix, AZ, September 3, 1986

OVER the course of our nation's history, the spirit and resources of the American people never have been more unified then when directed against a common enemy during a declared war. Today, the nation is under attack — the people, our values and institutions — from an insidious invasion of illegal drugs that threaten the very fabric of American society.

And once again, the spirit of America is beginning to rally behind the efforts to defeat this monstrous menace as part of a nationwide "war on drugs." This call to arms is being echoed in Congress in the form of an omnibus anti-drug bill, drafted under the direction of House Majority Leader Jim Wright, D-Texas, and Minority Leader Robert Michel, R-Ill.

The legislation is a comprehensive and coordinated approach to what is now considered the nation's biggest social problem. A product of 11 House committees working together, the bill authorizes and mobilizes new weapons to be launched on five fronts:

● Eradication — In a carrot-and-stick approach, the bill creates greater incentives for foreign nations to cooperate with the United States in eradicating drug crops and apprehending smugglers.

● Interdiction — The bill authorizes the use of various federal agencies, including military units, to detect and stop incoming air, land and sea shipments of illegal drugs. The measure also expedites the sharing of information from country to country on the issuance of visas and other information useful in monitoring drug trafficking and narco-terrorism.

● Enforcement — The legislation puts new teeth in narcotics enforcement by increasing penalties throughout, providing mandatory minimum sentences for trafficking in most dangerous drugs, cracking down on the laundering of drug money and coordinating local, state and federal efforts.

● Education — Federal assistance is provided to the states for programs of drug-abuse education and prevention, covering classes from kindergarten to college. The measure also sets up various federal commissions and programs designed to collect and distribute drug information and technical assistance.

● Rehabilitation — The bill strengthens federal drug- and alcohol-abuse prevention programs and assures the states adequate resources to provide treatment and rehabilitation services.

The cost of the legislation — reportedly as high as $1.4 billion — is small when compared with the profits generated from illicit drug trade in the United States — estimated to be a $230 billion industry — and the terrible toll illegal drugs are inflicting upon lives, property, productivity and resources in our society.

While the omnibus act provides some of the firepower necessary to wage the war on illicit drugs, the enemy, entrenched deep in society, will never be defeated until all Americans join the effort to rid themselves, friends and family from the pernicious alliance with drugs.

The Des Moines Register
Des Moines, IA September 14, 1986

The U.S. House of Representatives the other night displayed the closest thing to mob hysteria in a lawmaking body that Americans should ever want to see.

In a frenzy of get-tough posturing on drugs, no amendment was too extreme. How about the death penalty for some drug-related crimes? You bet, fry 'em. How about allowing illegal searches to obtain evidence? Hey, no problem, forget the Constitution. What about using the military to enforce civilian laws? Yeah, that old tradition of separating military and civilian authority is for wimps.

The unreality evoked the memory of the Vietnam commander who said he had to destroy the village to save it. The House would destroy the liberties of Americans to save them from drugs.

Is the United States to become a Chile, with the military patrolling the streets? Is it to become an Iran, to execute drug dealers? Is it to become a Soviet state, where the police need not bother to follow the rules to get evidence?

Yes, there is a drug problem, but not so great as to warrant the extreme measures approved by the House and other erosions of Americans' liberties, such as President Reagan's plans to subject millions of innocent Americans to drug tests as the price of retaining their jobs. What country is this anyway?

The House mood was so manic that it's as if the members themselves were high on something — re-election fever, perhaps.

House members can now head into the election pretending they have done something. What they've done is look real macho on drugs. That's a lot easier than balancing the budget, curing the trade deficit, rebuilding the nation's infrastructure, creating jobs or providing an upward path for the Americans who are most susceptible to the allure of drugs.

Cool the frenzy. Stop and think. A little common sense, please. Provide more money for law enforcement, prosecution and border patrol. Step up efforts to educate people about drugs. Work to create a society in which other pathways are more alluring than drugs.

The Washington Post
Washington, DC, September 10, 1986

THE TROUBLE with the drug problem is that there are no quick fixes. Surely, after all these years, members of Congress know that. What, then, is going on in the House this week? A mammoth bill and a set of amendments full of all sorts of proposals—some good, some doubtful and some really awful—are up for consideration. Yes, the war on narcotics is a hot political issue, but before this package is pushed through on the eve of national elections, legislators should take a deep breath, count to 10 and look critically at this legislation.

The rush to legislate began only six weeks ago when Speaker O'Neill announced a major bipartisan initiative on the drug problem. Each House committee with narcotics jurisdiction—there are at least nine—was asked to report a package of drug bills before the Labor Day recess. These bills were then rolled together into a single proposal and sent, via the Rules Committee, to the floor. It's a wish list, really. It contains a little something for everyone who has a plan for fighting drugs. Some of these ideas, such as long mandatory prison sentences for pushers, have been tried in the states and failed. Others look like window dressing. Do we really need a new White House Conference, a study by DOT on the relationship between drugs and highway safety (yes, a study) or a federal Advisory Commission on the Comprehensive Education of Intercollegiate Athletes? Then there are the "beefing-up" proposals: more coordination, more confiscation of assets, more pressure on drug-producing countries. Is any of this in response to a thoughtful and considered analysis of what is already being done?

Some zealots believe that even this package isn't enough. They propose to offer amendments on the floor that would bring the armed forces into the law enforcement effort, create a good-faith exception to the exclusionary rule and institute a federal death penalty to deal with traffickers. The fear of more reasonable members is that in this can-you-top-this atmosphere, just about anything will be passed and quickly considered by the Senate, where a comprehensive bill was introduced yesterday.

There is no doubt that narcotics are a major national problem in our society and that much can be done to address it. Education programs seem to be making a dent, for example, and should be continued. Results will be slow in coming, but we believe they will be steady. Activities in support of this trade by banks and individuals who handle the enormous amounts of money involved must be curbed. And law enforcement must be firm, well funded and well organized. There is much that is good in the House package, but the pressures of time and politics behind this rush are dangerous. It may take some political courage to challenge any part of it, but if legislators aren't careful, an awful lot of bad law could slip through in the guise of a tough and popular assault on narcotics.

House Backs National Assault on Drugs

The House of Representatives Sept. 11, 1986 approved a sweeping legislative package targeting the problem of illegal drugs. Backed by both the Democratic and Republican leadership, the bill passed 392 to 16. The speaker of the House, Rep. Thomas (Tip) O'Neil Jr. (D, Mass.), had called for preparation of the bill less than two months before. Public feeling against drugs was running high throughout the country. Senate Democrats had unveiled a similar bill before the House vote, while the Reagan administration and Senate Republicans were each working on packages of their own. The House bill was expected to cost as much as $6 billion over the next several years. It would provide new funds for local and federal enforcement of drug laws, as well as for state and local programs to counsel drug abusers and educate the public on the dangers of narcotics. No means of paying for the measures had been worked out. The bill also stiffened trafficking penalties and gave prosecutors new tools to fight money laundering, a method of concealing the source of funds or evading federal reporting requirements. In addition, it provided for economic sanctions against drug-exporting nations that did not try to eradicate their drug crops.

The bill's three most sweeping and controversial provisions were amendments proposed by House Republicans. The measures attracted the opposition of civil libertarians. One amendment, for instance, would require the Defense Department to use whatever military resources where needed "to halt the unlawful penetration of United States borders by aircraft and vessels carrying narcotics." Normally, the U.S. allowed no rule for the military in law enforcement. Another amendment would allow prosecutors to use illegally acquired evidence in some drug trials so long as the officials who had gathered the evidence had not realized they were breaking the law. Under the so-called exclusionary rule, courts normally barred evidence gathered in violation of defendants constitutional rights. In all, 31 amendments were attached to the bill. Describing the voting, Rep. Brian Donnelly (D, Mass.) said, "It's a mob mentality in there. It's just become the single biggest issue in the country." Donnelly added that he supported the measures being adopted.

The Miami Herald

Miami, FL, September 12, 1986

DRUG USE is this year's political red flag, and the legislative bull on Capitol Hill predictably is charging toward it. The House's bipartisan bill, a $1.4-billion package of new money bringing the three-year total spending to about $3 billion, emphasizes Federal law enforcement. It includes several hundred million for prevention and education but little for treatment. The November election sets a deadline for Senate action, for neither party wants to be blamed for failing to pass a drug bill this fall.

The haste mirrors the quick-fix mentality that is at the heart of America's drug problem. Americans by the millions, in proportions greater than those in any other Western nation, turn to pills, drinks, snorts, smokes, or shots to get instant "fun" or to banish the normal rough spots of everyday life. Now, faced with public outcry in an election year, the Administration wants to compensate for six years of consistent cutting of Federal support for community drug-treatment and prevention programs. Congress, which has done little better, is playing the same game.

Drug and alcohol dependency are linked inextricably to every category of white-collar and blue-collar crime, domestic violence, family disintegration, and decline of economic productivity. Yet the person who slips into chemical dependency, typically as an immature teen-ager or young adult, stands very little chance of getting help from the Government in straightening up.

Medicaid is the state-Federal health-insurance program for the poor. Its recipients can use their 45 days per year of hospital coverage for substance-abuse treatment. However, Medicaid in Florida excludes most adult males, no matter how poor they are. Congress has not defined addiction to drugs or alcohol as a disabling condition that makes a penniless adult eligible for care. Thus, of the $12 million that Medicaid spent in Florida last year on community-based mental-health care, only 11 percent went for substance-abuse treatment.

Some Federal dollars come to the states through block-grant programs rather than Medicaid. In general, though, state and local governments are on their own in treating the chemically dependent. The loss of Federal revenue sharing has killed many locally funded programs. Users who can buy private treatment can get it. The others, including many prisoners, often don't.

If the President and the Congress are as serious about drug use as they are about votes, they will take the time to forge Federal programs to guarantee medical treatment — as well as punishment — for the millions of Americans who endanger themselves and their communities with drugs or alcohol.

The Washington Times

Washington, DC, September 12, 1986

It's not every day that you can be proud of Congress, but most Americans appreciate the anti-drug work our legislators have thrown themselves into this week. The $3 billion, three-year anti-drug bill provides a combination of civil rights, law and order, and morality. A three-front war is under way, with no conscientious objectors in sight.

Drugs do their damage to all classes, races, and ages, and it is a source of shame that this country did not attack the problem when heroin and marijuana were more nearly confined to the ghetto. We have paid the price for dillydallying and for glamorizing drugs. A country that began as a safe haven from persecution is now under siege from within.

Without an intensified anti-drug effort, history will record that a great and powerful country was devastated by the effects of addiction and abuse, not by the nuclear winter about which Carl Sagan drones. Already our hospitals are filled with overdose victims and other drug cripples. Who knows the number of careers delayed or destroyed by drugs? How many families have been torn apart?

During the '60s, responsible citizens reassured themselves that drug abuse was just a phase, that the rebellious youth would grow up, have children, and stop living their psychedelic fantasies. In the '70s, marijuana laws were softened in hopes that, as with the end of Prohibition, those who wanted to ruin their health could do so without facing time in jail and the rest of the country could get on with its business.

Now the '80s have arrived, and illicit drug use has expanded exponentially. We've graduated from LSD and pot to crack and PCP — substances known to create addicts within hours. Such drugs can be fought only with strong medicine.

And so we have Rep. Don Edwards, the California Democrat, noting that President Reagan does not want a death penalty provision included in the bill, which draws accusations that the president is too soft. Another amendment establishes criminal penalties of up to three years in jail and fines up to $100,000 for those using the Postal Service to transport drug paraphernalia. Yet another amendment, though not binding, urges Hollywood to de-glamorize drug use.

Times change, and $3 billion will help fight the rising tide of zombieism. Yet the drug dealers, most of them deserving a few moments at the end of a rope, make far more. Consider the new bill a down payment.

The Union Leader

Manchester, NH, September 16, 1986

If there are, anywhere, citizens who remain blissfully unaware of the truly shocking dimensions of the drug problem threatening to destroy America from within, their number must be exceedingly small in the aftermath of President and Nancy Reagan's dramatic Sunday night appeal to the American people to declare all-out "war" on drugs and drug pushers.

Granted, the President and Mrs. Reagan proposed no new ways of fighting the drug menace; that's probably because there are none. Rather, theirs was an unprecedented call by the nation's most prominent mother and father for a total commitment by every segment of our society to the anti-drug "war" in much the same manner that the entire nation rallied to defeat the menace of Nazism and Fascism during World War II.

But "war," of course, entails self-sacrifice and unrelenting commitment to victory. The cynics, therefore, will scoff. They will say sneeringly that "we've heard it all before," that words, even when spoken in dramatic fashion by the President and First Lady, are no substitute for action and that, in the "war" against drugs, most Americans are pacifists. They will contend that the problem is too big, that "everyone's doing it," that the past glorification of the drug culture (for which we can thank principally the news and entertainment media) is woven inextricably into the national fabric. They will cite the obvious: that at best our past response to the menace was weak, platitudinous and hypocritical. And time may well prove that the presidential call for an end to moral neutrality concerning this issue was foredoomed to have few practical results.

We should not have to wait long to see whether such cynics are right. If the nation's school and legal authorities do not demonstrate to the nation's youth that *they* accept the President's reminder that "drug abuse is a repudiation of everything America is," if they act as if they do not really believe that "the destructiveness and human wreckage" of drug abuse "mock our heritage," then young people, most of whom really do want strong corrective action consistently applied against drug and alcohol abuse, will not be convinced either.

"Drugs out of the schools" should mean precisely that. Let there be no temporizing with the costly (estimated at $60 billion annually) problem, no inconsistency in applying anti-drug policies, no discriminatory favoring of superior students over those less intellectually endowed, no legal gimmicks that allow convicted druggies to "beat the system" and continue to stroll the corridors of the nation's schools with impunity.

Here in New Hampshire, we believe there is one easy yardstick to apply to determine just how seriously school authorities view the drug problem beyond the bounds of mere rhetoric: Let us see how many communities across the state follow the example set by the Portsmouth School Board and mandate the suspension of students apprehended with illegal drugs and alcohol. Let us see whether Manchester, Concord, Nashua and other cities and towns will follow suit.

Then let us see whether effective follow-up programs are put into effect to rehabilitate the drug- and alcohol-crazed outcasts.

Only those who fail to comprehend the nature of the drug-alcohol problem, who refuse to face the fact that students have a *right* to function during school hours in a drug-free atmosphere conducive to serious education, a right that is being outrageously violated, only these head-in-the-sand types will regard the Portsmouth policy, put into effect on the first day of this month, as too harsh.

Oh yes. Did we fail to mention it? The biggest cynics of them all when it comes to viewing the practical effects of dramatic warnings against drug abuse are young people, the principal target of the drug pushers. And they are cynical with good cause: They are accustomed to adults promising much and delivering little.

The Burlington Free Press

Burlington, VT, September 18, 1986

As one of the hottest issues in an election year, drug abuse has drawn the frenetic attention of politicians from all points on the political spectrum.

Democrats and Republicans are trying to outdo each other in their efforts to introduce proposals for curbing drug usage in the country. At times, it indeed appears as if their zeal borders on hysteria.

Several politicians want to put the country on a war footing to combat drug trafficking. With President Reagan playing the role of the general and a bipartisan group of congressmen his lieutenants, the battle to eradicate the drug scourge in the country is being plotted.

An arsenal of weapons, including mandatory drug testing of federal workers in "sensitive" jobs, capital punishment for some drug-related crimes and more research and treatment programs, will be used as a means of curbing drug use.

The House passed a bill last week which would require Reagan to send U.S. military forces within 45 days to halt the drug traffic along the nation's borders. Secretary of Defense Caspar W. Weinberger was a vehement opponent of the proposal.

Yet all the grandiose and politically popular schemes, some of them questionable, will be meaningless if a massive grassroots educational effort is not launched to impress young people with the harmful consequences of drug abuse.

Drug dealers cannot flourish and foreign suppliers cannot survive if the demand for such substances is drastically reduced. However undramatic that it may seem to many politicians, the place to begin the war is in the nation's schools.

What is equally important is that people assume responsibility for their actions. If they choose to use drugs, no amount of Big Brotherism is going to change the fact that addiction is the inevitable outcome.

Treatment programs certainly could help many people but the amount of money allocated in the House bill is niggardly in comparison to the amount that will be spent on halting the drug traffic.

The dollars spent on education and treatment undoubtedly will be more effective than some of the other measures advocated by the White House and Congress.

To win the drug war, it will be necessary to use those measures which will cut down the demand for drugs to such a point that drug dealers will find it unprofitable to do business in this country.

THE ☐ SUN

Baltimore, MD
September 15, 1986

Sometimes good motives move the wrong mountain. Congress and the White House, weighing initiatives on the burgeoning drug abuse problem, are vying for first place in the who-really-solved-it sweepstakes. But while events such as the death of Len Bias give poignant testimony to the breadth of the drug epidemic, sober analyses by health, law-enforcement and social-service agencies make it clear there is more than enough of this problem to go around:

☐ A federal General Accounting Office report showed that drug seizures and arrests are up, but the flow is unabated. From 1983 to 1985, 13 Organized Crime Drug Enforcement Task Forces convicted 2,453 people and gained more than $440 million in fines, seizures and forfeitures of property and cash, enough to pay about one-third of their operating costs.

☐ Total U.S. consumption of illegal drugs was 3 billion doses in 1984, a 15-percent increase from 1983, the GAO said. Later figures are not yet available, but if law-enforcement officials are right about the increasing flood of drugs on the street, consumption is still climbing.

☐ In Maryland alone, state health department figures show that an estimated 153,610 people, 5 percent of all Marylanders aged 11 to 65, abuse drugs. More than two thirds are addicted to cocaine (58,528) and heroin or other opiates (50,804). A state bar association report noted the deadly reach of drug pushers among the young, and called for a drastic shift in societal responses.

☐ Contraband drugs fuel a $110 billion a year industry, the GAO says, and "drug abuse is unlikely to be eliminated by domestic law enforcement efforts . . . ."

That last point is worth remembering as Congress stiffens penalties for drug possession and dealing, expand Drug Enforcement Administration, Coast Guard and Customs Service enforcement activities, build new prisons, establish an Agency for Substance Abuse Prevention and beef up state drug education programs.

Earlier, it was noted that federal drug treatment funds total $230 million, but enforcement monies come to $1.8 billion. Federal support for treatment and prevention has dropped 46 percent since 1980. The new bill puts some of this back: $350 million for treatment and $180 million for the prevention agency, but the disparity continues.

If the drug epidemic is ever to be contained, the war must shift some emphasis to the user front: patterns of addiction must be readily identified; businesses, schools, agencies and institutions of all kinds must learn to spot them and provide early help for abusers and their families; people must be weaned from experimenting with drugs. A real push toward these goals will be welcomed. Election-year sound and fury, followed by quiet neglect, will be worse than a waste of time.

The Virginian-Pilot

Norfolk, VA, September 15, 1986

The nation is having another fit of drug mania, judging by behavior in Washington in recent days. The president and Mrs. Reagan are speaking out forcefully against drugs. And Democratic and Republican leaders in Congress are speeding through House and Senate legislative mills with "comprehensive" and costly anti-drug packages.

Washington, collectively, ought to take a deep breath. Action against drug abuse is commendable. But rushing in with political quick fixes is not.

To be sure, some knowledgeable lawmakers have studied the problem and proposed programs — unsuccessfully — for years. But for most members of Congress, comprehension of the drug issue is largely limited to opinion polls that report widespread concern among constituents, anecdotes about deaths of well-known athletes, and the Nov. 4 elections. A deeper understanding is needed.

The current approach to drug abuse is reminiscent of earlier government reactions. In 1971, for example, the Nixon administration declared "war" on drugs. Funds for prevention and enforcement were doubled. Federal agents were empowered with "no-knock" and wiretap search powers. Border and coast patrols were beefed up.

But by the time Mr. Nixon's successor was in office, the roughly $3 billion effort was a noted failure. "Recent evidence suggests an increase in the availability and use of dangerous drugs in spite of the creation of special federal agencies and massive federal funding," President Gerald Ford declared in 1975.

Last week Congress considered familiar proposals — stiffer sentences for drug-related offenses, including death sentences; use of the armed forces in enforcement; use of illegally obtained evidence; eradication efforts; and so on. Cost: $1.5 billion to $3 billion, varying in direct proportion to the amount of expressed political concern. Some provisions have merit — notably, drug-abuse education programs run by state and local governments, and federal grants to states for drug-treatment and -prevention programs. But they may not offer enough political prevention against the dreaded "soft-on-drugs" taint for some incumbents.

Furthermore, some provisions are downright dangerous. Suspending guarantees against searches and seizures — in effect, the House of Representatives voted to override U.S. Supreme Court decisions that prevent illegally seized evidence from being used in court — is unwise and likely to be declared unconstitutional.

A few members are cautious. "I'm always a little skeptical about issues that get 30 seconds of attention, then become the most important issue in the nation," says Rep. Leon Panetta, Democrat of California. Adds Republican leader Robert Michel of Illinois: "It must be asked if all this taxpayers' money is going to put a dent in the problem."

Good question. More members of Congress should ask it before passing "comprehensive" anti-drug legislation. Political quick fixes seldom produce lasting results.

THE ATLANTA CONSTITUTION

Atlanta, GA, September 15, 1986

Quick, round up the family and head for the basement. Fed up with drug pushers, Congress has pulled its musket down from the mantel and started to fire wildly. The House's little tantrum last week, if indulged by the Senate, promises trouble for admirers of the U.S. Constitution and druglords alike. There should be a sense of urgency on the drug issue, but hysteria helps no one.

OK, maybe it helps politicians. Maybe a mad spasm of Draconian legislation can show the homefolks that Rep. Windbag is an ardent opponent of drug abuse.

Then again, maybe the homefolks aren't so gullible. They surely know, for example, that smuggling and drug abuse have been a problem for years now and that Congress, while concerned, never saw fit to put the matter at the top of its must-solve list until now, which happens to be the heart of election season.

In any case, some of this legislation would pose real dangers if it became law.

The strangest part of the House-passed bill is a section giving the president 30 days to deploy the military to halt smugglers at the border and arrest them when in pursuit. Within 45 days, our solons instruct, "the president shall substantially halt the unlawful penetration of United States borders by aircraft and vessels."

Oh, sure. All the House needs to do is decree, "45 days!" and then sit back and watch drug trafficking stopped forever. And never mind whether we really need martial law on our borders. Even the Reagan Justice Department finds this one hard to swallow. For his part, Defense Secretary Caspar Weinberger has tried to explain that it's a bad precedent to use soldiers as cops.

Then there are terrible ideas of a more conventional stripe. The House would allow imposition of the death penalty for murders that take place in drug-related crimes. Which means federal prosecutors would be burdened with the same endless death-case battles that now ensnare their state counterparts. The House would also permit courtroom use of evidence improperly obtained in warrantless searches. And so on.

In all, the House would toss $6 billion worth of programs at the problem over five years. Some might even succeed; not all of the package is harebrained. Yet the overall cost of this plan is outrageous, a heedless budget-buster.

Pressure against drugs, especially cocaine, is called for, but is it necessary for Americans to sacrifice their constitutional principles in the fray? No. With solid support from Washington, police work can be improved in ways that leave dopers defeated and the Constitution intact.

Nobody's saying the fight will be easy or quick, but this much is clear: Drug traffickers will only be stopped by canny, steady law enforcement. Dollar-mad hysteria may help in elections, but it won't win drug wars.

Mike Keefe THE DENVER POST

DESERET NEWS
Salt Lake City, UT, September 12, 1986

With elections coming up, politicians on both sides of the aisle are falling over each other in their rush to sign up for the latest war on drugs.

Talk about a safe issue. Who could possibly be faulted for voting for more drug education, beefed-up law enforcement, increased penalties for drug crimes?

The only area of much controversy until now has been mandatory drug testing, and that's one that should be susceptible of fairly easy compromise.

The House of Representatives passed Thursday night an omnibus drug-fighting bill with 300 cosponsors, carrying an estimated price tag of $3 billion over three years. The Senate and the Reagan administration also have their own packages.

The House bill would escalate the war on drugs by pouring billions of dollars into enforcement, education, rehabilitation, crop eradication, and withholding of aid from recalcitrant countries that won't stop growing the crops used to produce drugs. Among the measure's provisions is a particularly controversial one that would authorize U.S. troops to be sent to the nations borders and give them power to arrest drug smugglers. There are serious doubts about the constitutionality of giving troops civilian police enforcement authority.

It's hard to believe that all 300 cosponsors of the House bill have studied the drug issues in depth. Though some know whereof they speak, many seem to be joining just because it is a popular

and attention-getting cause. Some, no doubt, will be campaigning this fall on their law-and-order voting record.

A report of a 14-month investigation by the General Accounting Office, suggests, however, that neither well-meaning but uninformed votes nor electioneering is what's needed.

Although there's been a lot of talk about fighting a stepped-up war on drugs, the report concludes that the federal drug agencies have not been given the resources they need, and their effectiveness has been diminished by sometimes an almost total lack of coordination.

GAO investigators found, for example, that U.S. radar used to spot smugglers' airplanes isn't coordinated with the interceptor planes that are supposed to catch the smugglers.

Democratic Rep. Glenn English, of Oklahoma, said that the Reagan administration has called for the reduction of 770 Customs agents, and that White House chief of staff Donald Regan took millions of dollars away from gas and oil accounts for drug-fighting agencies to refurbish Treasury offices.

Fighting the pervasive influence of drugs on society has been and will continue to be a discouraging, difficult job, requiring a multifaceted approach and longterm commitment.

If all of this election-year hoopla leads toward a more coordinated, concentrated and better-funded effort, great! But why does that seem unlikely?

Newsday
Long Island, NY, September 12, 1986

Of all the cockamamie ideas that have sprung from Congress' rush to do something big about illicit drugs before the election, the worst has got to be a plan to let taxpayers earmark a portion of their income taxes to fight drugs. The second

Rangel

worst is a proposal to have taxpayers donate part of their tax refunds for the same purpose.

Senate Majority Leader Robert Dole (R-Kan.) advanced the first notion following a meeting on drug abuse at the White House. After some reflection, he switched to the second.

But anyone who wants to donate money to the government is already free to write a check. To clutter up tax refunds and burden the overworked and understaffed Internal Revenue Service with collecting contributions for drug-control — or any other purpose, if it comes to that — is plain silly.

As for the check-off, other proposals have been advanced to use this seemingly innocuous way of raising money for a pet cause. Rep. Charles Rangel (D-Manhattan) has a check-off bill ready to go in the drug fight. But no matter how worthwhile the purpose, it's still a bad idea.

It may well have been a mistake in the first place to rely on a check-off to fund presidential elections. Public financing has helped to level the playing field for candidates. But there's no reason that money shouldn't be appropriated along with everything else in the federal budget.

If Congress and the president decide a program is worthwhile, it should be funded through the normal budget process. Rangel and Dole should drop their check-off proposals before they go any further.

Study Finds Drug Use in Most Arrested

A Justice Department study released Jan. 21, 1988 found that half to three-quarters of men arrested for serious crimes in a dozen U.S. cities had used illegal drugs shortly before their arrest. The study, sponsored by the National Institute of Justice, the research arm of the Justice Department, was reportedly the first national study to test criminal suspects for drug use at the time of arrest. The results were based on urine samples collected voluntarily from 2,000 criminal suspects arrested between June and November of 1987. The survey tested for 10 drugs, including marijuana, cocaine, heroin and amphetamines. Most of those tested had been arrested for serious street crimes such as burglary, grand larceny and assault. Men charged with drug-related offenses were kept at less than 25% of the sample.

The results were "substantially higher than what we had anticipated," said James K. Stewart, director of the National Institute of Justice. They were higher than some earlier estimates, which, however, had been based on interviews with suspects rather than on urine tests. The new findings, Justice Department officials suggested, strengthened the case for increased funding of drug-treatment programs as a form of crime prevention, particularly at a time when most states faced court orders to relieve prison overcrowding but could ill afford to build new prisons, the estimated cost of which was $50,000 to $75,000 a cell.

An internal Justice Department memorandum, disclosed by the *Baltimore Sun* Feb. 25, urged top department officials to "polarize the debate" on issues such as drugs, crime and capital punishment in President Reagan's last year in office. On the drug issue, the memo urged the "hard, tough approach that emphasizes strong law enforcement measures and drug testing."

In a significant international development on the drug issue, the U.S. Justice Department Feb. 5 unsealed two indictments charging Panama's military leader and de facto ruler with involvement in international drug trafficking. The indictments were returned Feb. 4 by federal grand juries in Miami and Tampa. They charged the Panamanian, Gen. Manuel Antonio Noriega, with violating U.S. racketeering and drug laws. Noriega was accused of providing protection and other services to international traffickers, who used Panama as a transshipment point for cocaine and marijuana. The indictments also charged Noriega with permitting the laundering of drug profits through Panamanian banks. The indictments provoked a strong reaction in the U.S. Congress. At the time Noriega was said to have been profiting from the narcotics trade, he had a close relationship with the U.S. Defense Department and with the Central Intelligence Agency, particularly during the the directorship of the late William J. Casey. The intelligence relationship reportedly dated back to the 1970s. Some U.S. lawmakers suggested that the U.S. had overlooked or even covered up accusations against Noriega because of Noriega's usefullness to the U.S. The U.S. had for some time been pressing Noriega to resign, in the wake of domestic protests against his rule that were sparked by allegations of corruption made by former aides.

In other developments:

■ A New York City police officer was killed March 7, 1988 while guarding the home of a witness who had testified about gang violence in his neighborhood. The killing of officer Edward Byrne sparked widespread concern regarding law enforcement's inability to control the narcotics trade throughout the country. "If our son Eddie, sitting in a police car, representing and protecting us, can be wasted by scum," Byrne's father said, "then none of us is safe. And I don't care where you live."

■ Gang violence in Los Angeles, was reported at an all-time high. Gangs in the area were said to control large portions of the city and were implicated in nationwide narcotics trafficking.

THE PLAIN DEALER
Cleveland, OH, March 2, 1988

President Reagan says "the tide has turned" against drug abuse. Nancy Reagan accuses all casual drug users of being "accomplices to murder." Obviously, the Reagan White House wants to rejuvenate its sputtering war against drugs—a welcome development in a program that, two years ago, had all the hallmarks of election year lip-service. But has the tide turned? Has Mrs. Reagan's campaign to "Just Say No actually worked?

For the answer, just look at the daily news. The nation's most affluent suburbs play unwilling host to open-air drug markets in which crack, cocaine and other lethal drugs can be purchased. In Cleveland, 40% of last year's homicides were drug-related. Nationally, one-third of the inmates in federal prisons have been convicted of drug-related crimes. Internationally, the drug warlords are more pernicious than ever. High-ranking officials in Central and South American nations are either co-opted or assassinated. In Panama, the Bahamas, Mexico, Bolivia, Peru and Haiti, evidence links the drug trade to the loftiest levels of government.

Although the White House can exhort teen-agers and children to "Just Say No," it seems largely unwilling or unable to do the same. Under a 1986 law, drug-trafficking nations must be certified by the president to be making satisfactory efforts against the illicit drug industry. If they are not certified, they risk a host of economic punishments. But out of seven nations currently liable for such punishment, none feels its full weight. The countries either are exempted for national interests, or have so little economic strength that their drug production is more valuable than trading privileges.

Yesterday, for example, Reagan "decertified" Panama—a nation that is a rats' nest of drug trafficking and corruption. Yet military and economic aid was cut off last year, along with Panama's share of America's sugar quotas. So why should Panama's drug kingpins, including military strongman Gen. Manuel Antonio Noriega, care about American sanctions? Such people have scant interest in diplomatic pleasantries. Certainly, they don't care about the people they are supposed to serve. After all, the profit margin in foreign aid is too small to satisfy their lusts.

Mrs. Reagan's high-minded campaign to encourage self-discipline among young American drug users sounds good. But to be brutally frank, it is square—most effective on those who are not otherwise disposed to drug abuse in the first place. As for her "accomplice to murder" rhetoric: Such overreactive guilt trips establish implausible standards of judgment. It is preaching to the converted. Of course, any assault on drug abuse is welcome, but the problem is much bigger than casual users and teen-agers. Until the United States produces a cohesive campaign of diplomatic, penal, *and* moral suasion—combined with vigorous new efforts to rehabilitate drug users—American and hemispheric interests will remain hostage to a tide that has indeed turned . . . against us.

The Washington Post

Washington, DC, March 13, 1988

ONE OF THE MOST effective weapons available to the government in the fight against organized crime, and the narcotics trade in particular, is the forfeiture of assets that have been either the instruments or the fruits of criminal activities. Forfeiture provisions were greatly strengthened by Congress in 1984 and again in 1986, and in recent years law enforcement authorities have seized many hundreds of millions of dollars in property either in civil proceedings or as penalties after conviction. Last November, for example, federal authorities in Miami took possession of $15 million in assets, including real estate and racehorses, belonging to members of the Medellin drug cartel. A federal task force in Detroit took over a small chain of sporting goods stores. Large numbers of automobiles, mansions, yachts and airplanes have also been confiscated.

What happens to all this property? Initially, it has to be managed. Someone has to feed the racehorses and find a place to keep the yachts. But ultimately, tangible assets are sold and cash is deposited in a special fund in the Treasury. Monthly deposits are currently averaging $21 million. The attorney general has the authority to share some of these proceeds with state and local law enforcement agencies that have cooperated with federal task forces on cases which result in forfeitures. Deputy Assistant Attorney General Joe Whitely recently told a congressional subcommittee that more than $117 million has gone to the states in the last three years, with California alone receiving $48 million.

The main purpose of the forfeiture laws, of course, is deterrence. If the kingpin's castle and the pusher's costly sports car can be confiscated, some of the incentive for accumulating these status symbols in the drug trade will evaporate. An incidental benefit is that the program is self-sustaining. All training programs, administrative expenses, management services, legal advice and sales expertise needed in the handling and conversion of these assets are more than paid for by the money generated. And still there is more. So much more that Congress has begun to look at the forfeiture fund as a source of money for other federal programs. Legislation was recently passed to earmark 50 percent of the reserves for the Bureau of Prisons, for example. With the prison population at an all-time high, the needs of the bureau are acute. It is ironic that the fund might be tapped to support, in prison, some of the very gangsters whose assets were used to create the fund, but it's probably appropriate too. For once the taxpayers might have the last laugh on the thugs.

THE SACRAMENTO BEE

Sacramento, CA, March 4, 1988

The State Department's annual report on international drug trafficking paints a bleak picture. Despite strenuous global efforts, drug crops are bigger and drug use, particularly in other parts of the world, is growing. "Corruption of government officials and law enforcement officers, bribery, trafficker intimidation and violence and the stark fact that nations are outmanned, outgunned and outspent by narcotics traffickers, continue to undermine global efforts to stop narcotics production and trafficking," the State Department says.

Those facts produce political outrage on Capitol Hill, where lawmakers attack the president for having "certified" as adequate the anti-drug efforts of nations such as Mexico and Colombia. Yet who can "certify" that the United States is meeting its own anti-drug obligation? The economics of the drug trade is driven from the demand side. Some officials in drug-producing nations use that fact to excuse lackluster enforcement on their own soil. It's no excuse, but it's reason for honest Americans to look first to their own efforts.

Can drug-producing nations, working in cooperation with the United States, do more to cut the supply of drugs? They can and must. Increased efforts to eradicate drug crops, stop money laundering and strengthen the police and military forces arrayed against growers and traffickers are necessary.

But like other evidence before it, the State Department's report raises doubts that the supply of drugs can be substantially decreased while Americans are willing to squander billions of dollars to buy them. And as long as there are huge profits to be made from growing, processing and exporting coca and opiates, there will be peasants to grow them, well-armed drug traffickers ready to challenge the state, politicians prepared to wink at the drug trade that sustains their constituents and Gen. Noriegas wanting a cut of the action. If a nation as rich and well-organized as the United States cannot suppress drug smuggling at its border or drug sales on the streets of its major cities, it's unrealistic to expect poor nations with weak governments to be more effective in controlling their mountain outbacks and coastlines.

The big victories in the fight against drugs will be won, not in Pakistan or Colombia, but here, where user demand and legal prohibition combine to make the drug trade economically inviting. But they will come only slowly. Americans are morally opposed to ending drug prohibition and fiscally unprepared to back laws against drug use with all the police patrols and prison cells needed to arrest tens of thousands of illicit drug users and thereby deter millions of others.

What they will countenance are less dramatic but effective measures: beefed-up law enforcement aimed at drug smugglers and gangs; economic alternatives for poor neighborhoods caught up in the drug trade; more treatment for users wanting to get off drugs; and a sustained effort, at all levels of society, to discourage drug use through education and moral disapproval. But the federal government, for all its anti-drug rhetoric, has hardly taken up the fight, to judge by the resources it devotes to the battle. Until it does, let American politicians be less quick to point fingers at others.

DESERET NEWS

Salt Lake City, UT, March 23, 1988

The assassination of a New York City police officer last week while he was guarding the house of a witness in a drug case ought to evoke outrage all across the nation. This was not merely an isolated criminal act — it was a brazenly bold attack on the system of law and order in the United States.

The shooting of Officer Edward Bryne did not occur during an arrest or a raid. Instead, it was a deliberate murder with no other object than to intimidate and threaten potential drug witnesses and the police themselves.

This is particularly disturbing because it echoes the chilling example of the nation of Colombia, where drug kingpins have murdered police, witnesses, government officials, and judges, and have succeeded in effectively destroying the justice system and government opposition in that country. Some of that same Colombia-connected drug cartel is operating in the U.S.

Emboldened by what has happened in Colombia, some drug dealers evidently are using those same tactics in New York City, where several drug witnesses have met violent deaths in recent months.

New York Mayor Ed Koch put his finger exactly on the problem when he spoke at the slain officer's funeral this week. As Koch noted, "If drug trafficking has become so bold that they can engage in the assassination of a police officer, then our whole society is at risk."

The phrase, "war on drugs," has been used to describe attempts to halt the flow of cocaine into the U.S. But Officer Bryne's death is war in the real sense — a violent attack on a society and government. New York City clearly has become one of the major battle zones.

So far, government efforts have made the war look like a minor skirmish. Like any other war, the one against drugs is going to take money, commitment, more lawmen, tougher border controls, and perhaps even a deep sense of national outrage.

The Atlanta Journal
AND
THE ATLANTA CONSTITUTION
Atlanta, GA, March 5, 1988

In Washington, the State Department reports that production of coca, marijuana and opium poppies worldwide is beyond the ability of any single government to control. In Panama, dictator Manuel Noriega faces a U.S. indictment for his involvement with drug traffickers. In Atlanta, violence related to drug-dealing drives our homicide rate to an eight-year peak.

Can anything be done? Yes — but any solution will require more backbone and less hysteria from Congress and the Reagan administration.

For starters, the government must stop suckering for the grand gesture that solves nothing. Massive drug testing for federal employees and transportation workers falls into that category. Drug abuse takes its worst toll on the urban underclass — not bureaucrats and flight attendants. Why cede civil liberties for a negligible return?

Similar problems plague the Customs Service's plan to confiscate passports of travelers accused — but not convicted — of possessing illicit drugs as they enter the country. This might crimp the style of petty users, but it won't bother major traffickers. Both ideas offer little more than perilously false illusions of salutary action.

What can work? New attitudes, first. Here the Reaganites and their preachments have been somewhat successful. Studies show that drug abuse is declining among middle-class Americans. No longer are drugs widely regarded as chic. But here, too, the administration has failed. For all its talk, it apparently tolerated drug-thug Noriega for a time solely because he was sufficiently anti-Communist. That is some message to send our drug-fighting allies in this hemisphere.

A real commitment to law enforcement might help, too. The White House is trying to fight drugs on the cheap. Item: In 1986, it sought to halve the Customs Service budget for interdicting airborne smugglers. Item: In 1987, barely six months after the president asked for a "national crusade against drugs," the administration sought sharp cuts in federal money for drug education and aid to local law enforcement agencies.

The slight to local police is especially galling. As the administration correctly notes, drug trafficking threatens our very national security. Yet the administration would blithely leave most of our defense to local cop shops. In 1986, the locals shelled out 80 percent of money used to fight drugs. The bill came to $4.9 billion, or 18.2 percent of their total budgets. As anyone can deduce, they need help.

Meanwhile, our allies need to see less hypocrisy from us. And American citizens need to see fewer cockamamie detection schemes that merely divert attention from the tough challenge that lies ahead.

THE TAMPA TRIBUNE
Tampa, FL, March 26, 1988

The crack cocaine epidemic is being cited as a primary factor in pushing the number of serious crimes in Florida last year over the 1 million mark for the first time. And there's no relief in sight.

Robert Dempsey, commissioner of the Florida Department of Law Enforcement, warns: "Anybody who tells you the drug problem is leveling off is in fairyland. They don't know what's happening."

What's happening is that this highly addictive form of cocaine is plentiful and relatively cheap. It has become the drug of choice for youthful social dropouts who are both dealers and users. Unlike the opium-based narcotics, such as heroin and morphine, cocaine is a stimulant that produces excitement, incoherence and delusions that can lead to violence.

The February 26 execution-style slaying of police officer Edward Byrne in New York City is interpreted there as a message of intimidation from drug dealers to the police and public. That slaying changed the rules of the game, in the opinion of a spokesman for the Federal Drug Enforcement Administration. Until then, it was generally understood, even among pushers, that premeditated cop-killing was taboo.

Crack cocaine possesses the capacity to generate false bravado that leads to reckless action. Dealing with this problem puts law enforcement authorities in uncharted waters.

The drug scene is further complicated by a proliferation of automatic and semi-automatic weapons that can't be spiked by grassroot campaigns. Many of these weapons are in the hands of drug-dealing immigrants from Caribbean and South American countries where contempt for authority is endemic. Nor does it help from Florida's viewpoint that the worst crack cocaine violence is centered largely among New York City's unstable gangs. Florida is the great cocaine gateway.

Thus, while the problem is on our doorstep, it is national in scope. It can't be managed here without substantial federal assistance. Indeed, there is a growing sense that the war against drugs can't be won, period. And once that is said, it's necessary to contemplate an alternative strategy that's being talked of more and more: Decriminalizing drug use and permitting the state to dispense what are now illicit substances. All the ramifications of such a departure can't be fully known, but it's an option that deserves public discussion.

ST. LOUIS POST-DISPATCH
St. Louis, MO, March 4, 1988

Drug dealers may well be accustomed to intimidating the public and police in some foreign countries, but they must not be allowed to succeed in doing so in the United States. The murders last month of a police officer in New York and of two women in the presence of toddlers in the nation's capital were said to have been committed by a new breed of drug thugs, mainly crack traffickers, who are part of a violent subculture that has no respect for law, public sensibilities or human life. That is all the more reason their despicable behavior and their illicit activities must be held in check. Otherwise, no U.S. city is safe from these new drug-related assaults.

The seriousness of the problem is mentioned by police in an interview in the *The New York Times*. In past years, the officers note, drug traffickers seldom killed police officers because they feared the unwanted publicity. The officers told the newspaper, however, that many crack distributors come from nations where violence against police and the public is not uncommon. In light of that, it should be no surprise to discover that last month's slaying of the New York officer was said to be aimed at intimidating the police and the public. The officer was shot in the head as he sat in his patrol car, guarding the home of a witness in a drug case.

In light of this enlarged menace, federal and local law enforcement authorities must be given adequate resources to halt the proliferation of so-called crack gangs that have spread beyond the streets of New

York. Authorities report, for example, that Jamaican-run crack rings already are trying to gain a foothold in Kansas City. Can St. Louis be far behind?

This administration doesn't help police officers, taxpayers or addicts by its strong talk and weak action against countries said to be involved in drug-trafficking. Shouldn't these nations be denied all U.S. aid? Moreover, what does it say about Washington's commitment to stamping out the drug plague when it will look the other way, as it apparently did in Panama, in the interest of other foreign policy goals?

In addition, the administration spends far too little money on drug problems in general and targets practically all it does spend on law enforcement. A new study by the General Accounting Office notes that only about 10 cents of each dollar spent on anti-drug programs since 1982 went to prevention and treatment. Local police officials complain, meanwhile, that even the billions spent in this decade have fallen short of arming them with the tools they need to take on drug traffickers.

Not much of a dent is likely to be made in the drug problem until the administration gets tough with countries implicated in the traffic and spends a lot more on drug treatment and prevention. It must do this even as it gives law enforcement authorities the resources to get across the message to traffickers that the violent behavior permitted in the streets of Jamaica, Colombia and Mexico won't be tolerated within U.S. borders.

Herald News

Fall River, MA, March 3, 1988

The drug menace is clear to everyone, but what is not clear is how to get rid of it.

By now the distribution and sale of drugs is so widespread and lucrative that dealers in crack are reported to have taken over an entire street in Queens. It was while he was keeping watch on a house in that street that a young rookie police officer, Matthew Byrne, was shot and killed last week.

Byrne was a victim of the criminals that are engaged in the traffic in drugs. The anger Byrne's slaying evoked was national. Thousands of police officers came from all over the country to attend his funeral.

Outraged by the tragedy, Mayor Koch of New York assailed President Reagan, for not taking stronger measures to end the drug trade here and elsewhere.

In particular, Koch and others criticized the President for limiting the official reaction to the Panama crisis to verbal disapproval.

The President's reluctance to impose sanctions on Panama is understandable in view of the still unsettled Nicaraguan crisis and the sensitivity of Central America as a whole to any kind of intervention by the United States.

But it is also understandable that officials in this country are increasingly skeptical about the war on drugs that the administration has declared. They point out that the countries where most of the drugs are produced are well known, but that the administration never takes strong enough measures to compel the governments of those countries, even those that are nearby, to end their growth and distribution.

The complicity of Panama's General Noriego in the drug traffic is well-authenticated. Apparently he has not been repudiated by the Panamanian people as a whole, but there is surely no reason why the United States should not impose economic sanctions on the country until he is forced out.

Grant what is true, that any such action by the United States will be labeled imperialistic by those whose hostility to this country blinds them to the fact that some effective steps must be taken to end the plague of drugs imported from Latin America.

In some instances, of which Panama is the most obvious, public officials are involved in this nefarious trade. Although that increases the political complexity of taking steps against them, it should not prevent the United States from ending all aid to their countries as well as ending trade with them as far as possible.

Something must be done to end what is fast becoming an intolerable situation, and the administration ahould take the lead in doing it.

The Times-Picayune
The States-Item

New Orleans, LA, March 3, 1988

The State Department's annual report on narcotics worldwide is certain to arouse Congress, but for the wrong reasons. Everyone is coming to recognize the report's blunt finding that production, consumption and trafficking now blaze out of control, beyond the ability of any single government to suppress. Drug racketeers like Colombia's Medellin cartel use their billions to corrupt and even take over Western Hemisphere governments.

Where Congress is apt to go astray is in how to respond. So far, it has focused on the discrepancy between this five-alarm problem and the trade and aid sanctions the Administration has proposed. The error is to remain transfixed by the sanctions issue instead of pressing the Administration to respond to its own report with a powerful program.

Colombia is not the only sovereign nation whose authority has been challenged by drug lords. The entire regime in Panama has been subverted. Key government sectors in Mexico, the Bahamas, Paraguay and Honduras are being infiltrated. Fragile democracies in Peru and Bolivia are threatened. Despite Washington's stuttering attempts at control, drug syndicates have "outmanned, outgunned and outspent" governments, according to the study.

What was once a vexing problem in narcotics law enforcement swells steadily into a first-order geopolitical peril, not only to Latin societies but now also to our own. The report follows Nancy Reagan's grim warning that "if you're a casual drug user, you're an accomplice to murder," and comes only days after New Yorkers were shocked by the execution, Colombia-style, of a young New York cop on a crack-plagued Queens block.

Governments like those of Colombia, Peru or Bolivia are overwhelmed more than corrupt. What is the sense of inflicting trade and aid sanctions that will further reduce their police powers and legitimate business profits while leaving drug lords untouched? The Administration is right to use its discretion to override sanctions in such cases, even as it errs in not applying maximum pressure on countries like Panama where the fight is already lost.

The State Department report calls for a far sounder approach: strengthening the economic and law enforcement capacities of those governments that still have a will to resist. That means helicopters, training and logistical assistance and significant economic support.

Drug barons have exploited the vacuum created by the Latin countries' austerity. That grew out of their heavy foreign debt, which has curtailed legitimate economic activity and weakened the political grip of governments. It's hard to resist dirty drug dollars in a depressed, impoverished economy. Peasants have turned over croplands to coca. Guerrillas of every stripe have joined gunrunning and protection rackets. Politicians and judges have been intimidated, bribed, killed.

For years, the Reagan Administration has been fixated on its crusade to extirpate Communist influence from the hemisphere. Incredibly, it continued to cooperate with General Noriega even after intelligence reports tied him to drug crimes. Now its own State Department report, like the First Lady, sounds the right alarm. The nation, and the hemisphere, are listening for the response.

Omaha World-Herald

Omaha, NE, March 7, 1988

People connected with the fight against illegal drug trafficking sound pessimistic these days, and for good reason. The international drug cartels appear to have grown almost too big and too powerful to control.

The State Department seemed to say as much with its annual report on narcotics. It said that nations attempting to stem the flow of drugs are being "outmanned, outgunned and outspent."

Drug barons operate with impunity in a number of Latin American countries. In the past, they bribed police and low-level government officials. Now they seem capable of co-opting entire governments.

After Colombian officials tried to crack down on the Medellin drug cartel, a number of the officials were assassinated. Other Colombian officials were either bribed or intimidated, and efforts to prosecute cartel members there have largely subsided.

Recent attempts by civilian authorities in Panama to oust Gen. Manuel Antonio Noriega, the country's top military authority, resulted in a military takeover of the government. Noriega had been indicted by two U.S. grand juries just weeks earlier for allegedly accepting bribes from traffickers.

Frustrating, too, have been efforts to keep drugs from entering the United States. Six U.S. cities — Los Angeles, San Diego, Houston, Miami, Chicago and New York — have been identified as trafficking centers. But drugs can enter the country anywhere along the thousands of miles of coastline and borders. It is impossible to watch everywhere.

The State Department report contained sensible recommendations. Particularly sensible is the proposal to bolster the police and military resources of countries that show the political "will" to oppose drug bosses.

Some members of Congress have been clamoring for economic sanctions against countries that don't cooperate. But helping those who cooperate holds more promise. Withholding aid from non-cooperating countries might serve to make them more dependent on the income from drugs.

Hope for a long-term solution, if there is any to be found, may lie in efforts to curb the demand for drugs. Customers willing to pay high prices keep the traffickers going.

Especially important are efforts to educate children about the harmful effects of drugs and to encourage them to resist temptation and peer pressure. Children represent the next generation of customers for illegal drugs. Whatever can be done to dry up that market now may well represent the best hope for ultimately putting the drug lords out of business.

Rockford Register Star

Rockford, IL, March 3, 1988

New York Mayor Ed Koch's characterization of President Reagan as a "wimp" for not being tough enough on foreign sources of drugs is only partially accurate. The administration has not, in fact, been tough enough. But neither should it be as tough as Koch seems to suggest.

Koch, angered by the apparently drug-related killing of a New York police officer, would have the United States impose stern sanctions against "places like Mexico, Panama and the cadre of other nations that supply this country with its heroin, its cocaine and its marijuana."

Well, yes and no. Drugs are not the only issue, or in some cases even the principal issue, in Washington's relationships with other nations. Moreover, diplomacy has its intricacies, which vary among governments. Hence, the administration must exercise discretion in getting tough on drugs. And Panama and Mexico, the two states Koch named, pose differing problems.

At this writing, President Reagan reportedly is prepared to announce that he will not impose extraordinary sanctions against Panama, despite all the clear evidence that that country has been up to its eyeballs in drug trafficking and the laundering of drug profits. This reluctance doubtless would strike Koch as wimpish, and we are inclined to agree.

Tough measures against Panama would serve the dual purpose of increasing pressure on embattled military strongman Gen. Manual Antonio Noriega and sending the world a message about Washington's seriousness about dealing with the flow of drugs into this country.

The case in Mexico, however, is somewhat trickier. Clearly, the running of drugs from and through Mexico is significant, and often it is abetted by government corruption. But the posture of the United States must take into account the risks of political upheaval and attendant economic chaos. Mexico simply is too big, too close and too important to treat recklessly in the name of stemming the drug trade. Jawboning, albeit adamant, may be the preferable course.

But, yes, Ed Koch is right that the Reagan administration for too long has failed to give enough diplomatic emphasis to the international drug trade, preferring instead to base relationships on a geopolitical view of East-West struggles. Meanwhile, drug cartels have become multinational titans, stronger than some nations.

AKRON BEACON JOURNAL

Akron, OH, March 3, 1988

THE STATE Department issued a grim report this week on the war on drugs. It concluded the problem has grown substantially over the last year. Production of coca, marijuana and opium poppies is up in drug-producing countries. Finally, the report admitted there's little one country can do to win the fight on its own.

It hardly takes a great leap to reach the report's next conclusion: A stronger international effort is needed. The report talked about the need for "political will" in countries burdened by the drug trade and the mobilization of economic and military resources by all affected countries. The problem is, can it be done?

The tone of the report suggested it must. It chronicled the corruption, crime and violence that has captured countries such as Panama, Mexico and Colombia. It described the destructive effect of drugs on all levels of society, from democratic institutions to the growing number of drug users and victims worldwide.

As is all too well-known, dramatic language is not enough. Coherent strategies are required even to begin to achieve small success. Unfortunately, the State Department has left itself open to skeptics who may wonder how effective it can be in this war. Although largely symbolic, economic penalties were promised against Panama, Afghanistan, Iran and Syria. However, Mexico, the largest single country supplying both heroin and marijuana to the United States, and Colombia, the home of perhaps the most notorious cocaine cartel, were not penalized.

The politics are obvious. It's easy to point the finger at Panama and the usual international outlaws. But that still leaves the administration with an enormous gap between its words and its actions; the report describes corruption in Mexico as "endemic" and "the single most important factor which undermines effective and meaningful narcotics cooperation with Mexico." Plainly, the position on Mexico reflects the difficulty of mounting an international assault.

No one can deny the insidiousness of the drug trade. A large factor — glossed over in the State Department report — is the demand for drugs in the United States. Greatest sympathy should go to the truly innocent victims, those who are robbed or even killed as junkies pursue money to pay for their habit. Nancy Reagan has done much to encourage young people to resist drugs. The current national advertising campaigns against drugs are most worthwhile.

Without question, it's important to define the problem globally, as the State Department has, and efforts should be made to shape an effective international strategy. But that has proved maddening. The message is frustrating but clear: The war against drugs is most realistically waged at home, against demand.

THE TENNESSEAN

Nashville, TN, March 12, 1988

THE nation's war on drugs is resulting in confiscation of larger and larger shipments of illegal drugs.

But the foreign sources of drugs seem to be inexhaustible. The more drugs that are seized by U. S. law enforcement agencies, the more there are sent in to replace them. Despite much success in intercepting drugs, the amount captured is only a small part of the total coming into the nation, and there is little indication that any headway is being made against the main problem.

The lack of progress is causing frustration in the national administration, putting Cabinet members at odds with each other and goading some into making unwise suggestions.

Education Secretary William Bennett called last week for the U.S. to use military force against producer countries that do not cooperate in stopping drug shipments at their source. This is against administration policy, and it quickly drew fire from Defense Secretary Frank C. Carlucci, who said he would oppose an active law-enforcement role for the military in the anti-drug campaign.

Mr. Carlucci is right. Mr. Bennett's proposal was absurd. It would be virtually impossible for the U.S. military to police all the drug-producing areas in all the countries from which drugs are shipped to the U. S. Besides, military action against uncooperative nations would involve this nation in all kinds of problems with much of the rest of the world.

The Defense Department already provides some support services in the campaign against drugs — such as sharing equipment and intelligence — and that is enough. The job of the armed forces is to defend the nation against military enemies. The nation should not set the dangerous precedent of calling on the military to enforce domestic laws.

Many experts are of the opinion that the drug problem can be fought successfully only by eliminating the demand for drugs — through education, the prevention of addiction, or the removal of profits from drug sales. That makes a lot of sense. It may be impossible to alleviate the drug problem — by arrests, interdiction, or any other means — as long as a substantial percentage of the population is determined to obtain drugs at any cost. ■

THE CHRISTIAN SCIENCE MONITOR

Boston, MA, March 7, 1988

ILLICIT drugs wreck lives. Drugs finance crime, tie up tens of thousands of police in largely futile law enforcement. Drugs infiltrate schools. They are parasites: They finish off dying neighborhoods; they unravel wealthy suburban families.

Don't get us wrong. America isn't about to succumb to drug use, any more than it is about to go belly up because of the federal budget deficit.

Nor is it fair to say that drug use – crack, cocaine, marijuana, or substances we have not even heard of – is the fault of weak public leadership, any more than widespread ignorance is the fault of failed public education.

Some official steps *would* help: Washington's efforts this past week to put the financial screws on Panama's drug-connected strongman Manuel Antonio Noriega show one course. But the administration has not fully used this form of pressure elsewhere. Explicitly linking aid for countries like Mexico to action against drug producers and traffickers is difficult. But it is a tactic that should be tried, even as the US keeps in mind the need to work cooperatively with these countries.

A way *not* to go is to crimp the effectiveness of services like the US Coast Guard, whose budget the Reagan administration has cut. And the Customs Service's new policy of threatening to seize passports of drug-bearing tourists probably is not the way to go either, for constitutional reasons.

Illegal-drug use is not much of a partisan issue. Nancy Reagan's nostrum – "Just say no!" – has become a vehicle for parody. The presidential candidates at best can use it as a cipher for alleging the failure of previous national leaders, however unfairly.

Individual and collective values, if advanced and encouraged, can help potential users be alert enough to resist drugs when they are made available. Here, at the demand side of the drug trade, the defense can be strengthened.

But the supply side too must be attacked, and the trafficking mechanism shackled. The State Department reported this past week that the production of coca, marijuana, and opium-poppy crops in most drug-producing countries has been multiplying, not receding. The producer countries cannot control their internal drug operations. Tightening surveillance of bank money-laundering operations would help, though much of the drug world's money moves through underground channels.

So it's tough to resist drugs. It calls for action, persistence at official levels, and a strong personal defense

---

The Wichita
Eagle-Beacon

Wichita, KS, March 4, 1988

THE United States' obsession with communism in Central America has helped blind the country to the greatest national security risk in the Western Hemisphere — illegal drugs. While the Reagan administration has waged ceaseless war against leftist insurgency in Latin America, it has not shown the same intensity against cocaine, heroin and other drugs that are destroying millions of American lives and undermining political stability throughout the hemisphere.

It's time that combatting illegal narcotics became a top U.S. foreign policy priority. Periodic declarations of a "war on drugs" and public relations photos of huge drug seizures are not a substitute for a comprehensive anti-drug strategy.

In many respects the drug problem is like terrorism. It can't be dealt with by conventional diplomacy. Like terrorist cells, the drug cartels don't respect international borders or national sovereignty. Their ability to offer huge bribes or to intimidate government officials means that there is scarcely a country in Latin America that has not been severely corrupted by the drug lords.

Defeating the drug cartels is one of the greatest challenges of American foreign policy. Clearly, the country can no longer play footsie with such drug-tainted leaders as Panama's General Manuel Noriega simply because they can be useful in the struggle against communism.

Mexico and Colombia, two of the biggest drug-producing nations, must be given greater assistance — morally and materially — to resist the drug traffickers.

Most importantly, the American government must work harder to close the largest market for illegal drugs — the United States. Law enforcement and drug abuse programs must be strengthened. Drugs must be attacked at both the supply and demand sides.

No American is immune to the scourge of drugs. In Wichita, for example, Sheriff's Deputy Terry McNett recently was slain in a drug-related incident. But that was only one tragedy caused by drugs, which has taken a huge toll in wasted lives, crime and tax revenue.

Drugs can't be seen as a "victimless" crime. They are jeopardizing foreign governments and ruining individual Americans. In their own way, drugs can destroy the United States as effectively as any weapon in the Soviet arsenal. But until drugs as seen to be as great a threat as the Red Army, the United States will be at risk.

DAILY ◼ NEWS

New York, NY, March 2, 1988

'THE RULES OF THE GAME HAVE been changed by the drug dealers," Rudy Giuliani declared at yesterday's Daily News Leadership Forum on narcotics. "We have to change the rules of the game for them."

He was speaking specifically of the murder of Police Officer Edward Byrne. He was referring directly to the widely held belief that Byrne's assassination was ordered by leaders of the narcotics underworld. That the killing was a political act, a declaration that the underworld is immune from effective investigation, arrests or prosecution.

Giuliani is right. Absolutely. But the point goes far beyond either the tragedy or the outrage that is Byrne's death.

There was not a word of dissent on that point from the three dozen leaders from law enforcement, politics, clergy and civic activism who took part in the forum. And although there was much disagreement on other points, some of it heated, there was none on the fact that the narcotics "problem" in New York and the nation has reached a catastrophic level. That it has become a crisis. That if, as President Reagan said Monday, America has "turned the corner" on drugs, it has only been to discover a monster that is uglier and deadlier than was even imagined short years ago.

BYRNE'S KILLING CLEARLY HAS galvanized both public attention and political recognition of the horror. There is only one fitting tribute to Byrne and other fallen warriors in the war against drugs.

That tribute must be for New Yorkers and Americans to act. To win. Today's peak of awareness must not be allowed to pass. The tears will dry. The rage must not fade.

That is particularly difficult because the best strategies for the war are far from clear. The most intense and immediate action now must be to bring focus to the realities of drug use and the narcotics industry. To fashion a strategy. Or parallel strategies. And to put it—or them—into practice with force, intelligence and appropriate resources.

Among the specifics that demand urgent consideration:

A political commitment must be made at every level. A war on drugs must become a major element of the 1988 presidential and congressional campaign debates, as well as in city and local contests. Candidates in the 1988 primary and general elections must give voters concrete strategies for winning the war on drugs.

Laws must be toughened, fast. Even among many opponents of capital punishment, there is growing support for imposing the death penalty for drug-related killing of law enforcement officers and/or witnesses. There are complex constitutional problems in that area, but there is impressive logic in the suggestion that death could be a strong deterrent in such crimes—they are almost invariably thought out and carefully planned. Additionally, extend to local levels the federal witness protection program, which has been highly successful against the Mafia and some other organized crime.

Pilot programs must be designed to eradicate drug-trade domination of communities, such as the Queens neighborhood where Byrne died. The experience must be used to devise even broader programs. The approach has been used before, but fresh efforts by every pertinent agency and element of the city could work wonders.

There is promise in the idea that if local and federal police authorities, courts, social agencies, clergy and political leaders can bring about a clearly defined drug-free neighborhood, the techniques they develop could be applied more widely. The proposal was made at the forum by the Daily News and subsequently advocated by Mayor Koch. The mayor deserves support in his commitment to create and direct such a program in Southeast Queens. He would do well to extend that to include one such campaign in each of the five boroughs of New York.

A massive campaign must be undertaken to educate every American, especially every schoolchild, to the evils of drugs—in concert with a national commitment to treat drug sale and *use* at every level as the dreadful, deadly crimes that they are.

Adequate resources must be dedicated to the war. Money alone will not bring victory. But the total national commitment of funds at local and national levels falls far short of the profits being reaped from cocaine alone by the Latin American kings of that trade.

THOSE SPECIFICS ARE BUT A sampling of the earnest and promising proposals brought up in the Daily News Forum. There will be other such forums. This newspaper's commitment to providing exposure and leadership will not be abandoned. But it will take a profound, sustained public resolve—which has been hitherto elusive—to begin to win the war. New York and America have no sane alternative to making that commitment.

Part V:
Victims, Child Abuse & Sex Crimes

Prior to the 1970s, few people paid much attention to crime victims. So much of the criminal justice system was focused so intensely on the rights of the accused that there was no time, funds or attention left for the victim. Until the emergence of feudal society, it was up to the victim of a criminal act to arrest, prosecute and perhaps even punish the offender. As feudal lords began to offer protection to vassals, however, the theory of social contract emerged and was pushed and shaped into a meaningful form by some of the great social philosophers of history including Locke and Rousseau. Basically, social contract theory calls for individuals to surrender some of their rights to society in exchange for society's promise to protect the individual. It became the duty of society to protect the individual, to arrest a person who unlawfully attacked a victim, to prosecute the offender and to punish the person convicted. In turn, the victim of crime gave up these rights.

Historically, police protection has been slow to develop. Prior to the 18th century there were few organized police forces in any society. Military authorities or the victim performed the now traditional police functions of prevention and detection of crime. The victim no longer had to apprehend the offender as police forces became part of the government. As with prosecution, the assumption of the government of policing responsibility may have protected the victim, but it also removed from the victim the power to arrest.

Today we accept the government's role to provide the physical requirements and personal services needed to operate the criminal justice system. As a consequence, the victim has had little or no say about whether a person would be arrested, prosecuted or punished. Until recently, the victim of crime was only a witness in the criminal justice system.

The bridge between victims' rights and the criminal justice system is perhaps best seen with regards to the crime of rape, an act more horrible than most other crimes. There are many rape victims. So many, in fact, that it is difficult to determine the number. In 1986, the latest year for which we have statistics, there were more than 90,000 cases of rape reported to the police. But because rape is a vastly underreported crime, it is generally assumed by law enforcement officials and scholars alike, that the actual number is much higher. The U.S. Justice Department estimates that 56% of all rapes get reported. However, victimization surveys conducted by the FBI, the Census Bureau and the National Opinion Research Center report that only between 3.5 and 10 percent of all rapes are actually reported.

Much ground has been gained in dealing with rape victims. Sexual assault victims are now given medical examination. More importantly, efforts have been made to help the victim with counseling or other professional help with problems induced by the assault. Though many victims have no post-assault disorders, some are moderately or severely depressed following the rape, while others suffer from physical and psychological disorders for a year or more. The major difficulties are fear and anxiety, with some vicitms also experiencing flashbacks or concern about sexual censure. Not surprisingly, many rape victims suffer from sexual dysfunction afterward, and a large percentage of all women who attempt suicide have been rape victims. Accordingly, rape victims may need counseling of some kind immediately following the assault and perhaps for some time thereafter. Most areas in the country have rape crisis centers that offer counseling, and moves have been made to encourage victims to seek this help. Rape crisis centers have proven to offer tremendous assistance. Not only do they provide information about the criminal justice system, they offer companionship and compassion when both qualities are desperately needed. In addition, rape crisis counselors have been responsible for many of the legal reforms that have benefited victims of all crimes.

Related to the plight of the rape victim is the tragic issue of child abuse. Since the victimization of children is perhaps the most underreported of all crimes, the youngest victims of crime may be so numerous that it is impossible to count them all. Though some special rules and procedures have evolved during the past few years to assist abused children, parents too become victims when their child is assaulted or abused. While the criminal justice system in many states has made accommodations for children, no such accommodations exist for their parents, who play an important role in helping the child victim through the intricacies of the system.

The first and perhaps most difficult issue facing parents of child victims is whether or not to deal with the criminal justice system. Will dealing with police, prosecutors and the courts cause even greater trauma for their child than did the crime itself? The choice of letting a child become a complainant is not an easy one, but experts contend that the more parents are willing to do so, the fewer child victims there will be.

The situation becomes more complicated if the child abuser is a member of the family. Every state has procedures to remove a child victim from the home. These procedures seek to balance the parents' rights to be free of governmental interference—and the similar rights of children—with the government's desire to protect children. Almost without exception, states permit the police to take a child victim into protective custody when his or her life or health is in danger. Some states permit health care professionals to refuse to release a child into the custody of parents following treatment when the professional believes the child is in danger.

Except for emergency situations, most states require a court order to remove a child from the custody of a parent, even if the parent is the abuser. Some states have emergency procedures that don't require a court order. However, a child removed from home goes to a shelter or foster home, which may provide an environment only slightly better than what the child has left.

Crime Victims Receive New Attention

It is hard to find an American household in which someone has not been the victim of a crime. According to the most recent U.S. Justice Department statistics, 57 million U.S. citizens will be the victims of crime this year. Although some will not report the crime, they will all experience the economic loss, the physical pain and the emotional upset the victimization can cause. For example, 20 women are raped every hour—over 175,000 a year. However, sexual assault of women, men, children and the elderly is usually an unreported crime. Unfortunately, victims of these crimes are reluctant to complain to police or anyone else. Several studies have revealed that fewer than 20% of the women who are sexually assaulted report the crime to a law enforcement agency. This does not take into account sexual assault and molestation of children, a crime all experts agree is even more underreported than the sexual assault of women.

Since the 1970s, individuals, institutions and legal scholars have examined the role of the crime victim and have almost unanimously concluded that the role of the crime victim has been poorly defined and, even worse, ignored. Only recently has serious thought been given to the appropriate role for the victim. Most criminal justice practitioners had failed to even think about the crime victim's needs. But that has begun to change.

In the 1980s, the federal government has addressed the rights of violent crime victims. In 1980, President-elect Ronald Reagan created a Victims of Crime Task Force, and subsequently a Presidential Commission of Victims of Crime. In 1982, Congress passed the Victim/Witness Protection Act. However, this act was applicable only to victims and witnesses appearing in federal courts. After numerous attempts to convince Congress to pass a federal victim compensation law had failed, such a law was finally passed in 1984. Critics of the federal government's inattention to the problems of crime victims point to the fact that between 1968 and 1980, the Law Enforcement Assistance Administration, a government grant agency, awarded approximately $7.5 billion in criminal justice grants. Less than 1% of the money—less than $50 million—was directed to help victims of crime. In the same period, over $1 billion was awarded to improve services for and conditions of persons convicted of committing crimes.

The cooperation of crime victims with the police is the single most important prerequisite to effective law enforcement. Conviction rates plummet and crime increases when crime victims are unwilling or reluctant to assist police. Studies have shown that of every 100 felonies committed in this country, only about one-third are reported to the police. Only 10 result in arrest, and only three result in conviction. Requiring police to investigate and, where possible, to arrest in every case would be impossible. But advocates of victims' rights say that requiring police to listen to victims, help victims and express concern for them is necessary.

Crime victims are better off today than they were only a decade ago. There are more services and professionals working at the local level to assist crime victims, and legislation has been passed to guarantee them certain rights. On the national level and in every state, the plight of the crime victim has been presented to the legislatures, the courts and the public. The achievements gained by the crime victims' movement have not occurred accidentally. Domestic violence shelters and rape crisis centers have established coalitions to coordinate state-level activities on behalf of victims of these specific crimes. In some cities formal and informal networks of victim service providers have been created to address local needs. A number of different national organizations have been instrumental in focusing public interest and attention on the needs of crime victims. Though these groups have different agendas and different priorities, as a whole they describe the broad range of crime victim interests throughout the country.

WINSTON-SALEM JOURNAL

Winston-Salem, NC, March 5, 1984

Among anti-crime bills being considered by the Senate — many worthy efforts to tilt the protection of law more toward victims than criminals — is one that should not be enacted.

It would allow the federal government to execute terrorists, spies and people who assassinate, or attempt to assassinate, a president.

The Senate has approved the measure 63-32 (Sen. Robert Kasten voted for it, Sen. William Proxmire against). It is before the House.

In any form, the death penalty is wrong.

There is no convincing evidence to show it deters crime. There is the danger that innocent people will be executed. There is a moral contradiction in society commiting legal murder in response to illegal murder.

This bill fails to address those problems, while raising new doubts about capital punishment. Is a mass murderer like Charles Manson more virtuous than a terrorist? Is it a greater crime to attempt killing a president than it is to succeed in killing any other public official — or private citizen?

Does the Senate believe that people insane enough, or committed enough to their "cause" to engage in terrorism, espionage or assassination are going to be deterred by the possibility of execution?

President Reagan, urging the House to follow the Senate's lead, argued that "the liberal approach of coddling criminals didn't work and never will."

It is wrong to coddle criminals, but that doesn't make it right to execute them.

The Washington Post

Washington, DC, February 23, 1984

THE CHANCE that you will be the victim of a violent crime this year is greater than the chance that you will be hurt in a traffic accident, get a divorce or die of cancer. Your risk goes up if you are young, black and male, a city dweller and poor. The possibility that you will be seriously injured is greater if your assailant is a friend or relative. You will have plenty of company: violent crime causes more than 2 million injuries or deaths in this country each year.

Fortunately, given this grim situation, more is being done to help crime victims, and courts are paying more attention to their needs and desires. California was the first state to enact a victims' compensation program. Now 37 states and the District of Columbia have them. Most jurisdictions direct help to victims who can demonstrate financial hardship. Awards up to $50,000 are available in some states and are usually applied to medical costs and reimbursement of lost wages. In 11 states, money earned by offenders as a result of their crime—income from books, for example— must be put into an account from which victims are compensated. In cases where money compensation is not sought, a great deal is being done to protect and assist victims through the judicial process and allow their participation in some deliberations.

State trial judges from every state met recently in Reno, Nev., under the auspices of the National Judicial College, the American Bar Association and the National Institute of Justice. They made dozens of recommendations, most of which can easily be adopted without legislation: prosecutors should explain criminal justice procedures and keep victims informed of developments in their individual cases; victims should be given an opportunity to participate in pretrial release hearings, plea bargaining and sentencing; separate waiting rooms, psychological counseling, transportation, child care and reasonable witness fees should be guaranteed; trials involving especially sensitive victims—children, the elderly, handicapped, victims of sexual abuse and the families of homicide victims—should be expedited.

None of this new attention to victims is designed to guarantee revenge or encourage vigalantism. No one is thinking about turning convicted criminals over to victims for quick, private justice. As the judges' proposals indicate, however, much can be done to aid and protect victims and to provide reassurance that they, as well as the accused, will receive justice. It is about time.

Houston Chronicle

Houston, TX, April 20, 1984

Justice, if properly served, must weigh the seriousness of the crime against the rights of the accused. In our criminal justice system, however, the concern for fairness often seems more directed toward the criminal, so much so that the victims who suffer at their hands are swept into the shadows.

Gov. Mark White has proposed legislation that would expand and strengthen the rights of crime victims and their families. The proposal would require district attorneys to be more aware of the victim in prosecuting criminals. Under the proposal, an impact statement filed by the victim would become part of the official court record and would be considered in sentencing and paroling criminals.

Texas already has an increasingly effective victim compensation program that has paid $3.5 million to over 1,300 claimants. The program is funded by fines and court cost fees. It has run short of money at times, but efforts are being made to increase the amounts of the fines and the number of cases in which they are assessed. In addition, restitution centers are being established to house probationers while they work to pay their debt to society.

Money, however, may not be the most important element in making sure that victims — as well as criminals — get justice. All too often, victims are dealt with brusquely by law enforcement and court officials and even suspected by society at large of being victimized more by their own carelessness than by the predatory behavior of criminals: They shouldn't have been walking alone along that dark street, or they shouldn't have opened their doors to strangers, or they shouldn't have gotten out of their cars.

Gov. White's proposal would ensure that victims have a say in what happens to the criminals who brought them grief and injury. It would expand the opportunities for victims to see that justice is done. That would be only fair — and just.

FORT WORTH STAR-TELEGRAM

Fort Worth, TX, February 2, 1984

Slow step by slow step, victims of crimes are getting some consideration.

First, Texas established a crime victims compensation program under which victims can apply for financial aid to help reimburse them for lost income, medical expenses and other costs related to the criminal acts committed against them.

Later, the program was improved, with measures being taken to bring more money into the pool from which payments are made to crime victims.

Now, some Texas counties have taken steps to fill another need — they have established programs to provide much-needed information to crime victims about their cases.

Tarrant County is the latest to do that.

Initially, the program here will be paid for with grant money. Eventually, county government will pick up the entire tab.

The program will offer informational assistance to crime victims. It will orient them to the criminal justice system, notify them of the status and progress of their case and help them get through the courtroom experience. Those working in the program also will refer crime victims to appropriate social service agencies and advise victims how to file claims under the Crime Victims Compensation Act.

The district attorney's office, under the program, will hire some additional staff members who will help close the communication gap between prosecutors and crime victims. It is also envisioned that some volunteers will help.

For example, one rape victim who said she received no information about her case and who volunteered to help another rape victim face her attacker in court said she would continue to serve as a volunteer under the witness assistance program.

The rape victim said inadequate information about their cases only fuels crime victims' fears and puts them through "emotional ups and downs." She added, "Being a victim is devastating and terrifying. But being a victim with no information from the district attorney's office only adds to your fear."

There is a national trend toward establishing a liaison with prosecutors' offices to help crime victims.

Texas and Tarrant County are keeping pace with the trend and the real winners should be the victims of crimes.

Much time, money and attention of necessity is spent on those who commit criminal acts.

Step by step, crime victims belatedly are getting some assistance, too.

This new victim assistance program will not meet all the needs of crime victims, but it will provide them with much helpful information.

It also will do much to let the crime victims know that society is concerned about them and their well being.

And that should go a long way toward helping them, too.

The Star-Ledger

Newark, NJ, April 25, 1984

Setting aside a week of the year to honor this or celebrate that has been an effective way to focus attention on a special cause.

Unfortunately, federal, state, county and local officials all suffer from a common political ailment. None can say no to requests from constituents when the request may be painlessly granted—and at negligible cost.

Gov. Thomas Kean, however, has now shown how to recapture the original impact of the practice. He used the occasion of proclaiming Crime Victims Rights Week to make public a package of bills his administration has put together for the benefit of relatives of murder victims.

The measures include a bill of rights for crime victims and mandatory restitution. Appropriately, the forum for the Governor's presentation was a day-long seminar on the rights and needs of families of murder victims.

Sensitivity and understanding are reflected in the various provisions of the proposed rights. For example, victims and witnesses would have to be informed each step of the way as the case progresses from scheduling to disposition. Property would have to be returned to victims once it is not needed for evidence. Judges would have to order restitution as part of the sentence in any case where a victim suffered a loss. And the courts would be empowered to collect an inmate's prison pay to offset fines and make good on restitution.

Implicit in the proclamation and the victims' bill of rights is a central theme that was verbalized repeatedly at the seminar. The relatives of a murder victim are just as much victims as the man, woman or child whose life was snuffed out by the killer.

In her keynote speech at the seminar, Dorothea Morefield of the National Organization for Victims Assistance emphasized that the criminal justice system and society have been slow to accept this grim reality.

Implementing the Kean administration's victims' bill of rights will help to restore judicial even-handedness, provide restitution to the victims of crime and ease the anguish of the surviving relatives of murder victims, who—it must be repeated—are as much victims as the murdered person.

THE KANSAS CITY STAR

Kansas City, MO, June 4, 1984

Crime victims, long considered the lost people in the criminal justice system, have been receiving more attention and assistance in recent years. Compensation funds, some financed by convicted felons, and restitution programs have been established.

Now, the U.S Parole Commission has adopted rules to allow victims to appear at parole hearings of federal inmates convicted of acts involving them. It is still another signal that the well-being and rights of victims are moving to the forefront. In the process, the accountability of criminals for their violations is becoming more personal to their victims, rather than to society as a whole.

Some civil libertarians object to a victim's appearance at a parole hearing because of the emotional impact it might create. Supporters of victims' rights counter that victims participate in other proceedings during a case so the parole hearing should not be treated differently.

Prisoners have had an alternative of having a representative speak for them at parole hearings since a revamping of rules in 1976. Two years ago Congress enacted a law to expand the process to include individuals who object to the release of a convict. Until now, however, notice of hearings has not been given. Victims may request notification under the new rules.

There's also another change in favor of victims. Parole hearing examiners will consider, as a condition for release, the intention of an inmate to comply with a judge's order for restitution to victims.

None of this should suggest any infringement on offenders' rights. The Constitution is clear on certain guarantees designed to prevent over-zealous law enforcement authorities from abusing those rights. It does suggest victims are entitled to inject their side as a matter of fair treatment.

Detroit Free Press

Detroit, MI, September 15, 1984

THEY SUFFER not once but many times — robbed, raped and beaten by criminals, ignored by an often halting and indifferent legal system, left to grapple alone for years with lingering problems. But more help could be on the way for victims of crime.

The U.S. Senate has approved a bill that would use money from federal criminal fines to compensate and assist crime victims in all the states. The House has held hearings on a similar bill, but has not yet passed it. It should.

Besides compensating crime victims, the legislation would let federal district courts seize book royalties and other payments to criminals and defendants who would profit from publicizing their stories. The fines for federal crimes would rise and crime victims could testify at federal parole hearings on how their lives have been affected by crime. Each state and the district of Columbia would get at least $100,000 yearly from the program. Michigan's share when the fund is fully operational could top $3 million.

Though not all aspects of the legislation have equal merit, it does reinforce crime victims' right to compensation for their expenses and the disruption of their lives. Such reinforcement is important because a federal presidential task force investigating the problem found that many victims regretted having reported crimes and felt co-operating with police and the courts had caused them additional pain.

The case for compensating crime victims is strong. Most suffer losses, which may not be completely covered by insurance. Many poor and elderly victims, in fact, have no insurance. A woman crippled by a robber told the task force she had had to borrow on her life insurance to pay her heating bills. Moreover, victims sometimes lose wages or even jobs when forced to make repeated court appearances because of delayed and postponed trials. For many rape victims, the indignity of assault is compounded when they are billed for the tests required as evidence for the crime.

Money from the federal crime victims compensation program would supplement victim compensation programs already existing in Michigan and elsewhere and spur other states to set them up. Seizing all royalties owed to criminals who tell their stories for publication is not necessarily the best approach to the problem, since it might inhibit the airing of stories the public has a right to hear. It would make better sense to funnel a percentage of such royalties into the victim compensation fund.

The most important thing the bill would do, though, is to establish the principle that crime victims are entitled to assistance, and that its cost ought to be borne by those who break the law. The New York Legislature has passed a measure allowing authorities to confiscate any property of a convicted felon equivalent in value to the fruits of a crime and to distribute proceeds from the sale of such property to his victim first. One day soon, more states, including Michigan, ought to follow suit. In the meantime, Congress could do much to restore faith in our legal system by passing a law providing federal assistance to crime victims.

The ☘ State

Columbia, SC, May 28, 1984

OFFICIAL state note of the rights of crime victims, in effect, sanctions a saner way of looking at crime and a more humane way of dealing with its consequences.

Newly agreed on legislation, called the Victims and Witnesses Bill of Rights, sets up victim impact statements. It requires that the state, not the victim, pay the cost of medical exams for rape victims and it spells out ways for prosecutors to work with victims.

The measure will correct errors of the past when defendants were sometimes virtually coddled while their innocent victims were ignored.

As Gov. Dick Riley pointed out, "The compensation of victims is critical to the administration of justice. Their willingness to help the criminal justice system is one of society's most valuable resources in fighting crime."

The reform is one of several promoted by the Committee on Criminal Justice, Crime and Delinquency. Indeed, as the Governor noted in announcing his approval of the measure, other key changes are needed to round out the picture of criminal justice reform.

Steps have been taken to alleviate the sardining of people in the state's prisons but they are mostly stop-gap. Emergency legislation that allows the Governor to release certain types of offenders to relieve prison population is just that — emergency and crisis-oriented.

The Legislature, aided by the criminal justice committee, needs to find a long-range solution that ties in with a total statewide philosophy on criminal justice.

That solution must dovetail with other elements of justice, such as training of officers, magistrates and others; the state's laws; sentencing guidelines; and probation and parole practices.

The Governor also pointed to a critical need to bolster the indigent defense system to ensure that the poor, as well as the better off, are adequately represented in court.

While much needs to be done in the area of criminal justice, the victims rights bill represents an important step.

The Miami Herald

Miami, FL, March 14, 1984

VICTIMS of crime too often are the forgotten elements in the criminal-justice process. At times they are neglected, insulted, ridiculed, or otherwise abused. In recent years, though, victims have fought back, asserting that victims have rights too, just as suspects do.

The push for victims' rights is widespread. A Presidential task force recommends that the Sixth Amendment to the U.S. Constitution, which guarantees fair trials, be augmented to include a victim-protection clause. Likewise, Dade County State Reps. Dexter Lehtinen, a Democrat, and Ileana Ros, a Republican, suggest amending Florida's constitution. Representatives Lehtinen and Ros also have sponsored legislation for a comprehensive "Victim and Witness Protection Act of 1984."

Those efforts to ensure protections for victims by changing state statutes and passing new ones are both long overdue and commendable. To the extent that they bring victims greater access and respect within the legal system, they deserve support.

Lawmakers must be wary, however, of reaching for those desirable goals by altering the state and national constitutions. This is particularly true in situations where statutory changes could guarantee protections.

A big obstacle to balancing the rights of victims with those of defendants is the lack of awareness. Existing Florida law allows restitution, compensation, and other protections for victims. Thus any push for change must be accompanied by appropriate efforts to enforce and use existing laws.

Representatives Lehtinen's and Ros's omnibus victim's package — and a similar bill offered in the state Senate — would make several commendable changes. The bill would, for example, allow victims to recover property much sooner by permitting photographs of it to be used as evidence in place of property. It would require uniform standards for notifying victims and witnesses of court proceedings. It would seek their advice at pleadings, sentencings, and parole hearings. The bill also would impose tougher penalties against persons who intimidate witnesses and victims.

Some provisions of the omnibus victims' bill are bothersome and should be corrected before passage. The Lehtinen-Ros proposal, for example, would prohibit criminals from "profiting" from the sale of information relating to their crime. It also would bar the release of victims' and witnesses' names and addresses. Such provisions are needlessly restrictive and of questionable constitutionality.

Removing them would enhance the bill's chances of getting the broad approval that it deserves.

The time has come for fuller attention to victims' rights. The Lehtinen-Ros measure, once its few objectionable features are removed, would help the law recognize victims as it does defendants.

FORT WORTH STAR-TELEGRAM

Fort Worth, TX, June 5, 1984

Slowly but surely, victims of crime are receiving consideration within the justice system, just as the criminals do.

The latest move in this direction was the announcement by the U.S. Parole Commission, which holds parole hearings for those convicted of federal crimes, that victims will now have a significant voice in those proceedings. Now, if such victims wish, they will be notified in advance of the parole hearing. When a parole date is set, victims will be notified of the decision and the reasons for it.

Also of interest to victims is a commission decision to consider, as a condition for parole, a prisoner's intention to comply with any order requiring restitution and to deny parole if a prisoner is believed to be concealing assets in an effort to avoid making restitution.

It is another step forward in the recognition of the party of the second part — the individual victim — in many crimes.

States, under whose jurisdiction most crimes fall, also have been under pressure to consider the rights of victims.

In Texas, for instance, there are now provisions for some restitution to victims.

But only three states, California, Arkansas and Arizona, now permit victims to testify or be represented in parole proceedings. Other states are considering such a change.

It should be considered seriously in Texas, too, where easy parole is already an issue.

Calling participation by victims in parole hearings "a conservative, Reagan trend," an American Civil Liberties Union official says, "Victims have been neglected by the whole process, and they deserve better treatment, but not at the expense of the Bill of Rights."

Yet recognition of the rights of victims is not a "Reagan trend" nor an interference with the rights of a convicted malfactor. It is rather an admission that crime is not only a societal problem but also an individual one, especially for those victimized by criminal activity, and it crosses party and philosophical lines.

The victimizer has his day in court, his rights are carefully protected and when convicted he is frequently enabled to regain his freedom much earlier than a jury intended. Yet his release or retention in prison, in many cases, is of vital personal interest to those who were his victims and might be again.

This active recognition of that fact, at the federal level, should add impetus to the victims movement at the state level.

And that's good.

The Union Leader

Manchester, NH, March 20, 1984

Crime's victims are society's biggest losers.

The nation's courts have done everything possible to hamstring law enforcement agencies, minimize punishment and protect the rights of criminals — to the extent that it is virtually impossible for a victim to get a fair shake.

In Pershing County, Nev., residents have donated $7,500 and must raise a total of $60,000 to prosecute an accused sex fantasy killer — but they would rather see taxes raised to finance the trial than risk having the accused killer tried in California where he almost certainly would escape the death penalty if convicted.

The realities of crime, and the frequent lack of punishment, cause many otherwise law abiding citizens to cheer when a victim strikes back. The case of the father of a 12-year-old kidnap victim who shot his son's suspected abductor in the head in a crowded airport last Friday night is a perfect example. Who, other than the courts, which will insist the father be rigorously prosecuted, can feel any real sympathy for the alleged kidnapper, who threatened to kill the child and subjected the father, mother and child to incredible mental anguish? By all societal standards, the father was wrong: But his frustration with "justice" is entirely understandable to any rational citizen in modern society.

Victims pay; criminals seldom suffer the pain, both physical and psychological, they force upon those whose rights they almost freely violate.

And the fault rests squarely on the courts and, to an only moderately lesser extent, on legislators for their abject failure to insure that punishment is swift, certain and commensurate with the crime committed.

New Hampshire is no exception. When was the last brutal murderer executed? When was the last chronic criminal given a life term that meant life in prison, rather than parole in a mere handful of years? When, indeed, were escalating mandatory minimum sentences employed to insure that repetitive offenders — career criminals — preying on society, received the punishment they had earned? Where is justice when a vicious killer like Edward Coolidge can be facing parole, long before serving his full sentence for a heinous crime? What father, in similar circumstances today, would not feel compelled to take the law in his own hands to prevent a recurrence of New Hampshire's Coolidge travesty?

The courts and legislators must soon face the realities, sense the growing frustration of the state's citizens at watching every advantage be given to the criminal. Soon, before it is too late, they must act to implement meaningful mandatory minimum prison sentences for criminals, sentences that insure the reality of punishment.

The function of criminal justice is not, first and foremost, rehabilitation of lawbreakers: The function of criminal justice is punishment, and it is a function increasingly ignored in today's courtrooms.

The courts, including those in New Hampshire, have made crime pay and have turned crime's victims into society's losers. How long must society wait before legislators begin taking the initiative in placing the heaviest burden where it belongs: Squarely on convicted criminals?

It is time to rewrite the criminal laws, to force judges to insure punishment through establishment of rigid mandatory minimum prison sentences, to make them more accountable for their rulings, to abolish parole, to limit bail, to restore capital punishment, to provide victim compensation. The burden rests heavily on the legislature.

Newsday

Long Island, NY, September 15, 1984

Even though an estimated 40 million Americans fall victim to crimes every year, it's only recently that many states have established programs to compensate them for injuries, medical treatment or property losses not covered by insurance. And the state programs that do exist usually fall far short of meeting the need.

Now help from Washington may be on the way. The Senate has passed and the House subcommittee on criminal justice is considering legislation that would use federal criminal fines to augment the states' efforts and to set up hotlines along with other programs for assisting crime victims.

The bills, which are fairly similar, would also establish the so-called "Son-of-Sam" provision on the federal level by authorizing the seizure of book royalties or other payments received by convicts. The purpose is twofold: depriving criminals of the fruits of their crime and adding some money to the victims' fund.

But there's also a danger that this provision would take away any incentive for people convicted of crimes to tell their stories. And as Sen. Charles Mathias (R-Md.) has noted, some of them "may have something to say that many of us wish to hear." Among those that come to mind are the Watergate conspirators, draft resisters and others involved in acts of civil disobedience.

Sometimes chronicles of crime — which often involve payments to defendants to help support their families or cover their lawyers' fees — can offer considerable insight into the nature of criminals and the whole justice process.

Such reservations aside, Congress ought to pass the bill as quickly as possible. The $100 million or so that the fund is expected to contain — private contributions would be encouraged — would go a long way toward helping countless crime victims, whose plight is all too often ignored by the criminal justice system.

the Charleston Gazette

Charleston, WV, February 11, 1984

IF A middle-aged adult were shot in the back of the head by a teenager, what would courts do with the youth (assuming he was past 17 and eligible for public justice)?

Five years in forestry camp? Ten years in Moundsville?

In an opposite case — a 64-year-old Putnam County man who shot a 16-year-old boy — the shooter received, in effect, no punishment at all.

The youth, Denny Alexander, was "mud-buggying" with chums in a four-wheel-drive vehicle at a construction site. The irate man, Waitman Kesling, annoyed by the teenagers, fired at their backs. Young Alexander came within millimeters of being killed. The boy spent two weeks in a hospital. The bullet still is in his head.

Kesling was indicted for felonious wounding but was allowed by assistant prosecutor Michael Fewell to plead to simple battery, a misdemeanor. Thursday, Circuit Judge James Holliday put Kesling on probation with no jail time.

"He shot my son in the back of the head and got away with it," the boy's mother said. "It's totally unjust."

Why does society shrug off attacks on teenagers? Did Judge Holliday and assistant prosecutor Fewell decide that it's forgivable to shoot rowdy teenagers?

Why is justice so unfair? Compare the Putnam outcome to a Pocahontas County case in which a village no-account spent seven years in prison for two trivial break-ins, then drew a life term for setting a jail mattress afire.

In Pocahontas County, a jail mattress is worth life in prison. In Putnam County, a bullet in a boy's head merits no penalty.

With such results, the American principle of equal justice under law becomes a mockery.

The Des Moines Register

Des Moines, IA, March 10, 1984

"The criminal is given the choice of the very best lawyers. ... The system ... forgets the victim and relatives of the victim. They have no choice; they take what they can get. I wish someone would tell us what rights the victim's family have...."

Those are the words of a woman whose niece was stabbed and strangled to death nearly three years ago. Since then, the family of Sherri Lyn Henderson has become the victim of an indifferent city and police bureaucracy.

Two years after the young woman was murdered in Des Moines, her 1969 Pontiac, which was impounded as evidence, had not been returned to the family.

The victim's mother, Beverly Summers of Albia, first was told that the city was owed $1,400 in storage fees on the impounded car; later she learned that the car had been sold by the city nine months earlier, *before* the trial of the accused murderer. (And why should the victim's family have to pay storage on the car? Surely protection of evidence is as much a cost of prosecution as, say, the county attorney's salary.)

City Attorney Philip Riley has conceded that the city screwed up, and has offered to recommend that it reimburse the family for the car and for mileage on trips to Des Moines on this matter.

The criminal-justice system has created counterbalances to the power of the courts to protect the rights of the accused. But who helps the victims of crimes, who must bear the grief of personal and financial loss, take time off work to testify, and confront insensitive bureaucrats, police and court officials?

In Polk County, a year-old "victim services" agency has been created out of existing programs for victims of sexual and violent crimes.

With a small staff and budget of just under $150,000 — made up of Polk County and United Way money and a private grant — the program is modest but is just what many crime victims need. A similar program operates in Scott County, and the state will help pay medical bills, burial expenses and wages lost while testifying.

But many victims need an advocate to help them deal with the police and courts. Polk County Attorney Dan Johnston, who was instrumental in establishing the Des Moines victim-services agency, said a federal crime survey recently found that many crime victims were more disturbed by the treatment they received from police and court officials than from their attackers.

It is fashionable to talk of victim restitution these days, as though a convicted criminal will recompense his victims; but in reality compensation is rare. What a person who has been assaulted or robbed needs is help paying medical bills, an advocate in recovering lost or damaged property, and counseling in overcoming emotional distress. This should be considered as much a priority of the criminal-justice system as ensuring fairness to defendants.

The Dallas Morning News

Dallas, TX, March 11, 1984

While the nation's streets keep getting meaner — between 1972 and 1982 violent crime in America increased 54 percent — some attitudes have been changing in the direction of common sense. Nowhere is this clearer than in the area of victims' rights.

The latest bill, the Victims of Crime Assistance Act of 1984, has just been sent to Congress by Atty. Gen. William French Smith. It would assist both public and private agencies of the 38 states that have victim-compensation laws. It would also preclude those charged with a crime, until acquitted, from profiting by selling accounts of it to the media.

Victims'-rights bills have been floating around Congress for the last couple of years. Budgetary constrictions are severe at all levels of government, but this cause is so worthy that Congress should not scrimp. Given the true needs of victims, this bill's estimated cost of $45 million-$75 million, tied to the amounts paid in criminal fines and bonds, seems pathetically inadequate.

The victim population is growing far faster than the criminal population, and is also growing more and more bitter. Victims need more than financial compensation for their losses; they also need rehabilitative therapy, protection against intimidation and the capacity to sue the state when it releases dangerous criminals back into society.

That victims, and not criminals, are starting to become the objects of compassion is encouraging, but now it's time for some compassionate *action*.

Arkansas Gazette.

Little Rock, AR, August 30, 1984

News that Bob Troutt and his beating victim Bob Spears have "settled" the $1,750,000 judgment awarded Spears for injuries and punitive damages is a reminder that Congress will almost surely pass a crime-victims compensation bill this year — one that makes compensation a part of the actual punishment of the criminal.

That, of course, isn't the case with Troutt. He does face a 12-year sentence for ordering Spears beaten, but Spears had to get a civil judgment against him for damages — and isn't at all certain of collecting.

The agreement is that he'll accept whatever payment Troutt's insurors may prove liable for under the terms of Troutt's homeowners insurance policy — and the insurors disclaim liability. They say intentional acts of violence aren't covered. So Spears may or may not get a dime.

Not that he'd get anything like the full $1,750,000 under the compensation bill now before Congress. First of all, the compensation is limited to victims of federal crime. Secondly, it isn't intended as a substitute for civil judgments. It's aimed at making the criminal pay in both prison time and money by means of a fine — all in the same proceeding. The proposal has a social rather than a personal thrust.

The compensation fund is expected to average around $100 million a year. What the individual victim gets will depend on the federal trial judge and the criminal's means — but the intention is that the victim shall get some compensation.

The bill is actually a refinement of a 1982 law, which authorizes but doesn't require federal district judges to order restitution for property loss and personal injury. That discretionary approach hasn't come to much, which is why the present bill proposes to make the fines automatic. It also carries a provision for seizure of any royalties a criminal might earn by "writing up" his crime for publication.

Some of the estimated annual $100 million raised for the victims fund (the public will be invited to donate to it) will go to victim-compensation programs in the states. Most states have such programs (Governor Clinton is considering one for Arkansas) but most are also very poorly funded, so the money would be most welcome.

Some look upon victim-compensation laws and programs — including the proposed federal one — as cosmetic, a sop for the public complaint that justice never concerns itself with the injuries and losses suffered annually by some 40 million Americans at the hands of criminals.

That's true in part. No program, federal or state, moreover, however funded, could substitute for civil damage suits or match huge settlements like Spears'. But as sponsors of the federal bill (which has already passed the Senate) say, it's making the criminal pay *something* that counts. We'd agree. That general social commitment alone makes the programs worthwhile.

Four Convicted in Mass. Rape; Trial Shown on National TV

Four men were convicted in March 1984 of joining in the 1983 rape of a woman in a New Bedford, Mass. tavern. Two other men were acquitted of related charges. The rape case had drawn national attention in March 1983 when it had been reported that as many as a dozen bar patrons had cheered on the accused rapists. Evidence at the trials, however, indicated that only 10 persons, including the victim and the six defendants, were at Big Dan's Bar on the night of the alleged rape. Three of the convicted defendants received sentences of nine to 12 years, and the fourth was sentenced to six to eight years. The widely publicized case spawned debate over the rights of rape victims and live media coverage of trials. The defense in the trials frequently tried to discredit the woman's character. She was described as being a welfare cheat and as having a "sexually related" psychiatric problem. Women's groups, many of which were closely monitoring the trials, decried the defense's attempts to disparage the victim.

The extensive media coverage of the trials was led by *Cable News Network*, which showed several hours of court testimony on many days of the trials. In the trials, the victim's name was used repeatedly and was relayed by the broadcast and cable coverages. It was the policy of many news organizations not to disclose the names of rape victims because of the additional stress such publicity could cause. In demonstrations March 22 and 23, groups in New Bedford and Fall River, where the trials took place, marched and held vigils to what they viewed as prejudice against the defendants, all of whom were immigrants from the Portugese Azores. About half of New Bedord's resident's, including the 22-year-old rape victim, were of Portuguese descent.

SYRACUSE HERALD·JOURNAL
Syracuse, NY, March 28, 1984

The verdicts are in and the sentences imposed but the jury is still out on one aspect of the New Bedford (Mass.) rape case — television coverage.

Cable News Network, the all-news network available in 25 million homes, televised more than 45 hours of live, unedited and uncensored coverage. It was an unprecedented event in the history of American criminal proceedings.

Was it a new form of video voyeurism or was it a valuable opportunity for Americans to see the criminal justice system at work?

The network said it gave viewers a chance to see how the judicial system really works. And Susan Brownmiller, author of a landmark study of rape ("Against Our Will") found that the coverage enabled society to learn something about itself.

"These seemed to be fairly ordinary young men in a bar under the influence of alcohol, and under the influence of what I would think to be very faulty notions of masculinity, and something happened. There was a group dynamic that was appalling and I think that's what captured the interest, first of the national press and then of the nation," she said Sunday on ABC-TV's "This Week with David Brinkley."

But others worried the intense coverage deprived the victim of rights and, in doing so, may discourage other rape victims from pressing charges.

Defense attorneys, in effect, put the victim's conduct on trial. She was, of course, questioned thoroughly about the rape on the pool table at Big Dan's tavern. However, she was also grilled about welfare payments she may have received illegally, whether she had been raped before, the last time she had sex with her boyfriend, her mental health and whether her grandmother called her a drunk.

The defense technique was nothing unusual; it happens, to one degree or another, in virtually every rape trial. The diffrence this time was television, and its ability to reach millions.

"Although the guilty decision might have a mitigating influence, I don't see how the woman can help but feel this is going to follow her for a long time. Several women who agreed to prosecute other cases have changed their minds" after seeing what the New Bedford woman went through, said Janice Davidian of the Coalition Against Sexist Violence.

Massachusetts law permits the use of cameras in the courtroom. (New York does not.) Coverage was unobtrusive, involving a single camera and available light. Moreover, the trial judge prohibited shots of the victim.

But the victim had no protection from the prying eyes of a nation or her community, where at least 40,000 homes received the televised trial coverage. Although her face wasn't shown, her testimony — and her name — could be heard while the camera was focused on other people in the courtroom.

Over the years, newspapers have been sensitive to the unique nature of rape cases. They know many victims dread public exposure. They also know there's a considerable number of people who believe women — especially modern, "liberated" women — frequently "invite" rape or do not act forcefully enough to prevent it. Accusing the victim is peculiar to rape and sexual abuse cases. That is why The Herald-Journal and most other newspapers routinely do not use names of victims. (Local newspapers in the New Bedford area used the victim's name in the barroom rape case after it was used on television.)

Some, including distinguished attorneys, argue that women accusing men of rape should enjoy no special protection because it tends to weight the case against the defendant.

"A rape victim should not be singled out for special solicitude. To not show the victim's face presumes she is telling the truth, and showing the six defendants leads the public to believe they are guilty before they are proven to be," says Harvard Law School professor Alan Dershowitz.

THE MILWAUKEE JOURNAL
Milwaukee, WI, March 28, 1984

The message from the gang-rape trials in Fall River, Mass., should be clear: When a woman says no to sex, she means no. If a man persists to the point of physical violation, he is breaking the law and risking years behind bars. That's as it should be.

Millions of television viewers and newspaper readers followed the trials of six men accused of participating in the rape of a woman on a pool table in a New Bedford, Mass., tavern. Four were convicted and sentenced to from 6 to 12 years in prison. All that should help deter rape of any kind, including the often hard to prove variety known as "acquaintance rape," wherein the victim had willingly associated with the assailant before the actual rape.

Generally, the defense in a rape case tries to show either that the victim was mistaken in her identification or that she consented. The New Bedford case is significant because the defense failed to convince the jurors that the victim consented — even though there was testimony that she had joked with men in the tavern and put her arms around one defendant before the attack.

Interestingly, a grand jury in New Jersey last week indicted three men in a similar attack at a bar Feb. 2. In how many similar cases over the years have victims declined to cooperate or prosecutors declined to press charges? The New Bedford case should give victims reason to believe that justice will prevail.

Unfortunately, the case was complicated by two additional factors. One involved allegations of prejudice against the Portuguese-immigrant defendants. That seems unfounded because the victim, a prosecutor and some of the jurors were themselves of Portuguese descent.

The second factor was inadvertent release of the victim's name. Some observers fear that the release will deter victims from testifying. We don't think so. The release was an accident, not an indication of a trend. The trials were broadcast live. Although the judge, William Young, rightly did not allow the cameras to show the victim, her name was uttered during testimony and over the air. The live broadcast should have been delayed by, say, 10 seconds to permit deletion of the victim's name. Judge Young ruefully said, "In the future, I will be quick to protect the name of the victim."

However, Judge Young will best be remembered for repudiating a defense plea for leniency based on a theory of consent. He declared that "to suggest that any course of conduct — however flirtatious or seductive, engaged in whatever locale — may reduce the sentence" for a rape, is to "virtually outlaw an entire gender for the style of their dress, the length of their skirts or their choice to enter a place of public refreshment." In other words, women may dress as they wish and go to taverns alone without giving up their right to refuse sex.

None of that means that rape cases will be vastly easier to prosecute. It still will take courage on the part of the victim to press the charge and endure cross-examination, as one must. And there will be special problems in sensational cases. Because of harassment, the victim in the New Bedford case has had to move to another town. Yet, as the battle against rape proceeds along a broken front, this case must be considered a gain.

THE ANN ARBOR NEWS
Ann Arbor, MI, March 22, 1984

What, really, did the nation learn from live cable and radio coverage of the New Bedford rape trial? That truth is "better" than fiction and that the stuff of real life is better than watching the soaps?

Did a significant number of Americans' attitude toward rape change to one of serious, concentrated outrage? Did TV perform a valuable service by educating the public about how rape victims are treated in court?

These questions concern us as journalists as they should you the reader. Far more than just the public's right to know is involved here. For example, many people would say that the intense media coverage of the New Bedford trial will discourage women from pursuing rape charges.

If that is true, justice is nowhere near being served and a criminal element will continue to brutalize women in the knowledge that the ill-defined "system" intimidates the victim. What kind of system that promises "equal justice under the law" is that?

The New Bedford trial dramatized the great difference between print and TV coverage of such an event. It is one thing to report relevant details on a printed page, quite another to show the victim, albeit not her face, in her agony in court. Going through a rape trial, some say, can be like going through a rape again.

And that brings up another point: The victim, already stigmatized by the assault, is generally cast by defense counsel as a willing partner. Despite such signs of progress as shield laws protecting rape victims from having their sexual history paraded before juries and despite society beginning to come around attitudinally on rape as an assaultive crime, it's still the woman being put on trial as well as her assailants.

It should make no difference at all whether the victim was drunk or flirtatious in these circumstances. (And in that regard, doesn't the double standard protect men when they become drunk and flirtatious?) The only thing that matters is the crime itself and, of course, whether the perpetrators are punished.

What else *should* New Bedford teach? That however the means of attack and whether by group or individually, that the non-involvement of witnesses — in this case, the patrons of Big Dan's — is a crime in itself. It is the same, in our opinion, as denouncing politics as a giant cesspool, but then having done so, to do nothing to change or improve politics.

What is on trial in the New Bedford case is not so much whether we should televise court proceedings (38 states already allow cameras in courtrooms, with varying restrictions) but whether such coverage serves the dual purpose of aiding justice and giving the public more information on rape procedures so that it can demand and enact tougher, victim-sensitive rape laws.

It all leaves us feeling very incomplete and worried that New Bedford may in fact set back society's treatment of women and deter rape victims from pressing their rights in court.

Detroit Free Press
Detroit, MI, March 28, 1984

THE TRIAL of the defendants in the Fall River barroom rape turned out, as usual, to be a trial of the victim as well. For all our supposed heightened sensitivity to the trauma of rape, it is still the only crime that can be excused on the grounds that the victim somehow "asked for it." It is still the only crime in which a clever lawyer can cast doubt on the victim's past and behavior, while defendants are quite properly protected against disclosure of any past criminal records, precisely so a jury will not be improperly influenced against them.

In Massachusetts, the guilty verdict against four defendants set off angry protests among Portuguese-Americans who believe the men were convicted because of their nationality. The early accounts of the rape and the "cheering crowd" of onlookers, which stirred so much outrage, did turn out to be slightly exaggerated. But the trial itself, for those who glimpsed it on cable TV, seemed fair and even tedious, rather than sensational. It ended up being more a testimonial to the need for rape shield laws than a testament of prejudice against the Portuguese. In Fall River and elsewhere, the most pernicious bias is still against the victims of rape.

FORT WORTH STAR-TELEGRAM
Fort Worth, TX, March 20, 1984

Televising the Fall River, Mass., gang rape trial now in progress does more than let many viewers watch that particular trial. It also gives them a better understanding of how courtrooms work.

And that is a valuable education to have, especially in these days of ever-increasing litigation. Sooner or later, many citizens will find their way into the courtrooms — as jury members or parties to lawsuits — and it is important that they know as much as possible about the courts. What we know, we can deal with, even appreciate. What we do not know, we might fear.

Televising trials, then, can be most useful.

But, unfortunately for Texans, the opportunity to see a trial on television comes only when some trial that catches the attention of the nation happens to be in one of the states that allow TV cameras in the courtroom. Such instances, such as the Fall River trial, are rare.

Texas, on the other hand, often has trials of interest to many Texans. Televising them would cause many citizens in this state to watch either complete or partial trial coverage or trial segments offered during regular TV news programs.

Unfortunately, that cannot be done in Texas. It is not permitted.

A few years ago, a special committee of attorneys, judges, news people and others looked into the matter and recommended TV cameras be permitted in Texas courtrooms.

But the idea failed to win approval. One reason revolved around actions of some in the television business itself. While the proposal to permit televising of trials was being presented to a group of judges, some TV news personnel covering the meeting made such a commotion that some judges feared the same thing would happen in the courtroom while trials were being televised and decided against the idea.

But the TV news people involved were not using the same type of equipment that would be used in courtroom coverage. Equipment is available that would not interfere with the orderly conduct of courts. It is being used in states that now allow TV in the courtroom.

It has been a while since the idea was proposed and turned down in Texas.

The Fall River trial is a reminder that citizens can learn much about our courts from television. We can learn how they work and what they do. We can learn to understand them better, and perhaps some citizens — who are yet to have occasion to go to a court — could even learn to be less intimidated by their formal trappings. That would help them should they someday have to go to court.

Texas should once again pursue the idea of letting TV into the courtroom, for there would be a great deal to be gained from it.

THE CHRISTIAN SCIENCE MONITOR
Boston, MA, March 26, 1984

AMERICAN society and its legal system continue to make measured progress in dealing with the crime of rape. But the need for more improvement remains.

Rape is against the law. It is a crime not of passion but of violence, against the person and will of the victim. It is in no way justified by the presence of alcohol, nor by the victim's past behavior, nor by any other supposedly extenuating circumstance.

Across the United States a larger percentage of rape cases than in the past are being reported to police. More are resulting in convictions, most recently a nationally reported case in New Bedford, Mass. Yet only a minority of incidents is even reported — by one estimate as few as 1 in 20. Many victims remain concerned about the treatment they would receive from law-enforcement and judicial systems, despite considerable progress in both areas.

Sixteen states, beginning with Michigan 10 years ago, now have strong laws to protect victims from intrusions into issues irrelevant to the rape incident. These laws sharply restrict courtroom questions about victims' past conduct and actions prior to the offense.

Another 26 states have modified laws, which still permit some testimony that can have the old-time effect of first putting the victim, not the persons arrested, on trial. The remaining states have no such laws.

All states would do well to adopt the principles of the Michigan law. The act of rape is a violation of the physical privacy of an individual: This should not be compounded by an investigative or judicial violation of other elements of privacy.

News coverage of rape trials should be handled straightforwardly and with restraint. Its focus should be on legal issues rather than on elements of prurient interest. Coverage of the New Bedford case has varied from responsible to exploitative.

Incidents of rape should be reported and prosecuted fully. At the same time sensitive and compassionate handling of each case is required, to differentiate between information that should remain private and that which belongs in the public domain so that responsible court decisions can be reached.

BUFFALO EVENING NEWS
Buffalo, NY, March 28, 1984

JUSTICE HAS been done in the nationally publicized New Bedford, Mass., gang-rape case. The juries appear to have reached their verdicts in an impartial, conscientious manner, convicting four of the accused while acquitting two others. And the court, stressing that the defendants had "brutalized a defenseless young woman," appropriately imposed the prison terms recommended by the prosecution.

It is hard to understand claims that the trials were examples of ethnic discrimination. While it is true that all six defendants are Portuguese-Americans, so too are the victim, the prosecutor and several of the jurors. Superior Court Judge William Young rightly observed that "these sentences are not passed on these individuals because of who they are, but because of what crime they stand convicted of."

Despite the conviction of four defendants, the case ironically appears to have had a chilling effect on the prosecution of rape cases around the nation. A rape crisis center in Boston reported that about a third of the women who had been considering prosecution had changed their minds and decided to drop charges. This was their reaction to seeing what the rape victim had to go through in court.

It is a formidable ordeal for any woman to have to relive such a humiliating, terrifying attack, and, as the main witness in such cases, the rape victim must necessarily face grueling cross-examination by defense attorneys. She should not, however, as the New Bedford victim was, be subjected to irrelevant questions regarding her personal life.

Possibly the most disturbing aspect of the trial for rape victims considering prosecution was the broadcasting of the trial proceedings on radio and television. It is unsettling enough to testify in open court, but the knowledge that every word is going out to millions of listeners could prove overwhelming.

This confirms the view that such broadcasting of trials tends to turn them into spectacles and impedes the process of justice. In this case, the rape victim was not shown on television screens, but since it was being televised live, her name was mentioned, and it was subsequently published elsewhere. It is the policy of The News not to publish the names of rape victims, and that policy was followed in this case. Our system of justice in recent years has gone to great lengths to uphold the rights of defendants; in rape cases, too often the rights of the victim are overlooked.

The Evening Gazette
Worcester, MA, March 22, 1984

Citizens everywhere should be proud of Judge Robert A. Barton of Middlesex Superior Court and his courtroom statement that society's attitudes on rape are changing significantly.

Barton, at the sentencing of three men convicted of gang raping a woman soldier, said that blaming the victim for provocative behavior "will no longer be tolerated by this society and jurors who are a cross-section of this commonwealth."

"No longer will society accept the (idea) that a woman, even if she may initially act in a seductive or compromising manner, has waived her rights to say 'no' at any future time. 'No' means nothing further . . .," the judge emphasized in pronouncing sentences to Walpole on the three convicted by a jury two weeks ago.

Barton has underscored a major change in attitude of a judicial system that has long allowed the rape victim to be put on trial through a defense tactic of trying to destroy her character.

Sadly there are still places where rape is considered the victim's "fault." Not too many months ago in Massachusetts, a group of men who pleaded guilty to rape changed their pleas when a trial was held. They were found guilty of damaging a woman's car but not her person because she was unable to testify. And more than 30 states still permit rape within marriage, even if the two technically married persons do not live together.

Barton's words do indicate, however, that attitudes are changing. Rape, especially of a woman or child, by a stronger individual or by more than one person, is a vicious and brutal assault, a heinous crime, and those convicted of it deserve what they get.

The Boston Globe
Boston, MA, March 28, 1984

No one outside a tight-knit minority community can fully understand the bitterness of the New Bedford Portuguese community and its sense that it was collectively a victim of the Big Dan's rape case.

Viewed from outside the community it is clearly evident that the woman herself, as well as many of the investigating police officers, witnesses and jurors were also of Portuguese descent, and that every attempt appears to have been made to minimize the ethnic aspects of the case.

Outsiders are mystified by the community's contention that media identification of the six defendants as "Portuguese immigrants" was improper and inflammatory. No more improper or inflammatory, outsiders would respond, as the similar identification of the defendants in other recent group rape cases as medical doctors or as members of the Grand Slamm rock band.

Outsiders familiar with Dist. Atty. Ronald Pina's distinguished service as a state legislator and as Bristol County's prosecutor are concerned that his career may have been jeopardized by his vigorous prosecution of this case involving members of his own ethnic community.

All these factors in the reasonable response of outsiders did not prevent a protest march through New Bedford or lessen the lingering bitterness. This situation can too easily be exploited by opportunistic politicians, but also can – and should – provide an opportunity to repair bridges to the city's Portuguese community.

Such efforts – and the passage of time – will allow the Portuguese community to understand that only six of their members were on trial, only four were found guilty and only one member of the community was the victim and can never outlive what happened at Big Dan's.

The Wichita
Eagle-Beacon
Wichita, KS, March 26, 1984

It's good the juries in the barroom gang-rape trials concluded last week in Massachusetts flatly rejected the notion that the 22-year-old victim was responsible for her own pain and suffering. This isn't to suggest the conviction of the victim's four attackers set a nationwide legal precedent for the prosecution and punishment of rape. It didn't. But it may help elevate to a cultural precedent an old but still not widely accepted idea: Rape is a crime of violence in which attackers assert their contempt for and physical superiority over victims.

Should such a precedent now start taking hold in the nation, at least some rape victims may be spared the ordeal of the Massachusetts woman, whose social background, brought out in great detail by defense attorneys, became better known than the backgrounds of her assailants. It would become widely understood that a victim's marital status, economic status, social and sexual habits, and her demeanor prior to the rape itself, are irrelevant. In a rape trial, the question at hand would be: Is there sufficient evidence to prove the defendant had sex with a person who didn't consent?

The pillorying of the victim at the Massachusetts trial can't be blamed on the defense attorneys alone. They tried to show the defendant "was asking for it" because their task was to gain acquittal for the attackers, and that tactic has been successful in winning rape acquittals in the past.

The irony inherent in that tactic — that a rape victim, not her alleged attacker, seems the one being tried — is largely responsible for the fact that authoritative estimates suggest more rapes are unreported that reported. One hopes the tactic's failure will give other rape victims the courage to report and vigorously press charges against their assailants.

It's good also that another defense tactic, portraying the rape prosecution as a vendetta against Portuguese-Americans, wasn't effective. The jurors, several of whom themselves were Portuguese-Americans, properly understood that an ugly, despicable crime of violence unquestionably had taken place, and ruled accordingly.

ST. LOUIS POST-DISPATCH

St. Louis, MO, March 26, 1984

Yet another proxy war has made headlines in recent days — one played out on no distant battleground, but right here in the U.S.: New Bedford, Mass. There, last March, on a pool table in a bar where she had gone to purchase cigarettes, a young woman was raped by a gang of tavern regulars cheered on by their drinking companions. To some Portuguese-Americans, the case came to represent yet another example of the discrimination immigrants must face. To some feminists, it was one more instance of the double indignity suffered by any woman who, after the initial outrage inflicted by the rape itself, seeks to prosecute.

And so the parties in this particular crime became stand-ins for greater causes. The woman who was so callously violated was swiftly championed by those who saw in her only the opportunity to decry, however legitimately, the scrutiny of the victim's character that a rape trial now entails. To give a serious hearing to testimony indicating the victim may have consented to intercourse with one of the defendants is out of the question for these partisans. On the other side of the issue are those who would see the case as a slur on all Portuguese-Americans. But in minimizing the actions of the defendants as only an appropriate response to the advances of their accuser, they have not yet satisfactorily explained why the victim, herself of Portuguese descent, should not benefit from their sympathy.

But however much the issues in the case have been muddied, the outcome of the legal process itself is reassuring. Tried by a jury of their peers, four of the six defendants have been convicted. One could argue that in such cases, it is impossible for justice to be done. Yet there can be no dispute that what transpired in the courtroom serves justice's purposes far better than what has been done outside it.

Rockford Register Star

Rockford, IL, March 29, 1984

There was, tragically, a fifth sentence in the Fall River, Mass., gang rape trial. It was imposed on the victim.

Now that the lurid story of rape has faded somewhat, a postscript seems in order regarding the trial of six Portuguese immigrants, four of whom have been convicted.

First, their victim should receive a medal for bravery because she insisted that the case go to criminal trial. Not only did she face a jury of her peers. She faced cable television cameras, some of whose editors allowed the use of her name — which the presiding judge said henceforth he would not permit.

In passing sentences of 6 to 12 years' imprisonment on the four who were convicted, the judge noted why this was important. He said the four men "brutalized a defenseless young woman and sought to degrade and destroy her human, individual dignity."

At the very least, this was true.

And finally, their victim's attorney made a pertinent remark: "There were five sentences in this case — one of them exile."

He referred to the fact that the victim and her children have moved from Fall River, Mass., rather than face the disdain of the convicted men's families. The reasoning also was that her children's young lives could be psychologically battered if they remained in Fall River, while their mother's future was not only impaired but physically threatened.

Fall River, Mass., is not the root of all evil. It is merely a mirror of what can happen anywhere when decency falls victim to animal behavior.

WORCESTER TELEGRAM

Worcester, MA, March 26, 1984

Massachusetts is travelling through a despicable period. In recent weeks, at least four rape cases have been making headlines. Two trials have just concluded.

Three members of the rock band Grand Slamm were convicted in Ayer of rape after they offered a young woman a ride back to Fort Devens in their bus. In Fall River, four men were convicted in the so-called Big Dan's rape case. The rape occurred in a New Bedford bar. The victim was carried to a pool table and assaulted.

A Shrewsbury policeman and another man were recently convicted of rape in Worcester. Two Boston policemen are charged with taking a woman to a private club and raping her. They picked up the woman on for being disorderly in a Boston hotel. Another pair of policemen, on the North Shore, are facing charges they used alcohol to drug a young woman before raping her.

The ugly crimes have an element in common — the issue of consent. The defense lawyers in the New Bedford case tried to argue that the woman in the case "led on" the defendants. Testimony was introduced in the Ayer case that was designed to show that the woman was a willing participant.

Since rape is a crime of force and a crime carried out against the will of the victim, consent is an important aspect of any defense.

Rape is a felony punishable by life in prison, though a lesser term may be imposed. Every city and town is required by law to have a rape reporting unit trained in evidence, counseling and prosecution. The district attorney's office and the state police provide that service in many cases. All reports of rape are held confidential, by law.

Even more important, in 1977 the state reversed the old rules for prosecuting rape. Where once a victim's reputation and prior sexual conduct often became part of the case for the defense, today, it cannot, except as the court determines such information relevant.

Today there are no excuses, no cloudy issues. In New Bedford, some of those taking the defendants' side say the Big Dan's case was not a rape trial so much as a trial on charges against an ethnic group. That's nonsense. In Ayer, the defense focussed on supposed provocative behavior on the victim's part. The judge in that case answered directly that a woman has a right to say "no," that she retains that right.

Society will not condone sexual assault. The law and the sequence of court proceedings reaffirm that assertion. A rape trial is just that, a trial on charges of a heinous physical assault — no more and no less. The work of the court and the jury is to determine guilt or innocence.

To say otherwise, no matter what the verdict, is to twist the truth. The issue is rape, a crime against a person.

Portland Press Herald

Portland, ME, March 24, 1984

Just verdicts are in on the trials of six Massachusetts men charged with raping a woman a year ago in Big Dan's Tavern in New Bedford while onlookers applauded: four convictions for aggravated rape and two aquittals.

Those are reasoned judgments, rendered by two separate juries. They reflect throughtful consideration of the testimony presented to the juries and, through live television coverage of the trials, to the nation.

Two juries have independently determined that the 22-year-old woman who entered Big Dan's on a March night last year wasn't a partner in sexual encounters, but a victim of rape.

Equally important, the verdicts acknowledge that rape is a serious crime of violence that merits serious punishment: even deportation or life imprisonment. The failure to extend guilty verdicts and the punishment they carry to two of the defendants demonstrates how seriously jurors took the nature of the crime.

More than any other event, the New Bedford trial may imprint the violent reality of rape on our national consciousness. Only such an imprint can counter the persistent falsehood that rape is a sexual misadventure that occurs when women are "asking for it."

It isn't. It doesn't. And it never did.

Rape is a criminal attack. Punishing it is a public responsibility. That's the issue at hand.

Public attention must not be drawn away from the fact that rape—not discrimination, not bigotry, not the anguish of immigrant poverty—is what the two trials—and the verdicts—in a Fall River courtroom have been about.

Coming to Grips with the Problem of Child Abuse

A rash of scandals involving day-care centers across the country focused national attention in 1984 on the problem of child abuse, and in particular on the sexual molestation of children. It is uncertain how prevalent this crime is or whether it is simply more likely to be discovered because of increased awareness on the part of parents, teachers and social workers. One of the most shocking aspects of child abuse is that in a majority of cases, the molester is well known to the child, and is often a respected member of the community. This point, made repeatedly by experts on child abuse, was brought home Oct. 1, 1984 when John Clark Donahue, the founder and artistic director of the Minneapolis Children's Theatre Company & School, pleaded guilty to three counts of criminal sexual conduct with his young students. Donahue, who had started the Minneapolis company in 1961 and built it into one of the nation's most prominent and respected children's theatres, had resigned his post May 12, 1984 after being accused of having molested three male students, aged 12 to 14. In August 1984, six day care center employees were arrested in New York City on charges of child molestation, and the district attorney in the Bronx said that some 60 children might have been the victims of molestation at seven different day care centers. These and other cases have made working parents afraid to rely on day care for their children, although sexual abuse is actually more likely to occur in the child's home than in institutions such as day-care centers. As awareness of the problem had grown, a new understanding of the nature of child abuse has spawned better ways of dealing with both victims and the accused in the law courts, as well as helping to prevent many such crimes in the future.

THE RICHMOND NEWS LEADER
Richmond, VA, September 4, 1984

A subcommittee of a task force set up by the state's Division of Children has been studying the problem of sex crimes against children, and it promises to have some useful proposals to offer the General Assembly. Protection of the young against sexual abuse deserves a high priority these days, for the headlines and newscasts report shocking stories suggesting a growing incidence of this kind of crime.

One of the subcommittee's proposals goes to the heart of the issue by recommending ·mandatory prison terms for a second conviction of sexually abusing children. Parents everywhere must be chilled by the routine report that police are searching for "known sex criminals" following a sex crime. Too often lenient judges impose only token sentences on first offenders, and not even second convictions guarantee long sentences. Perhaps the way to keep the number of sex criminals — especially those who prey on children — to a minimum would be to require a mandatory sentence on the *first* conviction.

A second proposal would permit child victims of sexual abuse to give their testimony via videotape or closed-circuit television. This idea makes a great deal of sense. Courtroom proceedings can confuse a child already frightened and traumatized by a terrifying experience. Psychologists have made much progress in eliciting credible testimony from children by using toys and play-acting — methods that do not lend themselves to a witness box. Imagine the confusion of a six-year-old, say, seated in a witness' chair before courtroom full of strangers and expected to relate the awful details of a sexual assault. Many adults — as any rape victim would attest — crumble in such a situation.

One proposal most likely to excite controversy would require a check of police records for any supervisor of child activities. That would be a broad requirement covering everyone from teachers to volunteers in programs for young children. No doubt the proposal will attract charges of invasion of privacy and so on, but it seems a logical step toward insuring the good character of those to whom children are entrusted. A bank doesn't lend money to a deadbeat, a brokerage firm doesn't want to hire an embezzler, and parents don't want sex criminals around their children.

These criminals naturally gravitate to situations where they find easy prey: Witness the series of recent scandals about sexual abuse of children in childcare centers. Maybe it would be inconvenient to run police checks on everyone involved in children's activities, but it's a sure bet that no applicant for such a post would 'fess up voluntarily that he has a sex offense conviction or two. The requirement would have an added benefit in deterring sex criminals from applying for such positions in the first place.

Given the seeming epidemic of sexual abuse of children, it would be easy to go overboard in trying to protect children from such crimes. Civil libertarian Nat Hentoff, for instance, tells of a Midwestern couple who ran afoul of a strict law on child abuse. They innocently photographed their nude five-year-old daughter after her bath, and the photo-developer turned them in. The task force's subcommittee, however, sticks to logical proposals to strengthen enforcement of the law, and it offers recommendations only the guilty need to fear.

The Union Leader
Manchester, NH, August 30, 1984

The alarming increase in proven cases of major physical injuries and abuse of children in New Hampshire in 1983, and the corresponding increase so far this year, is genuinely disturbing. It requires immediate, and substantial, public attention.

Major physical injuries in child abuse include burns, bruises, cuts and welts — significantly more than the casual slap of an angered parent who temperorarily loses control.

It might be possible to convince people a single year 24 percent increase represented better reporting, better investigating or perhaps even an abberation, but that hope of consolation is shattered with the realization that figures for 1984 show reports of suspected child abuse will be 24 percent higher *than in 1983.*

Worse still, although the number of founded reports of child abuse rose, the total number of reports continues at a steady level: 2,979 in 1982; 2,973 in 1983.

What's happening? And why?

In 1982, proven cases of major physical injuries represented only 2 percent of the types of abuse in founded cases. In 1983, it represented 22 percent.

And still worse: Sexual abuse of children also is climbing, up 6 percent during 1983, accounting for 20 percent of all founded reports in 1983.

The statistics are stark and they are frightening — and clearly society is not doing enough.

Children are victims, and they are being victimized, the statistics clearly suggest, at a sharply increasing rate. It would appear, beyond any rational doubt, that society has failed, dismally, to attach sufficiently high penalties to such instances of abuse to discourage their perpetration.

The primary responsibility of the state, of government, must be the protection of those unable to protect themselves, and highest on that list ranks the children, not yet capable of defending themselves against the physical attack of adults.

Child abuse is a despicable crime, no matter the justifications abusers use to lessen their punishment.

Courts have no business considering "mitigating" circumstances — there can be none — when children are threatened.

It is time for a thorough review of the problem, and more new — and decidedly tougher — laws to deal with abusers. If the state cannot protect its children, it is failing its first fundamental purpose of existence.

The London Free Press

London, Ont., October 1, 1984

Is raising children too important to be left to parents? Should couples be screened before they have children to determine their qualifications? Should the right to have and raise children be limited by legislation?

Merely asking the questions reveals a lot about the direction of society today, most of it discouraging. Experts with authoritarian solutions are taking over, ready to impose them on us. They're now addressing the question of what constitutes good parents.

Good parents will always elude precise definition and defy arbitrary categorizing, despite conferences like the recent International Congress on Child Abuse and Neglect in Montreal where a scholarly speaker suggested that perhaps the time has come to license parents. In other words, society should make sure men and women are fit for the role before they're allowed — by whom? — to become parents.

"We say parenthood is the most important activity but we just let it come naturally . . . it should be considered a profession," said David Roy, founder of the Montreal Centre for Bioethics.

Yes, a child-care worker agreed, couples should have to prove they've developed "coping skills" before they have children. And if they muck up as parents, they should be forcibly sterilized, added a west coast academic.

Ordinary parents who are meeting the challenges and frustrations of their responsibilities without the professional credentials to fit them for their role don't appear to have been represented at the conference. They were probably too busy coping.

Child abuse, a distressing social problem with defenceless victims, needs thoughtful, humane responses, including community alertness and tough law enforcement — not decrees on who can have children. That would in turn be an abuse of a basic human right; it trivializes the problem.

Besides, a licence provides no assurance of competence. Instead of testing and licensing aspiring parents for coping skills, why not test and license the Montreal experts for common sense? Licence denied.

THE ANN ARBOR NEWS

Ann Arbor, MI, September 20, 1984

The statistics are alarming, shocking: Child sexual abuse is a growing national problem.

This week, a series on that subject is airing on PBS. Recently, sex crimes against children in day care centers were reported in California and New York, with several other child sexual abuse cases cropping up in between coastlines. It takes a lot to shock Americans these days, but if nothing else does, these hideous acts should.

Child sexual abuse takes many forms, the subtle as well as the obvious. In the former category is a case in Lexington, Ky., in which detectives used a minor as a decoy for homosexuals trying to pick up underage prostitutes.

The stories from day care centers in Minnesota and California sicken. Can allowance be made for exaggeration and imagination? It certainly doesn't seem so.

Cases of child sexual abuse reported to government protection agencies increased 649 percent in six years — from 7,559 in 1976 to 56,607 in 1982 — according to the children's division of the American Humane Association, a national child welfare organization. How many more cases go unreported? That figure might be even more shocking.

Congress has reacted predictably and, as usual, belatedly. Sen. Paula Hawkins, R-Fla., deplored a child care market that is poorly regulated.

"We pay more attention," said she, "to regulating racetrack workers, bank employees and real estate brokers." Another critic, Rep. Patricia Schroeder, D-Colo., said "we are paying more money . . . to kennel a dog than we are day care for our children."

But is throwing a lot of money at the problem and rushing to regulate the child care industry thoughtfully addressing the issue? Or does it go deeper than pushing for more training for child care and law enforcement officers?

In the past, there has been discussion — and only limited at that — of tax incentives for employers who provide day care facilities for their employees' children. Perhaps, in light of these sexual abuse statistics, we have already moved beyond that to the need for a national child care policy.

Clearly, more public education on child abuse is a priority. Sensible, honest talk with children about various sexual abuse prevention techniques ought to be encouraged. Children should be taught that potential abusers can be trustworthy types as well as suspicious-looking strangers.

Beyond that, the danger in cutting rather than expanding federal funding for qualifying day care centers ought to be apparent. We ought to consider federal aid to school districts which set up after-hours programs for school-age latchkey children.

Those who still deplore government involvement in this area should consider the economic necessity today of a two-breadwinner household, or in the case of the single parent, the need for safe, dependable child care with its accompanying peace of mind for the working parent.

It is often glibly said, children are our most precious asset. You wouldn't know it from those shocking child sexual abuse statistics. It's important to remember that not all child care centers fit that picture of abuse and exploitation, but a nation has been jolted into thinking about and doing more for the well-being of its children.

The Philadelphia Inquirer

Philadelphia, PA, September 13, 1984

From the first intuition by policeman James Keating, checking out a burglary false alarm, through hundreds of hours of what now appears to be very professional investigation by all elements of the Philadelphia Police Department's Sex Crimes Unit, it was the kind of performance that distinguishes a police force and the best of its men and women.

The results were dramatic. The 16 men arrested, and any more who are drawn in, are constitutionally entitled to the presumption of innocence, of course. But there can be no question that the crimes are among the most brutalizing known to civilized society. They also are among the most difficult of all truly heinous crimes to detect and prosecute.

All kinds of legal terms are used for them, in the arrests Tuesday and in subsequent prosecutions and in pending legislation, but the crimes are one thing: the sexual abuse of children.

There is no creditable body of psychological or psychiatric theory or practice that does not recognize that sexual contacts between adults and children are profoundly damaging.

The nuances of the theories are intricate. All rest, however, on the truth that such contacts invariably involve the imposition of power and exploitation, in the most fearfully private of all ways.

Such contacts are unrelated to healthy sexuality among adults, just as rape of adults has nothing to do with the act of love. Those impositions of power dehumanize children. They leave emotional scars, distrusts, self-contempt that last through lifetimes. A high proportion of perpetrators of sex crimes against children were victims themselves.

The arrests Tuesday involved child prostitution, production of pornography and other forms of sexual exploitation. The victims were boys, from 12 to 17 years old. The defendants are men, aged 18 through 61.

That does not mean that child sexual abuse is primarily homosexual. To the contrary, a growing body of serious research in the area of child abuse seems to demonstrate that sexual victimization preponderantly involves men abusing girls. Pathological pedophilia is neither gay nor straight. It is sick. It is poisoning. It is criminal.

There are substantial numbers of homosexual men and women in Philadelphia, Pennsylvania and throughout the world. Gradually and often with great difficulty, they are gaining legal rights and public acceptance and dignity that they deserve. They are no more to be identified with pathological, and criminal, pedophiles than all heterosexual men are to be equated with rapists. It would be tragic if, in a misplacement of zeal to prosecute true sexual offenders and to protect children, innocent gays became victimized, by official overreaction or by public scapegoating.

•

Because of the youth and fears and confusion of the victims of child sexual abuse, those crimes are inordinately difficult to investigate and prosecute. Many — almost certainly, most — occur within families.

There is grave need to improve, through legislation and public administration, proper methods for dealing with child sexual abuse. A Pennsylvania Senate subcommittee is studying proposals by Sen. Stewart J. Greenleaf (R., Montgomery) and others to strengthen the state laws. Other efforts are going forward at national and local levels.

Those efforts deserve — demand — the most serious attention.

That attention most critically must include awareness of the dangers inherent in the entire area. High among them is the susceptibility of children to the pressures of parents and other adults — not only to sexual exploitation, but to influences to lie or stand silent. Equally dangerous is the potential for demagoguery, for righteous scapegoating.

Los ANGELES
HERALD EXAMINER

Los Angeles, CA, September 19, 1984

Child abuse is one of America's fastest-growing and most painful social problems. Growing awareness undoubtedly has increased the case loads of already overburdened social workers and confronts families and agencies alike with terrible dilemmas.

An encounter by one local family — Bill and Cindy Williams of Pomona and their infant son, Cary — with the L.A. County Department of Social Services was recounted by staff writer Janet Kaye in Sunday's Herald. Cary, then 4 months old, had been hospitalized with se- vere seizures. Although the parents deny abusing their son and don't know what caused his illness (he is still undergoing treatment), hospital personnel suspected abuse. They reported their suspicions, as required by California law, and law-enforcement and social service officials followed up by placing the child in protective custody.

The Dependency Court in Los Angeles later put the boy in a relative's custody, and the Williamses were required to spend a month and thousands of dollars in legal fees to get him back. Only last month, after three more court appearances, were the charges dismissed. Today, while county officials won't discuss the case, they point out that dismissal doesn't necessarily mean the charges were unfounded.

Any way you look at it, this is a sad story. Was the baby in fact abused? Or were the doctor and social agencies wrong in their initial assessment? There is no way for an outsider to know. But the story nevertheless suggests that the county's child-abuse system is under such strain that there are real questions about how thoroughly it can investigate and treat cases of suspected abuse. Officials admit that innocent families sometimes are caught up in the process, either by coincidence or by groundless accusations of a kind that sometimes characterize divorce cases.

Every instance of suspected child abuse poses painful questions. First, should the child, for his own protection, be taken summarily, if temporarily, from the parents' custody? We think it is generally wise to err on the side of vigilance. If a child is being abused, immediate emergency action is required. If a decision to take a child from his parents turns out to have been needless, it's a terrible mistake — but less terrible than leaving the child in a dangerous, possibly deadly, environment.

Next, if a child is taken from his parents' custody, how much time should elapse before the facts of the case are determined in court? At present, a Dependency Court hearing must decide within 72 hours of putting a child in protective custody whether that custody should continue. The court's decision in this and subsequent hearings may be based on objective evidence — medical reports, for example — or on subjective judgments by trained social workers. And this is where heavy caseloads tend to complicate matters.

At last report, L.A. County had more than 16,000 child-abuse cases under investigation, twice as many as a year ago, and each social worker was juggling about 100 cases at any given time. With that kind of load, there's no way every case can get the attention it deserves. The task is even more difficult in an atmosphere of public hysteria like that surrounding the McMartin Pre-School case. Some child-abuse experts say, for example, that doctors or social workers may become overly zealous not so much to protect children as to protect themselves or their institutions.

How can we make the system work better? There is no avoiding the fundamental child-abuse dilemma: If officials are too lax, a child may suffer; if they are too restrictive, an innocent family may be put through hell. It helps for officials to issue warnings against hysteria, and some have. But the real answer is that the public must give public agencies the resources they need, and the agencies must then do the job that's expected of them. In L.A. County, however, budget increases have been too little and many children's programs have been criticized as poorly administered. More can, and should, be pro-vided. More can, and should, be done. ∎

TULSA WORLD

Tulsa, OK, September 1, 1984

HORRIBLE stories of abuse in New York, Minnesota and California child care centers garner front page headlines, then just as quickly move to the back pages before disappearing from sight — and public consciousness.

It is important that this issue not fade quickly from our thoughts.

A series of programs to be aired by the Oklahoma Educational Television Authority aims at doing just that.

OETA, in a project coordinated with the state Department of Mental Health, Department of Human Services and the Oklahoma Institute for Child Advocacy,

will air eight hours of special programming next month focusing attention on problems facing families and children.

Throughout the week of September 17, OETA will air two specials. The first, "Your Children, Our Children," will examine the status and well-being of children in America. The second, "Child Sexual Abuse," examines this explosive subject in a calm, educational way.

OETA and the Public Broadcast System have shown again the value of television when it is used intelligently to to address a critical public issue.

THE LOUISVILLE TIMES

Louisville, KY, September 4, 1984

The ubiquitous nature of violence in American society is one of our most disturbing phenomena. When violence reaches children through adults in positions of responsibility, it produces a profound sense of outrage, fear and powerlessness to protect those who are most dear.

Unfortunately, events both here and across the nation over recent months have brought this issue to the fore. In California and New York, workers in a preschool and a day-care center have been accused of sexual abuse against children left in their care. Closer to home, charges of sexual abuse have been leveled against parents in two Bullitt County foster homes. In June a Fort Knox elementary school principal was dismissed after pleading guilty to sexually abusing children. At about the same time, a former choirmaster and music teacher in Louisville was sentenced for similar crimes against children cared for in his home while their parents worked.

Child abuse and the sexual exploitation of children are, to some degree, the fad crimes of the 1980s. That sounds flippant but is not intended to be. It means that, like rape a few years ago, much more attention is focused on those assaults today than previously.

The increased attention may make such crimes seem more prevalent today than ever before, although that is not necessarily true. Also because of the attention, it probably is true that more adults who are guilty of such crimes are caught and convicted.

But the prosecution of adults who violate children won't be enough to restore the confidence of parents who must wonder how to raise their children without paranoia, how to teach them to make adult friends and how to feel secure about their safety.

Given the rise in the number of single parent families and the number of families in which both parents work outside the home, the dilemma of choosing someone to care for even very young children is rising. Incidents such

as those alleged in the California and New York cases can make parents wonder how they can be sure their children are in good hands.

And, of course, that fear — and the cases that provoke it — unfairly damages the thousands of wonderful, caring people who work for very low wages providing excellent child care in all sorts of settings.

The real danger, however, is not that such cases will make parents more aware of the dangers their children can face — and therefore more vigilant. The real danger is that such cases will not generate more attention to the quality of care society provides its young children. As education specialist Fred M. Hechinger recently observed in *The New York Times*, the issue goes deeper than the capture and punishment of individuals guilty of a most heinous crime:

"It is this country's refusal to look at the development and education of children as a continuum that should begin as soon as children require care outside the home, care that should, therefore, be carefully regulated and supervised."

In short, if this nation wants to ensure that all of children receive high-quality care in an environment where both they and their parents feel safe, it must provide more public and private resources than it ever has devoted to young children.

It must substitute the sort of care that is available in the best child care centers for the patchwork of make-do arrangements that provide care for the largest number of young children while their parents work today.

Thus far this society has not shown much interest in doing that. On the federal level, during the Reagan administration, it has moved further away from that goal, not closer.

Until that changes, the news stories that strike terror in the hearts of American parents probably will go on and on.

THE INDIANAPOLIS STAR

Indianapolis, IN, August 29, 1984

One of the many disturbing aspects of the case of Larry Eyler, charged in the dismemberment murder of a Chicago teen-ager, is that he worked for a short time recently at a state-licensed facility for developmentally disabled children in Chicago.

Eyler is a suspect in numerous homosexual-related murders in Indiana and was free on bond on another murder charge when arrested. Yet it was not this background that got him fired. It was a four-day absence from the job. His references were not checked until two days after he requested reinstatement.

Given the luxury of hindsight, it seems incredible that a facility caring for disabled children would not have investigated Eyler *before* hiring him. Yet the institution appears to have acted in fairly routine fashion.

Eyler's case reinforces growing concern about employees of agencies and facilities that deal with children. Shocking revelations regarding sexual abuse of very young children have put the spotlight currently on day care centers. Though Marion County has experienced no scandals in that area, officials are justifiably concerned and are stressing the necessity of prevention.

Prosecutor Stephen Goldsmith last week said he would send letters to day care centers and similar agencies reminding them that Indiana law permits them to check police records of present and prospective employees.

Goldsmith also proposed a statewide computer reporting system through which child care agencies could check criminal histories, including reports of child molesting. One questionable part of that proposal is that Goldsmith would include cases not yet prosecuted and employ a six-month purge of information not substantiated.

That smacks of conviction without trial. It seems obvious that any conscientiously cautious agency would fire or refuse to hire anyone listed in the system merely on the basis of an unproven complaint. Exposes elsewhere and an increased filing of charges here ought to alert officials, but what Goldsmith suggests is going too far. Basic legal rights must be protected.

Because most molesting doesn't comes to light until a child reveals it, a series of programs educating children about sexual abuse, what it is and how to report it, could be helpful. But the suggestion from the prosecutor's office that Indianapolis Public Schools adopt the programs should be examined on two scores.

Schools are already charged with too many extra-curricular duties. They should not be burdened with yet another, particularly one that demands considerable sensitivity. Also many parents may be uncomfortable or anxious about how such a program is presented. Parent-teacher organizations, rather than classrooms, would seem a more appropriate channel for such programs.

Responsible public officials should be outraged and shocked at the child abuse being uncovered among staffs and institutions entrusted with the care of our children. Every decent person is. Informational networks and preventive programs are in order. But so is a judicious concern for rights and for the sensibilities of both children and parents.

Sentence Commuted by Illinois Governor in Recanted Rape Case

After having served six years of a 25-to-50-year sentence for rape, Gary Dotson, 28, was freed on bail April 4, 1985 from the Joliet Correctional Facility in suburban Chicago. His release came after his accuser, Cathleen Crowell Webb, testified that the rape had never occurred. Webb filed an affidavit stating that in 1977, fearing that she was pregnant from her first sexual experience at the age of 16, she had invented a rape story to prevent her foster parents from throwing her out of their Chicago-area home. She had torn her clothes and cut her body, she said, to make the story appear authentic. Dotson, whose photo Webb selected from a file of police mug shots, had been convicted after a three-day trial in 1979.

Webb, who had since married, claimed that what had finally led her to tell the truth was her having become a Christian. Her story was found to lack "sufficient corroboration" by the judge who had originally sentenced Dotson, and who now rejected Dotson's petition to have the conviction overturned. The case then went before the Illinois Prisoner Review Board on a petition for executive clemency from Dotson's lawyers. Illinois Governor James Thompson sat in with the board when it met May 9-11; a former prosecutor, the governor himself questioned many of the 24 witnesses, including Webb and Dotson. Thompson and the panel also heard an array of medical evidence, much of it appearing to indicate that Webb had indeed been raped. Thompson decided against a pardon for Dotson, saying he had been "proven guilty beyond a reasonable doubt at his 1979 trial." But he commuted Dotson's sentence after the conclusion of the hearings, although the review board reportedly recommended against clemency. Invoking the need for "mercy," Thompson contended that Dotson had already served more time in prison than the average rapist convicted in Illinois, and that "no good purpose would be served" by his return to prison.

The Hartford Courant

Hartford, CT, May 14, 1985

Illinois Gov. James R. Thompson handled the case of Gary E. Dotson as a sophisticated politician could have been expected to do.

His compromise may delight no one, but it isn't likely to outrage anyone, either, and most people probably will be satisfied.

The governor, who rushed into the controversy by joining the board that heard Mr. Dotson's clemency petition, decided that Mr. Dotson was guilty but that he should be released. The original sentence, 25 to 50 years in prison for rape and aggravated kidnapping, was commuted to the six years Mr. Dotson has served. Without the governor's intervention, or an acquittal in a new trial, he would have remained in prison at least until 1988, when he would have been eligible for parole.

Mr. Dotson, who was accused of raping Cathleen Crowell Webb in 1977, was properly convicted, the governor said, and he found Mrs. Webb's claim to the contrary unbelievable. "If anything," he said, "the evidence at the hearing before the board and me was stronger than at the trial." So why did Mr. Thompson, a former federal prosecutor, commute the sentence?

The governor mentioned mercy, compassion, the longer-than-average term served by Mr. Dotson and his good prison record. But he wasn't kidding anyone. The biggest factor was the enormous outcry that followed a judge's refusal to order a new trial.

Reason, and fairness, dictated treating Mr. Dotson like any other prisoner. That meant pardoning him if the evidence wasn't strong enough, sending him back to prison if he was guilty or commuting his sentence if it was excessively punitive. The governor's reading of the public reaction obviously dictated a fourth option: reaffirming his guilt, but turning him loose.

A new trial, if Mr. Dotson gets one, will demonstrate why he deserved not commutation but a pardon. The evidence simply no longer supports a conviction — there's enough doubt of his guilt, especially because of the recantation of the only state witness, that the prosecution couldn't hope to carry its burden of proof today.

Demanding attention as much as the wrongs done to Mr. Dotson is the criminal justice system that devalued Mrs. Webb's recantation because it came after the trial rather than during it. A heavy bias against recantations seems to exist in courtrooms.

It's there because of a yearning for finality — a need to believe that a crime has been solved, and the guilty party fairly tried and suitably sentenced. Judges and society seem uncomfortable with the notion that someone who was judged guilty and punished may not be guilty. The system minimizes that discomfort by shifting the burden of proof, after the trial, from the state to the person convicted.

There's a lot to be said for finality; if cases were reopened for frivolous reasons, the court system would be in chaos. But there's more to be said for truth and justice. Whenever a witness voluntarily recants decisive testimony in a criminal case, an open-minded reconsideration of the decision to convict is in order.

Chicago Tribune

Chicago, IL, May 14, 1985

The lurid televised hearings on Gary Dotson's clemency petition begged for a dazzling finish, somebody breaking down on the stand and sobbing out a confession or the introduction of a stunning piece of surprise evidence that made everything suddenly become clear.

But, of course, the melodrama didn't play itself out that way. The hearings only magnified the sense of doubt—doubt about what exactly happened the night Cathleen Crowell Webb claimed she was raped; doubt about why years later Mrs. Webb recanted her testimony against Mr. Dotson; doubt about Gov. Thompson's motives in commanding the center stage in the proceedings; doubt about whether all those exceedingly private, often sexually explicit details should have been set out under the unrelenting glare of live television.

As to the events of the night of July 9, 1977, if the clemency hearings had been Gary Dotson's trial, all that doubt should certainly have led to a verdict that Mr. Dotson was not guilty of raping Mrs. Webb. In a criminal case, the state must prove the guilt of the accused beyond a reasonable doubt. And in this case, the doubts were more than reasonable; they were downright haunting.

But the clemency hearings weren't like a criminal trial. When Gov. Thompson interrogated witnesses, he did not have to adhere to the strict judicial rules of evidence. He served as both Perry Mason and Hamilton Berger. And in the process, he made the case that everyone was predicting he would. He cast a shadow on Mrs. Webb's recantation and set the stage for granting a commutation of Mr. Dotson's sentence without determining that he was innocent.

In a clemency hearing, he said, doubts should be resolved against the defendant, whose burden it is to prove the "substantial likelihood" of his innocence. That is a legal point that the scholars probably ought to discuss. But it allowed Gov. Thompson to make a decision that freed Gary Dotson and yet asserted the fundamental fairness of the legal proceedings that had kept him in jail. Solomon might have seen the wisdom of such a judgment, at least if Solomon had had to stand for election.

And that, of course, is what gave rise to the skepticism about Gov. Thompson's performance. The televised hearings showed him still to be an expert litigator. His questioning was thorough—sometimes painfully, explicitly so. It was almost always to the point, though in a few telling instances he lapsed into making points that were overtly political and utterly inappropriate. Perhaps if he hadn't slipped, it would have been possible to resolve the doubt in his favor and say that he was not interested in the publicity. But the evidence of his motives was there for everyone to see. And happily, the law doesn't establish a burden of proof on that point.

It was a strange spectacle, one that no one ought to be eager to see repeated. Next Saturday morning, parents can feel comfortable letting their children watch television again without the risk that the cartoons of animals and imaginary creatures will suddenly be preempted by a detailed description of the sexual act. But perhaps there was a public value in the exercise, for it showed how difficult it is for the law to come to a judgment, how factually and psychologically complex a case like this can be. And that is the beginning of wisdom, not only about the law but about the secrets of the human heart.

THE ARIZONA REPUBLIC

Phoenix, AZ, May 16, 1985

AUTHOR Henry James thought there was a constant force in the universe that makes for muddlement. That force must have been at work in the Gary Dotson-Cathleen Crowell Webb case.

Like Alice's trip through the looking glass, it just keeps getting curiouser and curiouser.

Illinois Gov. James Thompson gave in to public pressure when he commuted Dotson's sentence to time served despite the fact that as a skilled prosecutor, Thompson found the case abounding with ambiguities and questionable motives.

Thompson said he did not believe Webb's story, although it is difficult to imagine what motive could be behind her insistence on holding herself up to public humiliation.

Thompson, despite his reservations about the recantation and Dotson's innocence, had little choice but to free the accused. Since Webb's accusation was, in absence of conclusive corroborating physical evidence, the chief evidence against Dotson, Thompson had to release the convicted rapist on the strength of Webb's claims.

When any reasonable doubt exists, it is always best to err on the side of releasing the guilty than imprisoning the innocent.

It should be carefully noted, however, that Thompson commuted the sentence and did not extend a pardon. A retrial could establish Dotson's guilt or innocence, although he cannot be sent to prison again even if he is convicted.

Perhaps the most troublesome aspect of the case — aside from any personal tragedy for the principals involved — is that the whole of the justice system may come under criticism because of the mess in Illinois. If Webb wasn't raped, justice surely was.

Already there has been another case of a rape conviction being recanted in Washington, Pa.

There exists the real possibility that such cases may cause police, prosecutors and jurors to view the accusations of rape victims with a greater degree of skepticism. Juries might in the future be less willing to believe the testimony of the rapist's victim, thereby making prosecutions and convictions even more difficult to obtain.

It may be that after all the TV and magazine contracts are signed, it will be future rape victims who will suffer the most as a result of the Dotson-Webb muddle.

The Dispatch

Columbus, OH, May 17, 1985

Illinois Gov. James R. Thompson decided that — guilty or innocent — Gary Dotson had had enough and commuted the convicted rapist's 25- to 50-year prison sentence.

That decision, probably the best under the difficult set of circumstances, rescued the Illinois criminal justice system from its trying ordeal in the court of public opinion.

What it did not do was resolve conclusively the questions of who did what to whom and will Dotson have to bear the stigma of a felony conviction for a rape the victim now claims he didn't commit?

Cathleen Crowell Webb, the pivotal figure in what has become a national soap opera, claimed that as a 16-year-old she fabricated the rape story to cover a pregnancy she feared had resulted from voluntary sex with her boyfriend — an act the former boyfriend told. Thompson never was completed.

The Illinois governor presided at a rare, public clemency hearing after the judge who originally heard the case and sentenced Dotson declined to overturn the conviction based on Webb's recanted testimony.

The public outcry was understandable. An act of rape is the most personal of violent crimes, but it has one victim and when that victim says it never happened, the public sympathy is with the person confined to prison for an offense that didn't occur or was commited by someone else.

But Webb's story — what story there was — was hardly convincing. She could recall little of the events leading up to Dotson's conviction. Where her memory of the details surrounding the rape and the injuries she suffered was explicit and unshakable six years earlier, now she could scarcely remember anything.

Thompson, a former U.S. attorney, grilled her relentlessly, but in the end admitted he wasn't convinced. Lacking vital testimony that might have enabled him to pardon Dotson outright, Thompson took the convenient route of commutation. It took the heat off him and Illinois, but upheld the dignity and findings of the court and jury that convicted Dotson.

"I believe Cathleen Crowell Webb was raped ... if anything the evidence before me was even stronger ... (and) I'm satisfied Dotson was proved guilty beyond a reasonable doubt," Thompson concluded.

Dotson and his mother, who would have had it otherwise, were nonetheless relieved that his prison days were over. He is free to seek a new trial or appeal his conviction to a higher court. It is doubtful any prosecutor would proceed with a new trial considering the burden of proving not only that Dotson had raped Webb, but that Webb was lying when she said he hadn't.

A curious public may never know what really happened or whether the trial court did its job well or poorly. Webb, a born-again Christian, said she was anxious to clear her conscience and right a terrible wrong, whatever embarrassment it caused her. But her insistence the rape never occurred was hampered by the inability to recall details that would have strengthened her denial.

Is she was raped, as Thompson is convinced, who did it and why isn't she saying? If she wasn't, why was the circumstantial evidence, including her injuries, her demeanor after the attack, her identification of Dotson and a companion, and the presence of semen on her undergarments so convincing?

Women who have struggled with the many miseries that extend beyond an actual rape — the stigma, the trial ordeal, the prejudice that the victims somehow provoked or encouraged their attackers — view the Webb-Dotson case as a setback. That seems unlikely. It was an isolated situation and a highly unusual one. Webb at 16 was by her own admission a confused and promiscuous adolescent. Her impact in reordering social attitudes toward rape is likely to be minimal.

As for Dotson, the wrong or wronged man — if he is indeed that — central Ohioans have seen similar scenarios played out twice in recent years. William Bernard Jackson served about five years for crimes of which Dr. Edward Jackson was subsequently convicted. Bradley C. Cox of Lancaster, Ohio, served two years for crimes later confessed by Jon B. Simonis of Lake Charles, La., the so-called "ski mask rapist."

On balance, Thompson did what was best for everyone concerned. While the public appetite for the real answers will remain, the potential for grave injustice — beyond the six years Dotson already served — has been erased and the opportunity for true vindication strengthened.

THE MILWAUKEE JOURNAL

Milwaukee, WI, May 27, 1985

The Illinois Senate apparently does not agree that Gary Dotson, the man convicted of a rape that may never have happened, has been punished enough.

State senators have passed a bill to prevent him from directly benefiting from selling his story. The bill would channel any money he receives into a special fund to help crime victims. Present law apparently would withhold any money from Dotson for two years, while funds were held in escrow for possible awards to his victim. In the special circumstances of the case, the change seems mean-spirited.

Cathleen Crowell Webb, who accused Dotson of raping her, now says there never was a rape. Dotson's sentence has been commuted to time served, but he insists that he wants to clear his name.

As a general rule, a wrongdoer should not profit from crime, Yet it is inappropriate to use Dotson's case to tighten restrictions. We think there is sufficient doubt about the evidence on which he was convicted — even apart from Webb's recantation — to justify a new trial. Moreover, in light of Dotson's proclaimed intention to use the money for legal expenses, lawmakers seem as bent on depriving him of needed resources as they are determined to help crime victims.

AKRON BEACON JOURNAL
Akron, OH, May 19, 1985

THE PUZZLING case of Gary Dotson and the recanted rape testimony of Cathleen Crowell Webb may ultimately have some significance for America's criminal justice system. But the case says something right now about our society: Anyone can be a celebrity if his name is repeated often enough.

What began as a matter of concern and sympathy — rape victim admits she lied and mounts a campaign to free her alleged attacker — has now become merely tiresome.

The new testimony of both Dotson and Mrs. Webb revealed serious credibility problems. One judge heard the recanted testimony and still declared that the conviction should stand. Illinois Gov. James Thompson conducted his own review of the case, didn't particularly believe either party, but decided — Solomon-like — to commute the sentence rather than grant a full pardon.

It's the type of notoriety that, in our culture, inevitably leads to celebrity status.

The evidence of this came last week as Mrs. Webb and Dotson made the rounds of national network morning talk shows. NBC's *Today* footed the bill to bring the two and their families to New York; but a limousine whisked them also to ABC's *Good Morning America* and *The CBS Morning News* so they could appear on all three on the same day.

In addition, Dotson has received 41 offers from producers interested in a television movie of his life. Fortunately, Illinois has an enlightened law that requires any earnings from crime ventures to go into a fund to compensate the criminal's victims. If Dotson can get a new trial and win an acquittal, presumably he can keep the money. If he doesn't, would the money compensate Mrs. Webb, who is technically — though reluctantly — the victim?

The case is a puzzle that may change the way we look at rape laws, at victims' testimony, perhaps at the jury system itself. But that doesn't solve the other matter of celebrity status, which has a life of its own.

When CBS co-host Phyllis George urged Dotson and Mrs. Webb to shake hands on the air, for instance, they complied. Fortunately they refused her urgings to hug each other, which only proves that there are some standards of dignity among celebrities if not among talk show hosts. Such spectacles, however, trivialize serious matters: a person's guilt or innocence, the integrity of our justice system, even the progress made in prosecuting rape. The glare of the spotlight sheds too little light on those concerns.

THE DENVER POST
Denver, CO, May 15, 1985

ILLINOIS Gov. James Thompson's commutation of the rape sentence of Gary Dotson was an appropriate easing of a penalty in a case afflicted with unending uncertainty.

After a meticulous review of the case, Thompson announced he believed Dotson was properly convicted in 1979 and that he does not believe the claim of the alleged victim, Cathleen Crowell Webb, that the rape never happened. Yet, he commuted Dotson's sentence to the six years Dotson already has served.

Thompson had good reason to doubt Dotson's innocence. The physical evidence in the original trial was impressive. The nature of the wounds on Webb's body belies her present claim that they were self-inflicted. A careful rehearing by the trial judge as well as three days of testimony before Thompson himself failed to shake the original evidence.

The sole new evidence in Dotson's favor is Webb's confused and contradictory recantation. But while Webb doubtless believes what she now says, her change of story could well spring from a deep psychological phenomenon. Her confused mental state probably makes it impossible ever to determine the truth in this case beyond a reasonable doubt. The six years Dotson already has spent in prison is longer than the average time served on rape convictions in Illinois, and his prison record was good.

On balance, Thompson concluded rightly that returning Dotson to prison would do even more harm to public confidence in the justice system.

The Oregonian
Portland, OR, May 17, 1985

Illinois Gov. James Thompson did Solomon a step better. Forced to decide whether convicted rapist Gary Dotson did the crime and belonged in jail or didn't do it and deserved to be free, Thompson split the baby in two, judging that Dotson did do it but nevertheless deserved to go free.

Given the conflicting testimony surrounding the recantation of the once-but-no-more victim, Cathleen Webb, Thompson's improvisation on Solomon is at least politically understandable. Nevertheless, the case has a potential for injury that far exceeds its principal players.

Attorneys and law professors are now predicting that the widespread publicity surrounding the strange and confusing case may make juries more skeptical of women who say they have been raped. Paul Rothstein, a professor at Georgetown University Law Center, suggests, "Juries are going to look at every rape victim . . . and say, 'Is this person we believed today going to make fools of us tomorrow?'"

Women have expended an enormous amount of effort to convince legislatures, law enforcement agencies and the public that rape is a serious crime that merits serious penalty. It was not so long ago that rape victims were often believed to have contributed to the commission of the crime against them. One aberrant case — no matter how perversely captivating it is — must not be allowed to turn the clock backward.

THE KANSAS CITY STAR
Kansas City, MO, May 22, 1985

The prison sentence of Gary Dotson for a rape the victim now says did not occur has been commuted by Gov. James Thompson of Illinois. That was an appropriate decision, given the circumstances of this highly unusual case, though if Mr. Dotson is actually innocent his case has not been fully resolved.

His request was rejected for an immediate hearing by the Illinois Supreme Court on appeal of the lower court ruling that upheld his 1979 conviction. He is also seeking a new circuit court trial on the rape charge. Meanwhile Illinois authorities are investigating the case, including comments of a former cellmate of Mr. Dotson.

Governor Thompson, in commuting the sentence, took the middle, logical ground. He could have granted Mr. Dotson a full pardon, an act that would have freed him from further punishment.

Conflicting testimony developed at the clemency hearing, personally attended by the chief executive. Yet it would have seemed unjust to keep Mr. Dotson in prison after Cathleen Crowell Webb recanted her testimony that led to Mr. Dotson's conviction in 1979. Further, the governor noted the six years that Mr. Dotson served is longer than many rapists are imprisoned.

The justice system can appear at times to be inflexible — as perhaps it should be. In this instance there was a procedure, ably handled by Governor Thompson, to provide an acceptable remedy.

The Providence Journal
Providence, RI, May 17, 1985

The most wretched person in the nation these days should be Cathleen Webb. She tried but failed to convince the governor of Illinois that she was telling the truth about lying eight years ago. Gov. James Thompson concluded after three days of testimony that, contrary to her story, she had been raped. Whatever the truth may be, her credibility has all but vanished.

Instead of retiring within her family for a bout of contemplation and contrition, however, Mrs. Webb has been cavorting about New York City with her erstwhile rapist Gary Dotson in tow. They have traded apologies and thank-yous on all the network morning talk shows.

Mrs. Webb put herself out on a pretty risky limb when she insisted that the plot of any future movie would have to ratify her version of events — that she was not raped, that she made it all up and, eight years later, decided to tell the truth. Not that she needed to worry: movie moguls tend to base even the most factually oriented films not on the most relevant facts but on the most

Mrs. Webb put herself on a pretty risky limb

entertaining facts. Still, for her to insist on *her* version of the facts speaks poorly of her own confidence in the credibility others place in that version.

And what are the facts? Governor Thompson heard three days of testimony and concluded she was not telling the truth, that her recantation was fiction and that her rape was real. So while Mr. Dotson is free, it is by no means clear that he did not rape Mrs. Webb back in 1977.

This leering media treatment that he and Mrs. Webb are receiving may seriously hinder the chances of future rape victims to obtain justice. This treatment is giving credence to the idea that Mrs. Webb's recantation was truthful, and that she lied about being raped because she thought she might be pregnant after having had sex with her boyfriend. This view may be true or false. Nevertheless, its constant reiteration on television and eventually in other media can easily weaken the credibility of rape victims in the minds of jurors who must seek the truth at trial.

Roanoke Times & World-News
Roanoke, VA, May 16, 1985

GARY DOTSON is free. In March, Cathleen Crowell Webb said that she lied in 1977 when she identified him as the man who'd raped her. Since then, we've seen a series of bizarre events and statements that have now led Illinois Gov. James Thompson to commute Dotson's sentence. In doing so, Thompson has not declared that Dotson is innocent; he has said that the six years Dotson has already served are enough punishment. In this instance, it was the easiest thing Thompson could have done. It was also the right thing for him to do.

This entire affair has been examined so closely and so much contradictory evidence and testimony have been presented that it's impossible to state a single indisputable, unequivocal version of what happened on July 9, 1977. There are too many doubts, too many subjective interpretations. The sensational aspects of the case were inevitable, because of the rollercoaster nature of the proceedings: Dotson's being released on bail, then sent back to prison and shifted from one jail to another. While he was being shuffled around, Webb was appearing on virtually all of the television talk shows and explaining that she'd lied before, but was telling the truth now. Was it that simple, though?

● Her stepfather, who was nominally in charge of her when the alleged rape occurred, called her a liar, and suggested that she was being manipulated by her lawyer. The lawyer does stand to gain through possible book royalties and the movie that will almost certainly be made for television. At the same time, though, the stepfather's tone seemed a bit vindictive, and whatever his opinions on the subject, he could hardly be expected to be objective.

● Webb said that her wounds were self-inflicted. But in 1977, she was diagnosed as having internal injuries that her new story cannot explain.

● She said that she invented the rape charge in the first place because she was afraid she was pregnant by her boyfriend. He claims, however, that they never completed intercourse, and the timing of their meetings was wrong for semen stain found on her underwear to have been his.

● All of the physical evidence, including the semen stain and seven pubic hairs taken from her body on the night of the rape, is inconclusive as to Dotson's guilt or innocence.

● Most rape recantation testimony is suspect, since it normally comes within a few days or weeks of the crime, but Webb's is different. She waited years before coming forward and claims that she's telling the truth now because of her recent religious conversion.

Thompson, a former federal and state prosecutor, heard all the evidence and decided to let Dotson go. He said that his decision has "nothing to do with guilt or innocence. It has to do with the larger quality of mercy, of compassion for one's fellow man." In the absence of convincing truth, compassion has to be the controlling factor. There's no reason to believe that Dotson is especially dangerous now. His freedom is subject to good behavior and, for the immediate future at least, all three networks and the Phil Donahue show will tell us if he so much as jaywalks. Also, there is no wronged victim demanding justice. Webb and Dotson have reversed those roles.

No, in the middle of all this uncertainty, it would be terribly unfair to leave him in jail and, possibly, just as unfair to exonerate him. From Thompson's point of view, it might have been more politically advantageous to pardon Dotson, but the conflicting evidence doesn't justify it. In the same way, the doubts raised by Webb's statements don't justify Dotson's serving more time. About all we can say for sure is that somewhere in the process, a mistake was made. At the very least, letting Gary Dotson go free now compounds that mistake less than any other course of action would.

THE LOUISVILLE TIMES
*Louisville, KY,
May 17, 1985*

As a former federal prosecutor, James R. Thompson was uniquely qualified to lead the inquiry into the case of convicted rapist Gary Dotson, whose accuser now says the crime never happened.

The result was a Solomon-like decision with which few can quarrel. In commuting Mr. Dotson's 25- to 50-year sentence to the six years served, the Illinois governor observed that "no good purpose" would have been served by keeping Mr. Dotson in prison. Yet, despite Cathleen Crowell Webb's recantation, enough doubt remains — based on evidence aside from Mrs. Webb's trial testimony — to suggest that Gov. Thompson was justified in denying Mr. Dotson a pardon.

In effect, the governor returned the Dotson case to the courts, where properly it should be decided. Mr. Dotson is expected to press for a new trial.

Although justice appears to have been well-served, this case is not without its troubling elements. Many of the early news accounts greatly oversimplified its issues. This led to widespread, uninformed criticism of the trial judge who refused to overturn Mr. Dotson's conviction. The news media and public both have now been reminded of some of the basics of the justice system.

Newsweek reports that Mrs. Webb's belated recantation is already having an effect on the conduct of rape trials that some fear may threaten victim-rights gains of the last decade. According to Prof. Susan Estrich of Harvard, "The whole effort at reforming rape laws has been an attack on the premise that women who bring complaints are suspect. There's no proof whatsoever that rape complaints are more unfounded than those of any other crimes. Now Webb will be used to lend credence to all the fundamentally sexist assumptions about women."

Much more will, undoubtedly, be heard in the months to come about the Dotson-Webb case. On Gov. Thompson's role, at least, the verdict is clear.

Supreme Court Upholds Georgia Sodomy Law

The Supreme Court June 30, 1986 refused to extend the right of privacy inherent in the Constitution to homosexual activity. Newspaper editorialists around the nation were quick to draw a connection between the ruling and acquired immune deficiency Syndrome (AIDS), which is often contracted through sodomy anal and oral sex. In addition, they focused their attention on the ruling, which, by a 5-4 vote, upheld a Georgia law that made sodomy a crime, punishable by as long as 20 years in prison. "We are quite unwilling," Justice Byron R. White said in the majority opinion, to assert "a fundamental right to engage in homosexual sodomy." Justice Harry A. Blackmun, in a heated dissent, said the case was not about whether there was a fundamental right to engage in homosexual sodomy but "about 'the most comprehensive of rights, and the right most valued valued by civilized men,' namely, 'the right to be left alone.' The right of an individual to conduct intimate relationships in the intimacy of his or her home seems to me to be the heart of the Constitution's protection of privacy," Blackmun said.

Although the Constitution contained no specific mention of a right to privacy, the Supreme Court had taken a stand since 1965 that it was implicit in the Bill of Rights. Thus a right of personal privacy had been recognized for married couples in a 1965 ruling. A woman's right to abortion also was based on the right of privacy. But the court ruled out any such right in this case. "Any claim...that any kind of private sexual conduct between consenting adults is constitutionally insulated from state proscription is unsupportable," White said. The privacy right did not "reach so far," he said.

The opinion rested mainly on the established precedent of state laws making sodomy illegal—from the 13 original states in 1791, when the Bill of Rights was ratified, to 1986, when 23 other states had laws similar to Georgia's outlawing sodomy. Blackmun said the long history of antisodomy laws did not mean that the laws were proper or the court should accept them. The court had held in other cases, he said, "that mere public intolerance or animosity cannot constitutionally justify the deprivation of a person's physical liberty." Actually, the Georgia law covered heterosexual sodomy as well as homosexual sodomy, a fact pointed out by Blackmun. The court's decision opinion did not rule out enforcement of the sodomy laws in Georgia and most other states against heterosexual activity. But this had not been the practice in the past.

The Record

Hackensack, NJ, July 2, 1986

In 1969, police raided a homosexual social club in Greenwich Village called the Stonewall. It was no different from anything they had done scores of times before. They would simply bust in, arrest the proprietor, disperse the patrons, and padlock the door. No rough stuff, nothing dangerous, just a clear message that the authorities would not sit idly by and allow their city to degenerate into a Sodom-on-the-Hudson.

But this time, instead of accepting their fate meekly as they had so many times before, the gays rebelled. After years of being shoved around by cops, sidewalk preachers, and streetcorner John Waynes, they shoved back. For two nights running, they threw bottles and stones and chalked "gay power" on the walls. The ferocity of the protest astonished the police and, for that matter, probably astonished the gays as well. In hindsight, Stonewall can be seen as a turning point in American social history. Not only was it the birth of the gay-rights movement; it was an affirmation, since widely accepted throughout society, that the sexual practices of consenting adults are their own business. The job of the police is to prevent crime and guard the public's safety, not to go snooping in bedrooms.

This week we had another turning point — in the opposite direction. By the narrowest of margins, the Supreme Court upheld a Georgia state law forbidding "sodomy" between consenting adult homosexuals. Not merely is it the state's job to "establish justice, insure domestic tranquility, provide for the common defense," in the language of the Constitution; Justices White, Burger, Powell, Rehnquist, and O'Connor have now told the states that they're free to supervise bedroom intimacies. From Atlanta to Boston, Trenton to Sacramento, legislatures may now draw up rules as to who may engage in sex and how they may do it.

What next? State laws on how often and in what position? A statute relegating sex to certain hours of the late evening? Perhaps an official handbook on sexual rules and regulations for Atlanta and portions of adjacent De Kalb County? Of more immediate concern, if gay sex is illegal in Georgia, can the authorities there now go after gay-bar owners for promoting a criminal conspiracy?

Seventeen years after Stonewall, it seems, we can expect more such raids, this time with the approval of the U.S. Supreme Court. You'd think that if the right of privacy means anything, it is the right to engage in consensual sex in the confines of one's home. But now the Supreme Court says no. It is a giant step backward.

THE INDIANAPOLIS NEWS

Indianapolis, IN, July 5, 1986

Indiana once had a sodomy law on its books that was similar to the Georgia law that the U.S. Supreme Court narrowly upheld earlier this week.

In its wisdom, the Indiana General Assembly repealed that law more than a decade ago. One of the incidents that led to the sentiment to repeal the law was the filing of criminal charges by a disgruntled wife against her husband, charging him with committing sodomy on her.

Legislators concluded that the state had no business in bedrooms of private individuals, refereeing their most intimate conduct.

From a strict constructionist point of view, the Supreme Court's 5-4 refusal to strike down archaic sodomy laws in Georgia and 23 other states is understandable.

As noted in the majority opinion, until the 1960s every state had an anti-sodomy law on its books; thus, there can be no claim that such statutes violate a traditional right to privacy. Furthermore, the U.S. Constitution does not expressly grant a right to privacy.

But clearly, a presumption of privacy permeates the Constitution.

As former Justice Louis D. Brandeis wrote many years ago, the right to be left alone is perhaps "the most comprehensive of rights and the right most valued by civilized men."

Another reason why sodomy laws should be stricken from the books has to do with selective enforcement of such laws.

According to various surveys, nearly 80 percent of all adults have at one time or another violated such strictures. Yet, virtually no one is ever prosecuted.

In Georgia, there had not been a prosecution for violation of the law in the last half century. The state even declined to pursue its prosecution of the individual whose arrest instigated the lawsuit challenging the sodomy statute.

And, finally, the Supreme Court would do well to practice a little consistency.

Only a few weeks ago the court struck down another state statute that required physicians to read a fairly innocuous statement about abortion procedures and alternatives to abortions to women seeking to undergo an abortion. The court ruled that such a requirement violated a woman's right to privacy.

How the court can square that decision with the reasoning in the Georgia case is a mystery.

THE SACRAMENTO BEE
Sacramento, CA, July 3, 1986

The Supreme Court's narrow decision to uphold Georgia's sodomy law is hardly surprising. This is not a court prone to assert socially controversial rights, much less open new constitutional territory. Nor, to be fair, was it an easy decision to make. The issue here, after all, was not the wisdom of a law forbidding oral or anal sex between consenting adults, but the question of whether such conduct — conduct offensive to many people — is nonetheless constitutionally protected in the privacy of one's own home.

But that makes the decision no less frustrating — frustrating not only because it's wrong but because it leaves so many other issues unresolved. The court's majority dwelt on the homosexual aspects of the Georgia law: It was a homosexual, Michael Hardwick, who brought the case, and Justice White, in his lead opinion, chose to emphasize again and again that none of its previous privacy decisions — in cases involving contraception and abortion, for example — "bears any resemblance to the claimed constitutional right of homosexuals to engage in acts of sodomy that is asserted in this case."

But the Georgia law does not single out homosexuals, nor, in fairness, could it really do so. It simply defines the act. As Justice Blackmun pointed out in his dissent, "The sex or status of the persons who engage in the act is irrelevant." Its targets, indeed, seem to have included both heterosexual and homosexual conduct. Hardwick's claim that the law involves an unconstitutional intrusion into his privacy, therefore, "does not depend in any way on his sexual orientiation."

Which is to say that the law could be applied to anyone, and thus opens what is probably a majority of sexually active adults to the danger of prosecution. The fact that such laws are probably used selectively — against homosexuals in most cases, against other unpopular or vulnerable individuals in others — doesn't mitigate that danger. On the contrary it makes enforcement of such statutes all the more invidious.

The real issue in this case, therefore, is not homosexual sodomy but, as Justice Blackmun said, about the right to be let alone. The right is essential because it constitutes "a central part of an individual life . . . The fact that individuals define themselves in a significant way through their intimate sexual relationships with others suggests, in a nation as diverse as ours, that there may be many 'right' ways of conducting those relationships, and that much of the rightness of a relationship will come from the freedom an individual has to choose the form and nature of these intensely personal bonds."

The majority in this case argues that if sodomy is constitutionally protected, then incest must be, too. But that analogy is patently false: Incest and the acts prohibited by the Georgia law don't fall into the same moral, political or medical categories. Where intimate sexual relationships are conducted in private and where they carry with them no greater social hazard, as incest surely would, the attempt of the state to interfere creates many more dangers — dangers to individuals, dangers of social controversy — than it prevents. The Hardwick decision ends a generation that enlarged the right of privacy and gave new heart to official tolerance in America. The eye of the state is back in the bedroom.

The Kansas City Times
Kansas City, MO, July 2, 1986

The Supreme Court has made a pronouncement in an area, that of human intimacy, which it has no business regulating. Neither majority behavior, nor the existence of old local laws, nor religious dictates is adequate defense for institutionalizing discrimination.

Now, unless state and municipal leaders are courageous in separating civil rights from sexual behavior through statute and ordinance, the fair treatment of homosexuals — and eventually, perhaps, heterosexuals — is at risk of moving backward.

If the Supreme Court ruling on homosexual conduct is to be applied narrowly and strictly to that minority in this society, such people may well face increased bias on many sides, from employment to housing. This upholding of the Georgia sodomy law can, at the least, lend its flavor to every public dealing with gays.

If the ruling is, however, as dissenting Justice Harry A. Blackmun wrote, not at all about homosexual sodomy but about privacy and people's right to be different, it is a sad Independence Day prelude.

Undoubtedly, justification for the court interpretation will be found on many sides by those who view intimacy between people of the same sex as abhorrent. What is anathema to the court will carry weight in ostracizing AIDS sufferers.

Moreover, thoughtful Americans will find more questions than solutions in this decision. Is similar heterosexual practice protected under constitutional guarantees when homosexual practice is not? Many state laws, including Georgia's, say it isn't. What other areas presumed to be personal might next be raised to the public stage? If intimacy and the home are not private, what is?

In its anxiety to avoid breaking new ground, or "discover new fundamental rights" in the Constitution, the court apparently has made exactly the mighty leap it said it wanted to avoid.

In upholding Georgia's way, the high court found no constitutional protection for this conduct by homosexuals. The law was challenged as an intrusion into individuals' right to privacy.

How are these lawbreakers to be discovered and charged? There is, after all, a Fourth Amendment in the Bill of Rights. It says that "The right of people to be secure in their persons, houses, papers and effects, against unreasonable searches and seizures, shall not be violated. . . . " Surely the Constitution takes precedence over the Georgia Legislature's notion as to what is immoral and therefore a crime.

FIVE members of the Supreme Court have ruled that states may punish homosexual conduct in the bedroom as a crime; four say the decision intrudes on privacy.

That division may be fairly close to the general split of public opinion on the issue, even though sex between persons of the same gender was once universally condemned by law throughout the United States. Now, 24 states and the District of Columbia still have laws against homosexual conduct, while 26 states have moved away from them.

IT IS UNCLEAR how the court majority's opinion affects certain sexual practices between consenting heterosexual couples.

The ruling in a Georgia case obviously was intended to apply to homosexual conduct. But the state law that the court upheld prohibits sodomy without reference to whether it is between homosexuals or heterosexuals.

In any event, the decision is unlikely to change sexual practices in the privacy of American bedrooms to any appreciable degree. Police will not be any more inclined now to peep into windows to see what sort of activity is going on than they were before.

In fact, the Georgia case came before the court largely by accident. The homosexual who challenged the law was arrested after a police officer saw him having sexual relations in his bedroom with another man when the officer came to serve a warrant on an unrelated legal matter.

What would be unfortunate is if the Supreme Court's action leads to a round of homosexual bashing and a circumscription of civil rights for a segment of the population whose sexual preferences are different from the norm. To some extent this is already happening because of the AIDS scare.

The majority opinion, written by Justice Byron White, said no judgment was being made on whether state laws against sodomy are wise or desirable. What White said the majority wanted to make clear is that the Constitution does not provide a fundamental right to engage in homosexual sodomy.

WRITING FOR the four dissenting members, Justice Harry Blackmun said that the majority misread what the case was about. He said the case is about "the most comprehensive of rights and the most valued by civilized men" — "the right to be let alone."

Recognizing that people can differ on such an emotional issue, we are inclined to believe that Justice Blackmun is on the better track. Sexual activities between consenting adults in the privacy of the bedroom should not be the government's concern.

The Chattanooga Times

Chattanooga, TN, July 5, 1986

The Supreme Court, in a bitterly divided 5-to-4 vote, has upheld a Georgia law that declares sodomy between consenting adults a crime. But the ruling rests on a shaky, if not fatally narrow, premise: that "the respondent (the original plaintiff in this case) would have us announce . . . a fundamental right to engage in homosexual sodomy." That was not the issue in this case at all. As Justice Harry Blackmun wrote in an eloquent dissent, quoting the late Justice Louis Brandeis from an earlier case, the litigation decided Monday is about "the most comprehensive of rights and the most valued by civilized men," namely "the right to be left alone."

It is easy, but intellectually lazy, to use this decision as a vehicle for condemning the practice of sodomy, which as defined by the Georgia law involved both oral and anal sex. But condemnation of such practices breaks no new ground. Many religions, including Judaism and Christianity, prohibit sexual relations between members of the same sex as violations of divine law. Such prohibitions still stand despite the seemingly increased prevalence of homosexuality.

But as Justice Blackmun pointed out, the Georgia law at issue does not address itself solely to homosexual activity; the language is broad enough to encompass such activity even if it is engaged in by a heterosexual couple. In that regard, therefore, the real issue becomes the extent to which a state can regulate private and intensely personal actions among adults. It is irrelevant that states are unlikely to set up "bedroom patrols" to search for instances of illegal sexual behavior. The point is that the court has dramatically restricted the rights of privacy it has previously enunciated — in cases involving decisions, such as contraception, that only individuals can make, and in cases involving certain

places without regard for particular activities engaged in by the occupants.

Georgia argued that its law should be upheld because the actions it prohibits have been condemned as "immoral" for centuries. But the mere fact that a majority of society condemns an essentially *victimless* act, and has done so for years, does not necessarily mean that the majority can impose that view on others, even if the view is rooted in a religious base. Justice Blackmun argues persuasively that"the legitimacy of secular legislation depends instead on whether the state can advance some justification for its law beyond its conformity to religious doctrine." And later: "A state can no more punish private behavior because of religious intolerance than it can punish such behavior because of racial animus."

The state's legitimate right to protect public sensibilities justifies laws barring sexual activities in public places. Similarly, it has the right to protect individuals, particularly minors, from actions committed in privacy, even in the home, such as sexual abuse of children. But there is a difference between those responsibilities, and attempts by the state to enforce laws against persons who happen not to accept the values of a majority of society.

Since 1961, 26 states have repealed laws prohibiting homosexual acts of the sort included in the Georgia law. Does that mean the residents of those states approve of such conduct? Of course not. It simply means they saw no point in retaining unenforceable laws and, more important, that the state has more important things to do than attempt to regulate what consenting adults do in private. The Supreme Court's decision is a regrettable step backward in the protection of privacy.

The Saginaw News

Saginaw, MI, July 7, 1986

Nowhere is a right to privacy mentioned in the U.S. Constitution. But a Supreme Court majority still reasons from those grounds in affirming, for instance, a woman's right to abortion.

Within the broad scope of the document, justices can usually find what they choose to find.

Last week Justice Byron White chose to be blind to the implications of his opinion upholding anti-sodomy laws in Georgia, and thus in Michigan and 22 other states.

Most immediately, the 5-4 decision has brought fears that the decision could validate, even encourage, campaigns of repression against homosexuals.

Gays have cause for concern. A Justice Department ruling appears to allow employers to fire homosexuals virtually at will. In California, a LaRouchite ballot initiative would authorize the quarantine of gays. Now, if legislatures can outlaw homosexual behavior, why not homosexuals?

Other adults, though, should not dismiss the ruling as of no concern to them. As an American Bar Association analysis stressed, "This is much more than a homosexual rights case. At stake is the question of how far a state can regulate all private, consensual, adult sexual behavior and whether a bedroom is safer from police intrusion than a bar room or the street."

No, it isn't, replied the court.

Over the past 60 years, the justices had created a "zone of privacy" where government cannot g ,

without compelling cause. The only cause cited by Georgia was that of "traditions and moral values."

But whose morality? What "tradition" can be forced on people who do not share it? Whose business is it, anyway, what adults do in their own homes — or, for that matter, in a private camp?

The argument, as the ABA summed up, comes down to "whether, in a free and pluralistic society, private morality is to be determined by the majority or the individual."

That's why the decision involves more than sodomy laws. Those are hardly ever enforced anyway. Even the Georgia plaintiff was never prosecuted. The bedroom police are not yet at the door. But if this case signals a new court direction, then it means any personal — and private — adult behavior could be banned.

The court majority may not intend such a broad reading of this ruling. But the Georgia law did not distinguish betwen gays and others. Neither do Michigan's related statutes.

The high court's verdict warns once again that restrictions against one group, no matter how despised, can limit the rights of all. And what's at stake here is nothing less fundamental than, as Justice Harry Blackmun said in dissent, "the right to be let alone." If the other justices look hard enough, they'll find that, too, is in the tradition of the Constitution.

ST. LOUIS POST-DISPATCH

St. Louis, MO, July 2, 1986

The U.S. Supreme Court's decision upholding a Georgia sodomy law is appalling for what it does to the right of privacy, which the high court over many years has been expanding. Twenty-three states besides Georgia — including Missouri — have sodomy laws, some of them applying to heterosexual as well as homosexual conduct. But for the most part, they are not enforced, because they are unenforceable without government intrusion into the bedroom. Now the Supreme Court has in effect given government a license to invade homes and police private morals.

As Justice Blackmun said for the dissenters in the 5-4 decision, the ruling is an attack on the most fundamental right of all — the right to be let alone. Besides threatening the right of privacy, the decision will help to legitimize discrimination against homosexuals. As one gay rights spokesman suggested, courts will find it easier to say

that a homosexual parent is unfit to gain custody of a child, or employers will say they don't want to hire would-be criminals.

In holding that consenting adults have no right to private homosexual conduct, the Supreme Court was dealing with a case involving conduct between two males. But the sweeping language of the decision indicated that states can police heterosexual sodomy — a practice that, however it may be condemned morally, simply cannot be controlled by government except in a police state. The upshot of the decision is likely to be that prosecutors and police will use sodomy laws to hunt selectively for unpopular groups, namely homosexuals.

Since 1961, when all 50 states had outlawed homosexual acts, 26 states, by legislation or court decision, have legitimized such conduct between consenting adults. The Supreme Court has turned back the clock on the right of privacy.

'Your papers appear to be in order. Apparently you are a heterosexual married couple. Sorry, we thought you might be a coupla gays.'

Wisconsin
State Journal
Madison, WI
July 2, 1986

Five of the nine members of the U.S. Supreme Court, the "conservative majority," have invited themselves into America's bedrooms. That is the bottom line in the court's 5-4 ruling that the Constitution does not protect private homosexual relations between consenting adults, even in their own homes.

The ruling is as spectacularly short-sighted as it is a corruption of the true spirit of conservatism, which in the days before the rise of the "New Right," used to hold sacred the idea that government should not meddle in personal practices that do not adversely affect others.

The court ruled a Georgia anti-sodomy law could be used to criminally prosecute homosexual conduct between men or women. Besides Georgia, the ruling could affect 24 other states where homosexual sodomy is a crime.

In Wisconsin, sexual acts between consenting adults in private are legal. Former Gov. Lee Dreyfus, a Republican and a conservative in the traditional sense, signed that act into law in 1982 with the following comment:

"As one who believes in the fundamental Republican principle that government should have a very restricted involvement in people's private and personal lives, I feel strongly about governmentally sanctioned inquiries into an individual's thoughts, beliefs and feelings."

Whatever happened to the notion that laws must be enforceable in order to be effective? It seems unlikely even Georgia will initiate "bedroom raids" in search of homosexual conduct, although the case that came before the Supreme Court did begin with just such an arrest.

The court ruling also assumes people choose to be gay or straight, when in fact, medical research indicates people have little or no control over their sexual preferences. It is as fundamental as being born black, blond or left-handed.

Would the nation's highest court rule in favor of a law that criminalizes left-handedness in the privacy of the home? We don't think so.

Those who are concerned about the growing visibility of homosexuality in America should not draw much comfort in the court's decision. It is possible gay people will migrate from states like Georgia to "safe" states or cities, thus swelling the size of gay communities in cities like San Francisco, New York or Madison.

"Georgia does not sound too peachy today," one prominent member of Madison's gay community said.

If there is a positive side to the court's ruling, it is the debate over sodomy laws will be shifted to the legislatures of the various states. Conservatives still believe in states' rights, don't they?

THE PLAIN DEALER
Cleveland, OH, July 3, 1986

Why did Supreme Court Chief Justice Warren Burger vote to reject a homosexual's challenge to the constitutionality of a Georgia state law against sodomy? Because, in part, "Homosexual sodomy was a capital crime under Roman law." That's an interesting fact, and you might think that any reference to "capital crime" is appropriate to a court that upholds the death penalty. But if modern justice is to find literal precedent in ancient Rome, then it will tolerate slavery, incest, the appointment of a horse to the Senate and the use of the White House as a brothel. During the reign of Caligula, the laws of ancient Rome tolerated all of that and worse.

Obviously, the issue of homosexual sodomy requires judicial awareness that is superior to that of demented Roman emperors. So Burger updates his precedents, writing that the 18th century English jurist William Blackstone described homosexual sodomy "as an offense of 'deeper malignity' than rape." That's another interesting fact, although the idea that any sexual act between consenting adults is less tolerable than rape makes you wonder how the English Reformation ever got off the ground.

Burger's point is that 2,000 years of moral teachings cannot be ignored. But it's not the job of modern law to affirm history. And it's not the job of the Supreme Court to rely on fusty, antiquated precedents to establish and defend modern rights. That's especially the case in Georgia, where the law against sodomy (by which is meant either oral or anal intercourse) appears to be selectively enforced only against homosexuals.

In this case, the Georgia law was challenged on the grounds that it violates the constitutional right of privacy. Five Supreme Court justices rejected that argument even though a vast body of recent legal precedent supports it. Like Burger, the majority opinion (his was separate yet consenting) mentioned history: "Proscriptions against (homosexual sodomy) have ancient roots." But more remarkably, the majority ruled that the Georgia case is not buttressed by other rulings that pertain to privacy and sexual conduct, specifically because even consenting homosexual activity is not connected to "family, marriage or procreation." The lack of such a connection made the court "unwilling" to establish "a fundamental right to engage in homosexual activity."

"Family, marriage and procreation" have nothing to do with private sexual activities between consenting adults. Had the court upheld the challenge, then it might have established a precedent for striking down laws exclusively based on homophobic prejudice. But the Georgia law applies equally to heterosexuals. Married couples can also be prosecuted for "sodomy," although by the Supreme Court's "family" standard, such activity would be constitutionally protected. The double standard is very clear, and so, apparently, is its genesis: the willingness of five Supreme Court justices to accept that homosexuals do not deserve the rights afforded to heterosexuals.

That narrow mindset does indeed justify the invocation of laws enacted by ancient Rome and 18th-century English puritanism. But it is antithetical both to the legal progress that the Constitution symbolizes and to the advancing sophistication of society. It's not likely that this decision will result in the reinstatement of anti-sodomy laws in the 26 states, including Ohio, that have abolished them. But it will slow the decriminalization of private sexual acts between consenting adults.

The court accepts that de-evolution of social standards because it fears getting too far ahead of society. Yet again, it's the court's job to keep the Constitution vibrant. The justices might not want to be made "vulnerable" by decisions that arouse political distress and subsequent efforts to stack the court. That obviously would undercut its credibility. But interpreting Supreme Court decisions is a popular political activity regardless of whether the rulings are viewed as liberal or conservative. To say that vulnerability is a legitimate reason for constitutional restraint is as feckless as citing ancient Rome as an appropriate model of morality.

Attorney General's Panel Links Pornography, Violence

The Attorney General's Commission on Pornography July 9, 1986 released the final draft of a report claiming that violent pornography probably led to sexual violence. The report called for a crackdown on obscenity by federal, state and local authorities. The report contradicted the findings of the 1970 President's Commission on Obscenity and Pornography, which had found no danger in circulation of pornography. Response to the new report ranged from praise to heated denunciation. The 1,960 page report had been prepared by an 11-member commission appointed in May 1985. The group, working with a budget of $500,000, had commissioned no new scientific research but had reviewed current findings, held public hearings in six cities, heard testimony from "victims of pornography" and other witnesses, read or viewed samples of pornography and visited "adults only" emporiums.

The commission report said it identified pornography as "sexually explicit" material "intended primarily for the purpose of sexual arousal." It listed three types: pornography that featured violence or its threat, pornography that did not show violence but did show one sex partner's degradation by another and pornography that featured only simple nudity or sex acts engaged in by apparently willing and equal partners. The report said commission members were divided on the effect of the violent pornography. It reported "no persuasive evidence to date" linking it to violence but said that the material did in all probability encourage promiscuity. In recent months, several scientists whose research was cited by the panel complained that complex and often inconclusive evidence had been willfully misread. One, Edward Donnerstein of the University of Wisconsin, was quoted May 19 as calling the draft report "bizarre."

Attorney General Edwin Meese 3rd repeatedly declined to comment on the report's proposals, saying he had not read them. But he assured listeners that "this department, as long as I am attorney general, is not going to encourage in any censorship that violates the First Amendment."

Los Angeles Times
Los Angeles, CA, July 10, 1986

The kindest thing that can be said about the 2,000-page report of the Attorney General's Commission on Pornography is that it's a joke. Not funny, but a joke. The commission's scholarship is ludicrous, its conclusions unsupported, its methodology zany.

In 1984 President Reagan declared, "It's time to stop pretending that extreme pornography is a victimless crime." Then Atty. Gen. Edwin Meese III, no fool, carefully selected an 11-member commission that spent a year and $500,000 chasing around the country, listening to crackpot testimony and reaching the conclusion that the President had ordained. The report is a miasma of misplaced morality and prudishness masquerading as social science.

Henry E. Hudson, the commission's chairman, was a county prosecutor in Virginia who made a name for himself waging war on adult businesses there. Just the right person to head this group. In releasing the report on Tuesday, Hudson disclosed his real agenda. "I, as well as all the other commissioners, believe that sexual promiscuity . . . is not something that should be socially condoned," he said.

The commission's "hearings" were scenes out of a Fellini movie. The majority of witnesses were cops, victims of sexual abuse and spokesmen for anti-pornography groups, who told the commissioners lurid tales of harm that started with pornography. There were also field trips to red-light districts and private screenings of X-rated films.

The commission's main conclusion—based on the flimsiest of evidence, none of it original—is that sexually explicit material, whether violent or not, can cause violence and other social harm. Even Hudson acknowledged that the case had not been proved. "If we relied on scientific data for every one of our findings, I'm afraid that all of our conclusions, or all of our work, would be inconclusive," he said Tuesday.

Fortunately, two of the commissioners would not go along with this. Ellen Levine, editor of Women's Day magazine, and Judith Becker, a Columbia University psychologist, said that "efforts to tease the current data into proof of a casual relationship" between pornography and sex crimes "cannot be accepted." They said that no "self-respecting investigator" could reach these conclusions.

Nonetheless, the panel recommends 92 tough steps that governments and citizens should take to quell the plague of pornography. For his part, Meese assured everyone that "there will be no censorship . . . in violation of the First Amendment." Meese wouldn't know a First Amendment violation if it bit him.

The commission has already done harm. In February it sent letters to two dozen retail chains encompassing 10,000 stores that sold Playboy and Penthouse magazines, telling them that they had been identified as smut peddlers. The letter threatened to name the retailers in the commission's final report. Many stores have withdrawn the magazines. Last week U.S. District Judge John Garrett Penn in Washington ruled that such a blacklist would be unconstitutional.

Now that this silly episode is over, it should be quickly forgotten. The commission's report should be consigned to the trash.

Detroit Free Press
Detroit, MI, July 12, 1986

A FEDERAL COMMISSION has spent one year and half a million dollars producing a report on pornography that is, at bottom, a sham. Though the report does focus on some important issues — including the sexual exploitation of women and minors — it doesn't offer much credible evidence to justify a crackdown on pornography that might approach censorship.

Many Americans will applaud the 11-member Attorney General's Commission on Pornography for proposing that citizens' groups begin working more vigorously to shut down pornographers. The report urges citizens to guard against the sale of sexually explicit material, including magazines, videotapes and even cable television programming, by setting up "citizens watch groups." It also calls for tougher enforcement of existing obscenity laws, a crackdown on child pornography, and stronger and better co-ordinated attempts by local, state and federal enforcers to break up the porno industry.

The most controversial part of the report, though, is its claim that exposure to sexually explicit material portraying the violent abuse of women by men can cause some people to commit "anti-social acts of sexual violence," sometimes including sex crimes. But where is the social science research to back up such a claim? No one has yet conclusively proven that a presidential commission was wrong when it decided in 1970 that erotic material was not a significant cause of crime or sexual deviancy.

The conclusion seems inescapable that some members of this current panel had difficulty separating their strong feelings about pornography from the actual facts. Six of the panel's 11 members had publicly stated their anti-pornography views before their appointment, and discouraging sexual promiscuity among Americans seems to have been one of the panel's goals.

The commission's report does raise some important issues, especially the need for stronger laws against child pornography in some municipalities. Its attempt to categorize the relative impact of sexually violent, degrading but not violent, and neither violent nor degrading sexually explicit materials also may turn out to be useful to researchers in the future. But it's hard to take too seriously a report that urges that the doors be removed from the peep show booths in "adults only" stores, to discourage sexual activity in those booths. "The need for research remains as compelling as ever," the panel acknowledged. That is surely the case.

The Miami Herald
Miami, FL, July 11, 1986

ALARMISTS view findings of the Attorney General's Commission on Pornography as tantamount to roving bands of vigilantes snooping in theaters and book stores and finding obscenity in every film, book, and magazine therein. Civil libertarians fret over potential First Amendment abuses if certain commission recommendations are enacted. Many religious leaders applaud the report as a return to decency. And the average citizen, what does he think?

Not much, probably. Quite often, high-level commissions' reports on national problems are news today, dust collectors tomorrow. This panel, established by former Attorney General William French Smith in 1985, studied pornography and decided that, no surprise, it is bad. Specifically, the 11 commissioners found child pornography pernicious in the worst sense. They recommended stringent enforcement of current laws and enactment of a few new ones such as making possession of child porno a felony. Agreed.

Agreed, too, that pornographic material portraying violence linked with sexual arousal is true depravity, as the commission states. But there is no scientific evidence that this obscenity and rape are directly connected, as the commission alleged while admitting that it had no proof.

A "Well, we *know* it but we can't *prove* it" reasoning is dangerous because it *would* jeopardize First Amendment rights if accepted as fact. One hopes that Attorney General Edwin Meese III sticks to his pledge that the Justice Department "is not going to engage in any censorship that violates the First Amendment."

The panel also alleged that "non-degrading, nonviolent" sexually explicit material causes promiscuity. Here the commissioners are way out of line, again cloaking mere opinion as fact. A sample of their moralizing: "There are undoubtedly many causes for what used to be called the 'sexual revolution,' but it is absurd to suppose that depictions or descriptions of uncommitted sexuality were not among them." Proof? None.

When the commission came down from the pulpit and stuck to analyzing the actual facts gathered during its hearings, it came up with the soundest recommendation — that the U.S. Justice Department vigorously enforce existing anti-pornography laws, which are plenteous. As to its other suggestions, such as forming local watchdog committees to seek out hard-core porn, let the average citizen — whose viewing and reading tastes are his own concern — make these private choices.

The Salt Lake Tribune
Salt Lake City, UT, July 11, 1986

The report of the Attorney General's Commission on Pornography holds no surprises. The commission did exactly what was expected of it: Conclude that pornography can cause sexual violence. It didn't, however, provide much scientific evidence that its conclusion is correct.

The conclusion was pre-ordained the day the commission was appointed. Its 11 members included six people who had previously taken strong, public anti-pornography positions. Two other members, both academics, had done work that could be used to defend censorship of sexually explicit material.

Additionally, the commission was created in response to pressure on the Reagan administration from the religious right in America, elements of which have been sharply and stridently critical of government, at all levels, for failing to move more aggressively against pornography.

A further suggestion that the commission was a sop to the religious right are the limited resources of time and money granted the commission. It was given only a year to do to its job, on a budget of a scant $500,000. That is half the time and one-sixteenth the money that the commission's 1970 predecessor was allowed.

Such severe restrictions of money and time automatically precluded the commission from conducting sound, independent and objective scientific research into the effects of pornography.

Instead, as it turned out, the commission had to rely extensively on such shaky information as the subjective testimony of law enforcement officials.

It is not surprising that two of the commissioners, Ellen Levine, editor of Woman's Day, and Judith Becker, a Columbia University psychologist, dissented from the report's central findings, deploring "efforts to tease the current data into proof of a causal relationship" between exposure to pornography and the commission of sex crimes.

"No self-respecting investigator would accept conclusions based on such a study, and unfortunately the document produced reflects these inadequacies," they wrote.

The document that has been produced is exactly what the Reagan administration, and its friends on the religious right, effectively ordered; a lopsided, unsubstantiated attempt to connect sexual violence with pornography. But what else could be expected from a biased, demonstrably anti-pornography commission predisposed to censorship that only had a year and a half-million dollars to do its job?

What the American public has received is a 2,000-page, two-volume, $35 a copy, sermon instead of the superior, scientific study it deserved.

The Forum
Fargo, ND, July 11, 1986

Pornography got a black eye from the Attorney General's Commission on Pornography this week.

A 2,000-page report links hardcore porn to sex crimes and contains 92 recommendations for federal, state and local governments to crack down on pornography.

We haven't read the report, but what we've been reading about pornography lately would make the Marquis de Sade blush. Pornographers have pushed too far, and as with any other kind of threat to civilized existence, there is a backlash by society.

We cannot put up with pornography that uses children, with depictions of sexual sadism against women, with showings of bestiality — most of it done exploitively to make a buck, or billions of bucks, as the pornography report states.

It calls pornography an $8 billion a year business.

There are those who say that pornography does not cause sex crimes. Well, when we get into cause and effect and whether or not certain sex crimes would have been committed anyway, we are dealing with hypotheses that could consume hours of debate and analyses.

The commission researched it, and came to the conclusion that hard core pornography — such as perversions and sadism — does endanger those who are depicted as the objects of sex crimes.

The commission states that, with regard to state and federal obscenity laws, there is "under-complaining, under-investigation, under-prosecution and under-sentencing."

Only 160 people have been indicted under the federal obscenity law since 1978.

The report has been condemned by civil liberties groups as a move toward censorship.

Attorney General Edwin Meese says, "I'm not concerned about any censorship being fostered by this. I can guarantee you there will be no censorship ... in violation of the First Amendment."

The U.S. Supreme Court has ruled that community standards define what is obscene and that action can be taken legally against obscenity.

Of course, there can be no pre-publication action against publications, whether they be movies or printed matter or any kind of taped or recorded material.

Once there is publication, then charges can be filed, and there is a time-honored, well-established, Supreme Court-validated procedure for this.

The fact that little has been done against pornography indicates that the public at large is broadminded and in no mood to interfere with the choice by adults of what they read or view.

The pornographers, though, have pushed beyond tolerable limits, and the call for action is justified.

The Star-Ledger

Newark, NJ, July 11, 1986

Predictably, the findings of a year-long national study on pornography have stirred a sharp, emotional controversy between conservative elements and civil libertarians. There are broad divisions reflecting concern over the potentially deleterious social implications of hard-core pornography and the possible unsettling intrusion of censorship raised by the tough law enforcement remedies proposed by the federal inquiry into pornography.

One point of difference involves a major conclusion of the commission, which found a direct causal relationship between pornography and violent sex offenses. This conclusion conflicts with findings by a presidential commission on pornography in 1970 and scientific studies that could find no such link.

Another troublesome factor in trying to address this volatile social issue was underscored by the inability of the commission even to define pornography, a dilemma that also has frustrated the nation's court system. In this void, a determination of what constitutes pornography essentially becomes a matter of community standards, creating a confusing melange of conflicting regulatory constraints on the multibillion-dollar pornography industry.

In this regional concept, there is a potentially inflammatory issue of vigilantism inherent in the commission call for citizens to act unilaterally against stores and other establishments that deal in adult materials. This is a responsibility better left in the hands of law enforcement authorities.

There is little doubt, however, that rigorous enforcement measures can be justified against pornographic entrepreneurs who prey on children for illicit gain. But a more reasoned, balanced official overview should be taken in government anti-pornography initiatives, given the ambiguities in trying to definitively ascertain what is pornography.

But what is clearly—and distressingly—apparent is that there have been radical changes in pornography in the 16 years since the presidential commission study. It not only has become markedly widespread, but it has taken on disturbingly darker forms of violent child pornography and sadomasochism. Sadly, there is a thriving market for this type of filth.

Unfortunately, the current panel has not made needed distinctions between erotica and hard-core pornographic materials. This kind of demarcation could have provided guidelines for effective law enforcement in checking the proliferation of the pornography commerce.

THE ATLANTA CONSTITUTION

Atlanta, GA, July 11, 1986

Forget for a moment the academicians and civil libertarians. The general public may have offered the most eloquent response to the overheated screed released this week by the Attorney General's Commission on Pornography: Z-z-z-z.

Employees of the Government Printing Office bookstore had expected brisk sales Wednesday when the panel's final report came out. Instead, they sold a measly 75 to 100 copies in three hours. People got more excited over copies of the president's budget. The reasons are plain enough.

At least the budget had an element of surprise and some anchor in reality. The porn report has neither. Its findings are about what one would expect from a panel tilted from the beginning to favor anti-porn crusaders. The 2,000-page tome serves mainly as a call to action.

The question is, against what? While the report rattles off scores of recommendations on how to curb "the spread of pornography," it never bothers to say what it believes "pornography" is. The panel must hail from the know-it-when-we-see-it school.

The commission said the "centerpiece" of its report is this: "Obscene publications which depict child pornography and violent and degrading behavior toward women are socially harmful." OK, but what is new about that? The link between depictions of violence and acts of violence is something of a given. As for child pornography, there are laws against it now.

Interestingly, two dissident panelists charged the examples of pornography put before the panel "were skewed to the very violent and extremely degrading." That notwithstanding, the majority went on to say (in a notably vague passage) that materials showing sex between consenting adults, even those without any hint of violence or degradation, harm society. That contradicts volumes of real research, and some researchers have protested that the commission twisted their conclusions.

Oh, well. The administration set out to give the religious right a buzz, and it did. But the results were not entirely harmless. For example, the commission convinced the owners of some 8,000 convenience stores they shouldn't sell mainstream publications like *Playboy*. How? It threatened to identify them (arbitrarily and unfairly) as distributors of pornography. It was a distinctly un-American bit of censorship-by-intimidation.

It is only reasonable to ask at this point. If the dread porn scourge has had its way in our society, what is the result? Do citizens clamor for relief? Do police reel from the struggle? Do judges beg for more authority?

Uh, not exactly. The report finds "under-complaining, under-investigation, under-prosecution, and under-sentencing."

Under-complaining? Well, at least the public is consistent. Z-z-z-z.

The Birmingham News

Birmingham, AL, July 13, 1986

The furor that liberals, led by the American Civil Liberties Union, have created following release of the Attorney General's Commission on Pornography report is a manufactured tempest in a teapot.

In view of Attorney General Edwin Meese's pledge that the study will not be used to promote an attack on the First Amendment, the shrill cries from liberal strongholds seem bogus and designed to distort Meese's intent as well as deform his character.

By inference, they also distort the First Amendment. Do liberals actually believe that the First Amendment was designed to include protection for the bestial fantasies contained in the kind of pornography the commission deplored?

Do liberals actually believe that the 10 words guaranteeing free speech and press were meant to include protection for the creators and dealers in pictures of children explicitly engaged in the sex act?

Do liberals actually believe that the amendment protects the publication and distribution of sadistic and masochistic, violence-ridden garbage that demeans all of humankind, especially women and children, and sex itself?

Do the outraged liberals believe the First Amendment was intended to work to provide organized crime with income with which to finance drug smuggling, prostitution and a host of other crimes?

Of course not. And censorship is not the real issue here. The real fear in the liberal camp is that Meese, the commissioners and their report will mobilize public opinion to suppress this outrageous transgression of the public good, not through censorship, but through expressions of public outrage.

Perhaps hard-core pornography does not encourage sex crimes, such as rape and molestation of children. But in view of the vast increase in these crimes since pornography became so widespread and readily accessible, the public will need more than the carping of psychologists to convince it that brutalized sex displays have played no part.

While this newspaper deplores any attempt to censor any political discourse, written or otherwise, news events or legitimate literature, we believe society has an obligation to defend itself against forces that tend to corrupt it or dissolve the glue which binds it together.

If Americans want to register their protest against hard-core pornography, they have every right to do so — through boycotts, picketing or critical comment, as Americans have done for numerous liberal causes — as long as they avoid violence and any illegal activity directed at the people who sell hard-core pornography.

And it can be argued that under the general welfare clause of the Constitution government is empowered if not obligated to warn the nation when it is on the wrong track. Is censorship involved in such a warning? How about the legislated warning on tobacco? Is the free speech of cigarette manufacturers compromised when they are prevented by law from advertising their products on television and radio? And what about the other numerous warnings issued by various government agencies on a variety of diseases, foods and consumer items?

The truth is, Meese is no threat to the First Amendment. Neither are groups which pressure stores to eliminate hard-core pornography from their shelves.

"THE REPORT OF THE COMMISSION ON PORNOGRAPHY WILL CAUSE NO CENSORSHIP..."

"NEXT QUESTION."

CHARLESTON EVENING POST
Charleston, SC, July 15, 1986

As syndicated columnist Andrew J. Glass reminds in an article on this page, pornography has a long history. So have concerns about it and attempts to control it. In consequence, the recent report by the Attorney General's Commission on Pornography is likely to be regarded by the record-keepers as just another brief footnote on the subject.

The commission report, which concluded that some forms of pornography cause sexual violence, has been criticized for leaping to conclusions unsupported by scientific findings. It has been assailed as a "lopsided, pro-censorship report." It also has been praised by feminists and hailed by religious groups as "the death knell for the criminal pornography industry."

Even though it runs to almost 2,000 pages, the report is unlikely to be even half the things some say it is. It can be said without fear of argument that the report offers no new data (because, the commission said, there wasn't money for original research). It likewise can be said that it plows no new analytical or philosophical ground, although it does its share of moralizing.

The report does, however, contain 92 recommendations for federal, state and local crackdowns on pornography, including that most loathsome aspect some label "kiddie porn." In discussing child pornography the commission recognized what law enforcement agents are up against. There are more amateurs engaged in the production of "kiddie porn" than there are professionals, which makes policing difficult. Even so, that's no reason to relax efforts to counter child pornography.

In setting priorities for combating pornography, we suspect most Americans would favor letting adults (including consumers) fend for themselves so resources can be concentrated on (a) curbing porn's most repulsive aspect, the sexual exploitation and abuse of children, and (b) keeping pornographic material out of young hands.

San Francisco Chronicle
San Francisco, CA, July 11, 1986

PERHAPS ONE of the most incisive criticisms of the $500,000, two-volume Meese Commission on Pornography report is contained in the report itself. The 11 members concluded that they could not define pornography. We're not sure what it is, the commission said in effect, but we're sure agin it.

Pornography can, indeed, be defined. But it cannot be defined in a way which is acceptable to all people, just as the conclusions of this wasteful and useless study will not be accepted by all people.

The commission was rigged at appointment. More than half of its members were veterans of anti-porno campaigns and the commission was obviously designed to appease conservative fundamentalists in general and smutbusters in particular.

ITS FINDINGS have led the commission to encourage picketing and boycotting of a variety of enterprises: book stores, video shops, sex theaters and magazine racks dealing in sexually explicit material. It is difficult to understand this declaration of holy war against an enemy which cannot be defined to the commission's satisfaction. The report advocates federal, state and local censorship, but we doubt this has much popular support.

The commission's conclusion that pornography is linked both to sexual violence and sexual discrimination runs contrary to the findings of a 1970 presidential commission which relied more heavily on expert testimony. We do not believe that such a casual relationship can be demonstrated scientifically. We do know one other thing about the report. It lists plot outlines of hundreds of blue movies with great explicitness; that is bound to help the sales of the report to the interested public.

Part VI:
Prison & Capital Punishment

The first penetentiary in the U.S. was established in Philadelphia in the early 19th century. The goal of incarceration then was to encourage criminals to ponder their acts, repent and reform. This result was supposed to be achieved by locking prisoners in cells and enforcing an atmosphere of solitude. Within a century, this ideal had degenerated into long, hard work-days of unrelenting labor, floggings and the actual contracting out of prisoners to private employers. Even though prisoners rightly did not enjoy the same rights as other citizens, by the 1970s these practices were, of course, a thing of the past.

The last two decades have seen the federal courts respond by frequently intervening to correct conditions that subject prisoners to inadequate medical care, unsanitary facilities, lack of physical exercise, loss of contact with family and overcrowding. However, the intervention of the courts in establishing a detailed constitutional code of prison administration has been mainly limited to those cases brought by pre-trial detainees who are presumed innocent. The position of prisoners convicted of crimes has a different order within the constitution. Constitutionally protected freedoms may be withdrawn or constricted as to state prisoners. Long periods of incarceration in solitary confinement with little exercise and minimal sanitary facilities have been found not violative of the Constitution. The reluctance of the courts to closely supervise the operations of state penetentiaries is the result of their stated opposition to becoming entangled in the professional judgment of prison administrators.

Recently, prisoner rights have been expanded somewhat. Court definitions of "cruel and unusual punishment," prohibited by the 8th Amendment, have halted corporal punishment and the beating of prisoners by guards. Other rights such as the right to receive and send reasonable amounts of mail, the right to reading material that does present "a clear and present danger" to the institution and the right to hold religious services of one's religious choice have won recognition. Prison inmates have made the most concrete gains in the area of the right to counsel and legal assistance. However, since a prisoner's behavior and life is controlled by wardens and guards, not federal judges, the possibility of unconstitutional abuse remains great.

But despite the moves toward prison and sentence reform, the present trend is to send convicted criminals to prison and for longer terms. In 1987 the U.S. prison population increased by 21,833 to a new high of 545,632. In fact, these figures are representative of the last decade, when a sharp reversal of the decline in prison population during the 1960s transpired. Not including those people being held for trial, 225 Americans are in prison for every 100,000 citizens. Except for South Africa, no other Western developed nation has so many of its citizens in jail.

Comparable figures for other nations per 100,000 population are 31 in the Netherlands, 58 in Sweden, 70 in Denmark, 50 in Japan, 74 in France, 85 in the United Kingdom, 113 in Canada and 175 in Israel.

The increased prison population has resulted in severe prison overcrowding throughout the nation. But the desire to use prisons as the primary tool of punishment is not equaled by the desire to underwrite the costs. According to the National Institute of Criminal Justice, the average cost of construction of a single new maximum security cell $50,000 while the maintenance of an average prisoner costs about $25,000 a year.

Crowded prisons frequently result in homosexual rape, shortage of rehabilitative programs and prison disturbances. The infringement of inmates' constitutional rights by overcrowding has led to critics to argue that overcrowded conditions create an environment that not only makes it impossible for inmates to to rehabilitate themselves but actually makes them worse. The crisis of overcrowding has been pinpointed as one of the reasons for the tragic Attica rebellion in 1971 and the grisly uprising in the Sante Fe, New Mexico prison in 1980. Overcrowding leads to greater use of lock-up; prisoners are required to stay in their cell because of the shortage of prison resources.

Perhaps the most hotly debated issue regarding crime and punishment in the U.S. involves the death penalty. Any understanding of the principles underpinning the rationale of the death penalty requires an analysis of the Supreme Court's definition of the ``cruel and unusual'' clause of the 8th Amendment. From the time of its adoption into the Constitution in 1791, the 8th Amendment and the cruel and unusual clause have evolved with the standards and are now defined by the prevailing sentiment of the populace and history of capital punishment. For example, Supreme Court Justice Byron White, who has held that execution is not a constitutionally impermissible form of punishment, believes that the dictionary would define it as cruel. Additionally, public opinion polls have revealed a dramatic shift in support for the death penalty; in 1966 40% favored it, in 1976 the figure was 60% and in 1986 the figure was 77%.

Public opinion aside, it is the behavior of the legislatures to which the majority of the Supreme Court looks for guidance in its definitions. Since the Court's 1972 decision in the case of *Furman v. Georgia* to strike down as unconstitutional the existing laws permitting capital punishment, 37 states have enacted statutes providing for the death penalty in crimes resulting in the death of a person. Since 1976, 100 prisoners have been executed as of June 1988. But the continued willingness of juries to impose the death penalty signaled to the court that contemporary values still supported use of capital punishment. The court's conclusive rejection of the argument that the death penalty was an unacceptable mode of punishment was not reached until 1976 when, in a complicated decision involving five states, it ruled that the death penalty was constitutional but insisted that specific due process safeguards be established to prevent the death penalty from being imposed ``so wantonly and freakishly.''

The procedural barriers constructed by the Supreme Court, desirous of eliminating capricious and arbitrary implementation of the death penalty, have not impeded the prosecutors. More than two thousand people now wait on death row. Nor has it seemed to eliminate the criterion of race in determining who shall die as more than half of those sentenced to die belong to racial minorities. However, the last 12 years have brought Americans the spectacle of state executions.

Autry Executed in Texas; Television Coverage Denied

Convicted killer James David Autry was executed by lethal injection at the state penitentiary in Huntsville, Texas March 14, 1984. He was the third person put to death in the U.S. in 1984. "Cowboy" Autry, 29, had come within 24 minutes of being executed in October 1983. His hopes of a permanent reprieve were dashed in January, when the U.S. Supreme Court ruled that a state was not required to review a death sentence to see if it was comparable to punishments meted out in similar cases. The Supreme Court March 13 had voted, 7-2, against issuing a stay of Autry's execution. Texas Gov. Mark White the same day turned down a plea for clemency.

Autry had made an unusual last request. The convicted killer sought to have his execution televised on the ground that it could spur a backlash against capital punishment and thus save the lives of other inmates on death row. The Texas Board of Corrections, however, had denied his request. A federal judge March 12 barred television cameras from the execution. Autry, only the second person ever to be executed by an injection of sodium thiopental, died at 12:40 a.m. March 14.

The State

Columbia, SC, March 21, 1984

THE 11th-hour request by James David "Cowboy" Autry that he be publicly executed in Texas so his death could be a deterrent to crime hit at the core of capital punishment.

The 29-year-old murderer's request was rejected by the Texas Board of Corrections, although the state's attorney general, Jim Mattox, said, "If executions serve as a deterrent, then there's some very logical argument that they should be done publicly."

Opponents of the death penalty agreed, apparently expecting a public execution to revolt citizens and lead to a repeal of capital punishment. A Death Row prisoner who is a registered lobbyist said, "If they think it acts as a deterrent, then why do they want to hide it?"

The chairman of the board of corrections had his answer ready: "An individual's death should be private. I think it would be in extremely bad taste to put it on TV, and I'll vote against exploitation or sensationalism of such a situation."

A Dallas TV station went to court some time ago asking the right to broadcast executions, but was turned down. The court said the state did not have to permit cameras in the death chamber.

Legislation was prefiled in the S.C. General Assembly last year to require public executions, but the bill has attracted little interest, which is just as well. There's enough crime and violence in our world today without making one act of violence — even though legal — a spectacular.

ST. LOUIS POST-DISPATCH

St. Louis, MO, March 17, 1984

The state of Texas killed James David Autry, a convicted murderer, by injecting him with sodium thiopental on March 14, without granting his request — and that of a television reporter — to have his execution portrayed on television. A court petition demanding the admission of cameras to the death chamber was turned down by a federal judge. Robert Gunn, the chairman of the Texas Board of Corrections, which voted 8-0 to continue a ban on cameras, said televising an execution would be "just in bad taste."

Mr. Gunn was only partially right. The televising of an execution would indeed be in "bad taste." But it would be much more than that; it would be transmitting nonfictional barbarism into most of the living rooms of America. And most television viewers — and most public officials, including those of the Texas Board of Corrections — would, by our guess, not want that. We share their revulsion but commend Texas Attorney General Jim Mattox for being candid. He put the issue in stark terms when he said if the public truly favors the death penalty, then it should be permitted to view the execution and "should be willing, frankly, to inject the poison, if necessary."

In Texas and elsewhere in the United States, the public does tend to favor the death penalty. But much of the public would be reluctant to view what is being done in its name — the deliberate, official killing of human beings under the concept that this deters homicides and serves justice. It does neither, but it does satisfy a public desire for vengeance as long as people don't have to watch.

The Oregonian

Portland, OR, March 14, 1984

Texas, like other states where the death penalty is ordered, exhibits at the final moment a sense of shame, hiding the act of taking a human life. But if the death penalty is to serve as a deterrent, a dubious notion, even this side effect is greatly reduced when the state holds its executions out of public sight and off-camera.

The Texas Board of Corrections voted 8 to 0 against permitting television cameras to record the execution of James David "Cowboy" Autry, convicted of killing the mother of five in 1980, a crime he continued to declare he did not commit. The Texas attorney general, Jim Mattox, argued that there is a logical argument for a televised, public execution if such events are to have much deterrent value.

Autry sought a public execution, including the right of television news to cover his death by drug injection, believing such scenes would so outrage the public as to bring about the repeal of capital punishment laws.

There was a time when hangings were public matters, done in the town square or the prison courtyard. But even for notorious killers, only a fraction of a state's populace saw the execution. Television has changed all that, and it would be possible for millions to watch a condemned man's last moments, to hear his final words and to see attendants delivering the ghastly final jolt, be it from drugs, electricity, gas or a rope. Seeing death on the nightly news made the Vietnam war unacceptable to millions.

Printed news pictures of executions, along with later discoveries that sometimes the wrong person died, shocked civilized people. Now the United States and a few authoritarian countries are among the last few nations where the state has the power of life and death over its citizens.

Those who espouse the barbaric death penalty should not object if official killings are given the widest possible displays.

Times-Colonist

Victoria, B.C., March 15, 1984

The Texas Board of Corrections refused to allow the execution of a convicted murderer Wednesday to be shown on television.

Too bad. There are two arguments to be made in favor of the practice.

The attorney general of Texas, Jim Mattox, makes one of them: "If executions serve as a deterrent, then there's a very logical argument that they should be done publicly."

In fact, executions do not serve as a deterrent, as statistics in Canada have shown. But the other, and the better argument for televising executions, we suggest, is that any society which supports capital punishment should have an opportunity to see the results of that horrific policy in action. Murder is murder — whether conducted by an individual or the state.

Roanoke Times & World-News

Roanoke, VA, March 13, 1984

JAMES David "Cowboy" Autry is scheduled to die of lethal injection before sunrise Wednesday in Huntsville, Tex. He says he wants to die in public — with television cameras in attendance. Wisely, Texas prison officials have vetoed the idea.

Three types of people would support televised executions:

✔ The morbid types who would pay to see movies about chain-saw murders and who would enjoy a televised execution even more because it would be the real thing.

✔ Sincere opponents of capital punishment, who want to bring home to death-penalty advocates the horror involved in taking a human life.

✔ Misguided advocates of the death penalty who believe a televised execution would enhance its deterrent value.

Among the latter seems to be Texas Attorney General Jim Mattox, who said: "If executions serve as a deterrent, then there's a very logical argument that they should be done publicly."

But the death penalty has not been shown to be a deterrent. Attempts at demonstrating a statistical relationship between capital punishment and the incidence of capital crime have been inconclusive. Most homicides are committed in the heat of passion by individuals who don't stop to calculate their chances of being caught, convicted and executed. The kind of willful, heartless murderer for whom the death penalty is appropriate punishment is unlikely to be deterred by the fact that others have died for murder. Some pathological killers may even have a subconscious desire to die.

James Q. Wilson, in his book, "Thinking About Crime," discounts deterrence as a reason for supporting the death penalty.

"The main issue remains that of justice," he contends. "The point is not whether capital punishment prevents future crimes, but whether it is a proper and fitting penalty for crimes that have occurred."

If capital punishment is to be justified, it must be justified on the ground that some crimes are so cruel, so inhuman, that they place the perpetrator well beyond the bounds of human tolerance. It is not enough that such murderers be put behind solid walls, to live and, perhaps, one day go free to prey again. They and the threats they represent must be irrevocably removed from human society.

An argument can be made that the state of Texas imposes death sentences too readily for crimes that do not reach the ultimate depths of human depravity. Its death-row population outnumbers that of any other state except Florida, although Georgia uses the death penalty more frequently on a per-capita basis.

But to address that problem should not require that society's nose be rubbed in the capital-punishment spectacle as if society itself were guilty for wanting to punish murderers.

"If they think it acts as a deterrent, then why do they want to hide it?" asked Billy Hughes, a death-row inmate and registered lobbyist in opposition to the death penalty.

Because, answers Texas Prison Board Chairman Robert Gunn, "An individual's death should be private."

And why should society have to partake of the unpleasantness of the punishment when it has already partaken of the unpleasantness of the crime? Should all of us be expected to make regular treks through prisons, eat prison food, lie on prison beds just so we'll know how terrible is the lot of those we punish through incarceration?

When a state takes a life in punishment for murder, it should do so only with the greatest of reluctance, after a full review of the facts of the case in the light of the narrowest of criteria. And it should do so with a solemn dignity that places the state on the highest moral ground.

A televised execution would turn the solemn occasion into a morbid sideshow for those who exult in the macabre. The criminal should not be permitted to make a spectacle out of his death, or to lay his guilt upon the conscience of the society he offended.

Fort Worth, TX, March 12, 1984

News out of Austin today that the Texas Board of Corrections unanimously voted "No" on allowing the televising of executions is welcome in that it should put an end to speculation about such a grotesque possibility.

The matter was first raised by condemned killer James David Autry, who is scheduled to die Wednesday for the murder of a convenience store clerk in Port Arthur during a 1980 robbery.

Autry, who has escaped execution on several previous occasions through judicial intervention, requested recently that his death be recorded and broadcast by a Texas television station.

Autry's is a position taken previously by advocates of abolishing the death penalty. They believe people would be so shocked by scenes of an actual execution that an overwhelming public outcry would be generated against the practice.

They well may be right in believing that, but that is hardly sufficient reason for subjecting the public to such horrors.

The ranks of both pro and anti-death penalty groups contain people of good faith and honorable intentions. Valid, logical arguments exist on both sides of the issue. Unfortunately, those arguments are frequently shunted aside by the emotions this topic generates.

Public telecasts of executions would merely pour fuel on those raw emotions while adding nothing in the way of logical argument, one way or the other.

Society has made great strides since the barbaric days of the Roman forum, where humans were pitted against animals or each other in duels to the death for the amusement of the bloodthirsty masses. Execution as a bizarre spectator sport could set us back a thousand years.

No worthwhile purpose could be served by televising Autry's death, or anyone else's. Let's hope the matter is closed and remains that way.

THE INDIANAPOLIS STAR

Indianapolis, IN, March 24, 1984

Prison officials usually grant the last wishes of a doomed man. But the Texas Board of Corrections refused J.D. Autry's request that his execution be filmed for television.

Autry, convicted of killing a mother of five, died from a lethal injection administered earlier this month in a Texas prison. But arguments about televising executions are still heard.

Autry said TV coverage would expose the cruelty of capital punishment and aid the cause of those on Death Rows across the country. There are many who agree. They argue that bringing state executions live and in vivid color into the nation's living rooms would cause such public revulsion that pressure would be brought to outlaw the practice.

Some supporters of the death penalty also promote TV coverage, but as a deterrence to crime. There is no better way, they argue, to convince a criminal he is asking for trouble than to have him witness an execution.

None of the arguments pass scrutiny. Public hangings used to be fairly commonplace in this country. In some areas they took on the unfortunate trappings of a carnival. Yet there is no evidence that they influenced legislative sentiment one way or another.

The prolonged moratorium on capital punishment doubtless persuaded many habitual criminals that they were safe from the ultimate penalty. That is no longer the case. But it isn't necessary to show an execution on the six o'clock news or make it the climax of a TV special in order to impress that fact on the criminal community. News of an execution travels fast — on the street, among jailhouse lawyers and in courtrooms.

A few TV officials have said that it is only a matter of time until executions are filmed. They take place, so they'll eventually be seen on the home screen. Let us hope those TV people are wrong.

It is ghoulish to contend that the public's knowledge or welfare can be enhanced by witnessing the contortions of a body jolted by electricity or studying the closeup of a terrified man strapped to a gurney, his veins open to a fatal dose of drugs.

But perhaps the best argument for not allowing the Autry execution to be filmed was given by one member of the Texas corrections board. He said it was impossible to show the other side of the story: the mother of five being shot between the eyes because Autry and his pal didn't want to pay for a six-pack of beer.

THE DAILY HERALD

Biloxi, MS, March 13, 1984

Members of the Texas Board of Corrections displayed great good sense yesterday when they decided not to permit the televising of the execution of murderer James David Autry. Had they decided otherwise, they would have done a disservice to the whole country.

Although the board has jurisdiction only in Texas, the decision would influence similar boards in other states. In a sense, the Texas ruling sets a precedent, although it is one other states are free to ignore. Even so, it is significant. While Texas has only 170 prisoners on death row, the country has more than 1,300 and recent Supreme Court rulings indicate that many of those death sentences, some delayed for a half-dozen or more years, will be carried out in the next few years.

The television question came before the Texas board at the instigation of Mr. Autry, who apparently takes a perverse pleasure in throwing obstacles into the path of justice. It was Mr. Autry who, last October, avoided execution when one of his lawyers, grasping for any straw with less than 30 minutes before his client was scheduled to die, hit upon a plea requesting requirement of a comparative proportionality review. The plea found favor with Supreme Court Justice Byron R. White, partially because the same issue had been raised on behalf of California murderer Robert Alton Harris.

The Harris case was decided last January with a 7-2 vote against Harris. The same Justice White who delayed Mr. Autry's execution wrote the majority opinion that has led to the end of the execution delays. The ruling, in essence, makes it easier for states to carry out the death sentences of convicted murderers. Texas accordingly then went forward, for the second time, with plans for Mr. Autry's execution.

Mr. Autry's request for television coverage gained impetus when attorney General Jim Mattox, rather than oppose the idea, found some merit in it. He reasoned that one purpose of executions is to provide deterrence to crime, therefore executions should be done publicly. In other states, his argument would carry more weight.

For many years, executions were indeed public in this country. In Texas, the hanging of one Roy Mitchell on July 3, 193 — 61 years ago — was the last public execution. Mitchell was convicted of five murders. Of course, there was no television coverage since there was no television then.

Among those opposing the idea of televising the execution was one of the five children whose mother was Mr. Autry's victim. She argued, and in this case her position is sensible, that there would be no dramatic impact — or very little, at most — in televising Mr. Autry's execution since the viewers would see only a man falling asleep after an injection. Not much deterrent in that, unless Autry could put on a pre-injection demonstration for the cameras, a distinct possibility considering Mr. Autry's penchant for public attention.

Watching a man receive an injection and fall into deathly sleep would not give viewers the same level of violence as, say, execution by firing squad or by guillotine, yet there are some television stations in Texas more than willing to titillate their viewers with the first live scenes of the death penalty in action.

Texas has 44 TV stations. A dozen of them said they would show the execution. Six were undecided. Twenty-six, bless 'em, had the decency to make a commitment not to show it, either live or as part of a news program. Make no mistake, however, about the national availability of the horror show; if even one station filmed the event, that film would be shown via networks to everyone curious enough to want to see it.

It would be a better world were capital punishment not necessary. However, as long as some members of society commit the most heinous of crimes, there must be the severest of penalties. But it is no more necessary to make public spectacles of the executions than it is to require the televising of the heinous crimes themselves.

The Houston Post

Houston, TX, March 16, 1984

A years-long King's X for killers has worn thin with many Texans.

James David Autry granted no clemency on April 20, 1980, when he fired a fatal bullet into the head of Shirley A. Drouet, a 43-year-old with five children. Nor, during the same petty robbery, did he think of giving a break to Joseph A. Broussard, a former Catholic priest described by a friend as being "a very sensitive person, creative, very loving." He shot and killed Broussard, too.

Outside the Port Arthur convenience store that he robbed of a six-pack of beer priced at $2.70, Autry shot a Greek seaman, Athanasios Svarnas, making him an invalid for the rest of his life.

No, Autry did not give any of his three victims — nor their survivors — a chance to shout for King's X, a cry in children's games to call time out or claim exemption from being tagged or caught.

Yet the American system of criminal justice gave Autry one month short of four years before it executed him early Wednesday morning by lethal injection. During that time, at taxpayers' expense, Autry finally exhausted his appeals processes.

One has to wonder whether the people on death row have it too easy. A more swift and sure justice for them may not be the answer, but it just might be worth a try as a more effective deterrent. Why should some death row inmates wait as long as four years — some much longer — before receiving their punishment?

The people of Texas have spoken loud and clear — they want capital punishment. They want it impressed upon the minds of the few people in our society who would wantonly murder innocent people, in a convenience store or anywhere else, that they will not get leniency.

Some laws read and quoted by civil libertarians help get more time for people like Autry, while the time for surviving families of his victims is long gone. "He'll die a lot easier than the ones he killed," one victim's relative said before Autry's execution.

A jury found that Autry would remain a danger to human beings if released into free society again.

The tide must turn back in favor of the law-abiding majority — people sick and tired of seeing their innocent relatives murdered. A sure-fire way to do it is to carry out the ultimate penalty without reservations — after a reasonable period for appeals. But not four years.

Victims never get a chance for a King's X. Neither should killers.

DESERET NEWS

Salt Lake City, UT, March 13-14, 1984

Convicted Texas murderer James Autry has a bizarre last request. He wants his scheduled excecution to take place on national television. Fortunately, the Texas Board of Corrections this week turned him down.

However, Autry received support from Texas Atty. Gen. Jim Mattox who was quoted as saying, "If executions serve as a deterrent, then there's a very logical argument that they should be done publicly."

But most Texas television stations, asked if they would carry the proposed broadcast of the execution, said they would not.

The television people may have made their decision entirely on the basis of propriety and good taste although current programming does not entirely justify such an assumption.

One can't help imagining that a sterile, clinical execution by lethal injection might get somewhat low ratings with television audiences accustomed to the usual prime time succession of violence — murder, bloody brawls and Monday night football.

The only audience for televised executions could be a coterie of hard-eyed female knitters. Such a narrow audience-appeal could discourage sponsors with ample cash in hand, the ultimate determiner of what is and is not suitable for the television audience.

Since Autry's crime consisted of attempting to obtain a $2.70 six-pack of beer by killing a convenience store clerk, those enthusiastic promoters of popular televised events, the brewers, would seem to have been the logical sponsors of Autry's denouement, but they did not leap forward to seize the opportunity.

Who knows? With their assurances of a generous payment for TV rights, the Board of Corrections at least might have given the matter a second thought.

Pittsburgh Post-Gazette

Pittsburgh, PA,

March 15, 1984

For believers in the deterrent value of capital punishment, this has been a mixed week. In Texas, James David Autry, a 29-year-old drifter and convicted murderer, became the 14th person to be executed in the United States since 1976 — but not before he embarrassed the system that killed him.

In a civilized world in which murder was always punished by life in prison, a criminal like James Autry would not be able to score a moral victory by the nature of his punishment. Here was no sympathetic figure. He was convicted of shooting to death a mother of five working in a convenience store. She had asked him to pay for a six-pack of beer.

Yet the rationale of capital punishment afforded him a chance to look like a victim. What he did — quite logically — was to try to get the Texas Board of Corrections and then a federal judge to allow television coverage of his execution.

This bit of mischief-making made an uncomfortable point to those who would argue the deterrent value of executions. Obviously, if deterrence is a part of the argument, then executions should be on television. But we all know America has not stooped so low as to go back to the days when executing people was a public entertainment.

Of course, his petition was denied — but the obvious point cannot be. Capital punishment, if it is to proceed, must occur behind closed doors — operating on the hypocritical basis that out of sight is out of mind, and what people don't know about the brutality of this punishment will not disturb them.

Before he died, James David Autry hoisted capital punishment on its own petard. A just alternative would not have allowed him that satisfaction.

The Birmingham News

Birmingham, AL, March 15, 1984

A society in transition more often than not loses its moorings. The visible result is a kind of madness. For signs, one need look no further than the case of James "Cowboy" Autry, a convicted murderer of a mother of five. He was accused of a second murder but not tried.

Autry had had full access to the justice system before, during and after his trial. He was granted three stays of execution, the last by U.S. Supreme Court Justice Byron White, exhausting the public if not the criminal justice system itself.

In a sort of mad defiance, before his execution Wednesday, Autry and television reporter Don Kobos filed suit in a Houston federal court seeking to force officials to allow videotaping of the execution. Kobos maintained restricting him from taking recording devices into the death chamber violated his constitutional rights. Autry simply wanted to make the tape as a statement against the death penalty.

The Texas Board of Corrections, after fully considering the matter, voted against allowing the execution to be videotaped. It would be difficult to believe that sane, responsible and decent citizens could have made any other decision.

TV reporter Kobos may have seen videotaping the execution as his big opportunity to go down in television history as the first person to record a live execution on videotape for public distribution. Someone should have the kindness to explain to Kobos that there would be certain differences between filming Autry's death and the fictional deaths of villains taken out by the A-Team.

But the real horror is that rational human beings as part of a rational system would even consider such a travesty. How far from our civilized moorings have we drifted when the merited death of a convicted murderer is considered suitable fare for television audiences?

However, we wonder, would television audiences be horrified and leap to turn the sets off, or would they simply view the execution as they would a piece of fictional hocus pocus from a James Bond movie? There is evidence to support the contention that the aura of reality in televised fictional violence translates into an aura of unreality by viewers of non-fictional violence.

In any case, the nation would not have gained from seeing in their living rooms in dramatic detail the last minutes of a killer's life. For this, we can thank the civilized members of the Texas Board of Corrections.

THE PLAIN DEALER

Cleveland, OH, March 19, 1984

The fight against capital punishment has been momentarily lost, in the state of Texas at any rate. But the fight against the salacious marketing of that ignoble legal concept is just beginning, as witness the remarks by Stanford Law School professor John Kaplan on today's Forum page.

Kaplan addresses the implications of a decision by a Texas judge to prohibit television coverage of the execution of J.D. Autry, which took place by lethal injection Wednesday in Huntsville Prison. Autry had requested the coverage, saying that if the nation is "serious about using the death penalty as a deterrent, they (legal officers) should let the public see it." Kaplan argues that the media was remiss in not objecting to the prohibition, producing a barrage of arguments about the "right to know," the hypocrisy of the media for objecting to the Grenada blackout but not the Huntsville one, the "increasing tendency of the government to make decisions about the flow of information" and so on.

There is a thin line between the sublime and the ridiculous, and it may be that Kaplan has crossed it. His contention that the government should have no precedent by which to keep secret what it does to its citizens is quite right, but there was precious little secrecy surrounding the government's plans for Autry. It hardly was privy information that, barring a last minute reprieve, Autry would be executed, that an eye would be rendered for an eye, that the legal system would itself kill.

Secrecy was not an issue, and neither was the right to know. How can it be argued that exposure to death is a right? It is, typically, an ugly and frightening experience. Even the words "right to know" are facile and misused. The nation's dignity is diminished by its support of what amounts to ritual sacrifice. Why demean it further by beaming it into households across the nation? There are no compelling "rights" in that, only the compounding of terrible wrongs.

It is not wrong to recognize that the broadcast of an execution may indeed help galvanize public opinion against capital punishment. But the ensuing groundswell would miss the point. America should be able to rise above court-anointed murder, just as it can rise above the use of pandering, shallow appeals to emotion and sympathy, appeals that sacrifice both life and the dignity that should accompany death.

A judicial decision to forbid public executions is not the tip of some government cabal to justify secrecy and obscurity. It is the reasonable decision of a reasonable man—supported, we hope, by the nation's media—that a chamber of execution is not the appropriate venue for a circus; that although the sentence may be public, the death need not be. This nation does not need to understand the moment of death. Rather, it needs to understand the legal philosophy that provides for the debasement of our basic moral imperatives.

Private Contracting Pursued for Prisons

The Reagan administration heightened its efforts to transfer a wide range of public assets and programs to private enterprise, the *New York Times* reported March 9, 1985, but the program had run into some criticism from both the left and the right. Among the cornerstones of the strategy was the privatization of prisons. Joseph R. White Jr., deputy director of the Office of Management and Budget (OMB), told the *Times*, "We came in to make a fundamental reform in the way we do business. Our philosophy is that we should not be competing with the private sector." The OMB contended that business and industry could often do a better and cheaper job than government could. Such programs had won widespread support among congressional Republicans. Stuart N. Butler, an official of the Heritage Foundation, a conservative thinker, noted, "Even the threat of contracting out improves efficiency in government."

A Feb. 11, 1985 news account had reported that about 24 major prisons and hundreds of smaller correctional facilities were operated by private companies. Both liberals and conservatives reportedly supported privitization as a remedy for prison overcrowding. Prison companies claimed their freedom from bureaucracy allowed them to operate more cheaply than the government could and to build more without a hike in spending. Critics argued that inmates of private prisons were liable to be mistreated to save costs.

THE LOUISVILLE TIMES

Louisville, KY, August 12, 1985

At the urging of the Reagan administration, state and local governments increasingly have been experimenting with the transfer of roles traditionally performed by the public sector to private industry.

Advocates of "privatization" insist that private-enterprise contractors can more efficiently provide certain services. Even if that doesn't prove to be the case, the experience can give government yardsticks by which to measure its costs and, perhaps, begin to gain control of them.

While accepting the potential for savings in such areas as vehicle maintenance and garbage collection, many critics of the trend would draw the line at such an essential, basic government function as operating a prison.

Their concerns are well-founded, but not so compelling that they should rule out an experiment here in Kentucky with private operation of a minimum-security or similar adult corrections institution.

It *is* new ground; the record *is* sketchy. Gerald W. McEntee, president of the understandably skeptical American Federation of State, County and Municipal Employees, recently observed, "As little as 12 months ago the idea of contracting for corrections services was being laughed off as a pretty hare-brained idea." But it is now a $200 million a year business — and growing — as governments at all levels look for ways to stretch their limited resources.

As a task force named by Gov. Martha Layne Collins pointed out, Kentucky cannot afford to ignore any of its options. The state, after all, is facing a crisis in corrections. State and federal courts have ordered it to control its prison population and to reduce the backlog of inmates being held in local jails awaiting transfer to prisons. Estimates last year were that the prison population, then around 5,000 and now closer to 6,000, would double in the next decade.

The state is weighing two proposals submitted by for-profit companies to locate what is being called a "community residential treatment center" in Louisville. Under Corrections Cabinet standards, whichever location is selected would house only non-violent offenders with otherwise good records. They would have to be eligible for parole or release in 60 days to one year. Their days would be spent in work or training programs to be developed by the contractor either on the "campus" or off. Guards would be unarmed.

The Corrections Cabinet has reviewed the proposals and found them "programmatically" acceptable. They are now in the hands of state finance officials.

Both the size — 200 beds — and the two proposed locations — in or near residential areas — prompt questions that, so far, have not been answered. Others such as neighborhood safety and contractor accountability will have to be addressed before the go-ahead can be given on either Louisville site.

It is too soon to be sold on the notion of private operation of adult correctional institutions. But that does not mean it is not worth a try.

THE ATLANTA CONSTITUTION

Atlanta, GA, September 16, 1985

Say a state pays a company a flat rate to manage its prisoners. The fewer inmates in the system, the higher the profits. Officials might be tempted to tilt disciplinary reports and other papers in an inmate's favor to hasten his release. Public safety could suffer.

Or say a state pays a firm expenses plus an allowance for profit. The more inmates a firm manages, the more money it makes. It has an interest in keeping people behind bars longer. This could jeopardize justice for inmates.

But couldn't state governments oversee prison administration, the way they check up on public utilities? They could, but they wouldn't. There is little public demand for prison oversight. Privatization is attractive to many politicians precisely because it would let them wash their hands of prisons.

Prison reform would be even harder if, instead of state employees, reformers had to keep contract workers in line.

Prisons today have near-absolute control over the constitutional rights of some half a million inmates nationally. Because most prisoners are freed sometime, everyone has a stake in how this control is exercised.

The administration of constitutional rights should not be subject to a corporate bottom line. It is a responsibility for government. Government should not shirk it.

For scandal-weary governments, it is a tempting proposition: Why not hire private firms to run the prisons?

States could wash their hands of some embarrassing messes and turn full attention to popular projects like roads and schools. Officials would only need to mail off yearly payments for the maintenance of prisoners.

Alas, this is a siren song.

Tennessee is the latest government to listen — and really, who can blame it? Recent riots at five of its facilities did $11 million worth of damage. Meanwhile, the federal courts are demanding reform. Not only is this hard to achieve, it costs a bundle.

Enter the Corrections Corp. of America. Its pitch: It would lease Tennessee's whole system for 99 years and run it for a yearly fee. The fee would not exceed the state's present operating costs (but payments would be adjusted for inflation).

The problem is not with Corrections Corp. or any other private firm. Corrections Corp. already has seven contracts to run penal institutions around the country. There is no reason to doubt its claim that it can turn a profit of 8-to-11 percent by tightening up management.

The problem is more fundamental. It is rooted in dangerous incentives that likely would face private prison wardens.

Roanoke Times & World-News

Roanoke, VA, January 30, 1985

WHILE CRIME rates decline, prison populations in the United States rise. Maybe there's a connection. Anyhow, state and local governments nowadays have more and more prisoners to house, clothe, feed and care for.

All that is costly, bothersome and thankless. It can be more expensive to keep someone locked up for a year than to send him to Harvard. No wonder that many of those governments are looking with increasing interest at a new free-enterprise phenomenon: prisons for profit.

There aren't many of these, a dozen or so across the country. They're still experimental, but — not to pun — their operators mean business. Corrections Corporation of America, based in Nashville, Tenn., was formed in 1983; it was financed by the same investors' group that started the Hospital Corporation of America. Nearly a year ago it opened a $4 million, 300-bed detention facility for illegal aliens in Houston, Texas.

Companies like that one are "popping up all over the place," says Mary Fairchild of the National Conference of State Legislatures. Even some conglomerates are attracted to the idea: Control Data Corporation, best known for computer operations, started a "corrections services division" last January to run prisons.

A number of states already have contracted for such services, and others are looking into the concept. Republican Dels. Kenneth E. Calvert of Danville and W.R. O'Brien of Virginia Beach are co-sponsors of a resolution in the General Assembly calling for a bipartisan study.

Philosophical objections can be raised to the idea of making money from locking people up. But no matter who runs the prisons, they can't go out and round up individuals to keep their cells full; it's still the courts that put people behind bars. And heaven knows, the public sector has been no shining example at running prisons. Would the "warehousing" factor, the discipline problems, the sexual abuses be any worse under free enterprise?

It's hard to imagine how.

In any event, ultimate responsibility for the way prisons are run remains with the government, which would have to set standards, make inspections, run down escapees, etc., etc. That can be an argument for giving business a chance. It can also be an argument for keeping prisons in governmental hands: If final responsibility can't really be delegated, why bother to deal in a middleman?

Those, however, are value judgments to be weighed later, when more facts are available. The commonwealth ought to take a serious look at this new option in incarceration. How refreshing to have someplace that *wants* to take in prisoners.

DESERET NEWS

Salt Lake City, UT, October 30-31, 1985

Can private companies operate jails and even prisons more cheaply than the government? They already are, in many cases:

● In Tennessee, a private contractor now operates a workhouse for 300 men and women who are awaiting trial, or who are serving sentences of less than six months.

● In Pennsylvania, a firm has been operating a state maximum security facility for juveniles since 1975.

● Some 28 states now use privately-operated pre-release, work release, or halfway house facilities.

Faced with burdensome taxes to construct new prisons and jails for a growing inmate population, Utah needs to look at this relatively new trend in privatization. Last year, the Legislature appropriated $32 million to begin the first phase of a master plan that will cost $67.3 million in the next 10 years. The Utah Foundation this week explored the role of private enterprise in prison operations, and found a growing private involvement in corrections programs — including operation of halfway houses and minimum-medium facilities, training, prison industries, and others.

Another area of increasing private participation is lease-purchase arrangements where private capital is raised to build facilities, which are then leased back to the state. After a specified number of years the state becomes the owner.

Then, too, private firms contract for a growing list of specific services in many states. One Minnesota firm provides food service at 11 correctional facilities, including the state prison — so successfully, in fact, that the quality of the food has increased while total cost has dropped 10 percent.

A Maryland firm has contracted to transport prisoners for court appearances at a substantial savings to the state. And health care services are provided under contract to several corrections institutions.

One caution, however: In most of these cases, economies of scale have been possible because companies were working with large institutions. With a prison population of 1,435, says one knowledgeable corrections official, Utah is below the threshold where considerable savings can be expected even with the best plans of shifting some responsibilities to the private sector.

As one example, Utah not long ago asked for bids on operating a halfway house for 12 inmates. One company bid $900,000 — or $205 per prisoner per day. The state can do that job for $23 a day, or if intensive psychotherapy and other services are required, for $43 a day. The idea is to save money by privatization — not spend more.

Another question is ultimate liability. Is the state still liable for mistakes private companies make in handling prisoners? If so, the state must carefully supervise such operations or risk a liability suit.

Even so, savings could be effected in many areas of the correctional program — such as food services or health care — by using private firms. Those areas need to be identified in future prison studies.

Supreme Court Rejects Race Bias Challenge to Death Penalty

The Supreme Court April 22, 1987 rejected a racial challenge to the death penalty as insufficient proof that the defendant in the case under review had been the victim of discrimination. The court in a 5-4 decision upheld a death sentence imposed in Georgia against a black man convicted of killing a white police officer in Atlanta during a robbery. The defendant, Warren McClesky, charged that the Georgia capital punishment system was tainted by racism in its sentencing procedures and therefore had unconstitutionally deprived him of the 14th Amendment's guarantee of "equal protection of the laws." McClesky also charged that the sentencing violated the Eighth Amendment's prohibition against "cruel and unusual punishment." In proof thereof, McClesky submitted an authoritative study by University of Iowa Prof. David Bladus showing that defendants who killed white victims in Georgia were 11 times more likely to be sentenced to death than those who killed blacks, and that blacks who killed whites were sentenced to die seven times more often than whites who killed blacks.

The court's majority opinion, written by Justice Lewis F. Powell Jr., did not dispute the statistical report but said it did not prove discrimination in McClesky's specific case. A generalized study showing "a discrepency that appears to correlate with race" was not enough, he said. There was no showing in the Baldus study, Powell said, of "a constitutionally significant risk of racial prejudice affecting the Georgia capital-sentencing process." Nor did the Constitution require, he said, that a state eliminate every "demonstratable disparity" in sentencing. "Apparent disparities in sentencing are an inevitable part of our criminal justice system," he said. "Discretion is essential to the criminal justice process," Powell said. "We would demand exceptionally clear proof before we would infer that the discretion had been abused." The court's previous decisions on capital punishment had been grounded on factors showing "the risk of imposition of an arbitrary sentence, rather than the proven fact of one," he said. And the evidence in this case "relentlessly documents the risk that McClesky's sentence was not influenced by racial considerations."

The Honolulu Advertiser

Honolulu, HI, April 24, 1987

The Supreme Court vote upholding the death penalty was narrow, just 5 to 4, but wide enough to disappoint opponents and open the way to executions of many more of the 1,850 some death-row inmates across the land.

This last legal attack on the death penalty was based on its undenied tendency to discriminate by race. Blacks who kill whites in Georgia are 11 times more likely to be executed than those who kill blacks. And blacks who kill whites are executed three times more often than whites who killed whites. Such statistics are apt to be matched to some degree in most states.

In Hawaii, it was realization that capital punishment was meted out more often to non-whites and the poor (which often means the same thing) that gave impetus to its abolition. Despite repeated attempts to reinstate it in some form, humane and responsible legislators — usually in the House — have stood against it.

But it's a struggle. Polls show that three-quarters of the American people favor the death penalty. It is now legal in 37 states, although only 11 have actually carried out executions since 1977.

This wide support and practice of capital punishment puts this country at odds with most western, democratic nations, which no longer use capital punishment or restrict it to crimes like wartime espionage.

The Supreme Court found the evidence of discrimination was not enough to invalidate the death penalty. But the national battle is not over. It now shifts to the states.

It is hoped that evidence of systematic if unintended discrimination in the application of the death penalty will have greater impact in some enlightened state legislatures than it did before the Supreme Court.

Richmond Times-Dispatch

Richmond, VA, April 24, 1987

The U.S. Supreme Court's 5-4 decision upholding the death penalty against a statistically based charge of racial discrimination is not likely to result in speedy execution of hundreds of death-row inmates across the country. Even the losing petitioner in this case, convicted cop-killer Warren McCleskey, has not reached the end of his potential appeals. And it has been nine years since Mr. McCleskey was convicted of killing Atlanta police officer Frank Schlatt during the robbery of a furniture store. Nine years!

But if the court had swung the other direction, all executions would have been halted for many years, and perhaps forever. For as Justice Lewis F. Powell Jr. wrote for the majority, states could have been required to eliminate all sorts of other variables before carrying out capital sentences, had the Supreme Court bought the argument that statistical disparities alone are sufficient grounds for stripping the death penalty from criminal codes.

Mr. Powell delivered this concise, much-needed admonition against criminal law-making by the Supreme Court: "It is not the responsibility or indeed even the right — of this court to determine the appropriate punishment for particular crimes." Arguments made on Mr. McCleskey's behalf that killers of whites are more often sentenced to die than killers of blacks "are best presented to the legislative bodies," Mr. Powell wrote. Since the court rein-

stated the death penalty 11 years ago in another Georgia case, 37 states and Congress have enacted death penalty statutes. And polls show that clear majorities of Americans support those legislative actions.

By no means does the Supreme Court decision mean that prosecutors, juries and judges are free to discriminate against defendants in capital cases because of their race. The Powell decision instead states that defendants must prove that there was actual intent to discriminate against them. In his long trail of rejected *habeas corpus* petitions — extending from several local courts to the Georgia Supreme Court to U.S. District Court to the 11th Circuit Court of Appeals — Mr. McCleskey never offered evidence that racial prejudice contaminated jury selection or jury decisions. He did not deny that he had shot and killed a policeman. His case was based wholly on statistics.

If the studies are correct in suggesting that the criminal justice system operates to place a higher value on white life than black, corrective action does not have to entail abolition of the death penalty. Rather, state and local lawmakers and jurists can rededicate themselves to the ideal of a colorblind system of justice, one in which the murderers of blacks would be just as likely to face the ultimate punishment as the murderers of whites.

the Charleston Gazette

Charleston, WV, April 28, 1987

IGNORING reality, the conservative wing of the U.S. Supreme Court has squeezed through a 5-4 decision saying executions in America aren't racially skewed.

Baloney. The death penalty is chiefly an instrument of Southern redneck justice, as many studies have proven.

In the 1970s, Northeastern University researchers found that blacks who killed whites in Florida were 40 times more likely to be sentenced to death than were blacks who killed blacks. No comparison could be made to whites who kill blacks, because no Florida white had drawn a death sentence for killing a black.

In the early 1980s, University of Iowa researchers found that killers of white victims in Georgia were 11 times more likely to receive death sentences than killers of blacks.

Dixie prosecutors argue that juries react more strongly to murders committed during holdups — and most store proprietors are white — hence the imbalance in sentencing. But studies of holdup murders including cases with black proprietors still find at least a 4-to-1 racial disparity.

The conclusion is inescapable:

Executions happen mostly in the South, where white society cares little about black lives. When blacks kill blacks, authorities shrug. When whites kill whites, it's taken seriously. When blacks kill whites, lynch mob reaction flares.

For the Supreme Court's conservative bloc to rule otherwise is to insult the intelligence of most Americans.

Harvard law Professor Alan Dershowitz called the decision "a throwback to the days of slavery and Jim Crow, when it was murder to kill a white but not murder to kill a black."

Oklahoma public defender Bob Ravitz says the ruling will cause a wave of executions, perhaps "100 to 150 between now and the end of the year," because it removes a major legal obstacle. In nearby Texas, 250 prisoners are waiting for the state to kill them.

During the Supreme Court's oral arguments, Justice Antonin Scalia made a revealing "joke": The next thing you know, he said, ugly defendants may claim that they, too, are more likely to draw the death penalty. In his innermost heart, Scalia knows that this prejudice also intrudes into justice.

Instead of concocting warped logic to justify executions, the Supreme Court should try to steer America in the direction of other enlightened nations.

Every industrialized democracy in the world has ended the death penalty — except America. All Western nations have concluded that it's wrong for governments to kill prisoners.

Just the Soviet Union, Iran, South Africa, Turkey, China, Libya and other dictatorial countries still have state killings. It's disgusting that America stands in such a group.

The San Diego Union

San Diego, CA, April 25, 1987

The 37 states, including California, that have authorized the death penalty were sanctioned anew last week by two landmark rulings from the U.S. Supreme Court.

On Tuesday, the high court held that capital punishment is not racially discriminatory just because a disproportionate number of blacks happen be on death row, or because a study shows that defendants who kill white victims are more likely to be sentenced to death than are those who kill blacks.

On Wednesday, the court said that persons who participate in a crime leading to murder can be put to death even though they did not intend that the victim be killed.

The ruling on racial bias is particularly significant because it removes the last major barrier to the death penalty in this nation. Indeed, had the decision gone the other way, all state capital-punishment laws would be thrown out as they were 15 years ago, when a court majority held the administration of the penalty to be "arbitrary" and "capricious." Closer home, it could have let Robert Alton Harris off the hook.

Harris, who is awaiting the gas

chamber in San Quentin for the 1979 murders of two Mira Mesa teen-agers, has appealed his death sentence to the federal courts because his victims were white. Although he was convicted of shooting the two in cold blood, he nonetheless sought refuge under the equal protection clause of the Constitution. Now it appears that Harris could be executed this year.

The high court's ruling on felony murder is also essential to California justice because it effectively negates a 1983 state Supreme Court decision that mocked the concept of criminal intent.

In *Carlos vs. Superior Court,* the state Supreme Court, under former Chief Justice Rose Elizabeth Bird, barred the death penalty or life without parole unless the jury found that the defendant had actually intended to kill. In 1984, the court used the Carlos decision to reverse 14 death penalties and it could reverse 29 more, according to state prosecutors.

The Bird Court's interpretation of the law was so generous that cold-blooded killers routinely evaded capital punishment even though it was clearly justified by

their heinous crimes.

Consider the case of Bernard Lee Hamilton. In January 1981, a jury found him guilty of felony murder of Eleanore Francis Buchanan. Abducted by Hamilton from a Mesa College parking lot, she was stabbed in the stomach and her body was subsequently found in Pine Valley with both hands missing. Even though the intent rule was not applicable when the Hamilton verdict was rendered, it was nonetheless applied by the Bird Court in 1986 because his case was still under appeal. The majority opinion overturning Hamilton's death sentence concluded that, however unlikely, Mrs. Buchanan's death could have been accidental, or at least unintentional.

To their credit, California voters turned three of the justices out of office last November. The newly reconstituted state Supreme Court is going to review some of the most outrageous cases where the death sentence was reversed on the "intent" technicality. The likelihood that these and other killers will receive what they richly deserve is much improved now that the U.S. Supreme Court has cleared the way for executions nationwide.

The Courier-Journal

April 24, 1987
Louisville, KY

IT'S a sad day when the U.S. Supreme Court all but gives a state the go-ahead to execute someone while acknowledging that our criminal justice system is racist.

Coupled with another decision this week in which the court made it easier for states to condemn to death people who aren't killers and never intended to kill anyone, the rulings amount to a terrible broadening of the death penalty.

In the race-related ruling, the court ruled 5 to 4 that Georgia's capital punishment law is constitutional even though killers of white people are far more often sentenced to die than killers of blacks.

The court acknowledged as valid a study by David Baldus, professor of law at the University of Iowa, that showed sharp racial disparities in the sentencing of killers in Georgia and found capital punishment far more likely in cases involving black killers of white victims. Baldus also found that racial disparities manifested themselves at every stage of the judicial process, from indictment to sentencing. That would seem to be all the more reason for the court to move with extreme caution before broadening the states' powers of execution. But it wasn't.

Justice Lewis F. Powell Jr., author of the majority opinion, dismissed the study's importance with a single damning word. He called the findings a "discrepancy." "At most," he wrote, "the study indicates a discrepancy that appears to correlate with race," adding that "apparent disparities in sentencing are an inevitable part of our criminal justice system."

It's hard to imagine that this court that calls discrepancies inevitable is the same court that 15 years ago struck down death penalty laws largely because they gave judges and juries too much discretion. The court argued then that a disproportionate number of poor people and members of racial minority groups were executed, while more affluent people, and especially whites, were more often given lesser sentences or reprieved.

Or perhaps the short memory of the five justices isn't so surprising. After all, the essence of their ruling is a repudiation of history.

The Georgia case was the last broad-based legal challenge to the death penalty. Its failure means this country can now expect a steady stream of executions.

Given the court's endorsement of a discriminatory system, those will be other sad days.

The Chattanooga Times

Chattanooga, TN, April 29, 1987

In two capital punishment decisions last week, the U.S. Supreme Court further muddled that sensitive area of criminal law, this time by demonstrating a serious lack of regard for fairness and consistency. The court upheld a Georgia law that a researcher had shown discriminated against black defendants, and agreed to permit capital punishment for accomplices in murder cases. If nothing else, the court paradoxically proved the best argument for eliminating the death penalty.

In a 5-to-4 decision by Justice Lewis Powell, the court ruled against Warren McCleskey. Mr. McCleskey, a black man, was convicted of fatally shooting an Atlanta police officer and sentenced to death. In his opinion Justice Powell contended that the risk that some racial prejudice could influence a jury's decision is acceptable, even when, in a capital case, the ultimate sentence is execution.

To reach this astonishing conclusion, however, the court had to ignore a body of research into Georgia cases which showed that killers of whites are more likely to be sentenced to death than killers of blacks. The study reviewed all convictions for murder in Georgia from 1973 to 1978. It found that 22 percent of blacks who killed whites received the death penalty. However, the same punishment was imposed on only 1 percent of blacks who killed blacks, 3 percent of whites who killed blacks and 8 percent of whites who killed whites. Justice Powell conceded that the study indicated apparent racial bias. But, he said, such bias does not compare with the "major systemic defects" that prompted the court to overturn all capital punishment statutes in 1972.

But where the court was willing to discount the validity of the research in the Georgia case, it accepted other research in agreeing, in yet another 5-to-4 decision, to expand the definition of persons subject to capital punishment. It said that accomplices in murder cases can be sentenced to death if their actions in the crime demonstrated a "reckless indifference to human life." Justice Sandra Day O'Connor's opinion was based largely on a survey showing that of the 37 states with death penalty laws, only 11 would prohibit the supreme punishment for accomplices in such murder cases.

She argued that recent state laws on this subject illustrate that society "does not reject the death penalty as grossly excessive under these circumstances. But using that logic, it would be easy for states to evade the constitutional prohibition of cruel and unusual punishment. They would merely have to expand the use of the death penalty through legislation, making more and more defendants subject to that punishment. The court could then point to the states' actions and declare that such laws are constitutional.

Justice William Brennan's dissent in the Georgia case was both eloquent and correct because it went to the heart of the manner in which the death penalty is administered in our society: The effort to eliminate arbitrariness in the infliction of that ultimate sanction, Justice Brennan wrote, "is so plainly doomed to failure that it — and the death penalty — must be abandoned altogether."

When the court approves of punishment that is imposed inequitably, it approves in effect of inequitable punishment. In the arbitrary lottery known as the capital punishment system in America today, it is not cynical to suggest that those with the best chance of beating the death penalty rap are blacks who kill blacks and whites who kill blacks or other whites.

THE DENVER POST

Denver, CO, April 28, 1987

IN UPHOLDING a Georgia court's death sentence against a black holdup man who killed a white policeman, the U.S. Supreme Court has spoken for law and order in a single case, but has certified that the court holds black life cheaper than white life.

The court's five-four decision rejected compelling statistical evidence that Georgia murder defendants, in cases where whites are victims, are 11 times more likely to get a death sentence than if the victims are black.

The court did not even question the validity of the evidence of racial discrimination in sentencing in Georgia — and in other states. The court, instead, just begged off its responsibility, offering the weak suggestion that if "disparity" in sentencing existed, it was a consideration for state legislatures, not the U.S. court.

What the court handed down amounts to an impossible "Catch-22": The remedy to racial discrimination in sentencing is in the states that insist there is no such discrimination.

The majority opinion by Justice Lewis F. Powell was challenged by Justice John Paul Stevens, who recalled the court's 1972 criticism of "standardless" death penalty laws in the states, a ruling that for a time blocked executions until state laws were rewritten.

The disparity of sentencing shown in the defense arguments, "is constitutionally intolerable," Stevens wrote. "It flagrantly violates the court's prior insistence that capital punishment be imposed fairly . . . or not at all."

We intend no defense for Warren McCleskey, the black man under a death sentence for the murder of an Atlanta policeman in 1978. The question posed to the court was not specifically on McCleskey's guilt or innocence, but whether, given the proof of discrimination in the Georgia courts, he'd been deprived of his constitutional rights. It was also an unusual appeal because, in effect, it turned the conventional legal approach around to argue a bias based on the race of the victim instead of the defendant.

We find the court's decision in the McCleskey case thoroughly bad — as a precedent now standing against future valid claims of discrimination and as evidence the court shirked its duty.

There's a suggestion in the decision that, in murder convictions, it makes no difference if some defendants are sentenced to death and others are not, even when race is a clear factor.

But it does make a difference. We struggle to be a fair and just people. It is our heritage. We stay committed to our Constitution and — in this case — to its uncompromising requirement that no state "shall deprive any person of life, liberty or property without due process of law; nor deny to any person within its jurisdiction the equal protection of the laws."

In the McCleskey case, the Supreme Court closed its eyes to the Constitution and the court's duty.

The Register

Santa Ana, CA, April 24, 1987

Many opponents of capital punishment are complaining loudly about the Supreme Court's decision Wednesday not to invalidate the death penalty on the basis of circumstantial statistics, but there really is no other conclusion the court could have reached.

The Constitution specifically allows capital punishment. And to argue that the death penalty should be abolished because bigotry may influence jurors in its application is to argue that juries are simply incapable of rendering fair judgments.

In the case before the court this week, a jury of 11 whites and one black had sentenced Warren McCleskey to death for killing an Atlanta policeman in 1978. Judicial activists challenged that sentence with statistics showing that black murderers are more likely to get the death penalty than white ones.

Rather than offer specific proof that McCleskey had been condemned to die by a jury of bigots, the activists hoped the court would rule that capital punishment is inherently discriminatory.

It isn't. If jurors are bigots, the fault is not in the law but in the way juries are selected. Perhaps the courts need to do more to screen out unworthy jurors, but they should not throw out laws instead.

The concept of executing criminals is troubling. Can any individual commit a crime so heinous that he forfeits his right to life? If not, should taxpayers be forced to pay for lifetime care and feeding in the penitentiary?

Those questions, however, were not before the court. It had been asked only to decide if justice should be handed out on some sort of quota system. On that narrow issue, the majority correctly ruled that affirmative action has no place in determining criminal justice.

WELL, GEE, IT MIGHT BE RACIST... BUT THEN AGAIN, IT MIGHT BE COINCIDENTAL.

SUPREME COURT

CAPITAL PUNISHMENT RACIST?

The Sun Reporter

San Francisco, CA, April 29, 1987

There was a hallmark five to four U.S. Supreme Court decision last Thursday, which denied that racism could be a factor in the 14th Amendment right to equal protection under the law.

Civil rights advocates felt that the U.S. Supreme Court would certainly find the State of Georgia's criminal behavior unconstitutional by condemning the universal practice in which a Black person who kills a white is usually given the death penalty, while a white person who kills another white does not receive the death penalty; moreover, in many instances, the life of a Black who kills another Black is spared — he might get a long prison term, but not the death penalty.

Even though the facts were statistically reliable, the judges, in their opinion, which was written by Justice Lewis Powell, said that for such behavior to be racist and unconstitutional it had to be proven by the felon that race is the reason that the prosecution asked for the death penalty, or that the jury decreed it, or that the judiciary upheld it. The Powell requirement would place an undue burden upon the defendant. It it well-nigh impossible to prove racial discrimination in each case. However, the justices made a mistake when they refused to decide this case as racist.

Two kinds of racism exist in the nation: the first is institutional racism, which provides an umbrella under which the individual racists can operate without being accused specifically of being racists in a particular case. In fact, institutional racism is so pervasive until it usually becomes low-keyed and generally accepted as a way of life by many of the majority and the minority peoples. However, we feel that this case is a glaring example of institutional racism.

Justice Powell, in a facetious aside, added, "Why the next thing you know ugly people will charge discrimination too!" — which is a covert way of denying the very existence of racism.

Justice William Brennan, in a dissent which even Justice Powell referred to as eloquent, said, "We cannot pretend that in three decades we have completely escaped the grip of an historical legacy spanning centuries. Warren McCleskey's evidence confronts us with the subtle and persistent influence of the past. His message is a disturbing one to a society that has formally repudiated racism . . ."

As students of racism, we deny the argument that the victim himself must prove without a shadow of a doubt that the jury and the presiding judge showed undeniable signs of racism in their courtroom behavior. This opinion on the part of the majority of the court represents an effort to challenge the very existence of racism, and especially to deny the possibility that a particular jury's behavior could be discriminatory and still not necessarily racist, and therefore be perfectly constitutional.

While Warren McCleskey had killed a white policeman during a holdup, he is the only one out of 16 cases in Atlanta to draw the death sentence in the last seven years. He and many of the nation's 1,900 Death Row inmates have reason to wonder what role race played in their trials. Although 60 percent of Georgia homicide victims are Black, all seven people put to death in Georgia's electric chair since 1976 were convicted of killing white people; six of the seven murderers were Black. McCleskey was sentenced to death by a jury of 11 whites and one Black.

Justice Brennan has uttered a phrase which might become as historic as the 1896 *Plessy v. Ferguson* decision: "We ignore him [McCleskey] at our peril, for we remain imprisoned by the past as long as we deny its influence in the present."

Portland Press Herald

Portland, ME, April 24, 1987

The Supreme Court has held that the death penalty can be used despite statistics suggesting it is imposed in racially biased ways. And in Maine the decision was enough to raise the chant to bring back the hangman.

The legislative sponsor of a capital punishment proposal believes the court's decision will increase support for the bill. "It will have a positive influence on the bill, with the court saying 'yes, that type of punishment is OK,' " says Rep. Michael F. Hepburn, R-Skowhegan.

How's that again? The Supreme Court ruled in 1976 that the death penalty was constitutional. But Maine has turned back effort after effort since then to reinstitute the capital punishment it outlawed a century ago. It's unlikely that a reaffirmation of the constitutionality — based on a narrow, 5-4 court vote — will increase support for what is essentially legalized murder.

Actually, the claim of racial bias was a weak reed upon which to rest a case against capital punishment. That's not much different than saying the death penalty is sexually discriminatory because most of those executed are males.

A better argument against the death penalty is the likelihood of the state, in its quest for vengeance, killing an innocent person. A national study just a year ago concluded that more than 340 persons were wrongly convicted of crimes punishable by death in this century — and that 25 were actually killed.

Mainers outlawed the barbaric death penalty in part because we were aware of the inevitability of error. Instead, we literally lock away our worst offenders for the rest of their lives.

That makes sense. A wrongly convicted person can always be released. But how do you apologize to a corpse?

The Star-Ledger

Newark, NJ, April 24, 1987

The U.S. Supreme Court has dealt the opponents of capital punishment an enormous setback. It has rejected one of the last—perhaps the last—remaining constitutional arguments against the death penalty that had not been dealt with in earlier decisions.

A narrowly split court ruled against a constitutional challenge to a death penalty law in Georgia on the basis of racial bias. The attack on the statute noted that the murder of whites was far more apt to be punished in Georgia by death than the murder of blacks. By a 5-4 vote, the high court held that this racial pattern alone did not render the state law unconstitutional.

The new ruling did not quite end the constitutional issue. In some states—New Jersey is one of them—capital punishment opponents will seek to overturn death penalty laws on the basis of the equal protection clause of the state constitution.

Beyond the constitutional issues involved—even beyond the much greater moral and ethical issues surrounding the taking of life—there are other reasons, however, for dissatisfaction with capital punishment. In many respects, it simply hasn't been an effective tool in dispensing criminal justice.

In most states, even states with capital punishment, the death penalty has existed in law but not in fact. Executions have been limited, for the most part, to a handful of Southern states. There still is enormous reluctance to practice the death penalty, even in areas where it has been reaffirmed by the legislature. It is problematical whether the new high court ruling will change this paradoxical situation.

In New Jersey, for example, there has been no execution for a capital crime since 1963. For about half that period, there was a death penalty law on the books. But while there were death sentences, they have not been carried out. The gap between the legality of the death penalty and the process of execution remains enormous. And even court rulings that are supposed to settle the matter usually end up only adding to the confusion.

For example, New Jersey's Supreme Court recently reaffirmed the constitutionality of the state capital punishment law, but at the same time set aside on procedural grounds its imposition on two convicts. There are 26 prisoners on New Jersey's death row, and the number will continue to grow.

The end of the constitutional argument against capital punishment could be a good time to find a legislative solution that will end the present intolerable jumble that is having a deleterious effect on our criminal justice system.

A system of punishing the most heinous capital crimes with a maximum sentence of life imprisonment without parole remains a reasonable alternative. Supporters of capital punishment, as well as its opponents, ought to recognize the failures of the present system and consider this solution to what will otherwise continue to be a legal, ethical and moral quagmire.

Edmonton Journal

Edmonton, Alta., April 29, 1987

The U.S. Supreme Court recently handed down ʹo decisions in support of capital punishment. Ironically, they give Canadians two more good reasons why the death penalty should not be restored here.

First, the court ruled the death penalty could also be imposed on associates of murderers who show "reckless indifference to human life". It sets a frightening precedent. Now, one need not commit murder to be executed — simply being a party to the offence may be sufficient.

Some Canadians say if the death penalty were restored, it would be reserved only for heinous crimes. But how long would it be before those assurances were compromised?

The court also endorsed capital punishment despite evidence of racial discrimination in its use. A study of 2,500 homicides in Georgia by University of Iowa professor David Baldus found blacks are more likely to be sentenced to death than whites. The court acknowledged that the justice system is inequitable and fallible: "Apparent disparities in sentencing are an inevitable part of our criminal justice system . . . ."

Yet it said Baldus's study did "not demonstrate a constitutionally significant risk of racial bias affecting the Georgia capital-sentencing process." The system is flawed, it says, but so what?

Fallibility is just one of many reasons capital punishment should be rejected. An innocent man can be released from prison. He cannot be raised from the dead.

The Birmingham News

Birmingham, AL, April 1987

The statistics looked damning, but the crime committed by Warren McCleskey was even more damning.

That, essentially, is what a majority of the U.S. Supreme Court said Wednesday in upholding Georgia's death penalty law against a claim that killers of white people were far more likely to be sentenced to death under the statute than killers of blacks.

The 5-4 decision was touted as the most important death penalty ruling since 1976, when the court upheld new death penalty laws four years after striking down the old statutes partially on grounds they had been applied in a discriminatory manner.

On the surface, McCleskey's attorneys presented substantial evidence that the Georgia law has been unfairly applied. Killers of whites in the state, said their study, are four times more likely to be sentenced to death than killers of blacks. While 60 percent of Georgia's homicide victims are black, all seven people put to death in the state's electric chair since 1976 have been killers of whites.

Even in accepting the validity of that study, the justices claimed it was no proof that McCleskey himself had been a victim of racial prejudice. McCleskey, said Justice Lewis Powell, writing for the majority, "must prove that the decision-makers in *his* case acted with a discriminatory purpose."

That would be far more difficult to do. McCleskey was convicted of the murder of a 31-year-old Atlanta police officer who was shot and killed while he was investigating a burglary at a downtown furniture store. We have serious doubts racial prejudice played any role in his sentencing.

The standard the court set in this case is a fair one. Those who can prove racial prejudice in their trial or sentencing do have a legitimate grievance against the justice system. An overall statistical analysis does not prove an individual case, however.

As Powell noted, had the court agreed with McCleskey's attorneys, it might have led to widespread challenges by others claiming all manner of racial or sexual disparities in all manner of sentencing, or even by defendants claiming they were treated harshly because of such traits as physical uattractiveness.

That doesn't mean Georgia officials have anything to be proud of. There appear to be serious flaws in either their law or the way it has been applied. They should work to correct them.

It does mean that Warren McCleskey should not be let off the hook for killing a police officer because of unfortunate statistics.

The News and Courier

Raleigh, NC, April 24, 1987

Standing eyeball to eyeball with racial discrimination in a death penalty case, a majority of the U.S. Supreme Court blinked the evidence away. States thus are free to go on taking people's lives in a capricious manner.

Speaking for the five-member majority in the case of McCleskey v. Georgia, Justice Lewis F. Powell Jr. brushed aside a study that convincingly indicts the state for unfairness in administering the death penalty. Someone who kills a white person in Georgia is 11 times more likely to receive the death penalty than someone who kills a black person.

Such disparity under the law is not a monopoly of Georgia's. A study of 489 homicides over a 12-month period in North Carolina found the death-penalty scales tilted heavily against blacks in capital cases, especially when their victims were white. It also turned up astonishing differences — from zero to 100 percent — among judicial districts in defendants' chances of being tried for first-degree murder and put at risk of a death sentence.

There's abundant evidence, then, that not only race but also sheer chance plays a vital part in state executions. And yet the Supreme Court's majority waved that evidence off. In effect, its decision says that this is a cost of doing business under the U.S. system of criminal justice. The "discretion" used by prosecutors and juries is bound to bring disparities in sentencing, it argues. If there's anything wrong with the way the law is implemented, it's up to state legislatures — not the judicial system — to set things right.

What a deplorable position for the Supreme Court to take. There's a life-or-death difference between "discretion" employed in capital cases and that used in other criminal cases. Disparity of treatment because of race, quality of legal help or whimsical prosecution may involve only a longer or shorter prison sentence in non-capital cases. But lives are at stake when "discretion" comes into play in murder cases.

As administered in this country, capital punishment is fatally flawed. Its uneven application means that only about 3 percent of those charged with first-degree murder eventually get sentenced to death. Further, there has been far too little improvement in applying state death laws since 1972, when the Supreme Court called the results "wanton and freakish."

Justice William J. Brennan Jr., dissenting in the McCleskey case, is right in asserting that capital punishment should be imposed fairly or not at all. But there's only one sure way of remedying what's wrong with the state lottery known as the death penalty. That's for the Supreme Court to throw it out on solid grounds: Cruel and unusual punishment that results from unequal protection under the law.

Newsday

Long Island, NY,
April 24, 1987

Nothing in Georgia's death penalty law suggests that courts or juries should take the race of a murder victim into account in meting out punishment. But statistics show that a killer in Georgia is far more likely to be sentenced to death if the victim is white. The disparity is especially striking if the killer is black.

Yet the Supreme Court ruled Wednesday that a death sentence need not be overturned on equal protection grounds unless the defendant could prove "purposeful discrimination" had affected his case. That's a much heavier burden of proof than has been required in cases involving voting, jobs or housing; it's usually sufficient to show a discriminatory effect rather than discriminatory intent.

The black defendant in the Supreme Court case, Warren McCleskey, had been sentenced to death for the murder of a white police officer. He based his appeal on a detailed study that examined every case in which a Georgia defendant had been eligible for capital punishment under the present statute. Hundreds of separate factors were considered in about 2,400 cases, and virtually every method of statistical analysis showed that race was a major factor in death penalty decisions.

Yet Justice Lewis Powell, who wrote the court's 5-4 majority opinion, didn't see it quite that way. "At most," he said, "the . . . study indicates a discrepancy that appears to correlate with race."

Noting that the Eighth Amendment's protection against cruel and unusual punishment "is not limited to capital punishment but applies to all penalties," Powell worried that "if we accepted McCleskey's claim that racial bias has impermissibly tainted the capital-sentencing decisions, we could soon be faced with similar claims as to other types of penalty." But justice is supposed to be colorblind, and it ought to be demonstrably colorblind when it comes to invoking the ultimate punishment.

Powell also feared that if the court ruled for McCleskey, "membership in other minority groups," and "even gender" or "physical attractiveness of defendant or victim" might be cited in other cases. The time to deal with such contentions is when they arise, not when a man's life is at stake. But if the justices weren't swayed by the strong evidence of de facto discrimination in this case, it's hard to see what might persuade them.

Yet it may well be, for the very reasons cited by Powell, that it's simply not possible to impose the death penalty in anything but an "arbitrary and capricious" manner. And that's something state legislators should consider in dealing with capital punishment.

THE ☀ SUN

Baltimore, MD, April 23, 1987

The Supreme Court Tuesday and again yesterday dealt sickening blows to those Americans who oppose capital punishment. First, the court by a 5-4 margin ruled that the death penalty may be imposed even on the associates of murderers if in the course of a felony they display a "reckless indifference to human life." The court's majority indicated it considers that a broad and encompassing phrase. The two Arizona men whose death sentences they upheld were partners in the armed escape from prison of their father, who later killed captives. The sons had agreed to participate in the escape only upon getting a promise from their father that no one would be harmed.

This decision turns sentencing back toward that past when human life was so little esteemed even such crimes as robbery carried the death penalty. It suggests a hardening on the part of the court's pro-capital punishment majority. One member of that block is Byron White, who in 1982 wrote a decision saying the death penalty could only be imposed on those who actually committed murder or intended that the murder occur.

As bad as was Tuesday's decision, yesterday's verdict was even worse. The same five-member majority of Mr. White, Chief Justice William Rehnquist and Justices Sandra O'Connor, Lewis Powell and Antonin Scalia turned a deaf ear and blind eye to the clearest evidence yet that the death penalty is being imposed in a racially discriminatory way. It was such discrimination that led the court in 1972 to throw out the death penalty. In 1976 when the court reinstituted the death penalty, it expressed the belief new sentencing procedures developed by states after 1972 would prevent such vicious "arbitrary" discrimination.

That expectation was overly optimistic. Of the 70 executions carried out since 1976, 60 percent were of blacks. That's six times the number one would expect. Even more striking and more convincing are the statistics on the race of the victims of those sentenced to death. Ninety-five percent of those executed killed whites, as did 69 percent of those remaining on death row. A study presented to the court showed that murderers of whites were four times more likely to get the death penalty than murderers of blacks.

We do not see how the majority could view this any other way but as a racist determination about the value of black and white life. This may be unconscious on the part of prosecutors and jurors. We believe it is. But it is no less real for that reason. No less unfair. No less unconstitutional. Statistical disparities of this magnitude in employment or education would be accepted as evidence of illegal discrimination. It certainly should be when the issue is life and death. We can only wait for the court to come to its senses.

Revived Cuban Immigration Pact Sparks Prison Riots

The United States and Cuba had agreed to reactivate a 1984 immigration pact that called for more than 2,000 "undesireables" who had traveled to the U.S. in the 1980 Mariel boatlift, the U.S. State Department announced Nov. 20, 1987. Under the pact, the U.S. would accept Cuban political prisoners and more than 20,000 Cuban immigrants a year. News of the pact sparked riots among Cuban inmates in two detention centers in the U.S. The Cubans took over the facilities and refused to end their rebellions until they received assurances that they would not be sent back to Cuba.

Under the immigration pact, the 2,746 so-called "excludeables" who were not eligible to remain in the U.S. would be returned to Cuba. They included former mental patients and those who had committed crimes either in Cuba or since their arrival in the U.S. Of those deemed excludeable, 201 had been returned to Cuba before the immigration agreement was suspended. Most of the remainder were being held in federal detention centers in Atlanta, in Oakdale, La. and elsewhere. Some were free on parole. In all, 3,751 Mariel Cubans were currently under detention by the U.S. Immigration and Naturalization Service (INS). A further 3,830 were serving sentences in state and county prisons for crimes committed while in the U.S., and on completion of their prison sentences they would become INS detainees subject to deportation. U.S. officials had said they hoped to send back to Cuba not only the 2,746 deemed excludeable at the time the pact was negotiated but also many of those being detained by the INS and in state and country prisons, as well as many of the 3,000 "Marielitos" who had already been released to halfway houses or to their families. In addition to the 20,000 Cuban immigrants annually who would be admitted to the U.S. under the pact, a further 3,500 political prisoners would most likely be allowed into the U.S. as some 3,000 immediate relatives of U.S. citizens.

Responding to the news that the pact had been revived, inmates at the Oakdale detention center rioted and seized the facility Nov. 21. The unrest spread Nov. 23 to a federal prison housing the Marielitos in Atlanta. At the Oakdale center, some 1,000 Cubans took over the prison and seized 30 hostages, 28 of whom were still being held Nov. 30. The inmates set scattered fires, destroying much of the facility. Some 30 inmates and workers were reported to have suffered minor injuries in the first two days of the uprising. As in Atlanta, the Cubans threatened to kill their hostages if authorities attempted a rescue. Some inmates, Cuban and American, were permitted to leave Nov. 22 and were transferred to another facility. In the Atlanta takeover, one inmate was killed Nov. 23, the result of gunshot wounds. The circumstances of the killing were not immediately divulged. A few staff members received minor injuries. Some 75 hostages were initially seized. A group of Atlanta inmates released five hostages late Nov. 24, but others took the prison hospital, capturing another 25 employees, one of whom was released early Nov. 25. As of Nov. 25, some 315 prisoners in Atlanta--Cuban and American--had surrendered.

Most of the inmates at Oakdale had completed sentences for crimes they had committed while in the U.S. but remained in prison because they were subject to deportation. Many had believed that their release to halfway houses was imminent. More than 300 Oakdale inmates had been sent to halfway houses in December 1986. The federal penitentiary in Atlanta held 1,392 Cuban prisoners, mostly those who had committed more serious crimes. Many had been held since their arrival in the U.S. in 1980.

U.S. Attorney General Edwin Meese 3rd Nov. 23 said he would declare a moritorium on the return of Cubans to their homeland pending a review of each case. He said a moritorium would take effect "if the uprisings end immediately" and the hostages received "fair and humane treatment." He pledged "no unlawful reprisals" against those who participated in the riots.

The inmates Nov. 29 ended an eight-day siege at the federal detention center in Oakdale and released their remaining 26 hostages after reaching a settlement with federal negotiators. The 11-day siege at the federal penitentiary in Atlanta ended with the release of 89 remaining hostages Dec. 4. At both institutions, the freed hostages were reported in good condition. The conditions in both settlements involved a government agreement to hold individual hearings for each of the detainees and an agreement not to make arbitrary changes in release decisions for those detainees who had families or sponsors in the U.S. and whose parole had already been approved.

THE INDIANAPOLIS STAR

Indianapolis, IN, November 25, 1987

Cuban prisoners greeted the U.S. repatriation agreement with Castro by bloodletting, burning, rioting and hostage-taking.

It is a splendid irony that so many prefer U.S. prisons to being sent back to Fidel Castro and the glories of their communist homeland.

What is not splendid is the weakness exhibited by the Reagan administration in its dealings with the Cuban deportees.

What is the attorney general doing offering criminals a moratorium on deportations if they will be so kind as to release the 103 hostages they took and cease the murderous rampage that has laid waste two federal prisons?

Why should this country be so namby pamby in its dealings with Castro that it would agree to take 20,000 new Cuban emigres each year if Castro will take back the rest of the 2,500 undesirables he foisted off on President Carter during the 1980 Mariel boatlifts?

The vast majority of the Cuban prisoners, say immigration authorities, are persons guilty of serious crimes, ranging from murder to drug offenses. There is no reason in the world why the United States should have continued to house, feed and clothe these criminals.

It is the height of absurdity to fear political backlash from civil rights groups for summarily deporting vicious criminals and psychopaths who entered this country illegally and at the behest of the leader of an enemy state.

A long time ago this administration should have undertaken a reverse boatlift, with or without Castro's consent and with or without the approval of the civil rights establishment.

Instead, under the new repatriation agreement, Castro promises to take his bad guys back and, in turn, send us another 20,000 emigres each year. And apparently nobody can guarantee that some, perhaps many, of those 20,000 a year Cuban imports will not be just as bad or worse than the 2,500 the Immigration Department finally expels.

This whole business is demeaning to the United States. After all the pussy-footing around the Mariel outrage, the Reagan administration has knuckled under to the tinpot dictator who orchestrated it.

In doing so it has sparked prison riots that have cost lives, the national integrity and, very likely, the respect of the civilized world.

THE ATLANTA CONSTITUTION
Atlanta, GA, November 26, 1987

As hours stretch into days, as families of hostages and families of inmates watch and wait and hope, an urgent question begs for an answer: What can the government do to end the riots peacefully? Can it credibly promise its Cuban prisoners anything more specific than "fairness"? The answer: yes.

It can promise them open and impartial hearings. Not hearings run by Border Patrol guards or other officials whose attitudes are likely to be biased against freedom. Not hearings in which the government does all the talking and inmates do all the listening. Not hearings in which inmates are presumed unreleasable until proven otherwise. The feds have already tried those methods. They have not won inmate confidence.

Instead, the government should dust off a 1983 ruling by U.S. District Judge Marvin Shoob — a ruling it successfully fought — and give the inmates limited constitutional rights to unbiased hearings. The Shoob plan sets out a reasonable way to decide who should be deported and who should become a candidate for American freedom. It's time the feds took advantage of it.

But wouldn't this plan obligate the government to give due process to anyone who washed up on our shores from now on? No. The Mariel Cubans are a unique category. Shoob was careful to note the government's right to exclude some aliens. Due process, he said, would be extended only after "an initial period of time during which detention may reasonably be imposed."

From the time it signed the deportation agreement with Cuba last week, Washington has bungled. First, it announced the deal in blithe disregard of how this crucial news might affect the pool of possible deportees. Moreover, it still hasn't explained exactly who is in that pool — not even the Justice Department seems to know. This uncertainty keeps inmate anxiety at a fever pitch.

Some 6,000 to 7,000 Mariel Cubans are in state prisons, federal lockups, county jails, halfway houses and the like. In 1984, 201 Cubans on a confidential list of 2,700 were deported before Havana halted the program. The new program apparently picks up where the old one left off — with 2,500 inmates scheduled for return. But does Washington plan to work from the old list of names? (We may assume that many of those people have since been freed.) Will Justice compile a new list? What happens to the 570 prisoners who were approved for freedom recently but are still incarcerated?

The situation cries for explanations. Yet even in Atlanta — at the embattled federal penitentiary — officials were close-lipped about the inmate takeover until an exasperated Rep. John Lewis (D-Ga.) finally placed a call to Attorney General Edwin Meese; an official briefing followed. Official silence in these circumstances is dangerous. Inmates monitor the media. Confused reports add to the tension inside the prison.

For almost eight years now, officials have obfuscated and neglected the plight of Cuban prisoners. The government must change. It has no choice.

The Philadelphia Inquirer
Philadelphia, PA
November 25, 1987

The most astonishing thing about the Cuban prisoners' rioting and taking of hostages in Atlanta and Oakdale, La., is that something of this magnitude did not happen sooner. There are 7,600 veterans of the 1980 Mariel boatlift in federal detention camps and prisons, half of whom already have completed sentences for the crimes that got them locked up in the first place. They are "excludable aliens," people who never should have come to this country and who are marking time behind bars until the government figures a way to ship them back.

It is well worth noting that the Cubans did not riot over prison food or capitalist oppression. They rioted when they learned that the State Department had cut a deal with the Castro regime to send 2,500 of them back to the motherland. Prison in America apparently holds more appeal than an uncertain homecoming in Fidel Castro's Cuba.

Mr. Castro, it should be remembered, is the principal author of this mess. He took advantage of the chaotic Mariel situation to empty prisons and mental hospitals and send some of Cuba's least savory citizens to these shores. When many of them took up their old ways in the new land, the public outcry was so great that the federal government had to take a hard line on their continued presence here. Their indefinite detention, while cruel and contrary to American values, has been upheld by federal courts.

Attorney General Edwin Meese 3d is doing the only thing possible under the circumstances. He has assured the prisoners that there will be no mass deportations and promised a case-by-case review. As the government can hardly guarantee that these people will not be persecuted on their return, it should only send them back for the most compelling reasons. That the Cubans are now risking their lives to stay here is a factor that cannot be ignored.

THE PLAIN DEALER
Cleveland, OH, November 25, 1987

One hundred and twenty-five thousand Cubans arrived in the United States during the 1980 Mariel boat lift. Of that number, a scant 210 have been refused American freedoms—and for good reason. Among the tens of thousands of immigrants, Cuban premier Fidel Castro tossed in several thousand ringers, clearing his jails and mental institutions at the expense of American hospitality. Even with histories that would be unacceptable if held by any other immigrant, most *Marielitos* eventually won some measure of freedom as immigration parolees. In the years since, several thousand who violated the terms of their parole were imprisoned and then further detained pending their return to Cuba.

Those who deserve American residency the least are protesting news of a renewed repatriation pact the most. In doing so, they emphasize their undesirability. Hostage-taking, rioting, arson and violence might bring attention to their status, but it stimulates no sympathy. Attorney General Edwin Meese has been remarkably fair in saying that before any deportations occur, each case will be reviewed again.

The new pact itself warrants a few compliments. In exchange for ridding itself of Cubans who do not deserve American residency, the United States has agreed to accept as many as 27,000 Cuban immigrants per year. That's a large-sounding number, especially in southern Florida where many of the new immigrants will settle. But compared to the number of Cubans who could make legitimate claims to American residency, it's not many at all. And apart from the numbers, America's obligation to protect, shelter and welcome freedom-seekers is most powerful nearest American shores. You might even say that the pact is a diplomatic victory. True, it can be criticized as an American acceptance of a Cuban solution to a problem caused by Havana in the first place. Yet it is more difficult to defend the continued breach in diplomatic relations.

There is little room to dispute the legal status of the incarcerated *Marielitos*. As "excludable aliens," they simply cannot lay claim to the vast range of rights that are guaranteed American citizens. They do have some rights, though, and those rights deserve to be defended even in the wake of rampage and ruin. At least a few of those in detention facilities and prisons are guilty of relatively minor indiscretions. Do some of the deportees deserve special consideration? Do the complexities of the Cuban-American relationship—split families, political intrigues and bizarre history and culture shock—mitigate their status? In a few cases, maybe, which is why the Justice Department's reviews need to be both stern and compassionate. Rioters, drug-traffickers, sex offenders and murderers deserve nothing more. But after seven years, some *Marielitos* deserve nothing less.

The San Diego Union

San Diego, CA, November 24, 1987

The violence and arson that broke out during the weekend at the federal detention center in Oakdale, La., ought to be a reminder that America's open-door policy needs a screen.

More than 1,000 Cuban prisoners at the compound rioted after they were told that many of them would be returned to Cuba. Who can blame them? Life in an American prison, even one so remote as Oakdale, is to be preferred over what awaits them in Fidel Castro's dungeons.

The prisoners at Oakdale were the worst of a bad lot. All were among the more than 125,000 Cubans who arrived in Florida during the 1980 boatlift from the Cuban port of Mariel.

Federal law-enforcement officials estimate that at least 7,750 of that number were undesirables whom Mr. Castro wished to foist on the United States. Many are hardened criminals, drug addicts, the dregs of Cuban mental institutions, or specially trained agents of the DGI, Cuba's KGB.

U.S. law officers report that the criminals and thugs among the *Marielitos* are the most ferocious in recent memory. The list of violent crimes in which they have been implicated runs the gamut from armed robbery and murder to drug trafficking and sales. Many of these felons are so dangerous that they have continued to be detained even after their sentences in this country have been completed.

Last week, Washington and Havana announced a new immigration accord that will permit 250,000 more refugees to leave Cuba and enter the United States by the mid-1990s. Unlike the haphazard manner in which the Mariel boatlift was handled, the new wave of immigrants will be processed for entry into the United States in an orderly, and secure, flow.

This time the feds vow they won't be caught flat-footed. The U.S. Immigration and Naturalization Service and the FBI have wisely sought the help of the large Cuban emigre communities in the Miami and New York metropolitan areas to help ferret out criminals, terrorists, and others.

It would have been impossible in 1980 to separate legitimate refugees from the refuse of Cuba's prisons without the assistance of the emigre community. The ties of Cuban-Americans to their homeland are strong, and they often have information about events and personalities in Cuba that is impossible to get elsewhere.

Utilizing this resource is one way Washington can prevent a repetition of the ugly events at Oakdale.

Newsday

Long Island, NY, November 25, 1987

It shouldn't have surprised anyone that the revival of a deportation agreement between the United States and Cuba would cause this country's big detention centers for Cuban refugees to erupt: Many fear a return to Cuba more than continued imprisonment here.

Prison authorities in Oakdale, La., and most certainly Atlanta should have been better prepared for trouble. But while rioting is never tolerable, this uprising has exposed the just grievances of many of the detainees and may result in the kind of treatment they should have received in the first place: The case-by-case review that Attorney General Edwin Meese has now promised — if the hostages are released and order is restored.

The deportation agreement stipulates that Cuba will accept 2,500 Cubans who came here during the Mariel boatlift in 1980 but were deemed "excludable" by the United States. This country, in turn, will admit 3,000 political prisoners plus up to another 20,000 "regular" immigrants from Cuba a year.

Hundreds of Cubans who came here during the boatlift have been held at detention centers in a sort of legal limbo since; others have ended up there as a result of crimes committed after they arrived. Civil libertarians have complained for years that many Mariel Cubans convicted of minor crimes have been imprisoned indefinitely pending deportation.

Their peculiar circumstances stem from having been granted "immigration parole" at the time of arrival, which means they are easier to deport than other aliens. Many had come to believe — rightly or wrongly — that they would be allowed to stay in this country.

The Mariel Cubans subject to deportation fall into three general categories: those who had been jailed in Cuba for serious crimes, along with mental patients hospitalized in that country; those who committed serious crimes after arriving in the United States, and those who are still doing time or remain imprisoned after completing their sentences for minor offenses committed here.

The United States has no legal or moral obligation to serve as a dumping ground for criminals or mentally ill people from abroad. Under different circumstances, members of the first group would never have been allowed to enter this country. Neither, given the conditions of the admission, does the United States have to put up with serious criminality by those it does admit.

But there's no reason to treat those among the Mariel immigrants who ran afoul of the law in some small way any differently than other immigrants. Many have sunk roots here in the seven years since the boatlift.

Forcing them to return to Cuba now could be a real tragedy for them and their families. Giving them an incentive to persuade the militants to give up may be the best way out of this mess. Meese's promise is a start. Now it's up to the negotiators to make it credible.

Newsday / M.G. Lord

AKRON BEACON JOURNAL
Akron, OH, November 25, 1987

THE VIOLENCE that has exploded in two federal prisons ha _____ n simmering for months.

The inmates are Cubans who came to America in the 1980 Mariel boatlift and now face deportation back to Cuba. In a rage against that deportation, Cuban prisoners rioted, took hostages and set fires at two federal detention centers in Atlanta and Oakdale, La. At least one inmate is reported dead in Atlanta.

Attorney General Edwin Meese has made the right gesture on behalf of the federal government by offering a moratorium on deportations until each case can be reviewed individually. Now it is up to the inmates to accept or reject the offer.

The roots of the trouble go back to 1980, when a one-time agreement between Cuban leader Fidel Castro and President Jimmy Carter allowed limited immigration from Cuba to the United States. Some 125,000 Cubans took advantage of the opportunity, sailing from the port of Mariel in a rag-tag "freedom flotilla."

Most of those who came to the United States joined family or friends and assimilated into American life with no problem. But Castro, cynically, sent several hundred convicted criminals or mental incompetents. In addition, another 3,000 of the Mariel group have been convicted of crimes since they got to the United States.

These have become "excludable aliens," subject to expulsion. But Cuba did not want them back. These "excludables" have had little hope of freedom; a U.S. court of appeals has ruled they have no constitutional rights. To try to break the deadlock, the Immigration and Naturalization Service recently announced that it would begin reviewing cases on an individual basis, believing that many, if not most, could be released to families. Soon after, however, word came that Cuba had agreed to take back 2,600 of the excludables. So the brief hope of review turned to rage.

There should be little sympathy for rioting prisoners. Yet many of Oakdale's inmates had served their time and were awaiting review; and many fear persecution if returned to Cuba. The Meese offer shows that the government realizes it made a mistake in announcing the deportation without clearing up the question of fair review of each case.

Those immigrants convicted of minor crimes may deserve another chance. But the United States is not bound to keep those who are clearly undesirable, or those who never should have been allowed entry. And now there is the added offense of prison violence.

Individual review is the only way to clear up the mess. But the reviews can't begin as long as the inmates hold hostages, endanger others and make angry demands.

The Miami Herald
Miami, FL, November 25, 1987

THANKS to the secrecy in which bilateral immigration issues were negotiated in Mexico City between Washington and Havana, the new agreement exploded emotionally into South Florida's headlines over the weekend.

Surely no rational person believes that taking hostages and burning Federal property proves one's worthiness as a free U.S. resident. Quite the contrary, the Oakdale, La., and Atlanta riots and the Texas escape serve only to strengthen the odious stereotype that for seven years has plagued Mariel entrants in general and Mariel offenders in particular.

Some Oakdale and Atlanta prisoners almost certainly are innocent of these outrages, and others may have tried to help the hostages. These distinctions should be made carefully, and individually, when Federal officials actually choose whether to file riot charges, to deport, or to parole Mariel prisoners. Individual parole reviews started for Mariel felons before the new agreement, and they should continue. Families should not be split needlessly if a prisoner has shown himself to be rehabilitated.

For most Mariel felons, however, deportation is the proper, legal, and necessary course. Foreign nationals convicted of murder, drug trafficking, armed robbery, rape, habitual thievery, or of using guns and other weapons, simply forfeit the privilege of joining their law-abiding compatriots in American society. That fact applies to *all* aliens in this country, not just to Cubans.

Similarly, U.S. citizens, or permanent U.S. residents born in other countries, have a right to apply for entrance visas for certain relatives — as immigrants, not refugees. There is a worldwide quota as well as a nation-by-nation limit, and the applicant must guarantee his relative's support. The immigrant must pass a physical exam and background check before he is allowed in.

The new agreement invokes that standard along with the threat of deportation that applies to all foreigners. If the Government requires a realistic commitment from the U.S. relative — not the worthless "sponsorships" that turned thousands of Mariel vagrants onto Miami's streets — the impact on local social services should be minimal.

It's understandable that some exiles decry any dealings with the despot who rules Cuba. Yet it's undeniable that the Freedom Flights of the '60s, the exodus of political prisoners, and most other migrations from Cuba occurred only after such dealings.

This agreement embraces both family reunification and deportation of undesirables. This is the only way to stabilize the Cuban-American family and the larger community to which it contributes so much. The pact thus should be welcomed by all of South Florida.

The Chattanooga Times
Chattanooga, TN, November 25, 1987

It is a measure of their fear of the future that hundreds of Cuban prisoners have protested their planned deportation to Cuba by staging riots at two federal prisons, taking hostages and setting major fires. A standoff between the prisoners and authorities at the prisons in Atlanta and in Oakdale, La., may be broken by Attorney General Edwin Meese's offer of a moratorium on the repatriation, but it's hard to be optimistic.

The inmates arrived here during the Mariel boatlift in 1980, when some 125,000 Cubans left their homeland for the United States. The inmates have existed in a legal limbo since then. Under the law, they were in the so-called "excludable" category, meaning that because of a history of mental illness or a criminal record, they were not eligible for immigration into this country. They're only here because Fidel Castro, in a cynical exploitation of our desire to reunite Cubans with their relatives in the United States, emptied his prisons and hospitals of "undesirables" and packed them onto the boats.

President Castro has said that the 2,700 inmates who are to be returned to Cuba will be treated leniently, but the prisoners are understandably suspicious of such a promise. Even so, their suspicion, even their objections to being returned to Cuba, are no excuse for wanton destruction of property and hostage-taking. Mr. Meese is correct to offer a moratorium to allow for a "full and equitable" review of the Cubans' plight on a case-by-case basis. But that doesn't mean the United States should have to accept criminals who would not have met U.S. immigration criteria in the first place.

When President Castro agreed in 1985 to take some 2,500 "excludables" back, the Reagan administration reciprocated, saying it would admit 3,000 political prisoners as well as up to 20,000 other immigrants. The deal fell through shortly thereafter but was reinstated this year as a way of improving relations between Cuba and the United States.

The effect of the riots on that agreement is unclear, but obviously it will be hard to justify allowing many of the prisoners to remain here under the circumstances. We have enough crime problems of our own without importing criminals from Cuba. Similarly, there's no reason why we should allow prisoners to remain in this country who have protested the administration's proposal by taking hostages and burning down prisons. Compassion for the petty criminals who can be expected to prosper in this country? Sure. But for the ringleaders of these riots, the best response is a ticket back to Cuba.

Index

A